SEPARATION OF INVESTMENT BANKING ACTIVITIES FROM UNIVERSAL BANKS

SEPARATION OF INVESTMENT BANKING ACTIVITIES FROM UNIVERSAL BANKS

Preventing Financial Instability
North America, Japan, United Kingdom and European Union

Nikitas E. Bompotis

INTERSENTIA
LEFEBVRE GROUP

Intersentia
Lefebvre Belgium SA
Avenue Jean Monnet, 4
1348 Louvain-la-Neuve
Belgium
Email: contact@larcier-intersentia.com

Distribution for the UK, Ireland and
Rest of the World (excl. France, Belgium and Luxembourg)
Ingram Publisher Services UK
1 Deltic Avenue, Rooksley
Milton Keynes MK13 8LD
United Kingdom
Tel: +44 1752 202 301 | Fax: +44 1752 202 331
Email: ipsuk.customercare@ingramcontent.com

Distribution for France and Other Countries (excl. Ireland and the UK)
Interforum Editis
92 avenue de France
75013 Paris
France

Distribution for Belgium and Luxembourg (excl. France, Ireland and the UK)
Larcier-Intersentia
Avenue Jean Monnet, 4
1348 Louvain-la-Neuve
Belgium

Separation of Investment Banking Activities from Universal Banks.
Preventing Financial Instability. North America, Japan, United Kingdom and
European Union

ISBN : 978-1-83970-577-9
D/2025/06040/0671
NUR 828

British Library Cataloguing in Publication Data. A catalogue record for this book is available from the British Library

To my beloved mother, Calliope.
Thank you for everything. We miss you.

TABLE OF CONTENTS

PART II
REGULATION THROUGH STRUCTURAL REFORMS: CASE STUDIES ACROSS THE WORLD

PART III
ANALYSIS OF THE INTERPLAY BETWEEN THE STRUCTURAL REFORMS AND THE FINDINGS FROM THE CASE STUDY JURISDICTIONS

PREFACE

It is with great pleasure to write the preface of this book on an aspect of financial regulation (namely, structural regulations), which remains debatable and (broadly) unresolved at global level. In the aftermath of the recent (2007–2009) global financial crisis (GFC) and of the March 2023 banking turmoil, the concepts of 'narrow banking', 'public banking', and 'ring-fencing' *vis-à-vis* the 'universal banking model' have been brought under the spotlight again.

I am also very glad, because this book was written by one of my former students. I well know that it is the culmination of a time-consuming academic process that started more than a decade ago from a Master's thesis that evolved into a PhD thesis and now is a well-structured scientific book. As an academic supervisor of both these theses, it is with great pleasure to realise that this book can serve as a solid basis for a continuous academic dialogue in the topic of (at least, partly) separating banks' investment banking from their commercial banking activities. Moreover, the book explores this extremely interesting topic of financial regulation under a different and original lens and reaches a conclusion that may not yet been given the proper attention in academia.

The research on which this book is based is excellent and comprehensive, as the relevant literature is vast and diverse, ranging from economic analyses to demanding legal research on the nature of the contested reforms. Of particular importance is the ambiguity of the various economic analyses and research on the topic, since the results are highly debatable and the academics in economics and finance have not (as yet) reached solid conclusions with respect to the effectiveness and impact of such measures on the profitability and business models of banks.

The author starts the analysis by explaining, in the **first chapter of Part I**, the role of banks within the complex structure of the international financial system and delineates the relationship between structural reforms and financial stability. Given that there is no commonly accepted definition of financial stability, he discusses its notion and elaborates on its various parameters. Understanding differs among various sciences (legal and economic); accordingly, based on the parameters taken into account, different conclusions can be drawn on what exactly this concept entails. Moreover, the author sets out the framework to understand the nature of structural reforms, which can be simultaneously micro- and macroprudential and can be further divided into soft and hard reforms. Examples and further references to academic research accompany the analysis.

The **second chapter of Part I** overviews the banking models currently used from the perspective of structural reforms and provides a detailed analysis of the various proposals that aim at 'breaking the banks' (meaning to separate certain activities, mostly related to the investment banking services), that are deemed to be riskier and, unfortunately, demonised by the proponents of separation. Although each bank adapts its business model based on country-specific parameters and the particular services it desires to offer, the analysis here captures the broad business models and how the proposals for structural reforms interact with them.

Furthermore, the author develops on the various separation proposals that remain purely academic and have not (as yet) been adopted by any jurisdiction, providing a cost-benefit analysis for each of them. He then discusses in depth the ring-fencing (separation) proposal, that up to date is the only one fully adopted and implemented by some jurisdictions. This is a novel element in his approach, and readers can benefit from such an overview of the relevant proposals, with further references to the relevant literature.

In **Part II**, the author thoroughly presents, in five dedicated chapters, the case studies of five jurisdictions (including also the EU as a single jurisdiction), which have adopted in the past or currently have in place structural regulations of any type. The sample countries are the US, the UK, the EU, Canada and Japan and were selected on the basis of their significant importance for international financial regulation and financial markets. Through a historical lens, the author deep dives in the evolution of the countries' banking (and in general financial) system and explores how and under which circumstances these jurisdictions adopted separation measures. In this respect, the author notes the following:

First, the US plays a predominant role in the discussion of structural reforms, since it was the first country to have adopted such measures, in the wake of the 1929 financial crisis; accordingly, the analysis of that era and of the measures that followed is more than important in order for the reader to fully understand the background event and the legal rationale behind such bold reforms.

Second, the UK provides a useful case study with its strict separation model (ring-fencing) based on the proposals included in the Vickers Report. Moreover, the UK remains the only jurisdiction that has concluded an official review of the post separation situation; the results, also discussed here, are very interesting and give 'food for thought'.

Third – and on the other hand, Japan is a textbook example of how a distorted deregulation process, coupled with good government intentions but with ill performed prudential supervision, can be the prefect recipe for a banking crisis.

Fourth, the EU, examined as a single jurisdiction, gives the opposite view: universal banking is (almost) predominant and deeply rooted in the tradition of European financial law. The Liikanen Report identified certain aspects of investment banking services that could be 'structurally separated' from universal banks but the legislative proposal from the European Commission failed to see the light of adoption. Highly debatable discussions and strong opposition from certain Member States forced the Commission to withdraw the proposal and it is only some Member States which adopted the Liikanen Report's key proposals (albeit watered down).

Finally, Canada seems to have found the 'Holy Grail' of financial stability: robust prudential banking regulation and supervision and a deregulation process, coupled by controlled competition on behalf of the Government, preserved the stability of the Canadian banking system during the GFC, providing for a successful blueprint on how to avoid instability and achieve long term growth.

The **first chapter of Part III** focuses on exploring the interplay between structural reforms and certain aspects of financial regulation such as the resolution regimes that are in place, the prudential supervision of banks, the rise of the so called Non-Bank Financial Intermediation entities and last but not least the interplay with the 'Too-Big-To-Fail' (TBTF) doctrine, which is the *raison d'être* of structural reforms. The analysis reveals that certain questions still remain unanswered and, thus, further research would be more than welcomed from both academics and regulatory/supervisory authorities. Resolution schemes and the use of bail-inable instruments from banks and financial firms offer a powerful combination for assurance that financial distress will not develop into a generalised financial turmoil/crisis. However, it is clear from the analysis that further research is required to fully understand what needs to be done and how these tools will work in tandem.

Ultimately, the second and **last chapter of Part III** provides a comparative analysis of national particularities with respect to structural reforms, while pointing out common elements and key differences. This approach is particularly interesting, as it allows us to understand the specificities of each regime. Furthermore, the author concludes with a comparative analysis of the findings from the fourth chapter, which further articulates the main idea/ proposal of the book. The example of Canada demonstrates the importance of 'proactive' prudential supervision by competent authorities; combined with a robust regulatory framework relying on tailor-made bank capital requirements reflecting the country's specificities, it allows Canada to claim that it has the relatively safer financial system among the countries used as a yardstick. In the US, the picture is quite different: formed from the outset as a 'dual banking system' with multiple layers of prudential supervision, both at state and federal level, the banking system comes as an alternative to the deep capital markets' funding options and the products offered therein. The GFC and the March 2023 banking turmoil clearly demonstrated the lack of efficient coordination among the various regulatory/supervisory authorities. With respect to Japan, we come across a very interesting finding: again, the importance of 'proactive' supervision is highlighted given the strict segregation and compartmentalisation of the financial system, and the banking system in particular. In the EU, the Liikanen Report-based proposals for regulation, that would introduce structural reforms, failed. The traditional universal banking system was only adjusted by some Member States with reforms at national level that did not alter the very essence of the business model. The EU was facing another type of problem due to the lack of a single supervisory and resolution framework for cross-border active banks. The creation of the Banking Union for (mainly) the Member States whose currency is the euro was a major step towards enhanced prudential supervision and resolution to ensure financial stability. Finally, in the case of the UK, the bold measure of ring-fencing came naturally after the proposals articulated in the Vickers Report. Today, it remains the only strict separation model and the results from the official review made by the UK Parliament and the Government remain of a mixed nature, demonstrating the need for further research on why such measures seem to not fully ensure financial stability.

The **concluding remarks** are of very significant value, demonstrating that, based on the author's original analysis, the structural reforms, if adopted, are not a panacea *per se* for any future turmoil that could develop into a full-scale crisis. Structural reforms have a positive impact on banks' resolvability and create, under certain circumstances, simpler structures, which, in theory, can be supervised more effectively and be resolved easier if compared to other complex structures. An insight though from the present book is that reality usually differs from theoretical approaches. The task of 'breaking the banks', and more specifically the large and complex ones, is far from a straightforward exercise, since several parameters should be taken into account. Furthermore, many questions deserve clear answers, and the present book tries to demonstrate that those answers are not yet convincing.

Undoubtedly though, even the simpler (banking) structures fail. Sometimes, they even fail with severe and long-term macroeconomic consequences or might have adverse effects on credit supply and on financial innovation. The case of Japan provides a textbook example of such a situation. Therefore, the author concludes that the 'one size fits all' approach is not the preferable solution for such a complex issue with such diverging directions in the jurisdictions examined. The author further supports that the key to financial stability is a credible resolution regime that can ensure, to the extent possible, that all financial firms, and banks in particular, will be allowed to fail without negative spillover effects to the entire financial system. The lessons from the GFC and the March 2023 banking turmoil must have been learned by now and an optimal balance between innovation, profitability and stability should be achieved. This is not an easy task for both regulators and supervisors.

I trust that this book will further promote the academic debate around the topic of separating investment banking from commercial banking activities, where these are being performed under the so-called universal banking model, prompt fruitful discussions in academia and beyond, and foster further analysis and research on the delicate outstanding questions.

Prof. Dr. Christos V. Gortsos
University of Luxembourg,
National & Kapodistrian University of Athens

TABLE OF ABBREVIATIONS

ABCP	Asset Backed Commercial Paper
ABS	Asset Backed Securities
BCBS	Basel Committee on Banking Supervision
BHC	Bank Holding Company
BHCA	Bank Holding Company Act
BIS	Bank of International Settlements
BoC	(Central) Bank of Canada
BOC	Bank of Cyprus
BoE	(Central) Bank of England
BoJ	(Central) Bank of Japan
BRRD	Bank Resolution and Recovery Directive
CBC	Central Bank of Cyprus
CBDC	Central Bank Digital Currency
CBI	Central Bank of Ireland
CDIC	Canadian Deposit Insurance Corporation
CDO	Collateralized Debt Obligation
CDS	Credit Default Swap
CFTC	Commodity Futures Trading Commission
CMO	Collateralized Mortgage Obligation
CRA	Community Reinvestment Act
CSC	Canadian Supreme Court
DTI	Debt (Service) To Income
DSIB	Domestic Systemically Important Bank
EBA	European Banking Authority
ECB	European Central Bank
ECJ	European Court of Justice
EEA	European Economic Area
EEC	European Economic Community
EIOPA	European Insurance and Occupational Pensions Authority
ELA	Emergency Liquidity Assistance

ESM	European Stability Mechanism
ESMA	European Securities and Markets Authority
ESRB	European Systemic Risk Board
EU	European Union
FCA	Financial Conduct Authority
FDIC	Federal Deposit Insurance Corporation
FHC	Financial Holding Company
FIRREA	Financial Institutions Reform, Recovery, and Enforcement Act
FSA	Financial Services Authority
FSB	Financial Stability Board
FSOC	Financial Stability Oversight Council
GLBA	Gramm-Leach-Bliley Act
GDP	Gross Domestic Product
GSA	Glass-Steagall Act
GSEs	Government Sponsored Enterprises
GSIB	Global Systemically Important Bank
ICB	Independent Commission on Banking
IMF	International Monetary Fund
IOSCO	International Organization of Securities Commissions
JFSA[1]	Japanese Financial Services Agency
JSBA	Joint Stock Bank Act
LTV	Loan to Value
MBSs	Mortgage-Backed Securities
MMMF	Money Market Mutual Fund
MoF	(Japanese) Ministry of Finance
MPoE	Multiple Point of Entry
NBA	National Bank Act
NBFI	Non-Bank Financial Institution
NCUA	National Credit Union Administration
NFB	Narrow Funding Bank
NRFB	Non-Ring-Fenced Body

[1] Although the official name of the current Japanese regulator and supervisor is 'Financial Services Agency' (FSA), we use the term 'JFSA' to avoid confusion with the 'Financial Services Authority' (FSA), predecessor of the current UK regulator and supervisor. Since we use both abbreviations in the text, for the purpose of the present book when we use 'JFSA' we mean the Japanese 'Financial Services Agency'.

NYSE	New York Stock Exchange
OCC	Office of the Comptroller of the Currency
OLA	Orderly Liquidation Authority
OPEC	Organization of the Petroleum Exporting Countries
OSFI	Office of the Superintendent of Financial Institutions
OTC	Over the Counter (derivatives)
OTS	Office of Thrift Supervision
PRA	Prudential Regulation Authority
RFB	Ring Fenced Body
RMBS	Residential Mortgage-Backed Securities
RWAs	Risk Weighted Assets
SCAP	Supervisory Capital Assessment Program
SCOTUS	Supreme Court of the United States
SEC	Securities and Exchange Commission
SIFI	Systemically Important Financial Institution
SMEs	Small and Medium sized Enterprises
SPoE	Single Point of Entry
SPE	Special Purpose Entity
SPV	Special Purpose Vehicle
SRB	Single Resolution Board
SRF	Single Resolution Fund
SRM	Single Resolution Mechanism
SSM	Single Supervisory Mechanism
TARP	Troubled Assets Relief Program
VaR	Value at Risk

INTRODUCTION

During the second season's 6th episode of the famous British sitcom 'Yes Minister', bearing the title 'The Quality of Life', Sir Humphrey Appleby (SHA), Secretary of the Ministry, privately meets Sir Desmond Glazebrook (SDG), a British banker, and the following hilarious dialogue occurs:

> **SHA**: 'Didn't you read the Financial Times this morning?'
>
> **SDG**: 'Never do.'
>
> **SHA**: 'Well, you're a banker. Surely you read the Financial Times?'
>
> **SDG**: 'Can't understand it. Full of economic theory.'
>
> **SHA**: 'Why do you buy it?'
>
> **SDG**: 'Oh, you know, it's part of the uniform. It took me thirty years to understand Keynes' economics. Then when I'd just cottoned on, everyone started getting hooked on these new monetarist ideas, you know, 'I Want to Be Free' by Milton Shulman.'
>
> **SHA**: 'Milton Friedman.'
>
> **SDG**: 'Why are they all called Milton? Anyway, I've only got as far as Milton Keynes.'
>
> **SHA**: 'Maynard Keynes.'
>
> **SDG**: 'I'm sure there's a Milton Keynes.'
>
> **SHA**: 'Yes, there is, but it's...' [he gives up disappointed].

The above dialogue, although written many years ago, where optimism and short-term vanity were the dominant sentiments in financial markets, can be better understood when associated with the recent global financial crisis (GFC) of 2007–2009 and to some extent with the March 2023 banking turmoil. These events brought under the spotlight, again, a very serious question regarding the efficiency of financial regulation and specifically that of banking regulation. Before the GFC, what was uncontestably accepted as 'orthodoxy', was the perception that the so-called 'universal banking model', with all its local variations, differences, parameters and aspects, was efficient and due to the effective diversification of banking and financial risks, through multiple sources of business and sophisticated risk management techniques, was also safe. This illusion (?) stopped abruptly when the GFC erupted causing a global financial turmoil that changed radically the way we understood how the modern financial system was functioning. It seemed that bankers, just like Sir Desmond Glazebrook in the famous British sitcom, financial and risk management experts, auditors, and investors were not in the position to fully understand the risks that had assume with these financial transactions. Moreover, the banking turmoil of March 2023 brought up again questions regarding the ability of the Sir Desmond Glazebrooks of this world to fully understand the novel risks they engage and assume. The banking sector was at the epicentre again, after the collapse of certain US banks and that of Switzerland's giant financial firm, Crédit Suisse.

Since the 1970s, restrictions on banks' business lines have been relaxed, in parallel with the deregulation of financial markets due to, mostly but non-exclusively, geopolitical events (collapse of the Bretton Woods system). Back then, there was a broad consensus that banks which offer a wide (full) range of financial services could better provide the largest economic benefits amid a rapidly growing and competitive global economy. Innovations in risk management practices, diversification of business lines, market-based pricing of risks and assets and market discipline were thought to be effective mechanisms to safeguard against risk associated with the rapid expansion of large, universal banks across the world. The universal banking model was put under exhaustive scrutiny; politicians, supervisors, regulators, practitioners and academics were fiercely criticising its inefficiencies and the calamity that imposed in the financial markets by 'big banks'. The events of the GFC were incontestable, leaving no room for constructive dialogue against the total criticism. High profiled investment and commercial banks have gone bankrupt or were forced to merge with other financial firms to avoid bankruptcy. Lehmann Brothers, Bear Stearns, Northern Rock, Dexia, Wachovia are only a few names from a big list of financial firms that did not manage to survive the crisis. Apart from bankruptcies, many nationalisations also took place (especially in the US and the UK), and the national governments became the principal shareholders of previously privately owned universal banks, financial firms and in the US also of almost the entire automotive industry.

The enormous failure of the financial system to both contain and manage effectively the shockwaves of the GFC gave rise to numerous theoretical proposals regarding how the system should be regulated and specifically how the banks should be regulated and supervised. The banking system, as part of the greater financial system, played and continued to play the most important role in the efficient function and performance of the financial system. As a result, banks found themselves at the epicentre of the discussions that were and still are extremely important and interesting. Among the various proposals regarding the regulation of the financial system, the present book will explore the so-called 'structural reforms' of the banks and their impact on the financial systems' stability. Since financial stability is considered to be a public good, states have a huge interest in adopting measures that aim to safeguard and enhance financial stability for the sake of their economic growth and prosperity. As such, it is very common for the states after every financial crisis to impose various measures on the banks, since usually the latter are involved in these events of financial instability. Measures of structural reforms were also adopted and enacted by various states in the aftermath of the recent GFC. The UK, the US and the EU were among the first to table proposals for structural reforms of their banking sector respectively. Some of them were finally enacted by laws while others failed mostly because there was not enough political willingness to adopt them. This happened because essentially structural reforms are introducing fundamental alterations to the banking models that, in certain places, are the result of many years of business practice and tradition. For this reason, we will use a 'historical lens' when examining the structural reforms, because their adoption has a deeper background, often historical, that must be properly understood in order to have a solid understanding of the rationale behind their adoption.

Among the various countries, the US has a long tradition of adopting structural reforms for their financial system. From a universal banking style regime before the financial crash of 1929, they moved to an extremely strict regulatory regime with the structural reforms imposed by the so-called Glass-Steagall Act (GSA) in 1933, followed again by a deregulatory movement in the late 1970s that culminated with the adoption of the Gramm-Leach-Bliley Act (GLBA) in 1999. The recent GFC signalled the reintroduction of structural reforms, albeit not as strict as the previous ones. As a result, the proposed changes do not go as far as the previous regimes in certain countries where a complete separation of banking and securities activities existed. On the other hand, for several countries, mostly Europeans, regulation through structural reforms is a novelty and the imposed restrictions will definitely place a burden on their banking sectors. The basic rationale behind the adoption of structural reforms in the banking sector is to 'tame the megabanks' as Prof. Wilmarth expressly supports on his book.[2] Taming the megabanks essentially means two things: a) to 'insulate certain types of financial activities regarded as especially important for the real economy, or significant on consumer/depositor protection grounds, from the risks that emanate from potentially riskier but less important activities' as Gambacorta and van Rixtel have written on their paper,[3] and b) to deal with the so-called 'Too-Big-To-Fail' (TBTF) issue, which touches upon the size, importance, and level of interconnectedness of these financial institutions that are perceived as impossible to fail, and the states are always obliged to bail them out. The aims of structural reforms are thus well defined, making the necessity of these measures seem uncontestable. This is exactly where the problems start with this type of regulation. Despite the fact

[2] See in A.E. Wilmarth Jr., *Taming the Megabanks, Why We Need a New Glass-Steagall Act*, New York, Oxford University Press, 2020, pp. 10-14.

[3] See in L. Gambacorta and A. van Rixtel, 'Structural bank regulation initiatives: approaches and implications', *BIS Working Papers*, no. 412, April 2013, Basel, Bank of International Settlements, p. 1.

that the noble aims of structural reforms are very clear, this is exactly where the problems start, since their application lacks both clarity and justification. Lack of clarity means that the line of reforms is drawn 'somewhere in between commercial and investment banking'[4] without clear lines of activities, entities or persons that should be affected by these measures. Lack of justification means that in most cases the measures are burdensome, incomprehensible, ambiguous, and without proper connection to other regulatory initiatives that in most cases have similar aims. As a result, proponents of structural reforms, usually motivated by misconceptions and blurred understanding of the modern financial system, are proposing measures that can backfire if not properly calibrated and analysed, creating more problems than originally designed to solve. The structural reform measures usually advocate for the separation of investment banking activities from the commercial banking ones as it is believed that investment banking activities are inherently riskier and with lower social welfare impact. What is difficult to define is which activities shall be separated and how this separation will ultimately work towards a better and more stable financial system.

With the present book, we will try to present, explain, and analyse the structural reforms that aim to regulate the financial and the banking system particularly, while also trying to provide a framework for assessing their effectiveness in preserving financial system's stability from events of instability. We will use specific countries as case studies and through a historical evolution of their financial and banking systems we will explore how, and to what extent, these countries adopted, or not, structural regulations to their financial and banking systems. These countries were chosen based on their importance as international financial centres with a global role in the international financial system. Among them, by far the most important and influential is the US, playing an important role as the most important financial centre of the world. Canada, was chosen based on the fact that its financial system is neighbouring, therefore closely related to the US, based on geographical and other historical reasons. Japan was chosen because of the influential role the US played during the occupation period on the aftermath of World War II and the separation doctrine that was instilled during that time. The UK is an equally important financial centre with influential financial legislation and being the only country that has adopted and currently has in force the strictest separation regime among the countries we used as yardsticks. Finally, the EU was chosen not only because of its importance as a financial single market but also because in the aftermath of the GFC and the subsequent Eurozone crisis, took the bold initiative to propose legislation that would separate certain investment banking activities from the universal bank style credit institutions. The fact that this

[4] Ibid.

proposal failed reflects the strong tradition that the EU has towards the model of universal banking system.

An interesting parameter is that these countries have adopted structural reforms for their financial and banking systems and will provide us with important information regarding the function of these reforms, as a yardstick, to assess how successful these reforms were or still are. Finally, we will try to answer the fundamental question that the present book poses. Are structural reforms effective in preserving the stability of the financial system? Can they also act in a precautionary way? This last question is an important parameter of our analysis, since we should be also able to understand if these measures can be imposed ex-ante or ex-post, on the grounds that the supervisor might ask the banks to adopt such measures on a precautionary basis to increase the resilience of the system and to facilitate its tasks.

My PhD thesis, defended successfully in March 2024, in the Law School of the National and Kapodistrian University of Athens, forms the backbone of this book which significantly expands and updates the existing academic literature and events so far. Therefore, I could not omit expressing my sincere gratitude to those people who stood behind me and provided their support by discussing, reading and commenting both on the thesis and the book. I am highly indebted and immensely grateful, as always, to my PhD thesis supervisor, Professor Christos Gortsos, for being a great teacher, an excellent supervisor, and above all a true mentor. I owe him the most, since he continuously expressed his support, in various ways, through the long journey of researching, studying, and writing my doctoral thesis. He has been a true inspiration. I am also deeply thankful to Professor André Prüm, Full professor in Law at the University of Luxembourg, Professor Dirk Andreas Zetzsche, Head of Department of Law of the University of Luxembourg, and also Julia Sinnig, Assistant Professor at the University of Luxembourg, who not only accepted me as a postdoctoral researcher at the University of Luxembourg, but also supported the project of writing this book.

Finally, I would like to thank the publisher, Intersentia, for taking care of all the necessary steps for this book to see the light of the academic world, with their high professionalism and excellent support. Special thanks to Mr Nicolas Cassart and Ms Sophie Joiris for their continuous support.

It goes without saying that all errors and/or omissions are entirely of my own as well as the opinion and ideas expressed therein.

Luxembourg, May 2025

PART I.

Structural Reforms, Banking Models and the Financial System

CHAPTER 1
BANKS AND STRUCTURAL REFORMS WITHIN THE FINANCIAL SYSTEM: SETTING THE SCENE

1 FINANCIAL SYSTEM AND THE ROLE OF BANKS

Traditionally, any financial system, either domestic or international, is designed to perform a double task. Firstly, offers the necessary channels to transfer the funds from the 'positive savers'[5] (households, firms, individuals, and governments), which have a surplus of funds by spending less than their income and want to do something with their excess funds, to the 'negative savers'[6] (firms, households, governments, and individuals), which are in need of extra funds to invest, spend, buy, pay and honour their financial commitments.[7] Secondly, the financial system performs payment transactions without the use of coins and fiat money. This task is performed via technologically complex payment systems that are coordinated at international level to ensure the efficiency, safety, and stability of this task. The channelling of funds between positive and negative savers occurs either directly or indirectly. Directly, also known as 'direct finance', occurs when savers with negative surplus (borrowers) borrow funds directly from positive savers with surplus (lenders) in financial markets by selling them securities (also called financial instruments).[8] The second route to obtain funds occurs indirectly, also known as 'indirect finance', because it involves a financial intermediary that stands between the borrower and the

---

[5] Also known as 'Suppliers'. See in R.S. Carnell, J.R. Macey, G.P. Miller and P. Conti-Brown, *The Law of Financial Institutions*, 7th ed., Aspen Casebook Series, New York, Wolters Kluwer, 2021, p. 11.

[6] Also known as 'Users'. Ibid.

[7] See in F.S. Mishkin, *The Economics of Money, Banking, and Financial Markets*, 7th ed., The Addison-Wesley Series in economics, Boston, Pearson, 2004, p. 23; in R.S. Carnell, J.R. Macey, G.P. Miller and P. Conti-Brown, *The Law of Financial Institutions*, 7th ed., Aspen Casebook Series, New York, Wolters Kluwer, 2021, p. 11; in C.V. Gortsos, *Introduction to International Financial Law*, Athens, Nomiki Vivliothiki, 2011, p. 15.

[8] See in F.S. Mishkin, *The Economics of Money, Banking, and Financial Markets*, 7th ed., The Addison-Wesley Series in economics, Boston, Pearson, 2004, p. 24.

lender and assists transferring the funds from the lenders to the borrowers.[9] A financial intermediary does this by borrowing funds from the lenders-savers and then uses those funds to grant loans to borrowersspenders. The process of indirect finance, using financial intermediaries, is called 'financial intermediation' and up to date is the primary route for channelling funds between lenders and borrowers, and a far more important source of funding for corporations than securities markets.[10]

Financial intermediation is very important because it provides answers to certain 'issues' associated with the existence of financial markets: risk sharing, transaction costs, and information costs. Transaction costs are the time and money spent in carrying out financial transactions and financial intermediaries can help reduce such costs because they have developed expertise in lowering them; their large size allows them to exploit economies of scale and ultimately reduce the cost per transaction in far lower levels than any other individual case.[11] Risk sharing is the process of reducing the investors' exposure to risk, where risk is the uncertainty about the returns investors will earn on their assets.[12] Financial intermediaries perform that function by creating and selling assets with risk characteristics people are comfortable with; financial intermediaries then use the funds they acquire by selling these assets to purchase other assets that may have (far) more risk.[13] The process of risk sharing is also known as 'asset transformation' because in a sense financial intermediaries turn risky assets into safe assets for the investors.[14] Finally, information costs are related with the level of knowledge each party of the transaction has. Often one party knows far more, or far less, compared to its counterparty to make accurate decisions and this inequality is called 'asymmetric information'.[15] Such a lack of information among the parties creates problems in two fronts of the financial system, before the transaction is entered into and after. When the problem occurs before the transaction is called 'adverse selection' and when occurs after the transaction is called 'moral hazard'. Adverse selection occurs in the financial markets when the potential borrowers, who are the most likely to produce an undesirable outcome (adverse outcome) are the ones who most actively seek for borrowed funds and are thus most likely to be selected.[16] On the other side of the transaction, moral hazard occurs when exists the risk that the borrower might engage in activities that are undesirable from the lenders' point of view because they make it less likely that the loaned funds will be paid

9 Ibid., p. 29.
10 Ibid.
11 Ibid., p. 30.
12 Ibid., p. 31.
13 Ibid.
14 Ibid., p. 32.
15 Ibid.
16 Ibid.

back when due.[17] Adverse selection and moral hazard issues can be alleviated by the financial intermediaries which have the resources to gather information and produce assessment regarding the trustworthiness of their borrowers, therefore securing investors' money.

At the epicentre of this complex financial system, tasked to intermediate between borrowers and lenders in order to efficiently perform the financial system's double task, are banks (or 'credit institutions' according to the European Union (EU) terminology).[18] Banks though are not the only entities that intermediate in the financial markets and according to Prof. Mishkin, those entities are organised into three broad categories: a) depository institutions (banks), b) contractual savings institutions, and c) investment intermediaries.[19] For our analysis, we will use this typology and examine those institutions to understand their function. Depository institutions are financial intermediaries that accept deposits from individuals and institutions and make loans and depending on their size can be either banks, with international and/or domestic presence, credit unions and savings banks, depending on each country's tradition, history and of course regulation (legal framework). 'Credit Unions' are smaller financial institutions, cooperative in nature, that are organised around a group: union members, employees of a particular firm and so forth.[20] 'Savings Banks' are financial institutions, usually smaller than banks, albeit this is not always the case, that offer savings deposits and usually provide residential mortgages. Finally, banks are financial intermediaries that raise their funds primarily by accepting various types of deposits and then use these funds to make loans. Banks usually can provide various types of loans, from consumer loans and residential mortgages to large corporate loans (business loans) and government funding, through government bonds purchases. Once again, what type of loans a bank can provide is a matter of legislation – regulation and history since in many countries that business was heavily divided among financial intermediaries, with Japan being a textbook example of such regulation. Unlike normal corporations, what makes banks unique entities (or 'special' according to many commentators and academics) is the structure of their balance sheet, with loans being held on the asset side of

---

17 Ibid., p. 33.

18 For the purposes of the present book, we will use the words 'bank(s)' and 'credit institution(s)' interchangeably and without difference in their meaning. Although we are aware that according to the national legislation and the regulatory framework there might be differences in the definition of a bank/credit institution, we believe that for our purposes these definitional or conceptual differences are not of importance. When this is not the case, and we need to demonstrate any difference between the terms we will explicitly mention it. Therefore, when we use the term 'credit institution' we mean a bank within the meaning of the EU legislation and for all the rest national legislations we will use the term 'bank'.

19 See in F.S. Mishkin, *The Economics of Money, Banking, and Financial Markets*, 7th ed., The Addison-Wesley Series in economics, Boston, Pearson, 2004, p. 34.

20 Ibid., p. 35.

the balance sheet and deposits held on the liability side of the balance sheet.[21] When a bank makes a loan to a home owner or to a legal entity, it is listed as an asset and its value is determined by the borrowers' ability to repay such loans. Moreover, the liability side of a bank's balance sheet is funded mostly through deposits; this amount is a 'loan' from the depositors to the bank and can be withdrawn on demand.[22] At the same time, the bank does not keep depositors' money at a vault; it uses them by providing loans at the asset side of the balance sheet that will mature after several years while the deposits remain redeemable at par and at any time.[23] Therefore, the main justification for protecting the banking system lies on the special role of the banks in relation to the deposits and their role in the payment system. Deposits are more than just a bank liability; they are the means of settling transactions across the world in the everyday life of the people.[24] Given the fact that deposits can be withdrawn at any time, the danger of massive withdrawals by the depositors at the same time (or at the course of certain timeframe) when they sense that the bank is in trouble is what we call a 'bank run'. Bank runs can threaten financial stability and negatively affect not only the bank at stake, but also the entire payment system, thus creating problems for the broader society.[25]

The second category of institutions that intermediate in the financial markets are the 'contractual savings institutions', such as insurance firms and pension funds that acquire funds at periodic intervals on a contractual basis.[26] The basic difference between them and the depository institutions is that they can predict, pretty accurately, how much they will have to pay in future benefits and as a result they do not have to worry much about losing funds and therefore about the liquidity of their assets.[27] Finally, the third category of financial intermediaries is the 'investment intermediaries' and includes finance companies, money market mutual funds (MMMFs), and mutual

[21] See in M. de la Mano, 'Bank Structural Reform and Too-Big-to-Fail', in P.S. Kenadjian and A. Dombret (eds.), *Too Big to Fail III: Structural Reform Proposals - Should We Break Up the Banks?*, Volume 16, Institute for Law and Finance, Berlin, de Gruyter, 2015, p. 52; also in S. Omarova, 'Public Banking as an Institutional Design Project' (2024) 41 *Yale Journal on Regulation*, p. 1139 onwards.

[22] See in M. de la Mano, 'Bank Structural Reform and Too-Big-to-Fail', in P.S. Kenadjian and A. Dombret (eds.), *Too Big to Fail III: Structural Reform Proposals - Should We Break Up the Banks?*, Volume 16, Institute for Law and Finance Series, Berlin, De Gruyter, 2015, p. 52.

[23] Ibid.

[24] Ibid.

[25] When someone makes a payment (using bank accounts), the transaction is settled by moving money between accounts from one bank to another. Therefore, if the value of bank deposits comes into question for any reason, the entire payment system of a country may go down, with unimaginable potential effects.

[26] See in F.S. Mishkin, *The Economics of Money, Banking, and Financial Markets*, 7th ed., The Addison-Wesley Series in economics, Boston, Pearson, 2004, p. 35.

[27] Ibid., p. 37.

funds. Finance companies are usually organised under a parent company to help their operations and raise funds by selling commercial paper, a short-term debt instrument, and by issuing bonds and stocks. They lend such funds to consumers that use them to buy consumer goods.[28] Mutual funds acquire funds by selling shares to many individuals and use the proceeds to invest in diversified portfolios of stocks and bonds. Shareholders can sell (redeem) their shares at any time, but they face one major risk: the value of their shares will be determined by the value of the mutual fund's holdings of securities and since they greatly fluctuate the value of the mutual fund's shares will also greatly fluctuate, leading to risky investments.[29] Finally, MMMFs is a relatively new type of financial intermediary that was created in the US as a result of the interest rate regulation. MMMFs share the same characteristics as mutual funds but also function as a depository institution since they offer deposit type accounts.[30] Like most mutual funds, they acquire funds by selling shares and then use these funds to acquire money market financial instruments that are considered both safe and highly liquid. The interest accrued from these assets is then paid to the shareholders.[31]

The importance of banks in the proper functioning of the financial system is recognised by the fact that financial intermediaries which are not qualified as banks, namely the second and third category, are collectively known as Non-Bank Financial Institutions (NBFIs). Based on this elevated importance of banks it is fully understood why they must be both well-regulated and well supervised; their potential demise would provoke a failure of the entire financial system. Since banks are businesses which also seek earnings and returns for their shareholders, they must be able to fail without putting at risk the entire financial system. Therefore, financial intermediaries and particularly banks must be regulated in order not to put the financial system at any risk. Many rationales have been proposed regarding why banks must be regulated but three reasons should be considered as the most important ones for imposing special regulations on banks:[32]

(a) The first reason has to do with the general safety and soundness of the banks themselves,
(b) The second reason has to do with consumer protection, and
(c) The third reason has to do with broadly interpreted law enforcement interests.

28 Ibid.
29 Ibid.
30 Ibid.
31 Ibid.
32 See in R.S. Carnell, J.R. Macey, G.P. Miller and P. Conti-Brown, *The Law of Financial Institutions*, 7th ed., Aspen Casebook Series, New York, Wolters Kluwer, 2021, p. 100.

Banks' safety and soundness is a generic term that embraces all the necessary (sub) rationales for bank regulations and initiates from the theoretical point that banks offer special services to both economy and society: they offer payment services, they act as financial intermediaries in providing credit and ultimately, they are important players in the conduct of monetary policy by central banks.[33] Moreover, since they turn to be unstable, due to panics, runs and financial distresses, they can jeopardise the smooth function of the above crucial services and therefore are in need of special regulation. The justification for protecting the general safety and soundness of the financial system is based on the role of deposits in the payment system; deposits are not simply a bank liability but the means of settling transactions in the economy.[34] Consumer protection is the second, broad, rationale for special bank regulation. Because banks conduct business with unsophisticated individuals and small businesses, that do not have abundant resources to spend into proper due diligence about the available banking services, there is always the possibility of abusive practices. This lack of sophistication and subsequent lack of information on behalf of banks' customers is the rationale for special consumer protection bank regulation.[35] Finally, banks are often engaged in business with customers that on their side might not have always been engaged in lawful businesses (money laundering activities, terrorism financing operations, etc.). As a result, banks have developed a unique information about these activities and persons, which can be a powerful tool for governments and agencies that are enforcing anti money laundering legislation, criminal legislation and antiterrorist financing legislation.[36]

2 FINANCIAL STABILITY AND FINANCIAL CRISES

On the aftermath of the recent GFC (2007–2009), a growing trend in justifying the need for extensive financial regulation has to do with the preservation of financial stability, which has become the dominant idea and paramount target of any post crisis reforms, both at national and international level.[37] The academic literature regarding financial stability is becoming extremely abundant but still

33 Ibid.

34 See in M. de la Mano, 'Bank Structural Reform and Too-Big-to-Fail', in P.S. Kenadjian and A. Dombret (eds.), *Too Big to Fail III: Structural Reform Proposals - Should We Break Up the Banks?*, Volume 16, Institute for Law and Finance Series, Berlin, De Gruyter, 2015, p. 52.

35 Ibid.

36 Ibid., p. 101.

37 See in M. Khair-Alshaleel and J. Hoekstra, 'A Decade after the Global Financial Crisis: New Regulatory Challenges to Financial Stability' (2021) 32(1) *European Business Law Review*, p. 122.

remains very young. Financial stability appeared as a concern the last 40years when, as a sub product of the financial systems' liberalisation and the trend for further integration into a global financial market generated the first 'problems' regarding the resilience of the financial systems themselves. Despite being of such importance there is not yet a generally accepted agreement on what, precisely, financial stability is, neither in law nor in economics. The lack of a common definition can be justified by the fact that someone can use various parameters and start from very different points when trying to understand and define this concept.[38] Financial stability and economic efficiency have been traditionally associated with the economic welfare of the state and as a result, they have been viewed solely as a privilege of national governments with limited desirability to share it at an international level. Apart from the EU, the importance of financial stability for domestic policy is that it has traditionally been excluded from any international obligations that states wanted to assume, and therefore monetary authorities are not legally constraint from adopting all the necessary measures in order to maintain a stable economy.[39] In terms of finance, national regulators and supervisors are, in principle, legally free to adopt or even ignore the international financial standards and enjoy a great degree of freedom to choose when and how they will intervene when a local banking crisis emerges.[40] Since finance has uncertainty as an endogenous characteristic, it is obvious that this uncertainty will create situations in which instability, at any form, may arise. These events of instability may provoke crises, and these crises may end up being serious or less serious. They may create problems for the participants in the (financial) markets, to entire sectors of the economy or even to the economy of a state. Furthermore, economic history offers many examples where crises arose from bad economic policies on behalf of states which end up causing instability and damage to the financial sector.

Recent events, especially after the liberalisation of international financial markets due to the collapse of the Bretton Woods agreement, showed that

---

38 In the economic science for example we can use numerous parameters to define what will be the content of the financial stability. Prices, indexes, bonds, macroeconomic level, microeconomic level, the level of non-performing loans, the situation of an economy in general (deficits, potential bubbles, etc.) etc. might produce a result that it will be constraint by the parameters that we will use.

39 See in F. Lupo-Pasini, 'Financial Stability in International Law' (2017) 18 *Melbourne Journal of International Law*, p. 2.

40 Since the international regulatory standards are considered as 'soft law', they are not legally binding. Some authors argue that due to the international pressure from the IMF, the World Bank, the international fora and the financial markets, non-compliance with the international regulatory standards has become obligatory, and they tend to be characterized as 'de facto hard law'. See in F. Lupo-Pasini, 'Financial Stability in International Law' (2017) 18 *Melbourne Journal of International Law*, p. 3 and further on the bibliography cited therein.

both stability and instability in the financial system can no longer considered as purely domestic matters, where national authorities do not have to be held accountable for their policy choices because their actions or inactions could have cross border repercussions. To name but a few, the adoption of unsustainable macroeconomic and fiscal policies from national governments that can transmit instability to neighbouring countries and losses to investors; the adoption of national solutions in relation to a banking crisis can lead to export the crisis to the countries where the banks operate, further spreading systemic risks and financial contagion;[41] the adoption of expansionary monetary policies that result in increased liquidity in international financial markets can also cause problems in other countries. These examples help us understand that in an integrated and interconnected financial system, as exists nowadays, the adoption and implementation of domestic fiscal, financial, economic, and regulatory policies by one state can have repercussions in other, neighbouring or not, states. Lupo-Pasini, conceptualises the international law of financial stability as a trade-off between a) domestic stability, b) global stability, and c) international financial integration, with the level of protection that law attributes to each of these priorities directly affecting the protection afforded to the other two.[42]

Reviewing the relevant financial stability literature, Khair-Alshaleel and Hoekstra, concluded that there are two predominant schools of thought trying to define financial stability, with the first trying to define financial instability, and the second trying to define financial stability.[43] According to the first school of thought, defining financial instability should include the potential impact of changes in financial conditions in the real economy while Mishkin suggested that financial instability should also take into account the various information failures that may harm stability and produce instability.[44] The second school of thought tries to define financial stability per se and while does not view financial stability as a static or single condition it stresses in a continuum while other authors focus only on two components of the financial system: institutions and markets.[45] Allen and Wood, tried to define financial stability as not merely the absence of crisis but also as the ability of the financial

---

41 The most illustrative example of nationally adopted measures aiming at resolving a banking crisis were those related to the failure of Fortis Group in the EU In 2008. Belgium, Netherlands and Luxembourg, together with France, failed to efficiently collaborate and take coordinated actions and measures, leading to the demise of the bank and further spreading systemic risk across the EU.

42 See in F. Lupo-Pasini, 'Financial Stability in International Law' (2017) 18 *Melbourne Journal of International Law*, p. 6.

43 See in M. Khair-Alshaleel and J. Hoekstra, 'A Decade after the Global Financial Crisis: New Regulatory Challenges to Financial Stability' (2021) 32(1) *European Business Law Review*, p. 122.

44 Ibid.

45 Ibid., p. 123.

system to absorb any (financial) shocks.[46] This applies not only in a situation where the financial system is not in stability and suffers from a crisis, but also when the financial system appears to work well but is operating in such a way that will produce a crisis or a shock in the future and its ability to perform its tasks will be constrained.[47] Furthermore, Schinasi, in a remarkable effort to define financial stability, proposed a set of key principles that could help further delineate the concept of financial stability. These principles are:

- Financial stability has a very broad meaning and encompasses many different aspects and parameters of finance and financial system. It engulfs the necessary infrastructures, the relevant institutions and of course the financial markets. Participators are both public and private entities, with states issuing bonds and other debt instruments, private companies issuing corporate bonds, shares and other instruments and natural persons (investors or borrowers) transact in various ways.[48]
- Financial stability implies that on the one hand finance efficiently allocates funds and risks, satisfying supply and demand, and on the other hand secures the smooth function of the payment systems throughout the economy, locally or internationally.[49]
- Financial stability implies not only that the financial system has no crisis events but also that it has the capacity to avert, limit, contain and/or to absorb any crisis that erupts or threatens to erupt because of imbalances, bad policy strategies, spillover effects, or any other reason. A crisis can erupt in various ways and not every crisis threatens financial stability. Some authors even argue that crises, up to a certain extent, are events that are welcomed since they provide the market with the opportunity to restore to more realistic values and dispose the least competitive participants increasing efficiency. Financial stability appears thus to have both preventive and corrective mechanisms to restore the smooth functioning of the system.[50]
- The penultimate principle is that financial stability appears 'occurring along a continuum'. An implication of that approach is financial stability is seen as 'spare tire' meaning that maintaining financial stability does not mean that all the components of the system must work at an optimum level.[51]

---

46 See in W.A. Allen and G. Wood, 'Defining and Achieving Financial Stability', Special Paper No. 160, *Special Paper Series*, LSE Financial Markets Group, London School of Economics, London, April 2005, p. 13.

47 See in H.J. Allen, 'What is "Financial Stability"? The Need for Some Common Language in International Financial Regulation' (2014) 45 *Georgetown Journal of International Law*, p. 944.

48 See in G.J. Schinasi, 'Defining Financial Stability', *IMF Working Paper*, WP/04/187, International Monetary Fund, 2004, Washington D.C., p. 6.

49 Ibid.

50 Ibid.

51 Ibid., p. 7.

- Ultimately, is the principle that financial stability can be seen also through the lenses of the real economy consequences Schinasi further believes that 'disturbances in financial markets or at individual financial institutions need not to be considered threats to financial stability if they are not expected to damage economic activity at large'.[52]

Schinasi finally proposed a, more generic, definition of financial stability, this time by not including on it what constitutes a financial system: 'Financial stability is a condition in which an economy's mechanisms for pricing, allocating, and managing financial risks (credit, liquidity, counterparty, market, etc.) are functioning well enough to contribute to the performance of the economy.'[53] This definition though seems to be precarious, as the exclusion of financial system from a financial stability definition creates problems since the financial system plays by far the biggest and most vital role in promoting economic growth. Therefore, a definition of financial stability, without considering the benefits but also the potential dangers arising from the financial system, does not seem to be workable and consistent in the long run. We are of the opinion that Schinasi's proposed approach creates a major misconception and the events during the recent GFC emphatically demonstrated that the international financial system is extremely interconnected and the linkages among the various participants must be taken always into account. The demise of certain US based investment banks created a chained reaction that almost halted any financial activity and led to major economic problems, by derailing national budgets due to subsequent extensive bailouts. Moreover, economic history is full of examples where many times financial stability is closely related to the economic stability and welfare in such a way that, in order to preserve financial stability, we have to take into account and evaluate many other factors and parameters, not necessary directly related to the financial system (housing policy, inflation rate, budget and current account deficits, etc.). Furthermore, a minor event in the financial sector can end up having a major impact and finally create a shock to a fragile economy. Financial stability and stable banking sector are concepts that are highly interrelated since both have a direct impact on the stability of the other. The presence of financial stability enhances the financial intermediation process and the efficient allocation of economic resources through the financial system, where banks play a pivotal role.[54] On the contrary, an unhealthy financial system with impediments and financially unsound players, especially unhealthy banks, is a constant threat to the stability of the financial system and the broader economy. What is, however, ironic is the fact that long periods of financial stability usually led

---

52 Ibid.

53 Ibid., p. 9.

54 See in K. Alexander, '*Principles of Banking Regulation*', Cambridge, Cambridge University Press, 2019, p. 47.

to excessive risk taking by banks, and the recent GFC is a casebook example. Banks took unprecedented risks following a long period of a generally stable financial system where everyone was pointing in the health of individual trees while the forest was unprepared for a disaster of this magnitude.[55]

Prof. Allen, supports that in the post crisis era there is 'some level of amorphous shared understanding of what kind of thing financial stability is about' and that many authors tend to view financial stability in diverging ways:[56] some view financial stability as a 'First World problem',[57] others view it as a matter of global concern, others as a synonymous to the 'too big to fail' issue and others argue for 'more imagination when anticipating the future instabilities'.[58] According to Prof. Allen, since there is no common ground regarding the notion of financial stability, international financial regulation needs to be more preoccupied with the content of the term, since a lack of clarity regarding the goal of financial stability 'undermines efforts to harmonise financial stability regulation'.[59] Two examples confirm Prof. Allen's view regarding the lack of common understanding for the content of financial stability. The first example is related to the Basel Committee on Banking Supervision (BCBS).[60] The Basel III standards, as promulgated by the BCBS, do note that their objective is 'to improve the banking sector's ability to absorb shocks arising from financial and economic stress, whatever the source, thus reducing the risk of spillover from the financial sector to the real economy'.[61] Prof. Allen sees the Basel III language as helpful but further points out that the Basel framework is narrowly focused on the banking sector and does not provide much guidance for the meaning of financial stability with respect to the rest financial system. Similarly, the second example is Article IV of International Monetary Fund's (IMF) Articles of Association, which states that

---

55 Ibid.

56 See in H.J. Allen, 'What is 'Financial Stability'? The Need for Some Common Language in International Financial Regulation' (2014) 45 *Georgetown Journal of International Law*, p. 930.

57 This view comes from John Coffee who believes that major financial nations, and most notably the US and Europe, suffered a lot from the last financial crisis, while other nations with much less sophisticated financial institutions, less developed financial infrastructures, and less developed economies escaped, almost unscathed, from its effects.

58 See in H.J. Allen, 'What is "Financial Stability"? The Need for Some Common Language in International Financial Regulation' (2014) 45 *Georgetown Journal of International Law*, p. 930.

59 Ibid., p. 931.

60 The Basel Committee on Banking Supervision (BCBS) was created on 8 October 1974 based on an informal decision of the Governors of G-10 members' central banks and the Governor of the Swiss National Bank, as a reaction to the systemic impact caused by the collapse of the German bank Herstatt. BCBS aim was to contribute to safeguarding the stability of the international financial system and of the banking system in particular. For a deeper analysis see in C.V. Gortsos, *The Basel Committee on Banking Supervision through the lens of its 2013 Charter*, electronically available at SSRN: https://ssrn.com/abstract=2900107.

61 See in H.J. Allen, 'What is "Financial Stability"? The Need for Some Common Language in International Financial Regulation' (2014) 45 *Georgetown Journal of International Law*, p. 934.

'a principal objective is the continuing development of the orderly underlying conditions that are necessary for financial and economic stability'[62] and again the text does not provide any analysis of what financial stability means.[63] These two basic international financial regulation bodies demonstrate, according to Allen, the lack of clarity on the financial stability's content.

Given the importance of financial stability as a public policy goal, it is important that we reach a consensus at international level about what is meant by international financial stability in order to shape and implement the necessary policies to achieve and maintain it. Furthermore, there may be times where national regulators will be asked, on the basis of international financial regulation, to sacrifice certain national interests for a broader 'financial stability' and such sacrifice will be difficult to explain and accepted in the absence of a credible explanation on what international financial stability actually is.[64] Moreover, reaching a consensus to a common definition of financial stability is a prerequisite for further harmonisation, the *raison d'être* of international financial regulation.[65] National regulators must always take into account that fates of even purely domestic financial institutions are inextricably linked with those of their foreign counterparties and when attempting to address situations of financial instability, they must be prepared that their actions might have possible adverse implications to institutions that operate on a cross border basis and for potential regulatory arbitrage. The same can be also said when national authorities are trying to implement internationally agreed standards, using national tools, and succumbing to national priorities. This situation could create regulatory confusion affecting proper implementation and might also alter the adopted measures *vis-à-vis* the internationally agreed standard.[66]

For all the above-mentioned reasons, we fully support the view that the notion of financial stability must acquire a clear and consistent definition

---

62 Article IV, Articles of Agreement of the International Monetary Fund, Washington D.C., available at: https://www.imf.org/external/pubs/ft/aa/pdf/aa.pdf.

63 See in F. Lupo-Pasini, 'Financial Stability in International Law' (2017) 18 *Melbourne Journal of International Law*, p. 13 and in H.J. Allen, 'What is "Financial Stability"? The Need for Some Common Language in International Financial Regulation', *Georgetown Journal of International Law*, Vol. 45, 2014, p. 934.

64 See in H.J. Allen, 'What is "Financial Stability"? The Need for Some Common Language in International Financial Regulation' (2014) 45 *Georgetown Journal of International Law*, p. 935.

65 International financial regulation arose as a response to national concerns about the globalization of capital flows (globalization of finance) and of several bank failures that occurred in the 1970s and greatly disrupted international finance. See also in C.V. Gortsos, *Introduction to International Financial Law*, Athens, Nomiki Vivliothiki, 2011, and in K. Alexander, '*Principles of Banking Regulation*', Cambridge, Cambridge University Press, 2019 for a more analytical presentation of the topic.

66 See in H.J. Allen, 'What is "Financial Stability"? The Need for Some Common Language in International Financial Regulation' (2014) 45 *Georgetown Journal of International Law*, p. 936.

so that any policies aimed at achieving and safeguarding it must be clearly articulated and founded in predefined steps on how they will be implemented. Furthermore, the adoption of a common understanding of what are the foundational elements of financial stability, how they interact and how they are defined, at an international level will allow states, including competent authorities and stakeholders, to adopt and implement all necessary measures in a coordinated manner. The important question that arises is whether financial stability must be protected by the states and if it is correct to be considered as a public good, and particularly a global public good. The basic concept of public goods was already perceived by thinkers such as David Hume[67] and Adam Smith,[68] who wrote about goods 'which though they may be in the highest degree advantageous to a great society are, however, of such nature that the profits could never repay the expenses to any individual or small numbers of individuals, and which it therefore cannot be expected that any individual or small numbers of individuals should erect'.[69] The concept of public goods was given vibrant economic expression by Paul Samuelson[70] in the 1950s and introduced in the political science by Mancur Olson[71] in the 1960s.

Broadly speaking, economic theory separates public and private goods based on two basic characteristics: a) their non-rivalry, and b) their non-excludability. The non-rivalry characteristic means that one person can use it without diminishing its availability to other potential users. The second characteristic, the non-excludability, means that people cannot be excluded from using it, thus it is available to anyone, whether they contributed to produce it or not.[72] The non-rivalrous and non-excludable characteristics of public goods create a tension because since, on the one hand, they are non-excludable they tend to

67 David Hume (1711–1776) was a Scottish philosopher, historian, economist, and essayist who was best known for his highly influential system of empiricism, philosophical skepticism and metaphysical naturalism.

68 Adam Smith (1723–1790) was a Scottish economist and philosopher who was a pioneer in the field of political economy. Seen by many as the 'father of economics' or the 'father of capitalism', he is primarily known for two classic works: 'The Theory of Moral Sentiments' (1759) and 'An Inquiry into the Nature and Causes of the Wealth of Nations' (1776).

69 See in D. Bodansky, 'What's in a Concept? Global Public Goods, International Law, and Legitimacy' (2012) 23(3) *The European Journal of International Law*, p. 652.

70 Paul Samuelson (1915–2009) was one of the most influential economists of the 20th century. He is often credited with bringing mathematical rigour to economics, helping to transform it into a modern scientific discipline. He became the first American that won the Nobel Memorial Prize in Economic Sciences in 1970 for his contributions to static and dynamic economic theory, including his analysis of how consumers and firms behave and how markets function over time.

71 Mancur Olson (1932–1998) was an influential American economist and political scientist best known for his work on collective action, interest groups, and the relationship between politics and economic performance. His ideas are still used to explain why governments fail, why lobbies dominate, and why some nations decline despite peace and prosperity.

72 See in G. Dellis, *An Economic Analysis of Public Law, Demos and Agora*, Cheltenham, Edward Elgar Publishing, 2021, p. 22.

be under provided and people usually free ride on other peoples' efforts when consuming it. On the other hand, since public goods are non-rivalry, efforts to encourage their production through exclusion of certain people are inefficient because they prevent people from getting the benefit from the consumption of goods, which involve no marginal cost.[73]

As it is obvious, the concept of public goods is an ideal one and both in real world and everyday life, few goods are considered to be fully non-rivalrous and non-excludable, and those that do not meet the non-rivalry and non-excludability test are usually referred as 'impure public goods'.[74] The economic analysis of public law, further distinguishes public goods in two subcategories: a) 'merit goods' and b) 'commons'.[75] Merit goods are not considered as purely public goods. Education is the typical example where it can be a public policy to ensure a common approach but also education can be privately provided through a different set of measures and initiatives. Obviously, such conditions do not effectively cover the needs of the entire society, and the state must intervene to preserve public availability.[76] On the other hand, commons are public goods that may involve some type of rivalry when they are used. A very illustrative example is the use of water from a river through drainage that might deprive other potential users of its use. Based on such an approach it is understood that commons tend to be more prone to abuse and that the state must again intervene to secure their availability to the public. The state may intervene in the market to secure the supply of public goods, particularly those that are not supplied in conditions that meet the excludability and rivalry criteria. Those goods are subject to 'missing market conditions', since no one has the incentive to produce such goods when the others are not obliged to pay a consideration to acquire them.[77] Therefore, public goods are exposed to the free riding phenomenon and their sufficient supply cannot be achieved through private initiative, forcing the state to step in and provide such public goods. Governmental intervention to preserve financial stability, if seen under this lens, also explains why the provision of public goods from the states has

---

73 See in D. Bodansky, 'What's in a Concept? Global Public Goods, International Law, and Legitimacy' (2012) 23(3) *The European Journal of International Law*, p. 653. In the economic theory, the marginal cost is the change in total production cost that comes from creating or producing one additional unit. To calculate the marginal cost, we divide the change in production costs by the change in the produced quantity. The purpose of analysing marginal cost is to determine at what point the producer (a state, a company, etc.) can achieve economies of scale to optimize production and overall operations, meaning that if the marginal cost of producing one additional unit is lower than the per-unit price, the producer has the potential to gain a profit.

74 Ibid.

75 See in G. Dellis, *An Economic Analysis of Public Law, Demos and Agora*, Cheltenham, Edward Elgar Publishing, 2021, p. 22.

76 Ibid.

77 Ibid., p. 75.

been traditionally the optimum field for public intervention; financial stability belongs to this category of public goods, requiring extensive public intervention from the states, mostly in the form of financial regulation.

Financial stability is a multi-level notion, and the interconnectedness of financial markets had rendered financial stability as a national, regional, and international or global public good that cannot be stopped at national borders or limited within enclosed areas.[78] This means that the effects of financial stability, or instability if this the case, usually tend not to be restricted in a certain geographical area but rather expand affecting, for good or for worse, neighbouring states. Certain academics are of the view that the public good nature of financial stability means that it is a potential source of market failure, and it combines the two basic elements of public goods: a) the non-exclusivity, and b) the non-rivalry. The non-exclusive nature of financial stability means that the states/jurisdictions that invest heavily to attain it cannot exclude other states and jurisdictions from enjoying some of the benefits that arise from financial stability.[79] While its non-rivalrous nature means that, its enjoyments by one state/jurisdiction will not reduce the amount available to the other states/jurisdictions.[80] Professor Lastra further argues that based on the previous analysis we can symmetrically construe financial instability as a 'global public bad' which shares the features of lacking rivalry and exclusion.[81] This very interesting approach has the meaning that when the state does not intervene to secure the basic elements of public goods, stability is then turned into instability and becomes a public bad that affects the entire public of a state. Financial instability has, by definition, a terrible impact on the economy, the welfare, and the general well-being of the population of a state, both in the long term and in the short term. Financial instability may be present in several different forms, but the results are more or less the same, with economic contraction and decrease of the economic productivity.

Similarly, and by stretching our analysis a step further, Crockett argues that the various crises erupted in financial systems have clearly demonstrated the existence of 'close linkages between financial stability and the health of the real economy'.[82] In order to support his position Crockett makes a distinction between the notions of 'monetary stability' and 'financial stability'. The first refers to the stability of the general price level within an economy, while the latter refers to the stability of the key institutions and markets that comprise

---

78 See in R.M. Lastra, 'Systemic Risk and Macro-prudential Supervision', in N. Moloney, E. Ferran and J. Payne (eds.), *The Oxford Handbook of Financial Regulation*, Oxford, Oxford University Press, 2015, pp. 310–313.

79 Ibid.

80 Ibid.

81 Ibid., p. 314.

82 See in A. Crockett, 'Why is Financial Stability a Goal of Public Policy?', *Economic Review*, Federal Reserve of Kansas City, Fourth Quarter 1997, p. 5.

the financial system of an economy. Crockett supports that although the two concepts are objects of different policies, 'the linkages between the two are now increasingly recognized'.[83] Despite the fact that Crockett's article is relatively old (written in 1997), the idea behind it is and will always be at the forefront. Financial stability must be seen under a broad lens since it embraces every aspect of economic life, despite being anchored around the parts of the financial system stricto sensu. The interlinkages described by Crockett between the real economy and financial systems are numerous and are constantly evolving since new products, norms, habits are incorporated into the function of the financial system, mostly under the generous support of technological advances.

Within this labyrinth, banks remain special entities, and according to Crockett the instability that will arise in the banking system has 'a greater capacity to generate systemic contagion than difficulties elsewhere in the financial system'.[84] Now, that distinctions between the bank and the non-bank entities are becoming more and more blurred, the potential instability events in the non-bank entities, that are considered as key institutions, can have greater spillover effects and cause significant damages to the financial stability. Moreover, when financial difficulties are becoming more serious, the impact on the Gross National Product (GNP)[85] can be much larger and more direct, whether the authorities decide to support the financial system.[86] The case of several EU Member States that did the same in the recent GFC gives us direct examples of that. Crockett concludes his analysis by proposing measures that will safeguard financial stability, targeted mostly on financial institutions since they have been subjected to a more coherent analysis; reliance on market forces, safety nets and regulation are the necessary tools that will ensure financial stability. Overall, Crockett believes that there is persuasive evidence that 'financial stability provides a favourable environment for efficient resources allocation and more rapid economic growth'.[87] At the same time, he supports that 'instability has been associated with lower levels of saving and investment, fiscal costs and setbacks to GNP' only to conclude that '[i]t is therefore unavoidable that securing stability should be a concern of public policy authorities'.[88] The reasons therefore for which financial stability is a

---

83 Ibid., p. 6.

84 Ibid., p. 7.

85 The 'Gross National Product' (GNP) is a key economic metric that measures the total value of all final goods and services produced by a country's residents in a given period of time (usually one year) regardless of where they are located in the world. While GDP has become the standard for most international comparisons (e.g., by the IMF, World Bank), GNP is still used by some economists and for specific purposes; especially in countries with significant cross-border economic activity.

86 See in A. Crockett, 'Why is Financial Stability a Goal of Public Policy?', *Economic Review*, Federal Reserve of Kansas City, Fourth Quarter 1997, p. 12.

87 Ibid., p. 21.

88 Ibid.

public policy concern and must be treated as a public good have been well established. It is in the state's best interest to treat financial stability as a public good and therefore intervene in order to safeguard it as it has an added value to the entire population and secures the prosperity and economic growth of the national economy.

Finally, the substantial costs imposed on the economies by banking and financial crises demonstrates that the overriding objective of financial and banking regulation should be to safeguard financial stability and build resilient systems and institutions that will be able to absorb shocks, whenever they come from, providing at the same time a sustainable source of credit, payment services and savings products to the broader economy.[89] Alleviating the burden of financial crises and continuing the supply of financial services to the broader economy is definitely a goal of public policy, and financial stability is a public good that allows the state to intervene and adopt certain measures, of administrative nature, aiming to safeguard financial stability. State intervention however, if not properly calibrated, can produce distortions and adverse results that will further interact with financial markets leading to potential instabilities, further externalities, and funds misallocations.[90] During the recent GFC, sovereign states had to intervened in the financial markets to save their banks and in some cases the entire banking sector, playing a role of *Stato salvatore* as described by Prof. Napolitano.[91] This role required many times difficult manoeuvres within tight constitutional and administrative boundaries that in many cases led to lengthy judicial proceedings from stakeholders that felt that the state was expanding ferociously in the fields of private economy.[92] The interpretation of their powers from the states, under the constitutional lens, was and in many cases still is, among the most important side effects of the post-financial crisis state interventions. The powers attributed to the states, either through independent authorities such as the central banks or through core state entities such as the Ministries of finance, came under fire during the stress period of the financial turmoil. How the states applied such powers evolved alongside the turmoil stages and in some cases offered salvation while in other cases offered a coffin for prestigious institutions. Prof. Posner describes remarkably the saga between the vested powers that the US Department of Treasury utilised in various ways to provide support to

[89] See in K. Alexander, *Principles of Banking Regulation*, Cambridge, Cambridge University Press, 2019, p. 47.

[90] Ibid., p. 48.

[91] See in G. Napolitano, 'Il nuovo Stato salvatore: strumenti di intervento e assetti istituzionali', *Giornale di diritto amministrativo*, N. 11, 2008, pp. 1083–1094.

[92] For a deeper analysis on the litigation related matters of the bailout programs in the US see in E.A. Posner, *Last Resort, The Financial Crisis and the Future of Bailouts*, Chicago, The University of Chicago Press, 2018.

the entire economy, in the name of financial stability.[93] In a similar pattern, the US Federal Reserve (the Fed), which used ambiguity on its decisions when the market was in need of stability and certainty more than anything else, its decisions were under heavy criticism for not helping during the acute phase of the turmoil and contributing to the general calamity by failing to prevent the crisis. The legal basis that each time was adopted, or not, especially on the Fed-Lehman saga, demonstrated the blurred lines between financial stability as a public good and state intervention as a tool to safeguard it.

Ultimately, another important aspect of state intervention is the interaction of the measures adopted by the governments and their approval or dismissal by the judicial authorities. Although a detailed analysis of the judicial review of the measures adopted in the crisis era is well beyond the scope of the present book, this interplay deserves a few words. It is true that during the recent GFC, the Courts had a limited role to play, since the timely adoption of state intervention measures was not necessarily in tandem with a proper judicial review that always requires time. During the acute phase of the turmoil, time was and always will be much of an issue since any delays could have devastating effects in the financial markets affecting not only domestic markets but also global ones. Courts usually do not have the chance to review ex-ante some of the various measures that states put forward during the acute phase of the turmoil. Furthermore, the discussion of whether these decisions that aim at safeguarding financial stability and allow for state interventions should be reviewed by the national Courts, and to what extent, is generating hot debates and shall be addressed under certain theoretical and normative parameters which are not examined herewith.

Having defined, or at least attempted to define, what financial stability is and why it is viewed as a public good, we now turn to examine the nature of financial crises. The basic theoretical approach towards financial crises was shaped by the so-called 'Monetarists', a school of thought that linked financial crises with banking panics. Monetarists viewed banking panics as events that contract money supply and thus create economic contraction in the aggregate economy.[94] On the opposite side of the theoretical pendulum were standing Prof. Minsky[95] and Kindleberger[96] who supported a broader

---

93 Ibid.

94 See in F.S. Mishkin, 'Anatomy of a financial crisis', Working Paper No. 3934, *NBER Working Paper Series*, National Bureau of Economic Research (NBER), December 1991, p. 1.

95 Hyman P. Minsky (1919–1996) was an American economist, professor of economics and a distinguished scholar at the Levy Economics Institute of Bard College. His research attempted to provide an understanding and explanation of the characteristics of financial crises, which he attributed to swings in a potentially fragile financial system.

96 Charles P. Kindleberger (1910–2003) was an American economic historian and author. His 1978 book *Manias, Panics, and Crashes*, about speculative stock market bubbles, was reprinted in 2000 after the dot-com bubble. He is well known for developing the

view of what a financial crisis is, with either involving sharp declines in asset prices, failures of financial and non-financial firms, disruptions in foreign exchange markets, deflations or disinflations or a combination of all of these.[97] However, according to Prof. Mishkin, both the above-mentioned economic theories suffer from certain inconsistencies and financial crises could be better explained by bridging the two theories with the problems that arise from asymmetric information situations. Consequently, Mishkin's theory suggests that financial crises are the result of asymmetric information between the participants in the financial markets and proposes the following definition: 'A financial crisis is a disruption to financial markets in which adverse selection and moral hazard problems become much worse, so that financial markets are unable to efficiently channel funds to those who have the most productive investment opportunities. A financial crisis then results in the inability of financial markets to function efficiently, which leads to a sharp contraction in economic activity.'[98] Prof. Mishkin further describes five factors that can lead to substantial worsening of adverse selection and moral hazard in financial markets, creating the conditions for the financial crisis to occur. These factors are:[99]

(1) Increases in interest rates:
Increases in interest rates will result in increased adverse selection problems and lenders will no longer be willing to lend. This will possibly lead to a steep decline in credit supply, which will lead to a substantial decline in investment and aggregate economic activity.[100]

(2) Stock market declines:
A sharp decline in the stock market, like a stock market crash situation, can lead to increased adverse selection and moral hazard problems in the financial markets due to the large decline in the market value of firms' net worth.[101] This will disincentivise lenders to expand credit because of the loss of the firms' net worth that plays a role similar to that of a collateral, providing less protection to the lenders, causing in turn investment and aggregate output to decline.[102]

(3) Increases in uncertainty:
Increased uncertainty in financial markets, due to potentially various reasons (failure of a prominent financial or non-financial firm, recession, stock

'hegemonic stability theory', arguing that a hegemonic power was needed to maintain a stable international monetary system.

97 See in F.S. Mishkin, 'Anatomy of a financial crisis', Working Paper No. 3934, *NBER Working Paper Series*, National Bureau of Economic Research (NBER), December 1991, p. 1.

98 Ibid., p. 7.

99 Ibid., p. 8.

100 Ibid.

101 Ibid.

102 Ibid.

market crash, crisis events such as war, geopolitical turmoil, etc.) will lead to increased adverse selection problems since lenders will be substantially hindered from screening out good from bad borrowers. Therefore, they will be more unwilling to lend, leading to declined investment and aggregate activity.[103]

(4) Banking panics:
A financial crisis that will result in a bank panic[104] and the simultaneous failure of many banks will reduce the amount of financial intermediation that is undertaken by banks, thus leading to a decline in investment and aggregate economic activity.[105] A bank panic might also lead to higher interest rates because the panic results in decreased liquidity since the supply of funds to borrowers has been reduced.[106]

(5) Unanticipated declines in the price levels:
Unanticipated declines in the aggregate price level also decrease the firms' net worth because debt payments are, usually, contractually fixed in nominal terms, the unanticipated decline in price level raises the value of the firms' liabilities in real terms but does not raise the real value of the firms' assets.[107] The sharp decline in price levels causes a decline in real net worth and simultaneously increases adverse selection and moral hazard problems with the same results mentioned above.

The asymmetric information theory can also provide a strong rationale for the existence and operation of the discount window by central banks including the Fed.[108] The discount window operations can be used to channel funds (liquidity) directly to the sector that is most in need of it and effectively complement the open market operations by the Fed and other central banks, aiming at reducing the effects of a financial crisis.

---

103 Ibid., p. 9.

104 According to Prof. Mishkin, the source of a bank panic is again asymmetric information since the depositors, out of fear for their deposits' safety, will withdraw them from the banking system causing a contraction in loans and a multiple contraction in deposits that ultimately lead banks to fail. Asymmetric information is critical in this process because depositors will rush to withdraw their deposits from both solvent and insolvent institutions since they simply cannot distinguish between the two. The result of banking panics is that they reduce the available funds for banks to provide loans and increase the cost of financial intermediation causing reduction in investments and decline in aggregate economic activity.

105 See in F.S. Mishkin, 'Anatomy of a financial crisis', Working Paper No. 3934, *NBER Working Paper Series*, National Bureau of Economic Research (NBER), December 1991, p. 9.

106 Ibid.

107 Ibid., p. 10.

108 Ibid., p. 18.

3 TOOLS FOR ENSURING FINANCIAL STABILITY

Before the recent GFC, both regulators and supervisors were of the view that financial health of the individual firms was enough to secure the safety and soundness of the entire financial system. Better known as the 'composition fallacy', this micro-prudentially oriented approach contended that safety and soundness of any financial system was the aggregate soundness of all its participant institutions and was not taking into account the interconnection level that had been increased among the participants in the financial system and the systemic risk that was accumulated in the system.[109] Micro-prudential regulation and supervision of all parts of the system would sum up to regulation and supervision of the entire system itself, but as Prof. Hockett points out, 'a financial system is more than the sum of its parts' since it also embraces the relations that are developed among its various parts and are mediated through the use of various transactional infrastructures and various, often complex, species of financial claim that institutions and individuals issue to one another.[110] Currently, regulators and supervisors across the world have at their disposal more sophisticated tools that help them preserve financial stability and ensure that the financial system will continue to operate at an optimum level carrying out its intermediation role. The available tools are both of macroeconomic and microeconomic nature and most of them can be applied at the simultaneously at both levels by simply changing their regulatory perimeter.

3.1. Macro-Prudential Tools

The macro-prudential policy must encompass tools for the entire financial system, including areas that usually tend to fall outside the regulatory radar, since the NBFI entities, formerly known as 'shadow banking system', the much necessary market infrastructures, the market participants and financial instruments can all pose significant systemic threats to the domestic and transnational financial stability.[111] Through the adoption of macro-prudential policies regulators aim to tame the two dimension problems that systemic risk

---

[109] See in R.M. Lastra, 'Systemic Risk and Macro-prudential Supervision', in N. Moloney, E. Ferran and J. Payne (eds.), *The Oxford Handbook of Financial Regulation*, Oxford, Oxford University Press, 2015, p. 310. See also in S.L. Schwarcz, 'Systemic Risk' (2008) 97 *Georgetown Law Journal*, pp. 193–249.

[110] See in R. Hockett, 'The Macroprudential Turn: From Institutional "Safety and Soundness" to Systematic "Financial Stability" in Financial Supervision' (2015) 9(2) *Virginia Law and Business Review*, p. 207.

[111] See in R.M. Lastra, 'Systemic Risk and Macro-prudential Supervision', in N. Moloney, E. Ferran and J. Payne (eds.), *The Oxford Handbook of Financial Regulation*, Oxford, Oxford University Press, 2015, p. 317.

poses: a) the 'time dimension', and b) the 'cross sectional dimension'. The first is the evolution of systemic risk through time and must be counter-faced with measures that reduce procyclicality,[112] while the second dimension is the distribution of risk in the financial system at any given moment of time. In the later, the aim of macro-prudential measures is to limit the concentration of systemic risk which might occur either because of the simultaneous exposure of multiple financial intermediaries in risks from homogeneous exposures, or due to the interconnectedness of such financial entities, especially if they are off systemic importance.[113] The set of measures that have been developed by the financial regulators for macro-prudential regulation purposes has been known as 'the toolkit', which when supplemented by necessary adaptations in the agencies that apply these tools can be an extremely resourceful and powerful toolkit.[114] The macro-prudential policy toolkit comprises the following tools:

(i) Cross sectoral leverage ceilings (LTV, DTI, and Margin Requirements):[115] The first tool aims to close the spread between borrowing costs and capital gains that make the participation in asset price bubbles financially rational for investors. The point is to make difficult the borrowing for purely speculative reasons and one way to succeed is to limit the amount of leverage that a borrowing buyer can assume by requiring more collateral and/or down payment or margin be supplied by borrowers.[116] Similar to margin requirements in securities transactions are maximum 'Loan to Value' (LTV)[117] and 'Debt (Service) to Income' (DTI)[118] ratios that will

[112] See in C.V. Gortsos, *Introduction to International Financial Law*, Athens, Nomiki Vivliothiki, 2011, p. 90.

[113] Ibid., p. 91.

[114] See in R. Hockett, 'The Macroprudential Turn: From Institutional "Safety and Soundness" to Systematic "Financial Stability" in Financial Supervision' (2015) 9(2) *Virginia Law and Business Review*, p. 219.

[115] Ibid.

[116] Ibid.

[117] The 'Loan-to-Value' (LTV) is a financial term used to express the ratio of a loan to the value of an asset purchased, typically used in the context of mortgages. It is an important measure for both lenders and borrowers because it helps assess the risk associated with a loan. If the LTV is high (i.e. above 85–90%), this may indicate a higher risk loan, and borrowers might be required to make a larger down payment or pay for mortgage insurance. To the contrary, a low LTV (such as 60% or 70%) is typically seen as safer for the lender and might qualify the borrower for better loan terms, such as lower interest rates.
While LTV is commonly used in mortgages, it can also apply to other types of loans, such as auto loans or business loans, where the asset being financed is used as collateral. In these cases, the ratio still indicates the amount of financing relative to the value of the asset.

[118] The 'Debt Service to Income' (DSI) ratio, also known as 'Debt-to-Income Ratio' (DTI), is a financial metric used to assess a borrower's ability to manage monthly debt payments relative to their income. It measures the percentage of a borrower's income that goes toward servicing debt, and it is commonly used by lenders when evaluating loan applications, especially for mortgages. From a risk assessment perspective, a higher DSI suggests that a borrower is spending a significant portion of their income on debt, which could limit their ability to manage other financial obligations or cope with unexpected expenses. On

restrict credit supply, together with tighter 'Margin Requirements'.[119] These types of leverage ceilings can be used as macro-prudential tools and can be effective also at cross sectoral level while being constantly recalibrated according to the economic state.[120]

(ii) Cross sectoral credit and credit growth ceilings:[121]
Similar to the first tool, but with more direct effects, is the placement of direct credit and credit growth limits aiming to increase the borrowing costs and reduce capital gains by simply imposing upper bounds on lending capacity, independently of capital buffers and reserves.[122]

(iii) Cross sectoral reserve and capital buffer requirements:[123]
The third tool is the use of reserve and capital buffer requirements that also have the same scope with the first two tools, to increase the borrowing costs for capital gains of speculative nature. Although such measure is of micro-prudential nature, because individual firms are required to hold buffers to prevent liquidity crises from counterparty failures, when used and applied system wide can be considered also for the macro-prudential level.[124] These requirements will naturally limit the amount of credit that institutions will extend and funds that would normally supplied to the economy will either be kept internally as reserves or will be limited by how much capital can be raised from equity and subordinated debt holders.[125] The level of such requirements can be also countercyclically adjusted according to the state of the economy, and be increased in boom period or reduced in periods of stress.

(iv) Cross sectoral liquidity *minima* and maturity mismatch *maxima*:[126]
This tool will prevent liquidity crises from morphing into solvency crises; a danger rooted in the maturity transformation function of the financial

---

the contrary, a lower DSI indicates that a borrower has more disposable income relative to their debt payments, signalling a lower financial risk. The DSI ratio considers all types of monthly debt obligations (mortgage or rent payments, auto loans, student loans, credit card payments, personal loans and any other recurring debt).

119 The term 'Margin requirements' refer to the minimum amount of capital that an investor must deposit with a broker to open and maintain a leveraged position in financial markets. The specific margin requirements can vary depending on:
- the type of account (cash or margin),
- the financial instrument (stocks, options, futures, forex, etc.),
- the regulatory body (e.g. FINRA, SEC, CME, etc.), and
- the broker's internal policies.

120 See in R. Hockett, 'The Macroprudential Turn: From Institutional "Safety and Soundness" to Systematic "Financial Stability" in Financial Supervision' (2015) 9(2) *Virginia Law and Business Review*, p. 220.

121 Ibid., p. 221.

122 Ibid.

123 Ibid.

124 Ibid.

125 Ibid., p. 222.

126 Ibid., p. 223.

institutions and particularly banks. Although by nature a micro-prudential measure it can be also used system wide by imposing liquidity minima and maturity mismatch maxima upon particular financial institutions, and especially banks.[127] The idea behind that tool is to limit the vulnerability arising from the maturity mismatch by requiring either that some portion of the institutions' assets to be kept in liquid (cash) or in readily liquid form (such as the US Treasury securities), that the degree of maturity mismatch between assets and liabilities be kept at sufficiently low level or a combination of both measures.[128]

(v) Cross sectoral dynamic and countercyclical provisioning:[129]
All the tools elaborated above can be used simultaneously both at macro-prudential and micro-prudential level. Thus, they can be used not only system wide but also countercyclically system wide in order to 'lean against the wind' and 'take away the punchbowl exactly when the party is getting good'.[130] The regulator can use all the above-mentioned measures by adjusting them according to the phase of the economy (boom or slump) so that can effectively control financial institutions from assuming unnecessary risks. Moreover, the idea of 'dynamic provisioning' suggests that institutions must set aside capital during the 'fat years' to provide for the subsequent 'lean years' and that approach can be used for the feeding of the deposit insurance system by member banks, according to the economic state.[131]

(vi) Cross sectoral surveillance and data collection:[132]
The need for robust and adequate cross-sectoral data collection and surveillance is of paramount importance. In several jurisdictions, supervision and regulation is separated across sectors of the financial spectrum and access to quality data is considered as *conditio sine qua non* for the efficiency of supervision and regulation of the financial sector. Since distinct sectoral regulators exist and must coordinate their actions, it seems that they would need access to the same data sets of information in order all of them to have the same picture in front of them and stay on the same page and moreover, they would be able to understand that any possible actions in one sector could have destabilising effects on other sector(s).[133] Therefore, centralisation of information (through efficient data collection and data sharing) is extremely important in regulatory systems that divide responsibility over multiple regulators, with the US and the EU being the most brilliant examples of such systems. The next step is of course the close

[127] Ibid.
[128] Ibid., p. 224.
[129] Ibid., p. 225.
[130] Ibid.
[131] Ibid., p. 226.
[132] Ibid., p. 227.
[133] Ibid.

collaboration of such sectoral authorities in a way that avoids overlapping situations and allows for prompt decision making and action taking when stress emerges.

(vii) Size mitigation:[134]

The tool of size mitigation is closely related with the perception that some financial institutions have become 'too … to fail'. Either too big, too important, too complex, or too interconnected to fail, such institutions forced taxpayers to bail them out during the last global financial crisis, out of fear that their potential demise would have created far worse problems and could had further aggravated the global turmoil.[135] The macro-prudential toolkit includes measures that are specifically designed to deal with such fears and try to eliminate the 'too … to fail' problem. Among those measures, the most important are the orderly resolution related measures and simple measures that try to downsize these institutions. Moreover, another measure is to label such institutions with a special designation (such as 'Systemically Important Financial Institutions' – SIFIs) that will automatically mean a special regulatory regime with increased prudential requirements.[136]

3.2. *Micro-Prudential Tools*

The micro-prudential toolkit applies at a firms' level regulation and is preoccupied with the individual institutions' safety and soundness. All the previously mentioned macro-prudential tools could be also used at a micro-prudential level, tailor made to institutions' individual needs. Therefore, the available tools for regulators and supervisors are almost the same and both can be familiar with the tools, since the only change is the regulatory perimeter within which the tool is applied. Therefore, it is unnecessary to analyse again the previous tools since the rationale behind them is the same and the only change is the level/perimeter of their application. What though deserves to be distinctively referred are two measures that are primarily micro-prudential by nature: a) the on-site examination of banks, and b) the stress tests and asset quality reviews (AQRs). The second measure is of particular nature since it is primarily used in a system wide level, but its results are assessed individually at firms' level.

Bank supervisors use two principal methods for assessing a bank's financial condition: a) on-site examination and b) off-site monitoring. An on-site examination is conducted by supervisors in the banks' premises and facilitates obtaining information beyond what the bank itself reports through the data

---

134 Ibid.

135 Ibid.

136 Ibid., p. 228.

collection requirements (supervisory reporting). Examiners can delve into specific bank data constructively assessing all the parameters of the business model, the quality of loans and other assets, looking for any abuses or frauds and understand better the banks' business model and associated risks.[137] On-site examinations (or inspections according to some jurisdictions), are complemented by off-site monitoring that is achieved mostly through data submissions that cover a large area of banks' activities. Supervisors use this data to monitor, usually on a quarterly basis, the banks' financial health and decide to conduct on-site examinations when further information is needed.

The second important tool is the stress testing procedure, and especially after the recent GFC, stress tests have become another tool of prudential regulation. Stress tests are procedures based on fictitious but plausible scenarios that simulate adverse economic conditions and are used to assess the ability of banks to withstand such negative events that are severe yet must be plausible. The idea behind stress tests is to create and develop a model of the bank, input stress scenarios into that model and then evaluate how, based on that model, the bank will react and perform in various future states of the world.[138] The stress tests are expected to provide regulators with 'forward-looking' information that will be useful for banking supervision, assessing banks' capital adequacy and risk profiles. Moreover, stress tests are also expected to provide support in the improvement of banks' internal assessments of their capital adequacy, and their overall capital planning. Scenarios of the stress tests are updated every year in order to reflect the current trends in financial markets and account for the supervisors' view of the current and near future economic conditions.[139] It goes without saying that when stress tests are performed on a system wide basis can also be considered a macro-prudential tool, but the results of the tests are used to assess the banks' financial health individually, usually through the established supervisory review processes, thereby ultimately acting as a micro-prudential tool. The Asset Quality Review (AQR) is one of the most important tools in determining the overall condition of a bank. The primary factor/parameter affecting overall asset quality is the quality of the loan portfolio and the credit administration program. Loans typically comprise a majority of a bank's assets and carry the greatest amount of risk to their capital. Securities may also comprise a large portion of the banks' assets and contain significant risks. Moreover, other items which can impact banks' asset quality are real estate related assets, other assets, off-balance sheet items and, to a lesser extent, cash and due from accounts, and premises and fixed assets. Prior to assigning an asset quality rating to the banks' assets, several factors should

---

[137] See in R.S. Carnell, J.R. Macey, G.P. Miller and P. Conti-Brown, *The Law of Financial Institutions*, 7th ed., Aspen Casebook Series, New York, Wolters Kluwer, 2021, p. 318.

[138] Ibid., p. 238.

[139] Ibid., p. 239.

be considered and be reviewed within the context of any local and regional conditions that might have an impact on bank performance. Furthermore, any systemic weaknesses, as opposed to isolated problems, should be given appropriate consideration when determining the overall asset quality. The examiners should never look at things in a vacuum, instead noting how the current level/status of assets could be possibly affected by adverse events and expected performance.

Both stress tests and AQRs can be applied both micro and macro-prudentially, since they can be used either to examine a particular bank/institution or to examine the health of the entire banking/financial system. Usually, the AQRs are targeted at specific institutions and the stress tests are used as a system wide tool but this should not be taken as written in stone, as flexibility and ad hoc use of the tools when required is usually a sign of active supervision. The purpose of these tools is to provide accurate information to both supervisors and regulators and thus should be used accordingly, under the specific circumstances.

3.3. *The Tool of International Cooperation*

The perseverance of financial stability does not rely solely on domestic actors as the level of interconnection in the current system's structure can transmit turmoil and propagate crises to neighbouring financial systems that in principle appear to be healthy. International cooperation plays a critical role in safeguarding financial stability, especially in an increasingly interconnected and globalised financial system. Given the spillover effects that could be produced from events of financial instability and turmoil, we understand how important the efficient cooperation and coordination among regulators and supervisors at every level, both domestic and international, is. International cooperation matters for financial stability for three main reasons:

(a) To prevent cross border spillovers.
As financial crises can start in one country and quickly spill over to other countries, both neighbouring and non-neighbouring, cooperation at international level ensures that there is an 'early warning' system, the responses from the competent authorities are coordinated and there are efforts to contain the contagion.

(b) Global presence of financial institutions.
As banks and other NBFIs operate internationally, with significant cross border activity and global presence, financial regulation and supervision should match effectively this footprint to prevent the regulatory arbitrage ('forum shopping' for the weakest regulatory frameworks) and ensure that there is in place a consistent risk management practice from the financial firms.

(c) Monitoring systemic risk.
Systemic risks[140] require collective monitoring efforts and joint action to manage. International cooperation should be focused on ensuring that these steps are always followed.

The key mechanisms through which the countries cooperate at international level can be summarised as following: a) regulatory coordination, with the aim to further harmonise banking, insurance and capital markets regulations; b) information sharing practices, in order for the competent authorities to have access to accurate financial data, stress tests results and other crises signalling information;[141] and c) joint crisis management practices, that during turmoil and crises countries will be able to act in a coordinated and coherent manner, thereby taking measures that will be based on common understanding of the situation and the solutions needed.

The key international institutions involved in ensuring an appropriate level of international cooperation are the IMF, the Financial Stability Board (FSB),[142] the Bank for International Settlements (BIS) and at the pinnacle of the structure are the political bodies of G7, G10 and G20 summits offering high level political coordination and decision-making during crises. Equally important are the Organization for Economic Cooperation and Development (OECD), the Word Bank Group and the various regional development banks.[143] Currently, the BCBS, within the BIS structure, is the major international forum that promotes international cooperation in the field of banking supervision and produces international, soft law standards that form the core, internationally

---

140 For an excellent analysis on the topic of systemic risk see in the seminal journal article of S.L. Schwarcz, 'Systemic Risk' (2008) 97 *The Georgetown Law Journal*, pp. 193–249.

141 Information sharing practices, in theory, can be a powerful tool in the hands of competent authorities, since they will have access to valuable data and they will be able to conduct various analyses with more accurate data. In practice though, access to such information can sometimes be 'tricky' as it can reveal malpractices on behalf of home-host authorities and further complicate the relations among competent authorities, particularly in the cases of financial firms that have a cross-border presence. Stress tests' results can also perplex relations among national authorities as they can reveal a different picture from is what is perceived with respect to the health of financial firms. Therefore, we believe that there must be a mutual trust among the national authorities as well as the same 'level of understanding' of how the international financial regulation should work for the information sharing to be a truly powerful tool. This mutual trust is usually embedded through bilateral and multilateral Memoranda of Understanding (MoU).

142 Within the FSB's structure there is the Standing Committee on Supervisory and Regulatory Cooperation (SRC), and it has, among others, the responsibility to 'assisting in managing the coordination issues that arise among supervisors and regulators on issues that have cross-sector implications and raise any need for policy development required to close regulatory gaps that pose risk to financial stability'. See on FSB's website: https://www.fsb.org/about/organisation-and-governance/.

143 For an excellent analysis on the international and supranational level of coordination with respect to financial regulation see in C.V. Gortsos, *Introduction to International Financial Law*, Athens, Nomiki Vivliothiki, 2011.

accepted, prudential banking regulations. International cooperation can be also seen as a special tool that helps to ensure financial stability through exchange of information, ideas, policies, practices, and decision-making processes that can be used across jurisdictions, aiming at streamlining regulatory and supervisory practices. Moreover, frequent exchange of best practices and knowledge results in better coordination among both supervisors and regulators, translated into better outcomes when crises are at gates.

Several examples from the recent GFC, but more importantly from the March 2023 banking turmoil, confirm our view. The spillover and the subsequent bank run that occurred in the less significant US banks led to the demise of relatively big banks which appeared to enjoy a successful and profitable business model. Moreover, the demise of the Swiss giant Credit Suisse and the need for state intervention on behalf of the Swiss government further demonstrated how crises can be transmitted and become cross border at a fast pace. More importantly though, they demonstrated why cooperation and coordination between the competent authorities is a critical parameter of financial stability. Especially after the recent GFC, as well as during the March 2023 banking turmoil, cooperation, coordination and information sharing among institutional players of the financial regulatory system has been enhanced and supported by the relevant international fora. The aim was, and remains yet, to promote cooperation and coordination among competent authorities (including central banks, supervisors and regulators) in overseeing international banking activity.[144]

3.4. *The Tool of Structural Reforms*

Another tool that can be used to safeguard financial stability is the tool of structural measures/reforms or broadly known as 'structural regulation measures'. Structural regulation was aggressively reemerged after the recent GFC, where various politicians, academics and regulators promoted it as a solution to the TBTF problem. The crisis demonstrated how large, multi-functional financial and banking institutions, that have adopted the universal banking model, could fail catastrophically in managing their risks and the associated failure by regulators and supervisors to impose market discipline on their management, shareholders, and creditors.[145] The TBTF problem imposed a heavy burden on public finances since those institutions were bailed out by the taxpayers.

Structural regulation measures are of a special nature because they can be utilised both individually, at a firm level, but also system wide, covering the

[144] See in K. Alexander, *Principles of Banking Regulation*, Cambridge, Cambridge University Press, 2019, p. 64.

[145] Ibid., p. 208.

entire financial system. Therefore, structural reforms are of macro-prudential nature when applied to all firms that operate across one state/jurisdiction (system wide application) and of micro-prudential nature when applied to a specific firm, a bank/financial institution in terms of the present book. At the micro-prudential level, structural regulation requires from that specific bank to adopt certain measures and change the way bank operates or restrict its access to certain activities. Structural reform measures can vary also across the period of their implementation. They can be imposed before the resolution of a bank, in good times, as a preventive measure but also after the resolution, requiring the bank to stop certain activities or to transfer them to another entity, or to impose similar requirements.

4 STRUCTURAL REFORMS: AN IN-DEPTH ANALYSIS

Structural reforms or structural regulation actually means 'breaking the banks', because essentially such measures separate/divide banks so they cannot offer all the financial services under a single roof ('financial supermarket's' business model). Structural regulation rationale starts from the point that certain financial activities are perceived as riskier compared to others and therefore banks, that accept deposits and participate in a deposit guarantee scheme, thereby enjoying a certain funding advantage, cannot engage in such risky activities. It is widely believed that if a bank has a financial supermarket business model and offers the full spectrum of available financial services, operating thus as a 'universal bank', it is jeopardising depositors' funds by engaging in capital markets activities that require to expose herself in unacceptable levels of risk. Regulators and supervisors are adopting legislation that will require from the bank to either not engage in certain activities that are deemed as risky, or to create such a corporate structure that will prevent the bank from a) jeopardise retail deposits, b) reduce the incentives to use deposits as funding source for speculative activities in the capital markets, and c) if fail, certain crucial and vital banking activities will continue to be available to the public, thereby reducing the need for bail out by the taxpayers.

Two of the trading activities that are of relevance regarding structural reforms regulation are: proprietary trading and market making. Proprietary trading can best be understood as the 'purchase and sale of financial instruments with the intent to profit from the difference between the purchase price and the sale price'.[146] This practically means that a bank uses its own money to invest in financial instruments and puts its own money at risk to profit from

[146] See in K. Oppolzer, *Ring-Fencing in Europe, The EU's Bank Structural Reform and a Legal Comparative Look at National Legislation in Europe's Three Financial Capitals*, Baden-Baden, Nomos Verlagsgesellschaft mbH & Co. KG, 2019, p. 47.

its investments. Market making is a trading activity that can be understood as the purchasing and selling of financial instruments by standing ready to trade for their own account or for a client's order, whenever such an order arrives.[147] A market maker could be characterised as a central counterparty which buys financial instruments at a certain price and sells them at another. A buyer may buy financial instruments at the market makers' ask price, while a seller may sell financial instruments at the market makers' bid price. Market makers are usually compensated by the spread between bid-ask, and they offer the so-called 'immediacy' to clients, i.e. 'the ability to immediately absorb a client's demand or supply of an asset into its own inventory' as it allows them to buy or sell immediately.[148]

Currently, the known approaches are three: a) the US approach, with the so called 'Volcker Rule', b) the UK approach with the 'ring-fencing' requirements, and c) the EU approach, as it was presented with the Liikanen Report in 2012. With respect to the later, the European Commission took over from the Liikanen Report's conclusions and presented a legislative proposal slightly amended compared to the 2012 Report. Ultimately, for reasons that we will explore later, the EU proposal failed to become a regulation, and some Member States decided to enact their own structural reforms (France, Germany, and Belgium) but without being successfully imitated by the rest. Regulation through structural reforms could impose two types of requirements: the 'hard requirements', and the 'soft requirements'.[149]

4.1. Hard Requirements

Hard requirements are those imposed either by law or by a supervisor's binding decision, with an effect similar to that of a law (usually an administrative act). Hard requirements have predefined content, specific form and must be adopted as such, leaving to the bank small, if at all, room for manoeuvring regarding their implementation. Therefore, structural regulation of that type is very precise as to what is required, and banks must comply with such requirements. Currently, and to the best of our knowledge, hard requirements are further grouped into the following categories, according to the nature of the requirements they impose.

---

147 Ibid.

148 Ibid., p. 49.

149 Currently, the academic literature does not present structural reforms under the separation in hard and soft requirements. We believe that although this separation has nothing to do with the meaning or the concept of the structural reforms' typology is a step forward to better understand the nature of those measures, given the difference in severity of their application and in the result, they have (i.e. is very different to impose internal firewalls than introduce strict requirements the ban certain activities).

4.1.1 Restrictions on Activities

This type of structural regulation imposes restrictions on the activities that banks may engage in. In other words, regulators define ex ante, which are the bank eligible activities, or it can be the opposite, defining which the bank ineligible activities are. Restrictions on banking activities are strict prohibitions that exclude activities from being offered by certain entities, usually banks. Therefore, the crucial point is to define the exact meaning of a 'bank' to find which entities are falling within the regulatory perimeter. The most illustrative example of such regulation is the so-called 'Volcker Rule', adopted in the US, that bans proprietary trading and hedge funds sponsoring for the banks that are participating in the federal deposit insurance scheme.

4.1.2 Restrictions on the Bank Entity's Structure

Such requirements impose restrictions on the way the bank entity is structured, requiring that certain activities must be performed by specific entities, usually through standalone entities under the holding company but within the same group or through a subsidiary of a bank or other group entity. This obligation might lead to alterations to the current structure under which a bank operates, and certain activities might have to be transferred to new entities that will be created. Moreover, these requirements might also define how the banking group must be structured around a holding company to be allowed to engage in the full spectrum of financial activities. The example of the ring-fencing regulation that was adopted in the UK is the perfect example that will help us understand this requirement. Ring fencing required that a separate, subsidiary company had to be set up in order for the banks to engage in certain activities (proprietary trading and securities underwriting). This restriction can be seen from the opposite, if the bank does not want to engage in these two securities-related activities, it is free to operate as a single entity, engaging freely in the spectrum of services that are available for that entity.

4.1.3 Restrictions on Banks' Size (Size Limits)

The last type of hard requirement is associated with imposing size limits on banking activities. Such limits will further trigger the structural reforms mentioned above and will require a bank either to stop further engaging in certain activities that will exceed the preset threshold (banking activities restrictions) and/or will require structural reforms to permit engagement in such activities above the predefined threshold (bank entity structure restrictions). Such limits are therefore clearly defined quantitative thresholds that create limitations on banks' size and may trigger other measures to be breached by the regulated entities. At the EU level, the Liikanen Report and the subsequent

European Commission's proposal had proposed certain quantitative thresholds that would have triggered the separation of certain activities from the bank that accepts deposits and grants loans.

4.2. *Soft Requirements*

Except from the abovementioned hard requirements, structural reforms can be also imposed or adopted through the alternative option of the so-called 'soft requirements'. These requirements neither impose restrictions on the banks' activities, and size, nor require the adoption of a certain corporate structure. Instead, they can be adopted easier, faster, and more effectively, compared to the hard requirements, even under stress periods, since they are not requiring radical changes to the banks' corporate structure, business models or activities. Therefore, soft requirements are usually internal measures that are imposed or adopted and applied by the firms either after a request from the relevant supervisory authorities or voluntarily, based on banks' own initiative (management body initiative or shareholders initiative) and alter the internal organisation of the banks. Such internal organisation requirements may affect either the personnel of the bank or the internal structure of the firm per se, in the way it conducts its business.

Obviously, both soft and hard requirements should not be seen in isolation from other regulatory measures and can be mixed and matched together creating various potential combinations for regulators and supervisors to achieve the best outcome. Competent authorities must be able to use at their discretion every possible measure under whichever combination in order to propose structural regulation that will have the best result without curbing much of the risk diversification's benefits. This flexibility allows regulators and supervisors to propose tailor-made solutions based on both types (hard and soft) of requirements, enabling them to better adapt their strategy to specific needs of the institutions they supervise/regulate.

Internal Organisation Requirements

Internal organisation requirements are soft requirements that impose structural reforms on the way banks operate and are internally organised. The most important types of such requirements are the so called 'Chinese Walls'.[150] The term is used to describe a virtual wall/barrier intended to block mainly the exchange of information between corporate departments if it might result in

[150] The term 'Chinese Wall' got its name from the Great Wall of China, the impervious structure erected in ancient times to protect China from its enemies. The term entered the language shortly after the stock market crash of 1929 when the US Congress began debating the need to put some sort of regulatory barriers between brokers and investment bankers.

business activities that are ethically or legally questionable and create conflicts of interest. In terms of the present book, a Chinese wall is an important element of broker-dealer regulation since it imposes an information barrier that prevents insider trading and is used to address conflicts of interest between multi service broker-dealers.[151]

A conflict of interest is a situation in which the self-interest of a person may conflict with a fiduciary duty that he owes to another, or in a situation which a person had potentially conflicting fiduciary duties to two or more persons.[152] According to Gorman, conflicts of interest exist in broker-dealers for two principle reasons: a) because of the special compensation scheme that applies to broker-dealers and b) because of the multiple functions the broker-dealers perform.[153] Regarding the first reason, since broker-dealers are compensated based on commissions, they have the incentive to maximise their commission income through encouraging their clients to perform transactions so they can earn based on such transactions. The broker-dealers' self-interest in maximising their profit from commissions will directly conflict with the customers' interest in maximising their return on their investments, usually done by holding a security for an extended period.[154] The second reason had to do with the fact that in today's complex financial world, broker-dealers engage in various financial activities, and therefore face numerous conflicts of interest, with the most pressing being the analysts' conflicts.[155] This type of conflict became apparent after the Enron and World Com scandals in the US[156] leading to the adoption of the Sarbanes-Oxley Act in 2002.

---

151 See in C.M. Gorman, 'Are Chinese Walls the Best Solution to the Problems of Insider Trading and Conflicts of Interest in Broker-Dealers?' (2004) 9 *Fordham Journal of Corporate & Financial Law*, p. 475.

152 Ibid., p. 480.

153 Ibid., p. 481.

154 Ibid.

155 This conflict arises from the difficulty in trying to serve both corporate and individual clients. Since broker-dealers provide research through their analysts, sales through their brokers, and underwriting services to corporate clients. Therefore, there is a concern that analysts' recommendations will be biased and coloured by their firms' investment banking ties and be persuaded to issue overoptimistic reports about a corporate client. On the contrary, issuing a negative report would obviously upset the corporate client who may threaten to take away its underwriting operation into another firm. Thus, the broker-dealer has a compelling interest in keeping its corporate client happy with analysts' reports while at the same time customers' have a strong interest in obtaining objective analysts' reports about corporate securities in order to decide whether they will invest. See in C.M. Gorman, 'Are Chinese Walls the Best Solution to the Problems of Insider Trading and Conflicts of Interest in Broker-Dealers?' (2004) 9 *Fordham Journal of Corporate & Financial Law*, p. 482.

156 Regulators discovered that famous Wall Street analysts were privately selling personal holdings of the stocks they were promoting and had been pressured into providing good ratings, despite personal opinions and research that indicated otherwise. Regulators also found out that many of these analysts, who personally owned pre-IPO shares of certain

Initially, Chinese Walls were voluntary policies and internal procedures established by broker-dealers themselves but the SEC made them a statutory requirement for all firms. Chinese Walls were first adopted in 1968, as part of a settlement between Merrill Lynch and the SEC after Merrill Lynch had abused inside information about future, substantially lower earnings that the 'Douglas Aircraft Company' would announce. Merrill Lynch, and its clients, timely sold their stocks to avoid substantial losses prior to the announcement. As part of the settlement reached Merrill Lynch adopted a Statement of Policy that 'prohibited disclosure by any member of the Underwriting Division of material information obtained from a corporation' that was not already disclosed to the investing public and established the first Chinese wall.[157] The 'Merrill Lynch settlement', as it is known, created a strong precedent and incentive for other broker – dealers to adopt similar practices to prevent the SEC from raiding their offices for unsound practices. History shows that such, initial, Chinese Walls proved futile since numerous allegations of insider trading continued to arise and litigated by the SEC.[158] The US Congress responded to the pressure by adopting the Insider Trading and Securities Fraud Enforcement Act of 1988[159] and making Chinese Walls a statutory requirement by amending Section 15(f) of the Securities Exchange Act of 1934. As it is currently into force, the law stipulates that: 'Every investment adviser [...] shall establish, maintain, and enforce written policies and procedures reasonably designed, taking into consideration the nature of such investment adviser's business, to prevent the misuse [...] of material, non-public information by such investment adviser or any person associated with such investment adviser. The Commission, as it deems necessary or appropriate in the public interest or for the protection of investors, shall adopt rules or regulations to require specific policies or procedures reasonably designed to prevent misuse [...] of material, non-public information.'[160]

Although Chinese Walls exist primarily to prevent insider trading their adoption can serve also other important purposes, such as reducing the cases of conflicts of interest. They can isolate certain parts of the bank from other operations that have access to critical information that could be abused or

securities and would earn massive personal profits if they were successful, gave 'hot' tips to institutional clients and certain 'favoured' clients, enabling them to make enormous profits at the expense of unsuspecting members of the investing public.

157 See in C.M. Gorman, 'Are Chinese Walls the Best Solution to the Problems of Insider Trading and Conflicts of Interest in Broker-Dealers?' (2004) 9 *Fordham Journal of Corporate & Financial Law*, p. 483.

158 See indicatively: a) *SEC v. Levine*, 689 F. Supp. 317 (S.D.N.Y. 1988), and b) *SEC v. Drexel Burnham Lambert Inc.*, 837 F. Supp. 587 (S.D.N.Y. 1993).

159 Insider Trading and Securities Fraud Enforcement Act of 1988, Pub. L. No. 100–704, 102 Stat. 4677 (1988).

160 15 U.S.C. § 80b–4a.

unlawfully used by other departments for selfish reasons. Therefore, such internal walls can be adopted/erected where there is a need to maintain confidentiality to prevent conflicts of interest. Obviously, the wall is not a physical one, albeit in some cases physical distance between the various departments can be fully understandable as part of a Chinese wall, but an ethical one intended to prevent the sharing of information that might lead to ethical or legal violations. Chinese Walls might be permanent or temporary solutions, just until the completion of a trade and their specific policies and procedures are left to each individual bank considering the nature of their business.[161] To achieve that goal, the bank must separate departments with frequent access to confidential information from other departments that trade securities or give investment advice to bank's customers. One method to achieve that is by restricting and/or forbidding access to files, offices, documents, data, and electronic systems so that the 'hot' information will remain strictly to those that are necessary for the completion of the task. Obviously, the most effective way to ensure such separation would be to locate the 'hot' departments into separate floors or even in separate buildings, but especially the second option is far more expensive and difficult to realise.[162] Moreover, all the traditional techniques of preventing access to classified information, such as using code names, passwords, shredding sensitive documents and electronic firewalls are equally necessary and can, to a certain extent, protect the classified data from being compromised.[163]

In the US, the SEC has emphasised that Chinese Walls must be accompanied by observance, continuing education and review of the broker-dealer's trading practices, therefore must be a 'living organ' of the firm.[164] Nevertheless, Chinese Walls are still a highly debated topic and has both opponents and supporters. Opponents believe that their adoption is an ineffective and inefficient method to deal with such serious problems and that better alternatives are available. Supporters believe that they are an effective way to prevent conflicts of interest and more importantly they allow banks and other firms to continue their operations while at the same time can apply the maximum available protection. While in principle we do support the soft requirements approach, as more flexible and business friendly solution, on the other side of the fence, we cannot ignore the fact that Chinese Walls, and soft requirements in general, protect only from the accidental flow of information across the various departments of a bank. Should bank executives, want to engage in unlawful trading on

161 See in C.M. Gorman, 'Are Chinese Walls the Best Solution to the Problems of Insider Trading and Conflicts of Interest in Broker-Dealers?' (2004) 9 *Fordham Journal of Corporate & Financial Law*, p. 485.
162 Ibid.
163 Ibid.
164 Ibid., p. 486.

purpose, nothing will stop them from doing so, and Chinese Walls will remain untouched, since they will have been intentionally compromised. The only exception that applies is when someone has been 'brought over the wall'. The phrase means that an employee in the research department of an investment bank, usually a research analyst, or any other expert from another department which is not primarily involved in the deal, is brought over to work for the underwriting department in order to focus on a particular company or provide his expertise in a particular topic, acquiring for this reason access to confidential information. The purpose of such a transfer is to add a knowledgeable opinion to the underwriting process, thereby adding value to it. Once the underwriting process is complete, the research employee who has been 'brought over the wall' is not allowed to comment on any information learned in the underwriting process until it has become public knowledge. Usually, such practices are quite frequent in everyday business life and the financial institutions that combine banking and capital markets related services have such internal processes that allow to 'bring people over the wall' and participate at a specific project or deal, thereby having access to confidential information. Such practices are usually accompanied by an internal process that requires multiple requests to internal departments and usually are also accompanied by notifications to compliance or another department that is the ultimate responsible for implementing the transfer. To conclude, the main disadvantages of Chinese Walls are:[165]

- They might prove to be unsuccessful because broker-dealers might not have strong incentives to enforce them and to establish strong compliance,
- The compartmentalisation of information accomplished by such a measure might increase rather than decrease the conflict-of-interest problems,
- They do not prevent the intentional flow of information across the departments nor prevent inside trading situations completely, and
- Compliance with them might be tricky in the sense that although the firm might have established Chinese Walls it might still face liability for not using the 'hot information' to prevent customers from assuming wrong investments within its fiduciary duty, creating a catch – 22 positions creating thus adverse consequences for the firm.[166]

Except from Chinese Walls, banks may take advantage of other internal organisational measures that will have similar effects. Tools like Code of Conduct and Code of Ethics that will be adopted by the banks, various trainings and seminars to enhance their knowledgeability and implementation among its employees are softer measures compared to the already soft, albeit more statutory, Chinese Walls. It goes without saying that the effective application

165 Ibid., p. 490 onwards.

166 In *Slade v. Shearson, Hammill Co., Inc.*, 517 F.2d 398 (2d Cir. 1974) the Court held that the firm still faced liability towards its customers for not using that information to withdraw its 'buy' recommendation on the failed company's stock.

of these 'soft practices' rests within the willingness of the financial institution and of its employees. It is for the institution to verify that its employees, and particularly those involved in the capital markets and trading related units, comply with the internal codes and practices. This should be in many cases accompanied by discipline measures that promote a certain behaviour and punish deviating actions.

CHAPTER 2
BANKING MODELS AND STRUCTURAL REFORMS: A GORDIAN KNOT?

1 INTRODUCTION

As we explored earlier, the banking business is essentially the management of the intermediation risks associated with the maturity transformation that takes place from the banks. The invention and expansion of the limited liability company created ideal conditions for the banks to leverage their balance sheets and expand credit to as much as possible, thus assuming even more risks. As a result, in most developed economies the conduct of banking business is done through limited liability legal entities, which are based on common equity shares or possibly other forms of participation.[167] The effective management of the banking risks or the failure to do so has created serious doubts, both in academic theory and in practice, regarding what should be allowed for banks to do. In other words, in which activities banks may engage and may not. Because of historical reasons, policy options and crises adopted measures, the banking models of operations are set up around two main available options: a) the 'universal banking' model and b) the 'non-universal banking' models,[168] with the last being further divided into various specific sub-models with one commonality: the structural characteristic of precluding banks from engaging in certain activities that are usually perceived as risky and/or irrelevant to the business of banking. Since the recent GFC that led to massive taxpayer funded government bailouts not only of banks but also of other non-financial corporations,[169] proponents of structural regulatory reforms brought up

[167] See in K. Alexander, *Principles of Banking Regulation*, Cambridge, Cambridge University Press, 2019, p. 27.

[168] Alternatively, the non-universal banking model has been called 'separated banking' or 'narrow banking' aiming generally to be distinct from the universal banking. Especially, the narrow banking model has been backed by a specific proposal for adopting a similar banking model that will be in depth examined in the present book.

[169] During the 2007–2009 global financial crisis, the US Government, intervened and decided the bail out, through the grant of financial assistance, not only of almost the entire financial sector but also of certain non-financial companies, with the US car manufacturing

again the discussion about eliminating the TBTF problem through structural regulation measures targeted for the financial industry. Structural regulation tries to limit the range of what type of services and transactions and what organisational affiliations are permissible for a financial institution in order to achieve the optimum level of financial stability and address systemic risk.

Prof. Omarova supports the view that the use of structural regulation aims at altering 'the fundamental pattern of interconnectedness in the financial system'.[170] Under this lens, structural regulation can be seen as a specific macro-prudential tool that complements the general macro-prudential regulatory approach.[171] Introducing structural reform measures is not an easy task. The failure of the EU Member States to move forward with the proposed legislation by the European Commission back in 2014 shows the high costs (both economic and political) and stakes that create a salient field of action. Structural reform legislations aim to break the TBTF universal banks into simpler structures that would ensure the safety and soundness of the financial system and the banking system particularly in various ways. Since there is no clear definition of the separated banking model, because of its various alternations and sub models, the author of the present book supports the view that the broader term 'Non-Universal Banking' model(s) must be adopted, to better reflect all the different types of structure that the business of banking may adopt. To that end, we will use the term 'Universal Banking' to describe the bank that offers every type of financial activity and under the generic term 'Non-Universal Banking' we will assign and use interchangeably all the variations of banking structure that we will discuss, without any difference in their meaning. On the contrary, when needed, we will clearly mention the type of specific non universal banking sub model that we will refer to. As a result, the terms 'Separated Banking' model and 'Non-Universal Banking' model have the same meaning and include any type of banking model which is different from the classic universal banking model (such as ring-fencing, utility banking, narrow banking etc.). It goes without saying that the degree and level of separation depends on the aims that each policy option is designed to achieve. Therefore, on the one hand we observe light structural reforms that offer a high degree of flexibility to the banks for their implementation and on the other hand very strict and rigid forms of separation that apply a strict blanket of separation among the various financial services. In between the two fundamentally different approaches we

companies being the recipient of billions of US dollars. Although all the 'Big Three' (General Motors, Ford and Chrysler) US car manufacturers asked for financial assistance this was not enough for them to avoid filing for bankruptcy (except Ford) in mid-2009.

170 See in S.T. Omarova, 'Central Banks, systemic risk and financial sector structural reform', in R.M. Lastra and P. Conti-Brown (eds.), *Research Handbook on Central Banking*, Cheltenham, Edward Elgar Publishing, 2018, p. 1.

171 Ibid.

have a variety of 'mid solutions' that combine various elements of the two models, such as the narrow banking or the ring-fenced banking that have their own specificities and shall be carefully examined. After the recent GFC, various ideas were tabled on how to regulate the structure of the banking sector. At the epicentre of most proposals was the idea that the bank structure should be the most important parameter for establishing a safer and more prudent financial system. The structural regulation approach is considered by many authors a sort of panacea for the stability problems of the financial and banking sector and most importantly of those banks who are considered to be either too big or too important to fail and thus can potentially pose serious threats to financial stability by their role and market power.[172]

2 BANKING BUSINESS' MODELS: A BRIEF ANALYSIS

Based on the distinction we made earlier on, the two systems of funding the economy are the 'bank based' and the 'market-based' one. In Europe and to a lesser extent in Japan, the domination of bank-based funding is evident since more than 75% of the funding needs are covered from the banking sector. On the other side of the fence, the market-based system is dominant in the United States and Canada, since the capital markets are more sophisticated, with huge liquidity and a general culture of market funding very well embedded to all economic participants for almost two centuries now.[173] Compared to Europe, in US and Canada, bank-based funding accounts for only 26% of the total funding provided. As a result, the European banking sector grew by creating big banking groups that offered 'under the same roof' the full range of banking services (retail deposits, payment services, investment banking services, insurance, etc.) based on a single legal entity. That model is called 'Universal Banking' and is the predominant model in Europe (Germany, Switzerland, Austria, etc.). The theory behind universal banking has that the single bank aims at achieving synergies by providing every type of financial service through cross selling of financial products and investment services while at the same time will reduce the risks associated with banking operations through diversification.[174]

---

172 The market power of a bank can be measured by using various parameters. Some of them are easily quantifiable (assets, liabilities, capitalization, liquidity, transactions volume, etc.) while others are harder to be quantifiable (level of interconnection of the bank within the financial system, exposure on derivatives and other sectors, etc.).

173 For a better understanding of the history and the origins of the market-based oriented funding in the US and Canada see indicatively in M.D. Bordo, 'An Historical Perspective on The Crisis Of 2007-2008', Working Paper 14569, *NBER Working Paper Series*, National Bureau of Economic Research (NBER), 2008.

174 See in K. Alexander, *Principles of Banking Regulation*, Cambridge, Cambridge University Press, 2019, p. 209.

On the opposite side, we have the 'Non-Universal Banking' (or 'Separated Banking') models[175] that preclude certain types of (financial) services from being offered by the traditional bank entity that accepts deposits and grants loans. Usually, banned activities are those related to the banks' presence in the capital markets, broadly known as the investment banking services and from a historical point of view, the main activity of investment banks is what today we call securities underwriting. Investment banks buy securities, such as bonds and stocks, from an issuer and then sell them to the final investors.[176] Today the investment banking business comprises a rather heterogeneous and complex set of mostly fee based activities, including a) underwriting and advisory services, b) trading and brokerage, and c) asset management, both traditional and alternative.[177] Nonetheless, underwriting and fee based advisory activities, are still considered as the traditionally core investment banking functions. With underwriting services, an investment bank helps firms to raise funds by issuing securities in the financial markets. These securities can include equity, debt, as well as 'hybrid securities' like convertible debt or debt with warrants attached. Investment banks are structuring the transactions by verifying financial data and business claims, performing due diligence and, most importantly, pricing claims. These services are labelled 'underwriting services' because investment banks actually purchase securities from the issuer and then resale them to the market participants.[178] Investment banks also provide (fee based) assistance to firms to use their assets to issue debt, in a process labelled 'securitisation'[179] and the securities issued are called 'asset backed securities' (ABS). Many commercial banks as well securitise their loans and indeed, in the last years the traditional commercial banking activity has been moving from an 'originate-to hold' model, where banks make loans and keep these loans on their balance sheets to maturity, to an 'originate-to-distribute' model, where banks make loans and then sell them to the market, through the securitisation

175 As we will explain below, the 'Non-Universal Banking' model is sometimes also referred as 'Separated Banking' and/or 'Narrow Banking'. For reasons of coherence, we will use both Non-Universal Banking and Separated Banking interchangeably without any distinction in their meaning. On the opposite, since the 'Narrow Banking' model has some distinct characteristics, we will examine it as a standalone banking model without mixing it with the previous two more generic terms.

176 For an introduction to the investment banking services, see indicatively in F.S. Mishkin and S.G. Eakins, *Financial Markets and Institutions*, 5th ed., The Addison-Wesley Series in Economics, Boston, Pearson, 2006 and in G. Iannotta, *Investment Banking, A Guide to Underwriting and Advisory Services*, Springer, 2010.

177 See in G. Iannotta, *Investment Banking, A Guide to Underwriting and Advisory Services*, Berlin, Springer, 2010, p. 3.

178 Ibid., p. 4.

179 For a description of the securitisation process see indicatively in S.L. Schwarcz, 'What Is Securitization? And For What Purpose?' (2012) 85 *Southern California Law Review*, pp. 1283–1299.

process.[180] From an organisational point of view, most of the investment banks provide their services though a '3D matrix' business model where basically each deal, an IPO or an acquisition, a right issue or a bond offering, is generated and managed by the interaction of three main groups: (a) the 'country group', which assures a broader geographical coverage (e.g. Italy, Germany, UK, etc., and a higher level Japan, USA, Latin America, Europe and Middle East, etc.), (b) the 'industry group', which contributes the industry-specific knowledge (e.g. telecommunications, media, energy, mining, etc.), and (c) the 'product group', which has the skills for the specific deal (e.g. M&As, equity markets, debt markets etc.).[181] Summing up, it is worth noting that, despite commercial and investment banks perform very different activities, their economic rationale stems from the same type of 'friction'. Information asymmetry. If firms and individuals were able to access the financial markets by issuing securities, there would be no need for commercial banks. Commercial banks acquire and process information about prospective borrowers, the 'screening process', and control their activities, the 'monitoring process'.[182] Why does a firm need an investment bank to sell its securities in the market? It is still a matter of information asymmetry, because if a firm were in position to credibly approach the financial markets and market its own securities without any certification of its securities' quality, investment banks would not exist. The same rationale applies also to advisory services: the role of investment banks is collecting and processing information, and, based on this information, credibly certify to the market participants the 'quality' of the deal. Different roles, same friction: information asymmetry.[183] That model was and still is the predominant model in the US (with the GSA and now the Volcker Rule) and since 2013 in the UK (ring-fencing model), and roots back in the financial crisis of 1929, the Great Depression that followed, and the legal separation between commercial banks and investment banks (broker-dealer entities) that was introduced in the crisis' aftermath.

The evidence from the 2007–2009 global financial crisis suggests that bank failures resulted from a combination of various risk factors and the studies performed during the preparation of the Liikanen Report found that no business model performed particularly well or particularly poor during the crisis.[184] Rather the conclusion was that trading in highly complex financial products and real estate lending combined with excessive leverage and short

180 See in G. Iannotta, *Investment Banking, A Guide to Underwriting and Advisory Services*, Berlin, Springer, 2010, p. 5.
181 Ibid., p. 6.
182 Ibid.
183 Ibid.
184 See in J. Vinals, C. Pazarbasioglu, J. Surti, A. Narain, M. Erbenova and J. Chow, 'Creating a Safer Financial System: Will the Volcker, Vickers, and Liikanen Structural Measures Help?', *IMF Staff Discussion Note*, SDN/13/4, May 2013, International Monetary Fund, Washington D.C., p. 11.

term funding from the wholesale markets proved to be a troubled option for many financial institutions. Systemic risk was exaggerated by the strong linkages between the financial institutions, and we had the general meltdown and the spread of the crisis worldwide.[185] This analysis helps us understand that banks' business models are not one-dimensional and by adopting simplistic labels, such as 'retail bank' or 'investment bank', do not adequately describe the business model of a bank, its performance and its riskiness. These labels typically focus only on one or two of the numerous dimensions along which different bank business models may differ. Rather business models are diverse along different key dimensions, such as size, activities, income model, capital and funding structure, ownership, corporate structure, and geographic scope, including how cross-border operations are legally and operationally structured, and have evolved substantially over time.[186]

The Liikanen Report further discovered that the lack of diversity between the big banks' business models was a factor that aggravated the effects from the financial crisis: 'Lack of diversity can also apply to large banks and the current financial system as a whole. [...] over the last decades, financial institutions – especially the large ones – have become more similar to each other. They operate in the same global markets and undertake similar activities. Risk management systems used by these institutions have converged, resulting in near-identical assessments of risks which in turn cause homogeneous behaviour (including similar trading strategies) and amplifying the impact of shocks. The banks have also become increasingly reliant on the same funding sources, which makes them all vulnerable to the same shocks in funding markets. Homogeneity also arises indirectly though interlinkages among institutions (e.g. lending relationships, securitisation activities, etc.).'[187] Thus, although there are clear advantages of banks engaging in providing similar services to customers, for example through enhanced competition that leads to better and maybe cheaper options for end users, a lack of diversity among these banks also presents risks for the stability of the system. Since the decline in diversity has made the system more intertwined and hence more prone to contagion effects, the proper policy reaction to this trend is that diversity may be a good thing, and that targeted measures should be adopted aiming at fostering diversity in banking. The Liikanen Report further found that bank's size was not a critical determinant for the survival of the bank.[188] Some large, diversified banks, survived the crisis relatively well, especially those that were mainly focused on commercial banking and geographically diversified, as

---

185 Ibid.

186 See in High-Level Expert Group (HLEG), *Reforming the structure of the EU banking sector*, Brussels 2 October 2012, p. 32.

187 Ibid., p. 34.

188 Ibid., p. 37.

opposed to those banks that had built their business models around investment banking, the structuring of complex derivatives and proprietary trading as the main drivers of growth. By contrast, some of the smaller and less diversified banks, particularly those with business models focused on mortgages and headquartered in EU Member States where real estate bubbles burst, suffered significant losses. Therefore, the funding structure of a bank is an important determinant of its resilience, and some (large and small) commercial banks failed because of their over-reliance on short-term funding from wholesale markets (such as Northern Rock and Dexia).[189] Finally, the Liikanen Report provides us with some EU based banks' business models that failed during the recent GFC. While all banks were affected by the crisis, given its systemic nature, certain factors make certain banks more vulnerable than others:

- losses on trading activities and/or on investment portfolios (Lehman Brothers, Northern Rock, RBS, selected German Landesbanken),[190]
- aggressive expansion of their business (Lehman, RBS) and/or departing from their traditional function (selected German Landesbanken),[191]
- overreliance on short-term wholesale funding (Northern Rock, selected public finance banks),[192]
- poor lending decisions, including significant exposures to the property and construction sector (Northern Rock, RBS, Spanish cajas),[193] and
- high leverage (all the above) and, in the case of the Spanish cajas, constraints on external capital raising due to their legal structure.[194]

Against this brief overview of the banks' business models, we now must delve into and connect them with the structural reforms regimes that were proposed to address the concerns that arose mostly from the recent GFC. At the same time, we will try to understand their main characteristics, how they operate and what makes each proposal so special.

2.1. The 'Universal Banking' Model

The universal banking model is based on a straightforward idea; it allows for a single legal entity, usually a (commercial) bank that accepts deposits and provides loans, to engage in and offer a wide variety of financial services across various sectors of the financial system. Insurance activities, securities trading and underwriting, proprietary trading, mortgages, investment banking services and credit cards business, to name but a few possible activities that

189 Ibid., p. 38.
190 Ibid., p. 58.
191 Ibid.
192 Ibid.
193 Ibid.
194 Ibid., p. 59.

a universal bank may offer and engage. In some jurisdictions, with Germany being the textbook example, banks are even allowed to acquire and manage voting rights derived from equity stakes participations in non-financial sector corporations.[195] By using the voting rights, universal banks may influence the decisions of a company's management board, affecting thus the business model of that company. The German universal banking model has been the predominant banking model across Europe, although with some variations regarding the structure of the group level companies. Close to the German model's philosophy is the so-called 'keiretsu' system in Japan but with different restrictions imposed on it, as we will explore later. The continental Europe model has significant degrees of freedom to choose the best option compared to the more rigid US bank holding company structure.[196]

2.1.1 Theoretical Background and Legal Rationale

Universal banks constitute 'multi-product firms'[197] that are trying to offer their clients 'one stop shop' solutions related to financial services. Benston defined universal banks as these financial institutions that may offer the 'entire range of financial services'.[198] These financial services are conducted either by a single entity or by the affiliated entities that coexist within the same conglomerate structure. The ideology behind the universal banking model is one of the most hotly debated and in practice has to do with the optimal bank structure and the efficiency of financial regulation. This policy debate has always been the same: maximum efficiency gains within a political and economic model of stability and equity.[199] In this equation, we should also add the parameter of global competitiveness, both in terms of financial services and of the national economy in general. Since the late 1970s, international finance was in the pace of liberalisation and abolition of various protective measures, and this inevitably led to the creation of big financial firms that were trying to exploit all the possible synergies available across the globe. Within this environment, universal banking, which was already a tradition in Europe, and to a certain extent in the UK, appealed as the very prominent banking model that combined various efficiencies 'under the same roof'. Furthermore,

---

195 See in K. Alexander, *Principles of Banking Regulation*, Cambridge, Cambridge University Press, 2019, p. 229.

196 See in S.T. Omarova, 'Central Banks, systemic risk and financial sector structural reform', in R.M. Lastra and P. Conti-Brown (eds.), *Research Handbook on Central Banking*, Cheltenham, Edward Elgar Publishing, 2018, p. 3.

197 See in I. Walter, 'Universal Banking: A Shareholder Value Perspective', *New York University Working Paper* No. FIN-96-040, 1996, p. 1.

198 See in G. Benston, 'Universal Banking' (1994) 8(3) *Journal of Economic Perspectives*, p. 121.

199 See in A. Saunders and I. Walter, *Universal Banking in The United States-What Could We Gain? What Could We Lose?*, New York, Oxford University Press, 1994, p. 3.

the 'financial supermarket' logic behind universal banking ultimately has a positive impact on customers since the cost of obtaining credit, either from banks or from securities issuance, will be lower, compared to non-universal banking structures.[200] The universal banking model became the prominent model because the radical changes in the financial landscape helped establish its dominance. Until the early 1980s banks were mostly organised around two parts: a) the consumer bank, which provided banking services to the public at large and b) the private bank, that provided specialised services to high-net-worth individuals and families.[201] The changes in technology, the new regulatory landscape and the growth of securities markets changed the above well-established model forcing banks to adapt to a highly competitive environment. The increased competition for assets by institutional investors put a downward pressure on the spread of credit risk that banks were exposed to. Moreover, as credit opportunities across countries became easily available to investors and lenders from other countries, because of the technological and informational advances, the credit risk spreads were furthered pressed and narrowed.[202] The increased competition for better and better credit risks fuelled the transformation of traditional commercial banks into entities that were in need of new sources of rewarding activities since the traditional commercial banking was gradually becoming less profitable. As a result, the response of the sector was to expand into securities activities and into new 'territories' mostly uncharted. The universal banking model was gaining in popularity since it would allow for maximum efficiency and for faster structural adaptation. It was a period of 'aggressive market driven pursuit [...] of broader scope of activities [...] and greater geographical reach'[203] which would abruptly stop in 2007 when the first signs of the crisis appeared.

2.1.2 Forms of Universal Banking Structure

According to Prof. Walter, universal banks are usually organised based on 4 distinct types of corporate/business structures:

- Type A: the 'full integration' model[204]
  This model is the purest form of universal banking structure. It is comprised of only one entity, the bank that undertakes the full spectrum of financial

200 See in K. Alexander, *Principles of Banking Regulation*, Cambridge, Cambridge University Press, 2019, p. 209.

201 See in F. Sotelino and R. Gonzalez, *Universal Banking Post Crisis: Past and Future of International Corporate and Personal Banking*, 2012, p. 5, available at SSRN: https://papers.ssrn.com/sol3/papers.cfm?abstract_id=2102863.

202 Ibid.

203 Ibid., p. 9.

204 See in A. Saunders and I. Walter, *Universal Banking in The United States-What Could We Gain? What Could We Lose?*, New York, Oxford University Press, 1994, p. 85.

services. As a result, bank activities, securities activities, insurance activities and any other activity is offered from the same corporate entity using also the same (single) capital base.

- Type B: the 'partial integration' model[205]
  Under this model, the universal bank conducts the banking and securities activities under the same corporate entity, while the insurance activities, the mortgage banking related activities and any other activities are offered through distinct and separately capitalised subsidiaries. The activities undertaken by the subsidiaries are designated as such because either they are separately regulated, or they appear to have a significant potential for conflict of interest, or due to a combination of both. The parent -universal bank- company has a single capital base to support its banking and investment banking activities. The most prominent example of such a structure is the German Deutsche Bank.
- Type C: the 'bank parent company structure' model[206]
  This model has a parent company that offers only the traditional banking activities of accepting deposits and providing loans, while all other financial services (securities, insurance, etc.) are offered through the separately capitalised subsidiaries. As a result, the combination of parent and subsidiaries allows the financial group to be engaged in the full spectrum of financial services.
- Type D: the 'holding company structure' model[207]
  Finally, in this model we observe the creation of a holding company that controls subsidiaries engaged in various financial activities such as commercial banking, investment banking, insurance services and possibly various other types of financial or even non-financial businesses. Examples of this model include the big US banks that have adopted the bank holding company structure such as Morgan Stanley and Goldman Sachs.

Universal banks tend also to be internationally active and thus they become systemically important at an international level. Their expanded geographical network of services through subsidiaries, branches and representative offices and their high level of interconnection with other participants in the financial system, such as payment systems and clearinghouses, makes them important for the stability of the whole financial system. As such, any event of instability could have adverse effects for the entire financial system since it could be transmitted through the various interconnection points. Based on the analysis done by Gambacorta and van Rixtel, the Global Systemically Important Banks

205 Ibid.
206 Ibid.
207 Ibid.

(G-SIBs), a category where most of universal banks belong, can be classified according to their business model in four broad categories:[208]

(a) Investment Banks (IBs),
(b) Investment Banking oriented universal banks (IBU),
(c) Commercial Banks (CBs) and
(d) Commercial Banking oriented universal banks (CBU)

The first category includes the pure investment banking banks that are specialised in investment banking services, and their universality is derived from the fact that they operate on a global scale and not necessarily from offering the full service of financial services, at least in some of the countries in which they operate. The second category includes the universal banks that are mostly concentrated in investment banking activities, in the sense that most of their business is related to the investment banking activities, while the commercial banking activities comprise an important part of their total income. The third category includes the pure commercial banks that focus solely on the commercial banking activities and do not offer investment banking activities. Their universality comes from the fact that they operate in various jurisdictions across the world or because they have a significant market share in a particularly important jurisdiction. Ultimately, the fourth category includes the commercial banking oriented universal banks. These banks are mostly concentrated on commercial banking services, but they also have a significant participation in investment banking operations.

The above classification is of course constructed using various parameters and factors which can produce different results if mixed with other factors that determine the business model of a bank. Consequently, the classification of a bank as pure commercial and not as commercial oriented can be contested accordingly given the assumptions and the parameters on which the classification has been made.[209]

2.1.3 Evaluation of the Universal Banking Model: Benefits and Drawbacks

The advantages of the universal banking model are well documented in the relevant academic literature and include economies of scale and scope, risk diversification, ties with commercial firms and efficient allocation of funding. We will now discuss them in more depth.

---

208 See in L. Gambacorta and A. van Rixtel, 'Structural bank regulation initiatives: approaches and implications', *BIS Working Papers*, no. 412, April 2013, Basel, Bank of International Settlements, p. 7.

209 Ibid.

2.1.3.1 *Economies of Scale*

The existence of scale economies in finance (and banking in particular) produces intense debates at both academic and professional level, given that various research papers have tried to discuss this issue. Economies of scale are associated with the potential reduction in unit costs that the big universal banks can achieve by spreading the fixed costs over a larger customer basis.[210] Fixed costs can be considered those related to the payment systems, access to market infrastructure and technology. These costs can be of significant size thus affecting the business model of the bank. The debate becomes even fiercer when combined with the optimal firm structure of a bank entity that is supposed to exploit the expanded balance sheet to achieve these synergies. The main rationale behind scale economies is that a universal bank will achieve these economies when will combine various services offered to various clients and the funding cost (cost of borrowing) will be pushed down while at the same time its balance sheet will keep expanding. Size can also enhance the ability of banks to realise economies of scope, as large banks are more likely to achieve scope in multiple activities while at the same time maintaining scale in an individual activity, but scope economies will be discussed below under b. The existence of economies of scale differs between bank activities. For example, scale economies are more prominent in payment and clearing services, which require heavy fixed-cost investment in technologies and building up the relevant networks than in securities underwriting which requires a more individual risk assessment of the relevant deal.[211] Within the Liikanen Report, we found evidence from mergers in the banking sector that is also not overwhelmingly in favour of ever-increasing economies of scale. There is no strong evidence of increased bank efficiency after a merger or acquisition nor is there convincing evidence that cross-activity mergers create economic value with the crisis experience also suggesting that few (forced or unforced) mergers and acquisitions outperformed following their final consolidation.[212]

2.1.3.2 *Economies of Scope*

Economies of scope are related to the efficiency gains derived from diversifying the banks' business activities across products, geographies, and services or from any combination between them.[213] Generally, we further identify two subtype economies:

---

[210] Ibid., p. 8.

[211] See in High-Level Expert Group (HLEG), Reforming the structure of the EU banking sector, Brussels 2 October 2012, p. 131.

[212] Ibid.

[213] See in L. Gambacorta and A. van Rixtel, 'Structural bank regulation initiatives: approaches and implications', *BIS Working Papers*, no. 412, April 2013, Basel, Bank of International Settlements, p. 8.

(i) 'Revenue economies of scope'[214] or 'demand-side economies of scope'.[215] Such synergies from scope economies arise mostly from the cross-selling of various types of financial services to bank customers when they will be able to have access to a bucket of financial services from the same bank under a lower cost than acquiring them separately from different service providers. Clients may value the 'one-stop-shopping' offered by a bank with diversified services. In addition, by providing a service, banks gain valuable information on their clients that might provide advantages in the provision of other services, such that these banks may better serve their clients.[216]

(ii) 'Cost economies of scope'[217] or 'supply-side economies of scope'.[218] The bank achieves them when it can downsize its costs through sharing technology, infrastructure, know-how, common use of outsourcing service providers and generally becomes a more cost-efficient firm.[219]

Special attention must be paid also to the so-called network economics', mostly associated with the abovementioned demand-side scope economies. Network economics are associated with the expansion of the bank's clients' network, where any additional client linkage adds value to the existing network and thereby reduces the cost of accessing these clients. These so-called network externalities' have the tendency to increase alongside the increase of the network size in absolute terms.[220]

2.1.3.3 *Risk Diversification*

One of the most important arguments in favour of universal banking model is the opportunity for better risk diversification. Banks providing diversified services, with less than perfectly correlated income streams, may be able to diversify the overall risk of their operations and thereby reduce funding costs.[221] If the bank is allowed to expand its balance sheet into new financial services and

---

214 Ibid.

215 See in I. Walter, 'Universal Banking: A Shareholder Value Perspective', *New York University Working Paper* No. FIN-96-040, 1996, p. 7.

216 See in High-Level Expert Group (HLEG), *Reforming the structure of the EU banking sector*, Brussels 2 October 2012, p. 132.

217 See in L. Gambacorta and A. van Rixtel, 'Structural bank regulation initiatives: approaches and implications', *BIS Working Papers*, no. 412, April 2013, Basel, Bank of International Settlements, p. 8.

218 See in I. Walter, 'Universal Banking: A Shareholder Value Perspective', *New York University Working Paper* No. FIN-96-040, 1996, p. 7.

219 Ibid. See also in High-Level Expert Group (HLEG), *Reforming the structure of the EU banking sector*, Brussels 2 October 2012, p. 132.

220 I. Walter, 'Universal Banking: A Shareholder Value Perspective', *New York University Working Paper* No. FIN-96-040, 1996, p. 7.

221 See in S.T. Omarova, 'Central Banks, systemic risk and financial sector structural reform', in R.M. Lastra and P. Conti-Brown (eds.), *Research Handbook on Central Banking*, Cheltenham, Edward Elgar Publishing, 2018, p. 3 and in High-Level Expert Group (HLEG), *Reforming the structure of the EU banking sector*, Brussels 2 October 2012, p. 132.

products (portfolio diversification) the overall risks that will be accumulated will be spread out in a much richer portfolio with different maturities and returns, thus different risks. Evidence from the period prior to the adoption of GSA demonstrates that less diversified banks, concentrated into specific operations, observed higher rates of failure compared to other more diversified ones.[222] Furthermore, Benston supports that by introducing limitations on banking, with the separation between commercial and investment banking being one of them, we do not make financial system safer by reducing risk taking among its members.[223]

2.1.3.4 *Ties with Commercial Corporations*

Universal banks tend to create strong and deep linkages with commercial corporations because of their investments in their capital. The example of German universal banks' participations in the capital of commercial corporations and the Japanese keiretsu system are two illustrative examples of that tendency. Through those links, the banks have an in-depth knowledge of the companies to which they invest and most of the time provide financial services too. As a result, they can provide credit and other services on favourable terms and manage effectively all the risks that arise from their exposure to the companies. Furthermore, the fact that banks also participate in the management board of these corporations, exercising their voting rights, grants an obvious advantage in shaping business plans in a way that is, at least, favourable to their long-term interests. Via that participation, universal banks may be better positioned to evaluate and monitor the financial health of these corporations as well as the effectiveness of the management team[224] while being able to offer them tailored solutions to their financial needs. In both the German and the Japanese version of direct participation in commercial corporations, universal banks are better positioned when adverse events may occur than any other specialised bank of financial entity. This is derived from the fact that since universal banks are exposed to these corporations through various lending agreements, they have an extra motivation to provide support, by enhancing credit and liquidity arrangements in rough times, thus helping them adjust to the new conditions.[225]

---

[222] See in G. Benston, 'Universal Banking' (1994) 8(3) *Journal of Economic Perspectives*, Summer 1994, p. 125. The scientific evidence demonstrates that prior to the passage of the Glass-Steagall Act, commercial banks with active engagement into the investment banking business experienced lower rate of failures.

[223] Ibid.

[224] See in G. Benston, 'Universal Banking' (1994) 8(3) *Journal of Economic Perspectives*, p. 129.

[225] Ibid.

2.1.3.5 *Efficient Allocation of Funding*

By allowing universal banks to operate it is expected that the capital allocation will take place more efficiently since the banks will be able to move capital across their structure and to deploy it where and when it will be needed the most. Banks have the expertise to understand and evaluate accordingly all the business opportunities that will allow them to realise capital gains. Complemented with effective risk diversification, capital allocation will try to profit from higher margins in sectors that are performing better compared to others. If we could use an example to better understand that process let's imagine a situation where capital markets suffer from low returns while there is a high demand for real estate loans or corporate lending. Universal banks could exploit that chance and channel funds towards the most profitable sectors while deleveraging from positions and low return activities in the capital markets. The same approach can be used also for a geographical recalibration of activities that require capital investments.

Drawbacks of the Universal Banking Model

While it comes with undoubted benefits for the banks, the universal banking model comes also at certain costs. The drawbacks of this model are exactly what structural regulation initiatives are expected to tame:

2.1.3.6 *The 'Too-Big-to-Fail' Issues*

Allowing banks to grow their balance sheet size through permission to offer diverse financial products it is translated into assuming more risk. Growing beyond a centre point might pose serious threats to financial stability since these banks will be too big or too important to fail. As a result, taxpayers' money will continue to be ready for use to either assist or even bail out those entities that are considered too big to be left to fail. Big universal banks (usually the ones with global presence and systemic importance) with participation in a variety of financial markets are thus exposed to a variety of risks that can ultimately bring them down jeopardising thus financial stability potentially transmitting shocks to the real economies.

2.1.3.7 *Systemic Risk*

Individual diversification by banks can make the financial system, as a whole, less diversified. Since universal banks will be allowed to offer a wide variety of services/products it means that they will be part of various subsections of financial markets. They will participate in the banking system, in the payments system, in the capital markets and in the insurance market.[226] Their

[226] See in High-Level Expert Group (HLEG), *Reforming the structure of the EU banking sector*, Brussels 2 October 2012, p. 133.

simultaneous participation in so many parts of the financial system has the potential effect that in an adverse event these entities can transfer and spread the instability from one part of the system to other, healthy parts. As banks diversify into each other's traditional areas, and especially in the capital markets business, the system can become less diverse overall and potentially more vulnerable to common shocks. Due to their interconnectedness with various other entities and institutions, these firms might pose a serious threat to the whole system. Thus, they become of systemic importance from the moment they pose systemic risks to the financial system.[227]

2.1.3.8 *Conflicts of Interest*

Conflicts of interest are one of the most common fears of the universal banking system opponents and its probability of appearance increases with the breadth of the various financial services that the bank offers. Bearing in mind that the Great Depression was created, among other reasons, from the exploitation of the then commercial (universal) banks wrong incentives to sell to investors securities issued by companies to which they were lending creates understandable fears for a *déjà vu*. According to Prof. Walter, the conflicts of interest danger is 'endemic in universal banking'.[228] The major types of conflicting situations that a universal may engage in are the following:

- **Salesman's stake**: in this situation conflict arises when the bank has the right to sell financial products of its affiliates. Therefore, the managers of the bank will try to promote and sell 'house' products, possibly to the customer's detriment, since they will have a salesman's stake to these products.[229]
- **Stuffing fiduciary accounts**: in this situation conflict arises when the bank, aiming to ameliorate a securities underwriting process that is not performing well, decides to exploit the accounts managed by its investment department and the bank has a discretionary authority, by 'stuffing' them with unwanted securities as an effort to mitigate the potential losses from the underwriting process.[230]
- **Bankruptcy risk transfer**: in this situation the bank, knowing privately that an entity to which an outstanding loan appears to have an increased bankruptcy risk, decides to prompt that entity to issue securities that the bank will underwrite by its securities unit, to an unsuspecting public. Since the proceeds from the issuance of the securities will be used to fully pay the outstanding loan and while at the same time, the bank will earn the fee from

227 Ibid.

228 See in I. Walter, 'Universal Banking: A Shareholder Value Perspective', *New York University Working Paper* No. FIN-96-040, 1996, p. 18.

229 Ibid.

230 Ibid.

the underwriting process and/or the potential spread of the securities price, as a result, the bank has transferred the credit risk to the public.[231]

- **Third party loans**: in this situation, a bank that wishes to ensure that securities underwriting will be successful, may provide loans with preferable terms (below-market loans) for any third-party investors, under the condition that these investors will purchase securities underwritten by the securities unit of the bank.[232]
- **Tie-ins**: In this situation, conflict arises when a bank may attempt to use its lending power to compel or tie-in a customer to its own securities products offered by its own securities units.[233]
- **Information transfer**: in this situation when acting as a lender a commercial bank may obtain certain confidential and inside information about a certain customer and/or its rivals. This information may be used by the securities business departments to fix or set prices for the securities underwriting business. It is obvious that this kind of inside information also can flow the opposite way towards the commercial bank.[234]

2.1.3.9 *Complexity and Resolvability Issues*

Diversification and balance sheet expansion of large banks tends to increase their complexity, which may raise their risk management cost, reduce transparency, and complicate their resolution.[235] Where we all agree is that growth is an imperative for financial firms and particular banks. But an uncontrolled growth without continual pruning and streamlining of the structure and processes is a potential recipe for disaster and the mess after the Lehman Brothers failure brought up once again the fears about how complex the big financial entities can become. The lengthy processes of bankruptcy courts and the complexity of the structure that Lehman has at that time has pushed the academic debate towards the various issues that a universal bank may pose to the financial system's stability.

2.1.3.10 *Market Power and Competition Issues*

Many opponents of universal banking have expressed the fear that if we allow the formation of big banking groups that will combine under a single roof all financial services, these entities will increase their market share and power at such a level that competition will be distorted. Other financial institutions,

---

231 Ibid., p. 19.

232 Ibid.

233 Ibid.

234 Ibid.

235 See in High-Level Expert Group (HLEG), *Reforming the structure of the EU banking sector*, Brussels, 2 October 2012, p. 132.

including banks and non-banks, less powerful and less diversified compared to big universal banks, will be forced out of business by either predatory pricing, limit pricing and other unfair practices.[236] The banking sector's consolidation that occurred in the US financial market on the aftermath of the global financial crisis of 2007–2009, mostly with the acquisitions of failed banks from the healthy ones, demonstrated a clear path towards greater market share and power. The same path was followed after the enactment of the Financial Markets Modernization Act in 1999 (better known as Gramm-Leach-Bliley Act) that repealed certain provisions of the GSA and of the Bank Holding Company Act of 1956, paving the road for a wave of mergers and acquisitions in the financial services sector.[237] The ultimate saying in this field belongs to competition law that has all the necessary tools to regulate and supervise the abuse of market power and any unfair practices by legal entities, in tandem with bank supervisors and other designated authorities.

2.2. *The 'Non-Universal Banking' Models*

With respect to the non-universal banking models, we observe a variety of different approaches and structures. These policy options vary from complete separation systems, like the US system introduced under the GSA, to very strictly defined banking activities that comprise only deposit taking and payments activities. Prof. Alexander defines four types of advantages that a separated banking model would have:[238]

(a) Enhanced separability and therefore better resolvability for financial institutions,
(b) Different business activities would enjoy different levels of governmental guarantees,
(c) Structural regulation would be possible to resolve a time inconsistency problem in the TBTF problem, and
(d) Structural regulation reduces complexity and overall, the single entity's size by promoting transparency, resolvability and ultimately market discipline since the relevant state authorities will have more option than an 'all or nothing' approach.

---

236 See in G. Benston, 'Universal Banking' (1994) 8(3) *Journal of Economic Perspectives*, pp. 121–134.

237 Among the most important mergers and acquisitions of the post-deregulation era, to name but a few, were the formation of Citigroup from the merger between Citicorp and Travelers, the merger between Bank of America and Fleet Boston and the merger between Wells Fargo and Norwest Corporation.

238 See in K. Alexander, *Principles of Banking Regulation*, Cambridge, Cambridge University Press, 2019, pp. 229–230.

Although the advantages of structural separation regulatory measures are considered as straightforward, the disadvantages on the other hand are, in many cases, not well articulated in the academic dialogue. The sirens of separation doctrine condemn a priori the riskier operations of investment banking but almost fail to acknowledge and consider in depth the benefits of universal banks. Synergies in many sectors, economies of scale and scope, better risk mitigation and diversification for the bank itself and in many cases, this can be translated into better and cheaper finance options for the clients. We will start our examination of these approaches from the narrow banking proposal, and we will proceed with the other options to better understand the specificities of each one of them and their interactions with the goal of financial stability.

2.2.1 The 'Narrow Banking' Proposals

Narrow banking is the typical proposal that becomes popular after every financial crisis and gives a very extravagant idea of how the business of banking shall be regulated. The idea of narrowing the scope of banking business is a quite old one; so old that its roots can be traced back in the era of Great Depression and in Roosevelt administration. Back then, it was called the '100% reserve banking' principle contained in some memoranda to the Roosevelt administration sent from a group of economists from the University of Chicago.[239] What later became known as the 'Chicago Plan' was in favour of: a) the adoption of a requirement that deposit banks holding 100% reserves and b) the investment trusts would perform lending through securities funding. The intention of the Chicago Plan was to contain as much as possible banking services to achieve financial stability and ultimately reduce the possibilities for devastating bank runs.[240] As a result, narrow banking services can be offered from 'narrow banks' which are banks that perform only the very specific tasks of accepting deposits and offering payment services. Narrow banks are prohibited or restricted from providing loans to the private sector and must invest all their liabilities (deposits) into high quality assets (highly liquid). Since these banks will be also members of the deposit insurance schemes then there is no need to worry about potential banking crisis since, with the narrow banking concept, insured deposits will be the equivalent of currency.[241]

---

239 The most prominent economists among that group were Henry Simons, Frank Knight, and Lloyd Mints. See in B. Bossone, 'Should Banks Be Narrowed?', *IMF Working Paper*, WP/01/159, International Monetary Fund, 2001, Washington D.C., p. 6.

240 For a thorough analysis of the 'Chicago Plan', see indicatively in 10. J. Bens and M. Kumhof, 'The Chicago Plan Revisited', WP/12/202, IMF Working Paper, International Monetary Fund, 2012, Washington D.C.

241 See in B. Bossone, 'Should Banks Be Narrowed?', *IMF Working Paper*, WP/01/159, International Monetary Fund, 2001, Washington D.C., p. 4.

Another important point to be clarified in the narrow banking theory has to do with the fact that this concept has never been adopted by any country so far. Consequently, there is no evidence that this policy option can be measured and evaluated, thus providing us with concrete conclusions for its potential effectiveness. The narrow banking models remain mostly an academic idea with limited acceptance, if at all, from the real business world because of the implications for the effectiveness of monetary policy as well as the negative externalities that may arise in the economic policy followed by a state due to the anticipated credit contraction that this system implies. These two factors remain strong brakes towards its adoption. The concept of narrow banking has many variations and multiple scholars have tried in the past to reincarnate it in an effective way. The two most important subcategories are the Utility Banking proposal and the Narrow Funding Banks.

2.2.1.1 *The 'Utility Banking' Proposal*

The utility banking model[242] is a proposal based on the premise that banks are offering a (public) service that must be protected and regulated by the state in a way similar to utility services. To a certain extent, this is true and as we examined earlier banks, because of their special position within the financial system, are heavily supervised and regulated. The difference with this proposal lies in the fact that banking should have social ends and by offering a service that is meant to serve public interests should be regulated accordingly. Many theoretical supporters of that idea found fertile land after the last financial crisis and proposed to 'make banking boring again'.[243]

The Supreme Court of the US (SCOTUS) has defined the social ends of public utilities in various occasions since the late 19th century. The SCOTUS decision in *Munn v. Illinois*[244] sketched the framework for the definition of public interest very early. The public interest in access and the affordability of the service outweighed the rights over private property while justifying the state price regulation.[245] Behind that early decision, we find two important principles: a) the principle of universal access and b) the principle of fair pricing for an essential service. The above judicial activism has since evolved and filtered by other decisions that reflected the economic evolution of the US.[246] Utility companies are regulated both in terms of price charged to

242 See in J.T.S. Chow and J. Surti, 'Making Banks Safer: Can Volcker and Vickers Do It?', *IMF Working Paper*, WP/11/236, International Monetary Fund, 2011, Washington D.C., p. 5.

243 See in A. White, 'Banks as Utilities' (2016) 90 *Tulane Law Review*, p. 1243.

244 *Munn v. Illinois*, 94 U.S. 113 (1876).

245 See in A. White, 'Banks as Utilities' (2016) 90 *Tulane Law Review*, p. 1246.

246 After the decision in Munn, the SCOTUS adapted its jurisprudence to the Fourteenth Amendment and the Due Process Clause in *Lochner v. New York* (1905) and made a landing to the New Deal era with the decisions in *Nebbia v. New York* (1934) and in *West Coast*

customers and of reliability of their services. One particularly illustrative example is the regulation of power companies, either private or public, that offer a good that is essential for the well-being of people. The same can be said also for water supply, postal services etc. Banking services are perceived as such and are regulated to offer reliable services (deposits and payments) and to all the people without excluding certain parts of the population that under a competitive free market would not be included in. Banking services are thus subject to strict regulation regarding the prices they charge to customers, the universality of the services offered, their non-discriminatory nature and the safety and reliability of the deposit and payments function. White further believes that US banking law in general is constraint by the narrowly defined social ends and at the same time misses the principle of universality offer of services within reasonable and non-discriminatory prices, because the only purpose of the regulatory framework is to protect the safety and soundness of the financial system.[247] White's belief requires a radical change in the regulatory ideology that is currently running through the financial system. It requires a change from the traditional approach of safety and soundness of the financial system, as overarching aims of state intervention, towards a more broadly defined range of goals, which are more suitable for public utilities.[248] The regulation of banks as utilities is primarily aimed at establishing specific social ends similar with other utility services and not that much to define a certain structure that the bank must have. As a result, utility regulation aims to maximise public profit and not to dictate what banks are allowed to do in terms of activities engaged.

Bearing in mind the above analysis we understand that regulating banks as utilities has a very different meaning compared to the current framework of banking regulation and requires a completely new approach to capture all the new parameters of that idea. Safety and soundness of financial system are not the ultimate objectives anymore and the principles of universality and affordability are well embedded as requirements of the new approach. The new approach understands the interplay between banks and states as a public private joint venture since the banking sector is heavily relied on the infrastructure provided by the states to perform at its ultimate capacity. Payment systems' infrastructure and deposit guarantee schemes are considered of extreme importance for the efficient performance of the banking sector. Since both are provided or at least supported by the state utility banking theory supports the idea that banks must serve more social aims in a way like electricity, water, and

Hotel Co. v. Parish (1937). For a more detailed analysis see in A. White, 'Banks as Utilities' (2016) 90 *Tulane Law Review*, p. 1247.

247 See in A. White, 'Banks as Utilities' (2016) 90 *Tulane Law Review*, p. 1267.

248 Ibid., p. 1271.

telephone services providers, with high quality of service at an affordable cost coupled with the universality of that service.[249]

We will now focus our analysis on the separation aspects of utility banking model. The separation is the breaking up or deconcentrating of the utility companies that are participating in the market. White supports the view that just as regulators have break up the utility monopolies in order to ensure reliable and universal service, the same must apply to banking business.[250] The rationale behind these necessary break ups is based on a double goal: a) to ensure reliable and universal service and b) to contain the ever-increasing political power of big companies that operate in an oligopoly. The breaking up of these companies is both vertically and horizontal. Vertical break up is an analogous to the ring-fencing of core banking business that must be offered reliably and universally at a fair price from other more dangerous banking businesses and services (for example investment banking). Vertical break up is translated into strict business lines and as a result precludes banks from participating in certain risky activities that can jeopardise the supply of universal and affordable banking services to achieve social ends. Horizontal break up of utility monopolies and oligopolies can be also applied to banking according to White who uses as example the breaking up of the highly oligopolistic electric power industry in the 20th century from the SEC and the US Congress.[251] Back then, the Public Utility Holding Company Act (PUHCA) of 1935[252] required utility holding companies 'to be limited to a single integrated public utility system'.[253] As a result, transposing horizontal breaking up in banking means essentially the imposition of geographical and/or market restrictions to the banks that are regulated as (banking) utilities. Once again, the social aims imposed on banks are the background reasons for this type of breaking up.

By distinguishing utility banking services, which are deemed to be non-risky from non-utility banking services which are deemed to be risky, utility banking regulation follows a path in which safety and soundness of the financial system is gradually replaced by more socially oriented aims of regulation. What is striking though is that from a theoretical standpoint the exact 'location' of the separation is not very clear because no one provides a detailed analysis of what type of banking services are deemed as less risky and thus could be offered by the strictly regulated utility bank entity. White tends to believe that the utility sector will include those services that facilitate

---

249 Ibid., p. 1272.

250 Ibid., p. 1278.

251 Ibid.

252 Public Utility Holding Company Act of 1935, ch. 687, 49 Stat. 803 (1935) (codified as amended at 15 U.S.C. §§ 79 to 79z-6 (2000)) (repealed 2005).

253 See in A. White, 'Banks as Utilities' (2016) 90 *Tulane Law Review*, p. 1279. This meant that the electric or gas network within which the company should be established was limited to a single geographic area or region, usually being a state or a local market within a state.

economic growth and 'real sector activity' but there is now clear evidence if the real sector activity has risks that can drive a bank into failure, under the classic bank crisis theory.[254] Risk concentration in bank entities could create severe problems if not properly diversified and hedged and any horizontal restrictions make banks vulnerable to local 'disruptions' and do not allow for an effective client diversification. While it is well known that certain client groups, that undoubtedly deserve reliable bank services, are carrying higher credit risk than others, the utility bank regulation approach does not seem to provide a very convincing argument for dealing with this issue. Finally, regarding the equally important issue of the structure of the utility bank there is no clear proposal tabled and the two entities, utility services entity and non-utility services entity, would be able to use a golden share approach in favour of the state, as many scholars support or would be permitted to be under a common holding company but there would be no shared capital nor liquidity transfers between them.[255] Once again the mixing of social aims in the banking services regulation needs to be well calibrated and be decided on well documented evidence that creates, overall, a safer system and not a Red Cross type of social benefits towards services that ultimately may pose certain threats that banking regulation tries to avoid in the first place.

Lately, the discussion around treating banks as utility companies has re-emerged and the academic debates are well on track. During 2024, Prof. Menand and Ricks, reinitiated the discussion around the model of utility banking with their academic proposal.[256] They propose targeted amendments to the US National Banking Act (NBA) in order to create public utility entities that offer essential infrastructure: the money supply.[257] These entities will be regulated as public utilities and will have a certain geographic area within which they will operate and will be allowed to earn 'no more than a fair return on their invested capital'.[258] Utility banks would function in a 'cap and trade' system with an adjustable cap on the supply of bank money, through making loans and buying bonds to increase the money supply and by selling loans and bonds they decrease it.[259] According to their proposal, this model requires the modernisation of the national banking system and restoring the structural separation regime is necessary step towards this direction. Menand and Rick's proposal for utility banking brings again the discussion for this model on the spotlight and therefore reopens the much-needed academic debate.

---

[254] See in F.S. Mishkin, 'Anatomy of a financial crisis', Working Paper No. 3934, *NBER Working Paper Series*, National Bureau of Economic Research (NBER), December 1991.

[255] Ibid., Figure 1 at p. 6.

[256] See in L. Menand and M. Ricks, 'Rebuilding Banking Law: Banks as Public Utilities' (2024) 41 *Yale Journal on Regulation*, pp. 591–651.

[257] Ibid., p. 612.

[258] Ibid.

[259] Ibid.

Another very interesting approach towards the concept of public/utility banking has been proposed by Prof. Omarova; In August 2024, she published an article[260] building upon her previous proposals,[261] offering a detailed conceptual framework for establishing public banks that prioritise public interest over profit. The primary goal of Omarova's proposal is to democratise the financial system by ensuring that public money is used for the public good. She argues that the current system disproportionately benefits private banks and contributes to economic inequality. By restructuring the financial system, she aims to create a more equitable and resilient economy. With respect to the institutional design framework, she emphasises the importance of carefully designing public banks by considering their core functions, funding sources, asset structures, and governance models. She identifies critical decision points in these areas to guide the creation of institutions that can effectively deliver public benefits.[262] When it comes to the creation of a public interest-oriented finance ecosystem, Prof. Omarova advocates a systemic approach to public banking, encouraging policymakers to focus on developing an ecosystem of financial institutions that serve public interests. This includes integrating public banks with other public financial entities to maximise their impact on societal goals.[263] With respect to governance and accountability, she discusses the governance structures necessary for public banks to ensure transparency, accountability, and responsiveness to public needs. She highlights the challenges and opportunities in establishing such frameworks within the broader financial system.[264] Finally, she advocates for further integration with broader financial reforms, as the article situates public banking within the context of broader financial reforms, such as the introduction of Central Bank Digital Currencies (CBDCs) and the establishment of entities like the National Investment Authority (NIA), suggesting that these reforms can complement public banking initiatives to create a more equitable and resilient financial system.[265]

Prof. Omarova's ideas have faced significant opposition, particularly from conservative lawmakers and banking industry groups, with critics arguing that her proposals would lead to excessive government control over the financial

---

[260] See in S.T. Omarova, 'Public Banking as an Institutional Design Project' (2024) 41 *Yale Journal on Regulation*, pp. 1128–1184.

[261] Professor Saule Omarova, from Cornell University, has proposed a comprehensive reimagining of the US financial system through her concept of 'public banking'. Her ideas, particularly outlined in her 2020 paper '*The People's Ledger: How to Democratize Money and Finance the Economy*', have sparked significant debate and controversy, both academically and politically.

[262] See in S.T. Omarova, 'Public Banking as an Institutional Design Project' (2024) 41 *Yale Journal on Regulation*, p. 1146 onwards.

[263] Ibid., p. 1154 onwards.

[264] Ibid., p. 1159 onwards.

[265] Ibid., p. 1162 onwards.

system and undermine the role of private banks. Supporters contend that her proposals are thought experiments aimed at addressing systemic issues in the financial system, rather than concrete policy recommendations. They argue that her ideas are part of a broader discussion on how to reform financial institutions to better serve the public interest. The academic debate seems to escalate into a full discussion about the future of banking and financial regulation in the US; as we will explore below, based on the history of financial regulation in the US, these discussions are more than welcomed.

2.2.1.2 *The 'Narrow Funding Bank' Proposal*

The Narrow Funding Bank (NFB) is another attempt to solve the issues that universal banking poses for financial stability. It complements the abovementioned utility banking approach in the sense that it allows a bank to engage in certain activities that are deemed forbidden for utility banks. Prof. Gorton and Metrick put forward this proposal in 2010[266] and their goal was to deal with the securitisation problems that arose during the recent GFC. To that end, they suggested bringing within the regulatory perimeter Asset Backed Securities (ABS) by allowing their purchase to institutions that would be licensed and regulated. Perhaps the most important aspect of their proposal is that these institutions should be granted access to the US Federal Reserve's (Fed) discount window because they would be regulated and supervised by the Fed.[267]

Furthermore, these institutions would be subject to the prudential requirements imposed by the legislation associated with maximum levels (ceilings) in leverage, liquidity, and market risk. These banks would be funded by issuing medium term notes that would turn into equity if regulatory capital falls below certain minimum levels in times of distress. Regarding their legal status and structure, NFBs would be structured as standalone, separately ring-fenced entities without any direct ownership linkages to commercial banks. They would accept deposits and provide payments, but they would be banned from granting loans or exposing their own funds to investment banking activities, derivatives, and proprietary trading.[268] The above proposal is highly concentrated on bringing within the regulatory perimeter certain aspects of the shadow banking industry. Indeed, simple banking structures with separated entities to undertake the various businesses are very helpful for resolution and

---

[266] See in G. Gorton and A. Metrick, 'Regulating the Shadow Banking System', *Brookings Papers on Economic Activity*, Fall 2010, pp. 261–312.

[267] Their proposal was originally addressed only to the narrow funding banks that were registered in the US and would be under the supervision of the Federal Reserve.

[268] See in J.T.S. Chow and J. Surti, 'Making Banks Safer: Can Volcker and Vickers Do It?', *IMF Working Paper*, WP/11/236, International Monetary Fund, 2011, Washington D.C., p. 12.

effective supervision but the present proposal ends in increasing credit risk that securitisation tries to spread and diversify in the first place.

2.2.1.3 *Evaluation of the 'Narrow Banking' Proposals: Benefits and Drawbacks*

Narrow banking proposals have been proposed and formulated precisely to create a safer financial system. The problem is that since we do not have any countries that currently apply such regulatory framework, we are not able to fully evaluate these proposals and understand their potential impact. What is understandable though is that we can delineate some very theoretical aspects of their impact, both positive and negative, that will help us reach the final conclusions. The benefits of narrow banking proposals are very clear and straightforward. Financial stability, reduce the need for public bailouts and increase the resolvability of banking entities if needed. Since the narrow banking approach requires banks to operate under a very strict and simple business model (acceptance of deposits and payment solutions), crises will be extremely rare phenomena and the system's stability will be enhanced. The deposit guarantee system will ensure depositors that banks will be robust enough to handle any adverse effects arising from their business. As a result, no bank runs will occur since no maturity mismatching will take place.

The costs of narrow funding proposals are associated with the credit provision mechanism that banks are participating in. As we have seen earlier on, in their traditional business model, banks are accepting deposits and provide loans, normally long-term ones. The maturity mismatch between liquid liabilities (deposits) and illiquid assets (loans) creates risks (bank runs) but also generates profits for the banks. Furthermore, the above maturity mismatch supplies the economy with much needed credit that fuels investments and ultimately supports economic growth. Another serious impact on banks from the above structural measures might be the difficulty implementing the narrow banking proposals into reality, since major adjustments would be required in terms of already established contracts which will be difficult to renegotiate and restructure to reflect the new regime.[269] The costs from that adaptation could be extremely high and the uncertainty would be unnecessary for the industry. These costs can become even higher when difficult structural arrangements might take place to comply with the regulatory requirements. New legal entities might become necessary to establish and various tax benefits from operations under the same roof might get lost with further cost saving actions.[270] This situation could drive upwards the funding costs of a bank holding company that would like to combine a narrow bank and other financial services under the same holding company structure. Adverse effects of the narrow banking

[269] Ibid., p. 8.
[270] Ibid.

model might also affect consumers, since they may suffer from lower deposit returns attributed to the much safer banking model and of reduction in utility from the absence of the 'one stop shop' approach that the universal bank offers.[271] In addition, credit supply might become tighter or at a higher cost for consumers since the non-bank entity that wish to provide loans will bear increased costs of borrowing as well. Lastly, the diversification benefits for the bank will be lost since the structural break-up will create a very different operational model with few, if at all, diversification benefits.

2.2.2 The 'Ring-Fencing' Model Proposal

Ring-fencing is another structural proposal to regulate the banking sector. On the aftermath of the global financial crisis, ring-fencing became a very fashionable word in the regulatory circles, both academic and professional. Many regulators across the world decided it was time to adopt structural reforms that were based on the ring-fencing of entities, activities, or sometimes both. Ring-fencing per se is not a novelty; it has been well known and already used, especially in the US, before it 'was cool' to discuss about it as a financial regulation policy option. Since ring-fencing does not apply only to the financial sector, a more holistic approach is required to understand how it functions and applies to the financial and non-financial sector.

2.2.2.1 *Theoretical Background and Legal Rationale*

Although it became widely known after the publication of Vickers Report in the UK, the legal idea behind the adoption of ring-fencing model existed already in various regulatory regimes, especially in utility companies, in asset securitisation and in certain US Congress proposals to regulate the insurance industry. Since using ring-fenced entities to enforce regulation was not widely commented by scholars and academics, at least until the final version of Vickers Report, and also because few crystallised definitions of ring-fencing could be found in the academic literature, we will base our analysis on Prof. Schwarcz's seminal paper to delve into the various aspects of this regulatory tool.[272] Schwarcz supports that ring-fencing actually means the 'legal deconstruction of a firm in order to more optimally reallocate and reduce risks'.[273] This deconstruction can occur in three ways:

(i) by protecting the firm from any affiliate and/or bankruptcy risks ('bankruptcy remote firm'),[274]

---

271 Ibid.

272 See in S.L. Schwarcz, 'Ring-Fencing' (2013) 87 *Southern California Law Review*, pp. 69–110.

273 Ibid., p. 3.

274 Ibid.

(ii) by preventing the firm itself from engaging in activities deemed to be risky and/or investing in risky assets,[275] and

(iii) by separating from the firm, the assets that are deemed to be risky .[276]

Therefore, we understand that the aim of ring-fencing is to create a 'bankruptcy remote firm' ensuring that it will be able to operate on a standalone basis even in the case of failure of its affiliates, without also be taken advantage by its affiliated firms. This isolated and protected firm shall be able to withstand shocks, risks, and bankruptcy proceedings that might occur and will preserve both the assets and its business.[277]

(a) Ring-fencing as a measure to create a 'bankruptcy remote firm':
The use of ring-fencing measures to create a bankruptcy remote firm is not a novelty. That technique can be, and indeed has been, used in covered bonds and securitisation transactions and in public utility companies. In securitisation and covered bond transactions, the ring-fenced entity is usually the Special Purpose Entity (SPE) that acts on behalf of an affiliated firm that wants to raise funding. To increase its creditworthiness and borrow from investors at a lower cost, the SPE is usually bankruptcy remote, increasing thereby risk allocation. The aim is the same, to protect the SPEs from either voluntary or involuntary bankruptcy and can be achieved through contractual or legislative means.[278] Bankruptcy remoteness is also a basic aim of the use of ring-fencing in the public utility companies. Since the utility company is usually part of a broader group, most of the time affiliated with a holding company, it is thus exposed to the risks associated with the holding company and its activities. Ring-fencing the utility company results in a bankruptcy remote structure and helps assume the vital role in providing the public with utility services, notwithstanding any bankruptcy proceedings against the parent or other group companies.[279]
Bankruptcy remoteness can be achieved either contractually or with the enactment of appropriate legislation. Utility companies, for example in the US, are owned by a parent company under a holding company structure. This structure is considered to provide a flexible operating mode since it might be the case that the parent company is not regulated as a utility company and as a result, she might be exposed to risks associated with her other activities. The scope is to create a bankruptcy remote subsidiary entity that will withstand and mitigate the risks arising from the parent holding company activities.[280] In the US, both the terms and the means under which this remoteness will be achieved are mandated by the utility

275 Ibid.
276 Ibid.
277 Ibid.
278 Ibid., p. 6.
279 Ibid., p. 7.
280 Ibid., p. 8.

regulator.[281] An important point that must clarified here is that banks or insurance companies are not usually under ring-fencing structure aiming to be bankruptcy remote. This happens because usually banks and insurance companies are not subject to the traditional bankruptcy law. Especially for banks, the resolution regime has completely substituted the traditional bankruptcy law due to the special nature of banks.[282]

(b) Ring-fencing as a measure for a firm to operate on a standalone basis and to preserve a firm's business and assets:
Another use of ring-fencing measures is the ability of the ring-fenced entity to operate on a standalone basis even if its affiliate firm fails. A useful explanatory example is the case of a utility company that relies on its affiliates for certain goods and/or services to such extent that the utility entity will face problems if the affiliate fails. In that case, ring-fencing acts as an assurance for the smooth operation of the ring-fenced entity under any circumstances.[283] Thus, the dependence on the affiliates will be mitigated and other providers will assume that role.
The tool of ring-fencing can be used also to protect the ring-fenced entity from being 'taken advantage of by affiliated firms'.[284] This can be achieved through transacting at 'arm's length' with the affiliates and with other types of restrictions. This type of ring-fencing can also be applied to banks through regulatory requirements to transact with their affiliates 'at arm's length'.[285]

(c) Ring-fencing as a measure to limit the risky activities and/or investments of a firm:
Perhaps the most important aspect of the ring-fencing model in banking regulation is the ability to limit the risky activities and/or investments that a bank entity undertakes, thus aiming at achieving financial stability. In this category, the Vickers Report and the Liikanen Report are the most illustrative examples that we should examine in more detail.
i. Vickers Report:
The banking failures that occurred in the UK during the recent GFC (RBS, Northern Rock, etc.) gave an alarming signal that the banking sector was in a critical condition. In response to these failures, the UK established

---

281 Ibid., p. 9. In 1997, Enron acquired *Portland General Electric* (PGE), which was subjected to the regulation of the Oregon Public Utility Commission (OPUC). The merger was contingent upon specific terms imposed by the OPUC, among which was the mandate for Enron to own PGE under a bankruptcy remote structure. Indeed, when few years later Enron filed for bankruptcy, the ring-fenced PGE was protected from Enron's bankruptcy proceedings.

282 See in S.L. Schwarcz, 'Ring-Fencing' (2013) 87 *Southern California Law Review*, pp. 69–110.

283 Ibid.

284 Ibid., p. 10.

285 The principle of transacting at arm's length was adopted by the UK ring-fencing solution in 2013. For more details see our analysis below in Chapter 3.

the 'Independent Commission on Banking' (ICB), which produced a final report, the so-called 'Vickers Report'. The ICB was mandated to consider structural and non-structural reforms to the UK banking sector that would promote competition and financial stability. The ICB's goals were the following:

- 'Reduce the probability and impact of systemic financial crises in the future';[286]
- 'Maintain the efficient flow of credit to the real economy and the ability of households and businesses to manage their risks and financial needs over time';[287] and
- 'Preserve the function of the payments system and guaranteed capital certainty and liquidity for small savers including small and medium-sized enterprises (SMEs)';[288]

Based on the proposal tabled with the final report, the UK enacted new legislation that adopted the ring-fencing model as the principal means for ensuring financial stability and credit and liquidity provision across the more vulnerable parts of its economy.

ii. Liikanen Report:

At the EU level, discussions for imposing structural regulation (separation) to the banking sector started after the publication of the famous 'Liikanen Report'. The report was published by a High-Level Expert Group (HLEG) chaired by the then Governor of the Central Bank of Finland Erkki Liikanen. The European Commission tabled a legislative proposal for a Regulation introducing the structural separation of banks regarding certain trading activities but due to high political concerns and strong opposition from the industry the proposal did not manage to succeed in the institutional trialogue. Because of the stalemate in the legislative process, the European Commission announced back in 2019 that the legislative proposal would be withdrawn.

It must be clarified that although the Liikanen Report does not refer to ring-fencing per se, it recommends that banks, under predefined conditions and certain thresholds, separate certain activities which deemed to be risky from the deposit taking entities.[289] This is clearly a form of ring-fencing, albeit a broad one, that seeks to protect the bank that accepts deposits from engaging in activities that again are perceived to be risky. Risky activities, according

---

[286] See in Independent Commission on Banking (ICB), the 'Vickers Report', 'Final Report – Recommendations', September 2011, available at: https://webarchive.nationalarchives.gov.uk/ukgwa/20131003105424/https:/hmt-sanctions.s3.amazonaws.com/ICB%20final%20report/ICB%2520Final%2520Report%5B1%5D.pdf, p. 20.

[287] Ibid.

[288] Ibid.

[289] See in S.L. Schwarcz, 'Ring-Fencing' (2013) 87 *Southern California Law Review*, pp. 69–110, p. 15.

to the report, are proprietary trading and certain market making aspects, especially taking asset or derivatives positions.

Ring-Fencing and its use in financial industry:

From the above analysis, we understand that ring-fencing, in various types and specifications, has been broadly used to protect entities that provide special services (utilities, secured transactions, banking services) from risks that are associated with the broader group entities that the ring-fenced entities belong to. A similar approach can be traced in the financial industry where ring-fencing is used to create financial entities that can withstand shocks from adverse events and avoid creating financial instability that could put in danger either the deposits of people or the credit supply to the economy. Since the use of ring-fencing is considered as a form of financial regulation, at the same time forms part of the broader economic regulation which has two main objectives:

A) to correct the market failures of the financial system,[290] and

B) to protect the system against risk that can harm the system itself at its entirety.[291]

Ring-fencing can be used therefore as an economic regulation tool to correct the following market failures:

(1) distortions of market competition,
(2) the so called 'public goods problem',
(3) information failure,
(4) agency failure, and
(5) externalities.

We will proceed now and examine these market failures to better understand their interaction with the ring-fencing measures.

(1) Distortions of market competition

Under this generic title, we will include the distortions that arise from monopolistic and other situations of non-competitive markets. In a market where a monopoly exists, economic regulation tries to eliminate the possibility for an unregulated monopolist to increase prices through restrained production. The result will be increased prices and underproduction that leads to the undersupply of goods and services.[292] Other market distortions of competition include an oligopolistic situation where the production and the prices of the market participants are interdependent and interrelated between them. In a situation like this, market participants usually collude to set prices, production levels and market shares aiming at maximising their profits through increased prices. The rationale for regulating an oligopolistic market is therefore the

---

290 Ibid., p. 18.
291 Ibid.
292 Ibid., p. 19.

same as in monopoly: to avoid undersupply and unfair pricing.[293] What is interesting though is that this kind of market failure does not apply to the financial system since the market for financial and especially banking services is highly competitive. On the contrary, the utility services market is traditionally subject to competition regulation because it is considered as monopolistic. The application of ring-fencing model in utilities regulation does not intend to control competition and pricing issues but mostly is associated with the holding company structure model and the potential risks that may arise from the fact that the ring-fenced utility company is part of that holding company structure.[294]

(2) The 'public goods problem'

For Prof. Schwarcz the public goods problem is as 'a collective action supply problem' that results in either undersupply or oversupply and the state intervention aiming at correcting this problem is the typical solution either directly, by providing the goods, or indirectly by requiring the goods to be provided by the private sector.[295] As previously mentioned, the public goods problem arises when the goods have two characteristics: a) they are non-rivalry in consumption and b) they present non-excludability. The first situation arises when the use of goods by one person or group of persons does not obstruct other person or group of persons from their use and the latter situation arises when the benefits of the goods cannot be reserved for use by one person or group of persons. The public goods problem has two forms: a) 'prisoner's dilemma' and b) 'free riding'. Prisoner's dilemma is a game theory problem where two persons or groups of persons are acting in suboptimal ways because they lack the ability to communicate and coordinate their willing.[296] Free riding is a situation where person(s) or group(s) of persons lack the incentive to, or, to the contrary, are not incentivised to contribute personal resources into common endeavours and are free riding other's people efforts.[297] The connection between public goods problem and ring-fencing of financial firms can be established by adapting our perception of public goods to include the relevant financial services. Among them, the most suitable 'goods' are the banking services that are qualified as important for societal needs and are usually provided by private banks. Acceptance of deposits, efficient function of payments systems and credit supply through maturity mismatch in the traditional banking function. Prof. Schwarcz further understands that only the service of deposit acceptance can be qualified and protected under the earlier

[293] Ibid., p. 20.
[294] Ibid.
[295] Ibid., p. 21.
[296] Ibid.
[297] Ibid.

mentioned public goods' problem.[298] Sometimes, consumers acting under a prisoner's dilemma situation can act sub-optimally and since banks that offer that service are not always in a position to self-discipline other banks can actually exacerbate the situation and end up in a classic bank run situation. In that precise point the state intervention through bank regulation and deposit insurance schemes acts in a way that alleviates the burden and calms down the depositors. Therefore, ring-fencing initiatives can provide us with a credible solution to the bank run problems by isolating and protecting the deposit acceptance function of a bank that is deemed to be of social importance and therefore is qualified as a public good. The legal isolation of deposit taking banks from activities and assets that suffer from higher risk and potential losses can certainly be a credible choice for the regulators.

(3) Information failures

Another type of market failure is information failure. It results from inadequate information that is inherent in financial markets. Information failure can be further divided into two subcategories: a) 'bounded rationality' and b) 'asymmetric information'. Bounded rationality starts from the point when people are acting in a way not wholly rational. For example, events that are unlikely to happen but if they happen will create devastating effects, tend to be ignored. This bounded rationality issue causes information failure because people are misinterpreting, under-relying, or over-relying on information. On the other hand, asymmetric information occurs when in a transaction one party has superior information over the other party. This information advantage of the one party over the other can end up harming the less informed party and bring benefits to the better-informed party.[299] Complexity of the financial system and the evolution of financial engineering have further exacerbated the problems of asymmetric information. Transactions, markets, and interconnections among the participants can even undermine the ability of disclosure regimes to alleviate the burden of asymmetric information. Among the proposed solutions for reducing the negative effects of complexity is to increase standardisation in financial markets. However, standardisation in financial markets can also backfire and finally reduce innovation and ultimately prevent market participants from having access to tailor-made financial products that are specifically designed for their needs and risk appetite. Since financial firms suffer both from bounded rationality and asymmetric information problems,

298 Ibid., p. 23.

299 The most illustrative example of such an asymmetric information is the case of securities issuance. The issuing party has better and more accurate information over the potential byers regarding the financial situation of the company. Without proper disclosure regimes, this asymmetric information can end up harming the investors that will buy the securities in a price that might not reflect accurately the financial health of the company.

ring-fencing could possibly be a solution to these problems by simplifying the type of investments that these entities may engage.[300] Asymmetric information appears mostly in securities and bounded rationality can be experienced by banks in the form of bank runs. As a result, ring-fencing can help financial firms address these problems. Essentially in the banking sector, by ring-fencing the deposit institutions and protecting deposits by not allowing the banks to invest in certain risky activities, will eliminate the incentives for depositors to run on the banks since they will be protected from insolvency and other risks. As a result, deposits will be more stable and this added stability will make them feel less likely to panic, ultimately reducing the risk of bank runs.[301]

(4) Agency failure

Agency failure is relevant to economics and thus to financial regulation since it affects the management of financial firms.[302] It is based on the principal-agent conflict, which in our case applies to the management and shareholders of financial firms. The same problem can also arise within the firms, between middle ranked and senior ranked managers due to their reporting relationships. Since these managers are compensated based on their short-term schemes and targets, they do not care that much about the long-term survival of the firm. Various legislative proposals seek to address the agency failure issues that arise. Ring-fencing does not seem to be the optimal solution for the agency failure problems[303] at least directly. Indirectly, it can be helpful since it will not allow many risky investments on behalf of the depositors. These managers will be restricted to their options by the ring-fenced entity that will be allowed to perform only certain activities, in many cases predefined.

(5) Externalities

When we refer to externalities, we mean the market failure situation in which a firm, partly or totally, externalises the costs of taking an action. As an example, we can imagine the failure of a bank from adverse economic events that evaporates an investment. Although the investment could be in favour of its shareholders, the result of failure can cause serious adverse effects to the public, resulting in economic contraction and a financial crisis. The recent GFC provide us with numerous examples of financial institutions that took sound business decisions but ultimately failed to understand the associated tail risks that the complex structured financial products were associated with. Since the risks were not properly understood they were also not properly hedged and when accumulated losses appeared,

---

[300] See in S.L. Schwarcz, 'Ring-Fencing' (2013) 87 *Southern California Law Review*, pp. 69–110, p. 27.

[301] Ibid.

[302] Ibid., p. 28.

[303] Ibid., p. 29.

bounded rationality did not allow for proper actions towards minimisation of risks. As a result, the housing market bubble burst and various firms were amid acute crisis that their 'sound' investment practices and sophisticated risk models could not anticipate.

The externalities from the failure of various financial firms (such as Lehmann Brothers, AIG, Northern Rock, Bear Stearns etc.) created a huge financial crisis and the associated costs ultimately were resumed by the states and taxpayers crippling the financial stability of the world economy. The most appropriate way to solve the externalities problem is to require financial firms to internalise these costs arising from externalities.[304] This can become easily understandable if we imagine a fund that will be fed from bank contributions and each time a crisis arises the fund will intervene to calm down the markets and help internalise the costs from the crisis. This solution would prevent public money from being used as a bail out tool. The real solution for internalising the costs associated with externalities from financial institutions is the adoption of credible resolution regimes that will allow the orderly liquidation or wound down of financial institutions. The bigger the financial institution, the more credible and feasible the resolution regime must be. Resolution regimes, with the various tools that are available will, if properly calibrated and used, create a true mechanism for internalising the costs associated with financial intermediation.

Ring-fencing could be a wonderful solution that coupled with the available resolution tools can ensure that financial institutions will be able to internalise the costs that arise from externalities embedded in the financial industry. Recalling that ring-fencing can safeguard deposit taking activities of banks, reduce asymmetric information and limit the ability of financial firms to undertake risky investments that have big risks. As such, ring-fencing helps reduce market failures and overall increases the efficiency and the stability of the financial system. Another important role of ring-fencing measures is to protect against possible systemic risks, in two possible ways: a) by minimising panics and b) by creating modularity. As is well known, panics are often in the financial systems and sometimes can be also systemic in nature, thus causing systemic threats with severe repercussions.[305] Minimising panics can thus be an important aspect of financial stability. In the modern financial system, with extensive use of shadow banking entities to intermediate in credit supply, market failures can evolve into full scale crises and create panics. Ring-fencing, by correcting market failures, will thus help achieve to minimise panics and overall to protect the financial system from panics that have the potential to evolve into full scale crises with devastating effects. Creating modularity in

[304] Ibid., p. 31.
[305] Ibid., p. 33.

the financial system will protect it from the case in which a crisis that arises in a certain part of the system will not to be transmitted to the whole system. Since the modern financial system has the characteristic of high complexity and failures are almost inevitable, ring-fencing modularity will decouple the various parts of the system and will isolate certain parts, protecting them from the transmission of the crisis.[306] By protecting and isolating the parts of the financial system, failures will not be that devastated and in case they will severely damage certain parts of the system, they will not spread out to damage and collapse the whole system.

The ring-fencing tools we referred to earlier are suitable to bring modularity to the financial system. Bankruptcy remoteness, ability to operate on a standalone basis, structural separation of certain risky assets and/or activities etc. will ensure that in case of failure of these firms, their affiliates or their counterparties will not create and transmit a major crisis into the financial system and more importantly crises will not allow the ring-fenced entities to fail while are entitled with crucial services in favour of public interest.[307] Authorities introduce ring-fencing regimes in their prudential supervision and regulation frameworks for a variety of reasons. Especially in the financial sector, ring-fencing regimes can be based on two main reasons: a) policy reasons, and b) structural reasons.[308] The policy reasons are further divided into three drivers:

(a) The lack of a globally enforceable resolution mechanism,
(b) The existence of information asymmetries, and
(c) The desire to protect credit supply for external events

The first policy reason is the lack of a resolution regime with global enforceability. The former Bank of England (BoE) Governor, Mervin King, epitomised this problem by saying that 'global banking institutions are global in life and national in death'. When a crisis occurs, national central banks will have to step in and provide public support, acting as lenders of last resort. Without a clear view on what will happen when a bank is failing or likely to fail, home and host supervisors will probably have divergent interests on how the situation needs to be treated.[309] Despite of their intentions for cooperation, home and host supervisors will each seek to minimise the losses for their stakeholders, in their own jurisdictions, that might arise from this distressed situation. Ring-fencing regimes bring immediate relief and comfort for the supervisors when uncertainty arises about how efficiently the resolution mechanisms will perform. Someone must see the broader picture to realise that

---

306 Ibid., p. 34.

307 Ibid.

308 See in K. D'Hulster and I. Otker-Robe, 'Ring-Fencing Cross-Border Banks: An Effective Supervisory Response?' (2008) 5(1) *Journal of Financial Perspectives*, p. 5.

309 Ibid.

ring fencing, especially when suddenly imposed amid a crisis, has the potential to lead to a 'scramble for assets', stress the entire banking group and prevent 'good crisis management'.[310] The intensity of the works done at international level, with the aim to coordinate their actions, will allow supervisors to be better prepared for a crisis as bank specific resolution strategies are prepared, cooperation agreements are signed and resolvability assessments for the GSIBs are performed. However, in practice many impediments might arise since the resolution mechanisms, and particularly the bail in tool, are unlikely to provide absolute protection to the host countries for several reasons:

(a) The risk of using public funds to preserve financial stability will be always present, even if only for liquidity reasons and for a short period of time.[311]
(b) These international policies remain 'soft law', therefore are non-binding and non-enforceable contracts that are based on intents.[312]
(c) The lack of harmonisation on creditors' hierarchy between the various jurisdictions remains an important impediment to the resolution of branches of international banks.[313]
(d) Penultimate, these reforms are still 'works in progress' and new implementation challenges will be raised for supervisors, central banks, and resolution authorities along the way to concrete regimes.[314]
(e) Finally, loss absorbing capacities are not, by itself, a sufficient condition for ensuring effective resolution of globally active large banking groups.[315]

The second important rationale for ring-fencing measures is information asymmetries in the absence of any adequate information exchange arrangements between the home and host countries.[316] Therefore, such initiatives are driven by lack of information, doubts about the reliability of the relevant information, or uncertainty about how the resolution process will be executed in the jurisdictions where the bank operates and is headquartered. Even the simple threat of ring-fencing can also be used by the host supervisors as a means to persuade home supervisors to enhance their cooperation by stepping up information sharing or to address any particular host concerns.[317] Finally, the third policy rationale for a ring-fencing regime is to protect the supply of credit to the economy. At the same time, it can also prevent excessive deleveraging trends in the host country resulting from parent companies that are pulling out funding and capital from their operations in the host country.[318] As a

310 Ibid.
311 Ibid.
312 Ibid., p. 6.
313 Ibid.
314 Ibid.
315 Ibid.
316 Ibid.
317 Ibid.
318 Ibid., p. 7.

result, host supervisors have the option to ring-fence local liquidity and capital to support local credit supply through 'trapped pools' of assets, to the host country's benefit.

In addition to the above-mentioned policy reasons, ring-fencing measures can also be adopted based on certain structural characteristics of the financial system that influence home and host countries' decisions. These characteristics are the following:

- The location of financial stress:
  Supervisors in the host country have a strong incentive to ring-fence when they suspect that problems might arise in the parent bank or in the home country. Host country's supervisors have legitimate interests to ring-fence to protect the safety and soundness of the financial system through effective firewalls between the parent bank and the domestic operations in the host country. At the same time, the home country's supervisors have their own legitimate interest in imposing ring-fencing when they suspect that problems might arise in the host countries.[319]
- The business model of the banking group:
  Banking models may vary. On the one end of the spectrum, we find the typical branch business structure, where they key functions are centralised.[320] These institutions use also funding surpluses to fill deficits that appear within the group structure and as a result, affiliates are not independent entities since they trade and lend using the funds of the parent company, operating under the jurisdiction of the home country.[321] On the other end of the spectrum is the stand alone subsidiary structure. These entities are self-sufficient, operate nationally, and have effective firewalls between other group entities to prevent any support from the parent entity or from any other group entity. These entities have their own capital and liquidity to survive in times of distress and rely heavily on local deposits for funding and their business models are tied to the host country.[322]
  In centralised business models, host supervisors will need to rely heavily on the cooperation with the home country authorities but as second line of defence, host supervisors may adopt ring fencing measures that will restrict the use of centralised business models or will require additional requirements

319 Ibid.

320 Centralisation of business can apply in various areas such as corporate control functions, strategy and business planning operations, brand name, operational functions (IT systems, back-office business, accounting, telecommunications, etc.), treasury functions and marketing.

321 See in K. D'Hulster and I. Otker-Robe, 'Ring-Fencing Cross-Border Banks: An Effective Supervisory Response?' (2018) 5(1) *Journal of Financial Perspectives*, p. 7.

322 Many institutions are situated between these two extremes with hybrid structures and business models adapted to each specific situation. However, the centralized structures are the most common ones.

(additional capital and liquidity buffers) especially if the banking entity is allowed to accept deposits.[323] Apart from centralised business models though, a very important parameter of concern for both home and host supervisors is the complexity of the banking group itself. Modern banking groups with a global presence often can consist of hundreds or even thousands of legal entities (including branches, subsidiaries, and various service providing entities) that belong to the same group. Complex financial flows between these group entities and the frequent use of guarantees among them, perplexes even more the task for supervisors and renders almost impossible to introduce effective firewalls. Ring-fencing presents a credible alternative to tame these complex banking groups in the name of financial stability.[324]

- The geographical risk profile of the banking group:
  Herring defines three cases that are associated with the geographical risk profile or the systemic importance of a banking group: a) whether the parent bank is considered of systemic importance in the home country; b) whether the foreign operations are of significance to the solvency of the parent bank; and c) whether the foreign operations are of systemic importance in the host country.[325] Host supervisors will adopt ring-fencing measures when the foreign operations of a banking group are of systemic nature in their country, as the failure of such a firm would have a bigger impact on the domestic financial system. On the other hand, home supervisors will more likely ring fence if the bank is of systemic importance in the home country and particularly if the group is exposed to significant foreign operations.[326]

2.2.2.2 *Evaluation of the 'Ring-Fencing' Model: Benefits and Drawbacks*

The advantages of ring-fencing can be broadly grouped in four main categories. Firstly, the firm's structure that ring-fencing proposes can enhance the separability of the firm and so its resolvability.[327] Since the mixing of various business lines in huge financial conglomerates that are offering integrated universal banking services creates an extremely blurred image of what type of activities are riskier than others and if these activities will be viable on their own. This results in creating a favourable environment for the efficient

---

323 See in K. D'Hulster and I. Otker-Robe, 'Ring-Fencing Cross-Border Banks: An Effective Supervisory Response?' (2018) 5(1) *Journal of Financial Perspectives*, p. 8.

324 Ibid.

325 See in R.J. Herring, 'Conflicts Between Home and Host Country Prudential Supervisors', in D. Evanoff, G. Kaufman and J. LaBrosse (eds.), *International Financial Instability, Global Banking and National Regulation*, Vol. 2, World Scientific Studies in International Economics, October 2007, p. 267.

326 See in K. D'Hulster and I. Otker-Robe, 'Ring-Fencing Cross-Border Banks: An Effective Supervisory Response?' (2018) 5(1) *Journal of Financial Perspectives*, p. 8.

327 See in K. Alexander, 'Regulating the Structure of the EU Banking Sector' (2015) 16 *European Business Organization Law Review*, p. 246.

imposition of the losses from failing commercial, investment, or wholesale banks to their shareholders by the competent authorities.[328] The imposed transparency regarding structure and activities will impose market discipline to creditors and investors that will be able to correctly price the associated risks. As a result, any expectations for government sponsored bailouts or other implicit or explicit guarantees will diminish. Ring-fencing will create simpler structures and ultimately safer structures that will ensure taxpayers that the states will no longer intervene in the financial system using their money.

Secondly, ring-fencing will create separate categories of activities that will enjoy different levels of state protection.[329] In contrast to the universal banking model, which combines every type of banking and financial services under the same roof, ring-fenced entities will allow the competent authorities to treat differently different types of activities when in resolution. Furthermore, competent authorities will be able to separate and distinguish between various types of creditors of the retail banking operations and creditors of other activities that should bear a heavier burden.[330] Thirdly, ring-fencing will help to solve the time-inconsistency issue when trying to solve the TBTF problem. The problem is that the competent authorities will always feel extreme pressure, in the pic of the crisis, to support failing or likely to fail banks aiming not to fuel panics towards the banks.[331] By imposing the separation of certain banking activities, the pressure will be diminished since the most valuable activities will be under the ring-fenced entity that will be easier to be supported. As a result, the riskier activities will be separated from the political pressure and will untie the hands of competent authorities. Lastly, ring-fencing will reduce the size of the banks' balance sheets and will enhance supervision, market discipline and resolvability of the firms by reducing complexity.[332] Complexity of the modern financial system requires sophisticated risk management on behalf of the financial firms and sophisticated supervisory methodologies on behalf of the supervisors. Ring-fencing could, at least for the retail and payments activities, reduce the burden of both supervisors and bank managers since the simple and transparent structure of the banks would be much easier to supervise and regulated. Clarity of the rules applying to simpler structures would be also enhanced leading to simpler but more straightforward requirements.[333]

Ring-fencing is a very controversial policy option, since usually both its opponents and supporters are not entirely happy with the solutions ultimately adopted. While ring-fencing may provide immediate benefits for the host

[328] Ibid.
[329] Ibid.
[330] Ibid.
[331] Ibid., p. 247.
[332] Ibid.
[333] Ibid.

supervisors it comes at a cost that is positively correlated with the severity of the ring-fencing regime. In other words, the stricter the ring-fencing regime is, the higher will be the costs for the adopting jurisdiction.[334] These costs are also to the detriment of the banking group, in terms of resilience, and to the broader financial system in general. Among the most important aspects of the critic against ring-fencing measures are the following points. Firstly, ring-fencing can result in regulatory arbitrage by the large financial conglomerates. These resourceful institutions can utilise techniques that will allow them to transfer assets and activities to a more supervisory and regulatory friendly environment or to shift them into the so-called shadow banking system. As a result, many financial activities that were performed by banks and were regulated under the banking supervision regime will now be operated under the roof of non-banking entities (such as the asset management firms) posing serious threats to the system. Furthermore, since the dominating perception is that trading and proprietary trading activities are perceived as more than other activities, banks will need to dispose of them to other entities with unknown results. Even fears of credit misallocation might come up when banks will have to comply with complex ring-fencing requirements. Most of the synergies will be lost and we can expect an increase in the cost of credit.[335] Although the shifting of the riskier activities into other entities will not be destabilising per se, the mass amount of trading activities that will finally transferred will create huge regulatory imbalances that might hinder the ability of the supervisors to understand the new structure that will be created in a *déjà vu* of the recent GFC.

Secondly, the ring-fencing measures will enforce to the public opinion the fundamental theory that investment banking activities are riskier per se than the traditional, commercial banking activities. This misconception tends to create the belief that since investment banking services are riskier, thus requiring to be treated in a very specific way, they are socially burdensome and do not produce social welfare. This position has been shaped into a general attack to investment banking services, especially after the recent GFC that revealed the role of many investment banking practices in fuelling the crisis.[336] That position fails to consider the important synergies that we referred to earlier on and constitute the basis for the universal banking model. Economies of scale and scope are driving down the cost of credit for these giant conglomerates, allowing them to offer competitive financial services by

334 See in K. D'Hulster and I. Otker-Robe, 'Ring-Fencing Cross-Border Banks: An Effective Supervisory Response?' (2018) 5(1) *Journal of Financial Perspectives*, 2018, p. 14.
335 Ibid.
336 Ibid.

effectively combining risky securities activities and the less risky commercial banking activities.[337]

Thirdly, it must be expressly clarified that ring-fencing measures, and in general structural regulation in the banking sector, are not a panacea for safeguarding financial stability. Structural regulation initiatives must be complemented with a variety of tools that will act both macro-prudentially and micro-prudentially to achieve the social aim of financial stability. The fact that ring-fencing will create small and medium-sized banks, since certain activities will be abandoned or transferred to other entities, does not mean that these banks per se will not be vulnerable to other types of risks. The fact that these banks will not engage in investment banking means that they will not be able to diversify their portfolios effectively and efficiently since they will not have access to a deeper and wider financial market. Furthermore, their concentration in traditional and safer activities will make them vulnerable to risks arising from them, such as credit risk, since they will not be able to diversify their portfolio. Also, geographical restrictions in their activities will have similar effects with the 1920s financial crises that hit US banks. Unable to diversify their assets due to geographical restrictions, US banks suffered from local economic downturns and were exposed to the agricultural risks associated with bad weather conditions that were destroying harvesting and ultimately were driving borrowers bankrupt. An analogous situation might appear as well if ring-fencing is too strict. The perceived safer activities might create non-performing loans if an economic downturn will appear and will devalue the real estate assets that are used as collaterals for lending by the commercial banks. This lack of diversification combined with lending concentration to specific sectors and activities will create risks that might spread across the financial system, creating multiple adverse effects that the ring-fencing initiative was trying to avoid in the first place. Prof. Alexander provides further examples from the recent GFC based on UK findings. The collapse of Northern Rock, Bradford and Bingley and Alliance and Leicester in the 2007-2008 events in the UK demonstrate that banking crises might arise from poorly executed underwriting and suboptimal regulation in traditional banking activities, such as lending, and not necessarily from risky securities, derivatives, and trading activities.[338]

Ring-fencing, as has been discussed above, has a strict approach and clear aims. The use of ring-fencing is to protect what is perceived to be the most precious parts of a firm or the most important services from a provider and has nothing to do with the riskiness of the service or of the business per se. It simply tries to protect from risks what it has been chosen by the legislators. Ring-fencing proposals are extremely popular nowadays because their primary

337 Ibid.

338 Ibid.

objective is to create a safer financial system without limiting, to the extent possible, the benefits of the traditional financial intermediation role of banks. Given though the various, mostly unintended consequences that these measures might have, it is strongly suggested that ring-fencing and structural regulation measures in general should be adopted cautiously after being well calibrated and discussed among the various stakeholders for their consequences. Especially at an international level, regulation imposing structural reforms should be adopted after thorough examination and extensive discussion among the various regulatory *fora*. The purpose of this discussion is to inform in advance the counterparty states about the intention of a state to adopt such measures. Since the big financial conglomerates that are operating at a transnational level and have adopted the universal banking model are under constraint with the structural measures, the losers of this policy option might be both the firms and the states. The firms will lose their access at a minimum cost to deep financial markets and will have to adapt their operations in a new business model while on the other side of the fence the states that are adopting these measures might lose the beneficial operations of big universal banks that are providing capital, liquidity, and credit to their economies. Finally, another important aspect that must be considered when evaluating structural regulation measures is the fact that these measures do not offer complete protection to the financial system. Unless it is complemented with other, micro-prudential and macro-prudential measures, structural regulation is inadequate per se to address systemic risks that can create systemic instability and ultimately pose serious threats to the system and its components.

2.2.3 The 'Functional Separation/Subsidiarisation' Model

Another structural measure, with similar effects compared to the ring-fencing proposal but also with important differences, is the measure of separating certain (banking) activities that are considered riskier and thus posing a threat to the stability of the institution or the system in general. This approach is known as 'functional separation/subsidiarisation' approach (from now on 'FSS approach') aims to protect the firm, in our case the bank, from negative impacts arising from the business of banking or from certain businesses that are deemed to be riskier than others. As a result, the legislators decide which activities (banking services) are considered more important or riskier than others are and impose requirements for the separation of these types of activities from the bank entity that accepts deposits and provides vital services to society. Usually, the approach calls for the separation of the riskier activities to protect the deposit acceptance function of the bank. While traditional ring-fencing tries to isolate the activities that are considered of extreme importance for the social needs from the rest of the group, the FSS approach requires that the riskier activities shall be executed by another entity that might be part of the same group either as a standalone entity having no affiliation with the banking entity or as a subsidiary of the bank entity.[339]

The proposals of the Liikanen Report have the FSS approach at their epicentre, presenting both similarities with the Vickers Report and its ring-fencing concept but also important differences. Among the most important differences is that while the Vickers report proposed to carve out the domestic activities of deposit taking and payments services and to ring-fence them in a completely separately capitalised subsidiary entity of the banking group,[340] the Liikanen FSS approach aimed to carve out the functions of proprietary trading and certain aspects of market making activities from the rest of the banking activities. It recommended accordingly that these activities shall be performed by a legally separated entity and carried out on a standalone basis.[341] The Liikanen proposals would allow for the universal banking model to continue to exist as a broader financial group, but certain activities would be no longer able to be performed from the banking entity that accepts deposits and provides loans. This policy option would force the traditionally universal banks of the EU to adopt and operate under a holding company structure to continue to engage in the full spectrum of the financial industry. Under that structure, the subsidiaries of the holding company would be legally separated entities with their own capital, thus independently conducting their banking and trading activities.[342] From the preceding analysis, what is clear is that under the FSS approach, the activities perceived as riskier, and therefore need to be carried out by a legally separated entity to mitigate the risks arising from them, are not forbidden to be performed by the banking conglomerate. Therefore, the requirement imposed to the banks is a functional one, in the sense that it requires certain activities to be performed under certain requirements, and not a blanket style ban on these activities that a stricter separation regime requires.

Contrary to the regime of complete separation, that will be examined later, the FSS approach that the Liikanen report advocated for, accepts that the coexistence of certain activities within the same group would create advantages such as the facilitation of resolution, the simplification of risk management operations and would rand unnecessary for the investment banking activities to migrate to less regulated parts of the financial system.[343] As a result, the FSS approach seems to be less strict than the ring-fencing regime in the sense that it continues to allow certain activities to be performed by the banks since it

---

339 Ibid.

340 See in L. Gambacorta and A. van Rixtel, 'Structural bank regulation initiatives: approaches and implications', *BIS Working Papers*, no. 412, April 2013, Basel, Bank of International Settlements, p. 24.

341 Ibid.

342 Ibid., p. 25.

343 Ibid.

explicitly recognises the efficiency gains from the combination under the same roof of certain banking activities, despite being perceived as riskier.

Evaluation of the 'Functional Separation' Model: Benefits and Drawbacks

The main advantage of the FSS approach is that it allows the risky activities to remain within the banking group, albeit in a separate legal entity. It allows the continuation of the universal banking model, but it wouldn't be any longer possible to conduct a wide range of financial activities under a single roof, since these activities are perceived to be risky, or at least riskier than others, and must be performed through a separate legal entity, which is allowed to be within the same banking group. Universal banks, therefore, would be required to adopt a holding company structure with separately capitalised subsidiaries conducting (risky) banking and trading activities.[344]

Another advantage of the FSS approach is that the risky activities do not migrate to the shadow banking system. Remaining under the banking group umbrella they will be supervised together with the rest of the activities and therefore supervisors can monitor their riskiness. Should they discover evidence that such activities pose risks to the banking group or to the broader financial system they can intervene to mitigate such risks. The fact that these activities will be performed by a separately capitalised entity will provide extra safety since any potential losses will be absorbed by the capital of the subsidiary entity and will not infect the deposit taking entity. Overall, the FSS approach aims at achieving both advantages: a) facilitating resolution through a separately capitalised entity that will assume the risky activities, and b) keeping the benefits of diversification and scale and scope economies without allowing the migration of lucrative fee-based activities to the shadow banking sector.[345]

The main drawback of this approach is that it is based on the misconception that certain financial (banking) activities are riskier than others. Thus, the bank will not be able to enjoy the benefits of risk diversification and economies of scale and scope as described above. The evidence that some activities are riskier than others is difficult to be confirmed by scientific evidence and the economists are finding mixed results that do not explicitly support the need for separation of activities. Moreover, as the recent GFC has demonstrated, it is not unequivocally clear that the concentration of trading activities in separate entities will enhance financial stability and prevent crises from appearing since these firms may have access to less stable wholesale funding markets and be plagued by other issues (including traditional governance matters). At

---

344 See in L. Gambacorta and A. van Rixtel, 'Structural bank regulation initiatives: approaches and implications', *BIS Working Papers*, no. 412, April 2013, Basel, Bank of International Settlements, p. 25.

345 Ibid.

the same time, they will remain highly interconnected with other parts of the global financial system, and this could give rise to considerable contagion risk. Lehman Brothers is a seminal, case book example that supports that view.[346]

2.2.4 The 'Strict Structural Separation' Model

The last banking model regarding regulation through structural reforms, in a banking entity that offers the relevant services, is both a very clear cut and strict concept. The 'strict or complete structural separation' model (from now on the 'SSS model') can be illustrated by the GSA adopted by the US on the aftermath of the 1929 financial crash. The widespread belief that the big universal banks engaged in securities market created the financial crash by abusing investors and using their deposits to obtain cheap funding for speculative transactions forced legislators to introduce a SSS model between the deposit taking banking entities and the (pure) investment banks. As a result, the law imposed a total ban on the deposit institutions that had access to the discount window of the Federal Reserve, from engaging in securities markets. On the other hand, the investment banks were banned from accepting deposits and having access to the discount window, but at the same time they were protected from the competition in the securities markets. Specific exemptions were granted to the commercial banks allowing them to engage in a limited number of securities activities but generally the ban was complete and the structural regulation very strict, imposing a complete separation. That separation did not allow even for affiliation between the commercial and investment banks since it presumed that moral hazard and the conflict of interest would be a huge threat to the financial stability of the system.

The SSS model imposes strict requirements and bans certain types of financial institutions, banks in our case, from engaging in certain activities. The ban is usually very strict, in the sense that it can't be circumvent by using a holding company structure, thereby rejecting the possibility of establishing separately capitalised affiliates that would be allowed to participate in the securities markets and require enormous adaptation from the institutions to comply with it. Moreover, the ban on activities has a dual protection meaning; first, it protects the deposit taking institution from riskier activities that might have a negative impact on taxpayers' money and second it protects the different parts of the financial system from unfair practices and competition, since it allows specific entities to undertake specific activities.

---

[346] Ibid., p. 4.

Evaluation of the 'Strict Structural Separation' Model: Benefits and Drawbacks

The potential benefits produced from a SSS model can be grouped in two broad categories: a) the enhanced stability of the financial system and b) the enhanced resolvability of the financial entities. In terms of systemic stability, the much simpler structure and the rigid separation between the activities will create smaller institutions with smaller balance sheets consequently posing less risk for the entire system. The level of interconnection between the entities will diminish to far more manageable levels thereby simplifying the risk management requirements for the institutions at stake. On the other hand, the resolvability of the institutions is enhanced since there will be simpler, less complex institutions with no mixing of different activities that might perplex the effective resolution when needed. The complexity of the universal banking structure with countless subsidiaries and affiliated entities across the globe will not be worried since the banks will have to change their structure to better reflect the activities they want to focus on, divesting from the rest. Ultimately, the simplicity of the banks' structures will help the supervisors to better enforce supervision and moreover tailor their resolution plans for the specific needs of the banks, tasks that will be significantly easier to be accomplished.

Obviously, the adoption of the SSS model completely contradicts the theory of universal banking model we referred to earlier. The purported economies of scale and scope that support the business theory behind the universal banking model are no longer available and the benefits from risk and asset diversification cannot be applied since the combination of different streams of revenue is no longer possible. Perhaps the most important drawback is the fact that once diversification benefits will be lost, both commercial and investment banks will inevitably concentrate to business lines that have their one risks and will be exposed to higher risk that could only be mitigated had diversification across businesses lines be allowed. Taking as a hypothetical example the case of a universal bank that after the SSS model applies, is forced to abandon its investment banking activities, we can assume that the bank will inevitably shrink the size of its balance sheet, due to the loss of a considerable amount of income from its investment banking activities and will undertake only traditional banking activities (accepting deposits and providing loans). This will increase its exposure to the credit risk of its borrowers and will not be offset by another stream of revenue that could alleviate the potential burden from an increase in the non-performing loans.[347]

The same scenario could be also materialised for a bank that decides to abandon its commercial banking activities and because of the separation

---

[347] Any increase of the non-performing loans is a direct indication for deterioration of the bank's credit risk exposure.

requirement, will now shift her focus from universal banking to purely investment banking activities and the loss of deposit funding will increase its cost of capital, potentially leading to a shrink in activities and overall smaller value. It goes without saying that both the aforementioned examples will ultimately end up in a shrinkage of credit supply to the economy and at a higher cost. One final point which must be considered is the possibility that the SSS model might come also with geographical restrictions as was the case in the US with the restrictions on interstate branching. These types of restrictions can make banks even more vulnerable to adverse scenario events because they will be forced to focus their activities on areas that can suffer from area specific economic downturns.[348]

3 CORPORATE AND LEGAL STRUCTURES OF BANKING GROUPS: A BRIEF OVERVIEW

The corporate and legal structures among banking groups differ significantly. Bank groups are protean—not only are they very different one from another, but also, they may change significantly as the business of the bank changes. Although each banking group is to some extent unique, to a certain extent it is possible to categorise them into five broader types based on some common characteristics. To that end, we will use the 2012 study conducted by the Institute of International Finance (IIF), to replicate these types, excluding the cooperative and saving banks' models.

3.1. *The 'Holding Company (HoldCo) funded' model*[349]

In this model, a holding company (HoldCo entity) holds a bank and an investment business entity. A portion of the external funding of this entity – including equity, capital instruments and unsecured debt – is raised primarily at the HoldCo entity level. Business activities, such as commercial banking and trading activities, are conducted in the main bank or in another subsidiary. This model is not frequently used in Europe but is more common to the US and

[348] In the US, during the Glass-Steagall Act, banks were also facing geographical restrictions and were not allowed to expand into other states except under very specific circumstances. This fact made the US banking system extremely vulnerable to state specific economic downturns that were able to pose serious threats to state banks that were funding the economic activity of that state.

[349] See in Institute of International Finance (IIF), *Making Resolution Robust – Completing the Legal and Institutional Frameworks for Effective Cross-Border Resolution of Financial Institutions*, June 2012, Washington D.C., p. 52.

Japan[350] and the FDIC has pointed out certain useful features in their analysis. The liabilities most frequently cited for bail-in are concentrated in a single legal entity and the customer and counterparty relationships are typically conducted at a level below the HoldCo entity. This structure may allow resolution to take place using a 'single-point-of-entry' (SPoE) procedure at the HoldCo entity only, while the other legal entities stay in business. It is likely that at least one of these local entities has been adversely affected by recent events (as the cause of the stress on the group) and may need liquidity or capital to restore its position. This can be satisfied, when necessary, by down streaming any needed resources from the recapitalised HoldCo entity. Although this type of approach could reduce the amount of interjurisdictional coordination needed and simplify the resolution process it cannot be used for all institutions, as this initial organisation is not so frequently opted for systemically important banks outside the US.

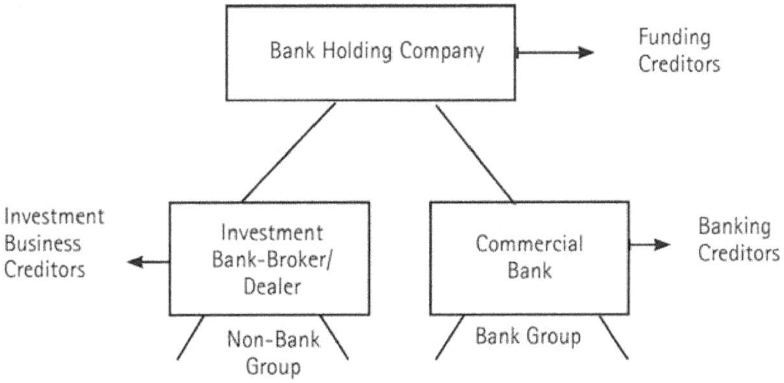

Source: Institute of International Finance (IIF),
Making Resolution Robust – Completing the Legal and Institutional Frameworks for Effective Cross-Border Resolution of Financial Institutions, June 2012, p. 53

350 In the US, about 84% of commercial banks form part of a Bank Holding Company (BHC) structure. More than 75% of small banks with assets of less than $100 million are owned by BHCs with this percentage increasing to 100% for large banks with more than $10 billion in assets. Finally, about 60% of minority-owned banks are owned by BHCs. Because of the global financial crisis of 2007–2009, almost all the independent investment banks that survived the turmoil (Goldman Sachs, Morgan Stanley, J.P. Morgan) adopted a holding company structure to have access in the Federal Reserve's discount window. Data available at: https://www.fedpartnership.gov/bank-life-cycle/grow-shareholder-value/bank-holding-companies.
In Japan, the most illustrative example is that of Nomura Group, one of the biggest financial services groups. Through a holding company structure, with *Nomura Holdings, Inc.* as the holding company, the group contains several subsidiaries that offer not only distinct services (*Nomura Securities Co., Ltd.*, *Nomura Asset Management Co., Ltd.*, *The Nomura Trust and Banking Co., Ltd.*, etc.) but also operates at various geographical areas (Nomura Americas, Nomura EMEA, Nomura Asia ex-Japan, etc.). For an overview of the Nomura Group structure see in their respective website: https://www.nomuraholdings.com/company/group/.

3.2. *The 'Big Bank' model*[351]

In this structure, an 'empty' holding company owns a bank with a large balance sheet; the assets not held within the bank itself are held by subsidiaries of the bank. Funding is often raised primarily at the bank level, since any funding raised at the holding company level is considered structurally subordinated to bank level funding. In general, the 'big bank' model is likely to conduct its derivatives, markets, and trading businesses outside of the main legal entity, since this will be the most creditworthy member of the group and will ensure that counterparties have the lowest risk exposure and therefore the lowest costs of dealing with it. A common variant of this structure is where the bank itself is the holding company for the group.

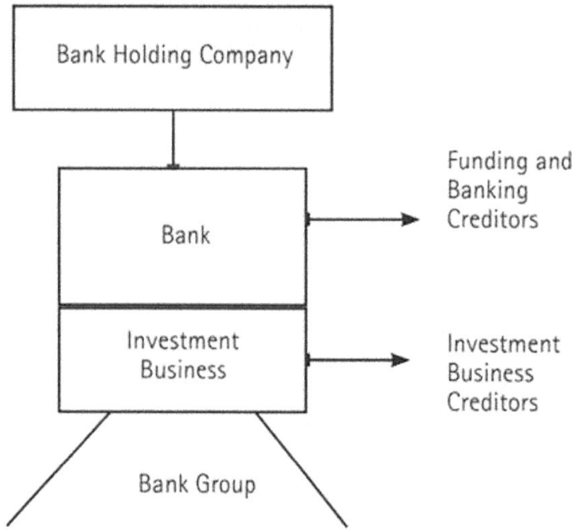

Source: Institute of International Finance (IIF),
Making Resolution Robust – Completing the Legal and Institutional Frameworks for Effective Cross-Border Resolution of Financial Institutions, June 2012, p. 54

3.3. *The 'Bank/Non-Bank' Model*[352]

In this model, a holding company owns a bank and a non-bank investment firm. There may be little interaction between these two group entities below the holding company level. In this case, it is possible that all three entities – the bank, the investment firm, and the holding company – may have raised

[351] See in Institute of International Finance (IIF), *Making Resolution Robust – Completing the Legal and Institutional Frameworks for Effective Cross-Border Resolution of Financial Institutions*, June 2012, Washington D.C., p. 53.

[352] Ibid.

senior debt. It is highly likely that the bank and the investment firm share the same branding, the same advertising campaign, and the same information technology, processing, and payment systems. As a result, it may well be the case that the survival of the brokerage will be entirely dependent on the survival of the bank.

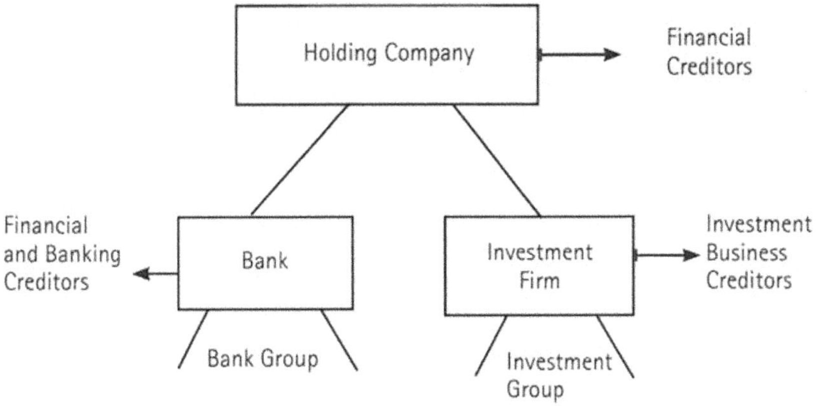

Source: Institute of International Finance (IIF),
'Making Resolution Robust – Completing the Legal and Institutional Frameworks for Effective Cross-Border Resolution of Financial Institutions', June 2012, p. 53

3.4. *The 'Global Multi-Bank' model*[353]

In this model, we assume that an 'empty' holding company owns several banks incorporated into different jurisdictions and subject to a certain degree of restrictions on their interconnection. In this case, a certain portion of debt might be raised at the holding company level, although it is likely that some, but perhaps not all, of the subsidiary banks will have also raised external financial debt. Each bank is also likely to have depositors covered by local deposit guarantee arrangements. Because we have assumed that the holding company is 'empty', it follows that the losses caused by the crisis must have been experienced in one or another of the bank subsidiaries. Moreover, this group is very likely to have an 'archipelago structure'—that is, to have specifically structured its activities so that they are not mutually dependent, and the structure is designed to permit a failure in one part of the group without affecting others.

353 Ibid., p. 54.

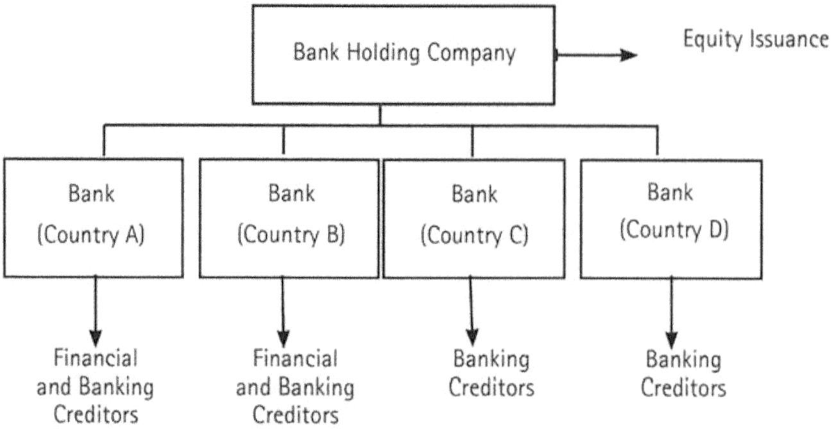

Source: Institute of International Finance (IIF),
'Making Resolution Robust – Completing the Legal and Institutional Frameworks for Effective Cross-Border Resolution of Financial Institutions', June 2012, p. 54

3.5. *The 'Financial Conglomerate' model*[354]

In this structure, an insurance company owns the bank entity. This is a very common type for the Dutch banking market where the insurance company is usually the biggest entity in the group.

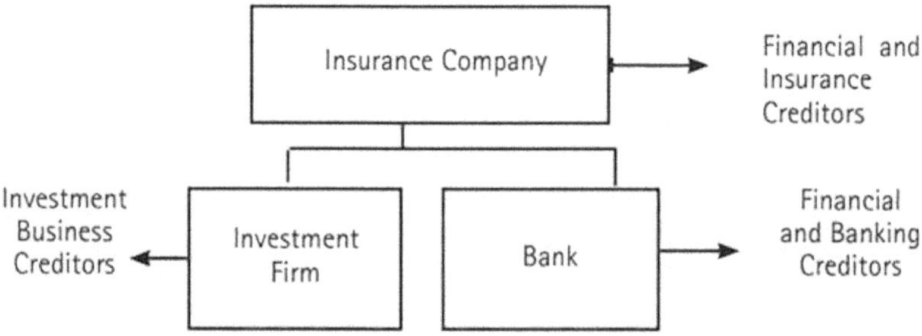

Source: Institute of International Finance (IIF),
'Making Resolution Robust – Completing the Legal and Institutional Frameworks for Effective Cross-Border Resolution of Financial Institutions', June 2012, p. 54

354 Ibid.

4 CONCLUDING REMARKS

From our analysis what became clear is that the term 'structural reforms' actually means breaking up the banks, and especially the big ones.[355] The common ground behind these approaches is that they try to solve the problem associated with the banks that are characterised as TBTF banks and, for good or for bad, dominate the modern financial system. The TBTF problem is real in the sense that it may arise at any time, and nobody knows how it will affect an interconnected financial system with many parts and stakeholders that look only for their profit maximisation. In this context, structural measures are understood as policy options that will allow supervisors to effectively manage and contain a future crisis before it will spread across the whole system (containment of spillover effects) and before it will damage the ability of the financial system to properly perform its tasks. Structural reforms have been adopted by various countries across the world. In the UK, in the US and in some EU Member States are already enacted by laws while other countries still do not support them (Switzerland).[356] Therefore, we should closely examine the reforms that have been adopted by these countries and have also a historical approach to our analysis since, especially in the US, structural reforms are an extremely hot debate since early 20th century.

[355] See in R.D. Guynn and P.S. Kenadjian, 'Structural Solutions: Blinded by Volcker, Vickers, Liikanen, Glass Steagall and Narrow Banking', in A. Dombret and P.S. Kenadjian (eds.), *Too Big to Fail III: Structural Reform Proposals - Should We Break Up the Banks?*, Volume 16, Institute for Law and Finance Series, Berlin, De Gruyter, 2015.

[356] Swiss laws do not impose explicit structural separation requirements, ban proprietary trading, specify the exclusion of certain services, or place restrictions on deposit takers regarding the type of customers that they can bank. In that sense, there is no ring-fencing regime in Switzerland. The Swiss resolution authority (FINMA) used its resolution powers to require two of its banks that were GSIBs, UBS and former Credit Suisse, to demonstrate that they have in place emergency plans to ensure the continuation of their systemically important functions in a resolution scenario. To comply with this requirement, both banks undertook changes to their corporate structures that somewhat resemble a ring-fence. The two banks transferred their Swiss domestic businesses into separate legal entities, designed to remain viable even if the rest of the group entered insolvency. The domestic entities are insulated from the rest of the group, and they have their own capital and liquidity requirements and service providers. These domestic entities are not authorized to provide investment banking services or engage in proprietary trading, apart from some market-making functions. For a better understanding of the Swiss legislation regarding structural separation, see in K. Oppolzer, *Ring-Fencing in Europe, The EU's Bank Structural Reform and a Legal Comparative Look at National Legislation in Europe's Three Financial Capitals*, Baden-Baden, Nomos Verlagsgesellschaft mbH & Co. KG, 2019.

PART II.

Regulation Through Structural Reforms: Case Studies across the World

CHAPTER 1
UNITED STATES: A GAME OF 'THRONES AND CRISES'

According to the most recent peer review from the FSB, 'financial markets in the US are the largest and most liquid in the world. In 2011, finance and insurance represented 8.3% (or nearly US$1.3 trillion) of US Gross Domestic Product (GDP)'.[357] The US banking sector is extremely important both in the real world and for the purpose of the present book. Its importance is undoubted due to its size, systemic importance and for reasons of regulatory importance. Insured depository institutions make up the largest group of financial institutions; these institutions accept deposits from both retail and institutional savers and, among other activities, make loans to businesses and consumers.[358] Moreover, 'as of end-2012, the US domestic banking industry was composed of 7,083 commercial banks and savings institutions. Approximately 2,205 institutions had assets under $100 million, while 4,216 institutions had assets between $100 million and $1 billion, and 662 institutions had assets over $1 billion. In addition, there were 6,819 credit unions in the fourth quarter of 2012. As of the fourth quarter of 2012, there were 1,014 top-tier Bank Holding Companies (BHCs) in the US, with aggregate assets of about $16.6 trillion.'[359] In addition to the US BHCs, foreign banking groups have a large presence in the US financial market and the US branches and agencies of foreign banks account for more than $2 trillion of banking assets. Furthermore, certain US government-sponsored enterprises (Fannie Mae, Freddie Mac, and the Federal Home Loan Banks) play an important role in the financing of residential mortgages and collectively hold more than $6 trillion in financial assets. These institutions facilitate liquidity in the secondary mortgage markets by guaranteeing and purchasing loans from mortgage lenders and by providing funding to financial institutions for mortgage lending.[360]

---

357 See in Financial Stability Board (FSB), *Peer Review of the United States, Review Report*, 27 August 2013, p. 39.

358 Ibid.

359 Ibid.

360 Ibid.

Although we will extensively present how the US banking regulation system was shaped, in a nutshell, and for purely introductory purposes, in order for an insured depository institution to accept customer deposits, it must be:[361]

- insured by either the Federal Deposit Insurance Corporation (FDIC) or the National Credit Union Administration (NCUA),[362]
- chartered respectively as a commercial bank, savings and loan association, credit union, or industrial loan company, and finally,
- be subject to the accompanying oversight, regulation, and activity restrictions.

A company must be either a Financial Holding Company (FHC), a Savings and Loan Holding Company (SLHC) or a Bank Holding Company (BHC) to own an insured depository institution, notwithstanding to some exceptions. Many of the largest insured depository institutions are part of BHCs and may be affiliated with non-depository institutions, such as security broker-dealers. Subsidiaries of FHCs, SLHCs and BHCs may also include investment companies, or insurance companies, however, there are rules that restrict the transactions that can occur between insured depository institutions and their affiliates.[363]

1 A BRIEF HISTORY OF THE US BANKING REGULATION REGIME

The current regulatory framework in the US has been the result of a more than 200 years evolution. The independence war, special interests, historical accidents, the civil war and exploration of wild west, (many) financial crises and panics, power of individual personalities and Congressional debates shaped the regulatory system that still today is based, and plagued, by the same principles and intense debates since its conception. The US financial regulation

361 Ibid.

362 Created by the US Congress in 1970, the National Credit Union Administration (NCUA) is an independent federal agency that insures deposits at federally insured credit unions, protects the members who own credit unions and charters and regulates federal credit unions. The NCUA protects the safety and soundness of the US credit union system by identifying, monitoring and reducing risks to the National Credit Union Share Insurance Fund (NCUSIF). Backed by the full faith and credit of the United States, the Share Insurance Fund provides up to $250,000 of federal share insurance to millions of account holders in all federal credit unions and the overwhelming majority of state-chartered credit unions. The NCUA also plays a role in helping to ensure broader financial stability as a member of the Federal Financial Institutions Examination Council (FFIEC), which is responsible for developing uniform principles, standards, and report forms, and for promoting uniformity in the supervision of depository financial institutions. The NCUA's Chairman is also a voting member of the Financial Stability Oversight Council. For more details see NCUA's official website: https://www.ncua.gov/about/mission-values.

363 See in Financial Stability Board (FSB), *Peer Review of the United States, Review Report*, 27 August 2013, p. 39.

system has many oddities, which are not only explainable from economic design, political debates, or legal specialties but to a great extent from history. We must understand, and therefore study financial regulation, using historical lens because understanding the historical background will allow us to place the current controversies in the right framework and understand the current transformation that takes place from top to bottom.[364]

1.1. From the Founding Years until the Second Bank of the United States

Soon after the end of the revolution and the enactment of the new Constitution, the US was in a terrible economic situation. The lack of a reliable currency and the inability of the Continental government to tax impeded commerce and made it extremely hard to pay the revolutionary government's bills. The 1787 adopted US Constitution, despite granting the federal government the power to regulate interstate and foreign commerce, stayed silent with respect to the US Congress's ability to charter a bank or any other corporation.[365] If the federal government had only the powers, which were specifically assigned to her by the Constitution, then silenced implied that the US Congress had not that ability. This situation became a very fruitful battlefield for almost a century and shaped the financial regulatory landscape in the US until nowadays. The need for a bank that would facilitate payments and tax collection, help the government finance its expenditures and issue a currency, acceptable to all as a means of payments, was of paramount importance.[366] Alexander Hamilton,[367] the then Treasury Secretary, sent to the US Congress a report on a national bank, privately owned but entrusted with extensive public powers. The bank would have an expiry after 20 years. Hamilton's proposal drew immediate opposition, and its plan was forcefully opposed by both James Madison[368] and Thomas Jefferson.[369] According to Madison's view, the Constitution granted only specific powers to the federal government with bank incorporation not

---

364 See in R.S. Carnell, J.R. Macey, G.P. Miller and P. Conti-Brown, *The Law of Financial Institutions*, 7th ed., Aspen Casebook Series, New York, Wolters Kluwer, 2021, p. 18.

365 Ibid.

366 Ibid.

367 Alexander Hamilton (1755 or 1757–1804) was an American revolutionary, statesman and one of the Founding Fathers of the United States. He was the first United States Secretary of the Treasury, in office from 11 September 1789, until 31 January 1795.

368 James Madison Jr. (1751–1836) was an American statesman, diplomat, and a Founding Father of the United States. He served as the fourth president of the United States from 1809 to 1817. He is hailed as the 'Father of the Constitution' for his pivotal role in drafting and promoting the Constitution of the United States and the Bill of Rights.

369 Thomas Jefferson (1743–1826) was an American statesman, diplomat, lawyer, architect, philosopher, and one of the Founding Fathers of the United States who served as the 3rd president of the United States from 1801 to 1809. He was previously the second vice president of the United States under John Adams and the first United States secretary of state under George Washington.

being one of them.[370] Despite the opposition, the bank succeeded in garnering 2/3 majorities in both houses of Congress, with Federalists and the Northerners fully supporting its concept and the Republicans and the Southerners overwhelmingly opposing her.

The difference between Hamilton and Jefferson, President's Washington Secretary of State, was simple but of fundamental importance. Jefferson feared the concentration of power in any form and Hamilton feared exactly the opposite, the lack of it. Jefferson argued that the bank was not 'necessary'; a term referred directly to the Constitution and therefore was unconstitutional.[371] Hamilton was reading the Constitution as trying to impose a 'workable' government and permitted the Congress to use all means 'fairly applicable' to achieve the purposes of that government, including those that were explicitly listed in the Constitution.[372] Since this debate regarding the powers granted by the Constitution is very important for the evolution and the application of the regulatory framework of the US financial industry, we will discuss it and analyse deeper on the present book. For the time being, we will close the first period by saying the conservative functioning of the First Bank of the United States successfully managed to provide a uniform currency, to help the government manage its public debt and regulate the money supply acting as the nation's central bank.[373] Despite that from a policy perspective, the bank was successful and that Jefferson, when he became president, he simply ignored it, Madison, who succeeded Jefferson, took the lead against the bank, and by attacking on its constitutionality led the Congressional debates. Even so, the final vote was a close battle, won by only one vote, in both Congressional Houses: re-chartering the bank failed and its dismemberment stated immediately.[374]

After the dissolution of the First Bank, banking flourished in the US with many of the bank's operations continuing under private initiative. The total banking business increased dramatically between 1811 and 1816, with double commercial loans and banknotes in circulation. Nevertheless, the new system soon collapsed. In 1814, the British burned Washington, D.C., and major bank runs occurred forcing the bankers to suspend redemption of the notes in specie. The federal government had to accept payments in depreciated bank notes leading to defaults over its debt. These conditions stimulated talks over the necessity of a new bank to improve the overall financial conditions of the state. In 1826, the Congress granted a 20-year charter to a new Bank of

370 See in R.S. Carnell, J.R. Macey, G.P. Miller, P. Conti-Brown, *The Law of Financial Institutions*, 7th ed., Aspen Casebook Series, New York, Wolters Kluwer, 2021, p. 19.

371 Ibid.

372 Ibid.

373 Ibid.

374 Ibid., p. 20.

the United States (Second Bank of the United States).[375] Since the nation was growing, the economy also grew and the demand for banking services was ever growing. However, things quickly changed, and the bank suffered from fraud, financial chicanery, and incompetent directorship.[376] The serious fraud case of an employee named McCulloch, led the state of Maryland to impose tax on the bank, but the case was overruled by the Supreme Court of the US (SCOTUS) on the famous case of *McCulloch v. Maryland*.[377] Apart from defining the sweeping federal powers, *McCulloch v. Maryland* also saved the bank from the hostile taxation and provide with a second life under the command of Nicholas Biddle.[378] Biddle managed responsibly the bank, protected the credit markets, stabilised the currency, and assisted the Treasury on its fiscal operations. The bank became popular but had the bad lack to see Andrew Jackson becoming the US President.[379] Jackson was against the bank and managed in 1832 to block the renewal of its charter under the veto procedure (the so called 'Bank War'), despite that the majorities in both Congressional Houses were in favour of the renewal.[380] Since the renewal failed, the Second Bank of the United States seize to exist when its charter expired in 1836.[381]

1.2. From the Free Banking Era (1836–1863) to the National Bank Act (1863–1864)

The era from the demise of the Second US bank until 1863 has been characterised by the free banking regime. In the free banking, no longer would each bank charter require a special legislature act and instead a state official would issue the charter to anyone who fulfilled certain predefined standards. Under such regime, the creation of many banks was facilitated, and the demise of the central bank left the states being solely responsible for the banking sector's soundness oversight.[382] Currency consisted mostly of bank notes issued by state banks and a noteholder had the right to redeem the note in specie at face value immediately upon demand if he succeeded to present the note at the issuing bank. Therefore, banks' notes traded at discounts from their

---

375 Ibid., p. 21.

376 Ibid.

377 *McCulloch v. Maryland*, 17 U.S. (4 Wheat.) 316 (1819).

378 See in R.S. Carnell, J.R. Macey, G.P. Miller and P. Conti-Brown, *The Law of Financial Institutions*, 7th ed., Aspen Casebook Series, New York, Wolters Kluwer, 2021, p. 21.

379 Andrew Jackson (1767–1845) was the seventh president of the United States from 1829 to 1837.

380 Although Jackson's political philosophy became the basis for the Democratic Party, his legacy is controversial. Jackson's famous quote has been the phrase '*I have always been afraid of banks*'.

381 See in R.S. Carnell, J.R. Macey, G.P. Miller and P. Conti-Brown, *The Law of Financial Institutions*, 7th ed., Aspen Casebook Series, New York, Wolters Kluwer, 2021, p. 22.

382 Ibid., p. 23.

facc value reflecting the issuing bank's location and reputation.[383] Counterfeit was rampant, and the lack of a single currency impeded again trade since the face value of the bank notes was not fixed. Another funny aspect of that era was the so-called 'wildcat banking', where wildcat banks located in remote areas and customers were able to hear wild cats and other mammals roaring into the wilderness. These banks were issuing banknotes backed by minimal specie, calculating in the extremely little demand for their bank notes to be redeemed by the noteholders. Free banking regime allow wildcat banking to expand, and these banks had a much higher fail rate than the rest, urbanised banks.[384] Since the Free Banking system failed to establish a safe and reliable banking system, the Treasury withdrew from the banking system altogether in 1846 establishing the so called 'Independent Treasury System' (ITS) and Congress prohibited the government from accepting bank notes or depositing public funds in banks. The ITS served the nation's fiscal needs adequately in a time of domestic tranquillity and passive government.[385]

The free banking system showed its limits when the American Civil War started in 1861, highlighting its defects, and when President Lincoln took office, the government was strapped for cash and unable to reach banks for loans. The situation became only worse and there was a specie shortage, forcing government and banks to suspend specie payments altogether. Lincoln government proposed a national banking system based on some elements of state banking statutes and some aspects of the old Bank of the United States. The main idea was that of a federal free banking regime with federally charted banks issuing a uniform national currency.[386] On 25 February 1863, the US Congress adopted and enacted the proposal as the National Currency Act of 1863. The biggest novelty of the Act was the establishment of the Office of the Comptroller of the Currency (OCC), charged with responsibility for organising and administering a system of nationally chartered banks and a uniform national currency.[387] In June 1864, the legislation underwent substantial amendments and refined in the National Bank Act (NBA) of 1864, which, with certain amendments through the years, continues to provide the basic governing framework for the US national banking system until today. Contrary to the expectations, state banks did not rush to convert into national banks through the adoption of a national charter; the vast majority of national

383 Ibid.

384 Ibid.

385 Ibid., p. 24.

386 Ibid., p. 25.

387 As we will see later, the OCC played and still does a very important role in the regulation of banking business in the US. Therefore, we could argue that maybe the most important aspect of this legislation was the creation of the OCC.

banks were new banks and not state banks.[388] Congress decided to press the situation and imposed a punitive and constitutionally dubious 10% tax on the state bank notes. The state banks challenged its constitutionality before the SCOTUS which, in a 7-2 ruling, asserted its legality in *Veazie Bank v. Fenno*,[389] establishing also an important precedent for 'the federal government's power to discriminate for regulatory purposes against an otherwise lawful industry'.[390]

1.3. *From the American Civil War to the 1907 Panic*

This period of almost 50 years saw three fundamental features that came to mark the financial industry and had a profound impact on its regulation, shaping it to the present. The first feature was the dual banking system; the second was the unit banking system and the last was the segmentation between commercial banks and thrift institutions.[391] The dual banking system was a reaction from state banks to the SCOTUS decision in *Veazie Bank v. Fenno*. The disputed tax in Veazie was actually precluding them from issuing bank notes, an activity perceived as fundamental to the banking business. Moreover, the tax proved ineffective because banks invented and developed the checking account as an effective alternative to the bank notes.[392] States offered bankers a more flexible regulatory environment compared to the national charters: a) no reserve requirements, b) much lower minimum shareholder's equity, and c) looser restrictions on the types of investments a bank could make.[393] It was this atypical competition between the states and the federal government that created this 'dual banking system', in which banks could choose between the state charters and the national ones, fuelling also the regulatory competition between states and federal officials that were looking for clientele.[394] The dual banking system remains today a distinct feature of the US banking industry and forms the core particularity of its regulatory system.

The second feature was the so-called 'unit banking system'. Unit banking was an American idea that banks should not be allowed to operate, simultaneously,

---

388 See in R.S. Carnell, J.R. Macey, G.P. Miller and P. Conti-Brown, *The Law of Financial Institutions*, 7th ed., Aspen Casebook Series, New York, Wolters Kluwer, 2021, p. 25.

389 *Veazie Bank v. Fenno*, 75 U.S. (8 Wall.) 533 (1869).

390 See in R.S. Carnell, J.R. Macey, G.P. Miller and P. Conti-Brown, *The Law of Financial Institutions*, 7th ed., Aspen Casebook Series, New York, Wolters Kluwer, 2021, p. 25.

391 Ibid.

392 Ibid. With the use of checking accounts, the bank could credit the amount of a loan into the borrower's account and then provide him with a block of checks allowing him to transfer his funds to others simply by giving them his checks. These checks, just like bank notes, were redeemable at par by the banks upon demand, giving clients flexibility, greater security and mostly avoided the 10% tax.

393 See in R.S. Carnell, J.R. Macey, G.P. Miller, P. Conti-Brown, *The Law of Financial Institutions*, 7th ed., Aspen Casebook Series, New York, Wolters Kluwer, 2021, p. 26.

394 Ibid.

at multiple locations, it therefore reminds us some sort of geographical restrictions. Back then, state laws varied a lot regarding the treatment of branches and state branching practices varied even within the same state.[395] The National Bank Act tried to converge these practices and contained two provisions that required a national bank to operate in a single location. Despite the fact that the true meaning of these provisions was to suppress the wildcat banking practice, the OCC took a different view and ruled that branching was not allowed for national banks.[396] To the contrary, the Act did not change anything for the state bank's branching practice, even allowing them to retain their existing networks when converting to a national bank charter.

From its establishment, unit banking vigorously opposed to branching liberalisation and the small banks, mostly state chartered, came to fear the intense competition from the big money centre banks, claiming that they serve far better the small communities and the rural areas than the big banks.[397] The charge that big city banks would drain rural capital was not entirely flawed since big banks were obviously able to use capital efficiently and secure bigger margins for profit compared to the rural unit banks. On the other hand, smaller banks had more deposits to invest than profitably lend to their local community, therefore were keen to invest them in big banks if only they would secure a profit margin share.[398] This resulted in a system of correspondent banking to facilitate the reallocation of deposits: smaller banks were investing their surpluses to the big banks and in return they were benefited from various services, such as investment banking, check clearing and securities brokerage. The rural capital was channelled towards the big cities, but the unit bankers had secured their cut.

The third and last feature was market segmentation. During this period, new types of banks were created, trying to secure market share. Since back then banks were not primarily designed to serve the needs of individuals, the thrift industry arose to fill this market need and secure access to credit for many individuals who were not enough privileged to have access to bank credit.[399] Several thrift types made their first steps during that period. Savings banks and savings and loan associations were usually organised under the mutual form and were owned by their depositors. Credit unions arose early in the 20th century, imported and influenced mostly from Canada and Europe providing credit to people who shared a common bond between them. This segmentation between various banking types and the growth of the thrift sector both in political and financial power profoundly affected the banking sector.

---

395 Ibid.
396 Ibid.
397 Ibid.
398 Ibid., p. 27.
399 Ibid., p. 28.

1.4. *The Federal Reserve Act (1907–1913)*

Even when the National Bank Act and the National Currency Act managed to create a uniform currency and the OCC to perform some oversight of the financial sector, the lack of a central bank remained a hot debate. There was no central bank to act as lender of last resort (function left almost entirely on private funds) and regulator of the money supply to the economy.[400] The American economy was hit multiple times by financial panics, in 1873, 1884, 1890, 1893 and in 1907. The panic of 1893 was particularly harsh and created several problems, highlighting the need for a centrally planned economy, at least to a certain extent. After the 1907 panic, which was spread also globally, the Jacksonian view of the central banking started to lose ground among its supporters. The US Congress formed the National Monetary Commission (NMC),[401] chaired by Senator Nelson Aldrich, who worked in close step with the banking industry to secure a deal that would leave all parties satisfied with the result.[402] After the 1912 presidential election, President Wilson agreed on an updated plan, based on the NMC's proposal, for the new monetary system. The functions of the new system were identical to that of the NMC's, but the structure was not. The new Federal Reserve System (the Federal Reserve or the Fed) included 12 regional Federal Reserve Banks (Fed Banks),[403] looking very similar to the bankers' clearinghouses,[404] where each Fed bank was enjoying a certain level of autonomy. Therefore, it was a system that blended decentralisation, government control and private ownership but most of all facilitated the rise of the United States as an international money centre and made the US dollar 'far better able to support international trade – the *sine*

---

400 Ibid., p. 30.

401 The National Monetary Commission (NMC) was a US congressional commission created by the Aldrich-Vreeland Act of 1908. The Commission issued 30 reports (1909-1912) that provided a detailed and authoritative survey of banking systems of the late 19th and early 20th centuries. The reports examine various topics such as US financial laws, US state banking statutes, Canadian banking history, and the banking and currency systems of England, France, Germany, and other nations.

402 See in R.S. Carnell, J.R. Macey, G.P. Miller and P. Conti-Brown, *The Law of Financial Institutions*, 7th ed., Aspen Casebook Series, New York, Wolters Kluwer, 2021, p. 31. The NMC's final plan, known as the 'Aldrich Plan', was the 'National Reserve Association', a New York dominated banker run syndicate that would regulate money supply and act as a lender of last resort, freeing the system from the specie and government securities. State and nationally chartered banks would have the option of subscribing to specified stock in their local association branch.

403 The twelve (12) Federal Reserve Banks created by the 1913 Act, were the Federal Reserve Banks of Boston, New York, Philadelphia, Cleveland, Richmond, Atlanta, Chicago, St. Louis, Minneapolis, Kansas City, Dallas, and San Francisco.

404 Bankers' clearinghouses were private arrangements by which the city banks cleared checks and made easily available other emergency loans.

qua non of an international financial centre'.[405] Finally, the Federal Reserve Act of 1913[406] required all nationally chartered banks to join the system and gave state banks the option to either join or stay out of the system. Despite optimism for the state banks' joining the system, this was not the case. State banks remained very reluctant and since the system of correspondent banking remained in place, motivation was lacking. As a result, national bank charters became less desirable due to the Fed system membership requirement, but the most severe repercussion was that state banks were vulnerable to bank runs since they were lacking access to the lender of last resort system.[407]

1.5. Industry Consolidation and Banking Crises (1914–1934)

The two decades following the passage of the Federal Reserve Act were a period of industry consolidation that led to the financial crisis of 1929 and the subsequent Great Depression. A bank with an integrated system of geographically dispersed offices could enjoy economies of scale and was better positioned compared to unit banks, even with strong correspondent banking relations.[408] Under this assumption it is not difficult to understand why unit banks were against the industry's consolidation. They feared competition from bigger, better diversified rivals and for this reason they exercised all their political influence to avoid further consolidation. Unit banks 'succeeded in maintaining many of the existing impediments to banking consolidation. But they could not reverse the underlying economic incentives to consolidate'.[409] The battle between these two contradictory forces gave rise to various compromises, the most notable of which were branch banking, the bank holding companies and chain banking.

During this period, the opposition against branching remained strong and some states even enacted anti branching statutes. Nevertheless, some states, pressed by state-chartered city banks that wanted to reach more retail customers in their home cities, began to permit branching by state banks. At the same time, National banks were bounded by the OCC's interpretation of the National Bank Act and were not permitted to branch.[410] The allowance of state bank branching destabilised the dual banking system since state banks previously were small unit banks and now, in those states that permitted branching had become much larger, giving a competitive advantage over national banks

---

405 See in R.S. Carnell, J.R. Macey, G.P. Miller and P. Conti-Brown, *The Law of Financial Institutions*, 7th ed., Aspen Casebook Series, New York, Wolters Kluwer, 2021, p. 32.

406 Federal Reserve Act, ch. 6, 38 Stat. 251 (1913) (codified as amended at 12 U.S.C. §§ 221–522).

407 See in R.S. Carnell, J.R. Macey, G.P. Miller and P. Conti-Brown, *The Law of Financial Institutions*, 7th ed., Aspen Casebook Series, New York, Wolters Kluwer, 2021, p. 32.

408 Ibid., p. 33.

409 Ibid., p. 34.

410 Ibid.

which were trying to protect it as their Holy Grail.[411] The major problem now was at the Fed's side, since the competitive advantage of branching has led many national banks to convert to state charters and therefore the Fed system was losing members because state banks were not participating in the federal system.[412] A temporary solution was given by the enactment of the McFadden Act of 1927[413] giving national banks limited branching rights within their home office cities. The Act allowed a national bank to operate branches to the extent permitted by state governments for state banks in each state. For example, in a state that prohibited branch banking, national banks could not open branches, while in a state that allowed state-chartered banks to operate branches in the same city as their headquarters, a national bank could operate branches in the same city as their headquarters. The Act's branch banking provisions were highly controversial and debatable and populist opponents of branch banking complained that the law gave too much power to big-city banks and hurt local communities. On the contrary, financial reformers claimed that the law did not go far enough and prevented banks from adopting safe, efficient, modern practices. This controversy continued for decades, until the reforms in the 1980s and 1990s finally allowed financial institutions to operate branches throughout the United States. Furthermore, the Act re-charted the Fed Banks in perpetuity,[414] and revised a wide range of laws related to the treatment of banks that were not members of the Fed. The original Federal Reserve Act of 1913 contained a sunset clause granting US Congress the power to reauthorise the Fed after 20 years, in 1933, amid the Great Depression, where most probably the Fed would have died being a victim of the financial crisis.[415] Finally yet importantly, McFadden Act authorised national banks to sell and buy investment securities that were deemed as 'marketable' by the OCC. These marketable securities included bonds and other debt securities but excluded equity stocks.[416]

Chain banking was an alternative idea to circumvent branching restrictions: instead of owing a bank with branches, it was better to own a set of separate banks. This trend remained largely a rural and small-town phenomenon mostly because of banks' corporate separateness and fiduciary duties to each bank's

---

411 Ibid.

412 Ibid.

413 McFadden Act, ch. 191, 44 Stat. 1224 (1927) (codified at 12 U.S.C. § 36).

414 The original charters of the twelve Federal Reserve District Banks were set to expire in 1934, twenty years after the banks began operations. This twenty-year limit mirrored the twenty-year charters given to the First and Second Banks of the United States, the Fed's 19th-century forerunners.

415 See in R.S. Carnell, J.R. Macey, G.P. Miller and P. Conti-Brown, *The Law of Financial Institutions*, 7th ed., Aspen Casebook Series, New York, Wolters Kluwer, 2021, p. 35.

416 See in A.E. Wilmarth Jr., *Taming the Megabanks, Why We Need a New Glass-Steagall Act*, New York, Oxford University Press, 2020, p. 29.

minority shareholders. Chain banks remained separate and independent banks sharing only a common individual owner.[417] Finally, the last feature of this era was the holding company structure. A bank holding company is a company that owns or controls one or more banks. In the same way as chain banking, the holding company structure circumvented rules against bank branching but compared to chain banking had three advantages: a) provided better access to capital markets because the holding company could sell its own securities to potential investors, b) facilitated entry into non-banking business lines, which were impermissible for banks themselves, directly or through subsidiaries, and c) facilitated centralised management because the holding company could oversee and guide the operations of all its subsidiaries.[418] Bank holding companies grew much later that chain banks, mostly in the 1920s, because of the corporate laws that were preventing one corporation from owning shares of another.

In the years leading to the financial crisis of 1929, many banks failed despite the general stability of the system. They failed mostly because they lacked a diversified asset portfolio and of inadequate supervision.[419] In addition, many thrift institutions failed, spreading questions of agony among the public for the general soundness of the banking system. In 1930, a rash of bank failures occurred in the Midwest and South, spreading a 'contagion of fear' among depositors. Public confidence was spiralling downward and state after state were forced to declare 'bank holidays' in an attempt to contain the crisis. The decision to impose a bank holiday relieved, temporary, the pressure to a bank or a banking system but in the long-run increased pressure to the banking system as a whole, since depositors would rush to withdraw their money, before their state would declare also a bank holiday.[420] On 4 March 1933, the banking system collapsed, forcing President Roosevelt to declare a nationwide bank holiday. All banking activities ceased, and banks began reopening after a week. Congress quickly enacted the Banking Act of 1933.[421] It was one of

417 See in R.S. Carnell, J.R. Macey, G.P. Miller and P. Conti-Brown, *The Law of Financial Institutions*, 7th ed., Aspen Casebook Series, New York, Wolters Kluwer, 2021, p. 35.

418 Ibid.

419 Ibid., p. 36.

420 Ibid.

421 Banking Act of 1933, ch. 89, §§ 16, 20, 21, 32, 48 Stat. 162, 163, 188, 189, 194 (codified as amended at 12 U.S.C. §§ 24 (Seventh), 78, 377, 378).
A very important clarification must be made in this point. The Banking Act of 1932 was also co-sponsored by Senator Carter Glass and Representative Henry Steagall and therefore was also known as the Glass-Steagall Act. The 1932 Act reformed the Federal Reserve's role in providing credit during economic downturns. The Banking Act of 1933, however, was also co-sponsored by Senator Carter Glass and Representative Henry Steagall, and four provisions from that act that limited commercial banks' activities in securities markets and relationships with investment banks have come to be commonly called the Glass-Steagall legislation. Nowadays, the Glass-Steagall label is seldom used for the earlier legislation.

the most widely debated legislative initiatives before enacted into law by President Roosevelt in June 1933, and among other things effectively separated commercial banking from investment banking and created the FDIC.[422] At the same time, fundamental legislation was enacted also for the thrift industry, securing their deposits and providing emergency loans when needed.[423] Finally, regulations were adopted for the securities industries with the creation of the Securities Exchange Commission (SEC) and relevant legislation to protect consumers.

1.6. Years of Stability (1935–1979)

After the crisis, a period of relative stability followed. The most important legislative initiative was the Bank Holding Company Act (BHCA) of 1956,[424] giving the Fed substantial supervisory authority over the banking structure of holding company, which was growing at a fast pace. After a decade, the US Congress passed three pieces of important legislation: a) the Financial Institutions Supervisory Act of 1966,[425] b) the Truth in Lending Act of 1968,[426] and c) the Bank Secrecy Act of 1970.[427] Apart from that, the stability of the period could be attributed to: a) the durability of the legislation adopted after the Great Depression era, b) the bankers of the post-Great Depression era had adopted a risk aversion culture, and c) bank failures became very rare, because the tsunami of the previous crisis had cleaned the banking system from the shakiest and least efficient banks.[428] This stability however does not mean that there were not any controversies. The issue of branching was still a controversial one and unit banks, faced with failures and with inflexible corporate laws, became supporters of a liberalised branching system. National banks were still not allowed to branch across state lines, when at the same

---

422 See in R.S. Carnell, J.R. Macey, G.P. Miller, P. Conti-Brown, *The Law of Financial Institutions*, 7th ed., Aspen Casebook Series, New York, Wolters Kluwer, 2021, p. 37.

423 Ibid.

424 Bank Holding Company Act of 1956, Pub. L. No. 84-511, 70 Stat. 133 (codified as amended at 12 U.S.C. §§ 1841–1852).

425 Financial Institutions Supervisory Act of 1966, Pub. L. No. 89-695, 80 Stat. 1028. This Act amended several earlier laws including the Federal Deposit Insurance Act, the Home Owners' Loan Act, and others, giving federal regulators (e.g. FDIC, Federal Reserve, and OCC) stronger enforcement powers.

426 Truth in Lending Act, Title I of the Consumer Credit Protection Act, Pub. L. No. 90-321, 82 Stat. 146 (1968) (codified as amended at 15 U.S.C. §§ 1601–1667f).

427 Bank Secrecy Act of 1970, Pub. L. No. 91-508, 84 Stat. 1114 (codified as amended at 12 U.S.C. §§ 1829b, 1951–1959 and 31 U.S.C. §§ 5311–5332). This Act was the foundational US anti-money laundering law requiring financial institutions to keep records and file reports that may be useful in detecting and preventing financial crimes.

428 See in R.S. Carnell, J.R. Macey, G.P. Miller and P. Conti-Brown, *The Law of Financial Institutions*, 7th ed., Aspen Casebook Series, New York, Wolters Kluwer, 2021, p. 40.

time foreign banks' branches were not facing such an issue. This unlevelled playing field allowed foreign banks to establish branches across multiple states and then take deposit and grant loans in ways indistinguishable to domestic banks.[429] The US Congress responded to the political pressures by enacting the International Banking Act of 1978,[430] eliminating most of foreign banks' interstate branching advantages.

The BHCA of 1956 allowed multibank holding companies to engage only in activities that are closely related to banking when at the same time, it prohibited holding companies from acquiring banks in other states, unless specifically authorised by statute in the state where the acquired bank was located. This provision was better known as the 'Douglas Amendment' and restricted even more the branching. However, the BHCA did not apply to single bank holding companies thus creating a loophole that big banks exploited during the 1960s by creating holding companies that would then engage, directly or indirectly, through non-bank subsidiaries, in various activities, which were not allowed to a bank. This loophole created fear that potentially, these holding companies would evolve into a Japanese zaibatsu style system of corporate power with big banking industrial conglomerates. In 1970, the US Congress enacted the Bank Holding Company Act Amendments (BHCAA),[431] extending the BHC regulation to the single bank holding companies and establishing the definition of 'non-banking activities' permissible for BHCs.[432] Within this period, thrift institutions thrived and started a rapid expansion until the mid-1980s. Several factors can explain this expansion: construction of new homes boomed, personal income and wealth grew rapidly, especially in the middle class, which was a traditional thrift institutions' client, the abolishment of the Regulation Q by the Fed, and the fact the traditional mutual ownership gave way into classic stock ownership, allowed thrifts to become more professional and better managed.[433] Penultimately, the liberalisation of the brokerage commissions, on 1 May 1975, propelled the stock market that were able to perform at a better cost. Furthermore, the creation of NASDAQ in 1971,[434] provided market making and clearance for shares that were more thinly traded compared to the NYSE's shares.[435] Lastly, at around the same time, the market for derivatives

429 Ibid., p. 41.

430 International Banking Act of 1978, Pub. L. No. 95-369, 92 Stat. 607 (codified as amended at 12 U.S.C. §§ 3101–3111).

431 Bank Holding Company Act Amendments of 1970, Pub. L. No. 91-607, 84 Stat. 1760 (codified as amended at 12 U.S.C. §§ 1841–1852).

432 See in R.S. Carnell, J.R. Macey, G.P. Miller and P. Conti-Brown, *The Law of Financial Institutions*, 7th ed., Aspen Casebook Series, New York, Wolters Kluwer, 2021, p. 41.

433 Ibid., p. 42.

434 Nasdaq was initially an acronym, which stands for the 'National Association of Securities Dealers Automated Quotations'.

435 See in R.S. Carnell, J.R. Macey, G.P. Miller and P. Conti-Brown, *The Law of Financial Institutions*, 7th ed., Aspen Casebook Series, New York, Wolters Kluwer, 2021, p. 43.

started to thrive. The Chicago Board Options Exchange started to trade stock options in 1973 and soon became a leading player in the market.

1.7. Years of Stress (1980–2006)

Since the late 1970s, the financial industry has undergone a profound revolution that altered completely the nature of financial intermediation. This revolution happened through agency action, judicial decisions, and federal and state legislation. Mostly though, it happened outside the legal and regulatory system, based on market forces and technological advances. In the early 1980s, due to the high interest rates, many thrift institutions went insolvent, and the federal authorities insisted on leaving these institutions to remain open hoping that the institutions would recover, and the situation would become better.[436] Thrift institutions ended up with an asset quality problem that falling interest rates could not cure and insolvencies mounted in the sector. The Federal Savings and Loan Insurance Corporation (FSLIC) itself became insolvent since it lacked reserves sufficient to protect insured depositors even on the 'most egregiously insolvent thrifts'.[437] The savings and loan crisis soon became one of the costliest regulatory failures in the US and the estimated taxpayers' costs amounted up to $125 billion leading to huge criticism of the government's reactions. US Congress reacted by enacting the Financial Institutions Reform, Recovery and Enforcement Act (FIRREA) of 1989,[438] which among other things:[439]

- provided $50 billion to protect thrift's depositors,
- abolished the Federal Home Loan Bank Board and the FSLIC,
- established the Resolution Trust Corporation (RTC) to close insolvent thrifts and dispose of their assets,
- made FDIC responsible for insuring deposits at the survived thrift institutions,
- assigned thrifts supervision to a newly created bureau of the Treasury, the Office of Thrift Supervision (OTS),
- required from thrift institutions to meet bank type capital requirements.

In 1991, Congress enacted also the Federal Deposit Insurance Corporation Improvement Act (FDICIA) of 1991,[440] which:

- greatly increased the FDIC's capacity to borrow from the Treasury,
- required the FDIC to set risk-based deposit insurance premiums,

---

436 Ibid., p. 44.

437 Ibid.

438 Financial Institutions Reform, Recovery, and Enforcement Act of 1989, Pub. L. No. 101-73, 103 Stat. 183 (1989) (codified in scattered sections of 12 U.S.C. and 42 U.S.C.).

439 See in R.S. Carnell, J.R. Macey, G.P. Miller, P. Conti-Brown, *The Law of Financial Institutions*, 7th ed., Aspen Casebook Series, New York, Wolters Kluwer, 2021, p. 44.

440 Federal Deposit Insurance Corporation Improvement Act of 1991, Pub. L. No. 102-242, 105 Stat. 2236 (1991) (codified at 12 U.S.C. §§ 1811 et seq.).

- attempted to curtail the practice of treating big banks as 'too-big-to-fail' entities, and
- established a system of prompt corrective action.[441]

The next major challenge was the deposits' interest rate deregulation, after certain macroeconomic factors significantly altered the economic environment. Thrift institutions and banks were offering regulated interest rates since they were bound by the Fed's Regulation Q, but when the economic conditions altered, the Regulation Q structure proved to be unsustainable.[442] Customers were unwilling to accept the administratively set interest rates and refugee to the Money Market Mutual Funds (MMMFs) which offered a safe and higher yield investment, directly competitive with the traditional banks' accounts.[443] The Depository Institutions Deregulation and Monetary Control Act (DIDMC) of 1980,[444] abolished the interest rate ceilings and all depository institutions were now free to compete on interest bearing checking accounts. Moreover, technological advances speed up the dismantling of geographical restrictions that were remaining in place. The rapid expansion of the Automated Teller Machines (ATMs) allowed customers to perform banking transactions at all hours from various locations. The US Congress accelerated that trend by enacting the Riegle-Neal Act of 1994[445] that repealed the Douglas Amendment and allowed the Fed to approve 'adequately capitalised, competently managed bank holding companies to acquire banks nationwide without regard to whether such transaction is prohibited under the law of any state'.[446] The Act also removed all the federal law impediments to establishing the new branches

---

441 See in R.S. Carnell, J.R. Macey, G.P. Miller, P. Conti-Brown, *The Law of Financial Institutions*, 7th ed., Aspen Casebook Series, New York, Wolters Kluwer, 2021, p. 44. The system of 'prompt corrective action' imposes increasingly more stringent restrictions and requirements as a depository institution's capital falls below the minimum required levels. The system's goal is to timely resolves problems, while these are still small and manageable, avoiding thus any regulatory procrastination.

442 See in R.S. Carnell, J.R. Macey, G.P. Miller and P. Conti-Brown, *The Law of Financial Institutions*, 7th ed., Aspen Casebook Series, New York, Wolters Kluwer, 2021, p. 44.

443 Ibid.
During the late 1970s, the MMMFs grew at an explosive rate, with assets under management increasing from less than $4 billion in 1978 to more than $60 billion in 1980.

444 Depository Institutions Deregulation and Monetary Control Act of 1980, Pub. L. No. 96-221, 94 Stat. 132 (1980) (codified in scattered sections of 12 U.S.C. and 31 U.S.C.).

445 Riegle-Neal Interstate Banking and Branching Efficiency Act of 1994, Pub. L. No. 103-328, 108 Stat. 2338 (1994) (codified at 12 U.S.C. §§ 1811 et seq.). The Act took its name from its sponsors, Senator Donald Riegle, a Michigan Democrat chairman of the Senate Banking Committee, and Representative Stephen Neal, a Democrat from North Carolina who headed the House Banking (now called Financial Services) Subcommittee on Domestic Monetary Policy.

446 See in R.S. Carnell, J.R. Macey, G.P. Miller and P. Conti-Brown, *The Law of Financial Institutions*, 7th ed., Aspen Casebook Series, New York, Wolters Kluwer, 2021, p. 47.

across state lines, by making such branching permissible when the host state had already enacted a statute that specifically authorised the branching.[447]

Finally, the last wall to be demolished was that of structural separation. The provisions of the GSA were preventing depository institutions and securities firms from entering each other's business. The US Congress enacted the Gramm Leach Bliley Act (GLBA) of 1999[448] to conclude this lengthy process of deregulation, since securities services had penetrated the core commercial banking business by helping their corporate clients to meet their short-term borrowing needs by issuing short-term commercial paper lending, and commercial banks had at the same time penetrated investment banking's core business by underwriting and dealing in securities with their securities firms subsidiaries and also helping their corporate clients to privately sell their commercial paper issuances.[449] The GLBA allowed the creation of the 'financial holding companies' (FHCs) by permitting banks' affiliation with companies that engage in the full spectrum of financial activities through these specially qualified entities. Nevertheless, not all restrictions were abolished, since: a) a bank can underwrite and deal only in a limited range of securities (government securities) and b) the same firm is not allowed to do both: accept deposits and underwrite securities.[450]

1.8. The Global Financial Crisis of 2007–2009 and the New, Post Crisis Landscape (2009 – Today)

The filing for bankruptcy by Lehman Brothers, on 15 September of 2008, was the culmination or the end of the beginning of the Global Financial Crisis (GFC) that shocked the global economy. Originating in the US subprime mortgage market and on the growing demand for securitised products based on subprime mortgages[451], it managed to spread across the world since the global interconnection level among financial institutions was big enough to spread the panic. Many financial institutions that had bet on these products, with the burst of the real estate bubble in the US, found themselves in an extremely difficult position to roll over their short-term debts and accounted huge losses. The low interest rates in the 2001–2004 period created enormous liquidity in the market which turn investors hungry for US mortgage-backed

---

447 Ibid.

448 Gramm-Leach-Bliley Act of 1999, Pub. L. No. 106-102, 113 Stat. 1338 (1999) (codified in scattered sections of 15 U.S.C., 12 U.S.C., and 31 U.S.C.).

449 See in R.S. Carnell, J.R. Macey, G.P. Miller and P. Conti-Brown, *The Law of Financial Institutions*, 7th ed., Aspen Casebook Series, New York, Wolters Kluwer, 2021, p. 47.

450 Ibid., p. 48.

451 A.E. Wilmarth Jr., 'The Dark Side of Universal Banking: Financial Conglomerates and the Origins of the Subprime Financial Crisis' (2009) 41(4) *Connecticut Law Review*, pp. 963–1050.

securities. The US Congress adopted the Troubled Asset Relief Program (TARP) to create a permanent solution as a backstop mechanism against the crisis and the Fed made use of the emergency lending authority (the so called '13(3) power').[452] After President Obama took office in 2008, the legislative process led to the Dodd–Frank Wall Street Reform and Consumer Protection Act of 2010, (the Dodd–Frank Act).[453] Capital regulation was also reinforced during and after the crisis. The BCBS updated almost immediately its capital requirements framework (Basel 2,5 framework) initially as a patchwork to the existed Basel II framework and then in the new Basel III framework, with a target on higher and of better-quality capital requirements.[454]

The post crisis environment in the US can be described as the 'Big Delegation', since the Dodd–Frank Act mandated the regulators to create and issue more than 250 substantive rulemakings and demanded around 100 studies to understand the market.[455] Recent changes, after the 2016 presidential election in the US, included the enactment of the Economic Growth, Regulatory Relief, and Consumer Protection Act (EGRRCPA) of 2017, (the 'Crapo Bill').[456] The Act obliged the Fed to use its prudential supervision authority over far less institutions compared to the initial approach of the Dodd-Frank Act.[457]

In March 2023, another banking crisis hit the US financial markets. This time the epicentre was on smaller, less significant banks, but the turmoil was big enough to generate discussions and most important saw certain banks go bankrupt again, the most important among them were the Silicon Valley Bank (SVB) and Signature Bank.[458] These events were triggered by a combination

---

452 Ibid., p. 52.

453 Dodd-Frank Wall Street Reform and Consumer Protection Act of 2010, Pub. L. No. 111-203, 124 Stat. 1376 (2010) (codified in scattered sections of 12 U.S.C., 15 U.S.C., 18 U.S.C., and 31 U.S.C.).
Named after sponsors Senator Christopher J. Dodd (D-Conn.) and Representative Barney Frank (D-Mass.), the Act's purpose was 'to Promote the Financial Stability of the United States by Improving Accountability and Transparency in the Financial System, to End "Too Big to Fail", to Protect the American Taxpayer by Ending Bailouts, to Protect Consumers from Abusive Financial Services Practices, and for Other Purposes'.

454 See in R.S. Carnell, J.R. Macey, G.P. Miller and P. Conti-Brown, *The Law of Financial Institutions*, 7th ed., Aspen Casebook Series, New York, Wolters Kluwer, 2021, p. 53.

455 Ibid., p. 54 and for an excellent analysis regarding the regulatory burden of Dodd-Frank Act see in P.A. McLaughlin, O. Sherouse, M. Febrizio and M. Scott King, 'Is Dodd-Frank the Biggest Law Ever?' (2021) 7 *Journal of Financial Regulation*, pp. 149–174.

456 Economic Growth, Regulatory Relief, and Consumer Protection Act, Pub. L. No. 115-174, 132 Stat. 1296 (2018) (codified in scattered sections of 12 U.S.C. and 15 U.S.C.).

457 See in R.S. Carnell, J.R. Macey, G.P. Miller and P. Conti-Brown, *The Law of Financial Institutions*, 7th ed., Aspen Casebook Series, New York, Wolters Kluwer, 2021, p. 55.

458 The March 2023 turmoil was not only centred in the US. The Swiss financial giant, Credit Suisse (CS), a global systemically important bank, also collapsed during the turmoil further aggravating the situation of stress in the global markets. Since Switzerland is not covered in our analysis and therefore it is not included in the book, we will not deal with this bank failure; we only mention it for coherence. For a more detailed analysis with respect

of rising interest rates, liquidity issues, and poor risk management. The US government stepped in quickly to prevent further panic, assuring depositors that their funds would be protected, even beyond the standard $250,000 insurance limit provided by the FDIC and the Fed introduced emergency lending measures to increase liquidity and prevent further banking instability. The crisis caused significant turbulence in global financial markets and raised concerns about the broader banking sector's health, especially regional banks that had similar risk profiles to SVB and Signature. Despite the turmoil, the Fed and Treasury worked to stabilise the situation, and the broader economy showed resilience in the face of the crisis. The crisis underscored the vulnerability of banks with concentrated business models and large unrealised losses in a rising interest rate environment.

2 THE US CONSTITUTIONAL DEBATE ON BANKING POWERS

The importance of the US system of financial regulation is well known to anyone who studies this legal field. On the contrary, what is less known is the lengthy debate between the supporters of the federal government and those who supported the states, regarding who has the right to regulate financial services, the federal government or the states. In other words, to what extent is the federal government entitled to regulate and pre-empt state powers in that field. Although the separation of powers in the US Constitution is well beyond the scope of the present book, it is important for reasons of coherence to dedicate few lines to this very important aspect of constitutional theory, since, at least in the beginning of the US's regulatory efforts this debate shaped not only the outcome of these efforts but also the whole process. Therefore, we will proceed with some theoretical aspects of the legal theory and then we will use specific examples as yardsticks to better understand the importance of the separation of powers between the federal government and the states.

The US legal system allows both the federal government and the states to regulate financial services. This particular legal structure sometimes is translated into a fruitful and passionate dialogue between the states and the federal government, sometimes creating tensions and conflicting interests. Financial institutions, and particular banks, are subject to a multitude of laws and regulations that vary by jurisdiction, both at federal and state level. Understanding each time which state and/or federal regulations shall apply and how to operate in compliance with these requirements can be a costly,

to the CS collapse see in Basel Committee on Banking Supervision (BCBS), *Report on the 2023 banking turmoil*, October 2023 and in Swiss Financial Markets Supervisory Authority (FINMA), 'Lessons Learned from the CS Crisis', *FINMA Report*, 19 December 2023.

burdensome, and often difficult compliance management process. Therefore, at any time it is important to clarify which regulation applies to each specific case: the state regulation, the federal one or is it a mixture of both?

The rules that allocate regulatory responsibility between the states and the federal government are embodied in the doctrine of 'pre-emption'.[459] The notion of pre-emption is unknown to those legal systems that have a central level of government determining the applicable law. A single, central government makes every decision and therefore there is no need for adopting and applying such a notion. Fundamental to the notion of pre-emption is the principle that the US federal government is a 'government of limited powers'.[460] The US Constitution creates an entity, the United States of America and gives to that entity powers that are deemed to be necessary for accomplishing the purposes of this entity. Therefore, any powers that are not delegated to the federal government by the US Constitution are retained by the states or the people. What is also very clear is that the notion of pre-emption applies only to those powers that are delegated to the federal government and not retained by the states or the people. The US Constitution apart from granting powers to regulate (banks) to the federal government, simultaneously contains the states' powers to regulate.[461] This happens even when the Constitution's wording is not explicit about the granting of powers or the retention in favour of the states or the people and the document is interpreted in such a way as to limit states' power in order to fulfil its basic purpose.[462] The Constitution contains the so-called 'dormant Commerce Clause' that precludes states from regulating commerce in such a way as to favour in state interests over out of states or federal interests or otherwise imposing a burden on the interstate commerce, implementing thus the basic purpose of the US Constitution, which is to bring the states together in a common economic market.[463]

The basic rule, therefore, has that, unless the US Congress, any other administrative agency, or federal officials take affirmative action, the states exercise their plenary power to regulate. This state power is of course subject to the federal constitutional protections but where the federal government has the power to regulate and chooses to exercise this power trumps the sovereign powers of the states.[464] This approach is derived from the US Constitution's Supremacy Clause in Article VI that provides that the US Constitution, federal laws made pursuant to it, and any treaties made under its authority constitute

459 Ibid., p. 59.

460 Ibid.

461 The US constitution grants the federal government the right to coin money but at the same time denies this right to the states.

462 See in R.S. Carnell, J.R. Macey, G.P. Miller and P. Conti-Brown, *The Law of Financial Institutions*, 7th ed., Aspen Casebook Series, New York, Wolters Kluwer, 2021, p. 59.

463 Ibid.

464 Ibid., p. 60.

the 'supreme law of the land'. This constitutional language is the foundation of the notion of federal pre-emption, which allows federal law to supersede state law when conflicting terms exist. The language of the Supremacy Clause implies that the US Congress is the 'the branch of the federal government that exercises the power to pre-empt state authority'.[465] With the evolution of the administrative state however, it became clear that certain administrative agencies are also necessary to regulate and therefore exercise lawmaking authority. This lawmaking capacity must be delegated by the Congress to the agency in question in order to be allowed to regulate an area of commerce, and as a result, this agency will enjoy a delegated authority to pre-empt the state law in the same manner, as the US Congress is able to pre-empt.[466] This is exactly when the problems start because the Congress must have actually delegated this authority to pre-empt, either expressly or by implication, and if not then the agency is not able to pre-empt state law even if Congress could do so.

The SCOTUS, through its rulings, has identified two ways in which federal law can pre-empt state law: a) 'expressly', and b) 'impliedly'.[467] Furthermore, the implied way of pre-emption can be further divided into two subcategories: a) the 'field pre-emption' and b) the 'conflict pre-emption'.[468] Pre-emption of a state law from a federal law can be characterised as expressly, when a federal statute or regulation contains 'explicit pre-emptive language'[469] which is translated in a clause contained in the federal legislation that explicitly provides that certain categories of state's law be displaced from the federal law.[470] The second case in which a federal law can pre-empt a state law is the implied pre-emption. The SCOTUS on its ruling in Gade v. National Solid Wastes Management Association[471] defined that the implied pre-emption '[...] is compelled whether Congress' command is explicitly stated in the statute's language or implicitly contained in its structure and purpose'.[472] With the same case the SCOTUS further defined the two subcategories of implied pre-emption, the 'field pre-emption' that occurs '[...] where the scheme of federal regulation is so pervasive as to make reasonable the inference that Congress left no room for the States to supplement it [...]'[473] and the 'conflict pre-emption' that occurs in two cases a) where 'compliance with both federal and

465 Ibid.
466 Ibid.
467 See in J.B. Sykes, 'Federal Preemption in the Dual Banking System: An Overview and Issues for the 116th Congress', *Congressional Research Service*, Report, R45726, 17 May 2019, p. 2.
468 Ibid.
469 Ibid.
470 Ibid.
471 *Gade v. National Solid Wastes Management Association*, 505 US 88, 108 (1992).
472 Ibid., at 98 (internal quotation marks and citation are omitted).
473 Ibid.

state regulations is a physical impossibility [...]'[474] or 'where state law stands as an obstacle to the accomplishment and execution of the full purposes and objectives of Congress [...]'[475]. The SCOTUS has repeatedly held that in both implied and express pre-emption cases, the cornerstone of its analysis is the 'purpose of the Congress'; therefore, it tries to discover and bring into light the true Congressional willingness as the steppingstone of its legal reasoning.[476]

Based on the above analysis we understand that if the US Congress or an administrative federal agency are duly authorised to pre-empt state powers and can regulate a certain issue, then state powers must give way to the federal governments' powers. In the same way, when the US Congress and the federal administrative agency explicitly disclaim their power and intention to pre-empt state powers, then the state sovereignty remains intact and the states are free to exercise their regulatory powers, always within the general limits imposed by the Constitution.[477] State legislation will prevail in the absence of federal legislation, or in such cases when state legislation provides more protection compared to what is available under existing federal legislation. However, determining whether federal legislation can override state legislation in each case is often a key point of contention and debate among regulators, financial institutions, and other stakeholders. Under the NBA, the OCC serves as the primary regulator for all national banks, thrift institutions and federal savings associations aiming at ensuring they operate in a safe and sound manner and that are in compliance with all applicable laws and regulations. Federal pre-emption permits national banks and federal savings associations, many of which have business across state lines, to operate under a uniform set of rules to support nationwide banking.[478]

Based on the above theoretical analysis of the doctrine of pre-emption, we can now delve into the specificities of the banking regulation within the US legal system. From the very beginning of the US Constitution's ratification, the banking business was based on a model of 'competitive dual federalism'.[479] While the Constitution had clearly allocated some powers regarding money supply regulation among governmental entities, banking business was

---

474 *Florida Lime & Avocado Growers, Inc. v. Paul*, 373 U. S. 132, 142-143 (1963).

475 *Hines v. Davidowitz*, 312 U. S. 52, 67 (1941).

476 See in J.B. Sykes, 'Banking Law: An Overview of Federal Pre-emption in the Dual Banking System', *Congressional Research Service*, Report, R45081, 23 January 2018, p. 4.

477 See in R.S. Carnell, J.R. Macey, G.P. Miller and P. Conti-Brown, *The Law of Financial Institutions*, 7th ed., Aspen Casebook Series, New York, Wolters Kluwer, 2021, p. 60.

478 For an interesting analysis of the notion of pre-emption and its application in the banking regulation field with further discussion in connection with the recent GFC, see in D.K. Bailey, 'A Defense of The Doctrine of Preemption: Revealing the Fallacy That Federal Preemption Contributed to The Financial Crisis' (2014) 16(4) *Journal of Constitutional Law*, pp. 1041–1108.

479 See in J.H. Gutwillig, 'Glass versus Steagall: The fight over federalism and American banking' (2014) 100 *Virginia Law Review*, Note, p. 772.

completely ignored by both the US Congress and states in the sense that no authority was allocated in either of them. The Constitutional text and the debates around it ignored banking and ultimately created an unhelpful silence that initiated a competition among the states and the federal government regarding who has the power to regulate banking.[480] The debate over the creation of the First Bank of the United States between Hamilton and Jefferson was actually an attempt to answer the critical question: who has the power to regulate banking when the Constitution says nothing about that? Since the credit supply had to do directly with the public finances, the international and interstate trade, and the federal government's right to coin money, banking became a field of public interest and of competition between the states and the federal government.[481] Hamilton's approach on the issue of banking regulation was in favour of the establishment of a national bank because he had the view that relying on state banks was imprudent for the US, since state banks simply 'happens to exist'. On the contrary, Jefferson was afraid that a national bank would create a financial monopoly that might undermine state banks and ultimately adopt policies that favoured financiers and merchants, who tended to be creditors, over plantation owners and family farmers, who tended to be debtors. This very first attempt of unification ended with the adoption of Hamilton's view for a more federal government even when the Constitution remained silent about that and was also supported by the SCOTUS decision in *McCulloch v. Maryland*. Chief Justice Marshall found that the Congress had the authority to establish a national bank, pursuant to the 'Necessary and Proper Clause'[482] of the US Constitution. Furthermore, the Supreme Court also found that the state of Maryland had no power to tax the national bank and its reasoning gave sweeping powers to the federal government.[483] According to Gutwillig, Chief Justice Marshall's reasoning relied on a creative reading of the Constitution in the sense that he construed the Constitution's silence as an affirmative statement that the federal government can't be dependent on the state government and therefore, the Congress was able to choose the means of creating a national bank in preference to state banks.[484] This position is also supported by Chief Justice Marshall's concluding opinion: 'It is of the very essence of supremacy to remove all obstacles to its action within its own sphere, and so to modify every power vested in subordinate governments as to exempt its own operations from their own influence. This effect need not be

480 Ibid.

481 Ibid., p. 779.

482 Article 1, Section 8, para. 18 of the Unites States Constitution ('To make all Laws which shall be necessary and proper for carrying into Execution the foregoing Powers, and all other Powers vested by this Constitution in the Government of the United States, or in any Department or Officer thereof.').

483 Ibid., p. 792.

484 Ibid., p. 793.

stated in terms. It is so involved in the declaration of supremacy, so necessarily implied in it, that the expression of it could not make it more certain. We must, therefore, keep it in view while construing the Constitution.'[485]

The second victory for federalism came again from the SCOTUS decision in *Veazie Bank v. Fenno*. According to Gutwillig, this time was the inversion of McCulloh's question: has the federal government the power to tax state banks?[486] The SCOTUS answered yes and signified a complete turn towards the increase of the federal powers granted to the Congress. The federal state taxation to the state banks had the intention to create a single uniform currency and retire the state bank notes already in circulation. The decision in Veazie Bank brought a shift in the competition between state and national banks that coexistence of the two schemes was untenable. The same view was also shared by the OCC.[487]

The third and the last attempt to unify the banking system came almost 50 years after the second. In 1913, the enactment of the Federal Reserve Act established a federal system of controlled money supply through quasi-public private federal banks and to supervise the banking sector more effectively.[488] The reform can be conceptualised as be comprised of two parts. Part A aimed at ensuring the circulation of the national currency more effectively by creating a more elastic one and by spreading the risks by restructuring national banks into a branching system. Part B of the reform plan aimed at securing that the new money supply would be properly regulated under the Federal Reserve banks' scheme.[489] According to Gutwillig the two parts were equally reincarnations of the Veazie Bank and McCulloh decisions, since the first part was insisting on the creation of the federal currency, in the spirit of Veazie Bank and the second part was insisting on making banking a federal business, in the spirit of McCulloh.[490]

Apart from the above historical events, the US Dual Banking System that was established with the NBA of 1863 and 1864, continues to shape the doctrine of pre-emption even in the recent era, reaching new conflicting levels with the enactment of Dodd-Frank Act. The Dual Banking System reinforces the necessity of the pre-emption doctrine in the US legal system since it divides chartering and regulatory authority between states and the federal government.[491] The reasoning behind a bank's decision to choose a national or

485 *McCulloch v. Maryland*, 17 U.S. (4 Wheat.) at 427.
486 See in J.H. Gutwillig, 'Glass versus Steagall: The fight over federalism and American banking' (2014) 100 *Virginia Law Review*, Note, p. 793.
487 Ibid., p. 794.
488 Ibid., p. 795.
489 Ibid.
490 Ibid., p. 796.
491 See in J.B. Sykes, 'Banking Law: An Overview of Federal Preemption in the Dual Banking System', *Congressional Research Service*, Report, R45081, 23 January 2018, p. 5.

a state charter are varied and may change over time together with the evolving regulatory landscape. A national charter may offer the benefit of federal pre-emption over state legislation and regulations, to avoid certain aggressive actions taken by the state regulators and supervisors and to achieve greater simplicity and uniformity of national regulation when it operates on a cross state basis.[492] At the same time, state charters may be preferred to avoid the higher supervisory fees charged by the OCC or because the bank is of the view that national regulation is more demanding and burdensome over the state one.[493] What is also important and must be pointed out is that by choosing the chartering authority, the bank chooses also its primary regulator, since the OCC serves as the primary regulator for the nationally chartered banks and the state banking authorities are the primary regulators for the state chartered banks.[494]

According to Sykes, although the regulatory treatment of national and state banks has accordingly converged, the doctrine of federal pre-emption confers to the national banks certain 'unique benefits'.[495] Federal legislation that grants national banks the power to engage in specific activities impliedly pre-empts the state legislation the 'significantly interfere' with the national banks' ability to engage in those activities. This wording has been used by the SCOTUS in the *Barnett Bank of Marion County, N. A. v. Nelson, Florida Insurance Commissioner, et al.*[496] The importance of this decision is undeniable since it created the yardstick of 'significant interference' when assessing whether a state law must be pre-empted by a federal one.[497] The Barnett's precedent has been strong and followed by lower courts providing for a stable and clear rule that absent any indications to the contrary, federal laws and regulations granting national banks the right to engage in specific activities pre-empt state laws and regulations that 'prohibit or significantly interfere with those

---

492 Ibid.

493 Ibid.

494 For instance, the Pennsylvania Department of Banking and Securities (PDBS) is responsible for approving the charter applications for Pennsylvania state-chartered banks and the New Jersey Department of Banking & Insurance (NJDBI) is responsible for approving charter applications for depository institutions chartered in the state of New Jersey, as well as supervising these institutions. See also in E.A. Bogert, 'Anti-Federalist Banking Policy Under Dodd-Frank: The Case for the Liberal Pre-Emption of State Banking Law' (2020) 6(2) *University of Pennsylvania Journal of Law & Public Affairs.*

495 See in J.B. Sykes, 'Federal Preemption in the Dual Banking System: An Overview and Issues for the 116th Congress', *Congressional Research Service*, Report, R45726, 17 May 2019, p. 8.

496 *Barnett Bank of Marion Cty., N. A. v. Nelson*, 517 U.S. 25 (1996).

497 In Barnett Bank a 1916 federal law (Federal Statute) permits national banks to sell insurance in small towns, but a Florida law (State Statute) prohibits such banks from selling most types of insurance. When the petitioner, Barnett Bank, a national bank doing business in a small Florida town, bought a state licensed insurance agency, the respondent, Florida State Insurance Commissioner ordered the agency to stop selling the prohibited forms of insurance.

activities'.[498] Few examples of the Barnett's rule endorsement by the lower courts can be found in the following, indicative, cases:[499] *Wells Fargo Bank of Texas NA v. James*,[500] *Monroe Retail, Inc. v. RBS Citizens, N.A.*,[501] *Rose v. Chase Bank USA*.[502] While federal courts have adopted expansive views regarding the circumstances in which state laws 'significantly interfere' with national banks' powers, nonetheless they have also recognised certain, broad limits, on the extent of pre-emption allowed in favour of the federal laws and regulations. An illustrative example of these limits can be found in the case *Gutierrez v. Wells Fargo Bank, NA*[503] where the court found that eventually 'such an expansive interpretation—with no limiting principle—would swallow all laws'.[504] Such judicial limitations are trying to prevent the federal regulation to enter into every aspect of the banking business and pre-empt state rules that can coexist and offer a certain level of regulation without, according to the Courts, significantly interfere with the Congressional willing.

A few words must be also written about the OOC's rules for pre-emption. The US Congress formally recognised that the OCC has the ability to pre-empt state laws and regulations, through the promulgation of specific rules, under Section 114 of the Riegle-Neal Act which specifies the OCC's power to pre-empt state laws and the administrative process for the exercise of this power.[505] The OCC took advantage of this power and in the 1990s and 2000s exercised this authority by issuing a number of interpretative letters and legal opinions, adopting the position that federal law pre-empted state laws that limited national banks' ability to engage in certain activities, such as:[506] advertise, operate ATM machines, engage in fiduciary duties, finance automobile purchases and sell annuities. The big change in the pre-emption policy came in

[498] See in J.B. Sykes, 'Federal Preemption in the Dual Banking System: An Overview and Issues for the 116th Congress', *Congressional Research Service*, Report, R45726, 17 May 2019, p. 8.

[499] Ibid., p. 9.

[500] *Wells Fargo Bank of Texas NA v. James*, 321 F.3d 488 (5th Cir. 2003), holding that an OCC interpretative regulation allowing banks to charge fees to anyone who presents a check for payment pre-empted Texas 'par value' statute that prohibited banks from charging check-cashing fees for checks drawn against an account at the same bank.

[501] *Monroe Retail, Inc. v. RBS Citizens, N.A.*, 589 F.3d 274 (6th Cir. 2009), holding that interpreting an Ohio statute to prohibit banks from deducting service fees after receiving a garnishment order on an account held at the bank would allow state law to 'significantly interfere' with the national bank's ability to collect and set service fees.

[502] *Rose v. Chase Bank USA, N.A.*, 513 F.3d 1032, 1038 (9th Cir. 2008), holding that claims based on certain disclosure violations were pre-empted by the NBA.

[503] *Gutierrez v. Wells Fargo Bank, NA*, 704 F.3d 712 (9th Cir. 2012), finding that claims based on misleading statements in the defendant's overdraft fee policy were not pre-empted.

[504] Ibid. at 727.

[505] See in J.B. Sykes, 'Federal Preemption in the Dual Banking System: An Overview and Issues for the 116th Congress', *Congressional Research Service*, Report, R45726, 17 May 2019, p. 11.

[506] Ibid., p. 12.

2004, when the OCC issued its 'sweeping'[507] pre-emption rules,[508] introducing a general pre-emption standard based on an expanding reading of the Barnett Bank case.[509] The OCC rule tested the Barnett Bank case rule in two ways: a) by omitting from its 2004 standard the word 'significantly' as articulated by the SCOTUS in the Barnett Bank case, and b) by requiring with the 2004 standard that national banks must be able to 'fully' exercise their powers, a phrase that does not appear in Barnett Bank rule.[510] According to the OCC's ruling, 'The pre-emption rule issued today builds on the current regulation by providing that state laws that 'obstruct, impair or condition' a national bank's powers in the areas of lending, deposit taking and other national bank operations are not applicable to national banks. The rule identifies additional specific types of state laws that apply to national banks and specific types of laws that do not apply'.[511]

The 2004 OCC's rules also defined general categories of state laws that survived the agency's interpretation of pre-emption doctrine. According to the rules, the NBA does not pre-empted state laws that are found to be consistent with federal law and particularly in the areas of: a) tort law, b) contract law, c) criminal law, d) rights to collect debts, e) acquisition and transfer of property, f) taxation, g) zoning and real estate lending, and h) certain homestead laws.[512] According to the OCC, 'The Final Rule also sets out examples of the types of state laws that are not pre-empted and would be applicable to national banks to the extent that they only incidentally affect the lending, deposit-taking, or other operations of national banks'.[513] The scope of the OCC was to exclude state laws from being pre-empted as long as they 'do not regulate the manner, content or extent of the activities authorised for national banks under federal

507 For a more detailed analysis on the matter see in A.E. Wilmarth Jr., 'The OCC's Preemption Rules Exceed the Agency's Authority and Present a Serious Threat to the Dual Banking System and Consumer Protection' (2004) 23 *Annual Review of Banking & Financial Law*, pp. 225–364.

508 See in Office of the Comptroller of the Currency (OCC), 'OCC Issues Final Rules on National Bank Preemption and Visitorial Powers; Includes Strong Standard to Keep Predatory Lending out of National Banks', Press Release, 7 January 2004, available at: https://www.occ.gov/news-issuances/news-releases/2004/nr-occ-2004-3.html.

509 See in J.B. Sykes, 'Federal Preemption in the Dual Banking System: An Overview and Issues for the 116th Congress', *Congressional Research Service*, Report, R45726, 17 May 2019, p. 12.

510 Ibid.

511 See in Office of the Comptroller of the Currency (OCC), 'OCC Issues Final Rules on National Bank Preemption and Visitorial Powers; Includes Strong Standard to Keep Predatory Lending out of National Banks', Press Release, 7 January 2004, available at: https://www.occ.gov/news-issuances/news-releases/2004/nr-occ-2004-3.html.

512 See in J.B. Sykes, 'Federal Preemption in the Dual Banking System: An Overview and Issues for the 116th Congress', *Congressional Research Service*, Report, R45726, 17 May 2019, p. 13.

513 See in Office of the Comptroller of the Currency (OCC), 'OCC Issues Final Rules on National Bank Preemption and Visitorial Powers; Includes Strong Standard to Keep Predatory Lending out of National Banks', Press Release, 7 January 2004, available at: https://www.occ.gov/news-issuances/news-releases/2004/nr-occ-2004-3.html.

law'.[514] Critics against the OCC's 2004 rules were targeted on the fact that as a result many state laws were pre-empted, mostly on the field of consumer protection, leading to an aggressive expansion of subprime mortgages that ultimately created the global financial crisis of 2007–2009.[515]

The above perception regarding the OCC's rules attempted to be repaired by the Dodd-Frank Act, through its section 1044 provisions. The Dodd-Frank Act made two important, targeted amendments to the pre-emption standards. First, it revised the scope of those state laws that affect the national banks' operations under the NBA and second, it mandated courts to follow the Skidmore deference doctrine[516] when they are evaluating rules promulgated by the OCC that attempt to pre-empt state laws.[517] Section 1044 of Dodd-Frank Act, set out three alternative criteria for the state laws pre-emption in the field of consumer protection. The first criterion stipulates that a state consumer protection law could be pre-empted if it had a discriminatory effect on national banks compared to the effect, the same law has, on a state-chartered bank.[518] This criterion clearly attempts to display an interest in securing parity between the state and the national bank charters, just as the Riegle-Neal Act attempted regarding the interstate branching. The second criterion sets that a state consumer finance protection law could be pre-empted by applying the Barnett Bank case rule, of preventing or significantly interfering with the exercise of national banks' powers.[519] The US Congress clearly believed that the OCC's 2004 rules were beyond the standard established by the Barnett Bank case law. As Bogert notes, this provision also limited OCC determinations that a state law was pre-empted under the Dodd-Frank Act to case-by-case evaluations and only after having consulted with the newly created Consumer Finance

---

514 See in J.B. Sykes, 'Federal Preemption in the Dual Banking System: An Overview and Issues for the 116th Congress', *Congressional Research Service*, Report, R45726, 17 May 2019, p. 13 and also in E.A. Bogert, 'Anti-Federalist Banking Policy Under Dodd-Frank: The Case for the Liberal Pre-Emption of State Banking Law' (2020) 6(2) *University of Pennsylvania Journal of Law & Public Affairs*, p. 319.

515 For a criticism against the OCC's rules see in A.E. Wilmarth Jr., 'The Dodd-Frank Act's Expansion of State Authority to Protect Consumers of Financial Services' (2011) 36(4) *The Journal of Corporation Law*, pp. 895–954. For an opinion against the criticism towards the OCC, see in D.K. Bailey, 'A Defense of The Doctrine of Preemption: Revealing the Fallacy That Federal Preemption Contributed to The Financial Crisis' (2014) 16(4) *Journal of Constitutional Law*, pp. 1041–1108.

516 *Skidmore v. Swift & Co., 323 U.S. 134 (1944)*, holding that although the rulings, interpretations, and opinions of the Administrator under the Fair Labor Standards Act do not control judicial decision, they do constitute a body of experience and informed judgement to which courts and litigants may properly resort for guidance.

517 See in E.A. Bogert, 'Anti-Federalist Banking Policy Under Dodd-Frank: The Case for the Liberal Pre-Emption of State Banking Law' (2020) 6(2) *University of Pennsylvania Journal of Law & Public Affairs*, p. 321.

518 Ibid.

519 Ibid.

Protection Bureau (CFPB).[520] Finally, the third criterion sets that a state law could be pre-empted if it was pre-empted by federal law, not belonging to the Title 62 (where the Dodd-Frank Act is housed).[521] Overall, Section 1044 of Dodd-Frank Act aimed clearly at restricting the extent of the OCC's ability to allow national banks to operate without complying with state legislations in the field of consumer finance protection.

3 THE 1929 FINANCIAL CRISIS

The 1929 financial crisis that erupted in the US stock market in 1929 is an event of major importance, both scientific and historical. Scientific because for economists was and still is a highly debatable issue and historical because its repercussions can be found across the world, since they crossed the Atlantic and hit Europe and other major economies of the world because national economies were linked together by the fixed exchange rates of the gold standard.[522] Apart from the above considerations, the 1929 crisis is also important for its social repercussions since it forced many people in unemployment and had serious social side effects, mostly attributed to the subsequent 'Great Depression'. With this term, we define the longest and deepest downturn in the history of the US and the modern industrial economy.[523] This period lasted for more than a decade, beginning in 1929 with the stock crash and ending during World War II in 1941. Apart from the stock market's crash in 1929, which undoubtedly propagated the crisis, Eichengreen believes that the basic parameters that led to the crisis by changing the general economic structure of that period could be summarised as follows:

- Changes in the composition of production with an expanding production of consumer durables,[524]
- Changes in the labour markets' operation with a declining flexibility to wage adaptation, particularly in the US,[525]
- Changes in the operation of the international monetary system with a growing fragility,[526] and

---

520 Ibid.

521 Ibid.

522 See in B. Eichengreen, 'The origins and nature of the Great Slump revisited' (1992) 45(2) *Economic History Review*, p. 225.

523 For a further analysis see also in C.W. Calomiris and J.R. Mason, 'Fundamentals, Panics, and Bank Distress During the Depression' (2003) 93(5) *American Economic Review*, pp. 1615–1647.

524 Ibid., p. 214.

525 Ibid., p. 216.

526 Ibid., p. 218.

- Changes in the pattern of international settlements with a dependence of those settlements to the US lending.[527]

These changes, magnified the initial impact from the stock market crash and together with a strict monetary policy followed by the Fed led to the deflationary economic effects.[528] With respect to the present book, the 1929 financial crisis is important for two reasons: a) because it was the starting point for the Great Depression and the regulatory tsunami that followed the myriad bank failures in the US, culminating with the enactment of the GSA, and b) because it provides us with useful similarities for assessing and analysing the financial crisis of 2007–2009, that also erupted in the US. Therefore, a brief analysis of the major events and government responses is necessary to better understand the driving power behind the discussion for imposing structural reforms in the banking sector.

3.1. *Brief History and Major Events*

Since a complete narrative of the 1929 crisis and the Great Depression's events and their impact is beyond the scope of the present book, we will make use of only the major events that had a crucial impact on the unfolding of the crisis and are in close connection with the subsequent regulatory measures adopted. The Great Depression began in August 1929, when the affluent economic expansion of the 'Roaring Twenties' came to an end. The financial boom occurred during an era of optimism where families prospered. Automobiles, telephones, and other new technologies proliferated, while ordinary men and women invested growing sums in stocks and bonds. A completely new industry of brokerage houses, investment trusts, and margin accounts enabled ordinary people to purchase corporate equities with borrowed funds, allowing purchasers to put down only a fraction of the price, typically 10%, and borrowed the rest. The stocks that they bought served as collateral for the loans and borrowed money poured into equity markets; stock prices soared. A subsequent series of financial crises punctuated the economic contraction. These crises included a stock market crash in 1929, a series of regional banking panics in 1930 and 1931, and a series of national and international financial crises from 1931 through 1933. The downturn hit bottom in March 1933, when the commercial banking system collapsed, and the newly elected President Roosevelt declared a national banking holiday.[529] The return of the US economy to its full output and employment occurred during World War II.

---

527 Ibid., p. 219.
528 Ibid., p. 236.
529 Ibid., p. 230.

3.1.1 Towards the Stock Market's Crash of 1929

The Great Depression started with the New York's stock market crash in October 1929. This event was the climax of a process that started five years before, in 1924, when the US stock market was under a euphoria facing a bull market[530] of 'unprecedented length and magnitude'.[531] Obviously, within such euphoric climate many investors were attracted to the market despite the fact that they had never before owned stocks. Commercial and investment banks continuously encouraged new investors to enter the market buying common stocks instead of bonds.[532] The bull market entered its last, frenzied, phase in 1928. Evidence of a speculative bubble in the stock market was a) the rapid increases in the trading volume of the New York Stock Exchange (NYSE), and b) the widening gap between stock prices and corporate earnings and dividends.[533] At the same time, call loans from brokers rose from $4.4 billion in 1927 to a high of $8.5 billion in October 1929.

The general optimism regarding the stock market conditions prevailed among the President's Coolidge administration, banks' executives, and prominent economists. On the contrary, the Fed was deeply concerned about the existence of a stock market bubble, mostly because of the stock prices and the accelerating volume of brokers' call loans and total credit provided. In early 1928, the Fed's Board supported decisions from the regional federal reserve banks to raise their discount window rates from 3.5% to 5% but did not raise the rates further in 1928 due to fears about the potentially disruptive impact that higher interest rates might have on business and agricultural production as well as the presidential elections in November of that year.[534] Despite the higher discount window interest rates, total bank credit and brokers' call loans continued to expand in 1928. In 1929 the Fed viewed the situation with great

---

530 According to *Investopedia*, the term 'bull market' is used to describe the condition of a financial market in which prices are rising or are expected to rise. The term is mostly used to refer to the stock market, but it can be applied to anything that is traded (i.e. bonds, real estate, currencies, and commodities). Since prices of securities rise and fall essentially continuously during trading, the term is typically reserved for extended periods of time, where a large portion of security prices are rising. Bull markets have the tendency to last for months or even years.
The opposite condition of a bull market is a 'bear market', which is characterized by falling prices and typically, pessimism prevails. The commonly held belief about the origin of these terms suggests that the use of bull and bear to describe markets comes from the way these animals attack their opponents. A bull thrusts its horns up into the air, while a bear swipes its paws downward. These actions are used as metaphors for the movement of a market. If the trend is upward, it is a bull market and if the trend is downward, it is a bear market.

531 See in A.E. Wilmarth Jr., *Taming the Megabanks, Why We Need a New Glass-Steagall Act*, New York, Oxford University Press, 2020, p. 70.

532 Ibid.

533 Ibid.

534 Ibid., p. 73.

alarm, however both the Fed Banks and the Board were not able to reach an agreement on the proper policy reaction. The Fed's Board and most of the regional Fed Banks were in favour of the so-called 'direct pressure' policy measure under which the Fed Banks would refuse to provide credit to banks if they planned to use it for making loans that finance trading activities.[535] In contrast, the NY Fed and some other regional Fed Banks opted for an increase in the discount window interest rates to restrain credit growth. The Board and its allies counter argued that this might have collateral damage since it would restrict credit availability for legitimate purposes.[536] The Fed's Board and its allies prevailed and applied their selected policy measure of direct pressure while refusing the NY Fed to raise its discount window interest rate to 6%. Ultimately, though, that policy failed to contain to bubble because the Fed missed the component of non-bank lenders which operated as a shadow banking system outside its regulatory perimeter, in a way similar to the 2007–2009 financial crisis. The direct pressure policy had its moment on March 25 and 26, 1929 when it came very close to bursting the bubble. On these two days, heavy selling occurred mostly due to the rumours that the Fed's Board would take more measure to curtail credit expansion and deflate the stock market.[537] Because of those rumours, call loan rates increased from 12% to 20% during the afternoon of 26 March and the situation looked grim, but the end of the bubble was far from present. The National City Bank's executive Charles Mitchell intervened, like *deus ex machina*, and announced a line of available new call loans up to $25 million with interest rates between 15% and 20%. This 'magic' intervention reassured investors, and the stock rallied again, capping also interest for call loans at 15%.[538] After Mitchell's intervention the Fed's Board abandoned the policy of direct pressure and allowed the NY Fed to increase the discount window interest rate at 6%. The interest increase was mostly symbolic since other Fed banks did not follow and let their rate at 5% while the NY Fed itself mitigated the potential effects of that move by reducing its discount rate for bankers' acceptances.[539]

The final stock market's spike occurred in the summer of 1929. During June, July, and August the New York Times industrial index rose by around 30% and

---

535 Ibid.

536 The Federal Reserve's decision to increase interest rates had unintended consequences and side effects. Because of the rigid international gold standard regime, the Fed's actions forced foreign central banks to also raise their own interest rates. Those tight-money policies tipped economies around the world into recession, contracted international commerce, and slowed the international economy. See also in B. Eichengreen, 'The origins and nature of the Great Slump revisited' (1992) 45(2) *Economic History Review*, p. 230 onwards.

537 See in A.E. Wilmarth Jr., *Taming the Megabanks, Why We Need a New Glass-Steagall Act*, New York, Oxford University Press, 2020, p. 74.

538 Ibid.

539 Ibid., p. 75.

everyone believed that better days were ahead. The bull market reached its peak on 3 September 1929, and the Dow Jones industrial index closed at 381, a six-fold increase from 63 in August 1921.[540] Despite the general optimism, the stock market was unable to sustain an upward movement during September and October, and stock prices began to decline. The epic boom ended in a spectacular and cataclysmic bust. After a sharp drop on 21 October, the market lost most of its gains since spring 1929. A few days before, on 15 October, the prominent Yale economist Irving Fisher, proclaimed, 'stock prices have reached what looks like a permanently high plateau'.[541] Despite the assurances from bankers and economists and Wall Street analysts, investors' confidence was shaking, and the Great Crash occurred the last week of October 1929. On 23 October, the stock market experienced a 'sudden avalanche of sell orders' and a 'perfect Niagara of liquidation'.[542] When trading began on 24 October, a wave of panic swept the market, and the ticker tape was delayed by more than 90 minutes by 1 p.m. Closing prices for stocks were not reported until 4 hours after the NYSE closed at 3:30 p.m. This day was the 'Black Thursday' and in the afternoon, a group of leading bankers met together and decided to intervene and save the situation. Their efforts stabilised the market by placing bids for leading stocks with total value up to $130 million, preventing an utter collapse.[543] This intervention managed to contain investors' fears and on 25 and 26 October's trading session prices remained relatively stable. Despite all the assurances from Wall Street executives on the Black Thursday's aftermath, a second typhoon of liquidation occurred on 'Black Monday', 28 October 1929, and the Dow Jones declined nearly 13%. This decline in stock prices was far more severe than on black Thursday and the Dow Jones drop was the largest recorded.[544] No sign of banker's intervention was available this time and the ticker tape was three hours late at the end of the NYSE trading session. Once the leading bankers had a meeting at the end of the stock market's session and informed the public that they would continue to provide support and act as stabilising factors 'as far as possible' while at the same they were not intend 'to maintain prices as such, but to insure an open and free market'.[545] On the following day, the famous 'Black Tuesday', trading volume was immensely grater compared to black Thursday and 'great block of stocks were offered for what they bring'.[546] Total losses for the day at the NYSE exceeded $8 billion and the market dropped nearly 12%. By mid-November, the Dow Jones had lost

540 Ibid., p. 76.
541 Ibid., p. 77.
542 Ibid., p. 78.
543 Ibid.
544 Ibid., p. 79.
545 Ibid.
546 Ibid.

almost half of its value. The slide continued through the summer of 1932, when the Dow Jones closed at 41.22, its lowest value of the 20th century, 89% below its peak and did not return to its pre-crash heights until November 1954.[547]

Funds that fled the stock market flowed into New York City's commercial banks that also assumed millions of dollars in stock-market loans. The sudden surges strained banks and as deposits increased, banks' reserve requirements rose; but banks' reserves fell as depositors withdrew cash, banks purchased loans, and checks (the principal method of depositing funds) cleared at slow pace. These counterpoised flows left many banks temporarily short of reserves. To relieve the strain, NY Fed sprang into action and started purchasing government securities on the open market, expedited lending through its discount window, and lowered the discount window's interest rate assuring commercial banks that it would supply the reserves they needed. These NY Fed's actions, although not without facing criticism,[548] had the following results:[549]

(a) Increased total reserves in the banking system,
(b) Relaxed the reserve constraint faced by banks in New York City,
(c) Enabled financial institutions to remain open for business and satisfy their customers' demands during the crisis, and
(d) Averted short-term interest rates from rising to disruptive levels, (frequently occurring during financial crises).

From the stock market crash of 1929, economists – including the leaders of the Federal Reserve – learned at least two lessons. The first lesson is that central banks – just like the Federal Reserve – should be very careful when acting in response to equity markets. Detecting and deflating financial bubbles is a difficult task and using monetary policy to restrain investors' exuberance may have broad, unintended, and undesirable consequences. The second lesson learned is that when stock market crashes occur, their damage can be contained by following the playbook developed by the NY Fed in the fall of 1929. The stock-market crash harmed commerce and manufacturing, since the crash frightened investors and consumers, both men and women lost their life savings, people feared for their jobs, and worried whether they could pay their bills. Fear and uncertainty reduced purchases of big-ticket items, like houses

547 Ibid., p. 80.

548 At the time being, the New York Fed's actions were controversial, and the Federal Reserve Board and several reserve banks complained that New York Fed exceeded its statutory authority, even though in hindsight these actions helped to contain the crisis in the short run. The stock market collapsed, but commercial banks near the centre of the storm remained in operation serving clients' needs. For a more detailed analysis, see in A.E. Wilmarth Jr., *Taming the Megabanks, Why We Need a New Glass-Steagall Act*, New York, Oxford University Press, 2020, p. 80.

549 See in A.E. Wilmarth Jr., *Taming the Megabanks, Why We Need a New Glass-Steagall Act*, New York, Oxford University Press, 2020, p. 80.

and automobiles that people bought with credit. Big firms – like Ford Motors – saw demand decline, so they decided to slow production and furlough workers. Unemployment rose, and the contraction that had begun in the summer of 1929 deepened across the country.[550]

3.1.2 The Banking Panics of 1930–1933

In the fall of 1930, the US economy appeared poised for recovery. At a historical coincidence, the previous three contractions, in 1920, 1923, and 1926, had lasted an average of 15 months and the downturn that began in the summer of 1929 lasted for 15 months. Therefore, a rapid and robust recovery was much anticipated, but in November 1930 however a series of panics among commercial banks turned what had been a typical recession into the beginning of the Great Depression.[551] The first major banking crisis occurred in the US in late 1930, triggered by the collapse of two major universal banking groups Caldwell and Company (Caldwell) and Bank of United States (BUS). Caldwell was following weak management practices by its executives (i.e. using it affiliated bank and insurance companies as 'last resort buyers' for any unsold stocks and bonds, requiring its bond underwriting clients to deposit the proceeds from the underwriting process in Caldwell owned banks, etc.) and had become a huge conglomerate with various subsidiaries and affiliated companies in every industry.[552] At the end of 1929, more than 4/5 of the securities held by Caldwell were defaulted bonds, securities issued by the companies under its control, and other illiquid securities that the company was unable to sell to customers. Caldwell was operating with an extremely low capital level since the assets to equity ratio rose to 21:1 by the end of 1929. Moreover, more than half of Caldwell's liabilities were due on demand and those on demand liabilities were as large as 9 times its liquid assets.[553] Caldwell's primary bank was Bank of Tennessee (BoT) which was also in deep troubles since it heavily relied on state government funds' deposits and most of its assets were unsold illiquid securities. In a last attempt to prevent the collapse, Caldwell's manager tried to merge with BancoKentucky Company (BKC), which controlled National

---

550 Ibid., p. 86.

551 Ibid., p. 90.

552 Caldwell was a rapidly expanding financial-industrial conglomerate and the largest financial holding company in the (US) South. It provided its clients with an array of services including banking, brokerage, and insurance through an expanding network of chain banks controlled by its parent corporation which was headquartered in Nashville, Tennessee. The parent entity got into trouble when its leaders invested too heavily in securities markets and lost substantial sums from the declined stock prices. To cover their own losses, Caldwell's leaders, drained cash from the corporations they controlled.

553 See in A.E. Wilmarth Jr., *Taming the Megabanks, Why We Need a New Glass-Steagall Act*, New York, Oxford University Press, 2020, p. 91.

Bank of Kentucky (NBK). NBK provided an emergency loan to Caldwell of up to $2.4 million but the relief was temporary and BKC suffered from its own problems.[554] Caldwell's problems were deepening in the second half of 1930, and amid the broader string economic conditions, on 7 November 1930, the Tennessee superintendent of banks closed BoT; six days later, the entire Caldwell group was put in a receivership.[555] On 12 and 17 November, 1930, Caldwell affiliates in Knoxville and Louisville failed. The failure of Caldwell banks triggered a correspondent cascade that forced around 100 commercial banks to suspend their operations (NBK was also a victim of this bank run) mostly in the Federal Reserve Districts of Atlanta, St. Louis, and Richmond. Those banks were either controlled by Caldwell or were correspondent banks of Caldwell affiliates.[556] In communities where these banks closed, depositors panicked and withdrew funds en masse from other operating banks, spreading the banking panic from town to town. Within a few weeks, hundreds of banks suspended their operations, and about 1/3 of these organisations reopened within a few months, but the majority were liquidated.

BUS was a state-chartered bank, member of the NY Fed.[557] By 1929, through a series of expansionary mergers and acquisitions had attracted more than 400.000 depositors (more than any other bank in the US) and had a balance sheet of $240 million of deposits funding a total of $315 million of assets.[558] BUS had two securities affiliates 'Bankus Corporation' and 'City Financial' that were actively trading on the NYSE and BUS was supporting their operations through large loans. At the same time, BUS was operating with more than 30 real estate companies that were receiving loans from BUS and issuing bonds to finance their construction operations. After losses from its trading activities during the market crash BUS was in a problematic situation and despite an effective campaign to attract new depositors on 11 December, BUS ceased operations.[559] BUS suffered $16 million losses from its trading operations, had $7 million of non-performing loans out of $23 impaired loans. Until the last moments a proposed merger between BUS and another bank was under discussion and the NY Fed had helped with the search for a merger partner. When negotiations broke down,[560] worried depositors rushed to withdraw funds, and New York's superintendent of banking closed the institution. Just like Caldwell, BUS collapsed because of its high-risk securities and real estate

554 Ibid.

555 Ibid., p. 92.

556 Ibid.

557 BUS was the 4th largest bank in New York City and the 28th largest universal bank in the US.

558 See in A.E. Wilmarth Jr., *Taming the Megabanks, Why We Need a New Glass-Steagall Act*, New York, Oxford University Press, 2020, p. 92.

559 Ibid.

560 Merger negotiations broke down when the New York Clearing House and the largest New York banks refused to provide a $30 million loan to finance the proposed merger.

activities, the bad management decisions and conflicts of interest coupled with self-dealing practices.[561] In a pattern similar to Caldwell, BUS failure triggered bank runs on three other smaller New York City banks having connections to BUS, including two of the banks involved in the failed merger negotiations. The smallest of those three banks ultimately failed and the rest of them were saved by the New York Clearing House. Overall, more than 15 banks failed during December 1930 and January 1931.[562] BUS's collapse received extensive media attention, both domestic and international, since it was also a member bank. Simultaneously, the failure of NY Fed to secure a safe merger that would prevent the banking crisis was highly criticised and shake public confidence toward the Fed. The differences across regional Fed Banks played an important role in making the banking crisis more acute.[563] The crisis began in the Sixth District, headquartered in Atlanta, Georgia and the leaders of the Atlanta Fed believed that their responsibility as a lender of last resort (LoR) extended to the broader banking system. The Atlanta Fed expedited discount lending to member banks, encouraged member banks to extend loans to their non-member respondents, and rushed funds to cities and towns beset by banking panics. The crisis also hit the Eighth District, headquartered in St. Louis, Missouri. Contrary to the Atlanta Fed's actions, the leaders of the St. Louis Fed had a narrower view of their mandate and responsibilities thereby refusing to rediscount loans for the purpose of accommodating the non-member banks. During the banking crisis, the St. Louis Fed limited discount lending and refused to assist non-member institutions. Consequently, a higher percentage of banks failed in the St. Louis Fed's district, compared to Atlanta Fed's district.[564]

The first major US banking crisis of 1931 occurred in Chicago, Illinois. The Chicago metropolitan area experienced a real estate boom in the 1920s, and the domestic banks had largely invested in residential and commercial mortgage lending together with real estate bonds, sold by the Chicago banks' affiliated securities firms. The Illinois state laws prevented intrastate branching, but this rule was circumvented through the establishment of chain banks.[565] The two largest Chicago based banks were Continental Illinois Bank (CIB) and the First National Bank of Chicago (First Chicago). In addition, other banking groups were operating their chain banks in the Chicago metropolitan area including Bain group, Foreman State group, Central Trust Company, and National Bank of the Republic group. In spring 1931, CIB and First Chicago responded to a sharp decline in real estate property values by announcing that

561 See in A.E. Wilmarth Jr., *Taming the Megabanks, Why We Need a New Glass-Steagall Act*, New York, Oxford University Press, 2020, p. 93.

562 Ibid.

563 Ibid., p. 94.

564 Ibid.

565 Ibid., p. 108.

they would no longer repurchase the real estate bonds issued by their securities affiliates.[566] This announcement alerted investors and depositors since smaller banks, which were heavily exposed to real estate loans, might be perceived as weaker thereby undermining public confidence in them. On 7 June 1931, First Chicago agreed to purchase Foreman State Bank and its affiliated trust company with support provided by the Chicago Clearing House. Central Trust agreed to merge with the National Republic at the same time, preventing them from collapse, as was the case with the Bain group of 12 banks that collapsed in late June 1931.[567]

The banking panics in 1930 and early 1931 were largely regional in nature. Unfortunately, the nature of the financial crisis changed in the fall of 1931, when the commercial banking crisis spread throughout the entire nation.[568] The hands-off approach adopted by the Fed's Board for the failing banks led several large cities to organise their own schemes of emergency mergers in order to prevent bank collapses.[569] In January 1932, based on President Hoover's initiative the US Congress created the Reconstruction Finance Corporation (RFC), which had the authority to lend up to $2 billion to banks, other financial institutions, and the railroads.[570] In addition, the Fed began a program of large-scale open market purchases in April 1932 with 'modestly

---

566 Ibid.

567 Ibid.

568 Professor Wilmarth writes that between June and August 1931, more than 400 banks with total deposits exceeding $400 million, failed. Moreover, between September and December 1931, almost 1500 banks with total deposits exceeding $1 billion, also failed. See in A.E. Wilmarth Jr., *Taming the Megabanks, Why We Need a New Glass-Steagall Act*, New York, Oxford University Press, 2020, p. 108.

569 Such emergency merger schemes were organized in Baltimore, where a consortium of Baltimore based banks and New York based banks rescued the 'Baltimore Trust Company', in Philadelphia where several leading banks saved the 'Integrity Trust Company', in Chicago as mentioned above, and in New York City where 'Manufacturers Trust' acquired 'Chatham Phoenix Bank'.

570 Initially, in October 1931, Hoover had asked the nation's largest banks to create a credit pool to supply with emergency loans the threatened banks. A group of large banks, members of the FED, organized the 'National Credit Corporation' (NCC) and promised to contribute $500 million for Hoover's credit pool. The credit would have been provided through local lending committees and would be backed by pledges of securities and other assets that were not eligible as collaterals in the FED's discounted window loans. Large banks were very reluctant to participate in the NCC mostly because they were trying to stay afloat themselves and did not want to share their resources with other banks. Hoover assured banks that he would set up another scheme of a new government-funding agency in case the NCC proven to be unsuccessful. Based on very conservative lending policies, the NCC approved only $10 million of loans by the end of November 1931, convincing Hoover that banks were unable to save themselves and the government had to intervene. See in A.E. Wilmarth Jr., *Taming the Megabanks, Why We Need a New Glass-Steagall Act*, New York, Oxford University Press, 2020, p. 110.

favourable effects'.[571] Economic conditions were slightly improved by the summer of 1932, but relief did not last. The Midwest and West, especially, saw an increase in bank failures towards the second half of 1932; Chicago once again was at the spotlight since the highly leveraged utilities' empire of Samuel Insull collapsed in June, and many Chicago based banks were heavily exposed. News about the bankers' trial in Chicago led people queueing outside bank branches, triggering a general run on Chicago's banks.[572] CIB and First Chicago were also victims of that run but managed to temporarily calm their depositors, unlike Central Republic Bank (CRB), which was in a very weak position. After negotiations and debates involving even the President Hoover, the RFC provided a $90 million loan to CRB together with another $5 million loan by Chicago's leading banks. Just four months after the RFC's loan CRB transferred all its deposits to a newly organised bank, City National Bank and Trust Co. and enter voluntary liquidation, demonstrating that RFC's loans were not enough to solve the US's banking problems. More than 350 banks failed during the last quarter of 1932 and almost half of them had received RFC loans. In December 1932, following the failure of a local chain bank group (Wingfield chain of banks) the Governor of Nevada declared a bank holiday to prevent a complete melt down of the state's financial system.[573]

In early 1933, a national panic arose. Many factors contributed to the national banking panic, including uncertainty over the economic policies of President Roosevelt, who was elected in November 1932 but did not take office until March 1933. Banks could have borrowed from the RFC but were reluctant to do so, in part because their names would be published and their action might be seen as a sign of weakness, which might then lead to a run on the bank.[574] After Nevada's bank holiday became clear that neither the FED nor the RFC were able to prevent banking crises from erupting anytime and a cascade of statewide bank holidays were approved. On 20 January 1933, Iowa's Governor declared a bank holiday after several Iowa based banks failed. In February 1933, the collapse of two Detroit banks triggered a nationwide banking panic. These banks were Guardian Detroit Union Group (Guardian)[575] and Detroit Bankers Company (DBC)[576] having took advantage of Michigan's industrial production (automobile industry) and created two holding companies that ended up in controlling Detroit's and Michigan's 3/5 of total banking assets and more

571 See in A.E. Wilmarth Jr., *Taming the Megabanks, Why We Need a New Glass-Steagall Act*, New York, Oxford University Press, 2020, p. 111.

572 Ibid., p. 112.

573 Ibid., p. 117.

574 Ibid.

575 Guardian was controlled by the Henry Ford family and held more than $379 million of assets.

576 DBC was controlled by a group of 12 Detroit business leaders, acting jointly as voting trustees for DBC's stocks and held more than $530 million of assets.

than 20 banks and several securities and real estate affiliates.[577] When the Detroit's booming car production plummeted these two banks encountered severe problems and both acquired several non-performing real estate loans and depreciated securities from their securities affiliates, following by the submission of deceptive reports towards the regulatory authorities.

The RFC loaned $16 million to Guardian in 1932 and in January 1933 the bank asked for another loan of $43.5 million. The RFC asked the Ford family to inject new capital to Guardian in an attempt to watered down its total financial support, but Henry Ford declined, and the RFC could not loan the total amount without adequate collateral after the CRB bailout.[578] At the same time, DBC asked for a $100 million loan from the RFC amid concerns that Ford would withdraw the deposits held also in DBC. The RFC declined to provide the loan and under the state of panic from the two banks' imminent collapse, federal and state regulators closed all banks' branches, and the Michigan Governor declared a statewide bank holiday, on 14 February 1933.[579]

3.2. US Government Responses and the Role of the Federal Reserve

The US government's responses and the Fed's role before and during the Great Recession were for decades a hot topic. Academic literature is extremely rich and only few decades ago economists managed to reach a consensus regarding the origins and the nature of the 'Great Slump'. Criticism follows both the US government under Hoover administration and the Fed because they underestimated the situation and did not take immediate action to counter the stock market's 1929 crash. Particularly the criticism towards the Fed must take into consideration certain limitations that back then formed important constraints on Fed's policy decisions. At the start of the crisis, the Fed's decision-making structure was decentralised and as a result, often ineffective. Each regional Fed district had a governor who set policies for his district, although some decisions required approval of the Board in Washington, D.C. The Board lacked the authority and the necessary tools to act on its own and struggled to coordinate policies across the regional Fed districts. At the same time though, the governors and the Board understood the need for coordination and frequently corresponded concerning important issues. This correspondence resulted in establishing procedures and programs, such as the Open Market Investment Committee, to institutionalise their cooperation. When these efforts yielded consensus, monetary policy could be swift and effective, but when the governors disagreed, districts could and in

577 See in A.E. Wilmarth Jr., *Taming the Megabanks, Why We Need a New Glass-Steagall Act*, New York, Oxford University Press, 2020, p. 117.

578 Ibid., p. 119.

579 Ibid.

many cases did pursue independent and occasionally contradictory policies. As the crisis was unfolding, among the governors, various approaches were promoted on how to deal with the banking crisis and to what extent the Fed should act as the lender of last resort, both for member banks and for non-member banks. Questions also arose as to what extent should the Fed lend money to non-banks. These differences of Governors' opinion contributed to the Fed's most serious sin of omission: failure to stem the decline in the supply of money. From the fall of 1930 through the winter of 1933, the money supply fell by nearly 30%, and this declining supply of funds reduced average prices by an equivalent amount. This deflation stemmed from the collapse of the banking system, increased debt burdens, distorted economic decision-making, reduced consumption, increased unemployment, and forced banks, firms, and individuals into bankruptcy.

The Fed could have prevented deflation by preventing the collapse of the banking system or by counteracting it with an expansion of the monetary base, but it failed to do so for several reasons. The economic collapse was unforeseen and unprecedented while at the same time decision makers lacked effective mechanisms for determining what went wrong and lacked the authority to take actions sufficient to cure the downward spiralling economy. According to Eichengreen, had the US abandoned the gold standard timely and the Fed adopted a more expansionary monetary policy, the result probably would have been different and the economic recovery much faster, compared to other countries that abandoned the gold standard earlier and adopted a more relaxed monetary policy.[580]

3.3. *The Pecora Committee Hearings*

During the last days of Hoover administration, Wall Street came to face another challenge. This challenge, ultimately, had both a profound effect on the future of financial regulation in the US and a name: the 'Pecora Committee'. The Senate Banking and Currency Committee, with President Hoover's support, authorised the creation of a new subcommittee to specifically investigate Wall Street's securities practices of short selling, bear raids, stock trading pools and other practices that were considered as manipulative. Initially created in March 1932 with the Senate Resolution 84, the subcommittee made little progress on its mandate during the first 11 months,[581] until it hired

580 See in B. Eichengreen, 'The origins and nature of the Great Slump revisited' (1992) 45(2) *Economic History Review*, p. 239.

581 The subcommittee was struggling to deliver results mostly because banking executives repeatedly denied committee's requests for bank records and internal documents. Witnesses easily evaded questions posed by counsels.

Ferdinand Pecora as its new chief counsel in January 1933.[582] As a result of Pecora's hiring, on 15 February 1933, the subcommittee launched a new stage of investigations into the Wall Street's securities practices, based on an expanded mandate according to the Senate Resolution 84. Pecora dominated the subcommittee's hearings, and his name has been synonymous with the subcommittee's very existence (Pecora Committee or Pecora Investigation). Using the power of subpoena, Pecora succeeded in obtaining the records of the nation's largest financial institutions, so that he and his staff pored over thousands of internal documents to be prepared for the testimonies that followed. Apart from accessing records and internal documentation, Pecora subpoenaed high profile bankers to testify in the subcommittee's hearings, calculating that their presence, appearance, and testimony would guarantee maximum press coverage. Indeed, national and regional newspapers carried daily front page accounts of the subcommittee's investigation.

Pecora started with the examination of Samuel Insull's utilities empire in 1932, and through the hearings successfully demonstrated that the Central Republic Bank and other, Chicago based, banks loaned huge amounts to Insull's companies violating both the spirit and the letter of the lending limits imposed under Illinois state law.[583] Moreover, some underwriting syndicates led by a leading Chicago investment bank, used high pressure marketing and deceptive advertising aiming at selling Insull's company securities to utility customers and other investors, which were classified as unsophisticated.[584] Pecora then subpoenaed National City Bank (NCB) and its securities affiliate, National City Company (NCC). Within only eight days of hearings, Pecora successfully destroyed the reputation of both NCB/NCC and of its chairman, Charles Mitchell, by focusing on NCB/NCC fraudulent and predatory sales practices by focusing on certain securities offerings that the two companies sold to their customers.[585] These transactions were associated with conflicts of interest, unethical sales practices and deceptive offering materials coupled with extensive self-dealing by senior officers and extremely high bonuses to the high ranked executives.[586] Moreover, it was demonstrated that NCB/NCC sold large stock blocks to a 'preferred list' of persons that probably posted high earnings from the initial price fluctuations. This form of transaction happened twice with the Boeing's stocks in October 1928 and January 1929,

---

582 Ferdinand Pecora served as the New York's deputy district attorney. See also in A.E. Wilmarth Jr., *Taming the Megabanks, Why We Need a New Glass-Steagall Act*, New York, Oxford University Press, 2020, p. 399.

583 Ibid., p. 124.

584 Ibid.

585 Ibid. Pecora examined the NCB/NCC trading practices in its own stock, the stock sales of Boeing and Anaconda Copper, the foreign bonds issuances of Peru, the Brazilian state of Minas Gerais and a Chilean industrial company producing nitrate.

586 Ibid., p. 125.

with NCB/NCC encouraging the public to invest and buy company's stocks.[587] Under Roosevelt's encouragement Pecora decided to inquire J.P. Morgan & Co. as the next subcommittee's subject.[588] Pecora examined J.P. Morgan across four lines of inquiry and managed to turn the public against the prestigious firm. Firstly, he demonstrated that Morgan's partners claimed losses from their investments, allowing them to pay extremely low taxes. Secondly, demonstrated that J.P. Morgan & Co. had granted financial favours to near 500 'friends of the firm', a list significantly larger that NCB/NCCs' similar attempts. Thirdly, Pecora uncovered the influential role of J.P. Morgan through an extensive network of relationships with many of the biggest and most influential companies and financial institutions in the US. These 'silken bonds of gratitude', as defined by Pecora, were reinforced by the participation of Morgan's executives in a variety of board member positions, favourable loans, and other similar practices. Lastly, Pecora demonstrated how J.P. Morgan undermined and compromised its code of ethics when it underwrites the securities of United Corporation and Alleghany Corporation.[589]

The subcommittee hearings continued even after the passage of the GSA and Pecora invited Dillon Read & Co., a private investment bank that proved to sell Latin America's bonds to American investors based on misleading information and prospectuses. Apart from the abusive practices towards customers, Dillon Read was sponsoring two large investment trusts and exercised complete control over them, extracting huge profits from them until the 1929 collapse where retail investors suffered huge losses.[590] After concluding with Dillon Read, Pecora subpoenaed Chase National Bank (CNB) and its securities affiliate Chase Securities Corporation (CSC). Pecora demonstrated that CNB/CSC used prospectus with falsifying and misleading statements to market Cuban government's high-risk bonds,[591] Canadian bonds, an infrastructure project company's bonds[592] and bonds of a real estate developer,[593] which all defaulted in 1933.[594] Moreover, Pecora demonstrated that Chase's chairman, Albert

587 Ibid.

588 Ibid., p. 130. Initially, the House of Morgan refused to cooperate with Pecora's request on the grounds that it was a private bank. On 4 April 1933, after Pecora's prompt actions the Senate approved a resolution that significantly expanded the subcommittee's power to investigate 'the business of banking, financing, and extending credit' conducted by any person, partnership of firm. In late May and early June, the subcommittee had convinced the House of Morgan to cooperate and participate in the hearings.

589 Ibid., pp. 130–131.

590 Ibid., p. 140.

591 See in A.E. Wilmarth Jr., 'Prelude to Glass-Steagall: Abusive Securities Practices by National City Bank and Chase National Bank During the "Roaring Twenties"' (2016) 90(5) *Tulane Law Review*, p. 1312.

592 Ibid., p. 1314.

593 Ibid., p. 1315.

594 See in A.E. Wilmarth Jr., *Taming the Megabanks, Why We Need a New Glass-Steagall Act*, New York, Oxford University Press, 2020, p. 141.

Wiggin, took extremely bonuses and at the same time he was involved in a massive self-dealing, at the expense of Chase's, through a network of family owned Canadian companies when at the same time Chase was actively trying to stabilise the negative effects from the financial crash.[595]

The outcome of the Pecora Committee was issued on 16 June 1934, with a 400-page final report[596] offering a careful and detailed analysis of a variety of banking and securities practices, though it stopped short of making concrete legislative recommendations. This was attributed in part to the fact that Congress had already passed major legislation in 1933 and 1934 aimed at curbing some of the more egregious abusive practices uncovered by the Pecora Committee and the supporting investigative team.[597] Apart from is pure financial investigation character, the Committee on Banking and Currency's investigation of Wall Street established several historic precedents and became the benchmark for any future committee, since it regularised the practice of Senate committees subpoenaing materials from individuals as well as institutions. Under Ferdinand Pecora's direction, the committee staff had managed to set a high standard for thoroughness and offered a model of excellence for future Senate investigators.

4 THE GREAT DEPRESSION AND THE POST CRISIS LANDSCAPE

During Roosevelt's Presidency, and mostly because of the result of the Pecora Committee hearings, there was a broad consensus among the people that the practices of big US universal banks had triggered the Great Depression since their participation in the stock market led to its 1929 crash. Despite the fact that scientific evidence does not support this fallacy[598] the public was outraged from those practices and the Roosevelt administration supported the GSA proposal for a separation between the commercial and investment banks.[599]

---

595 Ibid.

596 See in Committee on Banking and Currency (CBC – the 'Pecora Committee'), *Stock Exchange Practices, Final Report*, No. 1455, Senate – US Congress, 16 June 1934.

597 Congress passed on 16 June 1933 the Banking Act, also known as the Glass-Steagall Act. In 1934, Congress passed the 'Securities Exchange Act' of 1934, also known as the Fletcher-Rayburn bill.

598 See in R.S. Kroszner and R.G. Rajan, 'Is the Glass-Steagall Act Justified? A Study of the U.S. Experience with Universal Banking Before 1933' (1994) 84(4) *The American Economic Review*, pp. 810–832, where they provide evidence that securities underwrote by commercial banks, overall, had a better quality of those performed by investment banks.

599 An important distinction must be made at this point. In 1932, the Hoover administration vote the Banking Act of 1932, also known as Glass-Steagall Act, since it was sponsored by Senator Carter Glass and Representative Henry Steagall. The 1932 Banking Act reformed the Federal Reserve's role in providing credit during economic downturns and included two

Apart from strict separation regime that was adopted in the post crisis era, another important legislation in the financial sector was the major overhaul in the securities market, and the enactment of the deposit guarantee scheme.

4.1. The Glass-Steagall Act

Broadly speaking and within a general regulatory framework, the phrase 'Glass-Steagall Act' (GSA) is understood as the legislation that effectively enacted the separation between commercial banking and investment banking activities and created the FDIC, among other things. As a result of the legislation, a commercial bank, member of the Federal Reserve System that accepts deposits (depository institution) is not allowed, with some exemptions, to engage in the securities market activities and an investment bank – a securities firm or a broker/dealer – is not allowed to accept deposits. The enactment of the GSA was the result of the Pecora Committee hearings and was perceived as a response to the allegations that commercial banks, through their affiliates, used depositors' funds to engage and finance their investment banking activities, jeopardising the fiduciary duty towards their customers. As will be further explored in the present book, GSA was eroded through the years and partially repealed in the late 1990s, in an attempt to create a more competitive and efficient US banking system. Despite proposals for its re-enactment after the resent financial crisis, the GSA remains a historic but extremely important legislation because it still perceived as a legislation that created a stabilised and prosperous financial system even though its enactment was not accompanied by scientific evidence for its necessity.[600]

For reasons of coherence and for simplicity, for the present book purposes we will use the term GSA to describe the specific parts of the 1933 Banking Act since from a technical perspective, GSA describes four sections (provisions) of the US Banking Act of 1933 separating commercial and investment banking. These provisions were sections 16, 20, 21 and 32 contained in the Banking Act of 1933, and were designed to prevent banks from engaging in speculative

major provisions. The first was that the Federal Reserve banks received authority to lend to member banks on assets not otherwise eligible for discount, with the approval of five members of the Federal Reserve Board and at an interest rate at least one-half of 1% higher than the highest regular discount rate in effect at that Reserve bank. The second provision was that the Federal Reserve banks received authority to use government securities as collateral for Federal Reserve notes, in addition to gold and commercial paper, which were the types of collateral authorized by the Federal Reserve Act. Both provisions expired after one year, although subsequent legislation extended these temporary provisions, which eventually became permanent.

600 For the debate around its necessity see in R.S. Kroszner and R.G. Rajan, 'Is the Glass-Steagall Act Justified? A Study of the U.S. Experience with Universal Banking Before 1933' (1994) 84(4) *The American Economic Review*, pp. 810–832.

securities market operations.[601] Two Democrats southerners Congressmen, Senator Carter Glass (D-VA) and Representative Henry Steagall (D-AL), sponsored the measure and on 16 June 1933, President Roosevelt signed the bill into law. The Pecora Commission identified on its hearings many banking practices that led to conflicts of interest, and abusive practices 'arising out of the interrelationship of commercial and investment banking'[602] that played a role in the 1929 financial crisis. These deficiencies were attempted to be repaired through the enactment of a series of laws in both banking and securities activities between 1932–1935. Of particular importance was the Banking Act of 1933 which intended to 'provide for the safer and more effective use of the assets of banks, to regulate interbank control, and to prevent the undue diversion of funds into speculative operations, and for other purposes'.[603]

Specifically, Section 16 of the GSA, which, even though it has been amended through the years is still in force, together with Section 5(c), preserve the national banks 'as creatures of limited authority'.[604] This means that according to the provisions of Section 16, national banks are only authorised to engage in the 'business of banking' and any 'incidental power' thereto.[605] Then come the two restrictions that are imposed: 'The business of dealing in securities and stock by the association shall be limited to purchasing and selling such securities and stock without recourse, solely upon the order, and for the account of, customers, and in no case for its own account, and the association shall not underwrite any issue of securities or stock;' and 'Except as hereinafter provided or otherwise permitted by law, nothing herein contained shall authorise the purchase by the association for its own account of any shares of stock of any corporation.'[606]

According to the wording of Section 16, national banks are precluded from the business of underwriting and dealing in securities, for their own account, but are allowed to do so on behalf of their customers. However, it is important to point out that Section 16 also included an exemption that allowed commercial banks to purchase, deal in, and underwrite certain, enumerated, securities without imposing any quantitative limitations on these activities. These were the so-called 'bank eligible' securities:[607] a) US government bonds,

---

601 Ibid.

602 See in Committee on Banking and Currency (CBC – the 'Pecora Committee'), *Stock Exchange Practices, Final Report*, No. 1455, Senate – US Congress, 16 June 1934, p. 113.

603 See in D.H. Carpenter, E.V. Murphy and M.M. Murphy, 'The Glass-Steagall Act: A Legal and Policy Analysis', *Congressional Research Service*, Report, R44349, 16 January 2016, p. 5.

604 Ibid.

605 12 U.S. Code § 24 (seventh).

606 Ibid.

607 See in O. McDonald, 'The Repeal of the Glass-Steagall Act, Myth and Reality', *Policy Analysis*, No. 804, November 2016, Cato Institute, Washington D.C., p. 4; and in A.E. Wilmarth Jr., *Taming the Megabanks, Why We Need a New Glass-Steagall Act*, New York, Oxford University Press, 2020, p. 139.

b) general obligations of state and municipalities (state and municipal bonds), c) securities issued by the government-sponsored enterprises Fannie Mae and Freddie Mac[608] and d) Canadian Government securities. These securities were not accompanied by any quantitative limit, leaving commercial banks to engage as much as they wanted. All other securities not enumerated in the 'bank eligible' securities were defined as 'bank ineligible' securities and national banks were banned from engaging with them.[609]

Section 20 of the GSA prohibited member banks[610] from affiliating with firms that were 'engaged principally' in securities activities (underwriting and/or dealing). Underwriting had the meaning of assuming the risk that an issue of securities might not be sold to the investors and dealing refers to holding securities for trading purposes.[611]

Section 21 of the GSA, which still exists today albeit in an amended form, stipulates that it is illegal for a firm to engage in both deposit-taking and investment banking, except from the 'bank eligible' securities that are allowed under the Section 16 provisions.[612] Therefore, securities firms and other non-bank entities are prohibited from accepting deposits. The drafting of the terms of Section 21 is broad enough to embrace all types of short-term debt instruments, payable by the borrower on demand and at par, upon creditor's demand.[613] Section 21 stipulates that: '[...] it shall be unlawful [...] for any person, firm, corporation, association, business trust, or other similar organisation, engaged in the business of issuing, underwriting, selling, or distributing, at wholesale or retail, or through syndicate participation, stocks, bonds, debentures, notes, or other securities, to engage at the same time to any extent whatever in the business of receiving deposits subject to check or to repayment upon presentation of a passbook, certificate of deposit, or other evidence of debt, or upon request of the depositor [...].'[614]

Finally, Section 32 of the GSA prohibited interlocking directorates between member banks and affiliated securities firms, sharing thereby directors,

608 Fannie Mae's securities were added as 'bank eligible' securities under the 'Federal Financing Bank Act' of 1973. Freddie Mac's securities were added as 'bank eligible' securities under the 'Housing and Community Development Act' of 1974.

609 See in D.H. Carpenter, E.V. Murphy and M.M. Murphy, 'The Glass-Steagall Act: A Legal and Policy Analysis', *Congressional Research Service*, Report, R44349, 16 January 2016, p. 6.

610 As 'member banks' are defined all national banks and state charted banks that are members of the Federal Reserve System.

611 See in O. McDonald, 'The Repeal of the Glass-Steagall Act, Myth and Reality', *Policy Analysis*, No. 804, November 2016, Cato Institute, Washington D.C., p. 4.

612 See in D.H. Carpenter, E.V. Murphy and M.M. Murphy, 'The Glass-Steagall Act: A Legal and Policy Analysis', *Congressional Research Service*, Report, R44349, 16 January 2016, p. 6.

613 See in A.E. Wilmarth Jr., *Taming the Megabanks, Why We Need a New Glass-Steagall Act*, New York, Oxford University Press, 2020, p. 139.

614 12 U.S. Code § 378(a)(1).

managers, officers, and employees.[615] Apart from the above-mentioned provisions, the GSA contained also Sections 11(a) and 11(b) that deprived commercial banks from the right to offer interest rates on their demand deposits (Section 11(b) of the GSA) and also prohibited member banks from acting as the medium or agent for investments by non-bank entities or individuals in margin loans made by brokers or dealers (Section 11(a) of the GSA).[616] The first ban aimed at securing that big, money centre banks were not going to cannibalise smaller banks through higher interest deposits and the later at preventing big banks from channelling funds from non-bank investors to margin and call loans.[617]

What the GSA aimed for was to separate banking and securities industry since it was perceived that conflicts of interest would be created, and depositors' money would be used for speculative investment banking operations. Furthermore, GSA imposed a strict wall between those two activities by not allowing banks and securities firms to enter each other's 'exclusive economic zone' (depository institutions not engaging in securities business and securities firms not accepting deposits). Supporters of GSA believe that it also aimed at and tried to prevent the Fed from providing credit in support of speculative activities related to securities, commodities, and real estate.[618] Moreover, big money centre banks would not be able anymore to supply credit in speculative activities related to securities taking advantage of their massive liquidity provided by the deposits.

4.2. *Securities Regulation on the Aftermath of the Great Depression*

After the stock crash in 1929, and the subsequent Great Depression, the US Congress, under the public angry fuelled by the Pecora Committee hearings, enacted legislation that regulated the securities market, aiming in creating a more robust and consumer safer securities market. Two, extremely important legislations were adopted in the aftermath of the crisis: a) the Securities Act of 1933,[619] and b) the Securities Exchange Act of 1934.[620] Both acts, imposed requirements for the efficient performance of the stock market and more

---

[615] See in A.E. Wilmarth Jr., *Taming the Megabanks, Why We Need a New Glass-Steagall Act*, New York, Oxford University Press, 2020, p. 139.

[616] Ibid.

[617] Ibid.

[618] Ibid., p. 140.

[619] The Securities Act of 1933, Pub. L. 73–22, 48 Stat. 74, enacted 27 May 1933, codified at 15 U.S.C. § 77a et seq. The Act is also known under various names; the 1933 Act, the Securities Act, the Truth in Securities Act, the Federal Securities Act.

[620] The Securities Exchange Act of 1934, Pub. L. 73–291, 48 Stat. 881, enacted 6 June 1934, codified at 15 U.S.C. § 78a et seq. The Act is also known under various names; the Exchange Act, '34 Act, or 1934 Act.

importantly, the Act of 1934 created the federal agency that still today dominates the regulatory mandate: the Securities and Exchange Commission (SEC). Congress created the SEC and empowered the agency with broad authority over all aspects of the securities industry.

The Securities Act of 1933, legislated pursuant to the Interstate Commerce Clause of the Constitution, aims at a) requiring that investors receive financial and other significant information concerning securities being offered for public sale, and b) prohibiting deceit, misrepresentations, and other fraudulent situations in the sale of securities. Under the Act, a firm that wishes to offer to the public securities must register those securities with the SEC, before they will be offered to the public.[621] Registration of those securities is based on the premise that extensive disclosure of information to potential buyers-investors in advance would enhance market integrity since investors would have access to all relevant information about both securities and the firms that offer them. Federal regulators were empowered to even block a public offering if the accompanied documentation (prospectus) was incomplete and/or misleading in any material respect.[622] This available information will enable investors, not the US government, to make informed judgements about whether to purchase a company's securities. Finally, while the SEC requires that the information provided must be accurate, it does not guarantee it. Under the Securities Exchange Act of 1934, a firm that has publicly traded securities is obliged to register with the SEC and also is subject to certain, periodic, reporting requirements and other disclosures.[623] Moreover, the Act creates civil liability for any false or misleading statements made in connection with the purchase or sale of a security, empowers the SEC to prohibit manipulation, deceptions and contrivances in connection with a securities purchase or sale and requires brokers and dealers to register with SEC, which assumes the duty to regulate them and supervise their self-regulatory organisations.[624] The Act provides also the SEC with disciplinary powers over regulated entities and persons associated with them.

Other important legislative initiatives in the aftermath of the Great Depression, and after any crisis that erupted until today, include:

- the Trust Indenture Act (TIA) of 1939,[625] which applies to debt securities (bonds, debentures, etc.) and notes that are offered for public sale. Even though

---

621 See in R.S. Carnell, J.R. Macey, G.P. Miller and P. Conti-Brown, *The Law of Financial Institutions*, 7th ed., Aspen Casebook Series, New York, Wolters Kluwer, 2021, p. 611.

622 See in A.E. Wilmarth Jr., *Taming the Megabanks, Why We Need a New Glass-Steagall Act*, New York, Oxford University Press, 2020, p. 132.

623 See in R.S. Carnell, J.R. Macey, G.P. Miller and P. Conti-Brown, *The Law of Financial Institutions*, 7th ed., Aspen Casebook Series, New York, Wolters Kluwer, 2021, p. 612.

624 Ibid.

625 Trust Indenture Act of 1939, ch. 411, 53 Stat. 1149 (codified as amended at 15 U.S.C. §§ 77aaa–77bbbb).

such securities may be registered under the Securities Act of 1933, they may not be offered for sale to the public unless a formal agreement between the issuer of bonds and the bondholder, known as the trust indenture, conforms to the standards of this Act.[626]

- the Investment Company Act (ICA) of 1940,[627] which regulates the organisation of companies, including mutual funds, that engage primarily in investing (investment companies), reinvesting, and trading in securities, and whose own securities are offered to the investing public. ICA is designed to minimise conflicts of interest that might arise in these complex operations and require these companies to disclose their financial condition, their company structure and operations, and their investment policies to investors when their stock is initially sold as well as information about the fund and its investment objectives. An important clarification must be made at this point though: the Act does not permit the SEC to directly supervise the investment decisions and/or activities of these companies and/or judge the merits of their investments.[628]
- the Investment Advisers Act (IAI) of 1940,[629] which regulates investment advisers. Notwithstanding certain exceptions, IAI requires that firms and/or sole practitioners compensated for advising others about securities investments must register with the SEC and conform to regulations designed to protect investors. Since the last amendments in 1996 and 2010, generally only advisers who have at least $100 million of assets under management or advise a registered investment company must register with the SEC.[630]
- the Sarbanes-Oxley Act (SOX) of 2002,[631] which mandated several reforms to enhance corporate responsibility, financial disclosures and combat corporate and accounting fraud. The Act also created the Public Company Accounting Oversight Board (PCAOB), to oversee the activities of the auditing profession.[632]

Securities transactions regulation also applies at state level, which regulated those transactions even before 1933. These state laws were called 'blue sky' laws and took their name from the Kansas legislation that aimed at preventing

[626] See in R.S. Carnell, J.R. Macey, G.P. Miller and P. Conti-Brown, *The Law of Financial Institutions*, 7th ed., Aspen Casebook Series, New York, Wolters Kluwer, 2021, p. 612.

[627] Investment Company Act of 1940, Pub. L. No. 76-768, 54 Stat. 789.

[628] See in R.S. Carnell, J.R. Macey, G.P. Miller and P. Conti-Brown, *The Law of Financial Institutions*, 7th ed., Aspen Casebook Series, New York, Wolters Kluwer, 2021, p. 612.

[629] Investment Advisers Act of 1940, Pub. L. No. 76-768, Title II, 54 Stat. 847.
This act was Title II of the same law that created the Investment Company Act, so it shares the same public law number (76-768).

[630] See in R.S. Carnell, J.R. Macey, G.P. Miller and P. Conti-Brown, *The Law of Financial Institutions*, 7th ed., Aspen Casebook Series, New York, Wolters Kluwer, 2021, p. 612.

[631] Sarbanes-Oxley Act of 2002, Pub. L. No. 107-204, 116 Stat. 745.

[632] See in R.S. Carnell, J.R. Macey, G.P. Miller, P. Conti-Brown, *The Law of Financial Institutions*, 7th ed., Aspen Casebook Series, New York, Wolters Kluwer, 2021, p. 612.

securities salesmen from selling to farmers a 'piece of blue sky'.[633] States traditionally enjoyed ample room to enforce their legislations since the Act of 1933 expressly did not pre-empt state laws but this was partially altered after the Congress enacted the 'National Securities Markets Improvement Act' (NSMIA) of 1996,[634] pre-empting state laws in an attempt to reduce litigation expenses. NSMIA exempted certain categories of 'covered' securities from reporting requirements and registration including those listed on the New York Stock Exchange (NYSE) and on NASDAQ.[635] The importance of the Pecora Committee hearings was reflected in the enactment of the GSA and both securities legislations (Acts of 1933 and 1934). Had those hearings not demonstrated the securities practices of the universal banks, the regulatory framework would have been altered in favour of those supporting the old regime.[636]

4.3. *The Specific Role of the FDIC*

The FDIC was created with the 1933 Banking Act and insures bank deposits with a pool of money collected from banks.[637] The creation of a deposit guarantee system was the most controversial issue at the time and even drew veto threats from President Roosevelt, a fierce opponent of a federally insured deposit system. This provision was included at the insistence of Representative Henry Steagall, who had the interests of small rural banks in mind.[638] Small rural banks and their representatives were the main proponents of deposit insurance while opposition came from large banks that believed they would end up subsidising small banks. Steagall's (and his supporters') view of the deposit insurance necessity could be summarised as follows: absent of a robust and credible federal deposit guarantee, business and consumers would never bring back the funds they had withdrawn from the banking system and if such a return of deposits didn't occur, banks could never be able to provide the

[633] Ibid., p. 613.

[634] National Securities Markets Improvement Act of 1996, Pub. L. No. 104-290, 110 Stat. 3416. The Act is not codified as a standalone section but instead amended several existing federal securities laws.

[635] See in R.S. Carnell, J.R. Macey, G.P. Miller and P. Conti-Brown, *The Law of Financial Institutions*, 7th ed., Aspen Casebook Series, New York, Wolters Kluwer, 2021, p. 613.

[636] See in A.E. Wilmarth Jr., *Taming the Megabanks, Why We Need a New Glass-Steagall Act*, New York, Oxford University Press, 2020, p. 142.

[637] According to the FDIC's official website, the FDIC receives no Congressional appropriations, and it is funded by premiums that banks and savings associations pay for deposit insurance coverage. The FDIC insures deposits in U.S. banks and thrifts - deposits in virtually every bank and savings association in the country. See in: https://www.fdic.gov/about/what-we-do/.

[638] For a deeper analysis in Henry Steagall's opinions regarding the deposit guarantee issue in the US see in J.H. Gutwillig, 'Glass versus Steagall: The fight over federalism and American banking' (2014) 100 *Virginia Law Review*, Note, p. 799 onwards.

much-needed credit for the economic recovery.[639] On the contrary, Senator Glass offered a much more limited proposal for a 'liquidating corporation' that would use funds provided by Federal Reserve Banks and Fed member banks to offer partial reimbursement for losses suffered by closed banks' depositors; this proposal would apply only to closed banks and not the open ones, thus preventing vulnerable banks from recovering.[640] Senator Glass's proposal must be understood under the light of his view that deposit guarantee is 'an undesirable subsidy to weaker banks'.[641]

In the years before the Banking Act, deposit insurance schemes were initially state attempts that, with the exemption of Texas deposit insurance scheme, were mostly unsuccessful because of moral hazard and because local banks were not diversified regarding their assets and branches.[642] After the bank holiday, the public showed vast support for insurance, partly in the hope of recovering some of the losses occurred during the crisis and partly because many blamed Wall Street and big bankers for the Depression. Although Senator Glass had opposed deposit insurance for years, he changed his mind and urged Roosevelt to accept it. Especially crucial was the bank failures in the state of Michigan, in February 1933.[643] This event is of particular importance since it brought the enactment of the 'Emergency Banking Relief Act' of 1933, and because of Senator Arthur Vandenberg's response. Senator Vandenberg suggested that the best way to reopen Michigan's banks was to pass a Congressional resolution authorising the OCC to issue the same regulations for the reopening of both national and state banks, in an attempt to calm the public and secure orderly transition to the next day.[644]

---

639 See in A.E. Wilmarth Jr., *Taming the Megabanks, Why We Need a New Glass-Steagall Act*, New York, Oxford University Press, 2020, p. 136.

640 Ibid.

641 Ibid.

642 The State of Texas was not the only state that enacted a system of deposit insurance in between 1910 and early 1920s. Those states were Oklahoma, Kansas, Nebraska, Texas, Mississippi, South Dakota, North Dakota, and Washington. The Texas plan for deposit insurance had two distinct features compared to other states: a) it had an established capital to deposit ratio requirement that resembles the modern federal capital to asset requirement, providing thereby an important constraint on irresponsible banking practices, and b) it had the highest assessments of any other deposit insurance plan; also, should a case of emergency appeared, or the fund depleted these assessments would be raised to 2%. Compared to the Texas plan, only Oklahoma had a 1% taxation on deposits and all other states that enacted deposit insurance funds had not such requirements. Although the Texas plan eventually failed it was a very robust model that when replicated and strengthened at the federal level would eventually work effectively. See in J.H. Gutwillig, 'Glass versus Steagall: The fight over federalism and American banking' (2014) 100 *Virginia Law Review*, Note, p. 790.

643 After failing to secure enough temporary funds to keep Michigan banks open, the federal and state officials agreed, on 14 February 1933, to impose an 8-day bank holiday for all Michigan based banks. See in J.H. Gutwillig, 'Glass versus Steagall: The fight over federalism and American banking' (2014) 100 *Virginia Law Review*, Note, p. 812.

644 Ibid.

Senator Vandenberg's role did not stop there. On 19 May 1933, he introduced an amendment to the pending Glass bill, the so-called 'Vandenberg amendment'. This amendment called for the creation of a temporary fund, the 'Temporary Bank Deposit Insurance Fund', that would immediately insure bank deposits up to the amount of $2.500 until a permanent solution was to be found.[645] The Vandenberg's amendment passed the voting procedures and met with Senator Glass bill that also passed the necessary voting. After a week of deliberations in the Congress and meetings within the White House, President Roosevelt accepted the temporary guarantee, through the Vandenberg amendment and signed the bill into law, on 16 June 1933.[646] The temporary fund became effective on 1 January 1934, insuring deposits up to $2,500 and permanent in July 1934, also raising the limit of protection to $5,000. This limit was raised numerous times over the years until reaching the current amount of $250,000.[647] The final form of deposit insurance adopted by the GSA was neither a limited, temporary fund, nor a full federal guarantee of all deposits, as Senator Steagall was advocating for.[648] The new scheme was initially funded by contributions from both the Fed Banks and Fed's member banks and later by premiums paid by banks that became FDIC members.[649] Fed's member banks on or before 1 July 1934, were required to become stockholders of the FDIC by such date. No state bank was eligible for membership in the Federal Reserve System until it became a stockholder of the FDIC, and thereby became an insured institution, with required membership by national banks and voluntary membership by state banks. Substantial federal oversight was also included in the new deposit insurance program since national and state banks were accepted to the scheme if only the Secretary of Treasury certified them as 'sound'.[650] State non-member banks were admitted to the insurance program if only, they were also certified as 'sound' by the respective state regulators and from the moment they were accepted they were supervised by the FDIC.[651]

Deposit insurance is still viewed as a great success, although the problem of moral hazard and adverse selection came up again during banking failures of the 1980s. In response, the US Congress passed legislation that strengthened capital requirements and required banks with less capital to close. Today, the

---

645 Ibid., p. 813.

646 Ibid., p. 814.

647 The $250.000 limit was adopted on 3 October 2008, amid the global financial crisis, when President Bush Jr. signed into law the '*Emergency Economic Stabilization Act*' of 2008, as a response to the crisis. Initially, the measure of increased deposit protection was perceived as a temporary, aiming to expire on 31 December 2009. President Obama, on 21 July 2010, signed into law the Dodd-Frank Act and made the limit permanent.

648 Ibid.

649 See in A.E. Wilmarth Jr., *Taming the Megabanks, Why We Need a New Glass-Steagall Act*, New York, Oxford University Press, 2020, p. 136.

650 Ibid.

651 Ibid.

mission of the FDIC is to maintain stability and public confidence in the US's financial system. In support of this goal, the FDIC:

- Insures deposits,[652]
- Examines and supervises financial institutions for safety and soundness and consumer protection,[653]
- Works to make large and complex financial institutions resolvable,[654] and
- Manages receiverships.[655]

5 THE DEREGULATION ERA

Perhaps one of the most important moments in the US's financial regulation history is when the so called 'deregulation era' begun. This was equal to a revolution that has dismantled or shaken every piece of the New Deal legislation and banking structure. This revolution occurred through judicial decisions, agency action and federal and state legislation. Above all, this revolution 'has occurred outside the legal system through fast paced market developments'.[656]

5.1. From the Money Market Mutual Funds (MMMFs) to the Abolishment of Regulation Q

The first major component of GSA that was repealed during the deregulation period was the interest rate ceilings on bank deposits imposed by the Fed's

652 The standard insurance amount is $250,000 per depositor, per insured bank, for each account ownership category. The FDIC insures deposits only and does not insure securities, mutual funds, or similar types of investments that banks and thrift institutions may offer. For more details see in: https://www.fdic.gov/about/what-we-do/.

653 The FDIC directly supervises and examines more than 5,000 banks and savings associations for operational safety and soundness and is the primary federal regulator of banks that are chartered by the states that do not join the Federal Reserve System and is the back-up supervisor for the remaining insured banks and savings associations. For more details see in: https://www.fdic.gov/about/what-we-do/.

654 Aiming at protecting insured depositors, the FDIC responds immediately when a bank or savings association fails. The FDIC is not primarily responsible to dictate the closing of institutions, power which lies on their chartering authority (the state regulator or the OCC). The FDIC has several options for resolving failed institutions, but the most common is to sell the deposits and loans of the failed institution to another institution. Customers of the failed institution automatically become customers of the assuming institution, and the aim is to secure, most of the times, a seamless transition from the customer's point of view. For more details see in: https://www.fdic.gov/about/what-we-do/.

655 In the event of a bank failure, the FDIC also acts as the 'Receiver' of the failed bank, assumes the task of selling/collecting the assets of the failed bank and settling its debts, including claims for deposits in excess of the insured limit.

656 See in R.S. Carnell, J.R. Macey, G.P. Miller and P. Conti-Brown, *The Law of Financial Institutions*, 7th ed., Aspen Casebook Series, New York, Wolters Kluwer, 2021, p. 42.

Regulation Q.[657] These ceilings became unviable for a long period of time before ultimately abandoned in the early 1980s. In the late 1960s and early 1970s inflationary pressures started to circle the US economy mostly because the Johnson and Nixon administration ran large federal budget deficits to finance the expanding presence of the US military in the Vietnam War and the ambitious domestic spending programs.[658] The deficits and the trade imbalances forced President Nixon to exit the Bretton Woods regime[659] in August 1971, suspending the dollars convertibility into gold. The US exit from the Bretton Woods regime drove the regime into collapse and resulted in much higher volatility for the currency exchange and for the interests' rates.[660] Furthermore, the two oil crises in 1973, due to Organization of the Petroleum Exporting Countries (OPEC) oil embargo,[661] and in 1979, due to the Iranian Revolution, drove the oil prices in unprecedented levels. The spike in oil prices helped the US inflation rate to reach also unprecedented levels in 1980 and obliged the Carter administration to appoint Paul Volcker as Fed chairman in August 1979. Volcker was a strong proponent of using more aggressive monetary policy to try to break inflation's stranglehold on the US economy and made taming inflation their top priority, even if this priority came at the detriment of short-term employment.[662] The policies adopted during Volcker's

---

657 The maximum interest rate that banks and other institutions were allowed to pay on deposits was regulated by the federal government under specific legislation, known as Regulation Q. In fact, banks were not allowed to pay any interest on checking accounts ('demand deposit' accounts), and the rate on savings accounts at banks was set at 5.25%.

658 See in A. E. Wilmarth Jr., 'The Road to Repeal of the Glass-Steagall Act' (2017) 17(4) *Wake Forest Journal of Business and Intellectual Property Law*, p. 456.

659 See in M.D. Bordo, 'The Operation and Demise of the Bretton Woods System; 1958 to 1971', *Economics Working Paper*, Hoover Institution, February 2017, p. 1. The Bretton Woods system was created by the 1944 Articles of Agreement with the aim to design a new international monetary order for the post war era at a global conference organized by the US Treasury at the Mount Washington Hotel in Bretton Woods, New Hampshire at the height of World War II. The Articles of Agreement represented the final compromise between the American plan of Harry Dexter White and the British plan of John Maynard Keynes. The compromise created an adjustable pegging system that was based on the US dollar convertibility into gold at $35 per ounce, along with capital controls. The system was designed to combine the advantages of fixed exchange rates, of the pre-World War I gold standard, together with some flexibility to handle large real shocks. The final compromise gave members both exchange rate stability and the independence for their monetary authorities to maintain full employment.

660 See in A.E. Wilmarth Jr., 'The Road to Repeal of the Glass-Steagall Act' (2017) 17(4) *Wake Forest Journal of Business and Intellectual Property Law*, p. 456.

661 On 19 October 1973, immediately after President Nixon's request for Congress to make available $2,2 billion in emergency aid to Israel for the Yom Kippur War, the Organization of Arab Petroleum Exporting Countries (OAPEC) instituted an oil embargo on the United States. The embargo ceased U.S. oil imports from participating OAPEC nations and began a series of production cuts that altered the world price of oil. These cuts nearly quadrupled the price of oil from $2,90 a barrel before the embargo to $11,65 a barrel in January 1974.

662 As the president of the Federal Reserve Bank of New York, Paul Volcker had been an outspoken proponent of using monetary policy to combat rising inflation.

tenure ultimately proved successful in breaking the cycle of stagflation in the US,[663] though the monetary contraction—combined with the impact from the oil price shock—pushed the economy into the most severe recession since the Great Depression and spurred strong popular opposition. By the moment the short-term interest rates rose above the Regulation Q established ceilings, depositors started withdrawing their funds from traditional bank accounts and searched for alternative options that would grant them higher yielding deposits, when at the same time, large banks tried to circumvent the Regulation Q ceilings to keep their clientele.

In the early 1960s, Citibank issued negotiable rate, large denomination certificates of deposits (CDs) through its domestic branches and started to accept Eurodollar deposits from its overseas branches. Both products were paying higher interest rates than those permitted by the Regulation Q ceilings. The Fed did not oppose Citibank's novelties and soon other large banks started to offer similar products. In the early 1970s, the financial industry came through a true revolution. The securities industry introduced its own innovative instrument, the Money Market Mutual Fund (MMMF).[664] MMMFs were short-term investment vehicles offering deposit-like features, but most importantly, they were not subject to the burdensome Regulation Q ceilings. Just like bank deposit accounts MMMFs allowed investors to withdraw their funds based on a fixed Net Asset Value (NAV) equalling the purchase price of 1$ per share.[665] An important aspect of their function was the fact that MMMFs were not federally insured like the traditional bank deposits but offered their investors the ability to withdraw their funds at par on demand. Furthermore, MMMFs were regulated by the SEC and were required to invest their funds into safe, short-term securities (US Treasury bonds and high-quality commercial paper).[666] Despite the lack of federal insurance, investors in MMMFs believed that the institutional sponsors of the MMMFs would stand up and back them, preventing their funds from 'breaking the buck'.

In 1977, Merrill Lynch, introduced a novelty that soon was followed by many securities firms. The novelty was the 'Cash Management Account' (CMA) which allowed their holders to write checks against their funds held in MMMFs sponsored by Merrill Lynch. Since the MMMFs were not subject to the Regulation Q requirements because they were classified as mutual funds and not as 'deposits' they were able to offer their clients many services that

---

663 Under the Volcker presidency, the Fed was guided in raising the federal funds rate from 11% at the time Volcker took office to a peak of 19% in 1981, and the policy moves successfully lowered the rate of twelve-month inflation from a peak of nearly 15% to 4% by the end of 1982.

664 See in A.E. Wilmarth Jr., 'The Road to Repeal of the Glass-Steagall Act' (2017) 17(4) *Wake Forest Journal of Business and Intellectual Property Law*, p. 458.

665 Ibid.

666 Ibid.

in practice were perfect substitutes for bank deposits (redemption at par on demand, check writing and higher interest rates).[667] This perfect substitution between traditional bank deposits and MMMFs drove many depositors to withdraw their funds from traditional banks and place them in MMMFs spiking their assets under management from $3 billion in 1977 to $235 billion in 1982.[668] MMMFs were able to pay higher interest rates because they were exempted from paying deposit insurance premiums or from satisfying capital and reserve requirements. As it was expected, this capital fly from deposit banks to MMMFs rang many bells within the banking sector. In October 1979, letters were sent to the US Attorney General and the SEC, claiming that MMMFs offering check writing services were in violation of Section 21 of the GSA.[669] The US Department of Justice (DOJ) replied by rejecting these allegations and concluding that an investor in a MMMF was not a depositor but rather he owned an equity interest in the MMMF with the potential to gain or loss capital on his investment.[670] The DOJ supported the view that an investor's ability to transfer his ownership in a MMMF by simply writing checks was 'a mere formality and serves in no way to alter the substance of his status as owner'.[671] Although not completely wrong from an academic and theoretical point of view, DOJ's reply to such claims was simply ignoring the practical reality that MMMFs with CMA features for their clients were actually a perfect substitute for bank deposits.

The expansionary growth of MMMFs together with the general macroeconomic environment made unviable for banks and thrift institutions to maintain the Regulation Q interest rate ceilings. This situation provided favourable arguments to abolish Regulation Q ceilings by the banking sector and the US Congress responded to this challenge by abolishing them gradually until 1986 allowing thrift institutions to attract and retain more deposits. In 1980, the US Congress enacted the DIDMC[672] and signed into law by President Carter on 31 March 1980. The aim of the Act was twofold. On the one hand tried to deregulate depository institutions in order to increase their deposits and on the other hand aimed at ensuring better monetary control of behalf of the FED. Title I of the act, (known as the Monetary Control Act of 1980), required all institutions that accepted deposits (depository institutions) to meet

---

667 Ibid.

668 Ibid., p. 459.

669 Ibid. The letters were sent by Maurice Crawford Jr., chair of the Board of the Bowery Savings Bank of New York.

670 Ibid.

671 Ibid.

672 See *supra* n. 432.

reserve requirements.[673] The act contained an eight-year phase-in period for the formation of new reserve requirements for non-member institutions. Moreover, any institution holding reserves would now be eligible to apply for discount-window borrowing, which had previously only been available to member banks. Title II of the act, (known as the Depository Institutions Deregulation Act of 1980), gradually phased out restrictions on interest rates that depository institutions could offer on their deposits and ensured an orderly transition to this new environment, by introducing the phase-out period which lasted six years. In 1982, the US Congress enacted the Garn-St Germain Depository Institutions Act[674] and signed by President Reagan on 15 October 1982. This act was the second in this legislative series for controlling the interest rates and aimed to ease the pressures on banks, thrifts, and their insurance funds by expanding the previous deregulation of deposit rates, authorising adjustable-rate mortgages (ARMs), allowing state-chartered savings institutions broader lending powers, expanding FDIC emergency powers and easing depositor and lender regulations. It also removed some Depression-era constraints on thrift asset holdings to facilitate higher earnings. At the same time nonetheless, it significantly increased the cost of deposits when thrifts' primary assets were long term low yielding fixed rate mortgages, creating thus a maturity mismatch the ultimately led the thrift industry into a deep crisis.[675]

Since the MMMFs were facing lower regulatory requirements even after the demise of Regulation Q, their expansion was rapid, and their total assets increased from \$235 billion in 1982 to \$740 billion in 1995 and to \$3.8 trillion in 2007. The result of this growth was the creation of a new, parallel system of financial intermediation, from non-bank entities, that was named 'shadow banking system'.[676] The shadow banking system comprises of securities broker-dealers, finance companies, and other non-bank entities that obtained short-term funds from investors and provided long-term credit to firms and individuals.[677] The crucial point in defining the shadow banking entities is the

---

673 Reserve requirements are an important tool of monetary policy the central banks (and the Fed) can use to achieve desired changes in the money supply. Back then, only commercial banks, that were members of the Federal Reserve System, were required to hold reserves, and by 1980, less than 40% of banks were members. Other depository institutions, such as savings and loans and credit unions, whose deposits are also part of the total money supply and therefore are crucial for the effective application of monetary policy, were not subject to the Fed's reserve requirements. As a result, this was limiting the Fed's ability to effectively control the money supply and tame the high inflation rate.

674 Garn–St. Germain Depository Institutions Act of 1982, Pub. L. No. 97-320, 96 Stat. 1469 (codified in scattered sections of 12 U.S.C. and 15 U.S.C.).

675 See in A.E. Wilmarth Jr., *Taming the Megabanks, Why We Need a New Glass-Steagall Act*, New York, Oxford University Press, 2020, p. 152.

676 Ibid., p. 154.

677 See in A.E. Wilmarth Jr., 'The Road to Repeal of the Glass-Steagall Act' (2017) 17(4) *Wake Forest Journal of Business and Intellectual Property Law*, p. 460.

fact that those entities are not banks, and therefore are not eligible to accept deposits from the public, in their traditional definition, but participate in the maturity transformation performed by banks. Securities firms set up MMMFs aimed at attracting huge amounts of funds from retail and institutional customers, siphoning this credit supply into the system, increasing as a result the available liquidity.[678] MMMFs were leading investors in two specific market categories: a) the commercial paper market[679] and b) the securities repurchase agreements[680] (repos) market. The excess funding provided by the MMMFs in the repos and commercial paper markets enabled securities firms and other shadow banking entities to provide credit in firms and individuals through the securitisation process.[681]

5.2. *The Bank Holding Company Act*

In 1956, the US Congress enacted the Bank Holding Company Act (BHCA)[682] attempting to reinforce the GSA separation regime. The objective was twofold. First, to prevent undue concentration of banking power and to prevent banks from getting too large and accumulate power through the holding company structure. Second, to prevent the mixture between banking sector and

---

678 For a well-documented explanation of how the shadow banking system participated in the maturity transformation process, see indicatively in T. Adrian and H.S. Shin, 'The Shadow Banking System: Implications for Financial Regulation', Staff Report no. 382, *Federal Reserve Bank of New York Staff Reports*, July 2009; and in S.L. Schwarcz, 'Regulating Shadow Banking' (2012) 31 *Review of Banking and Financial Law*, pp. 619–642.

679 According to Investopedia, a '*commercial paper*' is a form of unsecured (not backed by any type of collateral), short-term debt commonly issued by companies to finance their payrolls, payables, inventories, and other short-term liabilities. Maturities on most commercial paper ranges from a few weeks to months, with an average of around 30 days. Commercial paper is often issued at a discount without paying coupons and matures to its face value, reflective of current interest rates.

680 According to Investopedia, a 'repurchase agreement', or 'repo', is a short-term agreement to sell securities to buy them back at a slightly higher price. The one selling the repo is effectively borrowing and the other party is lending, since the lender is credited the implicit interest in the difference in prices from initiation to repurchase. For the party selling the security and agreeing to repurchase it in the future, it is a repo while for the party on the other end of the transaction, buying the security and agreeing to sell in the future, it is a reverse repurchase agreement. Repos and reverse repos are thus used for short-term borrowing and lending, often with a tenor of overnight to 48 hours. The implicit interest rate on these agreements is known as the 'repo rate', a proxy for the overnight risk-free rate. Upon the expiration a repo term, usually after a day or a few days, the parties either renew the loan agreement or the lender returns the posted collateral to the borrower and the last repays the cash loan with the accrued interest.

681 See in T. Adrian and H.S. Shin, 'The Shadow Banking System: Implications for Financial Regulation', Staff Report no. 382, *Federal Reserve Bank of New York Staff Reports*, July 2009, p. 11 and in A.E. Wilmarth Jr., 'The Road to Repeal of the Glass-Steagall Act' (2017) 17(4) *Wake Forest Journal of Business and Intellectual Property Law*, p. 462.

682 See in *supra* n. 412.

commerce.[683] The BHCA was a response to the rapid growth and diversification of Transamerica Corporation,[684] and other large Bank Holding Companies (BHCs), mostly after World War II. Already since 1938, President Roosevelt, in a special message to Congress, demanded 'greater curbs' upon BHCs after pointing out their evil characteristics, although the truth is that commercial firms began to acquire banks in significant numbers, much later, in 1945.[685] The BHCA regulated the BHC structure and required the Fed to approve proposed acquisitions of banks by BHCs authorising at the same time the Fed to supervise them and regulate their non-banking activities.[686] The BHCA also prohibited affiliations between a BHC and securities firms, insurance companies and commercial enterprises.[687] Of particular importance were two specific provisions of the BHCA: a) Section 3(d) of the BHCA, better known as the 'Douglas Amendment', and b) Section 4 of the BHCA. The Douglas Amendment prohibited BHCs from acquiring banks across states unless such acquisitions were specifically authorised by the laws of the state in which the acquired banks were located (interstate branching).[688] Section 4 of the BHCA allowed BHCs, under the Fed's approval, to own non-bank subsidiaries engaged in activities that were 'closely related' to banking; it also prohibited BHCs from controlling or being controlled by commercial or industrial firms. With limited exemptions, Section 4 effectively prohibited BHCs from owning subsidiaries that engaged in most types of insurance activities and on industrial or commercial operations. Simultaneously, Section 4 also worked the other way

683 See in C. Felsenfeld, 'The Bank Holding Company Act: Has It Lived Its Life?' (1993) 38(1) *Villanova Law Review*, p. 67.

684 In 1956, *Transamerica Corporation* controlled banks in ten states as well as insurance companies, commercial enterprises engaged in oil and gas development, fish caning and frozen food production.

685 See in C. Felsenfeld, 'The Bank Holding Company Act: Has It Lived Its Life?' (1993) 38(1) *Villanova Law Review*, p. 66 and in R.J. Philips, 'The Regulation and Supervision of Bank Holding Companies: A Historical Perspective', *Working Paper* No. 116, Jerome Levy Economics Institute of Bard College and Colorado State University, May 1994, p. 13.

686 The history behind Fed's assignment with the task to supervise BHCs is very interesting since the obvious policy choice would have been to empower the OCC with this role. In the Congressional hearings before the Senate Banking Committee, the then Comptroller of the Currency, Raymond Gidney, was generally in favour of BHCs and was not willing to constrain their activities. Moreover, he proposed that Fed should take over the task of their supervision instead of the OCC. Another important parameter of the decision was that the 1956 legislation was drafted from the Fed's Board in 1943, under the presidency of Mariner Eccles, a strong advocate of controlling BHCs strength. Since Gidney seemed unwilling to undertake the task this was given to the Fed. For a deeper analysis on these events see in R.J. Philips, 'The Regulation and Supervision of Bank Holding Companies: A Historical Perspective', *Working Paper* No. 116, Jerome Levy Economics Institute of Bard College and Colorado State University, May 1994, p. 13 onwards.

687 See in A.E. Wilmarth Jr., *Taming the Megabanks, Why We Need a New Glass-Steagall Act*, New York, Oxford University Press, 2020, p. 148.

688 Ibid., p. 149.

round since it effectively prevented insurance companies, and industrial and commercial companies from owning a bank.[689]

As of today, the BHCA is still into force, and defines a BHC as 'a company having control over a bank or over a company that controls a bank'.[690] Therefore, the important concepts of the BHCA are the notions of 'company, 'control' and 'bank'. The notion of company is broadly defined as 'any corporation, partnership, business trust, association, or similar organisation, or any other trust unless by its terms it must terminate within twenty-five years [...] and shall not include a qualified family partnership'.[691] A company has control over a bank under three basic circumstances:

(a) 'the company directly or indirectly or acting through one or more other persons owns, controls, or has power to vote 25 per centum or more of any class of voting securities of the bank or company,[692] (statutory control),
(b) 'the company controls in any manner the election of a majority of the directors or trustees of the bank or company,[693] and
(c) the Federal Reserve Board 'determines, after notice and opportunity for hearing, that the company directly or indirectly exercises a controlling influence over the management or policies of the bank or company[694] (controlling influence).

A company can have statutory control without having actual control and several companies can have statutory control of the same bank without any of them having actual control.[695] The Fed had always a more expansive view of controlling influence and in 2020 adopted a new framework aiming at defining in a clear and transparent manner the controlling influence of a company or a bank (first company) over another company or bank (second company). The Fed's presumption over exercising control could be summarised as follows:[696]

(i) 5% ownership of the second company's securities,
(ii) 10% ownership of the second company's securities,
(iii) 15% ownership of the second company's securities,
(iv) 'Total equity ownership', if the first company owns at least 1/3 of the second company's total equity,

---

689 See in A.E. Wilmarth Jr., 'The Road to Repeal of the Glass-Steagall Act' (2017) 17(4) *Wake Forest Journal of Business and Intellectual Property Law*, p. 451.

690 12 U.S. Code § 1841(a)(1).

691 12 U.S. Code § 1841(b).

692 12 U.S. Code § 1841(a)(2)(A).

693 12 U.S. Code § 1841(a)(2)(B).

694 12 U.S. Code § 1841(a)(2)(C).

695 See in R.S. Carnell, J.R. Macey, G.P. Miller and P. Conti-Brown, *The Law of Financial Institutions*, 7th ed., Aspen Casebook Series, New York, Wolters Kluwer, 2021, p. 268.

696 Ibid., p. 269.

(v) No Tied to Ownership', regardless of whether the first company owns any securities of the second company, the first company's controlling influence is triggered if a) the second company is included in the consolidated financial statements or b) agree to help manage the second company, and
(vi) Even if no presumption applies the Fed may still seek to prove control based on any other facts.

Finally, the notion of 'bank' is defined in the BHCA as a) 'An insured bank as defined in section 3(h) of the Federal Deposit Insurance Act'[697] (any FDIC insured bank) and b) 'An institution organised under the laws of the United States, [...] accepts demand deposits or deposits that the depositor may withdraw by check or similar means for payment to third parties or others; and [...] is engaged in the business of making commercial loans' (any US chartered institution).[698] The statute contains also a long list of exemptions and therefore are not banks, for the sole purposes of the BHCA,[699]

(i) A thrift institution,
(ii) A credit union,
(iii) A credit card bank,
(iv) A qualifying industrial loan company,
(v) A trust company that accepts deposit only as fiduciary and does not offer transaction accounts,
(vi) A company that does business in the US only 'as an incident to its activities outside the United States',
(vii) An FDIC insured branch of a foreign bank, and
(viii) A limited purpose financial institution.

The BHCA restricts the available activities that a BHC can conduct, either directly or indirectly, through non-bank subsidiaries. A general limitation applies to the company's activities which must be a) 'banking or of managing or controlling banks and other subsidiaries authorised under this chapter or of furnishing services to or performing services for its subsidiaries'[700] and b) activities 'so closely related to banking as to be a proper incident thereto'.[701] This provision was and remains today so for BHCs the most important source of BHCs powers and as it was stated by the Court (D.C. Circuit) in National Courier Association v. Board of Governors of Federal Reserve System[702] the Court deferred for the Fed to find the proper connection between the service

697 12 U.S. Code § 1841(c)(1).
698 Ibid.
699 See in R.S. Carnell, J.R. Macey, G.P. Miller and P. Conti-Brown, *The Law of Financial Institutions*, 7th ed., Aspen Casebook Series, New York, Wolters Kluwer, 2021, p. 270.
700 12 U.S. Code § 1843(a)(2).
701 12 U.S. Code § 1843(a)(2)(c)(8).
702 National Courier Association v. Board of Governors of Federal Reserve System, 516 F. 2d 1229 (D.C. Circuit).

and the level of connection to banking activity, 'in a reasoned fashion consistent with the legislative intent'.[703] Therefore the Fed had to find and 'determine, not arbitrarily or capriciously, that the connections are close'[704] to banking activity. Building on the Court's decision, the Fed issued Regulation Y, which contains 14 classes of activities that are closely related to banking. The list of permissible non-banking activities, according to Regulation Y, has as follows:[705]

(1) Extending credit and servicing loans,
(2) Activities related to extending credit,
(3) Leasing personal or real property,
(4) Operating non-bank depository institutions,
(5) Trust company functions,
(6) Financial and investment advisory activities,
(7) Agency transactional services for customer investments,
(8) Investment transactions as principal,
(9) Management consulting and counselling activities,
(10) Support services,
(11) Insurance agency and underwriting,
(12) Community development activities,
(13) Money orders, savings bonds, and traveller's checks, and
(14) Data processing

Obviously, all the above-mentioned broad categories of activities are further divided into more categories and specific subcategories to better describe the constantly evolving banking activities. The Fed cannot find any new, additional activities closely related to banking, but it can provide a broader interpretation to an activity that is already in the list mentioned above.[706] Moreover the Fed has the power to supervise the BHCs since no company can become a BHC without Fed's prior approval and an existing BHC needs Fed's prior approval to acquire control of an additional bank, own more than 5% of a bank's voting shares or merge with another BHC.[707] In 1999, the enactment of the GLBA created a new category of BHC, the Financial Holding Company (FHC), which is able to engage in abroad range of activities. A BHC that qualifies as a FHC may engage either directly, or indirectly through subsidiaries in 'financial activities' or in activities which are 'incidental' or 'complementary' to financial activities.[708] Therefore, important aspects of the Act are the financial nature of the activities, and the fact that they are incidental and complementary.

[703] Ibid., para. 38.
[704] Ibid., para. 39.
[705] 12 CFR § 225.28(b)(1)–(14).
[706] See in R.S. Carnell, J.R. Macey, G.P. Miller and P. Conti-Brown, *The Law of Financial Institutions*, 7th ed., Aspen Casebook Series, New York, Wolters Kluwer, 2021, p. 273.
[707] Ibid.
[708] 12 U.S. Code § 1843(k)(1)(A)–(B).

For a BHC to qualify as a FHC must meet certain three requirements. First, the holding company and each of its subsidiary FDIC insured depository institution must be well capitalised and managed, second, each of those institutions must have at least one satisfactory examination under the Community Reinvestment Act (CRA), and third, the holding company must file with the Fed a declaration that is elects to become a FHC (there is no necessity to obtain prior approval in contrast to the procedure when becoming a BHC).[709] These eligibility criteria aim at promoting safety and soundness of the institutions and also community reinvestment be applying a screening process for the low performing firms providing them at the same time with incentives to achieve and maintain a good performance. The Fed's supervision of FHCs is based on the concept of functional regulation. The Fed supervises the consolidated organisation, while primarily relying on the reports and supervision of the appropriate state and federal authorities for the FHC subsidiaries.[710] The law thus kept in place the existing regulators for financial subsidiaries of FHCs but gave the Fed the oversighting role of 'umbrella supervisor', a role that was seen as necessary because these large and complex financial institutions had risks spread across their subsidiaries but managed them at a consolidated level. Therefore, someone had to oversee the operation of all the moving parts that comprise the FHCs. Furthermore, the goal of the GLBA was to protect banks and their customers from risks taken on at financial subsidiaries, while ensuring that the protections for banks (e.g. deposit insurance) were not extended to non-bank affiliates, thereby creating perverse incentives for risk management. From the moment when a BHC qualifies as a FHC it may engage in – or acquire the shares of companies that are engaged in – activities that are a) financial in nature, b) incidental to such financial activity, and c) complementary to such financial activity. At the same time, these activities must not 'pose a substantial risk to the safety or soundness of depository institutions or the financial system generally'.[711] In the provisions of BHCA are defined nine classes of activities that are considered to be financial:[712]

(1) 'Lending, exchanging, transferring, investing for others, or safeguarding money or securities',
(2) 'Insuring, guaranteeing, or indemnifying against loss, harm, damage, illness, disability, or death, or providing and issuing annuities, and acting as principal, agent, or broker for purposes of the foregoing, in any State',

709 See in R.S. Carnell, J.R. Macey, G.P. Miller and P. Conti-Brown, *The Law of Financial Institutions*, 7th ed., Aspen Casebook Series, New York, Wolters Kluwer, 2021, p. 273.

710 The SEC would regulate the registered securities brokers, dealers, and investment advisers, state insurance commissioners would oversee licensed insurance companies, and the appropriate state and federal banking agencies would supervise banks and thrifts.

711 12 U.S. Code § 1843(k)(1)(B).

712 12 U.S. Code § 1843(l)(A)–(I).

(3) 'Providing financial, investment, or economic advisory services, including advising an investment company,
(4) 'Issuing or selling instruments representing interests in pools of assets permissible for a bank to hold directly',
(5) 'Underwriting, dealing in, or making a market in securities',
(6) 'Engaging in any activity that the [Federal Reserve] Board has determined, by order or regulation that is in effect on November 12, 1999, to be so closely related to banking or managing or controlling banks as to be a proper incident thereto',
(7) 'Engaging, in the United States, in any activity that a bank holding company may engage in outside of the United States and the [Federal Reserve] Board has determined, [...] (as in effect on the day before November 12, 1999) to be usual in connection with the transaction of banking or other financial operations abroad',
(8) Acquiring shares, assets or ownership interest in any company, both financial and non-financial, if a) the shares are acquired 'as part of a bona fide underwriting or merchant or investment banking activity, including investment activities engaged in for the purpose of appreciation and ultimate resale or disposition of the investment', b) the shares, assets and ownership interests are held by a 'securities affiliate', an insurance company – affiliated investment adviser or an affiliate of such entities – and not by a depository institution or a subsidiary of a depository institution, c) the shares, assets and ownership interest are 'held for a period of time to enable the sale or disposition thereof on a reasonable basis consistent with the financial viability', and d) 'during the period such shares, assets, or ownership interests are held, the bank holding company does not routinely manage or operate such company or entity except as may be necessary or required to obtain a reasonable return on investment upon resale or disposition',
(9) Investing in any entity through an insurance company in the ordinary course of the insurance company's business in accordance with relevant state laws and without 'routinely manage or operate such company except as may be necessary or required to obtain a reasonable return on investment'.

An additional set of potentially permissible financial activities was defined by the US Congress but were subjected to special treatment because of their potential breadth. Instead of defining the activities as financial, Congress required the Fed to specify, through regulation, the extent to which these activities are financial or incidental to financial activities.[713] These activities are the following:

[713] 12 U.S. Code § 1843(k)(5)(A).

(10) 'Lending, exchanging, transferring, investing for others, or safeguarding financial assets other than money or securities'[714],
(11) 'Providing any device or other instrumentality for transferring money or other financial assets'[715],
(12) 'Arranging, effecting, or facilitating financial transactions for the account of third parties'.[716]

Certain academics are of the view that the standards against which the Fed will assert that the above-mentioned activities are financial or incidental to financial activities are 'strikingly lenient and vague'.[717] The Fed has therefore a very broad discretion to consider when asserting the nature of these activities, but she must consider four specific factors:

(1) The GLBA purposes,[718]
(2) Any 'changes or reasonably expected changes in the marketplace in which financial holding companies compete',[719]
(3) Any 'changes or reasonably expected changes in the technology for delivering financial services',[720] and
(4) 'Whether such activity is necessary or appropriate to allow a financial holding company and the affiliates of a financial holding company to':[721]
    4.1. 'Compete effectively with any company seeking to provide financial services in the United States',[722]
    4.2. 'Efficiently deliver information and services that are financial in nature through the use of technological means, including any application necessary to protect the security or efficacy of systems for the transmission of data or financial transactions',[723] and
    4.3. 'Offer customers any available or emerging technological means for using financial services or for the document imaging of data.'[724]

Critics also claim that similarly vague requirements apply also when the Fed permits FHCs to engage in a non-financial activity that is found to be complementary to a financial activity. Such criteria will not impose any real

---

714 12 U.S. Code § 1843(k)(5)(B)(i).
715 12 U.S. Code § 1843(k)(5)(B)(ii).
716 12 U.S. Code § 1843(k)(5)(B)(iii).
717 See in R.S. Carnell, J.R. Macey, G.P. Miller and P. Conti-Brown, *The Law of Financial Institutions*, 7th ed., Aspen Casebook Series, New York, Wolters Kluwer, 2021, p. 278.
718 12 U.S. Code § 1843(k)(3)(A).
719 12 U.S. Code § 1843(k)(3)(B).
720 12 U.S. Code § 1843(k)(3)(C).
721 12 U.S. Code § 1843(k)(3)(D)(i)–(iii).
722 Ibid.
723 Ibid.
724 Ibid.

constraints on an FHC's potentially permissible activities, neither the safety and soundness criteria nor the risk to the financial system in general.[725]

5.3. *The Savings and Loan Crisis*

In the 1980s, the US financial sector suffered through a period of distress that was mainly focused on the Savings and Loan (S&L) industry. What has been known as the 'S&L Crisis' or the 'S&L Debacle', was a time consuming and slow-moving financial disaster, that came to a head and resulted in the failure of nearly a third of the 3,234 S&L associations in the US between 1986 and 1995. The problems began during that era's volatile interest rate climate, stagflation, and slow growth of the 1970s, and key to the S&L crisis was a profound mismatch between regulations and actual market conditions, speculation, moral hazard brought about by the combination of taxpayer guarantees along with fast and inefficient deregulation, as well as outright corruption and fraud, and the implementation of greatly slackened and broadened lending standards that led desperate banks to take far too much risk balanced by far too little capital on hand. The crisis, initially underestimated by the policymakers and the regulators, plagued the US financial system with mistrust and political scandals,[726] outright fraud and serious crimes that ended with jail convictions.[727] Ultimately, taxpayers were called upon to provide a bailout, and Congress was forced to act with significant reform legislation as the 1980s came to a close.

The S&L (also known as 'thrifts'),[728] even though are generally smaller than banks, both in number and in assets under control, nevertheless, were important conduits for the US mortgage market. Its existence has its origins in the social goal of pursuing homeownership and therefore became hugely popular amongst lower-income communities.[729] Almost a century after the

---

[725] See in R.S. Carnell, J.R. Macey, G.P. Miller and P. Conti-Brown, *The Law of Financial Institutions*, 7th ed., Aspen Casebook Series, New York, Wolters Kluwer, 2021, p. 279.

[726] During this S&L crisis, the US Senate's Ethics Committee investigated five US senators, widely known as the 'Keating Five', due to the $1.5 million in campaign contributions, they accepted from Charles Keating, head of the *Lincoln Savings and Loan Association*. These senators were accused of pressuring the Federal Home Loan Banking Board to overlook suspicious activities in which Keating had participated.

[727] Charles Keating, head of the *Lincoln Savings and Loan Association*, was convicted of conspiracy, racketeering, and fraud, and served time in prison before his conviction was overturned in 1996. In 1999, he pleaded guilty to lesser charges and was sentenced to time served.

[728] The term 'thrift' includes savings-and-loan associations, credit unions and savings banks, but it will be used interchangeably with the term savings and loan.

[729] The first S&Ls were established in Pennsylvania in 1831. These institutions were originally organised as social collectives by groups of people who wished to buy their own homes but lacked sufficient savings to directly purchase them. In the early 1800s, banks did not lend money for residential mortgages so the members of the group would pool their savings and

foundation of the first S&L, the Federal Home Loan Bank Act (FHLBA) of 1932,[730] formally established the S&L industry as a safe way for lower-income Americans to achieve homeownership. The S&Ls offer lower mortgage rates, compared to banks, in return for lower rates paid on customers' deposits. In 1934, the Federal Savings and Loan Insurance Corporation (FSLIC) was created to insure S&Ls' deposits and until 1989 S&Ls were regulated by the Federal Home Loan Bank Board (FHLBB or Bank Board) and insured by the FSLIC, within a legislative framework historically separate from the one that applied to commercial banks.

Inflation rates and interest rates both rose dramatically in the late 1970s and early 1980s, producing two main problems for S&Ls. The first problem was that the interest rates that S&Ls could pay on deposits were administratively set by the federal government (Regulation Q) and were substantially below compared to what could be earned elsewhere (such in MMMFs), leading depositors to withdraw their funds from the S&Ls.[731] The second major problem was that S&Ls, primarily, supplied long-term fixed-rate mortgages. While this might sound like a prudent and conservative business model, when interest rates rose, these mortgages lost a considerable amount of value, essentially wiping out the S&L industry's net worth. The relatively greater concentration of S&L lending in mortgages, coupled with a reliance on deposits with short maturities for their funding, made savings institutions especially vulnerable to increases in interest rates.[732] As inflation accelerated and interest rates began to rise rapidly in the late 1970s, many S&Ls suffered extensive losses. The interest rates they had to pay to attract deposits rose sharply, but the amount they earned on (long-term fixed rate) mortgages did not change. As a result, losses began to mount. As inflation and interest rates began to decline in the early 1980s, S&Ls began to recover somewhat, but the basic problem was that regulators did not have the resources to resolve institutions that had become insolvent.[733]

---

lend them back to a few of the members to finance their home purchases. As the loans were repaid, funds could then be lent to other members of the group. In 1980, there were almost 4,000 thrifts with total assets of $600 billion, of which about $480 billion were in mortgage loans, representing half of the approximately $960 billion in home mortgages outstanding at that time.

730 Federal Home Loan Bank Act, Pub. L. No. 72-304, 47 Stat. 725 (1932) (codified as amended at 12 U.S.C. §§ 1421–1449).

731 Banks and S&Ls could compete in the free market only when deposits exceeded $100.000 because the Regulation Q restrictions were not applicable above that threshold. See in C. Felsenfeld, 'The Bank Holding Company Act: Has It Lived Its Life?' (1993) 38(1) *Villanova Law Review*, p. 20.

732 Ibid., p. 19.

733 For instance, in 1983 it was estimated that it would cost roughly $25 billion to pay off the insured depositors of failed institutions. Nevertheless, the thrifts' insurance fund, the FSLIC, had reserves of only $6 billion.

Policymakers instead took steps to deregulate the industry hoping that it could grow out of its problems. The industry's problems, though, grew even more severe. Policymakers under Reagan administration responded by passing the earlier mentioned DIDMCA[734] and the Garn-St Germain Act.[735] While these changes were intended to raise thrift earnings, they often backfired when inexperienced lenders made mistakes, and weak thrifts used the new powers to gamble unsuccessfully for recovery. This strategy was aided by deregulation in the early 1980s, which gave the S&L industry greater scope to enter new business areas[736] to aid its return to profitability. Thrifts began lending into commercial real estate and doing so in substantially greater volumes than would normally have been considered prudent. As a result, many thrifts failed and those that survived started lending to riskier projects in increasingly desperate attempts to cut their losses and turn their businesses into profitability. As a result, the regulatory response was one of forbearance, since many insolvent thrifts were allowed to remain open, and their financial problems only worsened over time, leading to the creation of S&L that came to be known as 'zombies'. Moreover, capital standards were reduced both by legislation and by decisions taken by regulators, federally chartered S&L were granted the authority to make new (and ultimately riskier) loans other than residential mortgages, and a number of states also enacted similar or even more expansive rules for state-chartered thrifts. The limit on deposit insurance coverage was raised from $40,000 to $100,000, making it easier for even troubled or insolvent institutions to attract deposits to lend with.

As a result of these regulatory and legislative changes, the S&L industry experienced rapid growth. From 1982 to 1985, thrift industry assets grew 56%, more than twice the 24% rate observed at banks. This growth was fuelled by an influx of deposits as zombie thrifts began paying higher and higher rates to attract funds. These zombies were engaging in a 'go for broke' strategy of investing in riskier and riskier projects, hoping they would pay off in higher returns. If these returns did not materialise, then taxpayers would ultimately foot the bill, since the zombies were already insolvent, and the FSLIC's resources were insufficient to cover losses. In 1989, President Bush legislated

---

734 See in *supra* n. 432.

735 See in *supra* n. 662.

736 See in C. Felsenfeld, 'The Bank Holding Company Act: Has It Lived Its Life?' (1993) 38(1) *Villanova Law Review*, p. 23. The Section 401 of DIDMCA enabled S&Ls to lend and invest in a broad variety of areas; Section 402 of the same Act allowed them to issue credit cards; Section 403 authorized them trust powers and Section 501 removed any state usury law limitations regarding residential real estate mortgage loans.

sweeping regulatory changes to the S&Ls industry along with a bailout plan. With the FIRREA of 1989:[737]

- abolished the FHLBB and FSLIC and in their place, Congress created the Office of Thrift Supervision (OTS) and placed thrifts' insurance under the FDIC,[738]
- created the Resolution Trust Corporation (RTC) to resolve the remaining troubled S&Ls by reselling their assets and using the proceeds to pay back depositors,[739]
- injected $50 billion of new borrowing authority to close failed banks,
- financed the US DoJ for the prosecution of S&L related crimes.

By 1989, more than 1,000 S&L institutions had failed, while the crisis cost a total of almost $160 billion, of which a whopping $132 billion was injected by American taxpayers through a financial bailout initiated by the federal government via higher taxes and charges levied on S&L accounts. $20 billion was paid to depositors of collapsed thrifts by the FSLIC before it became insolvent. The S&L Crisis of the 1980s and early 1990s was the first large US banking crisis since the Great Depression and resulted in thousands of S&L institutions closing and billions of dollars lost, hurting both customers and taxpayers. The crisis led to extensive banking reforms, but not enough to avoid another (global) financial crisis that occurred between 2007–2009, leading to the Great Recession. Lessons are still being learned from the S&L Crisis and its importance is that it accelerated the deregulation of the financial sector with a double aim; first to help the thrift institutions to recover from the crisis and second to respond to the inflationary era with the high interest rates and the increased competition in the financial sector. Moreover, it was a demonstration of how catastrophic lax regulation and supervision could be, accompanied by good intentions' deregulation. At the end of the day, S&L institutions were victims of the US dual banking system and the restricted environment within which they operated, restricting their access to benefits of risk diversification and modern portfolio management theory.[740]

---

737 See in *supra* n. 426.

738 The FSLIC was replaced by the Savings Association of Insurance Fund (SAIF) of the FDIC. See in C. Felsenfeld, 'The Bank Holding Company Act: Has It Lived Its Life?' (1993) 38(1) *Villanova Law Review*, p. 18.

739 The RTC closed a total of 747 S&L with assets of over $407 billion and the thrift crisis came to its end when the RTC was eventually closed on 31 December 1995.

740 See in C. Felsenfeld, 'The Bank Holding Company Act: Has It Lived Its Life?' (1993) 38(1) *Villanova Law Review*, p. 11.

5.4. Judicial and Agency Interpretation of the Legal Framework

Commercial banks and especially the nationally chartered ones were constantly trying to find new ways to circumvent the separation regime imposed by the GSA, undermining thereby its ability to keep them away from the securities sector. In their efforts, they found useful and willing allies in both the US administration and the Courts. The national banks' primary regulator, the OCC, through its interpretations of the legal framework, favouring expansionary rulings allowing banks to constantly expand their activities in which they would engage in. At the same time, judicial review of such OCC's decisions, while initially trying to prevent the repeal of the GSA regime with a series of important decisions, ultimately certified them paving the way for the deregulation era.

By enacting the National Bank Act (NBA),[741] the US Congress established administrative procedures for the creation of federally chartered business enterprises;[742] more importantly, it also established the OCC as federal government agency within the US Department of Treasury, with the power to issue national bank charters and regulations and the power to incorporate domestic federal business enterprises.[743] Today, national banks' legal framework is derived from three sources: a) the NBA, b) the OCC regulations, and c) the federal courts. Congress has amended NBA many times to adapt it to modern business needs since, compared to modern corporation law statutes, the NBA is considered to be quite primitive. The OCC plays an equally important role in shaping the law applied to national banks since it issues administrative rules that interpret the 'corporate practices of national banks'.[744] It must pointed out that although the NBA does not grant OCC any specific authority to prescribe corporate law rules for national banks, OCC claims the power to do so under its general authority to 'prescribe rules and regulations to carry out the responsibilities of the office'.[745] The NBA grants national banks certain

---

741 As it was earlier referred to the present book, two different Acts are known as 'National Bank Act'. On 25 February 1863, Congress passed the 'National Currency Act' (also known later as the National Bank Act) in an effort to boost the demand for 'greenbacks', the non-interest-bearing notes in denominations as small as $5. The National Banking Act of 3 June 1864, specified the requirements for establishing a 'national banking association'. These requirements included minimum capital levels and reserve requirements based on the population and designation of the city where a bank was located.

742 D.K. Tarullo, 'Bank Supervision and Administrative Law' (2022) 1 *Columbia Business Law Review*, pp. 279–401.

743 See in L. Menand and M. Ricks, 'Federal Corporate Law and the Business of Banking' (2021) 88(6) *The University of Chicago Law Review*, p. 1374.

744 Ibid., p. 1378.

745 12 U.S.C. § 93a.

corporate powers just as all corporations have. Those powers are enumerated in 12 U.S.C. § 24; a national bank may:

(1) 'adopt and use a corporate seal',[746]
(2) have perpetual existence,[747]
(3) make contracts,[748]
(4) 'sue and be sued, complain and defend, in any court of law and equity, as fully as natural persons',[749]
(5) 'elect or appoint directors',[750] and
(6) 'prescribe bylaws'.[751]

Apart from these six basic powers, that all corporations have, NBA grants a seventh power which embodies a bank's *raison d'être*. It is the most fundamental and at the same time the most problematic statute in the entire federal banking law: the 'core banking powers'.[752] Core banking powers are further divided into two subcategories: 1) the enumerated powers, and 2) the non-enumerated powers. Section 24 Seventh confers on national banks the following (enumerated) banking powers:[753]

(1) 'Discounting and negotiating promissory notes, drafts, bills of exchange, and other evidences of debt',
(2) 'Receiving deposits',
(3) 'Buying and selling exchange, coin, and bullion',
(4) 'Loaning money on personal security', and
(5) 'Obtaining, issuing, and circulating notes'

These five enumerated banking powers depict a *numerus clausus* snapshot of banking as it was conducted back in 1864, when the Act was enacted by the Congress. Today, except maybe from the fifth power that is anachronistic, it can describe, more or less, a very simple bank business model. Although these powers appear to be limited in scope, 'artfully interpreted by courts and the OCC, they have allowed banks considerable latitude to keep up with technological and marketplace developments'.[754] The US Courts and the OCC gave national banks the necessary powers to evolve by using two techniques of interpretation: abstraction and prescription. By using abstraction, they were

---

[746] 12 U.S.C. § 24 first.
[747] 12 U.S.C. § 24 second.
[748] 12 U.S.C. § 24 third.
[749] 12 U.S.C. § 24 fourth.
[750] 12 U.S.C. § 24 fifth.
[751] 12 U.S.C. § 24 sixth.
[752] 12 U.S.C. § 24 seventh.
[753] Ibid.
[754] See in R.S. Carnell, J.R. Macey, G.P. Miller, P. Conti-Brown, *The Law of Financial Institutions*, 7th ed., Aspen Casebook Series, New York, Wolters Kluwer, 2021, p. 117.

generalising from an express power to a more comprehensive function while by using prescription they were deriving powers from custom and usage.[755]

We must now pose (and answer) the critical question: Section 24 Seventh listed powers are 'exclusive' or 'illustrative'? Are national banks allowed to conduct other activities as part of the 'business of banking'? The issue remained unresolved for decades and neither option seemed altogether attractive. In 1995, the SCOTUS provided an answer on its famous *NationsBank v. VALIC* case[756] upholding an OCC's opinion that allowed banks to sell annuities.[757] According to that opinion, the sale of annuities was an activity within the banks' 'traditional role as financial intermediaries' and therefore qualified as an 'incidental power ... necessary to carry on the business of banking'.[758] SCOTUS agreed with the OCC's position that the business of banking is not limited to the enumerated powers in Section 24 Seventh, and that the OCC has the power to authorise activities which are beyond those specifically enumerated in the NBA. Its famous footnote 2 has as follows: 'We expressly hold that the "business of banking" is not limited to the enumerated powers in § 24 Seventh and that the Comptroller therefore has discretion to authorise activities beyond those specifically enumerated. The exercise of the Comptroller's discretion, however, must be kept within reasonable bounds. Ventures distant from dealing in financial investment instruments – for example, operating a general travel agency —may exceed those bounds.'[759]

SCOTUS also held that by applying its Chevron decision,[760] granted the OCC's judgement 'controlling weight'[761] to define a term or to fill a gap in the legislation, but within certain 'reasonable bounds'. Unfortunately, though, SCOTUS did not articulate any test that would be able to delineate the outer limits of those reasonable bounds, and the OCC interpreted VALIC as full endorsement of its, long held, broad view of banking powers.[762] Apart from the

---

755 Ibid.

756 *NationsBank of North Carolina v. Variable Annuity Life Insurance Co. (VALIC)*, 513 U.S. 251 (1995).

757 Ibid., para. 2. NationsBank of North Carolina, N.A., a national bank, and its brokerage subsidiary sought permission from the OCC, for the brokerage subsidiary to act as an agent in the sale of annuities. 'Annuities' are contracts under which the purchaser makes one or more premium payments to the issuer in exchange for a series of payments, which continue either for a fixed period or for the life of the purchaser or a designated beneficiary. When a purchaser invests in a 'variable annuity', the purchaser's money is invested in a designated way and payments to the purchaser vary with investment performance. In a classic 'fixed annuity', in contrast, payments do not vary.

758 Ibid., para. 11.

759 Ibid., p. 258 fn. two.

760 *Chevron U.S.A. Inc. v. Natural Resources Defense Council, Inc.*, 467 U. S. 837, 842 (1984).

761 *NationsBank v. VALIC*, p. 257.

762 See in A.E. Wilmarth Jr., 'The Road to Repeal of the Glass-Steagall Act' (2017) 17(4) *Wake Forest Journal of Business and Intellectual Property Law*, p. 483; in S.T. Omarova, 'The Quiet Metamorphosis: How Derivatives Changed the "Business of Banking"' (2009) 63(4)

enumerated powers, Section 24 Seventh referred also to '... all such incidental powers as shall be necessary to carry on the business of banking'.[763] With the VALIC case national banks reached a peak were the OCC had finally full discretion to expand the available banking powers since the judicial control had performed a huge turnaround from previous efforts to repeal the GSA wall between the banking and the securities sectors. Initially, SCOTUS was very reluctant to accept that the meaning of 'incidental powers' included also the securities activities. The OCC in the VALIC case based its decision on the 'incidental powers' provision but SCOTUS did not necessarily ruled on that ground.[764] The provision of incidental powers seems to establish two categories of permissible activities: 1) the 'business of banking' and 2) other activities that even though they are not part of that business, nevertheless are necessary to carry on that business.[765] Obviously, the second category is wider than the first and its limits are only a matter of debate and market evolution. Within the ambit of the second category, many other activities fall but the most important and tricky one is the underwriting and distribution of securities.

The GSA and the BHCA had created a very strong wall separating the business of banking from the securities related activities. That wall effectively limited the contagion risks associated with the mixing of such activities, thereby ensuring that any problems potentially arising to one sector would not be transferred to the other.[766] As the general disintermediation trend put pressure on banks to be more competitive against new forms of credit supply, bankers and lawyers turned their eyes to the legal text separating banking and securities in order to find ways to set aside these restrictions. The demise of what was perceived as a near impenetrable wall was the result of both agency and banks' persistence, administrative deference, and legal ingenuity. Banks' willingness to enter the securities services found powerful allies since both the OCC and the Fed were in favour of an expansionary reading of the Section 24 seventh bank powers. The process of blurring the limits between banking and securities activities was gradual and allowed banks to enter securities business (underwriting, brokering, dealing, and investing) leading to a complete metamorphosis of the business of banking. What must be clarified though is that initially, the Courts were very reluctant to break down the separating wall between the two sectors and rejected many early attempts towards that

University of Miami Law Review, p. 1053; in A.E. Wilmarth Jr., *Taming the Megabanks, Why We Need a New Glass-Steagall Act*, New York, Oxford University Press, 2020, p. 445.

763 12 U.S.C. § 24 seventh.

764 See in R.S. Carnell, J.R. Macey, G.P. Miller and P. Conti-Brown, *The Law of Financial Institutions*, 7th ed., Aspen Casebook Series, New York, Wolters Kluwer, 2021, p. 122.

765 Ibid.

766 See in A.E. Wilmarth Jr., 'The Road to Repeal of the Glass-Steagall Act' (2017) 17(4) *Wake Forest Journal of Business and Intellectual Property Law*, p. 445.

direction. In 1971, SCOTUS decided the *ICI v. Camp* case.[767] Almost twenty years before the VALIC decision, SCOTUS rejected a 1966 OCC's ruling that initially allowed First National Citi Bank (FNCB) to create a collective investment fund under the name 'Commingled Investment Account'.[768] FNCB's fund pooled and managed investments made by its customers who received participating units in the fund, creating actually a mutual fund but under a different name.[769] In the Camp case SCOTUS found that the operation of a collective investment fund of that kind (already approved by the OCC), that is in direct competition with the mutual fund industry, involves a bank in the underwriting, issuing, selling, and distributing of securities, is in violation of §§ 16 and 21 of the GSA. The Court reviewed GSA's legislative history and concluded that Congress had decided to prohibit banks from engaging in certain 'hazards and financial dangers'.[770] In essence, SCOTUS upheld the idea behind GSA that banks would have to face intolerable conflicts of interest should they were engaged in the securities services, in this particular case a salesman stake in marketing securities that were underwritten by them or by their affiliates.[771] Their entry in the securities market would have forced banks to provide loans to support the sales of the securities in a way similar to the practices during the 'roaring twenties'. These fears led to the adoption of the GSA forcing SCOTUS to deny a judicial repeal since it accepted that FNCB's participation units were securities within the ambit of the GSA, further concluding that the proposed investment fund created a clear risk that all these 'subtle hazards' would actually occur.[772]

Another important judicial decision was the *Securities Industry Assn. v. Board of Governors, FRS*, (*Bankers Trust I*).[773] Thirteen years after the Camp decision, SCOTUS struck down a Fed's decision that allowed Bankers Trust to sell to investors commercial paper issued by its corporate clients. The Fed's Board concluded that such activity by state member banks is not prohibited by the Banking Act of 1933, because commercial paper is neither a 'security'

767 *Investment Co. Inst. v. Camp*, (*ICI v. Camp*) 401 U.S. 617 (1971).

768 Under the plan, Citibank's customer tendered between $10.000 and $500.000 to the bank, together with an authorization making the bank the customer's managing agent. The customer's investment was added to the fund, and written evidence of participation was issued which expresses in 'units of participation' the customer's proportionate interest in fund assets. The units of participation were freely redeemable, and transferable to anyone who has executed a managing agency agreement with the bank. The fund was registered as an investment company under the Investment Company Act of 1940. See *ICI v. Camp*, pp. 622–623.

769 See in A.E. Wilmarth, 'The Road to Repeal of the Glass-Steagall Act' (2017) 17(4) *Wake Forest Journal of Business and Intellectual Property Law*, p. 467.

770 *ICI v. Camp*, p. 630.

771 See in A.E. Wilmarth Jr., *Taming the Megabanks, Why We Need a New Glass-Steagall Act*, New York, Oxford University Press, 2020, p. 158.

772 Ibid., p. 159.

773 *Securities Industry Assn. v. Board of Governors, FRS*, (*Bankers Trust I*) 468 U. S. 137 (1984).

nor a 'note' within the meaning of that Act and therefore falls outside the Act's proscriptions. The District Court disagreed with the Board, but the Court of Appeals deferred to the Board's interpretation and reversed the judgment of the District Court. SCOTUS rejected Fed's attempt to distinguish commercial paper from other types of debt securities[774] and held that '[b]ecause commercial paper falls within the plain language of the Act, and because the inclusion of commercial paper within the terms of the Act is fully consistent with its purposes, commercial paper is a "security" under the Act, and therefore is subject to its proscriptions'.[775] Quoting its Camp decision, SCOTUS clarified that 'Congress acted to keep commercial banks out of the investment banking business largely because it believed that the promotional incentives of investment banking and the investment banker's pecuniary stake in the success of particular investment opportunities was destructive of prudent and disinterested commercial banking and of public confidence in the commercial banking system'.[776]

In the aftermath of Bankers Trust I, the Fed issued a revised order which allowed Bankers Trust to sell commercial paper but under a different legal base. Instead of claiming that commercial paper was not a security, Fed's revised order stated that Bankers Trust would not engage in prohibited underwriting as long as it was she was going to sell the commercial paper only to sophisticated institutional buyers – investors under private placements.[777] The District of Columbia's US Court of Appeals upheld the revised Fed's order and SCOTUS denied any further review with its Bankers Trust II decision.[778] The D.C. Circuit stated on its decision that it owed 'substantial deference' to the Fed's revised order in light of SCOTUS groundbreaking Chevron decision.[779] When applying the first step from Chevron's two-step formula,[780] the D.C. Circuit

---

774 See in in A.E. Wilmarth Jr., *Taming the Megabanks, Why We Need a New Glass-Steagall Act*, New York, Oxford University Press, 2020, p. 159.

775 Bankers Trust I, p. 139.

776 Ibid., p. 155.

777 See in in A.E. Wilmarth Jr., *Taming the Megabanks, Why We Need a New Glass-Steagall Act*, New York, Oxford University Press, 2020, p. 159.

778 *Securities Industry Assn. v. Board of Governors, FRS, (Bankers Trust II)* 807 F.2d 1052 (D.C. Cir. 1986), cert. denied, 483 U.S. 1005 (1987).

779 *Chevron U.S.A. Inc. v. Natural Resources Defense Council, Inc.*, 467 U. S. 837, 842 (1984).

780 In its *Chevron* decision, SCOTUS instructed circuit courts to apply a simple two-part test when reviewing an agency's construction of a law it administers. Under the Chevron decision, the Court continues to defer to agency actions when an agency is acting under an ambiguous law. The Chevron decision established a two-step approach for the Court, where the first step allows the reviewing Court to ask, 'whether Congress has directly spoken to the precise question at issue. If the intent of the Congress is clear, that is the end of the matter; for the Court, as well as the agency, must give effect to the unambiguously expressed intent of Congress' (Quote from *Chevron*, pp. 842–843). Under the Chevron's second step, if a court finds that Congress 'has not directly addressed the precise question at issue, the court does not simply impose its own construction on the statute, […]. Rather, if the

held that the applicable GSA provisions were ambiguous and that Congress, as a result, has not addressed the question at stake, decided by the Fed. Applying the Chevron formula's second step, the Court deferred to Fed's analysis and determination that the commercial paper at stake (through a private placement sale) were a) permissible brokerage transactions falling within the ambit of 'business of banking',[781] as it has been amended by Section 16 of GSA, and b) did not constitute a prohibited underwriting of securities under Sections 16 and 21 of GSA.[782] In essence, the D.C. Circuit upheld the Fed's position that it was reasonable to interpret GSA's prohibition of underwriting in such a way as to not forbid private placements while forbidding public offerings.[783] The D.C. Circuit's decision acknowledged that the private placement would involve at least one of the 'subtle hazards', as defined in Camp and Bankers Trust I decisions, namely the danger for the bank to lose its reputation and customer's confidence, but ultimately rejected them as an insignificant risk.[784]

As a practical matter, Chevron's two-step formula for deference over the federal agency's legal authority grants such agencies a very broad discretion to answer positively when they address a question about the scope of their authority, as long as the Congress has not explicitly limited the agency's scope of authority. With respect to our analysis, the Chevron deference test plays an important role since it allowed the regulatory agencies, mostly the Fed, and the OCC, to extensively expand their authority and interpret the legal framework in such a way as to constantly expand the available banking powers for national banks allowing them to enter new business activities previously considered as prohibited.[785] Moreover, Bankers Trust II and the Chevron deference provided a clear blueprint for subsequent courts' decisions, which upheld agencies' rulings opening additional loopholes to the structural barriers imposed by both GSA and BHCA. The US Courts frequently invoked the Chevron deference as a legal rationale to affirm agency rulings that relied on 'highly creative interpretations of ambiguous statutory provisions to circumvent these barriers'.[786] The evolution of Courts' decisions was overwhelmingly adopted by both the OCC and the Fed, that were finally free to expand the statutory limits of what activities can banks and BHCs undertake. Both the Fed and the OCC

---

statute is silent or ambiguous with respect to the specific issue, the question for the court is whether the agency's answer is based on a permissible construction of the statute' (Quote from *Chevron*, pp. 843–844).

781 12 U.S.C. § 24 Seventh.

782 See in A.E. Wilmarth Jr., 'The Road to Repeal of the Glass-Steagall Act' (2017) 17(4) *Wake Forest Journal of Business and Intellectual Property Law*, p. 469.

783 Ibid.

784 Ibid.

785 See in in A.E. Wilmarth Jr., *Taming the Megabanks, Why We Need a New Glass-Steagall Act*, New York, Oxford University Press, 2020, p. 159.

786 Ibid., p. 160.

used their powers in various cases, and the result was the gradual but constant expansion of the permissible activities.

Although an analysis of the Chevron deference doctrine and its importance for US administrative law is far beyond the purposes of our book, we must mention that until mid-2024, it was one of the most important legal tools to define the limits of federal agencies interpretations of laws. Currently, the SCOTUS decision in *Loper Bright Enterprises v. Raimondo*,[787] on 28 June 2024, marks a pivotal shift in administrative law by overturning the 1984 Chevron deference doctrine. Chevron doctrine had long required courts to defer to federal agency interpretations of ambiguous statutes, provided those interpretations were deemed reasonable. The US Courts used it extensively and the agencies relied heavily on the doctrine to expand their power, particularly the OCC. The SCOTUS ruling (6-3) now mandates that courts exercise independent judgement in interpreting statutes, even when they are ambiguous, thereby limiting judicial deference to agency interpretations. The ruling significantly curtails the power of federal agencies to interpret statutes, potentially leading to increased legal challenges against agency regulations across various sectors. This landmark decision reshapes the landscape of administrative law, emphasising judicial interpretation over agency expertise in statutory interpretation. Its long-term effects will unfold as courts apply this new standard to future cases involving federal agency regulations.

5.4.1 The 'Section 20 Subsidiaries' of Glass-Steagall Act

In December 1986, the Fed reinterpreted Section 20 of the GSA, which bars commercial banks from being 'engaged principally' in securities business, deciding that banks can have up to 5% of gross revenues from investment banking business. Although this interpretation seemed to directly conflict with the letter of the law, nevertheless the Fed argued that since GSA did not precisely define the meaning of 'engaged principally', this was open to Fed's reinterpretation. The Fed permitted Bankers Trust to engage in the earlier mentioned commercial paper transactions based on a decision, concluding that the phrase 'engaged principally' in Section 20 allows banks to do a small amount of underwriting, so long as it does not become a large portion of revenue. This was the first time the Fed reinterpreted Section 20 to allow some previously prohibited activities, and that initiative was a clear demarcation of the post Chevron deference environment.

In March 1987, the Fed approved an application by Chase Manhattan to engage in underwriting commercial paper, applying the same reasoning as previously expressed in its 1986 Bankers Trust decision, and in April 1987,

---

[787] *Loper Bright Enterprises v. Raimondo*, 603 U.S. 369 (2024).

continued losing the restrictions, when approved the request of several banks to participate in various underwriting businesses. The Fed's Board voted 3-2 in favour of further easing regulations under GSA, overriding the opposition of its Chairman Paul Volcker.[788] The vote came after the proposals from Citicorp, J.P. Morgan, and Bankers Trust advocating the loosening of GSA restrictions to allow banks to handle several underwriting businesses, including commercial paper, municipal revenue bonds, and mortgage-backed securities. The Fed's order (hereinafter the Citicorp decision)[789] allowed the so called 'Section 20 subsidiaries' to underwrite and trade, albeit to a limited extent, in four designated categories of 'bank ineligible securities' which were not lawful for banks to underwrite or trade in directly under the GSA restrictions.[790] These bank ineligible securities were municipal revenue bonds, private label RMBS, ABS backed with consumer loan receivables and commercial paper. With its Citicorp decision, Fed also explained to what extent those Section 20 subsidiaries would be free to engage in those bank ineligible securities, by stating that subsidiaries of BHCs would not violate Section 20 of GSA as long as they were not engaged principally in underwriting or trading ineligible securities. Therefore, Section 20 subsidiaries were required to focus most of their activities on underwriting and investing in bank eligible government securities. However, the Section 20 subsidiaries would be free to underwrite or to invest in the four designated categories of bank ineligible securities as long as those activities did not account for more than 5% of their gross revenues.[791] The industry challenged Fed's Citicorp decision but the 2nd Circuit upheld the order and SCOTUS denied to further review the decision.[792] The 2nd Circuit's decision applied the Chevron deference rule to the Fed's reasonable interpretation of an ambiguous statute and accepted its argumentation that Section 20 of GSA was ambiguous on whether the banks could affiliate with companies that carried on securities activities but were not 'engaged principally' in underwriting or trading bank ineligible securities. The 2nd Circuit concluded that the Fed was

788 Thomas Theobald, the then vice chairman of Citicorp, argued that three 'outside checks' on corporate misbehaviour had emerged since 1933: a) 'a very effective' SEC, b) knowledgeable investors, and c) 'very sophisticated' rating agencies. Volcker was unconvinced by such arguments and expressed his fears that lenders will recklessly lower loan standards in pursuit of lucrative securities offerings and market bad loans to the public. For many critics, it boiled down to the issue of two different cultures - a culture of risk which was the securities business, and a culture of protection of deposits which was the culture of banking. See in in A.E. Wilmarth Jr., *Taming the Megabanks, Why We Need a New Glass-Steagall Act*, New York, Oxford University Press, 2020, p. 160.

789 *Citicorp, J.P. Morgan & Co, and Bankers Trust N.Y. Corp*, 73 Federal Reserve Bulletin 487, 1987.

790 See in A.E. Wilmarth Jr., *Taming the Megabanks, Why We Need a New Glass-Steagall Act*, New York, Oxford University Press, 2020, p. 160.

791 Ibid.

792 *Securities Industry Association v. Board of Governors of Federal Reserve System*, 839 F. 2d 47 (2nd Circuit), cert. denied, 486 U. S. 1059 (1988).

reasonable in allowing BHCs to establish Section 20 subsidiaries that derived 5% of their revenues from bank ineligible securities activities.[793] While the Fed's Board remained sensitive to concerns about mixing commercial banking and underwriting, it stated its belief that the original Congressional intent of 'principally engaged' allowed for some securities activities.

In August 1987, Alan Greenspan, former director of J.P. Morgan and an ardent proponent of banking deregulation, became chairman of the Fed.[794] One reason Greenspan favoured greater deregulation was to help US banks compete with big foreign institutions. Under Greenspan's tenure the Fed pursued further deregulation and steadily expanded the scope of activities allowed for the Section 20 subsidiaries while it also indicated that it would raise the limit from 5% to 10% of gross revenues at some point in the future. In 1989, the Fed granted permission to Section 20 subsidiaries to underwrite and trade all types of debt and equity securities and also raised the maximum revenue limit from bank ineligible activities from 5% to 10%.[795] Once again the Fed's decision was upheld by the D. C. Circuit that deferred to the Fed's determinations.[796] The Fed's Board believed the new reading of Section 20 would eventually increase competition and lead to greater convenience and increased efficiency. Later, in 1996, the Fed's Board issued an audacious ruling, allowing BHCs to own investment banking operations that accounted for as much as 25% of their revenues and under such a measure virtually any BHC wanting to engage in securities business would be able to stay under the 25% limit on revenue.[797] Soon thereafter, the Fed also removed several firewalls that imposed tight restrictions on cross marketing and other transactions between BHCs and their Section 20 subsidiaries. The sector's reaction to these measures was a consolidation wave since large domestic and foreign banks rush to acquire dozens of small and midsised securities firms.[798] However, the law remains in the books, and along with the BHCA, does impose other restrictions on banks, such as prohibiting them from owning insurance-underwriting companies.

---

793 Ibid., p. 161.

794 A former student of Ayn Rand's 'objectivist' thinking, Greenspan would serve four terms, stretching three decades and four Presidencies, becoming the second-longest serving Fed Chairman in history.

795 See in A.E. Wilmarth Jr., *Taming the Megabanks, Why We Need a New Glass-Steagall Act*, New York, Oxford University Press, 2020, p. 161.

796 *Securities Ind. Ass'n v. Board of Governors*, 900 F.2d 360 (D.C. Cir. 1990).

797 See in A.E. Wilmarth Jr., *Taming the Megabanks, Why We Need a New Glass-Steagall Act*, New York, Oxford University Press, 2020, p. 161.

798 Ibid.

5.4.2 Derivatives

Apart from entering the securities sector, national banks expanded their powers also in the derivatives business with the OCC playing an extremely important role, since its interpretations of the legal framework were crucial in paving the road and securing national banks' interests. Prof. Omarova believes that the role of the OCC was crucial, and its policy decisions shaped the derivatives markets and overcame the generalised evolutionary forces that drove the market.[799] The unprecedented expansion of the derivatives market is a direct result of the OCC's interpretation of the Section 24 Seventh that defines the bank powers. Since the term was not defined in the statute, the OCC took advantage of that loophole and by its interpretive letters between the mid-1980s and 2008, greatly expanded the available derivative transactions that national banks may engage in, as incidental to or part of the business of banking.[800]

The OCC based its interpretations of banking powers on three principal tools-approaches: a) the 'look through' approach, b) the 'functional equivalence' approach, and c) the most radical one, the 'elastic definition' approach.[801] Prof. Omarova supports that through the OCC's interpretive methods, the final result was a radical but 'quiet metamorphosis' of the banking business from their basic statutory concepts, that took place mostly outside the financial sector and under the administrative procedures of mostly one agency; the OCC.[802] Since the 1960s, the OCC has adopted a favourable stance towards the broad interpretation of the Section 24 Seventh banking powers and derivatives were not included in the letter of the law. The agency had a broad view of the banking powers that was not delimited on the few articulated powers and therefore derivatives had to find their place in the universe of the available banking activities.[803] After the landmark ruling in the VALIC case, the OCC viewed the decision as a full endorsement of its approach and its staff expressed the agency's broad view in an article that introduced the so-called 'Williams-Jacobsen test' (WJ test).[804] Under the proposed test, the business of

---

799 See S.T. Omarova, 'The Quiet Metamorphosis: How Derivatives Changed the 'Business of Banking'', *University of Miami Law Review*, Vol. 63, No. 4, July 2009, p. 1044.

800 Ibid., p. 1046.

801 Ibid.

802 Ibid., p. 1048.

803 The agency, articulated its view on the matter on its *Interpretive Letter No. 494*, issued on 20 December 1989, explicitly stating that the banking business was not limited to the five enumerated powers but was comprised of all those powers that are recognized as being incidental or features of such business. See in S.T. Omarova, 'The Quiet Metamorphosis: How Derivatives Changed the "Business of Banking"' (2009) 63(4) *University of Miami Law Review*, p. 1051.

804 See J. Williams and M. Jacobsen, 'The Business of Banking: Looking to the Future' (1995) 50 *The Business Lawyer*, pp. 783–816.

banking includes activities that are: 1) 'functionally equivalent to, or a logical outgrowth, of recognised bank functions',[805] 2) 'benefit bank customers or … are convenient or useful to banks'[806], and 3) 'present risks of a type similar to those already assumed by banks'.[807] The OCC adopted the WJ test when assessing permissibility of the activity in question, and in particular in case of derivatives transactions.

Initially, the OCC used the 'look through approach' where it looked through the nature of the underlying asset itself in the transaction, ignoring thereby the form of the transaction and held that if banks were permitted to invest or trade in the underlying asset per se, then they were also permitted to trade in the related derivative transaction.[808] The main advantages of that approach were its simplicity and high degree of effectiveness while its key limitation was that it did not address the general issue of permissibility of derivatives transactions per se, as a new type of banking activity.[809] Therefore, the look through approach is the most conservative and least controversial approach in the OCC's interpretational toolbox. As a result, the first authorisations for derivatives transactions adopted based on the look through approach were low profile and straightforward decisions.[810]

From mid-1980s to early 1990s, national banks started moving into the commodity derivatives market, both OTC and exchange traded. To approve these types of transactions where the underlying assets were not eligible for the banks to trade in directly, the OCC utilised its second alternative approach, the 'functional equivalence approach'.[811] Functional equivalence stands exactly on the opposite of the look through approach since instead of disregarding the form of the transaction and analysing solely the underlying asset, it ignores the nature of the underlying asset and focuses on the form of the financial transaction. Under functional equivalence all that matters is the nature of the financial activity and the risks that are associated with the transaction and not with the underlying asset.[812] When applying the functional equivalence tool to various commodity derivative transactions, the OCC argued that these activities were functionally equivalent either to an expressly authorised banking activity, under the Section 24 Seventh enumerated powers, or to another banking activity that, while not expressly enumerated in the statute,

---

805 See in S.T. Omarova, 'The Quiet Metamorphosis: How Derivatives Changed the "Business of Banking"' (2009) 63(4) *University of Miami Law Review*, p. 1053.

806 Ibid.

807 Ibid.

808 Ibid., p. 1057.

809 Ibid.

810 Ibid.

811 Ibid., p. 1060.

812 Ibid.

was previously authorised by the OCC.[813] Under that approach the OCC approved perfectly matched commodity swaps,[814] commodity linked deposits,[815] unmatched commodity swaps and swap warehousing transactions.[816] Based on the functional equivalence tool, the OCC also paved the way for equity swaps transactions that were perceived as functionally equivalent to the already approved commodity derivatives.[817] According to Prof. Omarova, the OCC's basic principle was to represent such activities in a highly abstract and generalised way, as a series of fundamental risks combination and generic actions which then could be found as functionally equivalent to actions and risks that banks were involved due to their expressly enumerated banking powers.[818] Moreover, the OCC significantly reduced or downplayed the importance of market risk, or any other type of risks, associated either with the underlying assets or the form of the transactions. The OCC repeatedly argued that the only risk that banks were exposed to was solely the counterparty's credit risk, a bank's main risk management concern, and therefore a familiar type of risk.[819] Critics further argue that the Interpretive Letters were written with a specific external audience in mind, courts and lawmakers in case those cases were ever judicially challenged, and as a result, their analysis was to advocate a position rather than present a thorough analysis of the issue at stake.[820]

The last interpretive tool was the 'elastic definition approach', a radical and far-reaching interpretive tool, that aimed at expanding the notion of the 'business of banking' as to encompass any modern form of financial intermediation, broadly understood as involving exchanges of payments and assumption or transfer of financial risks for customers' account.[821] Starting from the mid-1990s the OCC used that approach to allow national banks to engage in physical hedging of commodity and equity derivatives, enter into equity options and forwards, trade derivatives linked to electricity prices, gas emission allowances, real estate and natural disaster risk indices and even operate as regional electricity marketers.[822] This 'infinitely elastic' concept of banking business served as a powerful mechanism that would constantly expand the available banking powers, ignoring the inherently present restrictions that are imposed by the strictly enumerated banking powers in Section 24 Seventh.[823]

813 Ibid.
814 Ibid., p. 1061.
815 Ibid., p. 1063.
816 Ibid., p. 1065.
817 Ibid., p. 1069 onwards.
818 Ibid., p. 1072.
819 Ibid., p. 1073.
820 Ibid., p. 1075.
821 Ibid., p. 1077.
822 Ibid.
823 Ibid.

Under the 'elastic definition approach' the OCC defined, in highly abstract terms, the business of banking as to encompass essentially any bank activity that involved exchange of payments between, or with, third parties. The OCC typically argued that each newly proposed derivative transaction was a 'logical outgrowth' of a previously authorised bank activity and was 'convenient or useful' to banks and their customers.[824] Furthermore, the OCC argued that such transactions, both derivatives and related hedging transactions, would potentially increase bank's profitability and competitiveness and provided customers with wider options for risk management tools without a further analysis of the associated risks.[825] The *ultimum refugium* for these transactions were the requirements to be 'customer driven' and 'non-speculative'. The OCC interpreted the customer driven requirement when a transaction was performed by the bank as if it was for customers' 'valid and independent business purpose'.[826] Meanwhile, the non-speculative requirement was interpreted in such a way as to require that the bank transacts with third parties seeking to manage their own financial risks or achieve their own financial goals so that the banks' primary goal it to earn fees from the provided risk management services to its customers rather than perform such transactions with the aim to invest in the underlying asset and profit from the movements in its prices.[827]

Although the OCC succeeded in expanding the available banking activities in the derivatives business it did so in a way not allowing much regulatory dialogue and offering a concrete analysis of the pros and cons of its interpretations. The aim was to allow national banks to compete effectively in the growing market of derivatives transactions and in a way that would be compatible with the letter of the 1864 NBA, but not with its spirit. Using the aforementioned interpretive tools, the OCC successfully expanded the perimeter of available activities but as the recent GFC clearly demonstrated, opened the floodgates for a regulatory approach that did not consider all the relevant risks associated with such transactions.

5.4.3 The Current Permissible Activities

GSA's Section 16, as it currently stands, imposes two key restrictions on securities investments by national banks and state member banks. The first restriction is that the bank must limit its 'business of dealing in securities and stock … to purchasing and selling such securities and stock without recourse, solely upon the order, and for the account of, customers, and in no case for

824 Ibid., p. 1096.
825 Ibid.
826 Ibid., p. 1097.
827 Ibid.

its own account'.[828] The second restriction is that the bank generally cannot 'purchase ... for its own account [...] any shares of stock of any corporation'.[829] What makes the situation tricky is that the first restriction (prohibition of investing in securities for its own account) has two important exceptions: a) a bank may invest in US government securities and general obligations of state and local governments,[830] and b) 'the association may purchase for its own account investment securities under such limitations and restrictions as the Comptroller of the Currency may by regulation prescribe'.[831] The second exception allows national banks to purchase corporate debt securities but the bank's investment in securities of any issuer cannot exceed 10% of the bank's capital. In addition, Section 24 Seventh contains a list of minor exceptions that allow banks to engage (deal, underwrite, invest) in various other securities, all of which have some governmental connection.[832] The issuers of such bank eligible securities include international organisations,[833] federal government corporations,[834] government sponsored enterprises[835] and the federal and provincial governments of Canada. Banks have also very limited power to invest in equity securities.

Despite the fact that a national bank generally cannot own corporate stock for its own account, it can own shares of its own subsidiary. Permissible subsidiaries fall into three general categories: a) operating subsidiaries, b) financial subsidiaries, and c) subsidiaries that are authorised under specialised statutes.[836] Operating subsidiaries engage only in activities that the bank can conduct directly, with the word operating emphasising the fact that the bank chooses to conduct some of its own operations through a separate corporate entity.[837] Financial subsidiaries engage in at least one activity that the bank cannot conduct directly although they can also engage in activities that are permissible for banks and the word financial emphasises the fact that such

---

828 12 U.S.C. § 24 Seventh.

829 Ibid.

830 Ibid.

831 Ibid.

832 See in R.S. Carnell, J.R. Macey, G.P. Miller and P. Conti-Brown, *The Law of Financial Institutions*, 7th ed., Aspen Casebook Series, New York, Wolters Kluwer, 2021, p. 136.

833 The International Bank for Reconstruction and Development, the European Bank for Reconstruction and Development, the Inter-American Development Bank, the Bank for Economic Cooperation and Development in the Middle East and North Africa, the North American Development Bank, the Asian Development Bank, the African Development Bank, the Inter-American Investment Corporation, or the International Finance Corporation.

834 The Tennessee Valley Authority or the United States Postal Service.

835 The Federal National Mortgage Association (Fannie Mae), or the Government National Mortgage Association (Ginnie Mae), or the Federal Home Loan Mortgage Corporation (Freddie Mac).

836 See in R.S. Carnell, J.R. Macey, G.P. Miller and P. Conti-Brown, *The Law of Financial Institutions*, 7th ed., Aspen Casebook Series, New York, Wolters Kluwer, 2021, p. 136.

837 Ibid.

a subsidiary cannot engage in real estate or in general commercial activities.[838] Specialised statutes authorise a national bank to own small business investment companies and bank service companies.[839] Banks usually wholly own most of their subsidiaries, but the OCC also permits a bank to own a minority stake at another firm under certain conditions: 1) the firm engages only in banking or activities that are incidental to banking; 2) the investment is convenient or useful in carrying out the bank's own business; 3) owners of the subsidiary have limited liability for the subsidiary's debt; and 4) the bank has the power to either prevent the firm from engaging in impermissible activities or withdraw its investment.[840] Finally, the limitations that apply to national banks regarding stock ownership bind also state banks in the sense that an FDIC insured state bank generally cannot 'acquire or retain any equity investment of a type that is not permissible for a national bank'.[841]

On its latest list of permissible activities for national banks and federal savings associations, the OCC states clearly that the list is not exclusive and includes among others:[842]

- Management consulting,
- Finder activities for both financial and non-financial products,
- Courier services,
- Inventory management services,
- Various types of insurance underwriting activities,
- Annuity sales,
- Asset securitisation,
- Various broker dealer activities,
- Telecommunication and computer equipment leasing,
- Providing electronic marketplaces for non-financial products (ex. virtual malls),
- Commercial website hosting and the associated web design and development services,
- Software development and production for financial services

We can easily understand from the above list that the outer limits of the business of banking have been expanded and now encompass a wide range of

838 Ibid.

839 Ibid.

840 Ibid., p. 137.

841 12 U.S.C. § 1831a(c)(1).

842 See in Office of the Comptroller of the Currency (OCC), *Activities Permissible for National Banks and Federal Savings Associations*, Cumulative, Washington D.C., October 2017, available at: https://www.occ.gov/publications-and-resources/publications/banker-education/files/pub-activities-permissible-for-nat-banks-fed-saving.pdf.

non-financial activities, particularly in the new technologies area.[843] Much of this transformation of the banking sector was justified on the grounds that technological advances had blurred the traditional demarcations between banks and non-banks and that liberalisation of the sector was much needed to prevent commercial banking from technological obsolescence.[844] What is also clear is that the OCC can continue to designate additional activities as part of the 'business of banking' and thus within the corporate powers of national banks, rending useless the Section 24 Seventh, since the real legislation is created by the OCC and not the US Congress, at least regarding the national banks.[845]

5.5. *Legislative Initiatives towards Further Deregulation in the Financial Sector*

Another important aspect of the deregulation trend is the various legislative initiatives during the late 1980s and early 1990s adopted by the US Congress under various presidencies. In 1991, the Treasury Department issued a blueprint for a comprehensive adaptation of the financial system in the deregulation era. Entitled 'Modernizing the Financial System', the blueprint was built around three core pillars. The first pillar was the promotion of a nationwide banking and branching, the second pillar was the repeal of certain provisions from the 1933 Banking Act (the GSA), and the third pillar was the removal of barriers to acquisitions of banks from commercial and industrial companies.[846] The first pillar of the blueprint, the nationwide banking and branching, was based on the premise that it would create stronger and safer banks through the benefits of geographic diversification. Moreover, the blueprint supported that nationwide branching and banking would create a more competitive, efficient, and profitable industry providing at the same time greater convenience to banks' customers (including large corporations, individuals, traveller, and residents of urban areas).[847] The Treasury urged Congress to repeal Section 3(d) of the BHCA and the Douglas Amendment,[848] which prohibited the interstate acquisition of a bank by a BHC unless specifically authorised by the laws of the state where the bank was located. Treasury's call was for a new statute that would remove all federal and state-based barriers to interstate acquisitions of banks by BHCs and for an amendment to the McFadden Act that would

---

843 See L. Menand and M. Ricks, 'Federal Corporate Law and the Business of Banking' (2021) 88(6) *The University of Chicago Law Review*, p. 1406.

844 Ibid.

845 Ibid.

846 See in A.E.Wilmarth Jr., 'The Road to Repeal of the Glass-Steagall Act' (2017) 17(4) *Wake Forest Journal of Business and Intellectual Property Law*, p. 503.

847 Ibid., p. 504.

848 12 U.S.C. § 1842(d).

authorise national banks to establish branches either through mergers with other banks or by establishing de novo branches across state lines.[849]

In December 1991, under the Bush Presidency, the US Congress enacted the Federal Deposit Insurance Corporation Improvement Act (FDICIA)[850] in response to problems in the banking and thrift industries.[851] FDICIA's main scope was to implement such regulatory changes that would ensure the safety and soundness of both the banking and thrift industries. The main overarching provisions of the act, which was implemented in 1994, include a) the Prompt Corrective Action (PCA) mechanism and 'early resolution' policies, and b) the 'least cost resolution' scheme.[852] The PCA mechanism was designed to force regulators to impose sanctions and penalties on undercapitalised banks and empower them with the capacity to close any weak banks, timely, before they become insolvent and more costly to the taxpayers.[853] The PCA mechanism requires federal banking agencies to take progressively severe, corrective, supervisory actions as an insured depository institution's (member bank) capital declines. The federal agencies must assign individual institutions to one of five capital categories (well capitalised, adequately capitalised, undercapitalised, significantly undercapitalised, or critically undercapitalised) as determined by selected capital measures. Consequently, when a bank falls into any of the last three capital categories, its primary federal regulator must take certain mandatory supervisory actions and may supplement these with further discretionary actions. Banks that become critically undercapitalised must be placed in conservatorship or receivership within ninety days unless they restore their capital, or their federal regulator and the FDIC believe other actions are warranted.

The second provision, that of the least cost resolution, required the FDIC to use the least costly method to resolve bank failures should needed. The 'least cost test' intended to stop the FDIC from protecting uninsured depositors in banks that were failing, increasing the total cost of the resolution process.[854]

---

849 See in A.E. WILMARTH Jr., 'The Road to Repeal of the Glass-Steagall Act' (2017) 17(4) *Wake Forest Journal of Business and Intellectual Property Law*, p. 504.

850 Federal Deposit Insurance Corporation Improvement Act of 1991, Pub. L. No. 102-242, 105 Stat. 2236 (1991).

851 Since the establishment of FDIC in 1934, the number of bank failures in the US averaged roughly fifteen per year until 1981, when they began to rise and reached roughly 200 per year by the late 1980s. The wave of bank failures occurred due to a surge and subsequent collapse in certain industries (including energy, agriculture, and real estate). From roughly the beginning of 1980 until the end of 1991, nearly 1,300 commercial banks either failed or required failing bank assistance from the FDIC, which took action and closed-down insolvent institutions. By 1991, FDIC had become severely undercapitalised.

852 See in A.E. WILMARTH Jr., 'The Road to Repeal of the Glass-Steagall Act' (2017) 17(4) *Wake Forest Journal of Business and Intellectual Property Law*, p. 507.

853 Ibid.

854 Ibid.

The most important parameter of the least cost approach though was the 'systemic risk exemption' that allowed the FDIC, the Treasury and the Fed, jointly, to decide to protect the uninsured creditors of a failed bank in order to 'avoid or mitigate serious adverse effects on economic conditions or financial stability'.[855] Proponents of the measure viewed this a first time that a clear, and statutory legal basis for the 'too big to fail' doctrine was provided.[856] Penultimate, another important aspect of the FDICIA, significantly expanding the federal safety net in favour of the securities firms and other non-bank entities, were the provisions of Section 473 of FDICIA, amending Section 13(3) of the Federal Reserve Act, authorising the Fed to provide emergency loans to non-bank entities secured by almost any collateral type that the Fed deemed to be of satisfactory quality, including securities and other financial instruments.[857] This extremely important amendment allowed the Fed, in the 2007–2009 financial crisis to provide enormous financial support to securities firms, to AIG and to other non-bank entities. Ultimately, the FDICIA did not propose any amendments in favour of the nationwide banking and branching, leaving the hot potato for the Clinton administration that took office in 1993.

In September 1994, President Clinton signed into law the Riegle-Neal Act[858] removing many of the restrictions on opening bank branches across state lines. These restrictions were largely the result of the 1927 McFadden Act and other laws, that attempted to address long-standing concerns about the concentration of financial activity and the level of adequate supervision for large banking organisations operating in multiple states. The Riegle-Neal Act allowed banking organisations to acquire banks in any other state under a uniform, nationwide standard, providing for uniform branching and interstate acquisition rules for the entire country. These new rules included the following:

- BHCs that were well-managed and well-capitalised would be allowed to acquire banks in any state, after 29 September 1995,
- BHCs could merge banks located in different states into a single branch network after 1 June 1997,
- States had until 1 June 1997, to choose whether to opt out of the new law's branching provisions,[859] and
- A BHC could not control more than 10% of the nation's total deposits, or 30% of any single state's total deposits, unless a state elected to establish its own deposit cap above or below this 30% limit.

855 Ibid.

856 Ibid. See also in A.E. Wilmarth Jr., *Taming the Megabanks, Why We Need a New Glass-Steagall Act*, New York, Oxford University Press, 2020, p. 179.

857 Ibid.

858 See in *supra* n. 433.

859 Initially, the only states the decided to opt-out were Montana and Texas, but both states eventually agreed to allow interstate branching.

The Act further fuelled the consolidation wave in the banking sector, that was already in existence across the country,[860] resulting in banks expanding their balance sheets and becoming bigger and bigger in size, enjoying at the same time a constantly growing political influence in the Congressional corridors. By the late 1990s, consolidation in the banking industry had been an ongoing trend for almost twenty years and the number of commercial banks in the US had fallen from more than 14,000 in 1984 to fewer than 9,000 in 1999, while the average size of those banks had grown. This was part of a broader trend of consolidation in financial services industries.

The second component of the Treasury's blueprint was the repealing of the Glass-Steagall provisions in the 1933 Banking Act and the BHCA's provisions regarding affiliation rules and to authorise the creation of financial holding companies that would be able to own banks, securities firms, and insurance companies under a single roof.[861] To the Treasury's view, legislation already permitted banks and BHCs to engage in certain securities activities but strong impediments were still in place, imposing strict requirements. The Treasury also supported that the agency ruling based deregulation was seriously flawed because it was based on 'a piecemeal, inefficient and often irrational manner'.[862] As previously mentioned the FDICIA didn't include the Treasury's financial holding company proposal mostly because the US Congress House Energy and Commerce Committee (HECC) imposed very strict requirements and limits on the securities and insurance activities that would be available for the non-bank affiliates of banks rendering them worthless for the Treasury's and big banks' ambitions.[863] In 1995, the midterm elections changed the power balance in the US Congress and the HECC had a new chairman; thus the banks decided to retry their attempt for further liberalisation in the financial sector. Strong opposition from both the insurance industry and from community banks cancelled once again the financial modernisation bills of 1995 and 1996.[864]

The US Congress failed to adopt financial modernisation bill twice, in 1997 and in 1998, but during those years occurred two major events that permanently shifted the political landscape in favour of the liberalisation process.[865] The first was an attitude change on behalf of the securities and insurance firms, deciding to join forces with the banking industry after a series of unsuccessful legal

---

860 Seventy-four megamergers occurred between 1990 and 2005 in which both the acquiring and the acquired banks were holding more than $10 billion of assets. In 1995, big banks announced nine mergers that were ranked among the fourteen largest bank mergers in the US, up to that time.

861 See in A.E. Wilmarth Jr., 'The Road to Repeal of the Glass-Steagall Act' (2017) 17(4) *Wake Forest Journal of Business and Intellectual Property Law*, p. 510.

862 Ibid., p. 511.

863 Ibid., p. 512.

864 Ibid.

865 Ibid.

challenges of federal agency rulings. Securities and insurance firms supported the repealing of GSA provisions and BHCA's anti affiliation rules because they realised that the proposed financial holding company would work as a 'two-way street', enabling them to enter banking services on equal footing with the traditional banks.[866] The second major event was the 6 April 1998, announced merger between Citicorp and Travelers Insurance, under the new name 'Citigroup Inc.', with shareholders of each partner owning 50%, creating the world's largest financial institution.[867] The basic argumentation behind the mega merger is that the new company would be so well diversified that would have been able to withstand severe adverse economic shocks. The Citigroup merger was a huge pressure towards the US Congress to repeal the existing requirements timely for the approval of the merger; had these requirements been in force the merger would not have proceeded. The proposed merger was violating both the regulatory spirit and the statutory letter of GSA provisions and the only possible solution was a temporary statutory exemption on BHCA that allowed a newly formed BHC to retain non-conforming assets for up to five years (initially the exemption is for two years, but the Fed's Board has the power to renew this exemption for a maximum period of one year up to three times) after its creation, before needed to divest them.[868] The purpose of this exemption was to provide an orderly mechanism for the newly created BHC to divest from these assets and not to allow the warehousing of these assets hoping for a change in the legislation that would allow the BHC to ultimately keep them.[869] The Citigroup executives had already consulted with the Fed's Chairman Alan Greenspan, the Treasury's Secretary Robert Rubin and President Clinton before announcing their merger plans, and all of them endorsed the proposed merger despite the legislation restrictions. Indeed, the Fed approved the merger, and the D.C. Circuit upheld that decision.[870]

---

866 Ibid., p. 513.

867 Citicorp was the largest bank holding company in the US, and Travelers Insurance was a major insurance company that controlled a large securities broker-dealer, the Salomon Brothers. Behind the plan was a bold bet that several big trends that have picked up steam in the 1990s, such as the melding of banking and securities, big brand names, globalization, and consolidation, will define who would survive in the increasingly complex and international world of financial services. Thus, the transaction hinged on the promising strategy of 'cross-selling' products. Citigroup would be a sprawling company serving more than 100 million customers in 100 countries. It would have market capitalization of about $140 billion becoming the no. 1 among the world's financial-services firms. The two partners had 1997 operating income of about $7.5 billion and 1997 net revenue of more than $48 billion.

868 12 U.S.C. § 1843(a)(2).

869 See in A.E. Wilmarth Jr., 'The Road to Repeal of the Glass-Steagall Act' (2017) 17(4) *Wake Forest Journal of Business and Intellectual Property Law*, p. 514.

870 *Ind. Community Bankers v. Bd. of Governors*, 195 F.3d 28 (D.C. Cir. 1999), upholding the Fed's decision based on the argument that the Fed's order to approve the merger was in literal compliance with the BHCA and the possibility that the proposed merger would put pressure on the Congress to repeal the BHCA provision was irrelevant to the case.

In November 1999, President Clinton signed into law the Gramm-Leach-Bliley Act (GLBA), with the aim to promote the benefits of financial integration for consumers and investors while safeguarding the soundness of the banking and financial systems. The primary novelty the law ushered in was the creation of a new kind of financial institution: the 'financial holding company (FHC). A FHC was essentially an extension of the concept of a BHC; an umbrella organisation that could own subsidiaries involved in different financial activities. Based on the 1991 Treasury's Blueprint, the new FHC would: a) 'earn higher profits based on favourable economies of scope and scale',[871] b) 'achieve greater safety by diversifying their activities',[872] c) 'offer one stop shopping that would provide increased convenience and lower costs for businesses and consumers',[873] and d) 'compete with foreign universal banks on equal terms'.[874] This was something of a compromise, as security and insurance underwriting and sales by depository institutions would still be restricted, but banks could be part of a larger corporation that was involved in those activities. While GLBA repealed portions of the GSA and BHCA, it created new regulations for FHCs and placed cross-marketing restrictions to prevent a bank and a non-bank subsidiary of a FHC from marketing the products or services of the other entity. These restrictions were intended to prevent banks from promoting securities underwritten by other subsidiaries to their customers. In addition, restrictions remained on financial transactions between banks and non-bank subsidiaries. Moreover, GLBA also placed size limitations on banks' financial subsidiaries. At the time the law went into effect, the total assets of the financial subsidiaries of a national bank were limited to the lesser of $50 billion or 45 percent of its total assets. To give these rules teeth, it was necessary to appoint a regulator that would have the power to enforce them, and that responsibility fell primarily upon the Federal Reserve. GLBA relied primarily on 'firewalls' to stop universal banks from transferring their federal safety net subsidies to their securities and insurance affiliates that were legally based on the separate corporate entities of banks and their non-bank affiliates and in two sections of the Federal Reserve Act; Sections 23A and 23B that imposed certain requirements. As we will discover on the upcoming pages of the present book, these firewalls proved to be almost 'water walls' since they were compromised many times by the regulators to assist banks to circumvent them and expand their available activities.

---

871 See in A.E. Wilmarth Jr., 'The Road to Repeal of the Glass-Steagall Act' (2017) 17(4) *Wake Forest Journal of Business and Intellectual Property Law*, p. 517.

872 Ibid.

873 Ibid.

874 Ibid.

5.6. *The Requirements of Federal Reserve Act Sections 23A and 23B: a Matter of Interpretation*

In the Federal Reserve Act, Sections 23A and 23B describe the requirements that govern the transactions between an FDIC insured bank and any affiliate firm. The main policy objective behind Sections 23A and 23B requirements is threefold: a) allow affiliations between banks and other companies, b) allow banks to have dealings with these companies, and c) maintain a 'meaningful economic separation' between banks and various types of affiliates.[875] These requirements apply only to 'member banks' but other statutes apply these requirements to all FDIC insured depository institutions.

The requirements of Section 23A are both quantitative and qualitative and set limits on certain types of transactions between a bank and its affiliates, known as 'covered transactions'. A bank engages in a covered transaction when it:[876]

(i) extends credit to, or for the benefit of an affiliate,
(ii) issues a guarantee or letter of credit for the benefit of an affiliate,
(iii) purchases assets from an affiliate,
(iv) invests in securities that are issued by an affiliate,
(v) accepts securities issued by an affiliate as collateral for an extension of credit to anyone, including someone which is wholly unconnected to the bank,
(vi) loans securities to or borrows securities from an affiliate, or when it
(vii) participates in a derivative transaction with an affiliate.

Section 23A uses a very broad definition of the word 'affiliate' to include as an affiliate of a bank any:[877]

(i) company that controls the bank,
(ii) company controlled by a company that controls the bank,
(iii) bank that is a subsidiary of the bank,
(iv) company controlled by, or for the benefit of persons who control either the bank or a company that controls the bank,
(v) company, a majority of whose board of directors constitutes a majority of the bank's board of directors,
(vi) investment fund for which the bank acts as investment adviser,
(vii) company, whose relationship with the bank may, in the Federal Reserve Board's judgement, detrimentally affect the company's covered transactions with the bank.

---

875 See in R.S. Carnell, J.R. Macey, G.P. Miller and P. Conti-Brown, *The Law of Financial Institutions*, 7th ed., Aspen Casebook Series, New York, Wolters Kluwer, 2021, p. 259.

876 Ibid., p. 260.

877 Ibid.

The very broad definition of 'affiliate' reaches common ownership (4th case) and allows the Fed to enjoy a 'catch all' authority over potentially problematic relations that can be classified as affiliates and therefore be bind by the restrictions.[878] Section 23A is built around four main rules, two of which are quantitative and two are qualitative. The first rule stipulates that a bank's total covered transactions with any one affiliate cannot exceed 10% of the bank's capital,[879] the second rule stipulates that the bank's total covered transactions with all affiliates combined cannot exceed 20% of banks capital[880] and the third rule stipulates that certain types of the covered transactions – the 'credit transactions' according to Fed's terminology – must be fully secured with qualifying collateral. Credit transactions comprise extension of credit, letters of credit, guarantees and credit exposure arising from a derivative or from lending or borrowing securities. Collateral of high-quality means that the collateral posed for these transactions must be worth of 100–130% of the amount of the transaction, with the percentage depending on the type of collateral.[881] Finally, the fourth rule stipulates that a bank cannot purchase a low-quality asset from an affiliate unless the bank, pursuant to an independent credit evaluation, committed itself to purchase the asset before the affiliate acquired that asset. A low-quality asset is classified as such when:[882]

(i) The bank examiners classified that asset unfavourably when most recently examined the bank,
(ii) The affiliate cannot treat accrued interest as income because of doubt about the obligor's credit quality,
(iii) Principal or interest payments on the asset are more than 30 days past due,
(iv) The obligor renegotiated the terms of the asset because the obligor's financial condition has deteriorated.

Section 23A and Regulation W[883] allow for certain transactions to be exempted from the basic rules of Section 23A. As a result, the following transactions are exempted from the quantitative limits and the collateral requirements:[884]

- Transaction with another bank if the same company owns at least 80% of each bank's voting shares (sister bank exemption),
- Transaction with another bank of one bank owns at least 80% of the other bank's voting shares,

878 Ibid.
879 Ibid. For the purposes of Section 23A, the capital consists of tier 1 and tier 2 capital.
880 Ibid.
881 Ibid.
882 Ibid., p. 261.
883 'Transactions Between Member Banks and their Affiliates (Regulation W)', 12 CFR Part 223.
884 See in R.S. Carnell, J.R. Macey, G.P. Miller and P. Conti-Brown, *The Law of Financial Institutions*, 7th ed., Aspen Casebook Series, New York, Wolters Kluwer, 2021, p. 261.

- Purchasing loans without recourse from an affiliated bank,
- Purchasing assets from an affiliate as part of a qualifying internal reorganisation of the bank's holding company.

The above-mentioned transactions remain subject to the low-quality asset prohibition and to the safety and soundness requirement.[885] The following types of transactions are enjoying even broader exemptions as they don't need to comply with a) the quantitative limits, b) the collateral requirement, and c) the low-quality asset prohibition, must still be safe and sound:[886]

- Credit transactions to the extent that they are secured by US government securities or by a segregated, earmarked deposit account in the bank,
- Purchasing assets having readily identifiable, publicly available market price quotation, at the market price,
- Repurchasing loans originated by the bank and sold to an affiliate with recourse or under a repurchase agreement,
- Giving immediate credit for items submitted for collection in the ordinary course of business,
- Making deposits in an affiliated bank in the ordinary course of correspondent banking business, and
- An extension of credit repaid on the same business day.

Finally, we must also refer to the special treatment Section 23A applies to banks' subsidiaries. A subsidiary must be further distinguished in 'operating subsidiary' and in 'financial subsidiary'. An operating subsidiary is an entity that engages only in activities that a national bank can conduct directly (e.g. origination of mortgages), and a financial subsidiary is an entity that only engages in services that a national bank cannot conduct directly (e.g. corporate securities underwriting).[887] In general, Section 23A treats operating subsidiaries not as affiliates but as an integral part of the parent bank, eliminating thus the application of the four basic rules to the bank's transactions with an operating subsidiary, but the rules do apply to the bank's transactions with the financial subsidiary.[888]

Section 23B is built around four rules that aim to prevent abuses that are not covered by the rules of Section 23A. The first rule stipulates the most important requirement that a bank must deal with an affiliate and with third persons – the last in certain types of transactions – at arm's length (aka on market terms).[889] If no such comparable transactions exist in the market, then

---

885 Ibid.
886 Ibid.
887 Ibid., p. 262.
888 Ibid.
889 Ibid., p. 263.

the bank must transact with the affiliate on the same terms that it would apply to unaffiliated parties. The arm's length requirement applies when a bank:[890]

(i) Engages in a 'covered transaction' (as defined in Section 23A),
(ii) Sells a security or other asset to an affiliate,
(iii) Pay money or furnish a service to an affiliate,
(iv) Engages in a transaction in which an affiliate acts as an agent or as a broker or receives a fee for its services to the bank or any other person, and
(v) Engages in a transaction with a third party if an affiliate has a financial interest in the third party or participates in the transaction.

The second rule stipulates that a bank may not, as fiduciary, purchase securities or other assets from an affiliate except as permitted a) under the instrument creating the fiduciary relationship, b) by court order, and c) by the law of the jurisdiction governing the fiduciary relationship.[891] The third rule stipulates that the bank may not, as principal or fiduciary, purchase securities while an affiliate is a principal underwriter for those securities, aiming at preventing the bank from increasing the price of securities, for which market demand is slack, by buying the securities for trust accounts or its own portfolio. The only exemption that applies to the third rule is if the majority of the bank's directors approved the purchase before the initial offering of the securities to the public.[892] Ultimately, the fourth rule stipulates that neither the bank nor its affiliates may publish any advertisement or make any agreement that the bank shall be liable for the obligations of its affiliates. It must be pointed out that such agreements' prohibitions do not preclude the bank from issuing guarantees or letters of credit.[893]

The enforcement of Sections 23A and 23B provisions is done through the Fed's examination process. When examining a member bank, the Fed reviews its internal controls and its transactions with its affiliates in order to assess the compliance with the provisions of Sections 23A and 23B.[894] Also, the BHCs must submit to the Fed a quarterly report detailing how the insured depository is in compliance with the two sections regarding its transactions with its affiliates and no affirmative filings are required to demonstrate compliance with Section 23B.[895] Apart from enforcement power, the Fed is also equipped with the power to grant exemptions from the abovementioned requirements, upon request from the banks, provided that such exemptions are

[890] Ibid.
[891] Ibid.
[892] Ibid.
[893] Ibid.
[894] See in R. Benjenk, 'Quixotic Regulation: Section 23A of the Federal Reserve Act and Containment of the Federal Safety Net Subsidy' (2012) 2 *Harvard Business Law Review*, p. 467.
[895] Ibid.

to the public interest and also consistent with the purposes of the provisions of Sections 23A and 23B.[896] The Fed is also empowered to issue rules and regulations that will implement the provisions of the two sections; pursuant to this authority, Regulation W was issued in 2002, further clarifying the necessary requirements and legal technicalities for the effective application of the two sections.[897] Regulation W also contains the requirements for the Fed to discretionary exempt transactions from the ambit of Section 23A. A bank may request an exemption from the quantitative and qualitative requirements by explaining to and providing the Fed with the following: a) the details of the transaction or the relationship for which the (member) bank seeks the exemption, b) why the Fed should exempt the transaction or the relationship, and c) how the exemption is in favour of public interest and also consistent with the purpose of the provisions.[898]

5.7. Technological Advances and Financial Engineering (Securitisation and Derivatives)

Another two extremely important parameters of the deregulation era were the technological advances, that changed radically the way financial markets functioned, and the invention of complex financial products that were the mere result of financial engineering and investors' willingness to diversify their risks. The benefits of technological advances are straightforward and do not need much analysis. The wide use of internet connected previously cut off clients with financial markets in unprecedented ways. Access to financial markets became easy and cost effective through the use of telecommunication novelties while at the same time adoption of computerised solutions from the firms allowed them to process and execute higher volumes of transactions in more efficient and cost-effective ways. Internet and telecommunications connected financial markets around the world and increased interconnection among financial firms increasing thereby systemic risks since all were connected in a constantly evolving manner. On the other side of the coin, financial engineering created complex products that proved to be double-edged swords since they allowed higher yields and risk diversification in theory but ultimately proved to be associated with risks that financial market participants were unaware of, and regulatory authorities failed to timely evaluate. Among these products

---

896 Ibid., p. 466.

897 It must be referred that originally, Regulation W categorically exempted derivatives transactions from the ambit of Section 23A but not from Section 23B. After the enactment of the Dodd-Frank Act, Section 23A has been amended in order to include derivatives transactions.

898 See in R. Benjenk, 'Quixotic Regulation: Section 23A of the Federal Reserve Act and Containment of the Federal Safety Net Subsidy' (2012) 2 *Harvard Business Law Review*, p. 466.

and processes the most important are securitisation and derivatives. We will therefore examine them separately to better understand their functioning and economic importance.

Securitisation is a 'financial transaction in which (1) a special purpose entity issues securities to investors and, directly or indirectly, uses the proceeds to purchase rights to, or expectations of, payment, and (2) collections on the rights or expectations so purchased constitute the primary source of repayment of those securities'.[899] From the securitisation process are created the so-called Asset Backed Securities (ABS) of which a big subcategory are the Residential Mortgage Backed Securities (RMBS).[900] A central insight of the structured finance machine is that by pooling together a larger number of securities in the underlying pool of assets, a progressively larger fraction of the issued tranches can end up with higher credit ratings than the average rating of the underlying pool of assets.[901] The use of securitisation had two major benefits; a) it allowed banks to transfer illiquid assets (loans) out of their balance sheets and free more capital to provide loans and expand their balance sheets, and b) at the same time reduced capital requirements to minimum levels since these assets were transferred to off balance sheet special purpose entities. In the US, securitisation of home mortgages started in the late 1960s and early 1970s when the GSEs began to structure their RMBS as 'pass through' mortgage certificates granting to investors pro rata interests to the pooled mortgages.[902] To attract investors, First Boston and Salomon Brothers, created in the early 1980s, the so-called Collateralized Mortgage Obligations (CMOs)[903] that unlike

---

899 See in S.L. Schwarcz, 'What Is Securitization? And For What Purpose?' (2012) 85 *Southern California Law Review*, p. 1288. Professor Schwarcz further acknowledges that in order to avoid confusion between the special purpose entity (SPE) that is used in a securitization transaction and the investment company SPE to the definition above must be clarified that the securitization SPE does not speculate in the rights to, or expectations of, payment it purchases. Ibid., p. 1296.

900 Residential Mortgage-Backed Securities (RMBS) are a type of fixed-income investment that is backed by a pool of residential mortgage loans. These loans are typically sold by banks or other lenders to a trust, which then issues securities to investors. RMBS are often structured in 'tranches' with varying levels of risk and return. The cash flows (interest and principal payments) from the underlying mortgages are passed through to the investors in the form of periodic payments. We further distinguish between two types of RMBS: a) agency RMBS: Issued by government-sponsored entities and typically have an implied government guarantee, and b) non-agency (or private-label) RMBS: Issued by private institutions and carry more credit risk.

901 See in J.D. Coval, J. Jurek and E. Stafford, 'The Economics of Structured Finance', *Working Paper*, 09-060, Harvard Business School, 2009, p. 7.

902 See in A.E. Wilmarth Jr., 'The Road to Repeal of the Glass-Steagall Act' (2017) 17(4) *Wake Forest Journal of Business and Intellectual Property Law*, p. 465.

903 A collateralized mortgage obligation (CMO) is a type of mortgage-backed security that contains a pool of mortgages bundled together and sold as an investment. Organized by maturity and level of risk (tranches), CMOs receive cash flows as borrowers repay the underlying mortgages that act as collateral on these securities. In turn, CMOs distribute

the first pass through certificates were organised into multiple tranches offering investors differing rights and priorities for payments of income and principal from the pooled mortgages.[904] The new products attracted many investors and paved the way for the creation of similar securitised products based on ABS and RMBS in a business that generated huge profits for the participants.

Derivatives are financial contracts whose value is determined by reference to another, underlying asset, obligation, index or rate (the 'referenced factor').[905] Derivatives are used to hedge against various risk types or to speculate about future changes in the value of the underlying asset, obligation, rate, or index. Exchange traded derivatives are standardised contracts that are publicly traded on futures and options exchanges while the so called 'over the counter' (OTC) derivatives are customised contracts, tailor made to each clients' needs, that are privately negotiated between dealers (large financial institutions that are specialised in creating and promoting OTC derivatives) and end users (usually industrial and commercial firms and institutional investors).[906] The most widely used categories of OTC derivatives are:[907]

- A forward, where the buyer is obligated to purchase and the seller is required to deliver some type of commodity or other physical asset at a future date,
- A swap, where the parties agree to exchange streams of payments based on the future value of the referenced factor,
- An option, where the option seller gives the option buyer the right – but not the duty – to buy or sell the referenced factor at an agreed price on or before a specified future date.

In 1974, the US Congress created the Commodity Futures Trading Commission (CFTC) to oversee the exchange traded derivatives markets established pursuant to the Commodity Futures Trading Act of 1974 which substantially revised and expanded the Commodity Exchange Act (CEA) of 1936.[908] Markets of OTC interest rate and currency swaps grew rapidly in

---

principal and interest payments to their investors based on predetermined rules and agreements. CMOs consist of several tranches, or groups of mortgages, organized by their risk profiles. As complex financial instruments, tranches typically have different principal balances, interest rates, maturity dates, and potential of repayment defaults with each tranche having a different maturity date and size and bonds with monthly coupons are issued against it, with the coupon making monthly principal and interest rate payments. CMOs are sensitive to interest rate changes as well as to changes in economic conditions, such as foreclosure rates, refinance rates, and the rates at which properties are sold. Source: *Investopedia*, https://www.investopedia.com/terms/c/cmo.asp.

[904] See in A.E. Wilmarth, 'The Road to Repeal of the Glass-Steagall Act' (2017) 17(4) *Wake Forest Journal of Business and Intellectual Property Law*, p. 465.

[905] Ibid., p. 477.

[906] Ibid., p. 478.

[907] See in A.E. Wilmarth Jr., *Taming the Megabanks, Why We Need a New Glass-Steagall Act*, New York, Oxford University Press, 2020, p. 163 onwards.

[908] Commodity Futures Trading Commission Act of 1974, Pub. L. No. 93–463, 88 Stat. 1389.

the 1980s and the CFTC attempted to try to regulate such derivatives but according to Prof. Wilmarth, the major swap dealers threaten to move their business overseas forcing CFTC to back down and instead issue in 1989 a policy statement that would provide for a 'safe harbour' solution.[909] That 1989 policy statement declared that the agency would refrain from regulating the OTC swaps that were qualified for the safe harbour. For an OTC derivative to qualify for the safe harbour was required: a) to have individually tailored terms, b) could not be traded on or connected to a clearing organisation or a margin system, and c) could not be marketed to the general market.[910] In 1992, the US Congress through amendments in the CEA expressly authorised the CFTC to exempt certain types of OTC swaps from regulation under the CEA. In 1993, the CFTC responded to the CEA amendments by issuing a regulation replacing its 1989 policy statement.[911] The 1993 rule exempted OTC swaps from regulation under the CEA if the swaps: a) were not standardised as to their material economic terms, and b) if the parties were eligible swap participants.[912] The OCC, following an expansive interpretation of the legislation, allowed national banks to enter into the derivatives activities, in the 1980s and 1990s and since then constantly expanded the available derivatives types. The OCC argued that such products were comparable to the traditional powers of national banks and opened the floodgates for an industry that at its peak counted for several trillion of dollars.[913]

6 THE 2007–2009 GLOBAL FINANCIAL CRISIS AND THE RE-ENACTMENT OF STRUCTURAL REGULATION

The period known as the 'Great Moderation' came to an end when the decade-long expansion in the US housing market peaked in 2006 and residential construction began gradually to decline. In 2007, losses on mortgage-related financial assets began to cause strains in global financial markets, and by December 2007, the US economy had entered a recession. That year several large financial firms experienced serious financial distress, and many financial markets experienced significant turbulence. When the financial market turmoil had subsided, attention naturally turned to reforms to the financial sector and its supervision and regulation, motivated by a desire to avoid similar events

909 See in A.E. Wilmarth Jr., 'The Road to Repeal of the Glass-Steagall Act' (2017) 17(4) *Wake Forest Journal of Business and Intellectual Property Law*, p. 479.

910 Ibid.

911 Ibid.

912 Eligible swap participants included regulated financial institutions, qualified business firms, state and local governments, institutional investors, and wealthy individuals.

913 See in A.E. Wilmarth Jr., *Taming the Megabanks, Why We Need a New Glass-Steagall Act*, New York, Oxford University Press, 2020, p. 164.

in the future. Several measures have been proposed or put in place to reduce the risk of financial distress. The Dodd-Frank Act also created new provisions for the prudential treatment of large financial institutions. Among the various measures adopted in the aftermath of the crisis, the present book tries to delve into the structural reforms' measures and in the case of US the Volcker Rule, which erects a wall and bans certain activities for the banks that are FDIC insured. Nevertheless, to assess the importance and the effectiveness of the Volcker Rule we must first understand how and why it was legislated and why the recent GFC is of particular importance for its understanding.

6.1. The 2007–2009 Global Financial Crisis

The global financial crisis that lasted from 2007 until 2009 was a marking point in the US financial history since its aftermath was a cataclysmic regulatory overhaul, not only domestically but also globally. The literature regarding the origins and the events of the recent GFC is vastly rich. While such a thorough presentation of the origins of the crisis is not within the present book's scope, for reasons of coherence we will try to briefly present the origins and the major events, since they are necessary to understand the impact on the reforms adopted on the aftermath and associate them with the (bank) failures that happened during the climax of the crisis.

6.1.1 Origins and Major Events

Certain academics, support the view that the recent GFC had similarities with the 1997–1998 Asian financial crisis, since both could be attributed, partly, to 'improperly designed regulatory systems supporting overinvestment in real estate'.[914] Moreover, they support that 'such overinvestment [...] provided the initial trigger in both cases'[915] and categorise the origins of the 2007–2009 crisis in five principal causes:[916]

---

914 See in R.P. Buckley, E. Avgouleas and D.W. Arner, 'Three Decades of International Financial Crisis, What Have We Learned and What Still Needs to Be Done?', *ADB Economics Working Paper Series*, No. 615, Asian Development Bank, June 2020, p. 10.

915 The same theory regarding the origins of the 2007–2009 global financial crisis and the nexus with the governmental policies that favoured the crisis is supported by various other authors. See indicatively in J. Norberg, *Financial Fiasco, How America's Infatuation with Homeownership and Easy Money Created the Economic Crisis*, Washington, Cato Institute, 2009; R.G. Rajan, *Fault Lines: How Hidden Fractures Still Threaten the World Economy*, Princeton, Princeton University Press, 2011; and in R. Posner, *The Crisis of Capitalist Democracy*, Cambridge, Harvard University Press, 2010.

916 See in R.P. Buckley, E. Avgouleas and D.W. Arner, 'Three Decades of International Financial Crisis, What Have We Learned and What Still Needs to Be Done?', *ADB Economics Working Paper Series*, No. 615, Asian Development Bank, June 2020, p. 10.

(a) Excessive leverage of the financial system fuelled by the lax monetary policies by the central banks,
(b) Risk underpricing by poorly functioning credit markets,
(c) A disconnect between regulatory structures and the financial systems,
(d) Misaligned incentives, and
(e) Increased interconnection that facilitated the global transmission of systemic risk.

From 2000 until 2007, there was an environment of low interest rates, very easily available capital and lax regulatory framework and oversight that pushed lending and borrowing to new levels of excess, notably in the US, UK, and certain Eurozone Member States. High leverage can be per se a destabilising factor for financial systems.[917] Excessive borrowing and lending were concentrated particularly in the real estate markets and even borrowers of lower quality had ample access to credit that fuelled a bubble in the US housing market. The perception that credit risk could be hedged at a portfolio level with the use of complex credit default swaps and the perceived benefits from securitisation further eroded lending standards and siphoned billions into low quality borrowers.[918] In the US, the two Government Sponsored Enterprises (GSEs), Fannie Mae and Freddie Mac, were securing the loans by guaranteeing their repayment under the assumption that they were quasi-governmental entities and therefore the US government would assist in any adverse scenario. When low quality borrowers started defaulting *en masse* these two GSEs were unable to honour their guarantees and faced bankruptcy, posing systemic risks due to their central role in the financial process of loans securitisation.[919] Apart from real estate lending, investors pursued higher yields with little consideration of risk and advisors and arrangers were more than willing to provide them with such products. Debt securities manufactured by the securitisation process were packaged together and resold to financial institutions and to other investors around the world spreading the risk of default across the globe. When the market for these products froze, the systemic repercussions reached every place of the world.[920]

The malfunctions of the credit markets during the financial crisis have been characterised by a run on the short-term funding markets (repo markets) that banks were extensively relying on to fund their day-to-day activities.[921] The resulting liquidity crunch did not allow the rollover of large volumes of short-term funding debts and sent shockwaves across the entire financial system

---

917 Ibid.
918 Ibid., p. 11.
919 Ibid.
920 Ibid.
921 Ibid. See also in G. Gorton and A. Metrick, 'Securitized banking and the run on repo' (2012) 104(3) *Journal of Financial Economics*, p. 425 onwards.

since investors were unwilling to assume default risks. Another manifestation of the malfunctioning was the market for ABSs where risk was underpriced, and underwriting standards had been compromised. Derivatives played also an important role because they were critical in supporting the securitisation structure since they were used to hedge or insure the credit risks associated with these transactions. Their use was amplified by the regulatory framework of Basel II that allowed the use of credit derivatives to mitigate the risks, resulting in a heightened counterparty risk among financial institutions.[922] The derivatives market lacked transparency, and this defect did not allow regulators to understand the level of exposure of institutions such as AIG and Bear Stearns. Finally, credit ratings agencies played an extremely important role since their ratings were adopted by investors and institutions as authoritative. The credit rating agencies supported the securitisation process by rating the securities produced based on conflicting interests since the issuer paid for the rating and therefore had incentives to secure a good rating. This 'ratings' shopping' resulted in biased ratings inaccurately reflecting the associated risks.[923]

The disconnection between regulatory structures and the financial system is evident from the regulatory gaps that were identified on the crisis aftermath. These gaps allowed for regulatory arbitrage on behalf of institutions that were looking to avoid burdensome regulatory requirements and adopted cherry picking practices. Moreover, financial regulatory structures did not reflect the structure of the financial system and the most evident example was the macro-prudential framework that failed to adequately capture the associated risks.[924] Before the crisis, the focus was on the micro-prudential level to ensure that financial institutions were safe, and sound and the framework neglected the systemic (macro-prudential) risk in both its dimensions: time dimension and cross-sectoral dimension. Furthermore, demarcations between financial services and products were extremely blurred and the previously segregated business models, especially in the US, among the financial institutions were non-existent allowing for the creation of entities that were actual financial supermarkets with flawed risk management practices and structures.[925] The TBTF doctrine was reinforced, and governments had to intervene and bail out the systemically important financial institutions. Ultimately, the pro-cyclical nature of regulation, such as the mark to market accounting principle and the

---

922 See in R.P. Buckley, E. Avgouleas and D.W. Arner, 'Three Decades of International Financial Crisis, What Have We Learned and What Still Needs to Be Done?', *ADB Economics Working Paper Series*, No. 615, Asian Development Bank, June 2020, p. 12.

923 Ibid.

924 Ibid.

925 Ibid., p. 13.

Basel II framework further amplified these structural weaknesses and required even more capital at a time when it was non-existent.[926]

Systemic risk was globally transmitted through the counterparty risk; the failures of AIG and Lehman Brothers in a time when market participants had already lost their confidence to each other, further spread anxiety and panic. These events, together with the absence on behalf of the government of a credible contingency plan, threatened a complete breakdown of the global financial system.[927] The proper reaction to such 'black swans' should have been an international coordination to extinguish the fires and calm the markets. Instead of such approaches, governments adopted domestically oriented solutions without considering the broader repercussions. Furthermore, this situation was amplified by the fact that international bodies setting soft law standards, lacked any authority to supervise the implementation of these initiatives and the cross-border cooperation systems were non-existent. The failure of large, complex, systemically important financial institutions stretched governmental systems to their limits since other modalities to deal with such failures were also non-existent.[928] Lastly, the focus on traditional micro-prudential regulation, with individual institutions' health as a primary concern, forced the regulators to lose sight on the markets and their funding role, leading to a liquidity crunch, and widespread anxiety regarding who has been more heavily infected by the toxic products. As market participants had begun to scrutinise each other's health in order to trust them and extend borrowing, the problems were revealed, and those institutions exposed the most had to face the consequences.

In June 2006, the US housing market prices reached their peak and started to decline. During the first semester of 2007, credit rating agencies started to massively downgrade the ratings of Mortgage Backed Securities (MBSs)[929] and on 27 February 2007, Freddie Mac announced that it would no longer buy the riskiest subprime mortgages and mortgage related securities.[930] Few months later, on 2 April 2007, New Century Financial Corporation, the second largest subprime mortgage lender, filed for Chapter 11 bankruptcy protection; on 7 June 2007, Bear Stearns, a top tier investment bank, informed

926 Ibid.

927 Ibid.

928 Ibid., p. 14.

929 A Mortgage-Backed Security (MBS) is a type of asset-backed security that is created by pooling together a collection of home loans (mortgages) and selling the resulting cash flows (from borrowers' mortgage payments) to investors. In essence, MBS allow investors to receive monthly payments derived from the principal and interest payments made by homeowners. There are two types of MBSs: a) Pass-Through Securities: Directly pass on mortgage payments to investors (most common) and b) Collateralized Mortgage Obligations (CMOs): Structured MBS divided into tranches with different risk/return profiles.

930 See in R.Z. Wiggins, T. Piontek and A. Metrick, 'The Lehman Brothers Bankruptcy A: Overview' (2019) 1(1) *Journal of Financial Crises*, p. 58.

investors that it suspended redemption from its High-Grade Structured Credit Enhanced Leveraged Fund, which had been heavily exposed in the subprime MBSs. Through the entire August of 2007, various problems impaired the performance of the interbank market with raises in collaterals' haircuts and problems on the rollover of ABCPs debts.[931] On 9 August 2007, the French bank BNP Paribas halted redemptions on three of its investment funds and the next day, 10 August, the Fed added $38 billion in reserves to enhance liquidity in the system. On 17 August 2007, a run on Countrywide Financial occurred, after Fitch Ratings downgraded their rating the previous day. Countrywide was the largest subprime lender in the US and many depositors sought to withdraw their bank accounts. On 15 December 2007, Citibank announced that it would take its seven structured investment vehicles onto its balance sheet, in a value totalling $49 billion.[932]

On 11 January 2008, Bank of America (BofA) announced that it would purchase Countrywide Financial in an all-stock transaction valued at $4 billion and two months later, on 16 March 2008, in a turbulent weekend, JPMorgan Chase (JPMC) announced that it would acquire Bear Stearns for $2 per share (less than 7% of its market value just two days before) with the NY Fed providing financial assistance of up to $30 billion.[933] On 13 July 2008, the Fed Board authorised the NY Fed to expand financial assistance to both Fannie Mae and Freddie Mac, if necessary. On 30 July 2008, the US Congress enacted the Housing and Economic Recovery Act (HERA) of 2008,[934] to address the subprime mortgage crisis. The Act established the Federal Housing Finance Agency (FHFA) and intended to restore the two GSEs but ultimately led them to conservatorship on 7 September 2008.[935] In the weekend of 12–14 September 2008, the CEOs of biggest Wall Street investment banks met at the NY Fed's premises in order to reach a solution to save Lehman Brothers, which was already under heavy fire. Despite their interest, Barclays and BofA failed to close a deal and the next day, 15 September 2008, Lehman Brothers filed for Chapter 11 bankruptcy protection.[936] The same day, BofA announced that it would acquire the problematic Merrill Lynch for $38.25 billion in stock. A group of banks, with Citigroup and JPMC included, set up a $70 billion fund to increase liquidity in the system. That day Dow Jones fell at 504.49 points (4.4%) its worst percentage decline since the 9/11 terrorist attacks in the US.[937] The next day, 16 September 2008, the Fed bailed out AIG, the largest US insurance

931 Ibid.

932 Ibid., p. 59.

933 Ibid.

934 Housing and Economic Recovery Act of 2008, Pub. L. No. 110-289, 122 Stat. 2654 (2008).

935 See in R.Z. Wiggins, T. Piontek and A. Metrick, 'The Lehman Brothers Bankruptcy A: Overview' (2019) 1(1) *Journal of Financial Crises*, p. 60.

936 Ibid.

937 Ibid.

company, in exchange for 79.9% of its shares and the Reserve Primary Fund, a money market mutual fund (MMMF) 'broke the buck' triggering a run on the MMMFs, forcing the Fed to intervene.[938] On 17 September 2008, Dow Jones further fall to 449.36 points and the SEC announced a temporary emergency ban on short selling in the stocks of all companies in the financial sector. The next day, 18 September 2008, the Fed coordinated with other central banks of the world to inject a total of $184 billion into the banking system to propel lending.[939] On 19 September the US Treasury announced a temporary guarantee of MMMFs, and the Fed activated a special facility to provide liquidity in the MMMFs sector. On 25 September 2008, the OTS seized Washington Mutual Bank (WaMu), the largest savings and loan in the US, from its parent company, Washington Mutual Inc., and placed it into receivership with the FDIC.[940] Few days later, the Fed announced assistance for the merger between Wells Fargo and Wachovia, back then the 4th largest bank in the US. On 3 October 2008, the US Congress approved the TARP which authorised expenditures of $700 billion while, on 14 October, the Treasury invested more than $250 billion in nine major banks.[941] Finally, on 23 November 2008, the Fed, the Treasury, and the FDIC agreed to provide Citigroup a package of guarantees, capital, and liquidity access.[942] In the first days of 2009, a similar to Citigroup's agreement came into force, in favour of BofA, totalling $118 billion.[943] In mid-February 2009, President Obama signed

---

938 Ibid.

939 Ibid., p. 61.

940 Ibid.

941 Ibid., p. 62.

942 See in J. Rhee and A. Metrick, 'Guarantees and Capital Infusions in Response to Financial Crises B: U.S. Guarantees During the Global Financial Crisis' (2020) 2(1) *Yale Journal of Financial Crises*, p. 59 onwards. Citigroup was experiencing growing losses in 2008, including on its mortgage-related assets portfolio. According to the agreement of 23 November 2008, the Treasury, the Fed, and the FDIC jointly announced that the US government would provide support to Citigroup. The Treasury and the FDIC provided protection against the possibility of unusually large losses on an asset pool of approximately $300 billion of loans and securities backed by residential and commercial real estate and other similar assets, which remained on Citigroup's balance sheet. As a fee for this arrangement, Citigroup issued preferred shares to the Treasury and FDIC. The New York Fed agreed to provide a backstop commitment to absorb residual risk in the asset pool through a non-recourse loan. In addition, the Treasury invested $20 billion in Citigroup from the TARP funds in exchange for preferred stock with an 8% dividend to the Treasury. In December 2009, the Treasury, the Fed, and the FDIC agreed to terminate the Master Agreement dated 15 January 2009, with Citigroup and in return for the termination of the agreement, Citigroup agreed to pay the New York Fed $50 million.

943 When BofA acquired Merrill Lynch in late 2008, it also assumed a large portfolio of mortgage-related assets, hold by the later. On 16 January 2009, the Treasury, the Fed, and the FDIC jointly announced that the US government would provide support to BofA, through an asset protection arrangement. Protection would have been provided against a pool of approximately $118 billion in assets, the large majority of which were inherited from the Merrill Lynch acquisition, on terms analogous to those previously extended to Citigroup,

into law the American Recovery and Reinvestment Act of 2009, including a variety of measures and tax cuts to increase spending and promote economic recovery. In May 2009, the Treasury announced the results of the Supervisory Capital Assessment Program (SCAP), the banking sector's stress test, where many banks are required to increase their capital, and in October 2009, the US unemployment rate peaked at 10%.[944]

6.1.2 Bank and Non-Bank Failures

The US financial market is the biggest of its kind in the world. The crisis hit financial markets as a whole and many firms, banks, and non-banks, that participated through various ways in the financial markets suffered or even failed. In the framework of the present book, we will examine specific examples of financial firms, both banks and non-banks, that had severe problems from the financial crisis due to the fact that there were important market participants (Bear Stearns and AIG), their failure was completely unexpected (Lehman Brothers), or they were side but serious effects of the generalised crisis (such as the US automobile industry).

6.1.2.1 *The Fannie Mae-Freddie Mac saga*

On 11 July 2008, the New York Times reported that amid the ongoing financial crisis and the plunge in home prices, the US government was planning to take over Fannie Mae and Freddie Mac.[945] These two firms were buying and guaranteeing residential mortgages, and after the freezing of the private label RMBS market in mid-2007 were the largest and most important sources of funding for new mortgages.[946] Their role was to buy and guarantee mortgages, converting them into securities that were distributed to the public. For their role, they were expected to make money, and they did it successfully until the crisis arrived, but they were also perceived to promote public interest, that of facilitating mortgage lending in the US.[947] For this reason, they were

---

and an investment by the TARP would have provided support to BofA. However, the full arrangement was never implemented, because on 7 May 2009, following the release of the results of the banks' stress test, BofA announced that it did not plan to move forward with the announced arrangement. In September 2009, BofA paid an exit fee of $425 million to the Treasury, the FDIC, and the Federal Reserve to terminate the arrangement.

944 See in R.Z. Wiggins, T. Piontek and A. Metrick, 'The Lehman Brothers Bankruptcy A: Overview' (2019) 1(1) *Journal of Financial Crises*, p. 62.

945 See in The New York Times, *Loan-Agency Woes Swell From a Trickle to a Torrent*, 2008, available at: https://www.nytimes.com/2008/07/11/business/11ripple.html?ex=1373515200&en=8ad220403fcfdf6e&ei=5124 &partner=permalink&exprod=permalink.

946 See in A.E. Wilmarth Jr., *Taming the Megabanks, Why We Need a New Glass-Steagall Act*, New York, Oxford University Press, 2020, p. 272.

947 See in E.A. Posner, *Last Resort, The Financial Crisis and the Future of Bailouts*, Chicago, The University of Chicago Press, 2018, p. 103.

securitising the mortgages and financed them through the bonds they were issuing to the public massively.

Fannie Mae traces her roots in the Great Depression era and to the unstable housing market that the financial crisis had created. In 1938, the US Congress established the Federal National Mortgage Association (FNMA or better known as Fannie Mae), through amendments in the National Housing Act of 1934,[948] as part of the so-called 'New Deal'. Fannie Mae's purpose was to buy the mortgages from the original lenders, thereby freeing capital that would be reallocated in new loans; therefore, it was established as a governmental agency funded entirely by the federal budget.[949] Originally chartered as the 'National Mortgage Association of Washington', the organisation's explicit purpose was to provide local banks with federal money to finance home loans in an attempt to raise levels of home ownership and the availability of affordable housing. Fannie Mae succeeded in creating a liquid secondary mortgage market and thereby made it possible for banks and other loan originators to issue more housing loans, primarily by buying mortgages insured by the Federal Housing Administration (FHA) and for the first thirty years following its inception, it held a monopoly over the secondary mortgage market. In 1968, Fannie Mae was privatised, in order to disconnect her activities and funding from the federal budget amid the Vietnam War increased spending, and split her in the current, privatised company, and the Government National Mortgage Association (GNMA or better known as Ginnie Mae).[950] Fannie Mae was therefore a semi private company with shareholders and private creditors but still carrying on a quasi-governmental role.[951] In 1970, the federal government authorised Fannie Mae to also purchase conventional loans (i.e. loans which were not insured by the FHA, VA, or FmHA), and created the Federal Home Loan Mortgage Corporation (FHLMC or better known as Freddie Mac), to compete with Fannie Mae and thus facilitate a more robust, competitive and efficient secondary mortgage market.[952] Both firms were widely believed to be backed by the implicit subsidy of the US government guarantee due to their special role in promoting the housing market, and the American dream of homeownership. They were privately owned, Government Sponsored

---

948 National Housing Act of 1934, Pub. L. No. 73-479, 48 Stat. 1246 (codified as amended at 12 U.S.C. §§ 1701–1750g).

949 See in E.A. Posner, *Last Resort, The Financial Crisis and the Future of Bailouts*, Chicago, The University of Chicago Press, 2018, p. 103.

950 Ginnie Mae remained a government organization and guarantees FHA-insured mortgage loans as well as 'Veterans Administration' (VA) and 'Farmers Home Administration' (FmHA) insured mortgages. As such, Ginnie Mae is the only home-loan agency explicitly backed by the full faith and credit of the US government.

951 See in E.A. Posner, *Last Resort, The Financial Crisis and the Future of Bailouts*, Chicago, The University of Chicago Press, 2018, p. 105.

952 Ibid.

Enterprises (GSEs), promoting special interests of the US government and the main reasons behind this belief were the historical association with the government and the fact that these two firms were federally regulated.[953]

In August 2007, Fannie Mae requested its regulator, the Office of Federal Housing Enterprise Oversight (OFHEO) for relief in the regulatory cap that limited the aggregate size of Fannie's mortgage portfolio. Fannie Mae wanted to buy and/or guarantee a larger volume of mortgages, thereby increasing its profits. Initially, the OFHEO was reluctant to allow the cap removal, especially amid a downturn in the housing market since prices were falling, but the Treasury supported the proposed removal because the GSEs were the only players on a market that was showing signs of collapse and the housing market should be supported in order for the mortgage owners to be able to smoothly refinance their loans.[954] In September 2007 the OFHEO removed the caps and allowed both GSEs to expand their portfolios.[955] Due to reported losses of $9 billion for both firms, their capital had fallen below 2% of their total assets and guarantees as of end 2007.

In early 2008, both the Treasury and the Congress continued to encourage both GSEs to provide support in the secondary mortgage market and despite the market's condition and the severity of the two firms' undercapitalisation instructed the OFHEO to further remove the regulatory caps. In March 2008, both firms raised $14 billion of new capital as requested by the Treasury.[956] Overall, the two GSEs had expanded their portfolio by more than $600 billion(!) between June 2007 and June 2008, rising their combined mortgage assets and guarantees to the astronomic amount of $5.5 trillion by mid-2008.[957] For the first half of 2008, they both reported losses of $14 billion and their capital levels fall below 1% of their total risk exposures. In early July 2008, their stock prices had plummeted and few days later, Secretary Paulson announced a plan aimed at strengthening the two firms by: a) increasing their lines of credit the Treasury, b) granting Treasury unlimited authority to invest in their stock, and

953 Ibid.

954 See in A.E. Wilmarth Jr., *Taming the Megabanks, Why We Need a New Glass-Steagall Act*, New York, Oxford University Press, 2020, p. 272.

955 During the fourth quarter of 2007, after the regulatory cap relief, both Fannie Mae and Freddie Mac purchased 76% of all newly originated home mortgages, increasing their numbers by 46% compared to 2006.

956 See in A.E. Wilmarth Jr., *Taming the Megabanks, Why We Need a New Glass-Steagall Act*, New York, Oxford University Press, 2020, p. 273. In January 2008, the Treasury had raised the maximum conforming limit for both Fannie Mae and Freddie Mac mortgages from $470,000 to $730,000 and to Treasury's instructions; the OFHEO removed the remaining regulatory caps reducing also at the same time their capital surcharges in exchange for their pledges to raise more capital.

957 See in A.E. Wilmarth Jr., *Taming the Megabanks, Why We Need a New Glass-Steagall Act*, New York, Oxford University Press, 2020, p. 273.

c) establishing a new regulator, the Federal Housing Finance Agency (FHFA).[958] The new agency had stronger powers including the right to place both firms in conservatorships or receiverships and the new plan was adopted through HERA. After close examination of both firms, the OCC and the Fed concluded in early August, that they were insolvent and on 26 August 2008, President Bush Jr. gave his approval to put them in conservatorship – meaning that the FHFA would operate the two firms. On 7 September 2008, the Treasury and the FHFA announced conservatorships for both GSEs.[959] Under the deal's terms, Treasury agreed to recapitalise each entity by purchasing up to $100 billion of its preferred stock (a limit later increased to $200 billion) to cover their losses between 2008–2011. Treasury also received warrants to purchase up to 80% of the common stock of both firms as the existing shareholders of common and preferred stocks were largely wiped out.[960] On 25 November 2008, the Fed provided extra support to both firms by announcing that it would buy up to $100 billion of their debt and up to $500 billion of their RMBS.

Critics of the two GSEs bailouts claim that the emergency of the bailouts caused many investors to have second thoughts about the overall situation in the mortgage related asset market. These thoughts were translated in the conclusion that the market values were not accurate and therefore prices would continue to fall leaving 'naked' the firms that were heavily exposed to those products.[961] Many litigation cases arose from the bail out agreements for both firms, since the Treasury imposed strict terms that initially were not able to achieve by the two struggling entities. As of January 2017, the Treasury had received payments worth $247 billion, exceeding the original invested amount by almost $70 billion.[962]

6.1.2.2 *The Case of Bear Stearns*

Bear Stearns was part of the 'Big Five', the five biggest investment banks in the US.[963] On 11 March 2008, the Fed announced that TSLF would begin lending Treasury securities to primary dealers on 27 March. It was a promise to lend up to $200 billion in Treasury bonds to investment banks for 28 days. In return, the Treasury would get securities backed by home mortgages with uncertain values and other hard-to-trade collateral. Unfortunately, this announcement

---

[958] Ibid.

[959] Ibid., p. 274.

[960] Ibid.

[961] Ibid. See also in E.A. Posner, *Last Resort, The Financial Crisis and the Future of Bailouts*, Chicago, The University of Chicago Press, 2018, p. 107.

[962] See in E.A. Posner, *Last Resort, The Financial Crisis and the Future of Bailouts*, Chicago, The University of Chicago Press, 2018, p. 111.

[963] The 'Big Five' US investment banks were Morgan Stanley, Merrill Lynch, Goldman Sachs, Lehman Brothers and Bear Stearns.

came too late for Bear Stearns. On 12 March, Bear Stearns' lawyers informed the then President of the NY Fed, Timothy Geithner, that the bank's situation was critical since hedge funds were pulling their funds out of the firm and repo lenders were not accepting anymore to roll over their loans.[964] At the same time, bank's liquidity reserves were plunged from $18 billion on Monday, 10 March to just $2 billion at the close of business on Thursday, 13 March. On Thursday evening, after customers had continued to pull their money out of Bear Stearns, the bank reached out to JPMC, looking to discuss ways the Wall Street giant could help ease Bear's cash crunch.[965] Bear Stearns's hope was that the Fed would make a loan from its discount window to provide several weeks of breathing room. That, the firm hoped, would perhaps halt a run on the bank but the Fed's preference was to first seek a private-sector solution, such as a sale or financing agreement. At 7:30 a.m., Bear Stearns would have to begin paying back some of its billions of dollars in repo borrowings. If the firm did not repay the money on time, its creditors could start selling the collateral Bear Stearns had pledged to them. Those sales might have turned into fire sales, and the implications went well beyond Bear Stearns: If other investors questioned the safety of loans they made in the repo market, they could start to withhold funds from other investment banks and companies as well.[966]

The situation continued to be critical; on Friday morning, at 5 a.m., Mr Geithner, Mr Paulson, and Ben Bernanke, Chairman of the Fed, joined a conference call to debate whether Bear Stearns should be allowed to fail or whether the Fed should lend enough money to the investment bank in order to get through the weekend. At 7 a.m., they compromised on the lifeline option. Mr Bernanke then assembled the Fed's other three available governors to vote for the loan, the first time since the Great Depression the Fed would use its extraordinary authority to lend to non-banks. The Fed decided to make an emergency loan of $12,9 billion to JPMC, the clearing bank for Bear's triparty repos, invoking Section 13(3) powers in order to avoid a filing for bankruptcy from Bear Stearns, a move that might trigger enormous turmoil in the repo market.[967] JPMC transferred the funds to Bear to keep it operating on Friday, 14 March.[968] The Fed announced that according to the plan it would lend Bear

964 See in A.E. Wilmarth Jr., *Taming the Megabanks, Why We Need a New Glass-Steagall Act*, New York, Oxford University Press, 2020, p. 266.

965 Ibid.

966 Ibid., p. 268.

967 According to their testimony before the US Congress and their memoirs, Bernanke, Paulson, and Geithner took the view that leaving Bear Stearns to file for bankruptcy was a very dangerous option due to the bank's interconnections with other counterparties. Bear Stearns had 750,000 derivatives contracts and other trading positions with more than 5,000 counterparties around the world and more than $100 billion of outstanding repo loans.

968 See in A.E. Wilmarth Jr., *Taming the Megabanks, Why We Need a New Glass-Steagall Act*, New York, Oxford University Press, 2020, p. 267.

money, through JPMC, for up to 28 days to relief the venerable investment bank from its cash crunch. However, the markets did not take well to the news that a major investment bank was on the brink of failure and stocks sank even more. Other investment banks were seeing lenders turn cautious. Fed officials began planning a more direct response: opening the discount window to all investment banks, a request the Fed had resisted for months. During the weekend of 15–16 March, the Fed approved a rescue plan that supported the acquisition of Bear Stearns from JPMC at a highly discounted price, through the creation of an off-balance sheet entity named 'Maiden Lane'.[969] According to the plan, the Fed provided a $29 billion loan to that entity under Section 13(3) powers while JPMC made a $1 billion loan accepting a 'first loss' position on that loan. With a total amount of $30 billion, Maiden Lane acquired the most toxic assets from Bear's balance sheet up to that amount. Based on the structure of Maiden Lane, the Fed would be exposed to losses if the entity failed to recover at least the original amount of $29 billion.[970] On 16 March, the Fed approved the salvation scheme and Bear Stearns was the first investment bank that collapsed, astonishing the Fed and other officials.

6.1.2.3 *The Case of Lehman Brothers*

The collapse of Lehman Brothers was an event of global importance for the evolution of the global financial crisis. Although Lehman was not a traditional bank, since it did not accept deposits, the repercussions from its demise had consequences that nobody expected. Lehman was a traditional investment bank; on the deregulation's aftermath had expanded its activities and became the 4th largest US investment bank with global presence and a high degree of interconnection. Despite being 'too-big-to-fail', the US federal government decided not to employ extraordinary measures to save the firm, in a case similar of Bear Stearns.[971] Lehman Brothers failed because of its exposure to the US subprime mortgage market and to the real estate market, because of its excessive leverage, risk taking and short term funding reliance, regulatory gaps in the regulatory and supervisory framework and because of the complexity of the financial products, its corporate structure and lastly because of the perceived opinion that the firm would not pose a systemic threat.[972] When Lehman Brothers filed for Chapter 11 bankruptcy protection on 15 September 2008, it initiated the largest bankruptcy procedure in the US history, with assets of $639 billion and debts of $613 billion.

---

969 Ibid.

970 Ibid.

971 See in R.Z. Wiggins, T. Piontek and A. Metrick, 'The Lehman Brothers Bankruptcy A: Overview' (2019) 1(1) *Journal of Financial Crises*, p. 40.

972 Ibid.

Lehman Brothers was founded in 1844 in Montgomery, Alabama, as a small dry goods shop selling groceries and tools to local farmers.[973] Since the farmers were paying their bills also in cotton, the three Lehman Brothers decided to expand their operations in trading cotton and in 1858, they established an office in New York and were instrumental in founding the New York Cotton Exchange, in 1870, commodifying the crop. The firm also dealt in the emerging market for railroad bonds and entered the financial-advisory business, while Lehman became a member of the Coffee Exchange as early as 1883 and finally of the New York Stock Exchange in 1887. In 1899, it underwrote its first public offering, the preferred and common stock of the International Steam Pump Company. In the early 1900s, the firm developed its banking practice by intermediating funding for the emerging group of retail, industrial and transportation firms that were founded during that period.[974] Robert Lehman, a grandson of Emanuel Lehman, took over and led the firm from 1925 until his death in 1969, establishing the firm as a well-known investment bank working with leading international and US firms in underwriting securities, providing financial advice, and helping in mergers and acquisitions. After Robert Lehman's death, the firm entered a period of strong headwinds amidst the difficult economic environment of early 1970s and the partners decided to hire Pete Peterson, chairman and chief executive officer of the Bell & Howell Corporation, to save the firm.[975] During the recession in early 1980s, internal conflicts arose between the investment bankers and the traders of the firm, with the later requiring bigger part of the profits. Peterson appointed in 1983, as co-CEO of the firm, Lewis Glucksman, a former trader who managed to seize control within a year and forced Peterson to retire. Ultimately, Glucksman did not succeed in healing the internal wounds among the partners and amid weakened profits the firm was sold to American Express (AmEx) in 1984, which merged the firm with its Shearson financial subsidiary to form Shearson Lehman Brothers.[976] Finally, just after ten years, AmEx decided to focus on its

---

973 In 1844, 23-year-old Henry Lehman, the son of Jewish cattle merchant, immigrated to the US from Rimpar, Bavaria, and he settled in Montgomery, Alabama, where he opened a dry-goods store, 'H. Lehman'. In 1847, following the arrival of his brother Emanuel Lehman, the firm became 'H. Lehman and Bro.' while with the arrival of their youngest brother, Mayer Lehman, in 1850, the firm changed its name again and 'Lehman Brothers' was founded.

974 See in R.Z. Wiggins, T. Piontek and A. Metrick, 'The Lehman Brothers Bankruptcy A: Overview' (2019 1(1) *Journal of Financial Crises*, p. 41.

975 Under Peterson's leadership as chairman and CEO, the firm expanded and acquired *Abraham & Co.* in 1975, and two years later, in 1977, merged with *Kuhn, Loeb & Co.*, to form *Lehman Brothers, Kuhn, Loeb Inc.*, the country's 4th largest investment bank, behind *Salomon Brothers*, *Goldman Sachs*, and *First Boston*. Peterson successfully led the firm from significant operating losses to five consecutive years of record profits with a return on equity among the highest in the investment-banking industry.

976 See in R.Z. Wiggins, T. Piontek and A. Metrick, 'The Lehman Brothers Bankruptcy A: Overview' (2019) 1(1) *Journal of Financial Crises*, p. 42.

core business, personal finance and travel, spun off and sell Lehman Brothers in an initial public offering which capitalised the firm at $3.3 billion, with Richard Fuld becoming Lehman's new Chairman and CEO. Under Fuld's management, Lehman expanded again into new services, including riskier and more complex financial products that were being developed during the 2000s in the aftermath of the industry's deregulation,[977] and aggressively pursued proprietary trading,[978] derivatives, securitisation, asset management and real estate opportunities.

By 2006, Lehman was operating along three main segments: a) capital markets, b) investment banking, and c) investment management providing the full spectrum of relevant services in equity and fixed income sales, trading and research, investment banking services, asset management, private investment management, and private equity.[979] Lehman had established a worldwide presence with its headquarters in New York and regional headquarters in London and Tokyo and was regulated mainly by the SEC and the British Financial Services Authority (FSA). In March 2006, Lehman announced a new business strategy aimed at capitalising its existing significant experience in real estate.[980] The firm started buying aggressively real estate-related assets throughout 2006 and by mid-2007 held significant positions in commercial real estate. In August 2007, Lehman announced that it would close its main subprime loans origination platform and its Korean mortgage business and suspended its wholesale and correspondent lending activities at its subsidiary, Aurora Loan Services. Nevertheless, in October 2007, it acquired Archstone Real Estate Investment Trust in a deal that raised eyebrows since investors and rating agencies believed that Lehman had overpaid to buy Archstone.[981] By the end of 2007, Lehman held $111 billion in commercial or residential real estate related assets and securities, more than double than it held a year ago (end of 2006) and more than 4 times its equity. The constant revaluation of these types of assets from Lehman, throughout 2008, would ultimately lead to its demise. In November 2007, Lehman reported a leverage ratio of 30.7% which allowed the firm to pursue growth, increased profits but kept capital at limited levels. Since Lehman was highly leveraged two choices were available to reduce its leverage ratio: a) sell assets, and b) increase equity. Lehman choose to sell assets even though in early 2008 raised $6 billion.[982] In January 2008, Lehman started to deleverage its balance sheet from real estate positions. For some

977 Ibid.

978 By 2006, Lehman's proprietary trading activities comprised 21% of the firm's revenue, when in 2000 the percentage stood at 14%.

979 See in R.Z. Wiggins, T. Piontek and A. Metrick, 'The Lehman Brothers Bankruptcy A: Overview' (2019) 1(1) *Journal of Financial Crises*, p. 43.

980 Ibid., p. 44.

981 Ibid.

982 Ibid., p. 45.

commentators, this strategy proved to be challenging because Lehman was unsuccessful at selling these assets at acceptable prices amid a general slowing of the relevant market. Moreover, Lehman was reluctant to sell these assets at discounted prices because doing so would risk taking losses on the assets sold and would also call into question the value of the similar type of remaining assets, forcing Lehman to mark them to market value, potentially recognising even more losses.[983] As solutions were hard to materialise, Lehman decided to buy time. It exceeded its internal risk limits and manipulated its liquidity pool, by including encumbered assets, and its internal stress tests, by not including certain risky assets, to appear in a better financial situation. Most importantly, Lehman used a lot of a particular type of repo transactions, 'Repo 105',[984] to manage its balance sheet and net leverage ratio.

By 2008, Lehman was part of the 'Big Five' US investment banks.[985] After the demise of Bear Stearns, Lehman began looking around for a long-term strategy that would secure the future of the firm and calm the markets. In June 2008, Lehman managed to raise $6 billion in equity despite a reported $2.8 billion 2nd quarter loss caused partly by a $3.7 billion write down on its mortgage-related assets and leveraged loans portfolios.[986] The days were advancing but a solution was far from sure. On 10 September 2008, Lehman announced that it expected $5.6 billion in write-downs on its toxic assets and a 3rd quarter expected loss of $3.93 billion. Lehman's executives came up with a new plan: to spin off $50 billion of toxic assets into a publicly traded corporation separating them from the remaining healthy firm. That day, Moody's announced that it would further downgrade Lehman's rating unless a strong financial partner was not to be found.[987]

Over the summer of 2008, Lehman executives had approached various partners to explore possible merger options, but in the end, only two remained in the field: Barclays and Bank of America (BofA). Lehman had approached BofA in July and again in August, but BofA's executives were tepid about

---

983 Ibid.

984 The 'Repo 105' was a particular type of repo transactions in which the collateral delivered equalled at least 105% of the loan. While most repos were treated as 'financings', with the collateral remaining on the borrowers' books, the repo 105 transactions were treated as 'sales' and hence the collaterals that were delivered to the lender were removed from the borrowers' books, thereby reducing its reported leverage ratio. Lehman used the repo 105 transactions to remove as much as $50 billion of assets.

985 These were, in order of assets: *Goldman Sachs* ($1.120 billion), *Morgan Stanley* ($1.045 billion), *Merill Lynch* ($1.020 billion), *Lehman Brothers* ($691 billion), and *Bear Stearns* ($395 billion). See in L.M. Ball, *The Fed and Lehman Brothers: Setting the Record Straight on a Financial Disaster*, Studies in Macroeconomic History, Cambridge, Cambridge University Press, 2018, p. 19.

986 See in R.Z. Wiggins, T. Piontek and A. Metrick, 'The Lehman Brothers Bankruptcy A: Overview' (2019) 1(1) *Journal of Financial Crises*, p. 48.

987 Ibid.

such an idea. Finally, after Secretary's Paulson insist, BofA initiated a due diligence review on Lehman's assets on 9 September.[988] Lehman was also in talks with Barclays, but its CEO initially was not interested due to a belief that the two banks were overlapping too much between them. Later he changed his mind, mostly because he saw the merger as a chance to acquire Lehman on a 'very, very distressed price'.[989] After Geithner's and Paulson's persistence for a possible deal, Barclays began its due diligence on 12 September 2008. Unfortunately, around that time BofA lost interest on the deal since it believed that Lehman's assets were overvalued and found more attractive to buy another investment bank, Merrill Lynch, whose CEO feared a similar run on his bank and quickly closed a deal with BofA on 13 September 2008.[990] Another obstacle to the Barclays deal was the fact that Barclays did not want to acquire some of Lehman's illiquid assets (commercial real estate and private equity). Similar to the Bear Stearns-JPMC merger deal, Barclays demanded that someone else should take the rejected assets. The basic idea was that the deal would be a private solution since no public funds were available, either from the Fed or the government, and banks had to finance a structure to buy the assets that Barclays would reject, since there was not in place a solution like Maiden Lane.[991]

On the weekend of 12–14 September 2008, Timothy Geithner organised a meeting on the NY Fed premises, in close coordination with Treasury Secretary Paulson and SEC's chairman Christopher Cox. The aim of the meeting was to bring together Wall Street's CEOs in a last attempt to find a solution for Lehman's problems and help the deal with Barclays.[992] On Saturday, 13 September, the deal was almost closed between Barclays, Lehman, and the rest of the Wall Street's banks[993] and nothing seemed to be wrong but the next day, 14 September, the deal was derailed. To approve the deal, the NY

988 See in L.M. Ball, *The Fed and Lehman Brothers: Setting the Record Straight on a Financial Disaster*, Studies in Macroeconomic History, Cambridge, Cambridge University Press, 2018, p. 37.

989 Ibid.

990 Ibid., p. 38.

991 Ibid.

992 The attendees of that meeting, apart from the government officials, were Morgan Stanley's CEO John Mack, Citigroup's CEO Vikram Pandit, JPMorgan Chase's CEO Jamie Dimon, Merrill Lynch's CEO John Thain, Goldman Sach's CEO Lloyd Blackfein, UBS's CEO Robert Wolf, and representatives from the Royal Bank of Scotland and the Bank of New York Mellon.

993 According to L.M. Ball, *The Fed and Lehman Brothers: Setting the Record Straight on a Financial Disaster*, Studies in Macroeconomic History, Cambridge, Cambridge University Press, 2018, Barclays would pay $3 billion to acquire all of Lehman's assets (*Lehman Brothers Holdings Inc.* – LBHI) except for a pool of assets that were illiquid (commercial real estate, private equity, and investments in hedge funds) valued at $40 billion. The Wall Street banks consortium would lend $40 billion to LBHI with the illiquid assets as collateral, taking the risk of assuming any losses in case the value of the assets fell. LBHI would remain as an

Fed required Barclays to immediately guarantee all of Lehman's obligations in the same way that JPMC did for the Bear Stearns deal. However, under the UK law, such a guarantee required Barclays shareholder's approval, and such an approval was impossible to be obtained at such time constraints.[994] Immediately, Geithner and Cox appealed to the UK regulator, FSA, to waive such a requirement by the FSA refused and the same did the UK's Chancellor of the Exchequer, Alistair Darling, after Secretary Paulson's direct phone call. The deal was already dead, and Lehman had no choice but to file for bankruptcy.[995] After Fed's insistence that no public money would be available, Lehman's Board convened on Sunday, 14 September 2008, late evening and voted in favour of the bankruptcy option since nothing else came up and the bank had not enough cash to open for business the next day. Lehman's lawyers filed for bankruptcy on Monday morning, 15 September 2008, at 01:45 am.[996] By doing so, Lehman was granted in theory the opportunity to have certain parts of its activities dismantled in an orderly manner under the Court's surveillance. In fact, though, large parts of its activities were not overseen by the bankruptcy process, such as the estimated 900.000 derivatives contracts, that triggered fire sales among its counterparties in an attempt to protect themselves from Lehman's failure.[997] Lehman Brothers passed in history by triggering complete financial chaos for only $40 billion.

6.1.2.4 *The Case of AIG*

American International Group, Inc. (commonly known as AIG) is a huge conglomerate with activities across the insurance industry spectrum. AIG was founded during the early years of 20th century and grew rapidly into the largest insurance company in the US. During the 2007–2009 crisis, the US taxpayers bailed out AIG without being a *stricto sensu* bank but mostly because of its extreme systemic importance. The vast majority of AIG's services were unconnected to the traditional financial services and all of its insurance

independent corporation, but its only assets would be the $40 billion of assets that Barclays rejected, plus the $3 billion Barclays paid for the rest of LBHI. Simultaneously, its liabilities would be the $40 billion debt to the consortium.

994 See in L.M. Ball, *The Fed and Lehman Brothers: Setting the Record Straight on a Financial Disaster*, Studies in Macroeconomic History, Cambridge, Cambridge University Press, 2018, p. 39.

995 Nevertheless, Barclays managed to acquire Lehman's US assets in a deal worth of $1.35 billion just a few days after filed for bankruptcy, after the Court's approval. See in R.Z. Wiggins, T. Piontek and A. Metrick, 'The Lehman Brothers Bankruptcy A: Overview' (2019) 1(1) *Journal of Financial Crises*, p. 50.

996 See in L.M. Ball, *The Fed and Lehman Brothers: Setting the Record Straight on a Financial Disaster*, Studies in Macroeconomic History, Cambridge, Cambridge University Press, 2018, p. 40.

997 See in R.Z. Wiggins, T. Piontek and A. Metrick, 'The Lehman Brothers Bankruptcy A: Overview' (2019) 1(1) *Journal of Financial Crises*, p. 50.

subsidiaries were closely regulated by the state regulators and were financially healthy and prudently managed.[998] AIG's major source of trouble was its financial subsidiary, the AIG Financial Products (AIGFP), which had issued many Credit Default Swaps (CDS)[999] against many of the Collateralized Debt Obligations (CDOs)[1000] that lost their value during the financial crisis. Many AIG's subsidiaries have also invested in MBSs that also lost their value.

AIG's financial problems were derived from two sources. First, from its involvement in the CDS market since AIGFP had sold insurance on CDOs agreeing to pay the par value of the bonds in case they were defaulted in return for a small premium. AIGFP, like other market participants, believed that the highly rated tranches of the CDOs were credit worthy and their credit risk was miniscule.[1001] AIGFP insured a large number of those products but left the market in 2005, when its executives realised that the total exposure to those products was high and the quality of the CDOs was constantly declining since banks had lowered the underwriting standards.[1002] AIG exited the market while other companies stayed in, but AIG did not manage to hedge its risks or to unwind them and by the end of 1007, its total exposure to CDOs amounted to $78 billion. Under the contractual agreements with its counterparts AIG was required to post cash collateral on the CDSs, and while before the crisis these requirements were minimal the agreements stipulated that AIG would be required to post additional collateral if AIG's credit rating would decline or if these instruments' (CDOs) market value or credit rating would decline.[1003] When the market value of the CDOs started to decline, AIG was forced to post additional cash collateral and its financial situation became more and

---

998 See in E.A. Posner, *Last Resort, The Financial Crisis and the Future of Bailouts*, Chicago, The University of Chicago Press, 2018, p. 75.

999 A Credit Default Swap (CDS) is a financial derivative that functions as a form of insurance against the default or credit event (e.g. bankruptcy, failure to pay) of a borrower, such as a corporation or government. In a CDS contract, the buyer of the CDS pays a periodic premium (like an insurance premium) to the seller. In return, the seller agrees to compensate the buyer if the underlying credit entity (called the reference entity) experiences a defined credit event. The payout typically equals the loss incurred (usually the face value of the bond minus recovery value).

1000 A Collateralized Debt Obligation (CDO) is a structured financial product that pools together a collection of income-generating debt instruments, (such as bonds, loans, or mortgage-backed securities) and repackages them into tranches that are then sold to investors. Each tranche (or layer) has a different level of risk and return, with senior tranches having the highest credit rating and lowest risk, and junior or equity tranches bearing higher risk but offering higher potential returns.

1001 See in E.A. Posner, *Last Resort, The Financial Crisis and the Future of Bailouts*, Chicago, The University of Chicago Press, 2018, p. 76.

1002 Under the contractual terms, the institutions that managed the CDOs were allowed to replace expiring prime mortgages with new, subprime mortgages. This practice further eroded the overall quality of the CDOs.

1003 See in E.A. Posner, *Last Resort, The Financial Crisis and the Future of Bailouts*, Chicago, The University of Chicago Press, 2018, p. 76.

more precarious as it was needed to post cash and the reserves were depleted. As the situation was worsening AIG had posted almost $15 billion in cash collateral and was facing severe liquidity problems and a constant market value decline that required more cash collateral.[1004] The second source of problems for AIG came from its insurance subsidiaries that had bought RMBS using the proceeds from their securities lending business. These securities lending transactions allowed AIG to borrow $75 billion of funds and reinvest them on RMBSs. Under the insurance legislation, insurance companies were required to invest their assets only in safe securities like corporate bonds. AIG had lent these securities out to hedge funds and other financial institutions in return for interest and believed that these transactions were safe since the RMBSs were highly rated and liquid assets, so at any time, AIG would be free to sell them in the market and raise the necessary cash to post it as collateral to the creditors.[1005] When the crisis struck however, AIG was not able to sell these securities at market prices since they were devalued and was forced to proceed into fire sales at a huge loss. AIG's exposure to the real estate sector, through these two channels, came to many people's surprises, especially of government officials and politicians. The interconnection among the financial markets' participants was enormous and a possible failure of the AIG would have created enormous repercussions for the financial stability of the entire system. AIG's troubles began in the summer of 2007, when Goldman Sachs issued a collateral call of $1.8 billion. In mid-august 2008, a team of NY Fed examiners reported that AIG was facing increasing capital and liquidity pressure and within less than a month, on 9 and 12 September, AIG executives informed the NY Fed that urgently needed financial assistance.[1006] It was also reported that AIG held $2.7 trillion of OTC derivatives and that twelve big international banks were counterparties to $1 trillion of those contracts.[1007]

The events were overwhelming and horrific. On 14 September, AIG's CEO informed Secretary Paulson and the NY Fed Governor, that the firm needed $60 billion of assistance while the next day, 15 September, JPMC and Goldman Sachs estimated the bail out cost at $80 billion rejecting thereby the idea for a private sector assistance program as 'far too large'.[1008] Later that day, AIG's credit ratings were reduced triggering new collateral calls of up to $13 billion from its derivatives counterparties. On 16 September 2008, amid a general panic in the financial markets, the Fed decided to provide financial assistance

---

1004 Ibid.

1005 Ibid., p. 77.

1006 See in A.E. Wilmarth Jr., *Taming the Megabanks, Why We Need a New Glass-Steagall Act*, New York, Oxford University Press, 2020, p. 281.

1007 Ibid.

1008 Ibid., p. 282.

of up to $85 billion in exchange for 79.9% of AIG's shares.[1009] Under the Credit Agreement between the Fed and AIG, the Fed opened a $85 billion credit line for AIG which was secured by AIG's assets, including its insurance companies. Moreover, AIG agreed to pay a 14,5% interest rate and grant the US government preferred stocks, convertible into 79.9% of AIG's stocks.[1010] The Fed was forced to provide a second, secured by AIG's assets, loan in October 2008, amounting to $37.8 billion, since the company's financial situation was getting worse. The credit extension did not satisfy the CDS counterparties since they renewed their demands for additional collaterals based on the low market valuation of the CDOs. The Fed decided to address that issue and established a Special Purpose Vehicle (SPV), named Maiden Lane III, which was financed by an equity investment of $29.3 billion ($5 billion from AIG and the rest $24.3 billion from the Fed) and bought the underlying CDOs that AIG had insured, leading to a $62 billion transfer in cash to the counterparties.[1011] The Fed created a second SPV, Maiden Lane II, which paid the AIG's insurance subsidiaries more than $20 billion for MBSs with par value of almost $40 billion. The Fed siphoned almost $20 billion to Maiden Lane II to finance these transactions while AIG put only $1 billion. Overall, the US government siphoned around $126 billion to prevent AIG's collapse.[1012]

In the days of AIG's bail out from the Fed, President Bush Jr. asked Secretary Paulson, 'How did we get to this point?'[1013] According to Prof. Posner, AIG's only mistake was that it took for granted the outstanding (triple AAA) grading from the credit rating agencies and accepted the representations from the underwriters and packagers, investing its money on RMBS, thus taking excessive real estate related risk on its balance sheet.[1014] To briefly answer the President's Bush question we must point out that AIG fell through significant regulatory cracks in the US system of financial regulation. AIG's insurance subsidiaries were regulated by state authorities which ensured that these entities themselves were adequately capitalised and sound managed but despite the fact that state regulators were aware of the securities lending business,

1009 Ibid.

1010 See in E.A. Posner, *Last Resort, The Financial Crisis and the Future of Bailouts*, Chicago, The University of Chicago Press, 2018, p. 82.

1011 Since AIG was not legally required to buy the CDOs, let alone to pay their par value, this transaction raised serious questions regarding the extent of the financial support and the indirect bail out of AIG's creditors. AIG could have kept posting the required collaterals, paying only if default of the CDOs actually took place and since its counterparties were desperate for cash it could have negotiated better haircuts on the CDOs values.

1012 See in E.A. Posner, *Last Resort, The Financial Crisis and the Future of Bailouts*, Chicago, The University of Chicago Press, 2018, p. 82.

1013 See in A.E. Wilmarth Jr., *Taming the Megabanks, Why We Need a New Glass-Steagall Act*, New York, Oxford University Press, 2020, p. 283.

1014 See in E.A. Posner, *Last Resort, The Financial Crisis and the Future of Bailouts*, Chicago, The University of Chicago Press, 2018, p. 79.

were unconcerned simply because these transactions were secured by adequate collateral, as the practice suggested.[1015] At the same time, the thrifts' supervisor, the OTS, was overseeing the AIG's holding company, since AIG owned a thrift institution, but did not decide to enhance its supervision on the mortgaged related insurance activities and underestimated the risks that these activities were posing to the firm as a whole.[1016] Ultimately, blames must be attributed to the AIG's risk management function that failed to detect and accurately valuate the risks associated with the CDOs and the RMBSs that the firm had insured and invested. Due to the firm's expansion, its risk management systems and personnel failed to monitor and process the risks that were correlated throughout its disparate business operations.[1017]

6.1.2.5 *The 'Bank Run' on the Money Market Mutual Funds (MMMFs)*

One day after Lehman Brothers filed for bankruptcy, on Tuesday, 16 September 2008, an important MMMF,[1018] the Reserve Primary Fund (RPF),[1019] was forced to 'break the buck', because of its holdings of Lehman's short-term debt (commercial paper). Reserve, a New York-based fund manager specialising in money markets, held $64.8 billion in assets in RPF. The fund had allocated $785 million to short-term loans issued by Lehman Brothers. RPF's holdings of Lehman's debt were only 1.2% of its portfolio, well below the maximum level of 5% of a single issuer, as set by the SEC's rules.[1020] RPF's main problem though was that it lacked a parent company that would have been able to guarantee its share price, and this made it especially vulnerable among MMMFs. Demands to withdraw money from the fund reached 25% of its assets by the afternoon and more than half on the following day, 16 September, as clients sought to exit the fund before its Lehman assets impacted on the share price. To respond

---

1015 Ibid.

1016 Ibid.

1017 See in J.C. Kress, 'Solving Banking's 'Too Big to Manage' Problem' (2019) 104 *Minnesota Law Review*, p. 198.

1018 '*Money Market Mutual Funds*' (MMMFs) are a special type of open-ended mutual funds which are valued based on the '*Net Asset Value* – NAV' of their portfolios. For reasons of convenience, MMMFs are valued at $1.00 NAV per share, unless and until their portfolio's actual valuation (actual NAV) falls below the $0.995, at which point the funds it is said to have 'broken the buck'. Breaking the buck may happen when the MMMFs' investment income does not cover their operating expenses or investment losses. This normally occurs when interest rates drop to very low levels, or the funds use leverage to create capital risk in otherwise risk-free instruments.

1019 The *Reserve Primary Fund* (RPF) was the original money market fund, created in 1970 by Bruce R. Bent and Henry B.R. Brown and managed by the *Reserve Management Company* and at its peak, RPF held more than $60 billion in assets. Since it was forced to lose the dollar value, or 'broke the buck', RPF was liquidated. The fund was ultimately dissolved in December 2015, having paid investors $0.991 per share.

1020 See in J.N. Gordon and C.M. Gandia, 'Money Markets Funds Run Risk: Will Floating Net Asset Value Fix the Problem?' (2014) 2014(2) *Columbia Business Law Review*, p. 315.

to its clients' needs, RPF had to liquidate its assets, with Lehman's commercial paper being among them. Unable to find a buyer for the assets, RPF declared them worthless by marking them to current market values and announced a share price of $0.97 (broke the buck) that led other MMMFs to experience similar runs and some of them even broke the buck also, forcing their sponsors to rescue them.[1021] Although the Lehman paper represented only a small portion of the RPF's assets, investors were concerned about the value of the fund's other holdings and amid fears for the value of their investments, pulled their money out of the fund, which saw its asset decline by nearly two-thirds in about 24 hours. Unable to meet further redemption requests, the RPF froze redemptions for up to seven days and when this decision proved inefficient, the fund was forced to suspend operations and commence liquidation. According to Gordon and Gandia, the pressure arose not from the bankruptcy of other issuers of MMMFs instruments but from the risk fleeing investors who desperately wanted to switch from those instruments to the safer Treasury securities and/or to cash.[1022] These immediate redemptions exhausted the available funds' cash and highly liquid reserves and as they accelerated amid a frozen interbank short term credit market MMMFs were facing the prospect of selling the remaining assets at fire sale prices, thereby meaning a below $1 net asset value for many of them. MMMFs were the largest buyers of commercial papers since they were using them to borrow short term based on their high liquidity. The US government intervened immediately to stabilise the markets and prevent the total collapse of the MMMFs industry.

On Friday, 19 September 2008, the US Treasury announced that it would temporarily guarantee the deposits in the MMMFs through a specially designed program (the 'Temporary Guaranty Program for Money Market Funds').[1023] The program, which would be guaranteed by the then $50 billion Exchange Stabilization Fund (ESF), offered a US government guarantee on all existing deposits in the participating MMMFs, in effect the entire $3.5 trillion MMMFs industry, in exchange for a small premium for the Treasury.[1024] On the same day, the Fed announced that it would use emergency powers to make available a credit facility to fund no risk bank purchases of ABCPs from MMMFs, the 'Asset Backed Commercial Paper Money Market Mutual Fund Liquidity Facility' (AMLF). Under the AMLF program, the Federal Reserve provided non-recourse loans to US depository institutions, US bank holding companies (including their broker-dealer subsidiaries), and US branches and agencies of

[1021] Ibid.

[1022] Ibid.

[1023] Ibid., p. 316.

[1024] Ibid., p. 317. See also in E.A. Posner, *Last Resort, The Financial Crisis and the Future of Bailouts*, Chicago, The University of Chicago Press, 2018, p. 67, for a deeper analysis on the legality of the use of ESF's funds to prevent the MMMFs collapse.

foreign banks to purchase, at amortised cost, eligible ABCPs from MMMFs. Borrowers under the AMLF, therefore, served as conduits in providing liquidity to MMMFs, and the MMMFs were the primary, but indirect, beneficiaries of the AMLF.[1025] Because of the shrinkage of the prime MMMFs assets and of the shift of those MMMFs to Treasury's securities, parties that counted on such financing method faced an immediate funding crisis forcing the Fed to create an additional emergency lending facility, the 'Commercial Paper Funding Facility' (CPFF). The aim of this program was to revive the commercial paper market by supporting commercial paper issuers, and in particular the asset backed securitisation vehicles which could no longer count on purchases from the MMMFs.[1026] These large-scale governmental interventions halted the run on MMMFs and stabilised the relevant market and to prevent similar runs from happening again, in 2010 SEC adopted new rules to better manage MMMFs, through amendments in the Investment Company Act of 1940. These rules were intended to provide more stability and resilience by placing tighter restrictions on portfolio holdings and introducing provisions for imposing liquidity fees and suspending redemptions. MMMFs can no longer have an average dollar-weighted portfolio maturity exceeding sixty days. They also now have limitations on asset investments. MMMFs must restrict their holdings to investments that have more conservative maturities as well as credit ratings. SEC's new rules aimed at raising the standards on portfolio securities, shorten maturities, increase liquidity requirements, and create proper liquidation procedures for those MMMFs that 'break the buck'.[1027]

6.1.2.6 *The Cases of Wachovia and Washington Mutual*

After the mortgage market meltdown, and in the meantime before Lehman's collapse, the FDIC was also dealing with two highly problematic bank cases: a) Wachovia, and b) Washington Mutual Inc., (WaMu). These two cases are of particular interest because their resolution came under a different approach adopted by the regulators.

Wachovia was a financial holding company headquartered in Charlotte, North Carolina, that provided commercial and retail banking services and other financial services both in the United States and internationally. It was formed in 2001 after merger of First Union Corp., based in Charlotte, North Carolina, and Wachovia Corporation, based in Winston-Salem, North Carolina. Between 2001 and 2007, Wachovia bought several other financial services companies in an attempt to become a national bank and a comprehensive financial services

---

1025 See in J.N. Gordon and C.M. Gandia, 'Money Markets Funds Run Risk: Will Floating Net Asset Value Fix the Problem?' (2014) 2014(2) *Columbia Business Law Review*, p. 317.

1026 Ibid., p. 318.

1027 Ibid., p. 320.

company.[1028] Wachovia provided a broad range of banking, asset management, wealth management, and corporate and investment banking products and services, and at its height, it was one of the largest providers of financial services in the United States, operating in 21 states and Washington, D.C., providing also global services through more than 40 offices around the world. The company was organised into four general divisions:

(i) the 'General Bank' division, offering retail, small business, and commercial customers,

(ii) the 'Wealth Management' division, offering services to high-net-worth, personal trust, and insurance business,

(iii) the 'Capital Management' division, offering asset management, retirement, and retail brokerage services, and

(iv) the 'Corporate and Investment Bank' division, offering capital markets, investment banking, and financial advisory services.

At the end of the second quarter of 2008, Wachovia held assets of $812 billion, making it the 4th largest banking organisation in the US in terms of assets. The holding company's principal subsidiary was Wachovia Bank, holding assets of $671 billion. Wachovia also had two insured, thrift subsidiaries with total assets of $105 billion, with a very large retail presence (serving more than 27 million deposit accounts totalling more than $400 billion) and operated a large mortgage business. These subsidiaries were supervised, examined, and regulated by the OCC and the OTC, respectively. Wachovia also operated a large retail-oriented securities broker-dealer network through its subsidiaries, Wachovia Securities and A.G. Edwards, Inc., providing a wide range of investment banking, private banking, and asset management services. These subsidiaries were supervised and regulated by the SEC and in early September 2008, the FDIC became increasingly concerned about the financial situation in Wachovia. The bank was facing problems because of its structured finance business and its participation in the mortgage market, resulting in

[1028] During that period, willing to expand its activities, Wachovia acquired or merge with the following companies: On 1 July 2003, *Wachovia Securities*, and the securities division of *Prudential Financial, Inc.* combined to form *Wachovia Securities LLC*; On 22 October 2003, Wachovia announced it would acquire *Metropolitan West Securities*, an affiliate company of *Metropolitan West Financial* adding a portfolio of over $50 billion of securities on loan to the Wachovia Global Securities Lending division; On 1 November 2004, Wachovia completed the acquisition of the Alabama-based *SouthTrust Corporation* in a transaction valued at $14.3 billion. The merger created the largest bank in the southeast US, the 4th largest bank in terms of holdings, and the 2nd largest in terms of number of branches; In September 2005, *Westcorp*, Western Financial Bank's parent company, *WFS Financial Inc.*, and Wachovia announced a proposed acquisition by Wachovia; On 7 May 2006, Wachovia agreed to purchase *Golden West Financial* for almost $25.5 billion, with this acquisition giving Wachovia an additional 285-branch network spanning across 10 states. Finally, on 31 May 2007, Wachovia announced plans to purchase *A.G. Edwards* for $6.8 billion to create the United States' 2nd largest retail brokerage firm.

holding a considerable volume of subprime mortgages, syndicated credits with collateralised loan obligations and commercial real estate credits that were either acquired or originated for inclusion in commercial mortgage-backed securitisations.[1029] Due to the worsening of market conditions all these assets were almost illiquid and could not be sold easily to raise cash. Apart from their illiquidity, these assets were also suffering from credit quality problems resulting in large mark-to-market revaluations reflecting the risks associated with them.[1030]

Earlier that year, depositors had withdrawn $15 billion over a two-week period after Wachovia reported negative earnings results in April 2008 and with the Fed's encouragement, Wachovia raised $8 billion in capital attempting to offset these losses. A second wave of withdrawals occurred in September 2008, following Lehman's demise, where Wachovia experienced significant deposit outflows amounting to almost $8.3 billion. The failure of WaMu, as we will see shortly after, triggered a third run on the bank, with outflows reaching $10 billion. This combined $18.3 billion represented 4.4% of Wachovia's depositor base with much of the withdrawals concentrated among commercial accounts with balances above the $100,000 limit insured by the FDIC. On 25 September 2008, Wachovia's management informed regulators that it was facing a near-term liquidity crisis, later viewed by the FDIC as a 'silent bank run',[1031] mostly from uninsured depositors and unsecured creditors.[1032] Wachovia's stock price declined sharply and credit default swap spreads on its debt surged. On 26 September 2008, a day after WaMu's closure, the FDIC, by invoking the 'systemic risk exemption' for Wachovia, based on the FDIC Act, decide its resolution. The FDIC Act mandates the FDIC to adopt and apply the least cost resolution approach when dealing with failing depository institutions. The systemic risk exemption however is allowed if both the FDIC Board and the Federal Reserve Board, by a vote of at least 2/3 of their members and the Treasury's Secretary, having consulted with the President, may determine that the compliance with the least cost resolution requirement 'would have serious adverse effect on economic conditions or financial stability'[1033] and

---

1029 See in J. Rhee and A. Metrick, 'Guarantees and Capital Infusions in Response to Financial Crises A: Haircuts and Resolutions' (2020) 2(1) *Yale Journal of Financial Crises*, p. 43.

1030 Ibid.

1031 A 'silent bank run' occurs when depositors withdraw funds in large volumes without physically entering the bank. Silent bank runs are like normal bank runs, except funds are withdrawn via electronic fund transfers, wire transfers, and other methods that do not require physical withdrawals of cash. The 2008 financial crisis saw several examples of silent bank runs occurring throughout the world (Wachovia, WaMu, Icelandic banks, etc.).

1032 See in J. Rhee and A. Metrick, 'Guarantees and Capital Infusions in Response to Financial Crises A: Haircuts and Resolutions' (2020) 2(1), *Yale Journal of Financial Crises*, p. 44.

1033 Ibid.

that adopting another action or assistance than the least cost approach, would 'avoid or mitigate such effects'.[1034]

In the meantime, both Citigroup and Wells Fargo performed due diligence to acquire Wachovia in a private solution transaction, but neither could reach a definite agreement. On 28 September 2008, the FDIC started negotiations with both banks, and both submitted open bank assistance bids. Only Citigroup's proposal resulted in serious negotiations and the next day, 29 September, the FDIC announced Citigroup's plan to acquire Wachovia's assets and liabilities, including five depository institutions, and assume Wachovia's senior and subordinated debts.[1035] The same day, the Fed's Board by unanimous vote determined that compliance by the FDIC with the least-cost requirements of the FDIC Act, with respect to Wachovia Bank and its insured depository institution affiliates, would have serious adverse effects on economic conditions and financial stability, and that action or assistance by the FDIC permitted under the systemic risk exception within the act would avoid or mitigate these adverse effects. Similar determinations were made by the board of directors of the FDIC and the Secretary of the Treasury, in consultation with the President, which allowed the FDIC to consider measures outside the least-cost resolution requirement to resolve Wachovia, including the provision of so-called 'open bank' assistance. The FDIC staff recommended on their memo to accept the Citigroup plan as 'the least cost available method of dealing with the systemic risk' but on 2 October during the period when Citigroup and Wachovia were negotiating a final merger agreement, Wachovia's BoD received a communication from Wells Fargo that included an offer to acquire all of Wachovia's stock by merger, a better deal that didn't require either an FDIC receivership or any FDIC assistance.[1036] Wachovia's BoD and shareholders accepted the proposal from Wells Fargo and approved the deal, with the transaction taking place immediately after the amendment of the tax regulation regarding the limits on the income that banks could shelter based on the losses of the acquired companies. Citigroup officially walked away from the deal on 9 October and subsequently filed a suit against Wells Fargo for tort and damages, later settled at $100 million.[1037]

Washington Mutual, Inc. was a savings bank holding company and the former owner of Washington Mutual Bank (WaMu), which was the largest

1034 Ibid.

1035 Ibid. Citigroup's plan was to absorb up to $42 billion of losses on a $312 billion pool of loans and the FDIC was to absorb losses beyond that amount. To compensate FDIC for bearing such a risk, Citigroup would grant FDIC $12 billion in preferred stock and warrants.

1036 Ibid.

1037 Ibid.

savings and loan association in the US until its collapse in 2008.[1038] WaMu expanded rapidly through a series of mergers and acquisitions that allowed expansion into new business and geographic areas. On 1 October 2005, WaMu entered the credit card lending business by acquiring Providian Financial Corporation. These acquisitions enabled WaMu to expand across the country, build its customer base, and become the largest savings and loan association in the country. As of 30 June 2008, WaMu had more than 43,000 employees, more than 2,200 branch offices in 15 states and $188.3 billion in deposits. WaMu was organised internally along four business segments:

- the Retail Banking Group,
- the Card Services Group,
- the Commercial Group, and
- the Home Loans Group

Beginning in late 2006, WaMu was proactively changing its business strategy to respond to declining housing and market conditions by tightening credit standards, eliminating purchasing, and originating subprime mortgage loans, and discontinuing underwriting option ARM and stated income loans. Management reduced loans originated for sale and transferred held for sale loans to the held for investment portfolio. WaMu focused on shrinking its balance sheet and developing a retail strategy through its branch operations. After the mortgage meltdown however, it suffered huge losses from its investments in risky products and especially from the 'Alt-A' residential mortgages[1039] and liberal underwriting. In December 2007, the subsidiary WaMu Bank reorganised its home-loan division, deciding to close 160 of its 336 home-loan offices and remove 2,600 from its home-loan staff (a 22% reduction).

In March 2008, on the same weekend that JPMC negotiated the takeover of Bear Stearns, JPMC's CEO secretly dispatched members of his team to Seattle to meet with WaMu executives, urging them to consider a quick deal with his firm. However, WaMu's Chairman and CEO, rejected JPMC's offer that valued WaMu at $8 a share, mostly in stock. In April 2008, the holding company, responding to persistent losses and difficulties, because of the subprime mortgage crisis, announced that 3,000 people companywide would lose their

---

1038 WaMu was incorporated as the '*Washington National Building Loan and Investment Association*' on 25 September1889. The newly formed company made its first home mortgage loan on the West Coast on 10 February 1890. It changed its name to *Washington Savings and Loan Association* on 25 June 1908, and by 12 September 1917, it was operating under the name *WaMu Savings Bank*.

1039 Alt-A is a classification of mortgages with a risk profile falling between prime and subprime. They can be considered high risk due to provision factors customized by the lender. This type of loan tends to be more expensive for the borrower, as they may carry higher interest rates and/or fees.

jobs, and the company stated its intent to close its approximately 176 remaining stand-alone, home-loan offices. Moreover, it recorded a net loss of $6.1 billion for the three quarters ending 30 June 2008. In the second quarter of 2008, WaMu's management disclosed that the its credit quality had deteriorated, and it might incur up to $19 billion in losses on its single-family residential mortgage portfolio, increasing thereby its loan loss provisioning in response to the deteriorating housing market.[1040] It also announced a $7 billion infusion of new capital by new outside investors led by Texas Pacific Group Capital (TPG). TPG agreed to invest $2 billion into the WaMu holding company, while other investors, including some of WaMu's current institutional holders, agreed to buy an additional $5 billion in newly issued stock.[1041] This move temporarily improved WaMu's liquidity position but angered many investors, as TPG's investment would dilute the holdings of existing shareholders, and as WaMu executives excluded mortgage losses from computing their bonuses. In July 2008, WaMu encountered difficulties since depositors were withdrawing their funds and the Federal Home Loan Bank of San Francisco began to limit WaMu's borrowing capacity.[1042] By mid-September 2008, WaMu's share price had closed as low as $2. It had been worth over $30.00 in September 2007 and had briefly traded as high as $45 in the previous year. While WaMu publicly insisted it could stay independent, earlier that month had quietly hired Goldman Sachs to identify potential bidders. To attract depositors and improve its liquidity, WaMu started to offer teasing interest rates above its competitors' but after the demise of Lehman Brothers however, it incurred a silent bank run leading to deposit outflows of up to $16.7 billion within a ten day period.[1043] This led the Fed and the Treasury to step up pressure for WaMu to find a buyer, as a possible takeover by the FDIC could have been a severe drain on the FDIC insurance fund.

On 25 September 2008, shortly after the close of business on the West Coast, the OTS seized WaMu Bank and placed it into FDIC's receivership. In a statement, the OTS said that the massive run meant that WaMu was no longer sound and viable. The FDIC sold WaMu to JPMC which acquired its assets, assumed the financial contracts, and made a payment of $1.9 billion. Certain liabilities, including preferred stock, common stock, subordinated debt, and senior debt were left in FDIC's receivership.[1044] Moreover, all WaMu's depositors were fully protected, and the qualified contracts included swaps,

---

1040 Loan loss provisions were increased from $1.6 billion in the fourth quarter of 2007, to $3.6 billion in the first quarter of 2008 and up to $6.0 billion in the second quarter of 2008.

1041 See in J. Rhee and A. Metrick, 'Guarantees and Capital Infusions in Response to Financial Crises A: Haircuts and Resolutions' (2020) 2(1) *Yale Journal of Financial Crises*, p. 42.

1042 Ibid.

1043 Ibid.

1044 Ibid., p. 43.

options, futures, forwards and repurchase agreements accordingly defined in the federal legislation.[1045] JPMC assumed all assets but only some liabilities (including deposits, covered bonds, and other secured debt) of WaMu Bank. Under the deal, JPMC acquired all the banking operations of WaMu, including $307 billion in assets and $188 billion in deposits, for a price of $1.9 billion plus debt assumptions. Any unsecured senior debt obligations of the bank were not assumed by JPMC, leaving holders of those obligations with little meaningful source of potential recovery. On the morning of 26 September, WaMu Bank customers were informed that all deposits held by WaMu were now liabilities of JPMC. Because JPMC bought WaMu's assets for a low price, WaMu's stockholders were nearly wiped out. Its stock price dropped to $0.16 a share, and the transaction did not require any FDIC insurance funds. Normally, bank seizures take place after the close of business on Fridays, so that the process can be concluded within the weekend in an orderly manner without any consequences for consumers. However, due to the bank's deteriorating condition and press leaks that a seizure was imminent, regulators felt compelled to act a day early. During the bankruptcy process, WaMu required seven different reorganisation plans, with the last one announced in February 2012 and the company finally emerged from Chapter 11 bankruptcy the following month as WMI Holdings Corporation. By 2015, WMI Holdings was able to raise $598 million and was looking for new acquisitions.

6.1.3 The Responses to the Crisis from the US Government and the Federal Reserve

Although an analytical presentation of the US Government responses to the financial crisis are well beyond the scope of the present book, for coherence reasons it is necessary to refer the role of the Fed and the US Department of the Treasury (the Treasury), since they were the most important players in critical moments where 'no fire station existed in town'. Therefore, we will briefly present the initiatives undertaken both by the Treasury and the Fed to understand the broad framework within which these two institutions acted with the aim of preventing the complete collapse of the US financial system, either by pumping enormous amounts of public money into the system or by orchestrating and backing bail outs of failing institutions.

The Treasury was pivotal to the containment of the 2007–2009 financial crisis. Secretary Paulson, a former Goldman Sachs executive, used his financial markets experience and connections within the sector to play a dominant role in the negotiations and decisions regarding actions that were about to be taken. He stepped in and played a major role in orchestrating the bailout of major

[1045] 12 U.S.C. § 1821(e)(8)(D)(i).

financial institutions, including non-bank entities, almost the entire US car industry and in passing the Trouble Asset Relief Program (TARP) measures. The Treasury was present in almost every important decision and in many times urged the Fed and other federal administrative authorities to act in a timely and concise manner. The Treasury was present in almost every Fed's extraordinary operation either by orchestrating such operations or by providing support to complement such efforts. It guaranteed all the MMMFs money to prevent a general run on them and played an important, but negative role, in Lehman's case. Treasury's actions were under criticism by many scholars for either being out of law or for going beyond what was necessary back then to prevent the financial meltdown and avert a collapse. The cases of AIG and the salvation of the US car industry bring to the surface several questions and criticisms for Treasury's actions and decisions since the rationale behind the intervention and the use of specific tools is still doubtful and the same applies also for the MMMFs extraordinary support which came under the Exchange Stabilization Fund (ESF) without any proper (legal) explanation for the use of such facility.[1046]

During the turmoil, the US Congress enacted the Emergency Economic Stabilization Act (EESA) in October 2008,[1047] and the TARP, with a 'financial bazooka' of $700 billion, to support the failing financial institutions but it ended up being used for the salvation of the broader economy since many of its funds were channelled towards other sectors (US car industry). On 13 February 2008, President Bush Jr. signed into law a $168 billion economic stimulus package, mainly taking the form of income tax rebate checks mailed directly to taxpayers, starting the week of 28 April, 2008, and on 17 February 2009, President Obama signed the American Recovery and Reinvestment Act (ARRA) of 2009,[1048] a $787 billion stimulus package with a broad spectrum of spending and tax cuts. Over $75 billion of the package was specifically allocated to programs that help struggling homeowners (Homeowner Affordability and Stability Plan).

Although there is a widespread belief that the Fed was running always behind the dominance of the Treasury and Secretary Paulson's initiatives, the truth is that the Fed played an equally important role, which has been characterised as

---

1046 See in E.A. Posner, *Last Resort, The Financial Crisis and the Future of Bailouts*, Chicago, The University of Chicago Press, 2018, p. 68.

1047 Emergency Economic Stabilization Act of 2008, Pub. L. No. 110-343, 122 Stat. 3765 (codified as amended at 12 U.S.C. §§ 5201–5261).

1048 American Recovery and Reinvestment Act of 2009, Pub. L. No. 111-5, 123 Stat. 115 (codified in scattered sections of the U.S. Code).

'unprecedented' by certain academics. According to Prof. Mishkin and White, Fed's actions can be grouped on seven broad initiatives-actions:[1049]

(i) Unusually Easy Monetary Policy,
(ii) New Non-Bagehot Liquidity Facilities,
(iii) International Central Banks' cooperation,
(iv) Non-Conventional Monetary Policy,
(v) Central Bank Rescues of Financial Institutions / Provision for Orderly Liquidations,
(vi) Collaboration with the Treasury / Intervention / Aid, and
(vii) Supervisory Actions

Regarding the first action, Fed reacted fast to the freezing of the interbank lending markets, by lowering the spread between the discount rate and the federal funds rate target by 50 basis points, on 17 August 2007.[1050] A month later, the Federal Open Markets Committee (FOMC), cut the federal funds rate target by 50 basis points, in a momentum where the US economy was quite strong achieving growth rate of 3%. In December 2007, when recession began, Fed lowered even more the federal funds rate target by 100 basis points, reducing it again in May 2008, in a decline of almost 325 basis points.[1051] In terms of the second action, the Fed created several new credit facilities that aimed at providing liquidity, but not at high interest rates, as the Bagehot rule suggests. To encourage additional borrowing and provide further liquidity in the system, Fed set up the following facilities:

(a) Term Auction Facility (TAF),[1052]
(b) Term Securities Lending Facility (TSLF),[1053]

1049 See in F.S. Mishkin and E.N. White, 'Unprecedented Actions: The Federal Reserve's Response to the Global Financial Crisis in Historical Perspective', Working Paper 20737, *NBER Working Paper Series*, National Bureau of Economic Research (NBER), December 2014, p. 8 onwards.

1050 Ibid.

1051 Ibid.

1052 TAF was a temporary facility set up in December 2007 to auction Fed funds. The Fed auctioned term funds to depository institutions. All depository institutions that were eligible to borrow under the primary credit program were eligible to participate in TAF auctions. All advances were fully collateralized, and each TAF auction was for a fixed amount, with the rate determined by the auction process subject to a minimum bid rate. Bids were submitted by phone through local Reserve Banks. The final auction was conducted on 8 March 2010. TAF became more widely used than the discount window because it avoided the stigma problem and at the same time enabled banks to borrow at a competitive and lower rate than the discount rate. See also in E.A. Posner, *Last Resort, The Financial Crisis and the Future of Bailouts*, Chicago, The University of Chicago Press, 2018, p. 43.

1053 TSLF was a weekly loan facility that promoted liquidity in Treasury and other collateral markets. The program offered Treasury securities held by the System Open Market Account (SOMA) for loan over a one-month term against other program-eligible general collateral. Securities loans were awarded to primary dealers based on a competitive single-price auction. The TSLF was announced on 11 March 2008, with the first auction conducted on 27 March 2008 and was closed on 1 February 2010.

(c) Primary Dealer Credit Facility (PDCF),[1054]
(d) Asset Backed Commercial Paper Money Market Mutual Fund Liquidity Facility (AMLF),[1055]
(e) Commercial Paper Funding Facility (CPFF),[1056]
(f) Money Market Investor Funding Facility (MMIFF),[1057]
(g) Term Asset Backed Securities Loan Facility (TALF)[1058]

1054 *PDCF* was established to encourage financial markets to function more effectively. Primary dealers borrowed overnight loans (that settled the same business day and matured the following business day) from the PDCF through their clearing banks at the primary credit rate offered by the Federal Reserve Bank of New York, in exchange for eligible collateral. A frequency-based fee was assigned to primary dealers who borrow from the PDCF on more than forty-five business days. The initial facility closed in 2010.

1055 *AMLF* was a lending facility that provided funding to US depository institutions and BHCs to finance their purchases of high-quality ABCP from MMMFs under certain conditions. The program was intended to assist MMMFs that held such paper in meeting demands for redemptions by investors and to foster liquidity in the ABCP market and MMMFs more generally. The AMLF began operations on 22 September 2008 and ran until 1 February 2010.

1056 CPFF was created by the Fed on 7 October2008, because of the credit crunch faced by financial intermediaries in the commercial paper market and was designed to increase the liquidity of the commercial paper market by providing funding to issuers. The program specifically provided a backup measure of liquidity for commercial paper issuers via a special purpose vehicle (SPV) which was a Limited Liability Company (LLC). The SPV created through the CPFF was financed directly by the New York Fed and was used to purchase three-month commercial paper, both secured and unsecured. The commercial paper that was eligible for purchase was newly issued, highly rated, US dollar-denominated, unsecured, and asset-backed commercial paper with a three-month maturity. Issuers whose commercial paper was purchased by the LLC were required to pay an initial facility fee as well as fees at the time of each purchase. This financing was then to be secured by the assets placed into the SPVs and by the fees paid by issuers of unsecured paper. The New York Fed closed the CPFF in February 2010 after it no longer became necessary as the financial sector and the broader economy recovered.

1057 MMIFF was a facility created in October 2008 to support a private-sector initiative designed to provide liquidity to US money market investors. Under the MMIFF, the New York Fed provided senior secured funding to a series of special purpose vehicles (SPVs) to facilitate an industry-supported private-sector initiative to finance the purchase of eligible assets from eligible investors. Eligible assets included US dollar-denominated certificates of deposit and commercial paper issued by highly rated financial institutions with remaining maturities of 90 days or less. Eligible investors included US MMMFs and other US money market investors. The MMIFF complemented the CPFF and the AMLF facilities and intended to improve liquidity in short-term debt markets and thereby increase the availability of credit. The MMIFF commenced operations on 24 November of 2008 and expired on 30 October 2009.

1058 TALF was a facility created by the Fed in November 2008 to boost consumer spending in order to help restart the economy. It did this by issuing loans to banks using asset-backed securities (ABS) as collateral. The collateral for these securities was made up of illiquid assets (auto loans, student loans, credit card loans, equipment loans, floor plan loans, insurance premium finance loans, loans guaranteed by the Small Business Administration (SBA), residential mortgage servicing advances, or commercial mortgage loans). This increased banks' liquidity as they issued more credit to consumers and small businesses, which increased economic activity. The backing for these loans came from funds provided

Moreover, the Fed increased its international presence during the 2007–2009 financial crisis since it became an international lender of last resort for other central banks. In December 2007, set up swap lines with the European Central Bank (ECB) and the Swiss National Bank (SNB) in order to allow them borrow dollars from the Fed so they could provide domestic banks with dollar loans.[1059] After the Lehman's demise, the Fed expanded its swap lines with the central banks of Japan, Canada, Brazil, Denmark, Mexico, South Korea, United Kingdom, Sweden, Norway, Australia, Singapore, and New Zealand. At their peak, in December 2008, these swap lines amounted up to $600 billion.[1060]

The Fed also adopted radical measures regarding its monetary policy, with non-conventional monetary tools. Its large-scale asset purchases (LSAPs) program aimed at lowering the interest rates for particular types of credit and its Government Sponsored Entities Purchase Program (GSEPP), peaked at $1.25 trillion aiming at supporting mortgage-backed securities market and lower interest rates on residential mortgages.[1061] This program had as a result the increase of the Fed's balance sheet and of the monetary base and was broadly perceived as the first quantitative easing (QE1). In 2010, the Fed further announced that it would continue its expansionary monetary policy by purchasing $600 billion of long-term Treasury securities at a rate of about $75 billion per month. The program aimed at lowering long-term interest rates and became known as the second quantitative easing (QE2). Finally, in September 2012, the Fed announced a third large scale asset purchase program, which combined elements of the QE1 and QE2 since it conducted purchases of $40 billion of MBSs and $45 billion of long-term Treasury securities, but also had differences since it was open ended, without a fixed dollar amount, and purchases would continue as long as the market needs required them. This program was known as the third quantitative easing (QE3) and in December, the Fed announced that this program would be gradually phased out.[1062]

Apart from providing liquidity to the system and conducting monetary policy the Fed was also engaged in rescues and liquidation of several financial institutions that failed during the financial turmoil. The Fed brokered the deal between Bear Stearns and JPMC by purchasing $30 billion of distressed assets

---

by the New York Fed, which lent up to $200 billion on a non-recourse basis to holders of certain AAA-rated ABS backed by newly and recently originated consumer and small business loans. The New York Fed extended loans in an amount equal to the market value of the ABS, less a retained percentage known as a haircut, and these loans were secured at all times by the ABS.

1059 See in S. Mishkin and E.N. White, 'Unprecedented Actions: The Federal Reserve's Response to the Global Financial Crisis in Historical Perspective', Working Paper 20737, *NBER Working Paper Series*, National Bureau of Economic Research (NBER), December 2014, p. 9.

1060 Ibid.

1061 Ibid.

1062 Ibid., p. 10.

that JPMC rejected and moreover, expanded the federal safety net to include insurance firms by providing $85 billion to keep AIG afloat.[1063] Penultimate, at the same time, was collaborating with the Treasury and the FDIC to ensure that their actions and initiatives were closely coordinated and lobbied Congress to ensure that legislation will be adopted in a timely manner.[1064] Finally, regarding Fed's supervisory actions, the Treasury announced in February 2009, that the 19 largest banking institutions in the US would be placed under the Supervisory Capital Assessment Program (SCAP). SCAP would administer stress tests, run by the Fed, in close cooperation with the OCC and the FDIC.[1065] The stress tests improved market confidence, encouraged the recapitalisation of the underperformed banks and generally stabilised the market.

6.2. *The Enactment of Dodd-Frank Wall Street Reform and Consumer Protection Act*

The US Congress, shocked by the enormous bailout bill, decided to take action to safeguard that similar situation will never happen again. In January 2009, the Treasury issued Obama's administration blueprint for financial reform. The most important legislative act was the Dodd-Frank Act[1066] that contains numerous provisions, spelled out almost in 900 pages, that were to be implemented over a period of several years. The Act describes and regulates almost everything: from mortgage lending to shareholder voting rights, and from resolution of financial institutions to derivatives clearing and systemic oversight and reshaped the nature of the US financial system. Even though a more systematic analysis of the Dodd-Frank Act's content is beyond the scope of the present book, we are obliged to write a few lines about it since it remains the cornerstone legislation of the US financial regulation. Therefore, it is important to briefly describe, even in bullet points, what the Act contains not only for reasons of coherence but also for having an overview of the regulatory framework. The Act:

- imposes more stringent prudential standards – including tougher requirements for capital, leverage, risk management, mergers and acquisitions, and stress testing – on BHCs and other financial firms whose failure could threaten the stability of the US financial system,
- gives the Federal Reserve more authority to supervise more effectively the activities of non-bank companies,

1063 Ibid., p. 11.
1064 Ibid.
1065 Ibid.
1066 See in *supra* n. 440.

- established within the SEC the 'Office of Credit Ratings' (SEC OCR),[1067]
- requires more transparent trading and clearing of derivatives and, through the so-called 'Volcker Rule', prohibits insured depository institutions, from dealing in derivatives for their own account,
- requires banks, lenders, and others, whenever they securitise an asset, to hang on to a portion of the credit risk (to put more skin on the game),
- to help ensure regulators don't lose sight of the big picture, it establishes the Financial Stability Oversight Council (FSOC), whose membership includes the heads of all the financial regulatory agencies,
- requires large banks and other financial institutions to submit so-called 'living wills',[1068]
- establishes the Orderly Liquidation Authority (OLA), a way to take systemically important non-bank financial firms that are on the verge of collapse, place them in government receivership, and unwind them in a way that insulates the US economy from the undesirable effects of their collapse,
- deprives the Fed from some autonomy to provide emergency credit assistance, since the Act allows the Fed to make emergency loans but only through programs that are broadly available to many firms, not only to a single firm,
- established a new regulatory agency, the Consumer Financial Protection Bureau (CFPB),[1069] engulfed within the Treasury Department, dedicated to financial consumer protection,
- requires lenders to verify a (mortgage) borrower's ability to repay a loan and establishes the concept of 'qualified mortgages',[1070] and
- bans yield-spread premiums, a form of incentive compensation that often, encouraged originators to steer prospective borrowers into more expensive loans,

---

[1067] The purpose of the office is to ensure that Credit Rating Agencies provide meaningful and reliable credit ratings of the businesses, municipalities, and any other entities that they evaluate.

[1068] 'Living Wills' are special documents, prepared by the firms themselves, to explain to the regulatory agencies how these firms would deal with their own demise in the absence of extraordinary government support.

[1069] The CFPB has the power to enforce most federal financial consumer protection laws and has broad new consumer protection authority over medium-sized and larger banks and financial companies, including powers to regulate basic financial transactions (deposit taking and check cashing) and to set and enforce rules against abusive acts or practices. The CFPB became a highly controversial element of the Dodd-Frank Act. The CFPB has a single director structure instead of the board structure that typically have the financial institutions regulators. In its 2020 decision *Seila Law LLC v. Consumer Financial Protection Bureau* - 140 S. Ct. 2183 (2020), the US Supreme Court found the CFPB's structure violates the separation of powers.

[1070] 'Qualified Mortgages' are mortgage loans that meet certain criteria and, as a result, are considered to satisfy the ability-to-pay requirement. Any violation of the qualified mortgage standard is a defence against foreclosure.

- strengthened and expanded the existing whistleblower program, as it has been promulgated by the Sarbanes-Oxley Act of 2002.

6.2.1 The Volcker Rule

The most important aspect of the Dodd-Frank Act, at least for our analysis, is the so called 'Volcker Rule', enacted as Section 619, of the Act. Former Fed chairman, Paul Volcker, proposed that banks should be barred from holding ownership interests in hedge funds and private equity funds and should not also engage in proprietary trading in securities, commodities, or derivatives. Volcker wanted to stop banks from using their FDIC insured deposits and the Fed discount window loans to fund their speculative trades and investments in financial instruments.[1071] His argument was that proprietary trading and investing by banks was a dangerous and unfair exploitation of the benefits provided by the federal safety net subsidies. Volcker's argumentation found its way to the Obama administration and in January 2010, his rule was endorsed by President Obama to rally for public support.[1072]

As enacted, the rule restricts the way banks can invest, aiming at limiting speculative trading and eliminating proprietary trading. Banks are not allowed to be involved with hedge funds or private equity funds, which are considered too risky and to minimise possible conflicts of interest, financial firms are not allowed to trade proprietarily without sufficient 'skin in the game'. The Volcker Rule allows banks to buy and sell financial instruments for three basic purposes: a) underwriting, b) risk mitigation – hedging, and c) market making. Moreover, it allows banks to invest up to 3% of their equity capital in minority interests in hedge funds and private equity funds. The problem with these three activities is that it will be extremely difficult to distinguish, in practice, between a prohibited and a permitted activity, but this will be further discussed below.[1073] The Volcker Rule generally prohibits a banking entity from a) engaging in proprietary trading[1074] and from b) sponsoring or having (acquire or retain) an equity, partnership, or any other ownership interest in a hedge fund or a private equity fund.[1075] On the above general prohibitions, certain clarifications must be provided regarding the ambit of the rule.

- The term 'banking entity' means any (FDIC) insured depository institution, any company that controls an (FDIC) insured depository institution, or that is treated as a bank holding company for purposes of section 8 of the

---

1071 See in A.E. Wilmarth Jr., *Taming the Megabanks, Why We Need a New Glass-Steagall Act*, New York, Oxford University Press, 2020, p. 302.

1072 Ibid.

1073 Ibid.

1074 12 U.S.C. § 1851(a)(1)(A).

1075 12 U.S.C. § 1851(a)(1)(B).

International Banking Act of 1978, and any affiliate or subsidiary of any such entity.[1076]

- The term 'proprietary trading', when used with respect to a banking entity or a non-bank financial company supervised by the (Federal Reserve) Board, means engaging as a principal for the trading account of the banking entity or non-bank financial company supervised by the Board in any transaction to purchase or sell, or otherwise acquire or dispose of, any security, any derivative, any contract of sale of a commodity for future delivery, any option on any such security, derivative, or contract, or any other security or financial instrument that the appropriate Federal banking agencies, the SEC, and the CFTC may, by rule determine.[1077]
- The terms 'hedge fund' and 'private equity fund' mean an issuer that would be an investment company, as defined in the Investment Company Act of 1940, but for section 3(c)(1) or 3(c)(7) of that Act, or such similar funds as the appropriate Federal banking agencies, the SEC, and the CFTC May, by rule determine.[1078]
- The term to 'sponsor' a fund means:
    - 'To serve as a general partner, managing member, or trustee of a fund',[1079]
    - 'In any manner to select or to control (or to have employees, officers, or directors, or agents who constitute) a majority of the directors, trustees, or management of a fund',[1080]
    - 'To share with a fund, for corporate, marketing, promotional, or other purposes, the same name, or a variation of the same name, except as permitted under subsection (d)(1)(G)(vi)'.[1081]

The Volcker Rule, apart from prohibiting, also makes a variety of exceptions. These exemptions are stipulated, as 'permitted activities', as follows:

- 'The purchase, sale, acquisition, or disposition of obligations of the United States or any agency thereof, obligations, participations, or other instruments of or issued by the Government National Mortgage Association (Ginnie Mae), the Federal National Mortgage Association (Fannie Mae), the Federal Home Loan Mortgage Corporation (Freddie Mac), a Federal Home Loan Bank, the Federal Agricultural Mortgage Corporation, or a Farm Credit System institution chartered under and subject to the provisions of the Farm Credit Act of 1971, and obligations of any State or of any political subdivision thereof.',[1082]

1076 12 U.S.C. § 1851(h)(1).
1077 12 U.S.C. § 1851(h)(4).
1078 12 U.S.C. § 1851(h)(2).
1079 12 U.S.C. § 1851(h)(5)(A).
1080 12 U.S.C. § 1851(h)(5)(B).
1081 12 U.S.C. § 1851(h)(5)(C).
1082 12 U.S.C. § 1851(d)(1)(A).

- 'The purchase, sale, acquisition, or disposition of securities and other instruments [...] in connection with underwriting or market-making-related activities, to the extent that any such activities permitted [...] are designed not to exceed the reasonably expected near term demands of clients, customers, or counterparties.',[1083]
- 'Risk-mitigating hedging activities in connection with and related to individual or aggregated positions, contracts, or other holdings of a banking entity that are designed to reduce the specific risks to the banking entity in connection with and related to such positions, contracts, or other holdings.',[1084]
- 'The purchase, sale, acquisition, or disposition of securities and other instruments [...] on behalf of customers.',[1085]
- 'Investments in one or more small business investment companies, as defined in section 102 of the Small Business Investment Act of 1958, investments designed primarily to promote the public welfare, [...], or investments that are qualified rehabilitation expenditures with respect to a qualified rehabilitated building or certified historic structure, or a similar State historic tax credit program.',[1086]
- 'The purchase, sale, acquisition, or disposition of securities and other instruments [...] by a regulated insurance company directly engaged in the business of insurance for the general account of the company and by any affiliate of such regulated insurance company, provided that such activities by any affiliate are solely for the general account of the regulated insurance company, if':[1087]
  - 'The purchase, sale, acquisition, or disposition is conducted in compliance with, and subject to, the insurance company investment laws, regulations, and written guidance of the State or jurisdiction in which each such insurance company is domiciled',[1088]
  - 'The appropriate Federal banking agencies, after consultation with the FSOC and the relevant insurance commissioners of the States and territories of the US, have not jointly determined, after notice and comment, that a particular law, regulation, or written guidance described in clause (i) is insufficient to protect the safety and soundness of the banking entity, or of the financial stability of the United States',[1089]
- 'Organizing and offering a private equity or hedge fund, including serving as a general partner, managing member, or trustee of the fund and in any manner selecting or controlling (or having employees, officers, directors, or

1083 12 U.S.C. § 1851(d)(1)(B).
1084 12 U.S.C. § 1851(d)(1)(C).
1085 12 U.S.C. § 1851(d)(1)(D).
1086 12 U.S.C. § 1851(d)(1)(E).
1087 12 U.S.C. § 1851(d)(1)(F).
1088 12 U.S.C. § 1851(d)(1)(F)(i).
1089 12 U.S.C. § 1851(d)(1)(F)(ii).

agents who constitute) a majority of the directors, trustees, or management of the fund, including any necessary expenses for the foregoing, only if':[1090]

- 'The banking entity provides bona fide trust, fiduciary, or investment advisory services',
- 'The fund is organized and offered only in connection with the provision of bona fide trust, fiduciary, or investment advisory services and only to persons that are customers of such services of the banking entity',
- 'The banking entity does not acquire or retain an equity interest, partnership interest, or other ownership interest in the funds except for a de minimis investment subject to and in compliance with paragraph (4)',
- 'The banking entity complies with the restrictions under paragraphs (1) and (2) of subparagraph (f)',
- 'The banking entity does not, directly or indirectly, guarantee, assume, or otherwise insure the obligations or performance of the hedge fund or private equity fund or of any hedge fund or private equity fund in which such hedge fund or private equity fund invests',
- 'the banking entity does not share with the hedge fund or private equity fund, for corporate, marketing, promotional, or other purposes, the same name or a variation of the same name, except that the hedge fund or private equity fund may share the same name or a variation of the same name as a banking entity that is an investment adviser to the hedge fund or private equity fund, if:
  - such investment adviser is not an insured depository institution, a company that controls an insured depository institution, or a company that is treated as a bank holding company for purposes of section 8 of the International Banking Act of 1978,
  - such investment adviser does not share the same name or a variation of the same name as an insured depository institution, any company that controls an insured depository institution, or any company that is treated as a bank holding company for purposes of section 8 of the International Banking Act of 1978, and
  - such name does not contain the word "bank"'
- 'no director or employee of the banking entity takes or retains an equity interest, partnership interest, or other ownership interest in the hedge fund or private equity fund, except for any director or employee of the banking entity who is directly engaged in providing investment advisory or other services to the hedge fund or private equity fund; and
- the banking entity discloses to prospective and actual investors in the fund, in writing, that any losses in such hedge fund or private equity fund are borne solely by investors in the fund and not by the banking entity, and otherwise complies with any additional rules of the appropriate

[1090] 12 U.S.C. § 1851(d)(1)(G).

Federal banking agencies, the SEC, or the CFTC, [...], designed to ensure that losses in such hedge fund or private equity fund are borne solely by investors in the fund and not by the banking entity'.

- 'Proprietary trading conducted by a banking entity [...], provided that the trading occurs solely outside of the United States and that the banking entity is not directly or indirectly controlled by a banking entity that is organised under the laws of the United States or of one or more States'.[1091]
- 'The acquisition or retention of any equity, partnership, or other ownership interest in, or the sponsorship of, a hedge fund or a private equity fund by a banking entity [...] solely outside of the United States, provided that no ownership interest in such hedge fund or private equity fund is offered for sale or sold to a resident of the United States and that the banking entity is not directly or indirectly controlled by a banking entity that is organised under the laws of the United States or of one or more States'.[1092]
- 'Such other activity as the appropriate Federal banking agencies, the SEC, and the CFTC determine, by rule, [...], would promote and protect the safety and soundness of the banking entity and the financial stability of the United States'.[1093]

Such a rich palette of exemptions undoubtedly masks the effectiveness of the Act. The simplicity of the proprietary trading prohibition, as a conceptual framework, has been blurred by all these numerous exemptions, that primarily aim to facilitate the rule's implementation. Moreover, to perplex even more the situation, the Act also contains exemptions to the permitted activities. As such, limitations on permitted activities apply, when 'the transaction, class of transactions, or activity':

- 'Would involve or result in a material conflict of interest [...] between the banking entity and its clients, customers, or counterparties',[1094]
- 'Would result, directly or indirectly, in a material exposure by the banking entity to high-risk assets or high-risk trading strategies [...]',[1095]
- 'Would pose a threat to the safety and soundness of such banking entity',[1096] or
- 'Would pose a threat to the financial stability of the United States'.[1097]

The rule's implementing regulation (Regulation VV) provides further exceptions for various types of funds that are exempted from the general prohibition for investing and sponsoring a hedge fund or a private equity fund, such as inter alia venture capital funds, ABCP conduits, family wealth

---

1091 12 U.S.C. § 1851(d)(1)(H).
1092 12 U.S.C. § 1851(d)(1)(I).
1093 12 U.S.C. § 1851(d)(1)(J).
1094 12 U.S.C. § 1851(d)(2)(A)(i).
1095 12 U.S.C. § 1851(d)(2)(A)(ii).
1096 12 U.S.C. § 1851(d)(2)(A)(iii).
1097 12 U.S.C. § 1851(d)(2)(A)(iv).

management vehicles, loans securitisations and small business organisations.[1098] The banking entity's combined investment in any one fund generally cannot exceed 3% of the ownership interests in the fund, and the (banking) entity's combined investments in all funds cannot exceed 3% of the entity's total tier 1 capital.[1099] Ultimately, the Volcker Rule does not apply to a) a banking entity with less than $10 billion in total consolidated assets[1100] and b) if the entity engages only in limited trading activities, the entity's total trading assets and trading liabilities can't exceed 5% of the entity's total consolidated assets.[1101]

The main idea behind the Volcker Rule's enactment was that proprietary trading is an inherently risky activity that institutions with access to the federal safety net, the FDIC, must not engage with. At the same time, sponsoring of hedge funds and private equity funds was also perceived as risky and barred insured banks from also engaging with. The rule, in its final form, creates an extremely complex environment for banks to comply with. Implementing regulations impose strict and burdensome requirements and the biggest issue is how regulators and regulated institutions will distinguish between activities that are permitted and activities that are non-permitted.

6.2.2 Other (Structural) Reforms

When Donald Trump was elected president of the US, back in 2016, he pledged to repeal the Dodd-Frank Act. On 24 May 2018, he signed a new law, the Economic Growth, Regulatory Relief and Consumer Protection Act of 2018,[1102] (better known as the Crapo Bill), which rolled back significant portions of Dodd-Frank Act. Among its provisions, the most important are the following:

- Easing of the Dodd-Frank regulations for small and regional banks by increasing the asset threshold, from $50 billion to $250 billion, for the application of prudential standards, stress test requirements and mandatory risk committees ('to big to fail' standards),
- Exemption from the Volcker Rule requirements, lenders with assets less than $10 billion and impose less stringent reporting requirements and capital norms on them,
- Requiring that the three major credit reporting agencies allow consumers to freeze their credit files without any charge as a way of deterring fraud,
- Lower capital requirements and leverage ratios for institutions that have custody of clients' assets but do not function as traditional bankers or lenders,

---

1098 12 C.F.R. § 248.10(c).

1099 12 C.F.R. § 248.14(a)(2)(ii)–(iii).

1100 12 U.S.C. § 1851(h)(1)(B)(i).

1101 12 U.S.C. § 1851(h)(1)(B)(ii).

1102 Economic Growth, Regulatory Relief, and Consumer Protection Act, Pub. L. No. 115-174, 132 Stat. 1296 (2018).

- Directs the FHFA to set up standards and for Freddie Mac and Fannie Mae to consider alternative credit scoring methodologies, and
- Exemption from the escrow requirements for residential mortgage loans that are held by a depository institution or credit union under certain conditions.

Since these amendments are relatively new their impact will take some time before they are fully understood. Moreover, the ensuing Trump, Biden and the current second Trump administration have its own impact on the financial sector and must be given also the necessary time to make a real impact in the new environment which is characterised by a turn towards protectionism.

7 THE MARCH 2023 BANKING TURMOIL

The March 2023 banking turmoil is considered as the most significant system-wide banking crisis since the 2007–2009 global financial crisis in terms of scale and scope. The bank failures, while having largely distinct causes, triggered a broader crisis of confidence in the resilience of banks, banking systems and financial markets across multiple jurisdictions, most notably the US and Switzerland. In response, wide-scale public support measures were deployed by some jurisdictions to mitigate the impact of the stress. The reason we examine this banking turmoil within this section is twofold. On the one hand the US financial system was again at the epicentre of the turmoil, demonstrating once more its inability to supervise its banks properly and actively, particularly those which are perceived as less significant and/or less important in terms of financial stability, and on the other hand because we can again evaluate the structural reforms regulation using that turmoil as a yardstick for their necessity.

7.1. Events and Actions Taken

7.1.1 The Case of Silicon Valley Bank

The first victim of the turmoil was, on 10 March 2023, Silicon Valley Bank (SVB), a subsidiary of the Silicon Valley Bank Financial Group (SVBFG), a large bank holding company with almost $212 billion in assets when it failed in March 2023 and was closed by the California Department of Financial Protection and Innovation (CADFPI). SVBFG provided financial services predominantly to companies from the technology and life sciences sectors.[1103] Between 2019 and 2021, SVBFG tripled in size as it benefited from rapid deposit

[1103] See in Basel Committee on Banking Supervision (BCBS), *Report on the 2023 banking turmoil*, October 2023, p. 6.

inflows during aggressive venture capital (VC) and technology sectors' growth amid a period of exceptionally low interest rates. These deposits were largely uninsured, and SVBFG invested them primarily in securities with longer-term maturities. In 2022, as interest rates began to rise, SVBFG saw deposit outflows and a rapid increase in unrealised losses on those securities.[1104]

Given that the risks to its balance sheet mounted, SVBFG decided to address the issues, and on 8 March 2023, announced a plan to restructure its balance sheet and seek fresh capital from investors.[1105] The next day, 9 March 2023, SVB experienced a bank run as withdrawals of uninsured deposits rapidly accelerated, losing over $40 billion in deposits, and SVBFG management expected to lose over $100 billion more on 10 March. These deposit outflows were remarkable in terms of scale and scope when compared with other episodes of banking stress and reflected fundamental concerns about the bank and appear to have been sparked by several interrelated factors:[1106]

- heightened uncertainty and changing sentiment around the technology sector;
- potential negative action from credit rating agencies; and
- highly correlated withdrawals from SVBFG's concentrated network of VC investors and technology firms who, fuelled by social media, withdrew uninsured deposits in a coordinated manner at an unprecedented rate.

In response to these actual and expected outflows SVB failed on 10 March, which in turn led to the later bankruptcy of SVBFG. During the final days before its failure, SVB's operational weaknesses became apparent as it struggled to execute on its contingency funding plans. SVB had two major shortcomings that set the stage for its loud collapse: a) its risk management framework, which failed to keep up with its expanding business operations and rapid asset growth, and b) its failure to develop a sufficient contingent funding capacity.[1107] Therefore, its demise can be attributed directly to a lack of proper functioning of its Board of Directors and senior management, because collectively they failed to 'effectively oversee the risks inherent in SVBFG's business model and balance sheet strategy'.[1108] Moreover, supervisors also bare an important share of the blame because they failed to timely identified and appreciate the material issues that plagued SVBFG's internal governance framework. The Federal Reserve's review of SVBFG's supervision and regulation demonstrated that 'supervisors identified some of the material issues, but also underappreciated

---

1104 Ibid.

1105 SVBFG had sold $21 billion in available-for-sale (AFS) securities, was booking a $1.8 billion after-tax loss, was planning to increase term borrowings by $15 billion to $30 billion and was seeking to raise $2.25 billion in capital.

1106 See in Basel Committee on Banking Supervision (BCBS), *Report on the 2023 banking turmoil*, October 2023, p. 6.

1107 Ibid., p. 7.

1108 Ibid.

important ones, particularly during the period of SVBFG's rapid growth'.[1109] Despite the clear evidence of the foundational issues that SVB was facing, supervisors were slow to their reactions and didn't timely downgrade the supervisory ratings or they didn't ensure that the Board of Directors and the senior management would took sufficient and timely decisions to address the issues identified.[1110]

SVB was also internationally active, with a subsidiary operating in the UK (SVB UK).[1111] The demise of SVB resulted in the resolution of SVB UK as well. The UK PRA understood that SVB UK was exposed to concentration risk, as it provided loans and took deposits from the same relatively concentrated client base in the innovation sector. These parameters drove the UK PRA, for the last 18–24 months, to focus its supervision on concentration risk, and on the overlap of clients on the asset and liability side of the balance sheet. These items (concentration in assets and the interest rate risk in the banking book (IRRBB)) were discussed with both the firm and the Federal Reserve and furthermore were recognised in SVB UK's Pillar 2 capital requirements.[1112] SVB UK failed because of its parent company failure and despite the fact the UK subsidiary was able to meet all the deposit outflow demands until Friday, 10 March 2023.[1113] The ongoing belief that the UK bank would not be able to continue meeting the withdraw requests should the run persisted, forced the UK authorities to take action and on Friday evening, the Bank of England (BoE), as the UK's Resolution Authority, after consulting with HM Treasury, the UK Prudential Regulation Authority (PRA) and the UK Financial Conduct Authority (FCA), decided to place SVB UK into administration, after taking into account that any such decision would not jeopardise the financial stability in the UK.[1114]

The UK authorities' decision to put SVB into administration and then sell all or part of the failed bank was timely and prudent and the conclusion of the sale to HSBC, early on Monday morning, 13 March 2023, secured the availability of deposits and the bank's business continuity under the new ownership.

1109 Ibid., p. 8.

1110 Ibid.

1111 SVB UK was focused on commercial banking in the innovation sector (technology, life sciences and healthcare). Among its clients were start-ups, large corporates, VC, and private equity funds, as well as the companies in which they have invested. SVB UK had operated in the UK since 2012, initially as a UK PRA-FCA dual-regulated branch, and then since July 2022 as a subsidiary.

1112 See in Basel Committee on Banking Supervision (BCBS), *Report on the 2023 banking turmoil*, October 2023 p. 8.

1113 SVB UK would not have been a standalone entity because of her reliance on its US parent company for the IT infrastructure and systems, including the payment infrastructure.

1114 See in Basel Committee on Banking Supervision (BCBS), *Report on the 2023 banking turmoil*, October 2023, p. 10.

7.1.2 The Case of Signature Bank

Signature Bank New York (SBNY) was a full-service, commercial bank founded in 2001 as a de novo bank.[1115] Its main business lines were commercial real estate and commercial and industrial lending, principally funded through uninsured deposits collected from mid-sized commercial companies. Starting in 2018, SBNY began to expand its business model by launching other lending and deposit taking initiatives, including a Fund Banking Division dedicated to providing financing and banking services to the private equity industry and a Digital Assets Banking Group to collect cash deposits and maintain operating accounts for various digital asset-related businesses.[1116] Similar to SVB, SBNY experienced tremendous deposit growth relying heavily on uninsured deposits relative to its peer banks. During the pandemic, the bank's size more than doubled, resulting in total deposits of $88.6 billion at the end of 2022 and with total assets of $110 billion was ranked as the 29th largest US bank.[1117]

The main reason behind SBNY's demise was illiquidity brought on by contagion in the wake of Silvergate Bank's self-liquidation on 8 March 2023 and of SVB's failure on 10 March 2023, but the root cause of its failure was its 'poor management'.[1118] Similar to SVB, the SBNY's board of directors and its senior management pursued the bank's rapid expansion without proper internal governance and risk management framework for the complexity, business model, size and risk profile of the bank, which grew more than 150% within 5 years (2017-2022).[1119] The lack of fundamental liquidity risk management controls and practices was a disastrous partner to an expansion fuelled by overreliance to uninsured deposits. Furthermore, the failure in understanding the risk associated with its exposure to the crypto assets industry deposits and the potential contagion from their activities further undermined its stability when the black swans of the crypto industry appeared. Like the SVB case, supervisors were not very prudent when assessing SBNY's vulnerabilities and business model. The lack of sufficient resources from their side combined with hesitance to take proper and timely actions resulted in a protracted period during which SBNY was expanding at a fast pace and the internal issues, although identified, were never properly addressed. FDIC in many times, failed to timely communicate to SBN's board of directors the results of the

---

1115 A de novo bank is a bank that has not been acquired through purchase and is newly chartered by the Federal Deposit Insurance Corporation (FDIC). A de novo bank can be a commercial, state, national, savings, or thrift bank, among others, or even a newly opened branch of an existing bank.

1116 See in Basel Committee on Banking Supervision (BCBS), *Report on the 2023 banking turmoil*, October 2023, p. 10.

1117 Ibid.

1118 Ibid., p. 11.

1119 Ibid.

supervisory examinations leaving them no space for prompt action. Lack of human resources from FDIC's side did not allow for consistent supervisory examinations since the responsible team was changing composition and adequate staffing was always a reason for not closely examining the spotted issues from a supervisory perspective.[1120]

Overall, SBNY's poor governance, inadequate risk management practices and rapid balance sheet expansion without proper controls and supervisory scrutiny created the lethal cocktail that led to its demise. SBNY was not in apposition to manage effectively its liquidity needs in a time of stress and the run which was produced from Silvergate's self-liquidation and the SVB collapse exposed her to the cruelty of crypto assets markets. The very large withdrawal requests from its crypto clients exposed liquidity risk management related problems and further increased anxiety in the US markets.

7.1.3 The Case of First Republic Bank

First Republic Bank (FRB), established in 1985, was a commercial bank and provider of wealth management services headquartered in San Francisco, California. It was focused on providing banking services to high-net-worth (HNW) individuals including residential real estate lending, private banking and wealth management services, business banking, trust, and brokerage services, while operating 93 offices in 11 states, primarily in New York, California, Massachusetts, and Florida. As of 31 March 2023, the bank's balance sheet mounted on $233 billion of assets with a total of $105 deposits, 49% of which were uninsured and was the 14th largest US bank and the 2nd largest under FDIC's supervision.[1121] Despite having good examination results and historically been a well-run bank with responsiveness to supervisory feedback and recommendations, FRB's business model and management strategies made her vulnerable to interest rate changes and to the contagion resulted from SVB and SBNY's demise. FRB's biggest issues were:[1122]

(a) Its rapid growth and loan and funding concentrations,
(b) Its overreliance on uninsured deposits and depositor loyalty, and
(c) The interest rate risk mitigation failure.

During the weekend of 10 March 2023, FRB experienced a sudden lack of market and depositors' confidence which resulted in significant outflow of uninsured deposits.[1123] This loss of liquidity was very similar to SVB's situation and together with the substantial value difference in the loans' fair value and

---

1120 See in Basel Committee on Banking Supervision (BCBS), *Report on the 2023 banking turmoil*, October 2023, p. 12.

1121 Ibid., p. 16.

1122 Ibid.

1123 Ibid.

book value further aggravated the balance sheet characteristics. The contagion effect from the SVB and SBNY collapses caused immediate liquidity stress to FRB with a mounted uninsured deposits outflow. This liquidity stress forced FRB to receive huge amounts from the Federal Reserve Discount Window as well as from the Federal Home Loan Bank. Few days later, on 16 March 2023, eleven American banks including JPMC, Bank of America, Wells Fargo, Citigroup, and Truist Financial, deposited $30 billion within FRB, succeeding to slower the deposits' outflow rate. Despite the deposits, shares of the company declined because of an earnings call that revealed a loss of over $100 billion in deposits during the first quarter of 2023.[1124] Since the majority of the bank's long term assets were comprised of municipal bonds, FRB was unable to make full use of the Bank Term Funding Program – an emergency lending program enacted after the collapse of SVB – as those assets did not qualify as an eligible collateral. Given the constant deterioration of bank's condition and the lack of progress in restoring its lost confidence the FDIC and the CADFPI decided to downgrade the bank to 'problem status' on 28 April 2023. This action further deteriorated market confidence and eliminated the bank from having access to Fed's discount window. On 1 May 2023, the CADFPI decided to close the bank and appoint FDIC as a receiver, which in turn through the purchase and assumption approach agreed with JPMC to assume all the deposits and assets of FRB and as part of the agreement, all offices in all states reopened the same morning as branches of JP Morgan Chase.[1125]

7.2. Lessons Learned (?) from the 2023 Turmoil

The Basel Committee on Banking Supervision (BCBS) on its Final Report for the 2023 banking turmoil summarises the lessons learned based on three broad categories:

(a) Bank risk management practices and governance arrangements,
(b) Strong and effective supervision,
(c) Robust regulatory standards.

From the facts presented above, it was demonstrated the need for the banks to have in place strong and effective risk management practices and governance arrangements that will understand the operating business model, the associated risk, and the expansion/growth of the assets. Big balance sheets and complex strategies and products require complex and sophisticated risk management practices as well as a governance body that is fully aware of all the risks of the strategy. According to the BCBS final report, the major fault lines were:

[1124] Ibid.
[1125] Ibid., p. 17.

- 'Fundamental shortcomings in basic risk management of traditional banking risks' (liquidity risk and interest rate risk, various forms of concentration risk),[1126]
- 'a failure to appreciate how the build-up of various individual risks were interrelated and could compound one another',[1127]
- 'Inadequate and unsustainable business models, including an excessive focus on growth and short-term profitability (fuelled by remuneration policies), at the expense of appropriate risk management',[1128]
- 'a poor risk culture, as well as ineffective senior management and board oversight',[1129] and
- 'a failure to adequately respond to supervisory feedback and recommendations'.[1130]

Moreover, the 2023 banking turmoil highlighted the need for strong, efficient, and effective supervision. The BCBS identified the need for enhanced supervision across various dimensions, including:

- 'The ability and willingness of supervisors not just to actively identify weaknesses in banks but also to take and enforce prompt actions',[1131]
- 'The need to ensure supervisory teams have the appropriate quantity and quality of resources',[1132]
- 'The need to continuously monitor exogenous and structural changes to the banking system and adapt supervisory approaches to overseeing risks, especially for banks that are rapidly growing in size or adopting novel business models'[1133] and the need for
- 'Maintaining effective and timely cross-border supervisory cooperation across a wide network'.[1134]

Finally, with respect to the regulatory standards, the BCBS opened the discussion for a critical review of the liquidity risk framework as well as the application of the Basel III framework to the smaller banks, which are not internationally active but as demonstrated from the recent turmoil can effectively contaminate other healthy institutions and lead to failures. In the BCBS own wording: 'The regulatory framework is not calibrated to produce "zero failures" but seeks to reduce the likelihood and impact of a banking

---

1126 Ibid., p. 1.
1127 Ibid.
1128 Ibid.
1129 Ibid.
1130 Ibid.
1131 Ibid., p. 2.
1132 Ibid.
1133 Ibid.
1134 Ibid.

stress, while facilitating financial intermediation and economic growth.'[1135] Against this background, the identified lessons could be highlighted as follows:

- 'the importance of a full and consistent implementation of Basel standards',[1136]
- 'the importance of a robust design and calibration of global standards for internationally active banks',[1137]
- 'the need for a balanced approach between Pillar 1 regulation and Pillar 2 supervision, with robust and rigorous Pillar 2 approaches pursued as complements, and not substitutes, to Pillar 1 requirements',[1138]
- 'the potential for banks that are deemed to be not internationally active in a jurisdiction to pose cross-border financial stability risks, including through indirect contagion channels',[1139]
- 'the need for proportionate regulatory frameworks to reflect the Committee's expectations – as set out in the Basel Core Principles (BCPs) – that any proportionate approaches are commensurate with a bank's risk profile and systemic importance'.[1140]

What the BCBS has identified as potential lessons from the recent turmoil surprisingly relates to the essence of banking business and has nothing to do with exotic and sophisticatedly structured high-risk products. Liquidity risk management, contagion and concentration risk and sound governance are banking business's essentials and are considered as fundamentals for every bank that takes its business seriously. Not to mention the need for sound and effective supervision where the public authorities perform their duties timely and with sufficient resources. Concluding our analysis, the 2023 banking turmoil demonstrated again what we support in this book. Banks fell victim to their own ambitions and of flawed supervision. The regulatory framework was in place and even after the last global financial crisis it has been substantially reinforced but without guarantee of success. The nature of business, and in our case the discussion about structural reforms, has nothing to offer as added value if the core risk management principles for the banking business are not in place and both banks and supervisors tend to ignore them or hesitate to take prompt actions to correct their failures. The simplest banking operations, such deposits acceptance, can have devastating effects if improper practices are in place, as shown by the recent turmoil.

1135 Ibid.
1136 Ibid.
1137 Ibid.
1138 Ibid.
1139 Ibid.
1140 Ibid.

8 CONCLUDING REMARKS

The US banking system was and remains unique; its 'dual banking' nature, both the state and the federal level, is a blessing and a curse at the same time. A blessing because they offer different banking products to different customers and effectively (?) compete with each other but at the same time create a regulatory architecture that imposes, by definition, several constraints. The reforms since the recent GFC put again the BHC at the epicentre of the regulation of banking sector but the Congress was unwilling to return to the old religion as many advocates of GSA would crave for. Such a return would be a highly dubious step for securing financial stability as long as US banks continue to play a leading role in the international financial system. The Dodd-Frank Act did not reinstate the complete separation between investment and commercial banks but adopted a narrower approach and simply banned, completely, proprietary trading for certain banks, both at state and federal level. The delegated regulations are extremely difficult to apply and compliance with their requirements is a heavy burden with consequences that are difficult to calculate.

The truth is that as long as the US financial system remains capital market based, commercial banks will always have to compete with securities firms and other shadow banking entities that offer similar, and less regulated products. The survival of the banking sector is crucial and will always try to implement legislation in ways that will provide some free room for manoeuvring to be competitive and follow the markets' trends. Studying and understudying the US financial sector regulation, and particularly the need, or nor, for separation between commercial and investment banks is of extreme importance for the present book since it is the basis for other case studies that we will examine (Japan) or is exactly the other side of the fence (Europe). Whether the recently adopted regulation, Volcker Rule, will be successful is only a matter of time. The fear that other non-bank entities will assume the proprietary trading part that banks left behind and will perform such a role in a less regulated environment is and will always be present, but for the moment the system seems to work. How efficiently or how effectively is a matter of another science to discover it.

CHAPTER 2
CANADA: THE IMPECCABLE NEIGHBOUR?

For the needs of the present book, Canada offers a great example of a country that managed to survive from the recent GFC almost unscratched, while at the same time maintains a high level of sophistication to its financial sector. Therefore, an analysis and deeper understanding of how the Canadian authorities succeeded in adopting and implementing such policies that prevented the Canadian financial system from contamination while being so closely related with the source of the turmoil. Furthermore, since no major crisis has happened to Canada for many years, we should examine if these unique(?) features of the Canadian financial system shall be attributed to the way authorities perform their tasks or to the structure of the financial system itself and of Canadian banks specifically.

Canada has a very interesting financial system. Perceived by many as a traditionally conservative banking system (with the classical/anecdotal 3-6-3 banking model),[1141] with a proven record of effective regulation and supervision, sharing its borders with the United States and at the same time having minor effects from the recent GFC and the turmoil of 2023, Canada appeared to be a lost paradise during these turbulent years.[1142] Canada was different and has been praised by stakeholders, press, and academics for its efficiency in managing the waves from the meltdown of the GFC and succeeding to maintain financial stability with minimum disruptions (ABCP market event). No Canadian bank failed or even needed a bail out from the government and some of them even posted healthy profits during the crisis contrary to its southern neighbour.[1143] The Canadian banking system followed the general trend in the 1980s towards greater liberalisation and moved from the so called '4 pillars' system to an integrated system, where the financial institutions were able to mix, under

---

1141 Anecdotally, the old 3–6–3 model of banking – take deposits at 3 percent, make loans at 6 percent, and be on the golf course at 3:00 p.m.

1142 See in P. Meredith and J.L. Darroch, *Stumbling Giants, Transforming Canada's Banks for the Information Age*, Toronto, University of Toronto Press, 2017, p. 3 onwards.

1143 See in M. Copelovitch and D.A. Singer, *Banks on the Brink, Global Capital, Securities Markets, and the Political Roots of Financial Crises*, Cambridge, Cambridge University Press, 2020, p. 88.

strict and specific conditions, the offered services (universal banking model). We will therefore proceed as follows: we will first examine the current state of financial system's regulation in Canada and then we will use a historical and legal approach to understand how the current style of regulation has been formatted and why Canadian banks appear to be more crises-avert than others. We will then specifically analyse the structural regulation measures that are into force and explore to what extent these measures are efficient and effective as a crisis prevention mechanism.

1 A CURRENT OVERVIEW OF THE CANADIAN FINANCIAL AND BANKING SYSTEM: THE REGULATORY AND SUPERVISORY FRAMEWORK

Canadian banks are traditionally characterised as conservatives and their results during the recent GFC have been praised from international community and many scholars as a very important lesson for the rest of developed countries. At the same time, the entire financial system in Canada seems to perform at optimum level with no major disruptive events. Although the few crises' events in Canada do not allow us to have a reach and solid bibliography based on a historical approach, it is important to understand the formation of the financial sector in Canada through a historical lens. Moreover, the federal system of Canada has certain limits on how rules are produced and applied, limits that play an important role in the shaping of the system's structure. As a compass to this research, we will mostly use the most recent peer review report from the Financial Stability Board (FSB) and when necessary, we will make a historical throwback to better understand how the structural reforms were implemented to the Canadian financial and banking system.

Canadian banks have a heritage that represents a structural advantage: their industry is an oligopoly anchored around a strong domestic universal banking model. During the 1980s, Canadian banks were permitted to acquire brokerages and trust companies leading to a consolidation of the financial industry together with business diversification through expansion in insurance asset management business.[1144] According to the FSB peer review, the Canadian financial 'is large compared to the economy' with total assets representing a 336% high of GDP.[1145] The financial system is primarily a bank-based one, with credit institutions possessing more than 74% of its total assets. Credit

---

1144 See in A. Docherty and F. Viort, *Better Banking, Understanding and Addressing the Failures in Risk Management, Governance and Regulation*, Wiley Finance Series, Chichester, Wiley, 2014, p. 233.

1145 See in Financial Stability Board (FSB), *Peer Review of Canada, Review Report*, 30 January 2012, p. 8.

institutions are comprised of chartered banks, credit unions and '*caisses populaires*' (credit unions in the French speaking communities).[1146] Anand and Peihani, based on more recent data, supported that currently (as of 2019) the Canadian financial system has grown more, holding assets totalling 500% of the Canadian GDP.[1147]

With respect to the Canadian banking sector is dominated by the so-called 'big-six', federally chartered banks.[1148] Together, they account for more than 90% of total banking assets and offer a full range of banking, investment, and other financial services to their customers.[1149] Canadian banks have access to an expanded network of branches across the entire country (nationwide branching). At the same time are internationally active banks with presence in many countries, the most important of them are US, Latin America, and the Caribbean.[1150] Canadian banks have succeeded generating half of their profits from their international operations while at the same time their domestic operations face increased competition from regional banks and credit unions.

1146 See in C. Kobrak and J. Martin, *From Wall Street to Bay Street, The Origins and Evolution of American and Canadian Finance*, Toronto, University of Toronto Press, 2018, p. 220. The *caisse populaire* was established in 1900 as a co-operative savings and loan company with non-fixed capital and limited liability in Lévis, Quebec, by Alphonse DESJARDINS, a journalist and French-language stenographer in the House of Commons. Desjardins used as models for his enterprise the European savings and loan co-operatives. He encouraged the working classes to save and plan their future and provided the credit they needed for economic recovery. Desjardins also hoped the *caisse* would contribute to the economic emancipation of French Canadians. The '*Caisse populaire de Lévis*' opened on 23 January 1901 in Desjardins's own home and 12 people paid a total of $26.40 as first payment of their share in the partnership. The first savings deposit, made on 7 February was for only 5 cents. By 1906, savings amounted to nearly $40,000. Within the same year, after vigorous lobbying by Desjardins and his friends, the Quebec legislature adopted the Act on co-operative syndicates and until 1920, when Desjardins died, 219 *caisses populaires* had been established in Canada, including 23 in Ontario and 9 in French-Canadian communities in New England, largely because of the clergy's unfailing support of and eager participation in this undertaking.
Through the years, *caisses populaires* have created or acquired many financial subsidiaries operating in the insurance, trust, and industrial and commercial investment sectors, as well as the funds management, securities brokerage, and banking services sectors. With some 40,000 employees, what is now known as the '*Mouvement Desjardins*' is currently the largest private employer in Quebec.

1147 See in A. Anand and M. Peihani, 'Regulating Systemic Risk in Canada', in D. Arner et al. (eds.), *Systemic Risk in the Financial Sector: Ten Years After the Great Crash*, Waterloo, Centre for International Governance Innovation, 2019, p. 13.

1148 The 'big six' federally chartered banks are: 1) Bank of Montreal (BoM), 2) Bank of Nova Scotia, 3) Toronto-Dominion (TD) Bank, 4) Royal Bank of Canada (RBC), 5) National Bank of Canada (NBC), and 6) Canadian Imperial Bank of Commerce (CIBC).

1149 See in A. Anand and M. Peihani, 'Regulating Systemic Risk in Canada', in D. Arner et al. (eds.), *Systemic Risk in the Financial Sector: Ten Years After the Great Crash*, Waterloo, Centre for International Governance Innovation, 2019, p. 13.

1150 See in Financial Stability Board (FSB), *Peer Review of Canada, Review Report*, 30 January 2012, p. 8.

At the same time, large Canadian corporations enjoy access to borrowed funds mostly through international capital markets and syndicated loans, led by foreign banks.[1151] Consequently, what remains to be their domestic business model is the consumer and mortgage lending. Particularly the credit unions, are competing with the big six on equal terms and in some provinces are serving half of the population by providing financial services to small businesses and households. This expanded credit union system is supported by eight provincial centres and one federal, aiming at providing liquidity and payment settlement services to the member credit unions. As of February 2018, total Canadian household credit stood at $2.1 trillion, and chartered banks accounted for more than 71% of that amount.[1152] In this environment we must also take into account the presence of the so-called shadow banking system, which according to the Bank of Canada's (BoC) estimates, its credit value amounts to $1.1 trillion, an amount roughly half the total bank credit.[1153] The most important components of the Canadian shadow banking system are investment funds, repurchase agreements (repos) and securities lending transactions.[1154]

Canadian banks are facing a complex regulatory framework regarding their supervision. Due to the federal nature of the Canadian state and legal system, financial and banking regulation applies at two different levels: the federal and the provincial level. At the federal level, the basic supervisor and regulator is the Office of the Superintendent of Financial Institutions (OSFI), which is assigned to act both as prudential regulator and supervisor for the financial institutions that are federally regulated (banks, trust and loan companies and insurance companies) and for the private pension plans.[1155] At the same time, many other important 'players' participate in this complex federal regulatory framework. BoC is responsible to provide liquidity to the Canadian financial system, to oversee key payment, clearing and settlement systems while also assesses the risks that threaten the entire financial system (macro-prudential oversight).[1156] Moreover, the Department of Finance (DoF) is responsible for the overall stability of the financial system and with an overarching authority over the financial sector legislation. Finally, the Canada Deposit Insurance Corporation (CDIC), insures the deposits of member institutions and is the competent authority for the resolution regime in Canada and the Financial

---

[1151] Ibid.

[1152] See in A. Anand and M. Peihani, 'Regulating Systemic Risk in Canada', in D. Arner et al. (eds.), *Systemic Risk in the Financial Sector: Ten Years After the Great Crash*, Waterloo,: Centre for International Governance Innovation, 2019, p. 13.

[1153] Ibid., p. 14.

[1154] Ibid.

[1155] See in Financial Stability Board (FSB), *Peer Review of Canada, Review Report*, 30 January 2012, p. 9.

[1156] Ibid.

Consumer Agency of Canada (FCAC) which is tasked with the protection of the consumers that make use of the various financial products that are available in the Canadian market, at federal level.[1157]

OSFI's approach towards the federally chartered banks facilitates to enact policies that are aimed at mitigating the systemic risk and are fully aligned with the international standards as produced by the BCBS. In March 2013, OSFI designated the 'big-six' as Domestic-Systemically Important Banks (D-SIBs), thus subjecting them to stricter capital requirements, more disclosure requirements and intense supervision.[1158] The banking system is also regulated at provincial level, especially for the banks that are not federally charted and thus operate locally in the various Canadian provinces. Provincial regulation applies to those banks that are engaging in securities markets and in trustee activities. At the same time, since most of the credit unions and *caisses populaires* are almost exclusively incorporated at the provincial level are thus also provincially regulated, both for prudential and market conduct purposes.[1159]

According to FSB's peer review, the life insurance sector in Canada is dominated by three internationally active firms, Manulife, Sun Life and Great-West Life, that at the same time they compete in the wealth management services field. What is also remarkable with this dual level of regulation is that life and health insurance companies and the trust and loan companies are regulated at federal level for prudential purposes and at provincial level for their market conduct behaviour. Moreover, pension plans are also regulated at a double level, with shared competence among provinces and the federal government.[1160] Of great importance is the securities regulation in Canada because banks are allowed to participate in this special sector and therefore are required to comply with special requirements. Canada has three stock exchanges: the Toronto Stock Exchange (TSX), the TSX Venture Exchange (TSXVE) and the Canadian National Stock Exchange which is an alternative option for emerging companies.[1161] The domestic Canadian debt market has a relatively large size and government debt represents a large part of it. The Montreal Exchange is the financial derivatives exchange for Canada and in total, the Canadian market accounts for approximately 2% of the global market.[1162]

1157 Ibid.

1158 See in A. Anand and M. Peihani, 'Regulating Systemic Risk in Canada', in D. Arner et al. (eds.), *Systemic Risk in the Financial Sector: Ten Years After the Great Crash*, Waterloo, Centre for International Governance Innovation, 2019, p. 16.

1159 See in Financial Stability Board (FSB), *Peer Review of Canada, Review Report*, 30 January 2012, p. 10.

1160 Ibid., p. 9.

1161 Ibid.

1162 Ibid.

Securities regulation is not assigned to the federal level and remains a provincial competence. Each province is responsible for the regulation and supervision of the securities activities that take place within the territory of the province.[1163] Laws and regulations are generally harmonised across the provinces even though provinces have their own regulatory authority. Special attention should be given to the coordination among the provincial authorities for the effective application of the legislation. The Canadian Securities Administrators (CSA) is an umbrella organisation of voluntary nature, that seeks to improve coordination, cooperation, and harmonisation of the Canadian capital markets regulation. In recent years, the CSA has developed a major solution to the regulatory fragmentation, the 'passport system' through which a market participant has access to securities markets in all passport-participating jurisdictions by dealing only with its principal regulator and complying with one set of harmonised laws. This system is a major step forward in improving Canada's securities regulatory system by providing market participants with streamlined access to Canada's capital markets and by alleviating to a certain extent the regulatory burden. Provincial and territorial securities regulators tend to rely on self-regulatory organisations (SROs) for the regulation and supervision of the market and its participants. The two most important SROs are the Investment Industry Regulatory Organization of Canada (IIROC) and the Mutual Fund Dealers Association of Canada (MFDAC).[1164] Furthermore, collaboration is facilitated by a network of several mechanisms, which stand between the federal level and the provincial level. These mechanisms include:

(i) The Financial Institutions Supervisory Committee (FISC), which is chaired by the Superintendent of the OSFI and with, at least, quarterly meetings, is mandated by the OSFI Act to facilitate the consultation and the exchange of information among the BoC, CDIC, OSFI, FCAC and the DOF, on matters relating to the supervision of financial institutions.

(ii) The Senior Advisory Committee (SAC), which is chaired by the Deputy Minister of Finance, acts as a forum for discussions regarding financial sector policy issues, including macro-prudential oversight and financial stability issues. The aim of the committee is to provide advice to the Minister of Finance regarding the optimal policy choices, and the membership is the same as the FISC, although, when necessary, other government agencies might be invited to participate in the deliberations.

1163 The provincial authorities for the securities regulation in Canada are a) AMF (Autorité des marchés financiers) for Quebec, b) ASC (Alberta Securities Commission), c) BCSC (British Columbia Securities Commission), d) FCNB (Financial and Consumer Services Commission (New Brunswick)), e) MSC (Manitoba Securities Commission), f) NSSC (Nova Scotia Securities Commission), and g) OSC (Ontario Securities Commission).

1164 Ibid., p. 10.

(iii) The Heads of Agencies Committee (HAC) is chaired by the BoC Governor, and its members are a) the four largest Canadian provincial securities regulators,[1165] b) the Chair of the CSA, c) OSFI, and d) DOF. The committee serves as a forum to exchange views and information, to coordinate actions and initiatives on mutual concern issues (hedge funds, derivatives, etc.).

(iv) Other mechanisms of coordination are the 'CSA Systemic Risk Committee', established in 2009, where identification and analysis of systemic risks takes place regarding the Canadian financial markets and the 'CDIC Board of Directors', where the possible resolution tools are explored when needed.

2 THE CANADIAN BANKING SYSTEM UNDER A HISTORICAL PERSPECTIVE

The Canadian banking system has the prestigious title of being one of the safest and soundness of the world. At the same time, Canadian economy has a smooth functioning with growth and ability to absorb crises that may arise without any major consequences. In complete contrast with its 'naughty' neighbour, the US, and even though both banking and financial systems are based on a federal state with separation of powers, Canada's banking system seems to have always been well regulated and supervised. This unique feature of Canadian banks was extremely important during the recent GFC, where the system performed at a very satisfactory level helped by the effective regulation and supervision. Therefore, in understanding why and how Canada managed to avoid major negative events from the recent GFC, we should look through the historical perspective and understand the origins of the creation and evolution of the banking system in Canada.

2.1. The Early Years (Prior to the 1867 Constitution)

Since the very beginning, Canada was settled from both French and English migrants. This 'dual ethnicity issue' had been always a crucial parameter in the formation of one and coherent state that should engulf all the population, irrespective of their origins. Differences in language, culture, legal systems (French civil law and the English common law) and of course policy priorities among the two communities had always to be considered when the state was trying to form a coherent policy agenda over a matter. During the earliest days of French settlement in Canada, barter was widely accepted as the general

1165 These regulators are the provinces of Alberta, British Columbia, Ontario, and Quebec.

method of trade and there was no local currency. The coins and merchandise customarily sent from France returned there for the purchase of imports. One year, when a shipment did not arrive, Intendant François Bigot issued signed playing cards, redeemable in coins and merchandise (when they arrived) and ordered the colonists to accept them as money. By 1760, the colony was 80 million livres in debt, much of it in worthless ordinances issued by Bigot. After the British conquest, the British used Mexican, Spanish, Portuguese, French and German coins to pay their troops, which, with trade goods, became the coin of the realm.

In 1792, nine merchants from Montréal established the Canada Banking Company, but because it could not obtain permission to issue bank notes it failed. Two other similar ventures, in 1807 and 1808 respectively, failed as well. During the War of 1812, the governor issued 'army bills' that bore interest and could be exchanged for cash, government bills of exchange in London or more army bills. In 1817, the Bank of Montreal (BoM), a joint-stock operation owned by 289 subscribers, opened its doors in Canada but did not get approval of its charter until 1822. Two other banks also received their charters about this time - the Bank of New Brunswick in 1820 and the Bank of Upper Canada (BUC) in 1821.[1166] The BUC was controlled by the Family Compact, and the legislature of the time refused charters to any group unless some of its members belonged to the oligarchy. BUC received its charter from the legislature of Upper Canada in 1819 and its royal assent in 1821 and had the expectation from the relevant provincial government to be a prominent holder of the bank's stock.[1167] In contrast, the BoM, chartered by the Lower Canada legislature in 1817 and granted royal assent in 1822, had significantly fewer formal ties to the government and according to its charter was permitted to establish branches in both Lower and Upper Canada.[1168] At the same time another bank, the Bank of the People, was established by the enterprising Francis Hincks, who became prime minister of the Province of Canada and was later Sir John A. Macdonald's finance minister. He was responsible for ensuring the passage of Canada's first Bank Act (1871)[1169] and was later named president of the Consolidated Bank. This patchwork of banks, operating in Canada, each had its own idiosyncratic procedures regarding the issuance of

1166 As *Upper Canada* (modern day Ontario) came to be known the area bordering the Lake Ontario, where the famous St. Lawrence River begins its journey towards the Atlantic Ocean. The name was used to honour the prime location at the top of the river. The area further downstream and extending to the north was known as the *Lower Canada* (modern day Quebec). For more details see in M. Copelovitch and D.A. Singer, *Banks on the Brink, Global Capital, Securities Markets, and the Political Roots of Financial Crises*, Cambridge, Cambridge University Press, 2020, p. 92.

1167 Ibid., p. 94.

1168 Ibid.

1169 An Act respecting Banks and Banking, S.C. 1871, c. 5.

bank notes and backing them with gold or government bonds.[1170] In 1850, the new legislation, the Free Banking Act, attempted to minimise the influence of provincial legislation in the banks' chartering process but the end result was to encourage the establishment of 'unit banks', banks with a single only location, and exacerbated the existed fragmentation of the banking system. Thirty years later, in 1880, the Act was repealed after only five banks were established under its provisions.[1171] At the same time, the provinces had strong interests in safeguarding their exclusive control over the process of bank chartering. Apart from receiving a steady flow of chartering fees, provinces also enjoyed a quid pro quo with the banks that they helped to create. The bank's founders would implicitly pledge their support to the government of the province in exchange for granting the necessary charter.[1172] Obviously, the charter would be accompanied by various strings attached, including the requirement to hold government bonds as backing for the issuance of banknotes. In such a case, the province would be able to rely on the bank as a buyer of its bonds, ultimately resulting in issuing more debt at a lower interest rate.[1173] This quid pro quo, had strongly linked together the bankers and the politicians in each province, thereby leaving no room for politicians to succumb to any incentives for allowing the chartered banks from other provinces to enter their and offer services. The banking landscape in both Canada and the US looked very similar by the middle of the 19th century and argue that the banking business was clearly a subnational phenomenon.[1174] The Canadian provinces – or in the case of the US the state governments – had the sole authority and responsibility to grant bank charters. A big difference although between the two systems was that, during these first years, the Canadian banking model, was more a copy of the English unlimited branching model, and therefore banks were facing no restrictions on expanding their presence within the territorial boundaries of the country. On the contrary, in the US, unit banking was more common. Overall, both banking systems were highly fragmented with limited involvement of the national government.[1175]

2.2. *From the 1867 Constitution to the Great Depression*

The modern Canadian banking system was born in 1867, with the British North American Act (BNAA) of 1867, or better known as the Constitution Act,

---

1170 See in M. Copelovitch and D.A. Singer, *Banks on the Brink, Global Capital, Securities Markets, and the Political Roots of Financial Crises*, Cambridge, Cambridge University Press, 2020, p. 94.

1171 Ibid., p. 95.

1172 Ibid.

1173 Ibid.

1174 Ibid.

1175 Ibid.

which created the modern Canada.[1176] Under the blessing of the British crown, Canadian political leaders agreed to create a national government granted with sweeping powers over the economic and commercial policy. Furthermore, the Act formalised the establishment of provincial governments and clarified the important powers that were delegated to them. Since the drafting of the Canadian Constitution coincided with the US civil war, Canadian politicians like Sir John Mcdonald,[1177] during the 1864 Quebec Conference, where the basis for the Constitution were led down in the form of the famous 72 Resolutions, opted for a more powerful central government to avoid the *bras de fer* between the provinces and the central government, that appeared to tear apart the US. Contrary to US Constitution, in which any unspecified policy was assumed to be within the jurisdiction of the individual states, the Canadian Constitution Act opted for any power not specifically delegated to the provinces to be retained by the national government.[1178] Against this background, Canada has granted to the national government exclusive control over its banking legislation and regulation, compared to the extremely fragmented among the states US option. The details of the banking were left to be determined later with separate legislation. The Banking Act of 1871 formalised every necessary detail and established such a solid regime for banking, parts of it are still in force today.[1179] The act introduced a few important rules that set the founding stones of banking in Canada. Firstly, it required that all new banks require national charters, and that Parliament would be responsible for granting them. Any bank created under the previous regime would be given enough time until 1881 to renew its charter, under the new process, by applying for a new national charter.[1180] Secondly, the new charters were coupled with high requirements regarding the capital that should be gathered by the founders,

---

1176 The British North America Act of 1867 is a major part of the Constitution of Canada. The Act created a federal dominion and defined much of the operation of the Government of Canada, including its federal structure, the House of Commons, the Senate, the justice system, and the taxation system. Canadian Confederation was the process by which three former British North American provinces, the Province of Canada, Nova Scotia, and New Brunswick, were united into one federation called the *Dominion of Canada*, on 1 July 1867. Upon Confederation, Canada consisted originally of four provinces: Ontario and Quebec (which had been split out from the larger Province of Canada), and the provinces of Nova Scotia and New Brunswick. Over the years since Confederation, Canada has seen numerous territorial changes and expansions, resulting in the current number of ten provinces and three territories.

1177 Sir John Alexander Macdonald (1815–1891) was the first prime minister of Canada, serving from 1867 to 1873 and from 1878 to 1891. He is considered as a dominant figure of Canadian Confederation and had a reach political career for almost half a century.

1178 See in M. Copelovitch and D.A. Singer, *Banks on the Brink, Global Capital, Securities Markets, and the Political Roots of Financial Crises*, Cambridge, Cambridge University Press, 2020, p. 98.

1179 Ibid., p. 99.

1180 Ibid.

in order to be eligible to apply for them.[1181] The measure of high capital requirements performed a double role. On the one hand it ensured that the banks would be large, thereby forcing them to open branches over large areas to secure adequate deposit and lending bases. On the other hand, it also served as an entry restriction with many commentators calling that system 'a cartel backed by the central government'.[1182]

The evolution of the Canadian banking system was performed across further integration. According to Copelovitch and Singer, from around 51 banks during the 1870–1920 period to less than 10 through the rest of the century, the trend was always towards 'fewer but more stable' banks.[1183] However, we must keep in mind for that period is that Canadian banks also failed, but to a much smaller extent compared to the US banks. Copelovitch and Singer further believe that it would be an exaggeration to claim that Canadian banks of that period were all equally sound and stable, as the Canadian myth around financial stability has. While legislation at that time encouraged geographical diversification across the country, banks still found themselves in trouble and failed for various reasons, other than portfolio diversification. Luminous examples of that reality were the Ontario Bank and the Home Bank.[1184] The first bank failed in 1906 due to fraud by the bank's managers and of catastrophic bets in the US stock market and the latter failed in 1923 for similar reasons, even though it accounted for 1% of national bank capital back at that time. Home bank failure was helpful overall, since it propelled the creation of the national bank regulator, two years after the event.[1185] The Office of the Inspector General of Banks was renamed to the current OSFI in 1987 when it assumed the insurance sector under its jurisdiction.

One aspect of the Canadian banking landscape that existed since its inception but with enormous importance even for today is the constant absence of important competition and pressure from the capital markets. Canadian financial system was and still is a bank based financial system since its nascent years. Even though nowadays the Toronto stock exchange is among the most important exchanges of North America, the pressure to the banking system was and still is of less importance compared to more mature, deep, and competitive markets such as in the US. From the very beginning, the endless Canadian landscape with the abundant natural resources was in dire need of capital to overcome the various transportation and logistics needs that should be dealt with for a country that is so big. Therefore, the

1181 Ibid., where the bank managers had to secure subscribed capital of at least $500,000 with at least $100,000 in hand before the bank could open its doors.

1182 Ibid.

1183 Ibid., p. 100.

1184 Ibid.

1185 Ibid.

rise of capital markets was a necessity that should complement the banking system in supplying the necessary amounts of capital needed. The Canadians had to face two major challenges: a) the need to create specialised markets where the exchange would take place and the participants would transact[1186] and b) the need to build trust among the participants that integrity would prevail for both markets and securities themselves.[1187] Canada's reaction to the above challenges was challenged by the fact that the constitution was not helpful towards creating a single exchange market. The result was to emerge an extremely fragmented stock market with a decentralised regulation assigned to the provinces. This geographic fragmentation is attributable to the high transactional costs of trading stocks back in the 19th and 20th centuries.[1188] The BNAA did little to prevent this fragmentation. Back in that time, no consensus among the politicians was reachable since the benefits from a fragmented and dispersed stock trading system could not outweigh the benefits from direct banking relations and political quid pro quo.

The market crash and the Great Depression, fuelled by drought conditions and a worldwide economic slump, contributed to a change in government and unprecedented public criticism of Canada's banking system. This was a nationwide shock for Canada which it also coincided with Prime Minister R.B. Bennett's concern that Canada lacked a direct means for settling international accounts. A national policy response was necessary to stabilise the entire financial system, and in this context the government established the country's first central bank, the BoC, in 1934.[1189] The BoC received its royal assent in 1934 and in 1935 opened its doors to the public. Compared to the centrally 'governed' banking system, the securities industry remained fragmented and without a single set of rules or even a centrally performed coordination

1186 Ibid., p. 103.

1187 Ibid., p. 104.

1188 Ibid., p. 105.

1189 The story behind the creation of Canada's central bank has as follows: In 1933, Prime Minister Bennett, set up a Royal Commission to study 'the organization and working of our entire banking and monetary system [and] to consider the arguments for or against a central banking institution'. The Royal Commission, headed by Lord Macmillan, recommended in its report the establishment of a central bank. A week after the report was made public, the Prime Minister announced that his government would adopt the recommendations put forward by the Royal Commission. An appendix to the report, titled 'Suggestions as to some of the Main Features of the Constitution of a Central Bank for Canada', became the framework for the Bank of Canada Act, which formally established the central bank. In March 1935, the Bank of Canada opened its doors as a privately owned institution, with shares sold to the public. Soon after the Bank opened, a new government introduced an amendment to the Bank of Canada Act to nationalize the institution. In 1938, the Bank became publicly owned and remains so today. Source: Bank of Canada official website, https://www.bankofcanada.ca/about/history/.

was resembled to 'a patchwork of idiosyncratic markets with widely varying rules'.[1190]

2.3. *From the Great Depression to Present: A Tale of (De)Regulation and Success*

Canadian financial system entered the modern years with relevant stability and optimism. The country's central bank managed to enhance stability in the system and the single set of banking regulatory legislation preserve the system from further turmoil. Historically, the Canadian financial system has been structured and evolved, through the years, around five separate and distinct principal groups: a) the chartered banks, b) the securities dealers, c) the credit cooperatives, d) the trust and loan companies, and e) life insurance companies.[1191] These groups were formatted-separated around their core business model and the mixing of offered services was not allowed. Moreover, the regulation of this system was shared among the federal and the provincial government or was explicitly assigned to one of them.[1192]

Chartered banks are incorporated and supervised by the federal government and have always been a crucial part of commercial lending operations. Since the mid-1950s, chartered banks have expanded their presence in the personal loans business as well as in that of residential mortgage credit. Moreover, as we saw earlier, they expanded their presence at an international level with significant exposure overseas. Securities dealers have traditionally operated under a provincial regulatory framework and various efforts, to upgrade into a federal one, have been rejected by the Canadian Supreme Court (CSC). Their core business consists of underwriting and selling of bonds and stock issues, offering investment advice and of course the trading of securities in the secondary markets.[1193]

Credit cooperatives, comprising of credit unions and *caisses populaires*, were and still are operating under the provincial regulatory and legislative framework. Their traditional business was to provide residential mortgages and personal loans but through the years, they also expanded their business lines

[1190] See in M. Copelovitch and D.A. Singer, *Banks on the Brink, Global Capital, Securities Markets, and the Political Roots of Financial Crises*, Cambridge, Cambridge University Press, 2020, p. 112.

[1191] See in C. Freedman, *The Canadian Banking System*, Technical Report No. 81, Staff Research, Bank of Canada, March 1998, p. 2.

[1192] Freedman provides an example where a bank was under the exclusive federal jurisdiction for its banking services while insurance companies and trust and loan companies could be incorporated either at federal or at provincial level. See in C. Freedman, *The Canadian Banking System*, Technical Report No. 81, Staff Research, Bank of Canada, March 1998, p. 3.

[1193] See C. Freedman, *The Canadian Banking System*, Technical Report No. 81, Staff Research, Bank of Canada, March 1998, p. 4.

into new services and products.[1194] Trust and loan companies were specialised institutions offering residential mortgage lending and term deposits. The federally incorporated and supervised institutions were controlling the bulk portion of the assets within this special sector, although it must be noted that many institutions were provincially incorporated. Over the years, and especially around the 1980s, these institutions moved into new business lines by offering consumer and commercial lending. Moreover, trust and loan companies were the only institutions that were allowed to offer fiduciary services to the public.[1195] Canada during the late 1980s followed the worldwide trend of deregulation in the financial services industry. Technological advances and the need for more sophisticated financial products forced Canadian banks to push collectively for new legislations that would allow them to diversify and expand into new business lines.

2.3.1 Amendments to the 1871 Banking Act

Gradually, with the aim of adjusting the banking system into modern trends and to international competition, the Canadian Parliament amended several times the 1871 Banking Act. Among the most important events in the Canadian banking regulation history, was the establishment, in 1961, of the 'Royal Commission on Banking and Finance', better known as 'Porter Commission', following the public disagreement of James Coyne, the then governor of the BoC,[1196] with the federal government's economic policies. The aim of the Porter Commission was to examine and to make recommendations for the improvement of 'the structure and methods of operations of the Canadian financial system, including the banking and monetary system and the institutions and processes involved in the flow of funds through the capital markets'. The commission, which included several representatives of banking institutions, made many recommendations in its 1964 final report, including the following:[1197]

- abolition of the 6% interest rate ceiling on bank loans,
- disclosure of bank-loan costs,

1194 Ibid., p. 3.

1195 Ibid.

1196 James Elliott Coyne, (born 17/07/1910 in Winnipeg, died 12/10/2012 in Winnipeg), was a banker and businessman, who served as governor of the Bank of Canada from 1955 until his resignation on 13 July 1961. Coyne's refusal to adopt the government's expansionist monetary policy irritated not only the then Finance Minister, Donald Fleming, but also many leading economists who signed an open letter calling for his resignation. Coyne initially refused but confronted with a bill firing him, he finally stepped down. Source: The Canadian Encyclopedia, available at: https://www.thecanadianencyclopedia.ca/en/article/james-elliott-coyne.

1197 Source: The Canadian Encyclopedia, available at: https://www.thecanadianencyclopedia.ca/en/article/royal-commission-on-banking-and-finance.

- entry of banks into conventional mortgage financing,
- enactment of legislation to prevent banks from agreeing to set common interest rates, chequing costs and other customer charges,
- recommended that trust companies, finance companies, creditors and other 'near-banks' be brought under the authority of the BoC,
- the Bank Act shall be amended so that the government can overrule the central bank on monetary policy issues, and
- government regulations shall be established to control mergers between banks and trust companies or bank takeovers of other financial institutions.

Some of the above-mentioned recommendations were incorporated into the 1967 Bank Act revisions.

2.3.1.1 *The 1954 and 1967 Amendments*

The most important change that the 1954 amendments brought in was the power given to banks to provide mortgage loans secure by the National Housing Association (NHA) and to make personal loans secured by mortgages on personal property. The NHA provided government guarantees to the banks for the loans made and these amendments permitted banks to enter the lucrative household lending business in a serious way.[1198]

The 1967 amendments were also important because, among other things, eliminated the 6% ceiling on the interest rate on the bank loans. This decision came naturally because the market interest rates had been already moved above 6% in the mid-sixties having the effect of forcing banks out of mortgage lending to households. Moreover, with these amendments, banks were prohibited from making agreements with any other bank on the rate of interest paid to deposits or the rate of interest that was charged on loans they provided.[1199] Another important amendment was the elimination of the restrictions on the banks' involvement in the residential mortgage financing as they were permitted to invest in non-insured or conventional mortgages.

Simultaneously, banks were prohibited from owing trust companies and at the same time a 10% ownership limit on the shares of banks was introduced with the dual aim to ensure that Canadian banks would remain under domestic ownership and control and that concentration of ownership would be also prevented.[1200] These limits also served as a way of preventing the commercial ownership of the banks and as a way to prevent self-dealing

[1198] See C. Freedman, *The Canadian Banking System*, Technical Report No. 81, Staff Research, Bank of Canada, March 1998, p. 7.

[1199] Ibid.

[1200] According to Freedman, that time was also introduced the 25% limit on aggregate ownership by the non-residents, that was subsequently removed in 1995. See in C. Freedman, *The Canadian Banking System*, Technical Report No. 81, Staff Research, Bank of Canada, March 1998, p. 8.

between a bank and its owners. The concentration limit was a clear reflection of growing competition concerns, and the ownership limit can be seen as a sign of protectionism towards the Canadian bank system, reflecting national priorities over the banking industry.[1201] At the same time, deposit insurance was also introduced in Canada for banks and for the loan and trust companies, following the failure of two small financial companies and the subsequent financial difficulties that were spread across the trust and loan sector.[1202] The federal government passed the act to establish the Canadian Deposit Insurance Corporation (CDIC) to provide CA$20,000 insurance for deposits in banks and federally chartered near-banks. Provincial near banks were included in most provinces by relevant provincial legislation. The maximum insurance coverage was raised to CA$60,000 in 1983, and then to CA$100,000 in 2005.

2.3.1.2 *The 1980 Amendments*

With these amendments, Canadian banks were allowed to have subsidiaries in various financial sectors, such as venture capital companies and mortgage loan companies, where the last were allowed to held deposits that were excluded from the reserves requirements.[1203] This allowed banks to compete effectively with trust companies whose deposits were not excluded from the reserves requirements. Furthermore, the 1980 amendments allowed foreign banks to establish subsidiaries in Canada, albeit under restrictions on their total size of business in Canada. These restrictions were removed for the US banks in 1989, as part of the Canada-US Trade Agreement, and in 1994 for Mexican banks as part of the North American Free Trade Agreement (NAFTA). In 1995, these restrictions were also lifted for the rest of the world, as part of the world trade negotiations.[1204] Also in 1980, the Canadian Parliament also passed the Canadian Payments Association (CPA) Act which took over the responsibility for running the cheque clearing system from the Canadian Bankers Association with the responsibility also to further plan the future evolution of the Canadian payment system. The CPA Act was binding upon both bank and non-bank deposit taking institutions.

1201 Ibid., p. 8.

1202 Ibid.

1203 Ibid., p. 8.

1204 According to Freedman, the initial ceiling was placed at 8% of total domestic assets of all banks in Canada but was raised to 16% in 1985, because it was believed that this ceiling might be a binding constraint. When the US banks were exempted from that ceiling in 1989, it was reduced again in 12% for the remaining foreign bank subsidiaries. See in C. Freedman, *The Canadian Banking System*, Technical Report No. 81, Staff Research, Bank of Canada, March 1998, p. 9.

2.3.1.3 *The 1987 Amendments*

Perhaps the most important amendments to the Banking Act were adopted by the Canadian Parliament in 1987. These crucial amendments in the Act and to the Province of Ontario legislation eliminated the similar Glass-Steagall type restriction that existed in the Canadian banking sector. Until 1987, the banking legislation kept the banks outside of the securities business in a way similar to the US. According to Freedman, a set of customs and law prevented banks from entering the securities business by imposing tight restrictions in both upstream and downstream linkages between banks and securities dealers. Moreover, explicit rules were shaping the framework of permitted activities for banks, by defining the types of securities that banks were allowed to engage in and the types of securities that banks were excluded from.[1205] Banks were permitted to invest in corporate securities, both debt and equity, but only for portfolio purposes. Also were able to participate in the underwriting process for government bonds, to buy and sell securities in general but on an agency basis and distribute corporate securities as members of a selling group.[1206] Subject to the selling group exemption the banking sector was prohibited from corporate securities underwriting until the 1987 amendments and the provincial regulation was imposing strict and significant market access restrictions to the foreign dealers. Finally, it is worth noting that a bank, until the 1992 amendments, could not engage in portfolio management or investment counselling by herself. The rationale behind the 1987 amendments was based on several key factors:

- The decline of bank lending to corporations that preferred market borrowing over the traditional channels of borrowed funds,
- The general trend towards globalisation and in particular globalisation of the financial markets across the world,
- The technological advances that created a friendlier and more modern investment environment,
- The fear and concern that securities dealers were not in a position to guarantee the generation and supply of the larger amounts of capital that would be needed in the future,
- The fact that banks and securities industry have already penetrated, one way or another, in the core business fields of one another.

Thus, the old regime of separating banks and securities industry was appearing to be under heavy pressure as banks were entering the securities fields and corporations were covering their short-term financing needs through the commercial paper markets and banker's acceptances. The changing trend in corporate borrowing was therefore the major force behind the two sectors'

[1205] Ibid.
[1206] Ibid., p. 10.

integration. Furthermore, traditional banking business was constantly losing market share from bonds, equities, paper market financing solutions and other innovative tools. Moreover, the international landscape was also changing with the Euro-Canadian dollar and the foreign exchange issues to further undermine banks' profitability and diminish their overall competitiveness against both domestic securities dealers and foreign banks and securities dealers.[1207] The same arguments that applied to achieve the repeal of the GSA in the US later in the century were used in the Canadian banks position to enter the securities industry. Synergies from an efficient, universal banking model, and the experience that would be gained from their investment banking operations would help them to regain their market share and increase their competition globally.[1208]

At the same time, Canadian securities dealers were facing increasing international competition and their capacity to stand at equal footing with their competitors was highly debatable. Furthermore, the structure of the Canadian securities market was dominated by relatively small securities firms within a highly protective environment in a highly competitive world.[1209] The principal argument was that securities firms needed a larger capital base to compete effectively in a world of 'bought deals' associated with greater risks, therefore more capital was in dire need, and the current Canadian market structure was not in the position to provide that capital. Furthermore, growing concerns that the Canadian securities market would be considered as a second-tier market if did not open to the world competition and provide motivations for the creation of innovative financial products, were catalysts towards the removal of the barriers. These concerns were exacerbated by the fact that foreign firms were possible to enter the Canadian securities market and by exploiting the various financial and technological innovations available would grab the lion's share from domestic firms. The pressure for changes in the market structure, drove the Ontario province to introduce new legislation, supported by governmental legislation aiming at opening the Ontario securities industry to outsiders. As a result, from 30 June 1987, the limit on investments in securities firms by Canadian financial institutions was eliminated and were able to acquire securities firms. Moreover, on the same day, non-residents were able to own up to 50% of an existing securities firm's capital and after a year, 30 June of 1988, the limit was set at 100%.[1210] Finally, direct entry into the Ontario market, by foreign securities firms, would be allowed without any limitations from that same day, 30 June 1987.[1211]

1207 Ibid., p. 10.
1208 Ibid., p. 11.
1209 Ibid.
1210 Ibid., p. 12.
1211 Ibid.

2.3.1.4 *The 1992 Amendments*

The 1992 legislative changes were also very important for the Canadian banking system. The outcome was almost a complete rewriting of the legislation applied to banks, trust, and insurance companies. The changes were focused mostly on the powers of the various institutions, their ownership status, and various ways of managing self-dealing and the relevant conflicts of interest. The 1992 amendments followed the same path and continued the breakdown of the previously existed traditional pillar system and allowed financial institutions to enter previously forbidden domains of business activities. The rationale for the legislative amendments was based on several underlined factors:[1212]

- A need for modernisation of the banking legislation,
- A desire to further break down the barriers that existed among the pillars of the Canadian financial system,
- The need and the pressure to further define the relevant business powers of each financial institution so that it would be clear which services were available for every institution,
- The need to deal effectively with the concerns raised by the increased potential self-dealing, conflicts of interest and ownership concentration among the financial institutions,
- The need to effectively respond to the concerns regarding the need for adequate and effective supervision and of the deposit insurance system's role,
- The need for further harmonisation of the provincial and federal legislation that governed the activities of non-bank financial institutions, especially after the recent legislative initiatives undertook by many provinces in that field,
- The recognition of the increasingly important role that securitisation and internationalisation played in the financial and banking sectors.

The first four factors were responsible for the initiation of the legislative amendments and the last three added to the impetus by changing the direction of the process.[1213] With the new legislation, the federal financial institutions obtained the power to diversify into new financial business through subsidiary entities, as well as with increased in-house powers. Another important aspect of the amendments was the fact that institutions with no fiduciary powers, such as banks and life insurance companies, were able to own trust subsidiary companies. At the same time, banks and trust and loan companies were allowed to own insurance companies while non-bank financial institutions were allowed to own 'Schedule II' banks, without having to comply with the requirement to

---

[1212] For a further analysis of the factors that motivated the 1992 legislation amendments see in C. Freedman, *The Canadian Banking System*, Technical Report No. 81, Staff Research, Bank of Canada, March 1998, p. 13.

[1213] Ibid., p. 14.

divest their significant positions within 10 years, as had the other entities.[1214] Trust, loan and life insurance companies, under the provisions of the 1992 legislative amendments were given more 'in-house' powers to enter into the consumer and commercial lending markets.[1215] At the same time, banks and loan companies were allowed to offer a number of 'in-house' activities, such as investment advice and portfolio management, in the same way as trust companies, life insurance companies and securities dealers were able to do so for a long time. Moreover, all financial institutions were permitted to network together most financial services offered by their affiliates or by independent financial institutions.[1216] The 1992 legislative amendments also further closed the gap between banks and other deposit-taking institutions by addressing the issue of imposing interest-bearing reserve requirements on non-banks deposit taking institutions but not on banks. This requirement was designed to be phased out over a two-year period aiming at a more level playing field competition for the same type of business.

Overall, with the 1992 amendments, the Canadian financial institutions were able, if they wish, to expand their offered business by developing themselves to financial conglomerates with involvement into various financial areas under, to a certain extent, the same roof. Although the model of classic universal banking seemed to be the ultimate destination after these amendments, this was not possible because of certain limitations on the investments in the non-financial business sector. Nevertheless, the new financial landscape was much closer to the universal banking model than the previous, separation-oriented, pillar system.

2.3.1.5 *The 1997 Amendments*

The 1997 amendments were aiming at fine tune the 1992 amendments and can be characterised as a response to certain problems that arose after the previous amendments. Apart from the legislative fine-tuning, the 1997 amendments also dealt with consumer issues, such as privacy, and with deposit insurance amelioration. Specifically, the banks which were not engaged in retail deposit taking were allowed to opt out from their participation in the deposit insurance membership.[1217] Further measures for foreign banks alleviate the burden of establishing presence in the Canadian market. Foreign banks were able to establish directly their presence through branches directly, under specific restrictions, instead of being required to operate a separately capitalised subsidiary. What must also be noted is that a year earlier, in 1996, the banking

[1214] Ibid., p. 14.
[1215] Ibid.
[1216] Ibid.
[1217] Ibid., p. 15.

industry had voluntarily set up an independent ombudsman's office to resolve customer complaints about banks and investment dealers. The Ombudsman for Banking Services and Investments (OBSI) operates with a board of directors and staff independent from the banking industry.

2.3.1.6 *The 2001 Amendments*

The 2001 amendments were based on the proposals of the Task Force on the Future of the Canadian Financial Services Sector. The Task Force undertook a comprehensive review of the financial sector and in September 1998 delivered its final report.[1218] The conclusion was that the financial system was strong, working well, and that institutions generally did a good job with the offered services.[1219] The task force identified several measures that could be further improved and proposed 124 recommendations for enhancing the competition among the institutions, improving the regulatory framework and further empowering consumers. The aims of the 2001 amendments therefore were wide ranging. Promotion of efficiency and growth of the financial sector, greater domestic competition, improvement of the regulatory framework and finally empowerment and protection for consumers. Especially for the federally chartered banks, the amendments provided for more freedom regarding the available activities. The broaden scope of investment activities that were permitted to be performed either in-house or through their subsidiaries provided them with more opportunities to innovate and offer new financial products to their customers. With the amendments was easier for these institutions to have significant partners in the joint venture operations and enhanced their ability to meet the constantly increasing technological and competition challenges from the 'monoline' and unregulated institutions that offered specialised businesses.

Another important aspect of the 2001 amendments had to do with the ownership regime of the banks. Since the 1967 amendments, the bank ownership regime in Canada was based on the 'principle of wide ownership' of the major banks. This principle had been construed as follow: Prior to 2001 and according to that principle, a distinction was made between two categories, the so-called 'Schedule I' and 'Schedule II' banks. In the Schedule I category, were included the six largest domestic banks and were required to be 'widely held'. The precise meaning of widely was that no single shareholder and/or group of associated persons could hold more than 10% of shares of any class. In the second category, the Schedule II banks were those banks, able to be

1218 The final report, titled 'Change, Challenge, Opportunity' was supported by 5 background papers and 18 research studies commissioned by the Task Force.

1219 See in F. Daniel, 'Recent Changes to Canada's Financial Sector Legislation', *Bank of Canada Review*, Bank of Canada, Winter 2002-2003, p. 8.

closely held and commercially linked, but only for the first ten years of their existence. After the 10-year period expired, these banks were obliged to become 'widely held' banks. Foreign banks and other eligible foreign and domestic financial institutions, that themselves were widely held, were permitted to acquire Schedule II banks as closely held banks.[1220] This policy facilitated and reinforced Canadian control over the banking sector but also was used as a method of dealing with the financial system's stability concerns.

The 2001 amendments maintained the wide ownership principle through a size adaptation for better reflection of the current challenges. According to the legislation, banks were classified as:

(i) Large banks: the banks that had more than $5 billion in equity,
(ii) Medium banks: the banks that had more than $1 billion but less than $5 billion in equity, and
(iii) Small banks: the banks that had less than $1 billion in equity

Large banks were required to be widely held just as they were before the 2001 amendments. The definition of 'widely held' was expanded to allow them more flexibility to enter new alliances and/or joint venture schemes and an individual investor was allowed to own up to 20% of any class of voting shares and up to 30% of any class of non-voting shares.[1221] Furthermore, the Canadian Minister of Finance had the power to subject to a 'fit and proper test' any investor proposal to acquire a significant stake in any large bank. This test was assessed against a guideline aiming to prevent these financial institutions from becoming closely held.[1222] Medium sized banks were allowed to be closely held, under the requirement to have at least 35% of publicly floating voting shares, while small banks were not subject to any ownership restriction. For further organisational flexibility, banks were allowed to incorporate one or more banking subsidiaries and to assign them specific business lines (for example, a bank could establish a retail and/or commercial banking subsidiaries with significant international investors).[1223]

Apart from the banking ownership regime, the 2001 amendments dealt also with the non-bank financial institutions and their ownership. In contrast to the banking sector, there has not been a rule regarding the ownership regime of insurance companies and of trust and loans companies. The Minister of Finance had to approve any shareholding of more than 10%. With the new legislation and the imposed restrictions, large banks were not permitted to acquire or to merge with large, demutualised insurance companies, and vice versa, with the same restriction applying also to the large bank holding groups and to large life insurance groups. The 35% public floating requirement applied

---

1220 Ibid., p. 9.
1221 Ibid.
1222 Ibid.
1223 Ibid., p. 10.

also for trust companies, stock life insurance companies and property and casualty insurance companies with mora than CA$1 billion in equity.[1224]

Perhaps the most important aspect of structural reform in the 2001 legislation was the holding company regime. This regime applied to Canadian banks and insurance companies and permitted the creation of regulated non-operating holding companies. One important parameter of that regime was that this structure did not expand the bank or insurance entities' powers, rather the aim was to provide them with more flexibility in the way they were structuring their operations and organisation. This reform would allow the banks to shift various business operations into the new subsidiaries of the holding company, but within the same organisation.[1225] The ideal scenario would allow the bank holding company to have a securities subsidiary, an insurance subsidiary, and a subsidiary for the unregulated business lines. Moreover, it would also allow a bank to separate various banking activities (retail banking, credit cards business, consumer lending, etc.) and shift them into separate subsidiaries. The holding company structure was targeting the international investors and was aspiring to provide them with a clearer structure of the Canadian banking and financial system in general, since more flexibility was available.[1226] The regulation of these holding company structures was falling under the Banking Act and were required to have investment in at least one bank. The same requirement applied mutatis mutandis in the insurance holding companies, requiring them to invest in at least one (life) insurance company. The permitted investments in the case of bank holding companies were the same that were allowed for a bank to invest in, under the Banking Act. Even though the list of permitted investments for banks and financial institutions was significantly expanded, the restrictions on investments in commercial companies still existed and posed hardships for the effective adoption of the holding company structure.

Finally, the 2001 legislative amendments made two important improvements in the overall streamlining of the regulatory approval process to further reduce the burden of compliance for the federally regulated financial institutions. First, several applications formerly requiring approval by the minister were transferred to the OSFI approval. Second, OSFI had implemented a deemed approval process, aimed at speeding up the supervisory approvals required for certain corporate actions.[1227] As an overall evaluation of the importance of the 2001 amendments, we would stress the fact that as a result, the four distinct pillars of the financial system envisioned by the 1964 Porter Commission proposals, — banking, insurance, trust companies and securities — became blurred into one financial services sector.

1224 Ibid.
1225 Ibid.
1226 Ibid.
1227 Ibid., p. 12.

2.3.1.7 *The 2010 and 2018 Amendments*

In 2010, the Canadian Parliament amended the Bank Act to allow federal credit unions to exist as a new class of financial institution. Credit unions differ from banks in that they are member-owned and governed by co-operative principles. The Bank Act allows that federal credit unions may either be created by five persons (three of which must be individuals), or through the continuance of one or more credit unions existing within provincial jurisdiction by transforming their charter into a federal one. The provisions came into force at the end of 2012.

In 2018, the Canadian Parliament amended the Bank Act, to allow for amendments providing greater flexibility for financial institutions to undertake Fintech related activities thus expanding the business of banking, providing prudentially regulated deposit-taking institutions (including credit unions) with the right to use generic banking terms ('bank', 'banking'), and permitting life and health insurance companies to make long term investments in infrastructure. The purpose of these amendments was to allow banks to make non-controlling investments in Fintech related companies in order to take advantage of technological progress in the financial sector.

2.3.2 Structural Regulation Measures

The effect of the above-mentioned legislative changes has been of utmost importance to the banking sector. The federally chartered banks entered the securities business in a major way following especially the 1987 amendments. Most of them bought an existing securities dealer, while the Toronto Dominion bank established a new subsidiary de novo. This resulted in a situation where the largest dealers are now part of a broader financial services group, with a bank at its forefront. The following table provides an overview of the strategic moves performed by the big five banks to secure their presence within the securities market:

Purchaser	Purchased entity	Date	Ownership%	Purchase cost
Bank of Montreal	Nesbitt Thomson	August 1987	75%	$291 million
Bank of Nova Scotia	McLeod Young Weir	December 1987	100%	$419 million
Royal Bank of Canada	Dominion Securities	March 1988	70%	$385 million
Canadian Imperial Bank of Commerce	Wood Gundy	June 1988	65%	$190 million
Toronto-Dominion Bank	Discount brokerage of Loewen, McCutcheon, Ondaatje & Co.	October 1984	100%	Not available

Source: J. Martin, 'The Toronto-Dominion Bank and Canada's "Little Bang" of 1987', Case Study, Rotman School of Management, University of Toronto, 2012

Among the banks, the degree of integration of the management of the bank and securities firms varies, with many relations based at an arm's length more than others. Apart from the entrance of banks into the securities business, many private securities firms still exist, either as boutique firms or as competitors of a significant size.[1228] Banks also entered the mutual fund market by offering, in a major way, a wide variety of bank-sponsored funds in their branches. Freedman supported the view that Canadian banks had been successful in marketing money market and mortgage funds but not that successful in bond and equity funds.[1229] Despite the important market share that banks occupied in the securities market, this was not perceived a posing severe problems in the competition, for two reasons: a) there existed a significant level of competition among the bank owned dealers, while at the same time the independent firms contributed importantly in keeping competitive the market, and b) the legislative proposals also aimed in permitting also to foreign institutions to enter into the market and perform an important role, that of securing a desired level of competition. Contestability was perceived as an important parameter of the liberalisation agenda and therefore securities markets were supporting a sufficient level of actual or potential competition.[1230]

3 THE 2007-2009 GLOBAL FINANCIAL CRISIS AND ITS IMPACT

During the financial crisis Canadian banks, were not immune to the turmoil. Profitability declined, funding conditions deteriorated, and there was even a freeze in the local commercial paper market.[1231] Despite a traditional business model, where the retail banking focus is intense, risks and blemishes were not completely absent from the Canadian banking industry. These can be attributed to the fact that Canadian banks have significant operations in the US and this interconnection cannot fail to encounter problems when the US banking industry faces a severe crisis.[1232]

1228 See in C. Freedman, *The Canadian Banking System*, Technical Report No. 81, Staff Research, Bank of Canada, March 1998, p. 29.

1229 Ibid., p. 30.

1230 Ibid., p. 31.

1231 See in A. Docherty and F. Viort, *Better Banking, Understanding and Addressing the Failures in Risk Management, Governance and Regulation*, Wiley Finance Series, Chichester, Wiley, 2014, p. 233.

1232 The worst affected Canadian bank was CIBC, which had to write losses of $7.3 billion in its CIBC World Markets division, in 2008.

3.1. *The Asset Backed Commercial Paper (ABCP) Market Turmoil*

A major implication for the Canadian financial markets that arose from the global financial crisis was the run in the Asset Backed Commercial Paper (ABCP) market. The structure of the Canadian financial markets came under severe threat and pressure when the fears for contagion from the US subprime mortgage market, combined with an uncertainty regarding the underlying assets and the associated leverage of the institutions, led to a rush by the investors to exit the ABCP market and dispose of their investments.[1233] At the epicentre of the ABCP crisis was $35 billion in non-bank or third party sponsored ABCPs that were frozen because of the inability of the conduits to rollover their debt (in the form of ABCP). The regulatory environment back then was quite fragmented, not permitting a coherent reaction to the problem. Regarding the ABCP sponsorship practice, the conduits sponsored by the Canadian banks were monitored by the OSFI, whereas the third-party conduits sponsored by foreign banks were regulated only by their home authorities.[1234] Therefore, these banks, with no retail presence in Canada, refused to support with extra liquidity the conduits they sponsored when the crisis was unfolding.

According to Anand and Peihani, various third-party conduits were exempted from the securities regulation in Canada since the Canadian prospectus requirements were not applying to them.[1235] The excellent credit ratings that the debt notes from these conduits had received made securities regulation inapplicable to their investors, as these notes were almost exclusively distributed in the exempted market where the issuers had the right to distribute securities without a fully disclosed prospectus and in some cases without a prospectus at all.[1236] These lax regulatory requirements allowed the expansion of the ABCP market into a fragile business model that ultimately proved to jeopardise the whole system's stability and ultimately forcing the federal and provincial authorities to pump into the system $14 billion of liquidity to restore trust and support the restructuring process. Five major factors help explain the magnitude of the Canadian ABCP market crisis:[1237]

(i) The exemption of ABCP issuers from securities law prospectus requirements permitted them not to disclose the full spectrum of relevant and much needed information that was necessary for the investors,

---

1233 See in A. Anand and M. Peihani, 'Regulating Systemic Risk in Canada', in D. Arner et al. (eds.) *Systemic Risk in the Financial Sector: Ten Years After the Great Crash*, Waterloo, Centre for International Governance Innovation, 2019, p. 23.

1234 Ibid.

1235 Ibid.

1236 Ibid.

1237 Ibid., p. 24.

(ii) The sponsors of the ABCP issuers or their activities in respect of them, were in many cases under no supervision from the relevant authorities, mostly because banks were treating these conduits as off-balance sheet activities which allowed them to escape from onerous capital requirements,
(iii) Domestic and foreign banks, as well as non-bank financial institutions who were acting as liquidity providers for these conduits, securing them with standby liquidity and credit lines, were also undercapitalised and badly regulated simply because it was not required,
(iv) Credit rating agencies, and particularly the Canadian rating agency, aggravated the situation since they had assigned lucrative ratings to these products and endorsed them for distribution to the public and the short-term duration of these notes swift the responsibility to oversight this market from competent authorities to the rating agencies and,
(v) The risks associated with the ABCP products were passed on to the public by the relevant distributors who were subject to various suitability/know your customer rules but not to any explicit fiduciary duty.

Collectively, the above factors contributed and help the turmoil to propagate in a systemic instability that forced the Canadian authorities, and particularly the central bank, to take measures to address the situation.

3.2. Navigating through Hell: The Success in Managing the Global Financial Crisis

According to the FSB report, the Canadian response to the financial crisis was 'swift and effective'.[1238] The adoption of a variety of macroeconomic measures and policies to limit the effects from the crisis 'increased supervisory vigilance, expanded liquidity facilities and pro-actively addressed emerging problems'.[1239] This approach allowed Canadian banks to continue to raise capital in the markets and no Canadian institutions failed or required external bailout.[1240] The Bank of Canada Act was amended at the outset of the crisis to increase BoC's flexibility to apply its operating framework and allow conducting open market operations with a much wider range of eligible assets.[1241] Moreover, new, extraordinary liquidity facilities were introduced and the eligible collaterals were expanded for the Standing Liquidity Facility and Term Loan

1238 See in Financial Stability Board (FSB), *Peer Review of Canada, Review Report*, 30 January 2012, p. 11.
1239 Ibid.
1240 See in M. Copelovitch and D.A. Singer, *Banks on the Brink, Global Capital, Securities Markets, and the Political Roots of Financial Crises*, Cambridge, Cambridge University Press, 2020, p. 88.
1241 See in Financial Stability Board (FSB), *Peer Review of Canada, Review Report*, 30 January 2012, p. 11.

Facility tools.[1242] The size, frequency, term, range of securities and eligible counterparties of its operations were constantly monitored and adjusted as conditions were evolving.[1243] In April 2009, the BoC reduced the interest rate in the all-time low of 0.25% followed by the commitment to keep it low until the end of the second quarter of 2010.[1244] In 2009, the federal government, together with the provincial governments, initiated a huge fiscal stimulus, totalling about 4% of GDP over two years. The fiscal stimulus included measures targeted at credit, labour, and housing markets. The stimulus was also coupled with the Extraordinary Financing Framework,[1245] put in place by the federal government.[1246] Furthermore, during the crisis, the Canadian dollar sharply depreciated against the US dollar, and this further helped the Canadian economy to manage the fall in global demand.[1247]

Another important factor that effectively mitigated the crisis was the relevant regulatory framework that was applicable to the financial sector requiring Canadian banks to have higher capital requirements than the minimum international standards.[1248] Moreover, the OSFI imposed an asset to capital multiple that set a cap on the total leverage level: for banks and for trust and loan companies, this multiple was set at 20 times the sum of their adjusted net total capital and under special authorisation from the OSFI this could be raised to 23 or could also be reduced, especially for fast growing institutions, after examination and scrutiny by the OSFI.[1249] Also interesting is the fact that OSFI guidelines do not set a minimum liquidity ratio and instead stress testing and contingency planning are used and emphasised. Despite

---

1242 Ibid.

1243 A September 2008 reciprocal swap agreement with the US Federal Reserve complemented the Bank of Canada's actions to address the elevated needs in USD short term funding markets. Additionally, on 30 November 2011, the Bank of Canada, along with five other central banks, agreed to establish a temporary bilateral liquidity swap arrangement, ensuring that liquidity would be provided in each jurisdiction, in any of their currencies, should market conditions required that.

1244 See in Financial Stability Board (FSB), *Peer Review of Canada, Review Report*, 30 January 2012, p. 12.

1245 Ibid. The framework, most of which was wound down in March 2010, included targeted measures that supported lending to households and business. Some of these measures were aimed at easing financial institutions access to funds.

1246 Ibid.

1247 Ibid.

1248 See in L. Ratnovski and R. Huang, 'Why Are Canadian Banks More Resilient?', *IMF Working Paper*, WP/09/152, International Monetary Fund, Washington D.C., 2009, p. 16. While Basel II capital requirements required banks to hold minimum TIER 1 capital level of 4% and total capital ratios of 8%, Canadian banks were holding higher amount of capital since 1999. The OSFI required banks and the federally regulated trust and loan companies to exceed 7% of TIER 1 levels and 10% of total capital ratio. Furthermore, the OSFI may direct a bank or a trust and loan company to increase its capital through institution specific measures, under the Pillar 2 process.

1249 Ibid.

this lack of liquidity ratio, Canadian banks did not face significant funding pressures during the crisis and this can be attributed to two factors: a) they were holding high levels of liquid assets – cash and government securities – when heading into the crisis, and b) their non-capital funding has traditionally been from wholesale and retail deposits, providing them with a long-term and stable funding basis.[1250] Compared to the US, where the money market funds' competition towards the traditional banking system was intense, Canadian banks did not suffer from this type of competition and were able to keep deposit funding as their primary source of funding, even after the liberalisation during the late 1980s.[1251]

Finally, equally important factor was that Canadian banks avoided the US subprime mortgage market, or anything equivalent in the domestic market. The strict and rigid regulation of mortgage market in Canada contributed significantly to the overall stability of the system during the crisis. Residential mortgages were held at banks' books, usually to maturity, instead of being packaged, securitised and sold, creating therefore strong incentives for the banks to apply robust underwriting criteria.[1252] According to the Canadian legislation, all high LTV ratio residential mortgages produced by the regulated institutions must be insured against default for the full amount either by the Canada Mortgage and Housing Corporation (CMHC) or by a private mortgage insurer.[1253] Finally, mortgages bearing a LTV ratio of 95% or more, cannot be underwritten by federally regulated institutions.

4 THE POST CRISIS PICTURE: STRUCTURAL REGULATION AND ONGOING CHALLENGES

The Canadian banking industry is facing major challenges in the post crisis environment. The regulatory challenges are numerous, both in the home jurisdiction and abroad. In home, the OSFI implements the Basel III framework with tight liquidity and capital requirements. These new requirements will impose further changes to the systems, accounting, and administrative practices of the banks. Canadian banks are also affected by the regulatory requirements in the US, where they have an extensive presence, and the extraterritorial

---

1250 See in Financial Stability Board (FSB), *Peer Review of Canada, Review Report*, 30 January 2012, p. 13.

1251 See in C. Freedman, *The Canadian Banking System*, Technical Report No. 81, Staff Research, Bank of Canada, March 1998.

1252 See in Financial Stability Board (FSB), *Peer Review of Canada, Review Report*, 30 January 2012, p. 13.

1253 Ibid. It is worth noting that all private mortgage insurers have guarantee agreements with the federal government stating that 90% of their value of insured residential mortgage loans will be protected against loss, should the private insurer fail.

reach of US laws and regulations will impose on them a further compliance burden because of the double requirements. Another important aspect of the regulatory challenges in the Canadian banking sector has to do with the prolonged period of law interest rates coupled with the concerns over the stability of the housing market. OSFI has taken specific measures to advocate to banks how to apply the new capital requirements regarding exposures that are secured by residential real estate.

4.1. The Banking Sector's Structural Reforms

As was referred earlier on, banking industry regulation falls under the exclusive jurisdiction of the federal government. Although provincial governments have jurisdiction to incorporate and regulate certain deposit taking institutions, such as credit unions, only a financial institution that is incorporated under the Bank Act can conduct business as a 'bank' in Canada. Currently, the Bank Act is the main federal legislative tool to regulate a) domestic banks,[1254] b) foreign subsidiary banks that are controlled by eligible foreign institutions,[1255] and c) bank branches of foreign institutions.[1256] The Bank Act regulates, inter alia, the ownership of banks, their capital structure, their corporate governance structure, regulates and prohibits certain business undertakings and associations, regulates the capital and liquidity requirements, the disclosure and transparency requirements. The Bank Act is supplemented by various other regulations, issued mostly by the OSFI, that define and set many other requirements regarding aspects of the banking business, while OSFI also publishes guidelines and advisories to provide further clarity and guidance for the participants. Federally regulated banks are prohibited from engaging in any business other than the business of banking.[1257] The second paragraph of section 409 of the Bank Act provides further clarity regarding what a bank can do. According to the provisions of that section, the business of banking includes: '(a) providing any financial service,[1258] (b) acting as a financial agent,[1259](c) providing investment counselling services and portfolio management services,[1260] and (d) issuing payment, credit or charge cards and, in cooperation with others including other financial institutions, operating a payment, credit or charge card plan.'[1261]

1254 As listed on Schedule I of Bank Act.

1255 As listed on Schedule II of Bank Act.

1256 As listed on Schedule III of Bank Act.

1257 According to Part VIII, section 409 (1) of Bank Act, 'a bank shall not engage in or carry on any business other than the business of banking and such business generally as appertains thereto'.

1258 Bank Act, Section 409 (2)(a).

1259 Ibid., Section 409 (2)(b).

1260 Ibid., Section 409 (2)(c).

1261 Ibid., Section 409 (2)(d).

In addition to the above basic services, a bank can perform additional activities that are defined in Section 410 (1) of the Bank Act. The list of additional activities is extremely reach and allows banks to engage in many activities, except for those that are strictly forbidden, according to section 410 (2). The forbidden activities restrict the range of activities by stating that 'a bank shall not deal in goods, wares or merchandise or engage in any trade or other business'.[1262] Furthermore, the Bank Act restricts the fiduciary activities[1263] and the deposit taking business of banks.[1264] Deposit taking is not allowed for a bank in Canada, unless (a) it is a member institution, as defined in section 2 of the Canada Deposit Insurance Corporation Act (CDICA),[1265] (b) it has been authorised under subsection 26.03(1) of that Act to accept deposits without being a member institution, as defined in section 2 of that Act;[1266] or (c) the order approving the commencement and carrying on of business by the bank authorises it to accept deposits solely in accordance with subsection (3).[1267] Further, Canadian banks 'shall not deal in Canada in securities to the extent prohibited or restricted by such regulations as the Governor in Council may make for the purposes of this section' according to the provisions of Section 415 of the Bank Act. Section 415.1 of the Bank Act lays down the general prohibition as follows:

> 'It is prohibited for a bank to issue a debt obligation in relation to which the amounts of principal and interest owing are guaranteed to be paid from loans or other assets held by an entity that is created and organised for the principal purpose of holding those loans or other assets and with the intention of legally isolating those loans or other assets from the bank, unless
>
> (a) the debt obligation is a covered bond as defined in section 21.5 of the National Housing Act;
>
> (b) the bank is a registered issuer as defined in section 21.5 of that Act other than one whose right to issue covered bonds has been suspended; and
>
> (c) the debt obligation is issued under a registered program as defined in section 21.5 of that Act.'[1268]

Then an exemption applies based on regulations that further regulates securities business as follows: 'The Governor in Council may make regulations exempting any type of debt obligation from the application of subsection (1).'[1269] The same applies also to the derivatives business and eligible financial contracts, where '[t]he Governor in Council may make regulations respecting a bank's

1262 Ibid., Section 410 (2).
1263 Ibid., Section 412.
1264 Ibid., Section 413.
1265 Ibid., Section 413 (1)(a).
1266 Ibid., Section 413 (1)(b).
1267 Ibid., Section 413 (1)(c).
1268 Ibid., Section 415.1 (1).
1269 Ibid., Section 415.1 (2).

activities in relation to derivatives and eligible financial contracts',[1270] and to the benchmarks, where '[t]he Governor in Council may make regulations respecting a bank's activities in relation to benchmarks'.[1271] The Bank Act provides detailed definitions of what a derivative,[1272] an eligible financial contract[1273] and a benchmark[1274] are. This delegated power to the Governor in Council has been translated into the 'Securities Dealing Restrictions (Banks) Regulations'[1275] where the following restrictions apply:

'A bank shall not deal in Canada in securities to the extent that the securities dealings consist of

- (a) the primary distribution of shares or ownership interests, or warrants in respect thereof;
- (b) secondary market trading in shares or ownership interests, or warrants in respect thereof;
- (c) the primary distribution of debt obligations of a body corporate, or warrants in respect thereof; or
- (d) acting as a selling agent in connection with the distribution of mutual funds.
  - **(1)** Nothing in section 2 prohibits a bank from dealing in securities for its own account or any account administered by the bank or providing investment counselling and portfolio management services.
  - **(2)** Nothing in section 2 prohibits a bank from dealing in securities where the securities dealings consist of
    - o **(a)** the primary distribution of debt obligations of, or warrants in respect of debt obligations of, or guaranteed by
      - **(i)** the government of Canada or a province or municipality, or an agency thereof,
      - **(ii)** a corporation that is a public utility that is directly or indirectly owned by a government referred to in subparagraph (i),
      - **(iii)** the government of a foreign country or a political subdivision thereof, or by an agency thereof, or
      - **(iv)** an international agency of which Canada is a member, including an international agency that is a member of the World Bank Group, the Inter-American Development Bank, the Asian Development Bank, the Caribbean Development Bank and the European Bank for Reconstruction and Development and any other international regional bank;
    - o **(b)** the primary distribution of debt obligations, or warrants in respect thereof, that are money market securities;

[1270] Ibid., Section 415.2 (1).
[1271] Ibid., Section 415.3 (1).
[1272] Ibid., Section 415.2 (2).
[1273] Ibid., Section 415.2 (3).
[1274] Ibid., Section 415.3 (2).
[1275] The official text is available at: https://laws-lois.justice.gc.ca/PDF/SOR-92-279.pdf.

o (c) the primary distribution of debt obligations, or warrants in respect thereof, of the bank or an affiliated entity that are guaranteed by the bank;

o (d) the primary distribution of shares or ownership interests, or warrants in respect thereof, of the bank;

o (e) the unsolicited participation in the secondary market trading of shares or ownership interests, or warrants in respect thereof, where the trade is effected through a securities broker who is registered under a provincial securities Act or under the laws of any other jurisdiction;

o (f) acting as a selling agent for mutual funds where the dealings relate to corporate sponsored accounts for pension plans, deferred profit sharing plans, retirement plans or other similar capital accumulation plans;

o (g) acting as a member of a selling group in connection with the underwriting of securities issued by a body corporate other than the bank;

o (h) effecting the private placement of securities on the same or a similar basis to that on which a member of a selling group participates in respect of an underwriting; or

o (i) the primary distribution of debt obligations, or warrants in respect thereof, in respect of syndicated or consortium loans, including securities that are issued in the form of securitised debt instruments.'

Therefore, chartered banks are permitted to offer and carry on a broad set of financial services in Canada, including certain securities and insurance related activities. Certain of these activities however must be conducted through separately regulated subsidiary entities, especially many securities related activities that are not part of the traditional treasury management activities of banks, and the insurance underwriting activities. In addition, restrictions apply to banks' activities in leasing,[1276] on insurance business,[1277] in acting as an agent,[1278] and in their residential mortgage business.[1279] However, banks in Canada are permitted to create affiliate entities through which various core-banking activities, except from deposit taking, can be conducted. A foreign bank can establish a full-service branch or a lending branch and in either case, the foreign bank is permitted to carry on the same business activities in Canada through their branches as the Canadian chartered banks. However, the branches of foreign banks are not permitted to accept retail deposits in Canada.

To the best of our knowledge, it is understood that Canadian regulators rejected Volcker Rule style measures that would restrict banks presence in the

1276 Ibid., Section 417.
1277 Ibid., Section 416 (1).
1278 Ibid., Section 416 (2).
1279 Ibid., Section 418 (1).

securities industry. The measures adopted by the US have an extraterritorial effect on Canadian banks with presence in the US, by imposing them very costly, restrictive and unnecessary rules, according to critics from Canada.[1280] In his speech at Harvard University back in 2013, the then Deputy Governor of the BoC Timothy Lane shared his thoughts on the landmark reform bill and the Volcker rule, by saying that: 'These proposed regulations have raised concerns that US law could dictate the structure of major financial institutions in many other jurisdictions. Other jurisdictions—including Canada—have objected, both because they do not wish to have US law applied to the primarily domestic operations of their institutions, and also because they do not agree that the Volcker Rule is the only—or the most effective way to prevent excessive risk-taking in financial institutions.'[1281] The Deputy Governor proposed an alternative that is based on a mutual recognition regime of equivalent measures that could rend extraterritorial effects almost out of scope. Each jurisdiction should have a sufficiently strong regime that other jurisdictions can accept as broadly equivalent that would eliminate the need for a jurisdiction to impose their own rules across borders and unnecessarily restrict banking activities in any possible way.[1282] According to Reinhardt, the problem is that the Volcker Rule applies to the US operations of all foreign banks, including Canadian banks, as well as and to even purely foreign operations that simply use US financial infrastructure (US stock exchanges, mutual and money market funds, or bond trading firms to name but a few). Therefore, Canadian banks would have to comply with the rules to carry on with their business in the United States.[1283]

Another major concern is that the Volcker Rule's ban on proprietary trading provides an exemption for US government bonds, but not for non-US government bonds. Therefore, US banks and US branches of Canadian banks would no longer be able to buy and sell Canadian government bonds as easily as before, potentially reducing the total volume of new Canadian bonds circulating through the financial system.[1284] The same view was also expressed

[1280] See in C. Reinhardt, 'Why Canada hates the Volcker Rule, the landmark U.S. financial reform imposes high costs north of the border, say Canadians. Americans don't think so.', article, *MACLEANS' Business column*, February 2013.

[1281] See in T. Lane, *Financial Stability in One Country?*, Remarks by Tim Lane, Deputy Governor of the Bank of Canada, Weatherhead Center for International Affairs, Harvard University, 11 February 2013, p. 10.

[1282] Ibid.

[1283] See in C. Reinhardt, 'Why Canada hates the Volcker Rule, the landmark U.S. financial reform imposes high costs north of the border, say Canadians. Americans don't think so.', article, *MACLEANS' Business column*, February 2013.

[1284] Ibid.

by the Deputy Governor on his Harvard speech.[1285] Critics from Canada fear that the rule could end up raising borrowing costs for Canadian companies, municipal authorities, and the federal government.[1286] If the Volcker Rule will impede US investors from buying Canadian bonds and makes it harder to use US financial infrastructure, some fear that it will reduce overall demand for those bonds, causing the interest rates (yields), on them to rise.[1287] Critics of the Volcker Rule also fear that the proprietary trading ban will hurt the liquidity of Canadian government bonds. Currently, the high volume of Canadian bonds in circulation means they are viewed as 'safe' and 'liquid' assets, meaning that financial institutions can sell them quickly when they need cash in a hurry. The concern is that reduced US bank involvement in the Canadian bonds market will reduce the speed and reliability with which these bonds can be sold. This situation could have knock-on effects for Canadian financial institutions that use these instruments for this purpose.[1288]

In striking contrast with the US approach regarding proprietary trading activities, Canada has vigorously opposed restrictions on the ability of financial institutions to engage in proprietary trading. Instead of adopting similar measures, Canadian regulators have favoured the use of prudential and behavioural regulation to promote responsible risk-management policies and conflict-of interest rules within these institutions.[1289] What lies under these differing approaches regarding the regulation of proprietary trading reflects the ongoing debate on what constitutes the proper use of bank capital and the amount of risk financial institutions should be permitted to assume.[1290] In order to facilitate the growth of global capital markets in the 1980s and 1990s these restrictions were gradually relaxed with Canada allowing the retail banks to acquire securities brokerages and investment banking firms with the 1987 and 1992 Bank Act amendments. The Canadian approach is not compatible with the US practice since it advocates that it may be more appropriate to consider specific behavioural reforms which target the impugned conduct of

1285 See in T. Lane, *Financial Stability in One Country?*, Remarks by Tim Lane, Deputy Governor of the Bank of Canada, Weatherhead Center for International Affairs, Harvard University, 11 February 2013, p. 10.

1286 According to Reinhardt (2013), for several provincial and municipal governments that have been running up increasingly large deficits in the last few years, the prospect of no longer being able to easily sell and refinance their debt to large US banks is perceived as at least 'troubling'. Even though American banks would still be able to act as intermediaries for transactions, under the new rules they would no longer be able to buy up excess amounts for their own account.

1287 See in C. Reinhardt, 'Why Canada hates the Volcker Rule, the landmark U.S. financial reform imposes high costs north of the border, say Canadians. Americans don't think so.', article, *MACLEANS' Business column*, February 2013.

1288 Ibid.

1289 See in P. Puri and A. Nichol, 'Developments in Financial Services Regulation: A Canadian Perspective' (2014) 55(2) *Canadian Business Law Journal*, p. 481.

1290 Ibid.

proprietary traders rather than adopting measures that impose a structural remedy which may affect the market making capacity, risk management and profitability of financial institutions.[1291]

4.2. *The Securities Sector's Structural Reforms*

The CSA has played a vital role in the coordination of securities industry policies. It has provided provincial securities regulators with a forum that coordinates and communicates their policies, aiming for better and more effective implementation. Under its auspices, many changes have been introduced to the industry, such as the OTC derivatives market, where the primary focus of these measures was on the central cleaning of OTC derivatives, enhancing market transparency through trade repositories and migrating standard transactions to exchanges and trading platforms. The measures were following the general trend set by the international community and especially the work done by the FSB and IOSCO.[1292] In the crisis's aftermath, the CSA established a systemic risk sub-committee to better monitor, mitigate and manage the systemic risk accumulated in the securities market. The Ontario Securities Commission (OSC) also established a new risk committee with the aim of strengthening its capability to detect and manage systemic risk, following the steps of CSA.[1293] The federal government also took a bolder step in 2014, by proposing the Capital Markets Stability Act (CMSA). This Act proposed the creation of a new body that would oversee the new framework, the Capital Markets Regulatory Authority (CMRA) that would deal with systemic risk in the capital markets, by designating a product, service, or benchmark as systemically important.[1294] Unfortunately, this important initiative did not move forward due to strict opposition from the provinces, on the basis of the federal nature of Canada.

The federal nature of Canada had been confirmed by the CSC in two landmark decisions: a) in the 2011 *Reference Re Securities Act*[1295] and b) the 2018 *Reference re Pan-Canadian Securities Regulation.*[1296] Despite the negative ruling of the CSC, the federal jurisdiction on matters of 'genuine national importance' has been confirmed,[1297] with data collection, and management

---

1291 Ibid., p. 483.

1292 See in A. Anand and M. Peihani, 'Regulating Systemic Risk in Canada', in D. Arner et al. (eds.), *Systemic Risk in the Financial Sector: Ten Years After the Great Crash*, Waterloo, Centre for International Governance Innovation, 2019, p. 19.

1293 Ibid.

1294 Ibid., p. 20.

1295 *Reference re Securities Act*, 2011 SCC 66, [2011] 3 SCR 837 [Securities Reference].

1296 *Reference re Pan-Canadian Securities Regulation*, 2018 SCC 48.

1297 See in A. Anand and M. Peihani, 'Regulating Systemic Risk in Canada', in D. Arner et al. (eds.), *Systemic Risk in the Financial Sector: Ten Years After the Great Crash*, Waterloo, Centre for International Governance Innovation, 2019, p. 20.

of systemic risk. Following the CSC's ruling, the federal government published an updated version of the Act, in January 2016.[1298] Since these two landmark rulings shape the framework for the regulation of securities, they deserve a closer analysis given their special importance and their impact. In November 2011, the CSC released a decision in which provided its opinion on a 'reference' question addressed to it. A reference asks the CSC to give an advisory opinion on a particular question.[1299] In this case, the question was whether the proposed Securities Act, as drafted back then, fell 'within the legislative authority of the Parliament of Canada'. The question for the CSC's consideration in this reference case was whether the proposed federal Securities Act falls within the legislative authority of the federal government as outlined in the Constitution Act of 1867.[1300] Sections 91 and 92 of the Constitution Act divide the power to legislate in specific areas between the federal and the provincial governments.[1301] This separation is referred to as the 'division of powers'. For such a federal system to function, it is necessary that some powers be allocated to the federal government and others to the provinces, in order to achieve this division. However, not all questions of jurisdiction are answered easily by the grammatical text of sections 91 and 92 of the Constitution Act. Interpretational questions frequently arise regarding how a particular subject or area should be classified in the ambit of this division of powers. The task of interpreting the Canadian Constitution Act falls to the courts.[1302]

In the Securities Reference, the conflict was between the federal power over 'the regulation of trade and commerce'[1303] and the provincial power over 'property and civil rights in the province'.[1304] Specifically, the key question was whether the words 'the regulation of trade and commerce' include the regulation of securities, or whether the regulation of securities is part of 'property and civil rights in the province'.[1305] The provincial governments of Alberta, Quebec, Manitoba, and New Brunswick – also supported by several

---

1298 Ibid.

1299 The reference question in this case was brought under section 53 of the Supreme Court Act, RSC 1985, c S-26, which permits the Governor in Council to refer a question regarding the interpretation of any federal or provincial legislation to the Supreme Court for its consideration.

1300 See in L. McDaniel, 'Reference re Securities Act (2011): Does Parliament Have the Power to Establish a Canada-wide Securities Regulator?', Article, Centre for Constitutional Studies, University of Alberta.

1301 Ibid. For example, the federal government has jurisdiction in areas such as banking and criminal law, while the provincial governments have retained their jurisdiction over other areas such as natural resources, securities, and hospitals.

1302 Ibid.

1303 Section 91(2) of the Canadian Constitution Act.

1304 Section 92(13) of the Canadian Constitution Act.

1305 See in L. McDaniel, 'Reference re Securities Act (2011): Does Parliament Have the Power to Establish a Canada-wide Securities Regulator?', Article, Centre for Constitutional Studies, University of Alberta.

interveners – argued that the proposed Act was unconstitutional because it constituted a clear intrusion into their exclusive constitutional authority over property and civil rights, pursuant to section 92(13) of the 1867 Constitution Act, which includes authority over the regulation of contracts, property, and professions.[1306] On the contrary, the Government of Canada, along with the government of Ontario and several other interveners, argued that the contested Act is a constitutional exercise of the federal government's general power to regulate trade and commerce, pursuant to section 91(2) of the 1867 Constitution Act. The federal government did not dispute that some aspects of securities regulation are within the power of a province to regulate, including the regulation of contracts and property, but instead argued that the securities market has evolved in such a way that it is now a matter affecting the country as a whole. Therefore, the 'general' branch of the federal trade and commerce power gives the federal government the jurisdiction to legislate trade that affects the entire country, as opposed to a specific industry. Finally, they argued that without a national approach to the regulation of securities, the securities industry might not be adequately controlled, putting the entire country's financial system at risk.[1307] The CSC concluded in a unanimous decision, that the proposed Securities Act was not part of the federal government's power to regulate trade and commerce. Accordingly, the proposed Act was not within the legislative authority limits of the Parliament and thus deemed unconstitutional.[1308]

With its 2011 decision, the CSC concluded that the day-to-day regulation of the securities industry remained a provincial concern. Nevertheless, it left the door open to federal legislation relating directly to the management of systemic risk and national data collection.[1309] This left open the possibility for both levels of government to exercise their powers collaboratively to implement a co-operative system that would be lying within the constitutional framework of their respective powers. This resulted, on the signing of a Memorandum of Agreement (MOA) in September 2014, among the federal government and the provincial governments of Ontario, British Columbia, Saskatchewan, and New Brunswick, formalising the terms of a proposed new co-operative regulatory regime for Canada's capital markets, the Cooperative Capital Markets Regulatory System (CCMRS).[1310] The MOA calls for a new legislative

1306 Ibid.

1307 Ibid.

1308 Ibid.

1309 See in A. Anand and M. Peihani, 'Regulating Systemic Risk in Canada', in D. Arner et al. (eds.), *Systemic Risk in the Financial Sector: Ten Years After the Great Crash*, Waterloo, Centre for International Governance Innovation, 2019, p. 20.

1310 Two new members, Prince Edward Island and Yukon, have since entered the MOA. There are however five provinces and two territories, including Quebec, Alberta, and Manitoba, that have not signed the agreement and were against this initiative.

framework consisting of a single set of regulations to be administered by a new, single and national regulator, the Capital Markets Regulatory Authority (the Authority). Supervisory oversight of the Authority would be provided by an independent board of directors, in turn accountable to a Council of Ministers, comprised of the Minister of Finance of Canada and a minister from each participating province or territory, responsible for the securities regulation in that province.[1311] Each participating province or territory would enact a Provincial Capital Markets Act (the Model Provincial Act) and would replace the existing provincial or territorial securities legislation. Administration of the Model Provincial Act would be delegated to the Authority by each province. The federal Capital Markets Stability Act (CMSA) would address the areas ruled by the Court to be under federal jurisdiction in the 2011 Reference and would also be administered by the Authority. The CMSA would give the Authority national data collection, powers to monitor activity in the capital markets and the requisite tools to manage systemic risk in the capital markets nationally, just as the 2011 judgement has described.[1312] The new mechanism that came up after the 2011 decision was also contested before the Supreme Court, this time by the Quebec province, in 2017. In its 9 November 2018 decision Reference re Pan-Canadian Securities Regulation, the CSC unanimously upheld the constitutionality of a national co-operative system for the regulation of capital markets in Canada, as proposed in a draft federal and model provincial legislation, overturning thereby the Quebec Court of Appeal's 2017 decision that found the proposed regime unconstitutional. On appeal to the CSC, two questions were brought before it: a) Does the Canadian Constitution authorise the implementation of pan-Canadian securities regulation under the authority of a single regulator in accordance with the terms set out in the MOA? and b) Does the most recent version of the draft of the CMSA exceed the authority of the Canadian Parliament over the general branch of the trade and commerce power under subsection 91(2) of the 1867 Constitution Act? The CSC, with its 2018 decision, found that the MOA did not improperly fetter provincial legislative sovereignty, and that the CMSA was *intra vires* the jurisdiction of Parliament under subsection 91(2) of the 1867 Constitution Act.

With these two landmark decisions, the CSC paved the road for a unified system of securities regulation, at least in terms of systemic risk and data collection. The administration of the new cooperative system remains fragmented because the jurisdiction of the MOA reaches only its members and has not enhanced application throughout the entire country. Therefore, enforcement of securities legislation requires coordination among the various

---

1311 See in A. Anand and M. Peihani, 'Regulating Systemic Risk in Canada', in D. Arner et al. (eds.), *Systemic Risk in the Financial Sector: Ten Years After the Great Crash*, Waterloo, Centre for International Governance Innovation, 2019, p. 20.

1312 Ibid.

provincial regulators and with the federal level. This inevitably leads to delays, inefficiencies, and increased costs for all the participants.[1313] It is worth noting that Canada, still today, remains the only developed country that is not represented through a national securities regulator in IOSCO, which represents securities markets in 115 countries across the globe.[1314] Banks participating in the Canadian securities market must comply with a complex regulatory framework, which is spread across territorial, provincial, and federal rules. This complexity undoubtedly leads to higher costs related to other securities markets with more uniformity and coherence. Higher costs are translated to inefficient markets with less transactions at higher costs and generally illiquid conditions. Despite their presence in securities markets, Canadian banks do not participate aggressively in closing deals and replace their traditional lending business with other means of financing.

5 CONCLUDING REMARKS: A BLUEPRINT FOR SAFETY AND SOUNDNESS?

For more than a century, Canadian governments have seen banking as a strategic sector. According to Meredith and Dorrach, the Canadian regulatory regime has been crafted to achieve the following objectives:[1315]

(a) Stability to encourage capital inward flow;
(b) Federally regulated chartered banks as the country's dominant financial institutions;
(c) Canadian control over the bank entities;
(d) An industry that facilitates trade and commerce;
(e) An infrastructure that supports government financing;
(f) A retail network that serves the entire population.

The FSB report highlighted several important lessons that other jurisdictions would learn from Canada. Especially, during the global financial crisis Canada proved to be resilient and ready to act in a proactive manner. The report emphasises the importance of having:[1316]

- Proactive and targeted macroeconomic policies that should be supported by adequate fiscal space together with a flexible exchange rate regime that will help to absorb the shocks,

---

1313 See in M. Copelovitch and D.A. Singer, *Banks on the Brink, Global Capital, Securities Markets, and the Political Roots of Financial Crises*, Cambridge, Cambridge University Press, 2020, p. 115.

1314 Ibid.

1315 See in P. Meredith and J.L. Darroch, *Stumbling Giants, Transforming Canada's Banks for the Information Age*, Toronto, University of Toronto Press, 2017, p. 179.

1316 See in Financial Stability Board (FSB), *Peer Review of Canada, Review Report*, 30 January 2012, p. 16.

- Prudent bank risk management and particularly a stable and well-diversified funding profile together with conservative loan underwriting standards and
- A comprehensive regulatory and supervisory framework that will effectively address prudential domestic concerns with the option to further adopt more strict policies that go beyond the minimum international standards.

These recommendations reflect the overall stability of Canadian financial system that has been proven during the recent GFC. Such performance however shall not hinder the major challenges that are lying ahead. Among them are the global challenges that may arise and hit the Canadian economy, exactly because of its openness level and the increasing levels of Canadian household indebtedness.[1317] The international presence of Canadian institutions with significant operations abroad together with a high level of openness of the Canadian economy 'mean that Canada is exposed to global economic developments'.[1318] At the same time, the report sets the alarm for the high levels of indebtedness among the households, due to increasing and strong growth in residential mortgages and personal lending markets. This trend is also observable in the profitability among credit institutions, despite the low levels of non-performing loans and bank losses.[1319]

From the above analysis, the conclusions are of particular interest and importance. The Canadian financial system remains a highly sophisticated and well-regulated system despite the obvious problems of consumers' high levels of debt and the lack of a centrally established supervisory system in the securities industry. The general conservatism that runs across the Canadian banking system is reflected in the policy options for higher capital requirements compared to the generally adopted international standards, on the clear state protectionism over the banking sector with controlled competition among the banks, and finally on the business models that Canadian banks are currently running. Their participation in the subprime madness back in 2007-2009 was particularly low, compared to their neighbour and apart from the ABCP disruption in 2007, no major events or external assistance was needed for them to survive. Nevertheless, the question arises all by herself. Were the above reasons enough for an entire banking system to acquire the fame of being the most stable and safe among the developed countries? We are of the view that Canadian banks are stable but not only for the above-mentioned reasons. The important parameter that usually slips of our attention is the fact that the lower development level of Canadian securities markets acts as a further stabilisation mechanism for the banking sector. Banks participate in the securities markets through their subsidiaries, but the securities markets do not perform such an important function, for the financing needs, as in

1317 Ibid.
1318 Ibid.
1319 Ibid., p. 17.

other countries. The difference can be understood only in comparison to the US securities market, where the level of obtained financing is much higher and deeper than in Canada. Therefore, the much-needed liberalisation in the 1980s and the structural reforms in the banks that allowed them to participate and compete in the securities market did not change the nature of the financial system, which remained a bank-based system without facing intense competitions from other types of financing methods.

Copelovitch and Singer support the same view and by extending their analysis agree that this was an intended policy option by the Canadian government. The difficulty of establishing a single securities supervisor for the entire country seems to be an important issue for the elected representatives but not of that much importance. Since the financial sector works at a point where economic growth is attainable and no major crises have arisen, it is perceived that there is no need to achieve something that might be of Pandora's Box. The growth of securities markets will inevitably press the banks to enter new business lines and create new products to secure their market share and their profits. This will obviously create a momentum for financial innovation and tailored products, but it might be proven to be also a reckless policy option, since instability will be much easier to appear. Therefore, our analysis demonstrates that Canadian banks are indeed well regulated and effectively supervised, since the OSFI acts in a way that secures financial stability without oppressing banks and their business models. Furthermore, the structural regulation measures currently in place do not allow banks to become truly universal banks by combining under a single roof all aspects of financial activities, thus adopting a more conservative business model with activities that are still excluded for them. Finally, the lower competition from the securities industry does not press Canadian banks to expand into unknown business lines to secure their profits and market shares, as appears to be the case in the US. The combination of these facts together allows for a financial system that is well controlled by the competent authorities and operates with a smooth functioning method.

CHAPTER 3
JAPAN: A TALE OF UNSUCCESSFUL SUCCESSES

For the topic of the present book, Japan offers a great example of how economic success and good intentions on behalf of the Japanese Government can lead to a financial disaster due to a rigid financial system, bad supervision and flawed liberalisation initiatives. Japan enjoyed economic growth, especially after the devastating World War II, suffered from major crisis events in its financial system and tried, unsuccessfully to transform its economy, while having a heavily, and obviously unorthodoxly structured, financial system. Japan suffered also from bad luck, since three major crises knocked its door while trying to structurally reform in its economy. These reforms were going to have a major impact also in its society by changing radically the Japanese (traditional) way of life. Crises, both locally[1320] and at international level,[1321]corruption scandals, major attempts for reforms, bureaucratic arteriosclerosis that ultimately led to a broken financial system and the 'Two Lost Decades'[1322] of economic growth due to intolerance and bad incentives comprise an amalgam of a country that can be an excellent model to understand why overregulation can be a suboptimal solution in the long run.

1320 The most important local crisis was the Japanese banking crisis that erupted in the mid-1990s and lasted almost a decade.

1321 At an international level we can observe the Asian crisis in 1997, which had a major impact on the Japanese economy and the recent financial crisis of 2007-2009, that although was a global crisis the impact in the Japanese financial system was not as severe as in other areas of the world.

1322 The 'Two Lost Decades' (失われた二十年, *ushinawareta nijūnen*) refers to a prolonged period of economic stagnation in Japan from the early 1990s through the 2000s, following the burst of a massive asset price bubble in the late 1980s. The two decades after the crash (1991–2010) were marked by low or zero economic growth, deflation (falling prices), weak consumer demand, rising government debt and a credit crunch, as banks became reluctant to lend. Also, structural issues like an aging population and low productivity growth further aggravated the situation.
Japan became a cautionary tale for other economies about the dangers of asset bubbles and deflation. The term 'Japanification' is now used to describe similar low-growth, low-inflation scenarios in other developed countries. Efforts like Abenomics (a policy package of monetary easing, fiscal stimulus, and structural reforms) were launched to revive growth.

1 A CURRENT OVERVIEW OF THE JAPANESE FINANCIAL SYSTEM

According to the most recent FSB's peer review report, the Japanese financial system is bank-dominated, with banks comprising about 50% of total system's assets as of March 2016. Insurance and pension funds comprised 17% of total assets while securities firms accounted for 5% of assets. The Japanese banking sector primarily consists of 10 major banks (including three mega-banks),[1323] 105 regional banks[1324] and 256 shinkin banks.[1325] While the total assets of major banks stood at ¥671 trillion as of 31 March 2016, the total assets of regional banks and shinkin banks' were ¥370 trillion and ¥147 trillion respectively.[1326] Though regional banks are individually small, as a group they are systemically important representing approximately 40% of banking system assets. Other (specialised) banking institutions include various Trust Banks (i.e. Nomura Trust Bank), the Japan Post Bank[1327] and the Norinchukin Bank. Banks headquartered in Japan account for 97% of banking sector assets and the foreign banks include 50 branches and 4 local subsidiaries (Citibank Japan, SBJ Bank, New York Mellon Trust Bank, State Street Trust Bank, etc.).[1328]

1323 The 10 major banks are Mizuho Bank, The Bank of Tokyo-Mitsubishi UFJ, Sumitomo Mitsui Banking Corporation, Resona Bank, Saitama Resona Bank, Mitsubishi UFJ Trust and Banking Corporation, Mizuho Trust and Banking Company, Sumitomo Mitsui Trust Bank, Shinsei Bank, and Aozora Bank. The three mega-banks are Mitsubishi UFJ Financial Group, Inc., Sumitomo Mitsui Financial Group, Inc., and Mizuho Financial Group, Inc.

1324 The 105 regional banks comprise the 64 member banks of the Regional Banks Association of Japan (Regional banks I) and the 41 member banks of the Second Association of Regional Banks (Regional banks II).

1325 'Shinkin banks' (信用金庫, *shinkin kinko*) are cooperative regional financial institutions in Japan. They have close similarities to credit unions in other countries, but with distinct characteristics tailored to Japan's economic and social systems. Shinkin are mutual institutions, meaning they are owned by their members (primarily small and medium-sized businesses and individuals). They serve local communities, typically within a defined region or prefecture, and the aim to support local economic development. They accept deposits, offer personal and business loans, and provide other banking services, much like a regular commercial bank, while they are regulated by the Japanese Financial Services Agency (JFSA) and overseen by the Shinkin Central Bank, which acts as a central bank for all Shinkin. Shinkin banks don't operate nationwide and aren't part of large financial conglomerates like MUFG or SMBC while they also focus on community service over profit, and mostly cater to SMEs and individuals, not large corporations. The 256 shinkin banks are holding current accounts within the Bank of Japan.

1326 See in Financial Stability Board (FSB), *Peer Review of Japan, Review Report*, 21 December 2016, Basel, p. 40.

1327 On 4 November 2015, Japan Post Bank Co, Ltd, which was formerly part of the government's postal division, had its shares listed on the First Section of the Tokyo Stock Exchange, concurrently with the listing of its parent company, Japan Post Holdings Co, Ltd and another subsidiary of the parent company, Japan Post Insurance Co, Ltd. See in H. Akagami and Y. Watanabe, 'The Banking Regulation Review: Japan', *The Law Reviews*, 4 May 2021.

1328 See in Financial Stability Board (FSB), *Peer Review of Japan, Review Report*, 21 December 2016, Basel, p. 40.

Although perceived as a modern economy and country, with extreme technological advantages, Japan must be studied and understood through a historical dimension, mostly because the evolution of the Japanese financial system was based on a historical perspective and under the heavy influence of the US, since the first day of Japan's opening to the world.[1329] Therefore, we need to make both a historical and legal analysis on the evolution of the Japanese financial regulation and also to delve into the major events that led to certain policy options that shaped the regulatory landscape in Japan. Public policy aims and political aspirations had influenced a lot the regulatory framework and as a result, we need to examine and understand them to better assess the Japanese choices. Furthermore, the similarities between the US and the Japanese regulatory framework, especially as regards the structural regulation that applies to the banks, are also better understood through historical lenses. The two countries had similar regime regarding what banks can do but this policy option was based on different grounds. Furthermore, Japan had and still has a very different corporate governance culture that influences a lot how banks operate, especially as part of broader economic groups. The Zaibatsu and Keiretsu structures are similar but different concepts and equally important to understand the Japanese experience of regulating banking services.

2 THE EVOLUTION OF THE JAPANESE BANKING SYSTEM

The prewar era of the Japanese banking system is a historically interesting period because it largely explains the formation of the basic patterns that apply to the modern, post war, banking and financial system. What is more interesting though is the fact that although the American occupation prioritises the destruction of the old regime and the democratisation of the economy, simply failed because the Japanese managed to preserve key aspects

1329 Until 1853, Japan was under a sui-generis isolation policy regime that supported limited interaction with the rest of the world. US were determined to change that situation, even by the force of guns. US President Millard Fillmore mandated the US Navy Commodore, Matthew Calbraith Perry (1794-1858), to establish (trade) relations with Japan. Perry's primary goal was to force an end to Japan's 220-year-old policy of isolation and to open the Japanese ports to American trade. The primary goals behind the US decision to 'explore' Japan were the growing commerce between the United States and China, the presence of American whalers in waters offshore Japan, and the increasing monopolization of potential coaling stations by European powers in Asia. Perry was free to make use of 'gunboat diplomacy' if necessary and anchored his armed squadron at the mouth of Tokyo Bay.
The successful Perry Expedition led directly to the establishment of diplomatic relations between Japan and the western Great Powers, and eventually to the collapse of the ruling Tokugawa shogunate and the restoration of the emperor. The signing of the Kanagawa Treaty, on 31 March 1854 was the official opening of Japan to the Western world and the beginning of a new era.

of their 'financial philosophy' by maintaining old relations inside 'fancy new clothes'. They followed the wording but not the spirit of the laws originated from the occupants. The most illustrative example is the perseverance of the old zaibatsu relations through the new keiretsu corporate style. As a result, understanding the prewar financial system is a prerequisite for someone who wants to understand the current framework. Although the present book is far from being a historical one, however is necessary to follow a historical style of study and events presentation because certain events and policy options must be understood and discussed under such a lens.

2.1. From the Meiji Restoration to World War II

The 'Meiji Restoration' in 1868 is considered as the turning point in Japanese history. Until then, Japan was a feudal regime with rural economy and society, governed by the chief warlord, the well-known 'shogun'. This restoration came a few years after Commodore Perry forced Japan to open its borders to the rest of the world. The Japanese, feared from the humiliating fact that their sovereignty might be at danger from other countries and intimidated by the Perry's expedition memories, decided to industrialise their economy, modernise their society, and catch up with the rest of the world. Their efforts were based on foreign models, mostly regarding their legal, political and social system. Among these models adopted were UK and US based laws with respect to the banking and financial system.[1330] The National Bank Act of 1872 was enacted based on the American model and propelled Japan into the new era.[1331] To the contrary, securities legislation with the Stock Transaction Ordinance of 1874, was based on the London Stock Exchange rules and helped Japan establish the first stock exchanges in Tokyo and Osaka. The problem with these stock exchange places was that they were of a speculative nature, thus lacking a true capital market function. As a result, the banking system was called upon to provide capital and, ultimately replaced capital markets to a big extent, listing Japan as a country with a bank based financial system.[1332] Since the modernisation period, the Japanese financial system, banking included, transformed into a highly specialised system, in which the various financial institutions were serving only limited sectors of the economy instead

---

1330 See in B.A. Pomper, 'The Japanese Financial Reform of 1993: Will Reform Spark Innovation?' (1995) 28 *Cornell International Law Journal*, p. 529.

1331 National Bank Act of 1872 (Japan).
The first bank in Japan was the 'First National Bank', founded in Tokyo in 1873. After undergone several transformations and mergers, over many decades, ultimately became the *Dai-Ichi Kangyo Bank*.

1332 See in B.A. Pomper, 'The Japanese Financial Reform of 1993: Will Reform Spark Innovation?' (1995) 28 *Cornell International Law Journal*, p. 529. According to Pomper, between 1965 and 1974 nearly 80% of corporate financing was in the form of bank loans.

of offering comprehensive services. The distinction between long-term and short-term banking, that played an important role even in the post war regime, was adopted back then with the aim to protect and regulate the channelling of funds to the long-term investment plans for industry and agriculture.[1333] Moreover, trust business was established as a district and separate service from banking industry, in which only trust companies and trust banks were allowed to enter.[1334]

The government intervention was very intense from the beginning of the modernisation period. Formed in the 1870s, the Japanese Ministry of Finance (MoF) not only stood at the apex of the regulatory system and represented the most powerful bureaucratic entity in a country full of bureaucracies[1335] but also was assigned with many tasks that in the US were, and still are, performed by various government entities and agencies. After the rebellion in Kyushu Island, the government decided to establish the Bank of Japan (BoJ) in 1882, and two years later assigned her the right to issue currency.[1336] Japan run for a further consolidation on its banking sector by updating its banking law in 1927. Following the adoption of the new act capital standards were raised and a 'further amalgamation process' of the banking sector was adopted that drove over half of the existing, back then, banks to exit the market either through transformations or simply because they didn't meet the new higher requirements.[1337] This consolidation was not pursued primarily for efficiency in the banking market but rather for further control over it. As Japan was shifting into a war economy the government's intervention in the market was equally intense, forcing commercial banks to transform into controlled conduits for channelling capital to industries involved in war preparations. Victim of that intervention was also the BoJ, which was forced to follow war policies and her independence ended in 1942 with the enactment of the law that ordered the

---

1333 See in B.A. Pomper, 'The Japanese Financial Reform of 1993: Will Reform Spark Innovation?' (1995) 28 *Cornell International Law Journal*, p. 529.

1334 Ibid.

1335 See in R.J. Brown Jr., 'Japanese Banking Reform and the Occupation Legacy: Decompartmentalization, Deregulation, and Decentralization' (1993) 21(2) *Denver Journal of International Law & Policy*, p. 364.

1336 According to Brown, the Japanese government owned 55% of the BoJ shares and had the right to appoint the Governor, Vice-Governor, and several other officials. The BoJ Governor was either a career employee in the BoJ, a retired MoF official or a private banker, where the tradition had to be typically from the Yokohama Specie Bank (YSB). The BoJ received the authority to issue currency when the Diet adopted the Convertible Bank Note Act of 1884 or Convertible Bank-Note Ordinance (Ordinance No. 18 of 6 May 1884, Japan), under which the national banks lost that authority, and all notes were unified under the BoJ notes.

1337 See in R.J. Brown Jr., 'Japanese Banking Reform and the Occupation Legacy: Decompartmentalization, Deregulation, and Decentralization' (1993) 21(2) *Denver Journal of International Law & Policy*, p. 370.

accession to the MoF of the authority to order BoJ to follow and implement special war policies.[1338]

Japanese governments had always been interventionists and since the first days of the Meiji era, the officials and the government bureaucrats decided that the economic development should not be entrusted solely to the free market. At the same time, they also realised that development and growth was not possible without the assistance of the private sector.[1339] What must be clarified at this point is the crucial parameter that back then Japan had almost no factories and economic activity in the Meiji era was relatively small if non-existent at all. The economy was based largely upon taxation revenue from farmers and the government used this income to adopt and implement modernisation policies, returning to the society the benefits from modernisation and investment.[1340] This had the effect that close ties with the government were considered an important tool of entrepreneurialism evolving to a policy better known as 'seisho'. Seisho 'consists of business-government relations wherein politicians and businesspersons having special relations with the government receive special rights and advantages'.[1341] Although Japan desperately needed foreign aid and knowledge for its modernisation policies, the Japanese government was very reluctant towards foreigners, and they were ultimately shut out from the domestic market. Ultimately, on 5 November 1880, the Great Council of State of the early Meiji government decided and ordered the relevant departments to sell enterprises under their own jurisdictions. Since the government had built close relations with private enterprises to help boost modernisation of the economy, many of these 'for sale' enterprises ended up to special oligarchies[1342] under privileged terms.[1343] Big economic groups that formed what has been known as 'Zaibatsu' entities engulfed the sold enterprises. The term Zaibatsu has no fixed meaning and ended up mostly to describe 'a diversified structure of management established under the control and ownership of families or clans of rich men'.[1344] Their formation was based on a pyramid style scheme, where the holding companies were exercising control over a large number of entities by occupying the foremost position in the governance structure of the scheme. Typically, these holding companies were the biggest shareholders in the other entities and were able to influence decision-making hence

1338 Ibid., p. 371.

1339 See in A.H. Thorson and F. Siegfanz, 'The 1997 Deregulation of Japan's Holding Companies' (1999) 8(2) *Pacific Rim Law & Policy Journal*, p. 266.

1340 Ibid., p. 267.

1341 Ibid.

1342 These chosen oligarchies of privately owned enterprises included the Mitsui, Mitsubishi, Sumitomo, Yasuda, Furukawa, Okura, and Asano economic groups.

1343 See in A.H. Thorson and F. Siegfanz, 'The 1997 Deregulation of Japan's Holding Companies' (1999) 8(2) *Pacific Rim Law & Policy Journal*, p. 266.

1344 Ibid., p. 265.

completely controlling them and ultimately protecting them from takeovers.[1345] This regime evolved over time in large, complex, and integrated enterprises having close ties with the government while enjoying certain privileges such as exclusive licenses, capital funding, and competition practices.[1346] From a practical perspective, the banking sector in Japan was formatted to perform specific tasks and under the Zaibatsu regime, banks were not at the centre of this complex corporate structure; rather were a humble group member under the command and control of the holding companies which were the major shareholders to the group entities, and they were exercising strong control over it. The bank was used as a vehicle to economically support, through bank loans, the rest group entities and to participate in the capital of the various group companies, an economic powerhouse that had to provide credit for the necessary expansion of the group activities. This pyramid-based management style of Zaibatsu structure was in striking contrast to the modern corporate style of Japan that we will discover later. However, all these were important up to 1945.

2.2. The Post World War II Era

By the end of the Second World War Japan had surrender herself to the Allied Forces and its economy was devastated. The need for rebuild and modernisation was dire and here comes the second miracle achieved by Japan, that is the rebirth of a nation from its ashes and the huge economic growth achieved after that. For many scholars, commentators and practitioners Japan was the archetype of economic growth and recovery in the post war era. Despite the efforts for democratisation and the measures adopted by the Occupation Forces, the Japanese economic system remained adapted to its prewar mentality of doing business. One striking example is the financial system, which followed the segmentation of the prewar era and led to the bubble economy, the banking crisis and the two lost decades with low growth and structural problems.

2.2.1 The US Occupation of Japan: Competition Concerns and the Holding Companies' Issue

The US occupation of Japan lasted from 1945 until 1952 after the surrender of the Imperial Japan under the terms contained in the Potsdam Declaration (or Proclamation Defining Terms for Japanese Surrender).[1347] Among these terms

---

1345 Ibid.

1346 Ibid., p. 268.

1347 The surrender of Imperial Japan was announced by the Japanese Emperor Hirohito on 15 August 1945, and was formally signed on 2 September 1945, ending the hostilities of World War II between Japan and Allied Forces. Few days earlier, on 6 and 9 August 1945,

was the request to democratise Japan so as to avoid any future ability to engage in military imperialistic expansion. According to the Declaration:

- 'The Japanese Government shall remove all obstacles to the revival and strengthening of democratic tendencies among the Japanese people. Freedom of speech, of religion, and of thought, as well as respect for the fundamental human rights shall be established.'
- 'Japan shall be permitted to maintain such industries as will sustain her economy and permit the exaction of just reparations in kind, but not those which would enable her to rearm for war. To this end, access to, as distinguished from control of, raw materials shall be permitted. Eventual Japanese participation in world trade relations shall be permitted.'
- 'The occupying forces of the Allies shall be withdrawn from Japan as soon as these objectives have been accomplished and there has been established, in accordance with the freely expressed will of the Japanese people, a peacefully inclined and responsible government.'

The above terms crystallised the next steps that occupation forces had to take to establish a new regime in Japan. Banking and the financial sector in general should be adapted also to the new reality. Initially, the US did not want any responsibility for the economic and social policy in Japan and occupation officials were explicitly instructed not to assume control of the financial system.[1348] Oversight of the Japanese financial sector felt over the Economic and Scientific Section (ESS) of the Supreme Commander of Allied Powers (SCAP). The ESS had responsibility for science, economics, finance, and labour but with respect to banking, its powers were limited. The SCAP worked hand in hand with officials from the MoF and BoJ and many times intervened directly, but the Japanese were mainly responsible for the shaping of their banking system. SCAP and ESS officials relied heavily on MoF officials due to lack of expertise and prudence. MoF remained the key player in banking and financial matters simply because if any objections were raised by the MoF and were not considered by SCAP, after the end of occupation they would be

---

the US had detonated two atomic bombs over Hiroshima and Nagasaki, forcing Japan to accept the surrender terms, as proposed by the Potsdam Declaration, by end of July 1945. On 26 July 1945, the US President Harry S. Truman, the UK Prime Minister Winston Churchill, and President of China Chiang Kai-shek issued a document, which outlined the terms of surrender for the Empire of Japan, as agreed upon at the Potsdam Conference. The ultimatum stated that, if Japan did not surrender, it would face 'prompt and utter destruction'.

1348 Military officials were in Japan to democratize the country and denude Japan from the means to make war again. Consequently, they were not assigned to assist with the economic recovery and reconstruction of Japan. See in R.J. Brown Jr., 'Japanese Banking Reform and the Occupation Legacy: Decompartmentalization, Deregulation, and Decentralization' (1993) 21(2) *Denver Journal of International Law & Policy*, p. 375.

reversed.[1349] This power game resulted in a rigidly and segmented banking market where a true and comprehensive reform never actually took place.

The request of democratising Japan, as ordered by the Potsdam Declaration, was accompanied by that of liquidating the large, complex Japanese enterprises and holding companies (Zaibatsu), since these entities were considered as a major impediment towards further democratisation as well as a connection with Japan's imperialistic past.[1350] The dissolution of Zaibatsu took place through concrete measures adopted from the occupation forces and by the Japanese Government. The first step was the adoption of the Act Concerning Prohibition of Monopolization and Maintenance of Fair Trade of 1947 (better known as Anti Monopoly Act – AMA), which aimed at regulating the concentrations of excessive economic power through the use of holding companies.[1351] The second step was the zaibatsu liquidation measures that were adopted between 1946 and 1951, under the auspices of the General Headquarters and were including: a) destruction of the pyramid formation of the Zaibatsu regime through liquidation, b) public disposition of the Zaibatsu-owned stocks from the companies that were controlled by the holding companies, c) reorganisation of the large monopolies under a new regime, aiming more in deconcentrating the excessive economic power and d) enhancing the antimonopoly measures so as to prohibit unfair competition and the creation of private monopolies.[1352]

Behind the dissolution of Zaibatsu was the idea that excessive economic power concentrations were unacceptable in the post war Japan. As part of that post war policy, Japan adopted and enacted laws that banned pure holding companies which controlled stockholdings in large stock companies and in companies engaged in financial business, particularly important for the present book. In the late 1990s, an orchestrated effort to amend AMA and its strict provisions was attempted. This effort was based on the grounds of a) general structural reform, b) stimulation of Japan's economy in the context of severe international competition, c) enhanced flexibility in the stock company

1349 See in R.J. Brown Jr., 'Japanese Banking Reform and the Occupation Legacy: Decompartmentalization, Deregulation, and Decentralization' (1993) 21(2) *Denver Journal of International Law & Policy*, p. 377.

1350 See in A.H. Thorson and F. Siegfanz, 'The 1997 Deregulation of Japan's Holding Companies' (1999) 8(2) *Pacific Rim Law & Policy Journal*, p. 261.

1351 Act on Prohibition of Private Monopolization and Maintenance of Fair Trade (Act No. 54 of 1947, Japan). According to Thorson and Siegfanz, the original AMA contained in Article 9 the prohibition of the establishment of pure holding companies and in Article 11 the prohibition for financial enterprises from acquiring stocks of competing companies that were offering same kind of business. Article 11 also prohibited finance enterprises with net assets more than ¥5 million from acquiring more than 5% of any company's stock. Moreover, the provisions of Article 10 absolutely prohibited enterprises outside finance business from acquiring stocks of other companies, although with some exemptions.

1352 See in A.H. Thorson and F. Siegfanz, 'The 1997 Deregulation of Japan's Holding Companies' (1999) 8(2) *Pacific Rim Law & Policy Journal*, p. 270.

management and d) prerequisite for efficient transposition of the Big Bang financial reforms of 1996. In June 1997, the Japanese Diet adopted the Act for Partial Amendment of the AMA, and since December 1997, the almost fifty-year-old ban on pure holding companies was amended.

When the Zaibatsu entities were over, Japan found another way to essentially protect its firms from hostile takeovers. In the mid-1960s, only a decade after the end of the American occupation, cross holdings among Japanese corporations reappeared albeit in a different structure and name. Under the name 'Keiretsu', the big company networks and the banks started an effort to increase their cross holdings among firms, mostly associated with them as a reaction against depressed stock prices and a threat for hostile takeovers. The aims of these cross holdings were to protect the companies from potentially hostile takeovers, a pattern that reappeared in the 1970s.[1353] Essentially a Keiretsu structure is a group of member firms with each group member firm owing a small percentage of the stocks of other group member firms. Because each group member firm owns stocks from other group member firms, between 30% and 90% of the group member firms' stocks will be owned by other group members.[1354] Typically, at the centre of the keiretsu structure stand the banks, which have seats on the boards of the group members firms and can exert pressure on management, particularly in the cases when financial situation becomes unstable. While at first glance, the bank gains from such a structure are not clear and evident, in such crossholding structures is embedded a stable equity ownership aiming at the elimination of hostile takeovers, thus jeopardising the banks participation, and causing unexpected problems and difficulties. As a result, banks can influence the management decisions of the group by controlling the total risks associated with the group while at the same time when a firm joins a keiretsu structure, they limit their ability to access credit from another bank, apart from the group's bank. This happens for two main reasons: a) outside lenders know that the equity cross holdings will induce keiretsu firms to elect strategies benefiting the keiretsu group members and not the outsiders and b) when a borrower will be associated with the keiretsu's main bank, the information effects from switching to a new bank will hamper the borrower's ability to select another source of credit.[1355]

1353 See in J.R. Macey and G.P. Miller, 'Corporate Governance and Commercial Banking: A Comparative Examination of Germany, Japan, and the United States' (1995) 48 *Stanford Law Review*, p. 83.

1354 Ibid.

1355 Ibid., p. 84.

2.2.2 The Post World War II Japanese Financial and Banking System

The post war banking system in Japan could be sketched out based on its two distinct characteristics. The first one is that it was a bank centred (oriented) one, since households and most firms relied on banks to secure funding. Especially for firms, the alternatives were very few, if at all since debt funding was almost non-existent and stock offerings heavily regulated. Furthermore, a large proportion of the publicly traded stock companies were held by banks and companies belonging to the same group (keiretsu style). The second characteristic was the heavy regulation that accompanied banks and securities firms' operations. The goals of this regulatory approach were twofold. First, to assist the country recover from the war and to channel the available funds and households' deposits to the sectors that the government perceived as the most crucial for the recovery; Second, to secure the stability of the financial system and to exclude any failures or events that would jeopardise this stability. To secure both goals the MoF took the view that it was necessary a) to restrict competition among banks and b) assume full control over every aspect of their operations.[1356] Restricting competition had a double meaning since it was not only addressed to the domestic banks but also to foreign bank entities that wanted to enter the Japanese market and provide services. This policy option was not only applicable to the banking sector; As previously described, restricted competition characterised Japanese economy since always and was reinforced from the very special cultural elements of Japanese people. What will be presented later is the undoubted fact that the banking crisis occurred when Japan decided to deregulate its market and be more open to international trade and competition. The wrong approach towards deregulation had many side effects, especially in the banking sector; The last, being protected and isolated from international competition, became a victim by being forced to dig the hole in which it was believed he could be safe.

2.2.2.1 *Financial Sector: Rigid Structures, Strict Segmentation and Compartmentalisation*

Among the most important measures, aiming at restricting competition in the Japanese banking system was the strict regulation, through rigid segmentation and compartmentalisation, of the services that each type of bank would offer and on what type of business would engage. The strict classification allowed the MoF to fully control the market by not allowing the mixing of banking

[1356] See in E.C. Sibbitt, 'A Brave New World for M&A of Financial Institutions in Japan: Big Bang Financial Deregulation and the New Environment for Corporate Combinations of Financial Institutions' (1998) 19(4) *University of Pennsylvania Journal of International Economic Law*, p. 974.

types. Broadly speaking, Japanese banks were classified based on which segment of the market they operated. This segmentation of financial services was founded in two basic legal texts, the Banking Act[1357] and the Securities and Exchange Act (SEA).[1358] Further segmentation was imposed through various other specific laws applying to special entities that offered financial related services and resulted in the existence of the following bank types:

- Ordinary commercial banks: these banks were established and licensed according to the provisions of Banking Act[1359] and were further divided, on a non-statutory basis, into the following subcategories:
  - City banks,[1360]
  - Regional banks,[1361]
  - Second-tier regional banks (formerly known as 'mutual/sogo banks')[1362]
- Foreign exchange banks: this type of bank was created with the goal of actively participating in foreign exchange market transactions by offering

---

1357 Banking Act (Act No. 59 of 1981, Japan).

1358 Securities and Exchange Act (Act No. 25 of 1948, Japan).

1359 Foreign bank branches were charted and regulated as ordinary bank branches under the Bank Law. See in E.C. Sibbitt, 'A Brave New World for M&A of Financial Institutions in Japan: Big Bang Financial Deregulation and the New Environment for Corporate Combinations of Financial Institutions' (1998) 19(4) *University of Pennsylvania Journal of International Economic Law*, p. 975.

1360 'City bank' was a term utilized by the MoF to describe those large ordinary commercial banks that were operating on a nationwide basis. These banks (10 in number) had located most of their branches in the three biggest cities and country's economic centres (Tokyo, Osaka and Nagoya) and were specialized in providing large firms with short-term operating funds. See in E.C. Sibbitt, 'A Brave New World for M&A of Financial Institutions in Japan: Big Bang Financial Deregulation and the New Environment for Corporate Combinations of Financial Institutions' (1998) 19(4) *University of Pennsylvania Journal of International Economic Law*, p. 984.

1361 'Regional bank' was a term utilised by the MoF to describe relatively small ordinary commercial banks operating on a regional basis. They were based each in a particular prefectural capital of Japan in their business was to provide launch two individuals and business corporations within their perfection. Furthermore, they were underwriting municipal bonds issued by their local government, also handling the receipt and payment of local government funds. See in E.C. Sibbitt, 'A Brave New World for M&A of Financial Institutions in Japan: Big Bang Financial Deregulation and the New Environment for Corporate Combinations of Financial Institutions' (1998) 19(4) *University of Pennsylvania Journal of International Economic Law*, p. 984.

1362 'Second-tier regional banks' were the banks that had been reclassified by the MoF as such after the amendment of the Japanese Mutual Banking Law (Law No. 187 of 1952, Japan). After the amendment, these Sogo banks were converted into ordinary banks and were permitted to offer services related with mutual instalment funds. Moreover, this type of banks was permitted, with various other exceptions, to engage in the same activities as ordinary banks. See in E.C. Sibbitt, 'A Brave New World for M&A of Financial Institutions in Japan: Big Bang Financial Deregulation and the New Environment for Corporate Combinations of Financial Institutions' (1998) 19(4) *University of Pennsylvania Journal of International Economic Law*, p. 985.

activities related to letters of credit and other instruments for international trade financing.[1363]

- Long term credit banks: institutions specialised in long term credit supply, mostly for large corporations with funding needs in long-term, large scale investment projects. These banks collected funds through the issuance of special debentures with maturity from two to five years and discount debentures with maturity in one year. Furthermore, legal restrictions were applied regarding their ability to accept deposits and provide short-term loans.[1364]
- Trust banks: they were able to engage in long-term credit, but they had to do so through trusts.
- Credit cooperatives and credit associations (also known as shinkin banks): these entities were specialised in SMEs and retail banking operations,
- Other specialised institutions: other specialised institutions included the labour banks,[1365] the 'Shoko Chukin Bank'[1366] and a 3-tiered agricultural banking system, which included the agricultural cooperatives and the fishery

1363 See E.C. Sibbitt, 'A Brave New World for M&A of Financial Institutions in Japan: Big Bang Financial Deregulation and the New Environment for Corporate Combinations of Financial Institutions' (1998) 19(4) *University of Pennsylvania Journal of International Economic Law*, p. 978. The merger between Bank of Tokyo and Mitsubishi Bank eliminated the category of foreign exchange banks, since the first was the only foreign exchange bank in existence at that time.

1364 These banks were established under the provisions of Long-Term Credit Bank Act (Act No. 61 of 1952, Japan). Only three such banks existed in the post war Japan. The *Long-Term Credit Bank*, the *Industrial Bank of Japan*, and the *Nippon Bond Credit Bank*. See in E.C. Sibbitt, 'A Brave New World for M&A of Financial Institutions in Japan: Big Bang Financial Deregulation and the New Environment for Corporate Combinations of Financial Institutions' (1998) 19(4) *University of Pennsylvania Journal of International Economic Law*, p. 978.

1365 Labour banks were also cooperative institutions whose primary activities consisted of instalment savings, lending and deposit transactions offered to labour unions and their members. See in E.C. Sibbitt, 'A Brave New World for M&A of Financial Institutions in Japan: Big Bang Financial Deregulation and the New Environment for Corporate Combinations of Financial Institutions' (1998) 19(4) *University of Pennsylvania Journal of International Economic Law*, p. 979.

1366 The 'Shoko Chukin Bank' (商工中金 / Shōkō Chūkin Ginkō) is a government-affiliated financial institution in Japan that primarily supports small and medium-sized enterprises (SMEs). It was originally established in 1936 to bridge the gap between commercial banks and small businesses by providing stable financing. Its focus is to offer long-term, low-interest loans and crisis support to SMEs, especially during recessions, disasters, or pandemics. With relation to its ownership, formerly a mix of government and SME cooperatives; now under increasing government control after several scandals. Shoko Chukin plays a public-policy role, acting as a safety net lender for SMEs that are vital to Japan's economy but often underserved by private banks.

cooperatives,[1367] organised under the 'Norin Chukin Bank' (the Central Bank of Agriculture and Forestry).[1368]

Supervision of the financial system was assigned to the MoF. Initially, the MoF had authority over both fiscal policy (tax and custom policy, budget planning and execution, international trade, fiscal investments, etc.) and financial policy (financial sector containing banks, securities firms, and insurance companies). In the field of financial policy, performed both regulation and supervision together with inspection of financial sector entities.[1369] MoF was regulating literally everything, from authorisation and establishment to capital requirements and inspections, meaning that nothing could change without its prior approval. Interest rates were administratively regulated by the government, allowing every bank to earn enough so as not to compete with others. Within the MoF, the Banking Bureau was responsible for the banks and the Securities Bureau was responsible for the securities firms.

2.2.2.2 *The Adoption of Structural Separation between Banks and Securities Firms*

Apart from type specific segmentation, Japanese legislation also promoted business activity type segmentation. The most important example of such segmentation was the complete ban for banks and securities firms to engage in each other's activities. There was a statutory wall erected between the two industries that was impossible to penetrate. The creation of this wall was modelled after the separation regime imposed in the US with the GSA. In Japan, the statutory separation was imposed by Article 65 of SEA. Its provisions restricted access to 'securities' business to licensed securities firms and imposed further

---

1367 According to the provisions of the Fisheries Cooperatives Law (Act No. 242 of 1948, Japan), fishery cooperatives were focused on lending their members' savings to their members. See in E.C. Sibbitt, 'A Brave New World for M&A of Financial Institutions in Japan: Big Bang Financial Deregulation and the New Environment for Corporate Combinations of Financial Institutions' (1998) 19(4) *University of Pennsylvania Journal of International Economic Law*, p. 979.

1368 According to the provisions of the Norin Chukin Bank Law (Act No. 42 of 1923), agricultural cooperatives were required to deposit a percentage of funds to their respective prefectural Federation of Agricultural Cooperatives, which in turn were obliged to deposit a percentage in the Norin Chukin Bank. The Norin Chukin Bank therefore performs the role of an agricultural central bank, which raises funds not only through collections from the prefectural federations but also through issuing debentures. These funds either were invested in the securities markets or lend to business engaged in agriculture, forestry, and fisheries. See in E.C. Sibbitt, 'A Brave New World for M&A of Financial Institutions in Japan: Big Bang Financial Deregulation and the New Environment for Corporate Combinations of Financial Institutions' (1998) 19(4) *University of Pennsylvania Journal of International Economic Law*, p. 979.

1369 See in R. Kamikawa, 'The Interaction between Financial Regulation and Financial Crisis in Japan: Change in Financial Administration and Two Financial Crises from 1980 to 2010' (2012) 59 *Osaka University Law Review*, p. 3.

regulations on these firms. With certain exemptions regarding transactions performed by certain approved financial institutions, financial institutions other than licensed securities firms were generally prohibited from dealing in the securities business. At the same time, the provisions of the Banking Act further bolstered this division by restricting access to banking business only to licensed banks and further restricted the allowed business of licensed banks to specific categories: a) 'core banking business', b) 'incidental banking business' and c) 'other banking business'. SEL Article 65 and the Banking Act provisions were a very powerful blockade towards universal banking model and combining financial services under the same legal entity roof.

From a historical perspective, the total separation of banking and securities activities has been eroded through the years, but not completely. According to Sibbitt, this erosion could be attributed to two factors (kokusai-ka, in the Japanese language): a) to the internationalisation of the financial services and b) to the increased use of government bonds in the Japanese financial market. Following the example of their US counterparties, Japanese banks have gradually won the right to engage in a limited number of services in the securities market: underwriting and dealing in government bonds, derivative activities related to domestic and foreign government bonds, and activities related to certain money market instruments (commercial papers and certificates of deposits).[1370] Moreover, banks began to establish, in foreign countries, locally incorporated subsidiaries through which they engaged in the securities business. At the same time, securities firms managed to enter closely related to banking fields by selling medium term government securities funds that were closely related to money market instruments and were competing with bank deposits.[1371]

Based on the analysis so far, the Japanese authorities designed their own Glass-Steagall type restriction with a different goal in their mind. It goes without saying that consumer protection was also a desired target, but it was not the main reason and appears more persuasive that the rationale behind SEA's Article 65 prohibition had to do with the fears of distortive competition among big financial firms. The heavily regulated banks were not allowed to participate in other firms through stockholdings. Until the 1992 Financial System Reform Act,[1372] holding companies were prohibited and holdings by financial institutions were limited to 5%, without special approval from the

---

1370 See in E.C. Sibbitt, 'A Brave New World for M&A of Financial Institutions in Japan: Big Bang Financial Deregulation and the New Environment for Corporate Combinations of Financial Institutions' (1998) 19(4) *University of Pennsylvania Journal of International Economic Law*, p. 983.

1371 Ibid.

1372 The 1992 Financial Reform Act in Japan is actually a collection of laws and amendments rather than a single statute with one act number. This reform was implemented through multiple legislative changes affecting various financial laws.

Fair-Trade Commission.[1373] The MoF was afraid that if banks were allowed to freely enter the securities market, securities companies would lose market share since they did not have access to deposits to secure their financing like banks did. Furthermore, if at the same time securities companies were not able to enter the banking market and compete with banks many of them would be forced to go out of the market leaving more market share to be grabbed by the big banks.

2.2.2.3 *The Japanese Deposit Insurance Scheme*

Deposit insurance system in Japan was established only in 1971, after the slow start of liberalisation process in the banking sector. It was considered as a necessary step since liberalisation has already started. The Deposit Insurance Corporation of Japan (DICJ) offered protection limited to ¥1 million and it was not until 1986 that the insurance model was changed by the regulators. The two methods that were included in the toolkit were the 'insurance payout' and the 'financial assistance' while the insurance limit increased to ¥10 million.[1374] Many commentators pointed out the fact that DIC's funds were not able to cover the banking sector's needs, especially during the crisis time, even after the mid-1980s reforms. Initially, the DICJ was in a position to cover only the depositors of a small bank's failure and not to offer a credible solution to the entire sector during a crisis.[1375] The Deposit Insurance Act (DIA)[1376] was substantially amended in 1996, during the peak of the crisis, aiming at preventing bank runs from depositors with the raise of insurance premia contributions from bank members, in order to increase the insurance capacity.[1377] Finally, with the 2000 amendments on DIA, new rules were introduced to make resolution tools more effective and to give greater flexibility to the DICJ.

1373 See in E.C. Sibbitt, 'A Brave New World for M&A of Financial Institutions in Japan: Big Bang Financial Deregulation and the New Environment for Corporate Combinations of Financial Institutions' (1998) 19(4) *University of Pennsylvania Journal of International Economic Law*, p. 987.

1374 See in I. Tirado, 'Banking Crises and the Japanese Legal Framework', Discussion Paper No. 2017-E-2, Institute for Monetary and Economic Studies, Bank of Japan, Tokyo, 2017, p. 3.

1375 Ibid.

1376 Deposit Insurance Act (Act No. 59 of 1971, Japan).

1377 See in I. Tirado, 'Banking Crises and the Japanese Legal Framework', Discussion Paper No. 2017-E-2, Institute for Monetary and Economic Studies, Bank of Japan, Tokyo, 2017, p. 3. It is worth noting that in the initial period of the crisis, in 1996, the DIC had ¥876 billion available, only the 0,158% of the total value of insured deposits at that time.

2.3. *The Post World War II Economic Miracle and the 'Plaza Accord'*

By the mid-1980s, the Japanese economy had achieved its second miracle. It was completely resurrected from the ashes of the Second World War and had become the second biggest economy in the world. The consistent growth strategy, followed by the Japanese governments, has created an export driven economy, which had already exceeded its sustainable economic growth limits.[1378] It has become a matter of geopolitical concern that the contained island country could not support such a policy.[1379] Two alarming signals could certify the above: a) the trade war with the United States and b) the fast appreciation of Yen. The trade war erupted because of the constantly growing trade deficit of the US with Japan. The war ended up in imposing retaliatory measures against Japanese exports towards the US, in 1987. Earlier, on 22 September 1985, in the Plaza Hotel in New York, a joint agreement was signed between West Germany, the UK, the US, France and Japan. That agreement has been famously known as the 'Plaza Accord' and allowed for state interventions in the currency markets (foreign exchange markets) aiming in restoring, by depreciation, the US dollar against the currencies of these countries.[1380] Indeed, to a certain extent, the agreement helped the US dollar to recover but since Japan was the main target of the accord, that didn't happen mostly because of the structural problems that the Japanese economy was facing and affected the US exports towards Japan.[1381]

Based on the agreement, the parties concluded that 'some further orderly appreciation of the non-dollar currencies is desirable' and Paul Volcker, the then US finance minister, recounts that the Japanese finance minister Noboru Takeshita offered himself to allow a yen appreciation towards the US dollar for more than 10%.[1382] The yen appreciation was very fast and created serious problems to the Japanese manufacturers who ended up struggling to stay afloat.[1383] The monetary policy became of extreme priority in Japan politics. The Yen appreciation against the US dollar required a holistic approach that forced Japanese governments to deeply alter their economy and the way they were doing business. A new national doctrine arose for Japan and based on

1378 See in R. Himino, *The Japanese Banking Crisis*, Singapore, Palgrave Macmillan, 2021, p. 9.

1379 Ibid.

1380 The currencies that should restore their value towards the US dollar were the French Franc, the West German Mark, the British pound sterling and the Japanese Yen.

1381 For an excellent and more in-depth analysis of the Plaza Accord see in J. Frankel, 'The Plaza Accord, 30 Years Later', Working Paper 21813, *NBER Working Paper Series*, National Bureau of Economic Research (NBER), December 2015.

1382 See in R. Himino, *The Japanese Banking Crisis*, Singapore, Palgrave Macmillan, 2021, p. 10.

1383 According to Himino, the Japanese yen was at 240 yen per dollar on Friday before the agreement and reached 152 yen per dollar a year later. By the end of 1987 stood at 121 yen per dollar.

the proposals of the 1986 'Mayekawa Report'[1384] it included various structural reforms, fiscal and monetary stimulus, deregulation of land use and government projects. As described, it was a 'historic transformation [...] of the lifestyle of the nation'.[1385] This transformation expected to happen through expanding the domestic demand and changing the export-oriented nature of the economy. The state commenced to massively sale state owned land to stimulate real estate demand and aggressively expand government projects. These government-oriented projects were supported by a low interest policy from the BoJ that reduced the basic interest rate from 5% in the beginning of 1986 to the historic low of 2.5% in February 1987, aggressively easing its monetary policy.[1386]

The expansionary monetary policy fuelled the real estate sector and drove the creation of a bubble, around the real estate prices. What also happened at the time was a deregulation in the financial sector that broke the 'protective glass' of the banks and opened them to competition. The stripping of the bank's protective legislation after almost 40 years changed radically the regulatory landscape and nobody was truly prepared for. The earlier mentioned, compartmentalised regulatory structure of various special banks that supply with credit not based on supply and demand but on state policies and state industry priorities could not follow the fast speed evolution. The effect of deregulation was to allow the Japanese corporates to seek credit also from international markets, through bond issuances, thus reducing their reliance from the banks. As a result, banks lost their traditional core clients, which were not building anymore factories in Japan but were seeking investment opportunities overseas. The bankers feared that the deposit rates deregulation would ultimately raise their funding costs and limit their lending margins. This situation created a sort of existential threat for the Japanese banks that in order to survive and continue their operations had to find new customers-borrowers, ready to obtain credit and pay interests at higher rates.[1387] On top of the traditional lending channels, at the same time, non-bank lenders expanded their lending while not being regulated (direct supervision and inspections) from the MoF as traditional banks. Furthermore, borrowers had the impression that these non-bank lending entities would be accompanied by implicit

[1384] The '*Mayekawa Report*' was the final output of the Committee on Structural Adjustment of the Economy for International Coordination, a committee of wise men, created by the Japanese Prime minister Yasuhiro Nakasone and chaired by the former governor of Bank of Japan, Haruo Mayekawa.

[1385] See in R. Himino, *The Japanese Banking Crisis*, Singapore, Palgrave Macmillan, 2021, p. 11.

[1386] Ibid., p. 13.

[1387] Ibid., p. 17.

guarantees from the affiliated banks and insurance companies, although the exact state of these responsibilities were largely unknown.[1388]

2.4. *From the Bubble Economy to the Banking Crisis*

The traditional mechanism of bubble creation was triggered under these circumstances. Backed by a constantly growing demand, the asset prices started to rise while the value of collaterals also rose, and the credit underwriting standards weakened. Further speculative investments prompted by credit expansion rose asset prices even more, fuelling the bubble and expanding it. Certain commentators support that the Japanese bubble was significantly bigger than the US housing market bubble in early 2000s, in terms of GDP. He estimates the capital gains in Japan between 1986 and 1989 as 4.8 times as large as the annual GDP of Japan, while in the US, in the same 4 years period between 2003 and 2006 was about only 1.6 times.[1389] In late 1980s and in early 1990s, we observe an alternation to the major preoccupation of Japan's policies. As a result, instead of dealing with the yen appreciation, the main task was to control the increased land prices and to mitigate the deflationary effects from the collapse of the growing bubble. A variety of measures were adopted from the Japanese government to support the economy and alleviate the upcoming burden and among them were also prudential measures aiming at effectively control the real estate lending. The task was assigned to the MoF (back then supervising the banks). From 1986 to 1989, MoF issued a series of qualitative administrative guidance that were imposing reporting requirements, on-site inspections, etc., but proved to be inefficient regarding the containment of the lending frenzy.[1390] The following table is very illustrative regarding the efforts to control the credit supply by the MoF:

[1388] Ibid., p. 19. Based on the numbers presented by Himino, the situation was further aggravated by the fact that not only credit was provided by the traditional banks but also from non-banks lenders. The total outstanding loan amount of non-bank lenders skyrocketed from ¥33 trillion in 1986, to the astronomical number of ¥135 trillion in 1991.

[1389] See in R. Himino, *The Japanese Banking Crisis*, Singapore, Palgrave Macmillan, 2021, p. 21.

[1390] Ibid., p. 29.

Date	Nature	Guidance	Content
April 1986	Qualitative	Circular issued by the MoF	a) Request to behave so as not to attract criticism that banks are encouraging speculative land deals b) Reporting requirements on land related lending to real estate and construction industries
December 1986	Qualitative	Circular issued by the MoF	Request to strictly refrain from financing short-term resale of lands
July 1987	Qualitative	Extraordinary interviews conducted by the MoF	Interviews on lending terms with banks making large amount of loans in regions showing conspicuous rise in land prices
		'Common Understanding' published by the Bankers' Association	Confirmation that land-related lending attitude shall be strictly rectified
October 1987	Qualitative	Circular issued by the MoF	a) Request to be without flows in not making loans to finance speculative land transactions b) Request to make sure that affiliated non-bank lenders shall do the same
		Voluntary Rules by the Bankers' Association	Elimination of lending to finance speculative land transactions
October 1989	Qualitative	Circular issued by the MoF	a) Expansion of the scope of extraordinary interviews b) Reporting Requirements regarding lending to non-bank lenders c) Mobilise on-site inspections to contain lending to finance real estate speculations
March 1990	Quantitative	Circular issued by the MoF	Quantitative Restriction Circular

Source: R. Himino, *The Japanese Banking Crisis*, Singapore, Palgrave Macmillan, 2021, p. 30

The circular issued by the MoF in 1990 was the only quantitative restriction imposed on bank lending that had a major impact; lending immediately shut down. The MoF circular was one page short and communicated the two following points:

- For the time being each bank shall restrain the growth of loans in the real estate sector so that it will not surpass the rate of growth of all loans,[1391] and
- For the time being reports on lending to the real estate and construction sectors, and to non-bank lenders shall be submitted to the Ministry of Finance[1392]

The land prices for six large cities of Japan, reached their pick six months after the issuance of the quantitative restriction circular (September 1990) and then started to decline. The land price index for regions other than the above six large cities, picked out in September 1991. After a thorough analysis of the land price index, the MoF lifted the quantitative restrictions in December 1991.[1393] In Japan, the land price reached its peak in 1990, but the systemic banking problems began only in 1997. This was an extremely long period, unusual for a financial crisis that typically lasts 2–3 years,[1394] but in the meantime, Japanese banks and bankers realised how much of bad loans they had accumulated on their balance sheets with public authorities unsuccessfully trying to guess the exact amount of non-performing exposures.

2.5. A Distorted Financial Deregulation Process

Japan followed the general trend in financial services in late 1970s towards deregulation. Restrictions on competition were significantly eased[1395] but the process was very lengthy, and the major drawback was the fact that the corporate sector deregulation did not move in tandem with the financial sector. The MoF advanced deregulation of the financial sector at a much slower pace compared to the corporate sector, which started in 1980s under heavy pressure from the US, especially regarding the trade-yen relation.[1396] The banking crisis in Japan has been attributed, to a certain extent, not to financial liberalisation per se but to 'distorted financial liberalisation' and after the bank failures of

---

[1391] Ibid., p. 31.

[1392] Ibid.

[1393] Ibid.

[1394] Ibid., p. 47.

[1395] See in R. Kamikawa, 'The Interaction between Financial Regulation and Financial Crisis in Japan: Change in Financial Administration and Two Financial Crises from 1980 to 2010' (2012) 59 *Osaka University Law Review*, p. 3.

[1396] See in R. Himino, *The Japanese Banking Crisis*, Singapore, Palgrave Macmillan, 2021, p. 15.

1997 libcralisation moved at a faster speed.[1397] Japanese banks were suffering from tight regulation, aimed at protecting competition and from a collusive relation with the MoF, which supervised and regulated literally everything.[1398] Expansion through branches was impossible for certain banking categories (city banks), transformation through mergers and acquisitions was also impossible for competitions reasons and prior approval from the MoF was needed, interest rates were administratively set and practically were cartelised together with securities trading commissions.[1399] On the other hand, financial deregulation regarding corporate finance moved faster leading banks to suffer from lower profit margins and losing traditional clients that were equipped with better, cheaper and more innovative methods to obtain credit. When ultimately the interest rates were liberalised banks started to sell high-interest rate certificates of deposit (CDs) and this further suppressed their profit margins, their prime source of earning.[1400] In such a dried environment, most city banks and long-term credit banks preferred to convert into universal banks, just like their European counterparties, but this was impossible until the late 1990s. Only in 1993 were banks allowed to enter the securities business, under strict conditions, by forming subsidiaries that would be independently managed. Segmentation of financial services, according to Kamikawa, was not deregulated faster for three reasons:[1401]

(a) Securities companies and trust banks strongly opposed the entry of city banks into their protected business fields,
(b) The MoF was deeply concerned that financial deregulation would increase competition among the various financial services providers and would drive some of them into bankruptcy and
(c) The MoF was also concerned about the possible conflicts of interest that could be created between banks and securities companies in a Glass-Steagall based theory.

This regime forced banks to look elsewhere for profitable margins, and the real estate sector was providing with many opportunities since it was favoured by the government aspirations for creating a new Japan. Even after the 1996 Japanese Big Bang financial reforms,[1402] banks were still facing regulatory difficulties to expand into new business areas and where under

---

1397 See in R. Kamikawa, 'The Interaction between Financial Regulation and Financial Crisis in Japan: Change in Financial Administration and Two Financial Crises from 1980 to 2010' (2012) 59 *Osaka University Law Review*, p. 2.

1398 Ibid., p. 3.

1399 Ibid., p. 5.

1400 Ibid., p. 6.

1401 Ibid., p. 7.

1402 In November 1996, the former Prime Minister of Japan Ryutaro Hashimoto, called for a Japanese Big Bang financial deregulation of financial markets, nicknamed and inspired after the similar British reforms of the 1980s. Based on the final report, the recommendations

the heavy regulation and oversight of the MoF. The Japanese Big Bang contained liberalisation of various regulations, such as on international capital transactions, on brokerage commissions and the full liberalisation of securities derivatives. At the same time, the strict segmentation among the financial services was greatly relaxed and banks were allowed to sell investment trusts and issue non-structured bonds, while securities companies were allowed to sell insurance products and insurance companies were equally allowed to enter into the business of banking. Particularly important was the liberalisation of the holding company structure under which a bank, an insurance company, a securities company (dealer), an investment trust company and a financial service firm could co-exist.[1403]

3 THE JAPANESE BANKING CRISIS (1997–2005)

The banking crisis in Japan was a very prolonged and painful series of events that forced Japan to use huge amounts of public funds and to design new tools and approaches when exactly the water was boiling hot. With no previous experience in banking crisis management the authorities were facing the failing of banks which had invested in real estate during the boom years and now have been defaulted. The most important impact of the crisis was the prolonged credit crunch that followed and pushed Japan in a spiral recession and anaemically growth for almost two decades.

3.1. Ineffective Regulation and Supervision of the Banking Sector

The post war banking system in Japan has been designed in such a way to supply with credit the Japanese economy under strict rules and heavy governmental intervention. The aim was to create a stable level of industrial production that would be able to support the recovery of the destroyed country. As a result, credit policy was dictated by the Government (through the MoF) based on policy priorities and not on a typical, western-based competitive system of credit allocation, where the most efficient provider earns a competitive interest rate versus the less efficient. The only preoccupation of the MoF was to exercise its duties and to keep the banking sector afloat by allowing a completely controlled function of banks under a strict separation

were: 1) liberalization and diversification of products, business, and organisational structures, 2) preparation of the infrastructure and rules for markets and transactions, and 3) secure of the financial system's soundness.

1403 See in R. Kamikawa, 'The Interaction between Financial Regulation and Financial Crisis in Japan: Change in Financial Administration and Two Financial Crises from 1980 to 2010' (2012) 59 *Osaka University Law Review*, p. 12.

scheme of 'who does what' principle. A rigid compartmentalisation allowed for easy oversight, guaranteed earnings and almost no competition among the participants. Foreign banks were facing extremely high barriers to enter the Japanese market, leaving the entire market for the local banks that were operating under the predetermined regime of government influenced credit policy.

The MoF has adopted the so-called 'convoy system' of regulation. Just as in a real convoy all the vehicles that participate on it must adapt and follow the speed of the slower vehicle to arrive safely at their destination, Japanese banks had to adapt and follow the 'speed' of the slowest/weakest bank, to arrive safely at their destination, which is the stability of the entire banking system. Since no banking failures were allowed, the supervision regime was adapted to absorb shocks and the rare failures through the forced mergers among the banks. The convoy system was based on the following principles:[1404]

(a) Survival of the weakest: the regulatory framework was set in such a way to support the survival of the weakest member of the banking sector and the high entrance barriers were keeping the number of banks at manageable levels.
(b) No exit (no failure): the no exit principle had the meaning that no bank failure was acceptable, and it was perceived as the corollary of the first principle. The only possible exit option was the merger with a stronger bank, an option that was aimed at enhancing stability by preventing failure and by increasing public confidence towards supervisors' capabilities.
(c) Responsibility and equitable subordination: this principle implied that when difficulties would appear, the parent or principal source of funding for the failing bank was expected to assume the debts and take responsibility by extending financial assistance and by subordinating its claims to those of other creditors even if not legally required to do so
(d) Implicit government insurance: the above norms led to an implicit government insurance that if stronger members would assist the weaker members and no failure would be accepted, then the government would step in and back up the strong members to perform their duty. Milhaupt supports the view that since the implicit insurance from the government was inherent to the functioning of the previous norms, this meant that the responsibility norm was extended to the government itself.[1405]

The above norms, for many years, were enough to secure the safety and stability of the financial system. Confidence was extended to the regulators and the supervisors because the whole system was perceived to be a partnership

1404 See in C.J. MILHAUPT, 'Japan's Experience with Deposit Insurance and Failing Banks: Implications for Financial Regulatory Design?' (1999) 77 *Washington University Law Quarterly*, p. 410.

1405 Ibid., p. 411.

between public and private actors. In practice, the safety net of Japanese banks was that implicit government support and not the DIC itself.[1406] Furthermore, the retired officials from the MoF were usually offered job positions in the banks, as managers or board members. Consequently, there were having legitimate interests to keep afloat the banks and the banking system in general, while at the same time, keeping good relations with the management of the banks, compromising their supervisory duties.

The rigid segmentation and the heavy regulation from the regulatory framework of Japan also affected the way supervision was performed by the MoF. Preoccupied with the aim of no failure policy, MoF was not able to understand the tectonic changes in the 1980s and 1990s related to financial services. As a result, the convoy style and the collusive approach towards the banks resulted in the huge amount of bad loans and ultimately the banking crisis. Furthermore, societal traditions between the MoF officials and the banks such the 'amakudari' and the 'MoF-tan' system were further obscuring the ability for effective supervision. The amakudari system, which is translated as 'descent from heaven' was an institutionalised system whereby senior bureaucrats from the MoF received high-level appointments in financial institutions after their retirement. Those officials were having strong interests in preserving this system and ultimately preserving financial institutions from failing. Moreover, another relation system among banks and MoF officials, was the so-called 'MoF-tan' system, where elite bank executives where exchanging information with MoF officials and entertained them by taking them to dinners and other related activities.[1407] Among the exchanged information were the dates of on-site inspections by the MoF officials, so the banks could be prepared, the release dates for new products by competitor banks and what kind of products these were, and trying to get first authorisation to sell their own products before their competitors.[1408] These ill relations would be strongly disapproved by the society in case of bank failures and the MoF officials would be blamed more than bank executives would. As a result, the MoF had been strongly opposed to the use of public money in saving the failed banks and preferred the 'wait and see' approach aiming in a slow, self-recovery process.

Apart from supervisory failure, Japan suffered also from ill competition among the financial institutions and particularly among banks. By applying the convoy style of supervision, MoF was not giving any incentive for innovation, thus the financial institutions were not offering products according to customers' needs but according to the government's general policy preferences.

1406 Ibid.

1407 See in R. Kamikawa, 'The Interaction between Financial Regulation and Financial Crisis in Japan: Change in Financial Administration and Two Financial Crises from 1980 to 2010' (2012) 59 *Osaka University Law Review*, p. 13.

1408 Ibid.

Bank customers had no incentive to change from one bank to another, in search of better yields or for services of better quality. Every service was the same among the various institutions and with centrally set interest rates which offered banks premium and standardised earnings no bank had any incentive to offer new products and new services with the aim of increasing its market share.

3.2. *Bank Failures and Government Reactions*

As previously mentioned, Japan had no previous experience of a major bank failure since the end of the Second World War. The heavy regulation under the convoy system and the strict compartmentalisation imposed by the MoF had created the sentiment of safety and the implicit guarantee that no bank would ever fail, since the authorities would always find a way to avoid any implications for the broader financial system.[1409]

3.2.1 Bank Failures

The Japanese banking system began to experience sporadic bank failures after the breaking of the bubble, in 1991, but these were small institutions and were perceived as isolated events without any further implications for the financial system. Even though stock prices were declining since the beginning of 1990, there was a general optimism that as soon as the bubble economy would be cleaned up from the repercussions the economy would be back on track and growth will continue.[1410] The Japanese authorities, misled by the fact that the Japanese economy kept growing, but at a slower pace, had the impression that recovery of land prices was only a matter of time. The collateral values would pick up again and banks would become healthy again. According to Nakaso, this was the main idea behind the 'wait and see' approach that was adopted, primarily from the MoF.[1411] The entire year of 1993 and the first half of 1994 passed by without any velar sign of economic recovery. At the same time, the Japanese authorities did not take any serious measures to address the situation. In October 1994, Yasushi Mieno, Governor of the BoJ[1412] delivered a speech on the financial system. The speech was perceived as a milestone for the BoJ's involvement with the crisis and financial stability. What Governor Mieno said was straightforward: 'It is not the business of the central bank to save all

1409 See in H. Nakaso, 'The financial crisis in Japan during the 1990s: how the Bank of Japan responded and the lessons learnt', *BIS Papers*, No. 6, Bank of International Settlements, October 2001, p. 2.

1410 Ibid., p. 3.

1411 Ibid.

1412 Yasushi Mieno was the 26th Governor of the Bank of Japan, from 17 December 1989, to 16 December 1994, having previously served as Deputy Governor from 1984 to 1989.

financial institutions from failure. On the contrary, failure of an institution that has reasons to fail is even necessary from the viewpoint of nurturing a sound financial system.'[1413] In reality, what Governor Mieno implied never happened. The BoJ was involved in a never-ending nightmare with major banking crises constantly erupting and almost non-existent economic growth, creating a lethal cocktail for the 'lost two decades'.

3.2.1.1 *The Case of Japanese Credit Cooperatives (1994)*

The first victims of the banking crisis, after the breaking of the bubble economy, were two urban credit cooperative banks in December 1994. The Tokyo Kyowa Credit Association (TKCA), and the Anzen Credit Association (Anzen) collapsed simultaneously with a combined ¥210 billion in deposits. Anzen and TKCA were the first urban deposit-taking institutions that failed, while being poorly managed and obviously badly supervised. The failure of the two credit cooperatives resulted in the resignation of two politicians while the investigations revealed various breaches of the regulatory rules and particularly those related to the limits towards lending to a single client. Since at that time a clear solution for the resolution of failed banks did not exist, the resolution had to be tailor made for each case by the relevant authorities.

The reaction of the Japanese authorities was shaped between two available options at that time. The first option was a traditional 'pay-off' approach where the failed institution would be liquidated, and the DICJ would intervene to cover deposits up to ¥10 million each.[1414] The second option, the 'financial assistance' approach, involved the transfer of liabilities and sound assets from the failing institution to another that would assume the operations and the DICJ would cover any losses incurred from the failing institution after the shareholders' capital would be wiped out.[1415] What must be clarified to this point is that these two options were available after the 1986 amendment to the Japanese DIA. Despite the amendment, several obstacles were still in place since the DICJ was constraint by the statutory limitation of the amount that could be used to cover the losses when the second approach was preferred. McNamara and Metrick support that under the Japanese law, the financial assistance approach had endogenous limits and as a result was a difficult option from the very beginning. The Japanese law required that the amount of money that the DICJ could provide for financial assistance would be limited

1413 See in H. Nakaso, 'The financial crisis in Japan during the 1990s: how the Bank of Japan responded and the lessons learnt', *BIS Papers*, No. 6, Bank of International Settlements, October 2001, p. 4.

1414 See in C. McNamara and A. Metrick, 'Restructuring and Forgiveness in Financial Crises D: The Japanese Financial Crisis of the 1990s' (2020) 2(1) *The Journal of Financial Crises*, p. 126.

1415 Ibid.

to the amount that it would have paid under the pay-off approach. This 'pay-off cost limit', as defined by McNamara and Metrick,[1416] was a critical constraint and was calculated 'by determining the amount of insured deposits held by a failed institution and subtracting any remaining value of the firm that could be used to satisfy such deposits prior to relying on the DICJ'.[1417] This statutory constraint was coupled with the general indifference of other banking institutions to assume the role of the bank that would accept the sound assets, even with the involvement of the DICJ. For the two cooperatives the funds were not sufficient since the pay-off cost limit was lower than the required funds and therefore someone had to provide additional funds. Acting as 'deus ex machina' the BoJ prepared a bailout plan that was formatted on the following principles:

(i) A new bank, namely the Tokyo Kyoudou Bank (TKB), would be established by the BoJ and a group of private financial institutions that each one of them would contribute ¥20 billion to create TKB's ¥40 billion required capital. The role of the new bank would be to assume the sound assets and liabilities of the two failed institutions.
(ii) The shareholders' capital would be used to cover the losses that the two cooperatives had and then the DICJ would provide with the necessary financial assistance, to cover the remaining losses up to the legally accepted amount (pay-off cost limit).
(iii) The management of the two cooperatives would be replaced as a measure to minimise the moral hazard, and
(iv) The ongoing operations of TKB would be supported through a low-interest loan from the private financial institutions, to support the profitability of the new bank.

In this way, all the depositors, including the large ones, were protected and were able to withdraw their deposits from the new bank. According to McNamara and Metrick, the above participation of the private institutions was the so called 'hougachou approach', used to describe the collective contribution technique that was adopted by the Japanese authorities to secure the participation of the private firms in terms of preventing the collapse of the system that could backfire on them and harm their own interests as well.[1418] This collective contribution scheme was organised for the first time and although the participation by private institutions was voluntary, after a request from the authorities it must have been very difficult not to participate.[1419]

1416 Ibid., p. 127.

1417 Ibid.

1418 Ibid., p. 128.

1419 See in H. Nakaso, 'The financial crisis in Japan during the 1990s: how the Bank of Japan responded and the lessons learnt', *BIS Papers*, No. 6, Bank of International Settlements, October 2001, p. 5.

What makes this scheme more interesting is the fact that participation was not limited only to institutions that had a special interest in the failed institutions but was open to virtually all financial institutions. Another novelty introduced was the use of funds from the BoJ. The capital contribution for the establishment of the TKB was used for the first time although the BoJ, as an established lender of last resort based on the provisions of Article 25 of the Bank of Japan Act, was allowed to provide not only liquidity support but also risk capital.[1420] The use of this discretion by the BoJ was very rare and the rescue of the two cooperatives was the first time that the BoJ had to provide capital.[1421] The use of public funds to support the failing institutions created a sentiment of criticism in the media against BoJ, since they felt that was contradictory with Governor's Mieno speech, in which he supported the view that it was necessary for the health of the financial system to let the institutions that deserve to fail to fail.[1422] McNamara and Metrick are of the view that despite the abovementioned criticism, the 'hougachou approach' accompanied with liquidity support and *ad hoc* capital contributions from the BoJ was the most preferable method for resolving failing institutions.[1423] This method was again used for the effective address of two other cooperatives that failed shortly after TKB and Anzen.

Apart from the above-mentioned criticism, the deterioration of the financial system continued. The two new credit cooperatives, victims of the bubble were Cosmo Credit Cooperative (Cosmo) in July 1995 and Hyogo Bank in August 1995. Apart from these two banks another one also failed in August 1995, and her size was well beyond the capabilities of the 'hougachou approach'. The Kizu Credit Cooperative (Kizu) failed in August 1995 with losses estimated at more than ¥1.000 billion, an amount that was considered too large for private institutions to assume, since they had already contributed enough funds to the rest bailout operations.[1424] For Cosmo and Hyogo, the resolution plans were basically the hougachou approach, as their assets were inside the perimeter of the approach. In the Cosmo case, many private financial institutions were called upon to provide support and cover losses beyond the amount that DICJ could cover. The deposits and sound assets from Cosmo were transferred to TKB. In the interim period between the announcement of the

1420 See in C. McNamara and A. Metrick, 'Restructuring and Forgiveness in Financial Crises D: The Japanese Financial Crisis of the 1990s' (2020) 2(1) *The Journal of Financial Crises*, p. 128.

1421 Historically, the BoJ has made use of the statutory power referred to Article 25 only in the stock market crash of 1965 when it lent funds to the securities firms and then only to provide liquidity support and not capital.

1422 See in C. McNamara and A. Metrick, 'Restructuring and Forgiveness in Financial Crises D: The Japanese Financial Crisis of the 1990s' (2020) 2(1) *The Journal of Financial Crises*, p. 128.

1423 Ibid.

1424 Ibid.

failure, in July 1995, and the day of the actual business transfer in March 1996, the BoJ provided liquidity based on Article 25 provisions, thus allowing Cosmo to continue operations and conclude the deposit repayments.[1425] With respect to Hyogo, the final solution was slightly different, since a new bank was established, the Midori Bank, to assume operations of Hyogo. Midori was established by private financial institutions and local industrial enterprises, having ¥80 billion in capital.[1426] The BoJ again provided ¥110 billion of subordinated loans, based on Article 25, to reinforce Midori's capital base and continued to provide liquidity support to Hyogo until the completion of the transfer to Midori, in January 1996. In both the Hyogo and Cosmos cases, the support provided from the BoJ was fully repaid using the funds provided from the DIC, in the form of financial assistance.[1427]

For Kizu, the situation was further complicated by the endogenous constraints imposed by the 'pay-off cost limit'; since the losses were above ¥1.000 billion the hougachou approach seemed pointless. The amount needed was so large that the authorities concluded it would be impossible to collect it from private financial institutions since they had already supplied much capital for the rest resolution efforts. Another important parameter was the assumption that the endless capital contributions from private financial institutions would ultimately erode their capital base up to the point of impairing their profitability and reputation.[1428] It was obvious that a new framework of resolution was needed. The difficulties posed by the failure of Kizu speeded up the discussions for a revision in the provisions of the Deposit Insurance Act, to facilitate the intervention to stabilise the financial system and more specifically to lift the limitation imposed by the 'pay-off cost limit'. On that basis, the Financial System Research Council, an advisory body to the MoF, started discussions on possible amendments to the DIA, targeting especially the 'pay-off cost limit'. The June 1996 amendments to the DIA included:

- The temporary lift of the pay-off cost limit, until March 2001,[1429]
- The increase of the insurance premiums on insured deposits from 0.012% to 0.084% resulting in an increase in the annual revenue up to ¥460 billion,[1430] and

[1425] See in H. Nakaso, 'The financial crisis in Japan during the 1990s: how the Bank of Japan responded and the lessons learnt', *BIS Papers*, No. 6, Bank of International Settlements, October 2001, p. 5.

[1426] Ibid.

[1427] Ibid.

[1428] Ibid.

[1429] See in C. McNamara and A. Metrick, 'Restructuring and Forgiveness in Financial Crises D: The Japanese Financial Crisis of the 1990s' (2020) 2(1) *The Journal of Financial Crises*, p. 128.

[1430] Ibid.

- The reorganisation of the TKB in the Resolution and Collection Bank (RCB), with a new broader mandate of assuming failed credit cooperatives for which there would not be available a private institution to assume the failed institution and to purchase the non-performing loans from the failed credit cooperatives, with the aim to make them more attractive to potential private banks[1431] and finally,
- A new Chief Executive Director has been appointed to the DICJ by the Minister of Finance.[1432]

According to McNamara and Metrick these measures were aimed at providing support for the failing cooperatives and were based on the general assumption that the small banks will continue to fail at the same rate as the previous years. The Japanese regulators never succeeded in foresee that also bigger banks could fail, and a financial meltdown was ante portas.[1433] The perception of market stakeholders was strikingly different though and resulted in the creation of the 'Japan premium' in the market. That premium was the additional amount that Japanese financial institutions had to pay for interbank loans, due to the country's risk. As a result, Japanese banks were borrowing the same amount of money with a higher interest rate compared to other financial institutions from the US or Europe. The obvious meaning of that premium was that interbank market participants were demanding extra security when borrowing money to Japanese financial institutions since they were afraid from the real impact of the bubble to the financial system.

3.2.1.2 *The Case of Jūsen (1995)*

The turmoil in the Japanese financial markets continued well after the failure of the credit cooperatives. It became bigger and more acute when the Jūsen companies started revealing their exposure to the bubble and ultimately began to fail.[1434] The Jūsen were non-bank housing loan entities, established primarily by major commercial banks and other financial institutions during the 1970s, to provide home mortgages and complement banks in their traditional credit provider role.[1435] The deregulation in the 1980s increased market competition

---

1431 Ibid.

1432 See in H. Nakaso, 'The financial crisis in Japan during the 1990s: how the Bank of Japan responded and the lessons learnt', *BIS Papers*, No. 6, Bank of International Settlements, October 2001, p. 7.

1433 See in C. McNamara and A. Metrick, 'Restructuring and Forgiveness in Financial Crises D: The Japanese Financial Crisis of the 1990s' (2020) 2(1) *The Journal of Financial Crises*, p. 128.

1434 The Jūsen problem first appeared in the headlines in 1993 but again became a major issue in 1995-1996.

1435 See in H. Nakaso, 'The financial crisis in Japan during the 1990s: how the Bank of Japan responded and the lessons learnt', *BIS Papers*, No. 6, Bank of International Settlements, October 2001, p. 6. Jūsen were founded to offer residential mortgages, since regular banks

and the Jūsen, in order to survive, pursued an aggressive strategy of providing loans to real estate developers. This strategy proved to be very effective during the boom phase of the cycle, when the increasing land values made this kind of lending attractive but ultimately exposed Jūsen to a huge amount of non-performing loans. Already in 1991, the non-performing loans level of Jūsen reached ¥4.600 billion, an amount equivalent to the 38% of their entire loan portfolio.[1436] In 1995, all the measures adopted by the MoF[1437] to restore Jūsen portfolios, failed and the non-performing loans skyrocketed to the 75% of all loans outstanding. What was even more shocking was the fact that 60% of these loans were considered unrecoverable.[1438] In the summer of 1995, the MoF closely examined the Jūsen and revealed that the aggregate losses of the seven Jūsen were ¥6,410 billion.[1439] The extraordinary amount of money that the examination revealed was highly problematic for the Japanese authorities. It was too much to be covered entirely from the founding banks. The MoF came with a new plan-proposal to the Japanese Diet.[1440] The proposed plan called for the taxpayers to finance a portion of the losses but amid fierce debate and deliberations, the Diet ended up with a complex structure of funds allocation among the original founding banks, agricultural cooperatives, taxpayers, and other lenders, as follow:[1441]

- The founding banks would pay ¥3,500 billion,
- The agricultural cooperatives would pay ¥530 billion,[1442]

---

were restricted in how much they could lend to individuals for housing. Their original role was to provide long-term housing loans to individuals and help promote home ownership during Japan's rapid economic growth.

1436 See in C. McNamara and A. Metrick, 'Restructuring and Forgiveness in Financial Crises D: The Japanese Financial Crisis of the 1990s' (2020) 2(1) *The Journal of Financial Crises*, p. 129.

1437 From 1991 already and in 1993, the Japanese MoF and the Jūsen founding banks, organized limited rescue plans in favour of the trembling industry. Among the measures adopted were interest rate reductions, cost cutting measures, new loans, and loans concessions.

1438 Ibid.

1439 See in H. Nakaso, 'The financial crisis in Japan during the 1990s: how the Bank of Japan responded and the lessons learnt', *BIS Papers*, No. 6, Bank of International Settlements, October 2001, p. 6.

1440 See in C. McNamara and A. Metrick, 'Restructuring and Forgiveness in Financial Crises D: The Japanese Financial Crisis of the 1990s' (2020) 2(1) *The Journal of Financial Crises*, p. 129.

1441 Ibid., p. 130.

1442 The participation of the agricultural cooperatives in the Jūsen salvation scheme could be explained by the fact that Jūsen were typically sponsored and owned by multiple banks. On average, a Jūsen borrowed 30% of its debt from a sponsoring bank, 30% from a non-sponsoring bank and the last 40% from agricultural cooperatives. This network of participations aggravated the situation since the downfall of the Jūsen would have multiple negative effects across the entire financial system. Himino, explains that sponsoring banks could have possibly been better off by simply allowing Jūsen to go bankrupt but then the cooperatives and the non-sponsoring banks, possibly feeling betrayed by that approach from

- The taxpayers would pay ¥680 billion and
- The other lenders would pay ¥1,700 billion

Additionally, to the above ranking, the BoJ decided to provide ¥100 billion for the capital of the newly established Housing Loan Administration Corporation (HLAC), an asset management company that would assume the sound and performing assets of the Jūsen. McNamara and Metrick, reveal two reasons for which the Jūsen failure was of particular importance within the Japanese banking crisis context. The first reason has to do with the fact that the use of taxpayers' money for the bail-out of the Jūsen entities was perceived as a big step-back from the government that was constantly proclaiming that public funds would not be used to solve the problems of banking sector. The portion that the taxpayers were called upon to assume, although relatively small, had tied governments' hands since it was almost impossible to request further funds from the public at the later stages of the crisis. The non-banking nature of the Jūsen entities, that were not accepting deposits, made them appear to be loosely connected with the taxpayers' daily lives.[1443] The second reason, is the adoption from the Japanese authorities of the so-called 'wait and see' approach for the adoption of necessary regulatory measures, that characterised much of the Japanese reaction in the early years of the crisis.[1444] This type of regulatory forbearance was preferred by the Japanese authorities as they didn't want to reveal the true size of the problem within the banking sector, aiming to avoid the cliff effects that might occurred and the following panic that could appear among the depositors. The Jūsen crisis became one of the first major signs of Japan's 'Lost Decade' – a long period of economic stagnation – and highlighted the weaknesses in Japan's financial oversight system.

3.2.1.3 *The Case of Nippon Credit Bank (1997)*

The 1997 should be considered as a cursed year in Japan. The authorities' perception of the soundness of the financial system collapsed together with the major bank failures that occurred that year. The persistent problem of non-performing loans, after breaking down the cooperatives and the Jūsen, started threatening the major banking institutions and the authorities were obviously unprepared to deal with such a problem. The design of the DICJ fund was not based on the assumption that a big institution could collapse, and its intervention should avert it.

---

sponsoring banks, would have run against the other Jūsen demanding liquidation of their participations, ultimately provoking a bank-run situation. See in R. Himino, *The Japanese Banking Crisis*, Singapore, Palgrave Macmillan, 2021, p. 51.

1443 See in R. Himino, *The Japanese Banking Crisis*, Singapore, Palgrave Macmillan, 2021, p. 51.

1444 Ibid.

The first victim of that 'annus horribilis' was the internationally active Nippon Credit Bank (NCB), with assets of ¥15.000 billion. NCB was the smallest of the three long-term credit banks operating in Japan, with the Long-Term Credit Bank (LTCB) and the Industrial Bank of Japan (IBJ) being the other two. NCB was heavily involved in real estate lending and its exposure was renting her as a potential danger for financial stability. On the investors eyes NCB was problematic and this was reflected on the downgraded ratings and the funding difficulties that NCB was facing. The time for the major banks has come and the non-performing loans levels at each bank were at the epicentre of the concerns. Amid an environment of growing concerns, the MoF decided to intervene and as a first step organised capital injections from both NCBs' shareholders and the two other long-term credit banks but proved to be inefficient. The NCB decided to organise a restructuring plan with ¥290.6 billion in new capital, provided from the BoJ (¥80 billion) and from private sources (¥210.6 billion).[1445] The funds that the BoJ provided came from the newly established New Financial Stabilization Fund (NFSF), a vehicle that was created amid the Jūsen crisis with ¥100 billion in capital. The purpose of this vehicle was to provide capital to ailing institutions. Even though NCB managed to overcome the immediate and acute crisis, in the end the recapitalisation was insufficient because of the asset deterioration that was always present. Following its constant asset deterioration, NCB was nationalised in December 1998, after the passage by the Japanese Diet of the Financial Revitalization Act.[1446] Earlier on, in March 1998, NCB had received another capital injection of ¥60 billion, comprised of Tier-2 subordinated debt. After all these efforts, nationalisation occurred based on the process that was created from the new legislation and concluded that NCB was insolvent, with its shares being worthless. As a result, the last capital injection from the BoJ (¥80 billion) in 1997 has been wiped out, and the new owner, a group of investors led by Softbank, acquired NCB for ¥1 billion adding also ¥100 billion in capital and the Japanese government providing another ¥260 billion.[1447]

3.2.1.4 *The Case of Sanyo Securities (November 1997)*

The effective, for the time being, stabilisation of the NCB managed to calm down the markets, but the November days proved to be a scary roller coaster with four major institution failures. The first of these failures was Sanyo Securities, a medium-sized securities firm, with approximately ¥2,700 billion in client assets.[1448] The firm was supervised by the MoF and was outside the

1445 Ibid., p. 131.
1446 Act on Special Measures for Strengthening Financial Functions (Act No. 111 of 1998, Japan).
1447 Ibid., p. 136.
1448 Ibid., p. 131.

coverage of the deposit insurance system. After evaluation of the situation, the MoF and the BoJ concluded that the systemic implications from a potential failure of Sanyo would be minimum since the firm was not of systemic importance and therefore could be allowed to collapse. On 3 November, Sanyo Securities filed for bankruptcy with the Tokyo District Court an application for the commencement of reorganisation proceedings under the Corporate Reorganization Law[1449] and automatically halt business as required by that approach under Japanese law.[1450] This suspension of business caused Sanyo to be unable to repay money it had borrowed from the interbank market. This default on obligations assumed in the interbank market was the first in the history of the Japanese interbank market. Despite the relatively small amount of default (¥8.3 billion) the effects were unexpectedly big. The first default of this kind was difficult to be understood by the rest participants and sparked the light of insecurity causing a run in the interbank market.[1451] Since there was no previous experience, the participants were not in position to fully understand the effects and some of them stopped lending in the interbank market and decided that it was safer to deposit their funds within the BoJ. Foreign banks squeezed their credit limits to Japanese banks in general, whose reputation had already been deteriorating from the overall market situation.[1452] According to McNamara and Metrick, this 'produced spikes in interbank interest rates that caused a significant widening of the spread between the lowest rate charged for overnight lending to the most creditworthy banks and the highest rate charged for overnight lending to the least creditworthy banks'.[1453]

Based on the above-described situation, it was now evident that liquidity in the interbank market was drying up resulting in its intermediary function being undermined. Once again, the BoJ decided, in late November, to step in by injecting, into the market, massive liquidity via purchases of eligible bills, repos and bilateral lending to banks against eligible collateral. Simultaneously, the BoJ absorbed liquidity from foreign banks by drawing bills for sale. As Nakaso points out: 'Such two-way operation by the Bank was in effect an exercise of

---

1449 Corporate Reorganization Act (Act No. 154 of 2002, Japan).

1450 See in H. Nakaso, 'The financial crisis in Japan during the 1990s: how the Bank of Japan responded and the lessons learnt', *BIS Papers*, No. 6, Bank of International Settlements, October 2001, p. 8.

1451 See in C. McNamara and A. Metrick, 'Restructuring and Forgiveness in Financial Crises D: The Japanese Financial Crisis of the 1990s' (2020) 2(1) *The Journal of Financial Crises*, p. 131.

1452 See in H. Nakaso, 'The financial crisis in Japan during the 1990s: how the Bank of Japan responded and the lessons learnt', *BIS Papers*, No. 6, Bank of International Settlements, October 2001, p. 8.

1453 See in C. McNamara and A. Metrick, 'Restructuring and Forgiveness in Financial Crises D: The Japanese Financial Crisis of the 1990s' (2020) 2(1) *The Journal of Financial Crises*, p. 132.

the function of market-maker of last resort.'[1454] Despite all these difficulties, the interbank market managed to continue functioning but the outstanding credit supply by the BoJ, through money market operations, reached as much as ¥22 trillion ($190 billion) in December 1997.[1455]

3.2.1.5 *The Case of Hokkaido Takushoku Bank (November 1997)*

Two weeks after the collapse of Sanyo, it was time for another bank to collapse. The Hokkaido Takushoku Bank (HTB) lost its ability to borrow funds on the interbank market and could not continue operations without government or any other support. HTB was of major importance for the economy of Hokkaido Island, the northern island of Japan, since with ¥9,500 billion of assets was playing a key role in the local economy.[1456] This resulted in the decision from the BoJ to allow HTB continue its operations until another bank could be found to assume its sound assets, liabilities, and operations.[1457] It must be referred at this point that an earlier attempt to merge HTB with Hokkaido Bank failed due to, apart from general cultural difference between the two institutions, concerns regarding the level of non-performing loans held by HTB on its books and the potential losses that night occur. By Friday, 14 November, the funding difficulties for HTB had intensified and all eligible bills for interbank funding had been exhausted. Furthermore, the bank failed to satisfy its reserve requirement with the BoJ. As Nakaso points out, it was at this point HTB understood that because of the accelerated deposit withdrawals it would be impossible to stand by herself and continue operations.[1458] After this fail, BoJ continued to provide support until another bank, willing to assume, could be found. Running against the time, the BoJ had to secure the presence of an assuming bank for the DICJ to intervene. Over the weekend, the authorities succeeded in finding an assuming bank. Hokuyo Bank, a regional bank in Hokkaido with assets of only ¥1.8 trillion, agreed to become the assuming bank for the business of HTB in Hokkaido Island. Bilateral talks between senior officials of the BoJ and the top management of Hokuyo Bank played a vital role in the timely formulation of the salvation package.[1459] Finally, on 17 November

---

[1454] See in H. Nakaso, 'The financial crisis in Japan during the 1990s: how the Bank of Japan responded and the lessons learnt', *BIS Papers*, No. 6, Bank of International Settlements, October 2001, p. 9.

[1455] Ibid.

[1456] See in C. McNamara and A. Metrick, 'Restructuring and Forgiveness in Financial Crises D: The Japanese Financial Crisis of the 1990s' (2020) 2(1) *The Journal of Financial Crises*, p. 132.

[1457] Ibid.

[1458] See in H. Nakaso, 'The financial crisis in Japan during the 1990s: how the Bank of Japan responded and the lessons learnt', *BIS Papers*, No. 6, Bank of International Settlements, October 2001, p. 9.

[1459] Ibid.

1997, the failure of HTB was announced. Again, the BoJ stood ready and began providing liquidity support, pursuant to Article 25 of the Bank of Japan Law, to finance massive deposit outflows and calm down the depositors and the markets. The uncollateralised liquidity support, provided from the BoJ to HTB, reached its peak of ¥2.6 trillion in early February 1998.

3.2.1.6 *The Case of Yamaichi Securities (November 1997)*

The third collapse of that month was that of Yamaichi Securities, one of the four largest securities firms in Japan. The firm was a financial conglomerate with clients' assets of ¥22.000 billion and many banking subsidiaries across Europe (Germany, Switzerland, United Kingdom and the Netherlands).[1460] The firm's collapse was attributable to the reveal of more than ¥200 billion in off-the-book liabilities. The BoJ concluded that the failure of the securities firm could possibly have a devastating effect on the market, both domestic and globally, since the size and the complexity of the firm were important parameters to the financial stability equation. Another important factor was the effects to the interbank market from the failure of the smaller and simpler Sanyo and the fears that the present case could destroy completely the market. Consequently, the Japanese authorities, rather than halting Yamaichi's operations, as was the case with Sanyo, preferred to orderly wind down the firm and do not trigger a normal bankruptcy procedure. The aim was to allow the firm to settle the claims arising from the existing contracts.[1461]

The government had to address the issue of the firm's funding and since Yamaichi had no access to the markets, another plan to secure liquidity should apply. This was the point where the problems began to appear. According to Article 25, the BoJ had the authority to provide liquidity support to a non-bank entity, with the aim to prevent financial instability, such an option was perceived as extraordinary for two reasons. First, the failure of a securities firm in normal circumstances would not trigger a systemic collapse and second, it was unclear whether Yamaichi was solvent or insolvent.[1462] Therefore, the true question was whether the BoJ would be able to recover the liquidity support that would provide since Yamaichi, as a securities firm, was outside the scope of the deposit insurance and leaving the BoJ with no recourse to the DICJ.[1463] After negotiations and certain assurances from the MoF that the BoJ would ultimately be reimbursed in case Yamaichi would become insolvent, the BoJ agreed to provide liquidity support to the firm. The support was unlimited

---

1460 See in C. McNamara and A. Metrick, 'Restructuring and Forgiveness in Financial Crises D: The Japanese Financial Crisis of the 1990s' (2020) 2(1) *The Journal of Financial Crises*, p. 133.

1461 Ibid.

1462 Ibid.

1463 Ibid.

and although the immediate needs were estimated to be ¥800 billion, peaked in December 1998, at ¥1.200 billion. As McNamara and Metrick are pointing out, this unlimited liquidity support provided by the BoJ, replaced the counterparties' exposure to Yamaichi, since all that amount was assumed from the central bank.[1464] The effect of that bold move was the full mitigation of the risks to the system but could not save Yamaichi from bankruptcy, which happened in June 1999, due to a continuous deterioration of her financial situation, with a loss of around ¥160 billion.[1465]

3.2.1.7 *The Case of Tokuyo City Bank (November 1997)*

The Tokuyo City Bank (TCB) was the fourth and the last bank that collapsed in November 1997 days. The collapse announcement occurred on 26 November and although TCB was a second tier regional bank in the northeastern city of Sendai, its failure was another important blow to the trembling financial stability and had a negative psychological impact to the market.[1466] TCB, suffering from the weight of ¥58.8 billion in non-performing loans announced it will transfer operations to Sendai Bank after handing over some of its assets and liabilities to other financial institutions. Because of the collapse, a bank run occurred to the rest of the regional banks and 26 November has been characterised as the worst day in the financial history of Japan because the system 'was closest to a systemic collapse'.[1467] In response to these fears, the BoJ and the MoF jointly declared that they were committed to the financial system's stability and that all deposits were protected because the BoJ was ready to provide liquidity support, in order to manage the massive withdrawal of deposits.

3.2.1.8 *The Case of Long-Term Credit Bank of Japan (1998)*

The Long-Term Credit Bank of Japan (LTCB) was established in 1952, under the Long-Term Credit Bank Act.[1468] According to its statute, LTCB had the privilege of issuing debentures and was financing investments in factories and equipment. It should be mentioned that according to the strict segmentation of the Japanese banking sector, the privilege of issuing debentures was of utmost importance since only a handful of banks were awarded. The name of the bank reflects the nature of the services provided. The funds from the issuance of debentures were channelled into long term investments for the purpose of rebuilding Japan's damaged industrial production. Until the mid-1980s,

---

1464 Ibid.
1465 Ibid., p. 134.
1466 Ibid.
1467 Ibid.
1468 Long-Term Credit Bank Act (Act No. 61 of 1952, Japan).

LTCB helped the industrial sector of Japan to claim the miracle of post war recovery and expansion. The problems began when the Japanese manufacturers stopped building new factories in Japan or expanding the present ones and large companies decided that it was more convenient to borrow from the international financial markets and finance themselves overseas.[1469] This change in the preferences of Japanese companies was very important because it reflected not isolated cases but a general trend that was radically reshaping the banking market. As a result of these trends, the bank had lost its unique *raison d'être*.[1470]

The above existential crisis of LTCB became worse in the summer (June) of 1998. An article in the Financial Times created a turmoil around the soundness of the bank and its overall viability. Although that LTCB was recapitalised with a capital injection in March 1998, the amount was seen as too little to absorb losses and turbulence from the markets. LTCB possessed ¥26.000 billion in assets and a derivatives book with ¥50,000 billion of contracts measured in notional value.[1471] The Japanese authorities understood that LTCB was posing a major threat to the financial system and decide to organise a possible merger with Sumitomo Trust Bank, but that attempt failed when the last remained doubtful about the actual levels of NPLs held by LTCB. Rating agencies and the stock market were sending signals that if the merger was to be concluded they would react against Sumitomo. Based on the above considerations Sumitomo decided to step back and rejected the deal. As an alternative, the Japanese authorities decided to pursue an orderly wind-down process aiming at selling the leftovers to a new buyer. The basic idea was to apply a process like that of Yamaichi. The basic difference with Yamaichi though was that LTCB was to be wound down to be sold to new investors. This decision was based on the fact that LTCB was offering a variety of financial services and the loss of these services was deemed as likely to put borrowers and customers of LTCB in difficulties.[1472] In addition, the active participation of LTCB in derivatives market, with an active and large portfolio, was posing systemic concerns that had to be taken into account before applying any particular solution. The concerns regarding the derivatives portfolio had to do with the fact that a significant portion of this portfolio contained interest rate and currency swaps with major foreign and domestic players as counterparties. This meant that direct links with domestic and overseas financial markets existed, posing

---

1469 See in R. Himino, *The Japanese Banking Crisis*, Singapore, Palgrave Macmillan, 2021, p. 67.

1470 Ibid.

1471 Ibid., p. 136.

1472 See in H. Nakaso, 'The financial crisis in Japan during the 1990s: how the Bank of Japan responded and the lessons learnt', *BIS Papers*, No. 6, Bank of International Settlements, October 2001, p. 12.

serious threats in case of disorderly failure.[1473] Japanese authorities were very cautious when drafting the law, fearing that a possible trigger of default clauses under the ISDA Agreements would have major impact with cross defaults, disruptions in other markets and mostly negative impact with upward pressure on yen interest rates and downward pressure on yen exchange rates.

Still Japan was lacking a coercive and consistent framework for the effective resolution of such complex entities. LTCB was the largest bank failure the authorities encountered, and no precedent was available.[1474] On 23 October 1998, the Japanese authorities, based on a recent law passed by the Diet,[1475] nationalised the LTCB and as a following step the management body was replaced, bad loans were removed from the balance sheet and the losses were covered both from BoJ and the DIC.[1476] The BoJ, steadily provided liquidity support that reached a pick of ¥3,700 billion in November 1998. Finally, the LTCB sold in February 2000 for ¥1 billion to a US investment group, with the purchaser investing ¥120 billion in new capital and the Japanese government providing another ¥240 billion of fresh capital.

3.2.2 Government Reactions to the Crisis

The Japanese Government realised that the 'wait and see' approach was completely ineffective to manage and overcome the current situation. On Wednesday, 26 November 1997, emergency morning phone calls rang within the MoF and the BoJ, from their local offices across the country. Bank branches across the country (Wakayama, Utsunomiya, Sapporo, Nagoya, Osaka, Fukuoka, and Tokyo), reported depositors that started queuing in front of banks, massive withdrawals and long queues, as depositors believed that the situation would only worsen.[1477] The BoJ pumped enormous amount of cash to the banks, the MoF gave instructions to banks how to contain the queues by giving people priority numbered cards and guiding them inside to the branches, and newspapers and tv stations all refrained from reporting the bank-run. Later the evening of that day, the minister of finance and the BoJ Governor issued a joint statement that confirmed the guarantee of all deposits and interbank exposures.[1478] The following political deliberation was very intense within the ruling party with different approaches proposed. Finally,

---

1473 Ibid., p. 13.

1474 Ibid., p. 12.

1475 Law Concerning Emergency Measures for the Reconstruction of the Functions of the Financial System (Financial Reconstruction Law) (Law No. 132 of 1998, Japan).

1476 See in C. McNamara and A. Metrick, 'Restructuring and Forgiveness in Financial Crises D: The Japanese Financial Crisis of the 1990s' (2020) 2(1) *The Journal of Financial Crises*, p. 136.

1477 See in R. Himino, *The Japanese Banking Crisis*, Singapore, Palgrave Macmillan, 2021, p. 63.

1478 Ibid.

the MoF officials submitted to the national Diet two proposals for reform, on 16 February 1998. The first law enacted by the Diet was the Financial Function Stabilization Act (FFSA),[1479] which made available for maintaining financial stability, ¥30,000 billion of public funds.[1480] This amount was split as follow: ¥17,000 billion was available for the protection of the failed banks depositors, and ¥13,000 billion was available for the necessary bank recapitalisations. The second legislative proposal that was enacted into law was the Prompt Recapitalization Act (PRA),[1481] which replaced the framework established by the FFSA. The PRA increased the available public funds to ¥60,000 billion allocated accordingly: ¥25,000 billion for bank recapitalisation, ¥18,000 billion available to nationalise the failed banks and ¥17,000 billion to secure deposits in the event of banking failures.[1482]

In the beginning, banks were very hesitant to participate in the recapitalisation process established by the FFSA. The stigma effect was certainly one major reason since the potential effects would be unknown and of course very difficult to manage. The signalling to the market could be that any bank participating in the process was in dire need of capital, thus in financial troubles. Another possible concern would have been the fact that after the recapitalisation process, the Japanese government was supposed to be given securities with seniority to the existing securities holders' claims.[1483] To bypass these concerns, the authorities managed to persuade the major banks to participate in the recapitalisation process only by giving them identical amounts of capital so any speculation would be worthless. This resulted in giving ¥100 billion in capital to eight of the nine largest banks in Japan, and ¥99 billion to the ninth one. The ¥100 billion amount was calculated based on the maximum amount that the healthiest of the biggest banks, the Bank of Tokyo Mitsubishi, was willing to ask for. This unorthodox approach resulted in an awkward situation in which many banks received much less capital than their actual needs.[1484] This clear suboptimal solution undermined the efforts to secure the trembling financial system from bank runs and to restore credibility to the markets. The recapitalisation provided by the FFSA resulted in 21 banks receiving a combined amount of ¥1,800 trillion and most of the banks received

---

1479 Act on Temporary Measures for Strengthening Financial Functions (Act No. 99 of 1998, Japan).

1480 See in C. McNamara and A. Metrick, 'Restructuring and Forgiveness in Financial Crises D: The Japanese Financial Crisis of the 1990s' (2020) 2(1) *The Journal of Financial Crises*, p. 134.

1481 Act on Emergency Measures for Early Strengthening of the Financial System (Act No. 132 of 1998, Japan).

1482 See in C. McNamara and A. Metrick, 'Restructuring and Forgiveness in Financial Crises D: The Japanese Financial Crisis of the 1990s' (2020) 2(1) *The Journal of Financial Crises*, p. 136.

1483 Ibid., p. 135.

1484 Ibid.

this amount in the form of subordinated debt having interest rates also tied with the perceived health of the borrower.[1485] Another, smaller, group of banks received the capital in the form of preferred shares that were convertible in common shares.

Under the PRA scheme, banks received a second round of capital injections in March 1999. The main difference from the March 1998 recapitalisation was the in-depth examination of banks' assets by the newly established Financial Reconstruction Commission (FRC).[1486] Under the examination process, FRC adjusted the banks' reported capital figures to correct them for any unrealised losses from securities holdings and for potentially under-reserving loan losses, to have a more accurate picture regarding the banks' actual capital needs.[1487] Another important difference from the March 1998 recapitalisation was also the fact that the second recapitalisation was accomplished mostly with preferred shares rather than subordinated debt. McNamara and Metrick refer that the fifteen major banks that applied for capital in the March 1999 recapitalisation had unrealised losses on securities holding levelling ¥2,700 billion and were under-reserved by ¥9,000 billion, resulting in a ¥11,700 billion gap covered as follow: ¥2,500 billion of net core operating profits, ¥7,500 billion in public funds under the PRA and ¥2,100 in private capital.[1488]

At the same time, the Tokyo Prosecutor's Office raided the MoF resulting in two bank inspectors being arrested on the charge of being entertained by banks, the resignation of the Minister and of the Vice-Minister and the suicide of one senior inspector.[1489] Since the situation with bank failures continued, the raids on the supervisors became more frequent. While the examination of banks' applications for capital injections were ongoing, two more officials from the MoF and a BoJ director were arrested and another MoF officer committed suicide.[1490] Pursuant to a raid in BoJ, the Governor and the Deputy Governor resigned, while one month after the capital injection to the banks the director general of the MoF's Securities Bureau was fired together with the deputy director general of the Banking Bureau, while disciplinary measures were imposed on 110 officers for being entertained by financial institutions.[1491] At the same time, BoJ took measures on 98 of its officers for misconduct.

[1485] Ibid.

[1486] Ibid., p. 136.

[1487] Ibid.

[1488] Ibid.

[1489] See in R. Himino, *The Japanese Banking Crisis*, Singapore, Palgrave Macmillan, 2021, p. 66.

[1490] Ibid.

[1491] Ibid.

3.3. *The Special Issue of Non-Performing Loans*

The Non-Performing Loans (NPLs), a legacy of the bubble economy, were a major problem for the Japanese banking sector. Although not the only one, it was by far the most critical, requiring immediate solution aiming at relieving the pressure from the trembling banking sector. The credit expansion that accompanied the bubble economy resulted in a huge amount of NPLs with little or non-existent chance to recover, while at the same time, property values were steadily declining forcing down the collateral values, in a downward spiral, further increasing the recapitalisation needs. In reality, the NPLs problem in Japan was much bigger than anyone could even anticipate, since the time lag was big enough to give the impression that the situation was under control.[1492] The roots of the NPLs problem in Japan are deeper and are related with the overall approach followed by the MoF, in its capacity as supervisory authority, who followed the 'wait and see' approach instead of adopting a more fast and interventional one.

In early 1992, the Japanese bankers slowly started to realise that NPLs could potentially destabilise the entire banking system with the same view being also shared by the regulators and, unfortunately, many journalists. To protect the system and their reputation, Japanese regulators carefully and narrowly defined impaired loans when they were publishing data or their amount. The problem was that their definition was covering only a portion of the problem without including the bad loans held by the non-bank entities affiliated to the banks (Jūsen). The issue of non-existent accurate statistics for the total size of the impaired loans aggravated the situation and made it even more difficult for the authorities to find a solution to the problem. In 1992, both the BoJ and the MoF, estimated the NPLs at ¥30-50 trillion. According to Himino, although this amount was impressive, it reflected only part of the real number, and the Japanese banks were facing four distinct problems that were aggravating the situation:[1493]

- In attempting to resolve the bad loans banks would have to foreclose the borrowers and sell the collaterals, a move that would further reduce land prices and increase the bad loans since the value of collaterals would further decrease.
- Apart from the issue of NPLs, Japanese banks were facing the decreasing value of stocks that they were holding (and crossholding due to the Keiretsu

1492 In October 1991, the Japanese government declared emphatically that the credit expansion was the largest since the end of World War II but had not realised that the business cycles had already peaked in February, thus giving the impression that everything was going great. See in R. Himino, *The Japanese Banking Crisis*, Singapore, Palgrave Macmillan, 2021, p. 48.

1493 See in R. Himino, *The Japanese Banking Crisis*, Singapore, Palgrave Macmillan, 2021, p. 51.

style corporate relations), further pushing down prices. As a result, banks were accumulating losses also from their investments.

- Non-bank lenders had provided loans amounting to ¥100 trillion. Since banks had financed almost 80% of their debt and the Jūsen were very aggressive lenders, banks were attached to the Jūsen and their huge levels of NPLs since they were financing them.
- Japanese regulators needed new resolution powers for the failing banks and new public funds to spent if they wanted to avoid a systemic crisis. The recent scandals involving bankers and the yakuza members had exactly the opposite result and therefore nobody was foolish enough to ask for more money from the taxpayers to bail out banks that were showing such an attitude during the roaring years of the bubble economy.[1494]

The MoF took a very cautious approach regarding the NPLs and decided to take the necessary time to resolve the situation. The common belief was that banks would have annual profits over the coming years and the unrealised capital gains on securities held by them would prove to be sufficiently enough for a smooth recovery.[1495] The deliberations in the Japanese Diet and the different approaches proposed even among the cabinet members proved to be a hurdle tall enough to bypass. The BoJ and the MoF frequently disagreed regarding how the NPLs, and the failing banks would be resolved. The following years were very difficult and as the crisis became acute, many approaches that were believed to be bulletproof had to radically adapt to the new conditions. What had become obvious was that MoF's decision to give time for a self-healing process by the 'invisible hand' was wrong. Maybe the MoF was afraid that if many well-established practices changed, there would be a major blow to its credibility and therefore the basic target was to defend itself from the humiliation of failing to efficiently supervise the financial sector. After the March 1999 recapitalisation the markets calmed down for a while and the Japan premium largely disappeared by April 1999. This elimination of the Japan premium reflects that, from a first sight, the measures were bold enough to bring back normality. Nevertheless, normality was far from being a reality.

The major issue now was the constant deterioration of banking assets due to the economic recession that Japan had entered after the collapse of the bubble economy. It became apparent that since the macroeconomic measures were not getting better at any time soon the capital shortage was at gates. The vicious circle between the events of financial instability and the economic

---

[1494] Back in 1991, Nomura Securities and other brokers were found to have compensated favoured clients for losses stemming from the decline in the stock market. Although those transactions were not illegal at the time, they gave rise to new regulatory initiatives against loss-compensation schemes provided by the stockbrokers. For a more detailed analysis on the matter see in: https://www.nytimes.com/1997/03/22/business/nomura-scandal-in-japan-hurts-plans-for-reform.html.

[1495] See in R. Himino, *The Japanese Banking Crisis*, Singapore, Palgrave Macmillan, 2021, p. 52.

downturns produced ongoing fresh losses that were making capital anything but sufficient.[1496] Another point of anxiety was the quality of the reported capital by banks, and the question was imminent: What is included in this reported capital? Many were afraid that banks included in their calculations deferred tax assets (DTAs),[1497] that if they could not manage to return to profitability within a given timeframe, these deductions would become useless and as a result their capital would be helpless from this contribution. Another important parameter of the discussion was the belief that banks were overestimating the quality of their loans, and either were not holding enough reserves or were holding inadequate ones for losses over their NPLs. Should they be obliged to hold adequate reserves their quality of capital would have been diminished with adverse effects.[1498]

Against this background, the next major step against the NPLs was the 'Takenaka Plan', named after Heizo Takenaka who took over the Japanese Financial Services Agency (JFSA),[1499] after previously headed financial reform efforts. Takenaka prepared and launched a targeted plan to end the NPLs problem based on six measures:[1500]

(i) The first measure required a more rigorous evaluation of assets using discounted expected cash flows or market prices of NPLs,
(ii) The second measure required the monitoring of cross-bank consistency in classifying loans to large debtors,
(iii) The third measure required the publication of the discrepancies between the evaluation performed by the JFSA and banks' self-evaluations,
(iv) The fourth measure was the injection of public funds if deemed necessary,
(v) The fifth measure was the prohibition of unrealistically large DTAs and
(vi) The sixth measure was the imposition of 'business improvement' orders to the banks that were underachieving.

1496 See in C. McNamara and A. Metrick, 'Restructuring and Forgiveness in Financial Crises D: The Japanese Financial Crisis of the 1990s' (2020) 2(1) *The Journal of Financial Crises*, p. 138.

1497 Deferred Tax Assets (DTAs) were tax deductions that could only be used if banks return to profitability within a 5-year timeframe.

1498 See in C. McNamara and A. Metrick, 'Restructuring and Forgiveness in Financial Crises D: The Japanese Financial Crisis of the 1990s' (2020) 2(1) *The Journal of Financial Crises*, p. 138, where they demonstrate that the reported capital of ¥30,200 billion from banks, after the necessary adjustments for NPLs provisions and tax deductions became only ¥12,800 billion. As a result, in March 2002, with total assets of ¥756,100 billion and ¥7,200 billion of government held capital, Japanese banks hold capital equal to less than 2% of assets, with almost no private capital.

1499 We should make an important distinction at this point. In order to avoid confusion with the pre-crisis supervisory and regulatory authority in the UK, the UK FSA (Financial Services Authority) and given that the Japanese authority has a very similar meaning (Financial Services Agency) we will use the abbreviation 'JFSA' to distinct it from the previous UK regulator and supervisor.

1500 See in C. McNamara and A. Metrick, 'Restructuring and Forgiveness in Financial Crises D: The Japanese Financial Crisis of the 1990s' (2020) 2(1) *The Journal of Financial Crises*, p. 140.

The bold initiative from Commissioner Takenaka occurred at the same time with a general reorientation in the governmental approach towards the non-performing borrowers. In April 2003, the Japanese government established the Industrial Revitalization Corporation of Japan (IRCJ) with the aim to purchase the NPLs from the secondary lenders and working in cooperation with primary lenders to reorganise the borrowers restoring their health.[1501] Simultaneously, the Resolution and Collection Corporation (RCC) was established in 1999 from the merging of two existing asset management companies, the HLAC and the RCB. Both entities managed to restructure and reorganise over ¥10,000 billion in assets from over 600 borrowers.[1502] Although the Takenaka Plan had a major impact on banks' efforts to reduce the NPLs, the fundamental disposal of NPLs was achieved in different ways from those initially expected.[1503] Firstly, although it had been thought that huge amount of capital would be needed to restore banks capital base, many major banks managed to clean their bad loans by themselves.[1504] Secondly, Minister Takenaka threatened to nationalise major banks and this was enough for banks to intensify their efforts to reduce NPLs that had been put off handling. At the same time, the Japanese economy experienced a recovery on its exports, based on increased demand especially from China. This allowed many ailing firms to recover and start repaying their debts, which had been previously classified as non-performing.[1505] Thirdly, the way Resona Bank was handled on its financial difficulties gave a sharp upward to stock prices and a crisis was averted.[1506]

4 THE POST BANKING CRISIS INSTITUTIONAL LANDSCAPE FOR THE REGULATION AND SUPERVISION OF THE JAPANESE FINANCIAL AND BANKING SECTOR: A MAJOR REGULATORY OVERHAUL.

Supervision of Japanese banks was at the epicentre of the banking crisis. The Japanese authorities failed to detect the critical situation of many banks that were overexposed to real estate lending, non-performing loans and were also suffering from an outdated competition system that was suppressing their profits and their capacity to expand. The convoy system that characterised the style of supervision was abandoned for a more modern and integrated system

1501 Ibid.
1502 Ibid.
1503 See in R. Kamikawa, 'The Interaction between Financial Regulation and Financial Crisis in Japan: Change in Financial Administration and Two Financial Crises from 1980 to 2010' (2012) 59 *Osaka University Law Review*, p. 19.
1504 Ibid. Only *Resona Bank* and *Ashikaga Bank* applied for public funds injection.
1505 Ibid.
1506 Ibid.

based on rules and principles. The tectonic changes in the Japanese system of financial regulation and supervision created a new world but most importantly they introduced a completely new style of supervision that Japanese banks and financial firms were not used to. The post crisis picture of the Japanese banking sector had nothing to do with the pre-crisis one. The most important change had been the transfer of supervisory duty from the MoF to the new authority. The JFSA tried to adopt a new, rule-based approach that was based on clear rules and regulations aiming to ameliorate the regulatory environment in general. From the late 1990s to early 2000s, the JFSA has made tremendous efforts to rebuild the public confidence in the Japanese financial system. This was done by such supervisory tools as rigorous on-site inspections for reviewing banks' asset quality, and rigid administrative actions against any violations of laws and regulations.

4.1. The Establishment of the JFSA and the New Roles of the MoF and of the BoJ for the Regulation and Supervision of the Japanese Financial and Banking Sector

As a result of growing criticism against the MoF, regarding its cozy relationship with the financial industry, separation of fiscal policy and financial administration was carried out in the 1990s. The powerful MoF of the pre-crisis era is now having a very limited role to the financial system's regulation. MoF is only involved with the government's budget management and maintaining stability in the currency markets.[1507] After the regulatory overhaul, the BoJ participates indirectly in the supervision of the financial system and its main responsibility is to carry out the monetary policy of the country and is also responsible for financial stability through:

(a) analysis and assessment of the financial system's stability,
(b) coordination with specific micro-prudential actions (on-site examinations and off-site monitoring),
(c) implementation of various measures to ensure the stability of the financial system, among them the most important function is the lender of last resort, and
(d) its duty to operate and oversight the sound performance of payment and settlement systems.[1508]

The BoJ, based upon Article 44 of the Bank of Japan Act, may submit the documents describing the results of the on-site examinations, as well as other related materials, to the Commissioner or have officials of the JFSA inspect

1507 See in E. Brown, 'Consolidated Financial Regulation: Six National Case Studies and the Experience of the European Union', Background Paper no. 2, The Volcker Alliance, 2015, p. 68.

1508 Ibid.

them. Regarding off-site analyses and at senior management level, there exists more regular information exchange between the JFSA and BoJ.

The major breakthrough though was with the establishment of the new agency, the JFSA, as the main supervisor (and in many cases also regulator) of the Japanese financial system. The JFSA, established in July 2000, succeeding its short lived predecessor, the 'Financial Supervisory Agency' (created in 1998),[1509] after the Japanese Diet approved government's decision to span-off the Banking Bureau and the Insurance Bureau from the MoF and transfer their duties to then newly created agency.[1510] In addition, the government also moved the Securities Exchange Surveillance Commission (SESC) from the MoF to the JFSA,[1511] and decided to give to the JFSA the supervisory authority and the relevant powers that were previously held by various other governmental agencies. The JFSA became thus responsible for supervising the agricultural cooperatives, together with the Ministry of Agriculture, Forestry & Fisheries (MAFF), while under the previous regime MAFF was solely responsible for the supervision of those cooperatives. The same applied also to the labour cooperatives, with the supervisory duty being assigned to both the JFSA and the Ministry of Labor, where prior to 1998, the latter was solely responsible. These policy options put more institutions under JFSA's supervision than the MoF was supervising before the radical regulatory overhaul, following the banking crisis.[1512] On July 2000, JFSA merged with the Financial System Planning Bureau of the MoF and together formed the JFSA, as it exists today. According to some commentators, this merger made the JFSA a more cautious agency because they didn't want to blame and embarrass the former Planning Bureau's executives that just joined them; thus, the FSA avoided undertaking of a bank closure, that could have been attributed to inadequate planning from the former MoF executives and a failure to set appropriate rules and

1509 Ibid., p. 65. The Financial Supervisory Agency was established as an administrative organ (external organ of the Prime Minister's Office) responsible for inspection and supervision of private sector financial institutions and surveillance of securities transactions. With the establishment of the Financial Reconstruction Commission (FRC) in December of the same year, the Financial Supervisory Agency became an organization under the jurisdiction of the FRC.

1510 Act for Establishment of the Financial Services Agency (Act No. 57 of 2000, Japan). The JFSA was established under the jurisdiction of the FRC through reorganization of the Financial Supervisory Agency. With this change, the JFSA became responsible for planning of the financial system for which the MoF had been responsible.

1511 The Securities and Exchange Surveillance Commission (SESC) is placed within the JFSA and conducts market surveillance and on-site inspections of securities companies. However, is not authorized to take administrative actions such as penalties; the JFSA is responsible for these actions based on the advice of the SESC.

1512 See in E. Brown, 'Consolidated Financial Regulation: Six National Case Studies and the Experience of the European Union', Background Paper no. 2, The Volcker Alliance, 2015, p. 65.

regulations.[1513] Moreover, the JFSA now had responsibility not only to exercise its supervisory duties but also to plan and design a more cohesive macro-prudential plan for the financial stability of the system. By the reorganisation of central government ministers in January 2001, the JFSA became an external organ of the Cabinet Office and, with concurrent abolishment of the FRC, the JFSA took over the business concerning disposition of failed financial institutions.

The JFSA is responsible for ensuring stability of Japan's financial system, protection of depositors, insurance policyholders and securities investors, and smooth finance through such measures as planning and policymaking concerning the financial system, inspection and supervision of private sector financial institutions, and surveillance of securities transactions. According to Article 3 of the Act for Establishment of the Financial Services Agency, the JFSA:

(a) has a mission to secure the stability of financial functions in Japan and protect depositors, policyholders, securities investors, and any equivalent persons, and facilitating financing;[1514]
(b) beyond what is specified in the preceding paragraph, has a mission to assist with affairs of the Cabinet concerning specific important policies of the Cabinet relating to the mission referred to in that paragraph;[1515]
(c) is to assist the Cabinet Secretariat in carrying out the mission referred to in the preceding paragraph.[1516]

The JFSA, according to Article 4 of the Act for Establishment of the Financial Services Agency, is responsible for:

- Planning and policy making of financial systems,[1517]
- Inspection and supervision of private sector financial institutions, including banks, insurance companies, and financial instrument business operators, as well as market participants, including stock exchanges,[1518]
- Establishment of rules for trading in markets,[1519]
- Establishment of business accounting standards and others concerning corporate finance,[1520]
- Supervision of certified public accountants (CPAs) and auditing firms,[1521]

1513 Ibid., p. 66.
1514 Article 3, Act for Establishment of the Financial Services Agency (Act No. 57 of 2000, Japan).
1515 Ibid.
1516 Ibid.
1517 Article 4, Act for Establishment of the Financial Services Agency (Act No. 57 of 2000, Japan).
1518 Ibid.
1519 Ibid.
1520 Ibid.
1521 Ibid.

- Participation in activities of international organisations and bilateral and multilateral fora on financial issues to develop an internationally consistent policy,[1522] and
- Surveillance of compliance with rules in markets.[1523]

The JFSA is mainly responsible for the early detection of banks distress through its 'general and *ad hoc* surveillance mandate'[1524] and adopts its decisions through a specific framework which covers the early action approach while is the driving force behind the plans to tackle capital and/or liquidity shortages/problems and finally is tasked to monitor the whole process of implementation of the recovery and/or resolution plans.[1525] The JFSA, although is an independent supervisor, constitutes part of Japan's public administration and its decisions are subject to the review from Japan's administrative law and Courts[1526] and is funded from the annual government budget, upon approval from the MoF and from the Minister for Financial Services. The Japanese Diet has also a saying over the annual budget and as a result, JFSA does not control its funding levels.[1527]

4.2. *The New Recovery and Resolution Framework*

Before the banking crisis, the legal framework regarding banks' recovery and resolution was almost non-existent in Japan. The convoy style of regulation and supervision was in place to secure the survival of the least healthy banks while the heavy regulation was guaranteeing a minimum earning for all in exchange for reduced competition. Therefore, the Japanese government had to create *ad hoc* and tailor-made solutions to each case without any coherence and general approach. The regulatory overhaul that changed radically Japan's legal framework for financial regulation affected also, many times, the resolution framework. From the initial 'wait and see' approach, we moved to the 'hougachou' and then the 'purchase and assumption' has also been tested.

Tirado has delivered an excellent analysis of the Japanese legal framework of resolution and in our analysis, we will only make a very broad reference for

1522 Ibid.

1523 Ibid.

1524 See in I. Tirado, 'Banking Crises and the Japanese Legal Framework', Discussion Paper No. 2017-E-2, Institute for Monetary and Economic Studies, Bank of Japan, Tokyo, 2017, p. 18.

1525 Ibid.

1526 Ibid.

1527 The IMF, back in 2012, had identify that the budget approval process could potentially harm the independence of the JFSA, because could be subject to budget cut decisions based on political reasons and without having any room for manoeuvring. See in E. Brown, 'Consolidated Financial Regulation: Six National Case Studies and the Experience of the European Union', Background Paper no. 2, The Volcker Alliance, 2015, p. 66.

reasons of coherence.[1528] The framework is divided alongside the importance of the failed institution and different processes apply to different cases. Therefore the 'one size fits all' is not preferable in Japan and dedicated resolution mechanisms exist for each bank categories and types of crises. Simple bank crises are confronted differently from enhanced non-systemic crises and different proceedings ensure the orderly resolution in each case. Systemically important financial institutions have special proceedings to follow whether they are solvent or insolvent, an important distinction. Finally, special crisis management for solvent and non-solvent institutions and early intervention measure at Prime Minister level secure that any crisis and any institution will not jeopardise the stability and soundness of the system.

4.3. Structural Regulation in the Banking Sector

Until 1993, Japanese banks were not able to expand into new services and particularly in the securities business. The cumbersome regulatory framework did not allow the establishment of holding companies (strict prohibition) and any holdings from financial institutions were limited to 5% without a special approval from the Japanese Fair Trade Commission.[1529] The framework imposed prohibitions on banking activities, by not allowing banks to engage in activities other than the banking business, defined as 'core banking business', 'incidental banking business' and 'other banking business'.[1530] According to Sibbitt, the strict regulation did not allow even indirect engagement in these activities (by a non-bank entity), through an affiliated entity.[1531] The 1993 Financial System Reform Act (FSRA),[1532] eased these restrictions but not in an effective way. By amending the laws that governed the statutes of most financial institutions, the FSRA took a bold approach in the de-compartmentalisation of the Japanese financial system, as it expanded the product areas in which different types of financial institutions were now able to compete with banks,[1533] allowing them,

---

1528 See in I. Tirado, 'Banking Crises and the Japanese Legal Framework', Discussion Paper No. 2017-E-2, Institute for Monetary and Economic Studies, Bank of Japan, Tokyo, 2017.

1529 See in E.C. Sibbitt, 'A Brave New World for M&A of Financial Institutions in Japan: Big Bang Financial Deregulation and the New Environment for Corporate Combinations of Financial Institutions' (1998) 19(4) *University of Pennsylvania Journal of International Economic Law*, p. 987.

1530 Ibid. Moreover, certain activities were perceived to be completely unrelated to the banking business, such as retail real estate business, travel agency, hotel and warehouse business, marine courier, and mining business.

1531 Ibid., p. 988.

1532 Financial System Reform Act (Act No. 87 of 1993, Japan).

1533 See in E.C. Sibbitt, 'A Brave New World for M&A of Financial Institutions in Japan: Big Bang Financial Deregulation and the New Environment for Corporate Combinations of Financial Institutions' (1998) 19(4) *University of Pennsylvania Journal of International Economic Law*, p. 988.

inter alia, greater degree of engagement in the securities market. Moreover, the FSRA amended the Banking Act, permitting all types of banks to engage in securities' private placements in the secondary markets, expanded the definition of a bank's primary activities from 'acceptance of term deposits' to 'acceptance of term deposits, etc.',[1534] and expanded slightly and clarified the definition of 'security'.[1535]

The next step towards decompartmentalisation was to allow certain financial institutions to create subsidiaries that would enable them to enter new and diverse business fields. This combination of different financial institutions and the integration of new areas of business was hoped to generate profits and increase innovation in the financial sector.[1536] Upon MoF's approval, Japanese banks were allowed to establish, acquire, and retain domestic securities and domestic trust banking subsidiaries, provided that the parent (bank) company owns at least 50% of the outstanding voting shares of the subsidiary.[1537] The Japanese SEA was amended to state that the prohibition against a bank to conduct business in the securities sector does not bar a bank's acquisition of a securities firm. At the same time, securities companies were able to establish and/or acquire trust and/or banking subsidiaries of their own, in an effort to effectively compete with other financial institutions.[1538] Even the smaller institutions were able to engage in certain trust and securities related activities, despite being perceived as too small to establish full subsidiaries.[1539] An interesting parameter of the FSRA was the possibility given to institutions to acquire failing or failed banking organisations, including deposit institutions, such as long-term credit banks and foreign exchange banks.[1540]

With the FSRA and the subsequent regulations, several firewalls were established to protect from conflicts of interest and other harmful situations, by imposing restrictions on personnel exchanges between parent and subsidiary company, dealings with common clients, transactions between parent and subsidiary company and the shared use of facilities.[1541] Furthermore, the MoF retained a great level of discretion to regulate and intervene when needed, including the option to prohibit and waive transactions with customers and subsidiaries for the sake of public interest and/or to potentially designate

---

1534 Banking Act, Article 10(1)(i).

1535 See in E.C. Sibbitt, 'A Brave New World for M&A of Financial Institutions in Japan: Big Bang Financial Deregulation and the New Environment for Corporate Combinations of Financial Institutions' (1998) 19(4) *University of Pennsylvania Journal of International Economic Law*, p. 988.

1536 Ibid., p. 989.

1537 Ibid.

1538 Ibid.

1539 Ibid.

1540 Ibid.

1541 Ibid., p. 990.

certain transactions with subsidiaries and customers as potentially hindering the parent bank's sound and proper operations.[1542] The MoF retained also the power to require prior approval before any acquisition or establishment of securities and/or trust subsidiary from a bank or from a securities company respectively. Moreover, this power included the right by the MoF to designate by a special ordinance which types of securities companies, trust banks, or any other banks could be acquired.[1543] The MoF also had the right to intervene when a bank was trying to establish a securities company or a trust subsidiary in a foreign country. Obviously, all these discretionary powers gave the MoF the ability to effectively control the degree of liberalisation in the financial sector, thus creating a situation where with the one hand gave its blessing to the process but with the other hand continued to pull the strings of the system, limiting its ability to reach the objectives of the 'big bang' reforms.

The mixing of the new freedoms, which were allotted to the financial institutions, gave them the impetus to rapidly expand their operations and acquire or establish subsidiaries that would take advantage of the new status quo. The MoF had set a timeline in which certain institutions were able to enter specific business lines in predefined time slots. For example, city banks were not able to set up securities subsidiaries until the summer of 1994, while the Industrial Bank of Japan, the Norin Chukin Bank and the LTCB opened securities subsidiaries in July 1993 and the trust banks began opening securities subsidiaries in late 1993.[1544] Finally, securities firms and commercial banks were able to set up trust bank subsidiaries from October 1995. The last step to be taken was the further relaxation of restrictions imposed on holding companies, including the financial ones. The revised antimonopoly law was enacted by the Japanese Diet on 2 June 1997, and on 17 December 1997, and removed the ban on non-financial holding companies.[1545] The government however did not lift the ban on financial holding companies because it wanted to enact first an investors' protection law, before lifting the ban. Finally, on 12 December 1997, the Japanese Diet enacted two laws[1546] that eliminated the restrictions on financial holding companies, based on the conclusions of the financial reform councils. The Maintenance of Bank Holding Companies Act amended

1542 Securities and Exchange Act Articles 10 and 16(2)(3), as amended by the FSRA.

1543 Banking Act Article 16-2(3), as amended by the FSRA.

1544 See in E.C. Sibbitt, 'A Brave New World for M&A of Financial Institutions in Japan: Big Bang Financial Deregulation and the New Environment for Corporate Combinations of Financial Institutions' (1998) 19(4) *University of Pennsylvania Journal of International Economic Law*, p. 990.

1545 Ibid., p. 993.

1546 The two acts were: the Act on Preparation of Relevant Financial Acts Accompanying Cancellation of Prohibition of Establishment, etc. of Holding Companies (Act No. 120 and 121 of 1997, Japan). Act No. 120 and Act No. 121 of 1997 are related but separate acts enacted around the same time addressing financial regulation and holding company laws.

Article 52 of Banking Act, introducing a new definition of a bank holding company and assigning bank holding companies to supervise the subsidiary bank's management and related business to maintain their soundness.[1547]

Furthermore, restrictions on the scope of bank activities, avoidance of excessively risky activities, prevention of unscrupulous trading and ensuring efficient performance of bank's business were imposed as requirements to these bank holding companies.[1548] Regarding scope restrictions, a holding company could own as subsidiaries banks and trust banks, long term credit banks, foreign exchange banks, securities companies and foreign subsidiaries engaging in banking or securities. The MoF was able to designate with ordinance, that institutions 'subordinate to, supplementary to, or relate to banking or securities' may also become subsidiaries of a holding company.[1549] The law limited the bank holding company's collective acquisition of shares, in excess of 15%, of companies belonging to unapproved fields (fields that are not subordinate, supplemental or related to banking or securities activities). In order not to become an impediment to the establishment of bank holding companies, the 15% rule would apply with exemptions to the holding companies that were exceeding the limit. These holding companies would still be approved, conditioned upon disposal of the exceeding number of shares within a period of five years, starting from the day the bank holding company is formed. However, in any case, was not allowed the shares in a 'general enterprise company to exceed 50% of the outstanding shares of that company.[1550] Again, the MoF had broad powers to regulate these holding companies (imposing arm's length rules, capital requirements, extensive disclosure requirements, annual and mid-year business plans) and if the bank holding company would violate any rule and/or commit any harmful action to the public welfare, the MoF had the power to dispose of the holding company by requiring the suspension of all or part of the holding company's subsidiary activities.[1551] The result of these reforms brought the Japanese financial sector in front of a new world and trying to achieve targets that were not easily combined without serious compromises. The means/methods to achieve this liberalisation were based on five different available options: a) the universal banking approach, b) the bank

[1547] See in E.C. Sibbitt, 'A Brave New World for M&A of Financial Institutions in Japan: Big Bang Financial Deregulation and the New Environment for Corporate Combinations of Financial Institutions' (1998) 19(4) *University of Pennsylvania Journal of International Economic Law*, p. 994.

[1548] Ibid.

[1549] Ibid.

[1550] Ibid., p. 995.

[1551] Ibid., p. 994.

holding company structure, c) multifunctional subsidiaries, d) a 'piecemeal approach', and e) mutual entry through wholly owned subsidiaries.[1552]

(a) The universal banking model approach

This method would have allowed financial institutions to engage in a broad range of activities without having to establish subsidiaries or use separate entities to perform part or all the offered activities.[1553] This approach was ultimately rejected by the Japanese authorities partly because it was difficult to achieve a level playing field for all the participants. This statement reflected the reality that large (city) banks supported the idea of universal banking but at the same time, the smaller banks and the securities firms were opposing it because they were afraid of losing their market shares from an intense competition.[1554] The small and specialised banks and the securities firms with the limited number of branches, under the universal banking model would have serious competition problems against large (city) banks who had access to a large branch network, across the country. Moreover, the securities industry insisted on imposing strict firewalls between different financial operations.[1555] From this standpoint, the universal banking model might not have provided sufficient safeguards against situations of conflicting interests and self-dealing.[1556]

(b) The bank holding company structure approach

The second option available was to allow financial institutions to mutual entry in the respective fields through the creation of bank holding companies, in a system like the US. Although it could be a working solution for the financial sector, the problem with this approach was the strong links with the relevant competition regulation, since Article 9 of Japanese antitrust regulation prohibited back then the creation of holding companies and the Reform Council did not want to amend the antitrust law only for the sake of banking industry.[1557]

1552 See in C.P.A Jones, 'Japanese Banking Reform: A Legal Analysis of Recent Developments' (1993) 3 *Duke Journal of Comparative & International Law*, p. 411.

1553 Under the universal banking approach, securities companies would be able to accept deposits and provide loans and banks would be allowed to deal in the securities markets and in trust business.

1554 See in C.P.A Jones, 'Japanese Banking Reform: A Legal Analysis of Recent Developments' (1993) 3 *Duke Journal of Comparative & International Law*, p. 411.

1555 These firewalls, which are in existence still today, are more about securing the level playing field between the market players than preventing the inappropriate exchange and use of information between parent companies and their subsidiaries. In essence, this is the main reason behind the heavy regulatory framework of the Japanese banking and financial system: prevent unfair competition and abuses of dominant positions.

1556 See in C.P.A Jones, 'Japanese Banking Reform: A Legal Analysis of Recent Developments' (1993) 3 *Duke Journal of Comparative & International Law*, p. 412.

1557 Ibid.

(c) The 'multifunctional subsidiaries' approach

The third option was again for mutual entry but through 'multifunctional subsidiaries'. This plan would involve different financial entities participating in each other's fields of business through a special type of subsidiary company.[1558] While this approach, if adopted would have been be able to offer institutions some advantages arising from synergies across operations, the Reform Council expressed certain concerns about potential conflicts of interests and self-dealing situations.[1559] These concerns were very similar to the universal banking model and ultimately resulted in making this option less appealing to the institutions as a method to enter other sectors.

(d) The 'piecemeal approach'

The fourth option available was the 'piecemeal approach' and was based on the idea of desegregating certain, individual, areas of business while leaving the rest of them still segregated and heavily regulated. This 'more of the same' approach, despite having some obvious political merits, since the impact on several financial sectors would be minimised, it was also rejected from the Reform Council because it estimated that it would be difficult to pursue a consistent and far-reaching mutual entry regime for the user's benefit.[1560] Despite the rejection, the merits of that approach were highlighted as appropriate for specific financial sectors, such as regional banks and small financial institutions.[1561]

(e) The mutual entry through wholly owned subsidiaries approach

The last option, which was ultimately endorsed by the Reform Council, allowed mutual entry through wholly owned subsidiary companies, which would specialise in offering the new business activities. This approach presented the fewest problems for its application, since the wholly owned subsidiary model would more effectively manage the harmful conflicts of interest compared to the multifunctional subsidiary, thus maintaining financial stability. Further advantages of this approach would be also fairer competition conditions thus

1558 According to commentators, the term 'multifunctional subsidiaries' would refer to subsidiaries established under the new legislation with special licensing criteria and certain permissible activities that would be in striking difference from the then existing types of financial institutions. This option would resemble more to an investment banking subsidiary limited only to wholesale activities. See in C.P.A Jones, 'Japanese Banking Reform: A Legal Analysis of Recent Developments' (1993) 3 *Duke Journal of Comparative & International Law*, p. 412.

1559 See in C.P.A Jones, 'Japanese Banking Reform: A Legal Analysis of Recent Developments' (1993) 3 *Duke Journal of Comparative & International Law*, p. 412.

1560 Ibid., p. 413.

1561 Ibid.

securing the much-debated level playing field, without any drastic effects on it.[1562]

Finally, the separate subsidiary model became law with the 1992 reforms. The reforms left a broad interpretational and regulatory authority to the MoF, which ultimately, as we have seen earlier, tried to continue the convoy regulation system and protect its acquis and power. The Japanese banks lost the chance to adopt a fully universal banking system and instead opted for the separate subsidiaries approach, keeping in their mind that bottom line was always to protect fair competition among the financial institutions and not to offer their consumers and businesses a modern financial system that would promote innovation and growth. Their legislative reforms were based solely on local competition concerns and on fears of exposing their, out of fashion, financial system to the modern world.

5 THE 2007–2009 GLOBAL FINANCIAL CRISIS: IMPACT AND NEW(?) STRUCTURAL REGULATION MEASURES

5.1. *The Impact of the 2007–2009 GFC in the Japanese Economy and Financial Sector*

The 2007-2009 GFC that originated from the US also hit Japan and although its financial sector proved to be resilient, overall, the economy suffered from a sharp decline in exported products, more than other countries, which ended in an economic contraction. The present book will focus solely on the impact of the global financial crisis in Japan's financial sector, but an important remark must be provided to have a broader view of the crisis' effects. What exactly Japan experienced in 2008 and 2009 was that Japanese stock prices reached a peak in the summer of 2007 and when the US subprime crisis started, they began a gradual and substantial decline.[1563] This decline on stock prices eroded the capital base of commercial banks and put a severe strain on their balance sheets, resulting in a general unwillingness to provide credit. The Lehman Brothers collapse in 2008 further depressed the stock market and put extra strains on Japanese commercial banks. This overall situation started to press industrial production since September 2008.[1564] According to the data provided by Kawai and Takagi, the biggest impact was in the exports towards western Europe and the US and although the decline was across the board of exports

1562 Ibid.

1563 See in M. Kawai and S. Takagi, 'Why was Japan Hit So Hard by the Global Financial Crisis?', Working Paper No. 153, *ADBI Working Paper Series*, Asian Development Bank Institute (ADBI), October 2009, p. 3

1564 Ibid., Figure 3.

it can be specified particularly to consumer durables, capital equipment and industrial supplies, Japan's main three categories of export products.[1565] The next step in our analysis is to understand why this contraction happened, since the financial sector performed almost without any major impact from the turmoil. Kawai and Takagi mention two main reasons to explain the negative effects that Japan experienced during the recent GFC. The first reason is related to Japan's trade structure and the second has to do with its industrial structure. Regarding the trade structure, over 90% of Japan's exports consisted of highly income-elastic industrial supplies, capital goods and consumer durables, hence a collapse of demand for these products in the US and the western European market was a serious negative impact on Japan's exports.[1566] Regarding now the Japan's industrial structure, the past twenty years major changes had been performed and had changed radically. The exchange rate fluctuation of the yen, especially after the Plaza Accord in 1985, had changed profoundly the trade pattern. Japan depended more on trade and this trend was reflected by a decline of non-tradable sector.[1567]

The Japanese banks, having learned from the previous domestic banking crisis, were much more cautious in investing and engaging in exotic financial products. Furthermore, the generally conservative banking environment in Japan together with the new style of financial supervision from the JFSA averted an expansion into deep and unknown financial waters. The recent experience from the enormous amount of NPLs and the failure of many credit institutions played an important role in proving the resilience of Japanese banks. As a result, Japanese banks were averted from inventing in securitised products, in structured financial products and in subprime mortgages on a large scale.[1568] Instead, they preferred to focus more on traditional banking services with small involvement in the production and distribution of securitised financial products and this attitude was translated in losses of only ¥1,038 billion.[1569] This limited exposure resulted also in small increases in funding costs to the interbank market and were considered as less volatile compared to Europe and US.[1570] The Japanese government had to intervene again in the banking sector,

---

1565 Ibid., p. 4.

1566 Ibid., p. 6.

1567 Ibid., p. 14.

1568 See in U. Vollmer and R. Bebenroth, 'The Financial Crisis in Japan: Causes and Policy Reactions by the Bank of Japan' (2012) 9(1) *The European Journal of Comparative Economics*, p. 58.

1569 Ibid.

1570 The Tokyo interbank market rate (TIBOR), a major reference rate for Japanese domestic banks, also remained stable during the global turmoil, attributed also to the fact that Japanese banks had a stable deposit base, which funded only 10% of their interbank market liabilities. See in U. Vollmer and R. Bebenroth, 'The Financial Crisis in Japan: Causes and Policy Reactions by the Bank of Japan' (2012) 9(1) *The European Journal of Comparative Economics*, p. 59.

to reduce the impact from the crisis, in a three-step approach. As a first step, the government urged banks to apply for public capital aiming in reducing banks' reluctance to provide new loans during the crisis. The second step was the easing of FSA's inspection standards, to a large degree, while asking banks to expand lending to small and medium sized enterprises. The third step was the government's decision to relax the current value accounting rules, as the same spirit as in Europe and US.[1571]

These interventions allowed Japanese banks to continue credit supply in the economy despite the global turmoil. Crucial was also the stance of BoJ, which also supported the economy with various monetary policy measures. Aiming at securing financial stability and facilitating corporate finance, the BoJ adopted many measures that eased its monetary policy and provided huge amounts of cash in the markets. With targeted interventions such as interest rates cuts, interest rates on the excess reserves, central bank swap lines with ECB and the Fed, expansion of the eligible collaterals, purchase of stocks held by financial institutions and outright purchase of government bonds, among various other measures, the BoJ succeeded to control the turmoil and provide a credible policy of mitigating the effects through both quantitative and qualitative easing measures.[1572]

5.2. The Current Japanese Structural Separation Framework: The 'Firewall Regulations' Regime

Since the recent GFC, Japan has been adapted to the new circumstances and the new regulatory framework. Currently, the legal framework for banking supervision in Japan is formulated on four levels:

(i) The first level (Level 1 legislation) comprises of the Banking Act that has been approved by the Cabinet and passed by the Diet.
(ii) The second level (Level 2 legislation) is the Orders for Enforcement of the Banking Act that have been approved and issued by the Cabinet.
(iii) The third level (Level 3 legislation) is the Ordinances for Enforcement of the Banking Act, which is issued by the FSA.[1573]

1571 See in R. Kamikawa, 'The Interaction between Financial Regulation and Financial Crisis in Japan: Change in Financial Administration and Two Financial Crises from 1980 to 2010' (2012) 59 *Osaka University Law Review*, p. 22.

1572 See in U. Vollmer and R. Bebenroth, 'The Financial Crisis in Japan: Causes and Policy Reactions by the Bank of Japan' (2012) 9(1) *The European Journal of Comparative Economics*, p. 66.

1573 The JFSA is substantially involved in the drafting of laws, orders, and ordinances.

(iv) The fourth level (Level 4 legislation) contains supervisory guidelines and inspection manuals that implement and reinforce the legal framework, developed, and published by the FSA.[1574]

The permissible activities of institutions that are licensed and subject to supervision as banks are clearly defined either by supervisors, or by laws or regulations. The principal source of regulation for banks doing in business in Japan is the Banking Act, to which all banks are subject. Banking Act regulates their corporate governance, banking business and capital adequacy ratios, as well as their principal shareholders and subsidiaries. The Banking Act also regulates holding companies that have banks as subsidiaries (bank holding companies).[1575] The Japanese regulatory framework still today regulates commercial banking activities and investment banking activities separately. The Banking Act is, in principle, applicable only to the former (i.e. acceptance of deposits, provision of loans and transfer of funds, which are deemed to be the core banking business). Many banks also engage in investment banking activities, which generally include securities and derivatives-related businesses. Article 10 of the Japanese Banking Act provides a specific list of available banking activities, while Article 11 refers to the requirements for undertaking business pursuant to the provisions of the Secured Bonds Trust Act or other laws.[1576] For this purpose, these activities are subject to separate requirements and restrictions, and these banks are concurrently regulated under the Financial Instruments and Exchange Act (FIEA).[1577] Some banks have affiliated securities companies engaging in investment banking business, with these companies are also subject to the FIEA's regulation.[1578] Overseas banks that are interested in doing business in Japan have two organisational structures available to offer the core banking business. The first option consists of the establishment of a joint-stock company with limited liability in Japan, as a subsidiary or affiliate, in accordance with the Companies Act of Japan.[1579] This entity, subsidiary, or affiliate must obtain a banking license from the Prime Minister of Japan, pursuant to the Banking Act (a local entity bank). The alternative option consists of the establishment of branches of the foreign bank within Japan

---

1574 In practice, the supervisory guidelines are mostly used in the assessment of offsite activities of the JFSA staff, whereas the inspection manuals are mostly used as guiding practice for the on-site activities of the JFSA ding their inspections. Supervisory Guidelines and Inspection manuals are frequently updated to consider recent developments in the banking industry and improvements in supervisory practices.

1575 See in H. Akagami and Y. Watanabe, 'The Banking Regulation Review: Japan', *The Law Reviews*, 4 May 2021.

1576 The activities a bank may undertake are specifically mentioned in the Banking Act. Other activities may not be conducted.

1577 Financial Instruments and Exchange Act (Act No. 25 of 1948, Japan).

1578 See in H. Akagami and Y. Watanabe, 'The Banking Regulation Review: Japan', *The Law Reviews*, 4 May 2021.

1579 Companies Act (Act No. 86 of 2005, Japan).

and obtaining a relevant foreign bank branch banking license. Regarding the foreign bank branch scheme, the opening of subsequent branches (also known as sub-branches) is also subject to prior approval by the JFSA. The granting of the necessary licenses and approvals is at the discretion of the relevant authority in each instance.[1580] For a bank to engage in investment banking activities, such as securities and derivatives business, must also be registered with the competent local finance bureau, pursuant to the FIEA.[1581] Registered banks are generally permitted to operate a wider range of derivatives and securities businesses, including brokerage of government bonds and sales of unit trusts or non-discretionary investment advisory services. However, for the historical reasons we referred earlier, banks are generally prohibited from engaging in certain categories of securities business, including brokerage, and underwriting of corporate stocks and corporate bonds, and discretionary investment management services.[1582] To be able to conduct these activities, banks must establish a subsidiary or affiliate that will be a separate legal entity, and register it pursuant to the FIEA as a financial instruments business operator. In this connection, the scope of business of a subsidiary or affiliate that a bank may have is restricted to certain financial and related businesses, but it has been expanded to some extent by an amendment of the Banking Act in 2016, to include fintech business.[1583]

Despite the problems from the banking crisis in the 1990s and from the recent GFC, Japan has still in force the structural measures that impede free access for banks to the capital markets. These are the so-called 'Firewall Regulations', introduced in 1993 and modelled after the US GSA, which were initially aimed at preventing market distortions caused by transactions exploiting parent-subsidiary relationships within the financial groups. Nevertheless, over time their purpose expanded to include protection of customer information, managing conflicts of interest, and preventing abuse of superior positions.[1584] Originally, these rules prohibited banks from establishing securities subsidiaries. However, the legislative changes in 1993 we examined earlier on allowed banks to create securities subsidiaries and securities firms to establish banking subsidiaries, under strict separation requirements. Since their inception, the firewall regulations have undergone several amendments, notably in 2009, 2014, 2021 and 2022, to relax restrictions and improve flexibility,

1580 Article 47-3 of the Banking Act.
1581 Article 33-2 of the FIEA.
1582 Article 33 of the FIEA.
1583 Articles 16-2 and 16-4 of the Banking Act.
1584 See in S. Ono, 'Japan's firewall regulation – a crackdown on undisclosed information transfer', *IFLR*, 1 February 2023.

especially for foreign corporations and listed companies.[1585] Responsible for the firewall regulation is the JFSA, through the relevant legal acts:

(a) the Financial Instruments and Exchange Act (FIEA),
(b) the Cabinet Office Ordinance on Financial Instruments Business (COOFIB),[1586] and
(c) the Comprehensive Guidelines for Supervision of Financial Instruments Business Operators, etc. of the FIEA (Supervision of FIBO Guidelines).[1587]

The current version of firewall regulations contains a 'Ginsho firewall regulation'[1588] which is an information sharing ban, meaning that as a general rule, pursuant to such regulations, no Non-Public Information (NPI) regarding a client (both as an issuer of securities or as an investor) may be shared between a bank and a securities company, within the same financial group, without that client's prior written consent. Within this context, NPI means:

(a) undisclosed and important information regarding a client's management, operations or properties which affects the investment decisions of a securities firm's client,[1589] and
(b) information regarding certain other matters such as the sale and other transactional trends in the securities-related orders of a securities firm's clients, where such information is obtained by officers or employees of a securities firm or its parent and subsidiary companies during the performance of their duties.[1590]

Although the definition of NPI is based on the view that such information that has not been made public should generally be treated as NPI, it is not clear what type of information falls within the NPI ambit, and therefore cautious judgement is required in practice by the financial entities.[1591] The firewall regulations regime also comes with certain exemptions and does not apply:

(a) to the transfer of NPI if the client gives consent in writing or by electromagnetic records in advance, to a securities firm and its parent and

---

[1585] See in Anderson Mori & Tomotsune, *Easing of Firewall Regulations under the Financial Instruments and Exchange Act of Japan*, Japan, September 2014.

[1586] Cabinet Office Ordinance on Financial Instruments Business Association, etc., (Cabinet Office Ordinance No. 53 of 7 August 2007), available at: https://www.japaneselawtranslation.go.jp/en/laws/view/2539/en.

[1587] See in Financial Services Agency (FSA), *Comprehensive Guidelines for Supervision of Financial Instruments Business Operators, etc.*, March 2024, available in English at: https://www.fsa.go.jp/common/law/guide/kinyushohin_eng.pdf.

[1588] In Japanese banking and finance regulatory framework, 'Ginsho Firewall' (銀行のファイアウォール規制, *ginshō fairuōru kisei*) refers to regulatory 'firewalls' between different types of financial institutions, especially between banks (銀行, *ginkō*) and their affiliated securities firms (証券会社, *shōken gaisha*).

[1589] See in Anderson Mori & Tomotsune, *Easing of Firewall Regulations under the Financial Instruments and Exchange Act of Japan*, Japan, September 2014.

[1590] Ibid.

[1591] See in S. Ono, 'Japan's firewall regulation – a crackdown on undisclosed information transfer', *IFLR*, 1 February 2023.

subsidiary companies to share NPI (the 'Written Consent'). In practice, however, comprehensive consent is obtained to allow the transfer of NPI over a wide range of areas in many cases, provided, however, that even if comprehensive consent is obtained in a case where the client states its intention not to allow the transfer of specific information, the transfer is not permitted.[1592]

(b) where the sharing of NPI is necessary for a securities firm and their 'Specific Affiliates'[1593] to coordinate their internal control functions (the 'Internal Control Exception' – ICE);[1594]

(c) where a client is given written notice stating, among others, that a securities firm and its parent and subsidiary companies will share NPI relating to the client (the 'Information Sharing Notice'), pursuant to which the client will, unless it expressly indicates otherwise, be deemed to permit such information sharing (the 'Opt-out').[1595]

With respect to the opt-out option certain clarifications are necessary, as this includes the scope of NPI to be transferred, the scope of the parent or subsidiary companies and the transfer method of NPI. Moreover, in cases where the opt-out option is used, it is necessary to have appropriate measures in place which might include a period of time necessary for judging whether the corporate client actually opts out or not or responding as promptly and appropriately as possible in cases where the corporate client opts out.[1596] Other exceptional cases in which the transfer of NPI is permitted include when it is transferred for the purpose of maintaining an electronic data processing system or when it is received or provided pursuant to laws and regulations.

After the 2009 reform, information sharing among the two entities, the bank, and its securities subsidiary, was permitted about corporate customers if they had been notified by the firms for their intention to share information and give them the opportunity to opt-out. Since these rules apply also to foreign financial groups, the management and compliance with these requirements is obviously a demanding exercise, mostly because they must maintain databases to comply with the requirements of firewall regulations and the opt-out policy exemption. With the 2014 amendments to the firewall regulations, it was introduced an expanded meaning of the Internal Control Exemption to include also the administrative functions of the firms, adding to the already existing

---

1592 Ibid.

1593 The meaning of '*Specific Affiliates*' includes a) the holding company of a securities firm, b) the parent companies of the securities firm which perform the internal control functions of the securities firm and c) the securities firm's parent and subsidiary companies which are financial institutions (such as banks or securities firms).

1594 See in S. Ono, 'Japan's firewall regulation – a crackdown on undisclosed information transfer', *IFLR*, 1 February 2023.

1595 Ibid.

1596 Ibid.

compliance control functions, risk management functions, internal audit and review functions, finance and accounting functions, taxation functions.[1597] Moreover, further amendments were adopted with respect to the opt out right as the Supervision of FIBO Guidelines proved to be cumbersome for the securities firms. The 2021 amendments aimed at excluding information relating to foreign corporate clients from the definition of NPI (Foreign Corporate Client Information Firewall) as well as amendments with respect to the consent to sharing of NPI relating to domestic corporate clients (i.e. excluding domestic clients who are individuals) is subject to an opt-out rule (Domestic Client Information Firewall). The framework was amended again in 2022 to permit the transfer of NPI of listed companies, in cases where the transfer of such information to the parent or subsidiary companies may be suspended upon request. In this case it is also required to take appropriate measures, but the requirements are more lenient than in the case of the opt-out mechanism.[1598] While relaxing the firewall regulations, would lift a serious impediment towards universal banking model, there are also concerns expressed by customers of financial institutions about undue influence resulting from the concurrent operations of bank and securities businesses by the same financial group. Such influence is aimed to be handled by adding regulations on customer information management, enhancing regulatory monitoring on conflict of interests, and implementing coordination measures between financial regulators and competition authorities regarding the abuse of dominant bargaining positions by financial institutions.

6 CONCLUDING REMARKS: THE 'TWO LOST DECADES' AND A NEW ERA OF FINANCIAL REGULATION

What are the lessons to be learned from Japan? The question is far from rhetoric. Japan had and still implements a sui generis regime regarding its banks. Firewall regulations are still in force and although the government constantly discusses the possibility of lifting them and coming closer to a quasi-universal banking system, this is far from sure as the holding company structure will most probably remain a prerequisite for banks. These reasons, as presented earlier, have to do with competition concerns among the various financial institutions and not so much with investor protection concerns or protection of depositors, as is the case in the US. The Banking Act obliges banks

1597 For a more detailed analysis of the 2014 amendments see in See in Anderson Mori & Tomotsune, *Easing of Firewall Regulations under the Financial Instruments and Exchange Act of Japan*, Japan, September 2014.

1598 See in S. Ono, 'Japan's firewall regulation – a crackdown on undisclosed information transfer', *IFLR*, 1 February 2023.

to carry on their business in compliance with various regulations, including a prohibition on abuse of a dominant bargaining position, the management of a conflict of interests, provision of an explanation of the risks associated with their products and other information to customers and the appropriate handling of personal information.[1599] Mostly for historical reasons, banks must have a separate subsidiary company to perform activities in the capital markets and strict firewalls apply between these two entities to prevent situations of conflicting interests.

The most important lesson though from the Japanese experience is undoubtedly the fact that even in the narrowest banking system, in terms of offered services and sectors of the economy served, strict regulation is not a panacea. It cannot avert crises and furthermore cannot avert systemic collapses that can jeopardise the stability of the system. Strict regulations must always be accompanied by effective supervision and credible resolution regime. In a modern and highly interconnected financial system, where banks are exposed to various risks, regulation is only one side of the coin. Rules must be applied in a consistent and clear manner, without any unlawful relations between supervisors and banks, and a credible resolution regime must be in place to secure that any bank can fail, orderly and according to the rulebook that the government has adopted. The Japanese experience demonstrates further the necessity for banks to have the possibility to effectively diversify their portfolios. Had the Japanese banks the ability to effectively offer services to wider variety of customers their exposure to real estate lending would have been much smaller than what actually were. Strict and regent segmentation on what banks can do and on what they cannot do has proven not to be the optimal policy option, at least in Japan. Furthermore, the strict regulation of corporate structure, mostly through the holding company restrictions, further shrunk the available options for the banks. In this critical mixture, the government's policy targets for growth and economic prosperity were dysfunctional since the structural deficiencies of the financial sector needed special attention and targeted measures to be fixed for the macroeconomic policies to be effective.

[1599] See in H. Akagami and Y. Watanabe, 'The Banking Regulation Review: Japan', *The Law Reviews*, 4 May 2021.

CHAPTER 4
UNITED KINGDOM: FROM UNIVERSALISM TO 'RING-FENCING'

The United Kingdom (UK) has been traditionally seen as one of the most important financial mega hubs of the world. With deep and liquid capital markets, big banks and financial institutions with an international presence and a judicial system that has extensive experience in disputes of financial nature, the UK had managed to become the second biggest market, just after the US. UK banking sector assets are the fourth largest in the world and include large domestic and foreign-owned financial institutions. The latter - consisting of both foreign branches and subsidiaries - accounts for one half of banking assets in the UK, while UK-owned banks have over half of their assets outside the country. The UK is also central in the sense of lying on the path between other nodes, reflecting its role as a financial centre where a bank from a second country raises money in a third country to lend to a fourth. On this measure of centrality, the UK exceeds all other financial centres, including the US.

1 A CURRENT OVERVIEW OF THE UK'S FINANCIAL SECTOR

Based on the latest available FSAP Report from the IMF, the UK hosts a large, complex, and globally interconnected financial system with the sum of financial assets owned by all financial institutions (excluding the central bank) standing at about £20 trillion; this amount is over ten times UK annual GDP and almost half of this is accounted for by banks.[1600] Furthermore, four banks and two insurers are classified as globally systemically important, its insurance sector is the largest in Europe and the third largest in the world and it hosts the largest fund management industry and many of the most important equity trading platforms in Europe, as well as two of the largest central counterparties (CCPs) in the world.[1601] The banking sector particularly

---

[1600] See in International Monetary Fund (IMF), *United Kingdom, Financial Sector Assessment Program, Financial System Stability Assessment*, IMF Country Report No. 16/167, June 2016, Washington D.C., p. 9.

[1601] Ibid.

is concentrated and the seven largest UK banks represent over 75% of total system assets and by this measure, sector concentration is higher than in Japan (71%), Switzerland (71%), Germany (48%), and the US (48%), though lower than in France (91%).[1602] Nevertheless, the market is becoming increasingly contested with smaller 'challenger' banks, focusing on certain market segments (especially retail), are growing, although they still represent only about 5% of total lending market share.[1603]

Although the picture might be slightly amended due to the Brexit referendum and the changes this decision brought, the importance of the UK as a financial hub is beyond doubt. The UK suffered enormously from the last global financial crisis. Classic bank runs, nationalisations of failed banks, excessive public spending to support banks and favourable treatment of mergers that stretch to the edge competition rules are some of the various issues that the UK had to come up to mitigate the effects of the financial meltdown. These problems forced the government to adopt strict 'structural measures' that aim to secure that the supply of critical banking services will continue even under harsh conditions. The supply of these services assumes that individuals and small businesses cannot afford to lose these vital services without any alternative options and without great repercussions for social welfare. The adopted solution is to 'ring-fence' certain activities that fall within the ambit of vital services aiming to protect the entity that provides these services from any adverse effects that may arise. Ring fencing legislation has already been into effect, and this allows us to attempt a very first evaluation of these measures, based on relatively limited data and evidence, that will help us understand what the overall benefit of the measures has been. In striking contrast with the other countries that we use as yardsticks for our research question, the UK has enacted a very clear and pure form of separation (ring-fencing regime) that allows us to present, analyse but also evaluate the regime based on an official review for the UK Parliament. Therefore, we will not attempt a similar historical approach to the structural reforms, as we do for the other jurisdictions since the regime at stake is the child of the last financial crisis, and the events are already well known.

1602 Ibid., p. 10.

1603 Ibid.

2 A HISTORICAL EVOLUTION OF THE UK BANKING SYSTEM

2.1. *From the Early Years until the 'Big-Bang'*

With respect to the UK, through the years, few entities were involved in the historical evolution of its financial regulation, since the Bank of England (BoE) and few elite firms formed a highly concentrated industry.[1604] The most important elements of prudential regulation in the UK were established in 20th century following the establishment of the main outlines of the banking industry in the 19th century. The BoE dominated the banking scene from its foundation, back in 1694 until well into the 19th century. Originally established as a commercial bank, the BoE enjoyed a wide range of privileges, governmentally conferred upon her, while at the same time all other banks in England and Wales were obliged to adopt the partnership legal form.[1605]

Until the first attempt of liberalising the sector, through the 1826 Joint Stock Bank Act (JSBA),[1606] banking outside London remained practically underdeveloped and the small expansion attempted during the Napoleonic wars resulted in a number of seriously undercapitalised banks, which ultimately failed creating a general crisis in the years 1825-1826.[1607] The 1826 JSBA paved the way for the formation of a more stable but highly concentrated banking system through the formation of joint stock companies commercial banks that were able to operate extensive branch networks across the country.[1608] The most important novelty that the 1826 JSBA introduced was that it extracted the BoE's legislative monopoly by permitting the creation of banks, with an unlimited number of partners or shareholders, outside a radius of sixty-five miles from London.[1609] The amendments through the 1844 JSBA imposed stricter requirements to these banks, implementing a new regulatory

1604 See in H.M. Schooner and M. Taylor, 'Convergence and Competition: The Case of Bank Regulation in Britain and the United States' (1999) 20 *Michigan Journal of International Law*, p. 605.

1605 Ibid., p. 606. The maximum number of partners that could join the partnership was limited to 6.

1606 Joint Stock Banks Act 1852, 15 & 16 Vict. c. 32 (UK).

1607 During that time, more than 90 banks in England and Wales found themselves unable to meet customers' demands for cash. See in H.M. Schooner and M. Taylor, 'Convergence and Competition: The Case of Bank Regulation in Britain and the United States' (1999) 20 *Michigan Journal of International Law*, p. 607.

1608 H.M. Schooner and M. Taylor, 'Convergence and Competition: The Case of Bank Regulation in Britain and the United States' (1999) 20 *Michigan Journal of International Law*, p. 607.

1609 Ibid.

framework,[1610] that ultimately led to a hiatus in establishment of new banks' without preventing though bank failures. The short lived 1844 JSBA was repealed already in 1857; a series of Acts between 1858 and 1862 extended the limited liability right to shareholders in general and culminated in the 1879 Companies Act.[1611] Despite the various amendments in the legal framework, the business of banking was not subject to a statutory authorisation process or to any on-going prudential supervision, nor was existed a clear definition of the banking business or of a bank.[1612]

The type of banking system managed to survive two world wars and the Great Depression without any fundamental changes, like the ones that occurred in the US. Banking supervision was driven by a strict hierarchy, at the apex of which were the large clearing banks, dominated by the so-called 'Big Five' (Barclays, Lloyds', Midland, National Provincial and Westminster) that had an extensive network of branches.[1613] The BoE created a relationship with the clearing banks that could be described as a 'bank-client relationship', effective for the implementation of its tasks. Apart from the clearing banks, in the UK's top tier system participated small, elite institutions known as 'discount houses or accepting houses'. These institutions, together with clearing banks, represented the core banking system over which the BoE was highly interested in exercising a tight grip. BoE's aim was to rather ensure stability than encouraging and improving competition and as a result encouraged the creation of cartels among them.[1614] Moreover, institutional links between banks, securities dealers, and insurance companies, although not specifically prohibited by law or other regulations, were discouraged and informal means were utilised to exercise control over potential bubbles in the stock market.[1615] The BoE conducted its informal supervisory function, primarily through the 'Discount Office' and through its own market operations, the BoE was able to exercise a big influence on all the banks' activities.[1616] Many authors took the view that this style of supervision had important limitations, since it presumed

---

1610 With the new framework, the prescribed nominal capital was raised to £100.000, with at least half of that amount to be paid up before the bank could commence its operations. Moreover, banks shares were issued at a denomination of £100 and a statement of assets and liabilities was required to be published once each month. The annual accounts were to be examined by auditors elected by the shareholders, and no bank was permitted to lend or to purchase upon the security of its own shares.

1611 See in H.M. Schooner and M. Taylor, 'Convergence and Competition: The Case of Bank Regulation in Britain and the United States' (1999) 20 *Michigan Journal of International Law*, p. 608.

1612 Ibid.

1613 Ibid., p. 609.

1614 Ibid., p. 614.

1615 Ibid.

1616 Ibid., p. 615.

that a 'trust & confidence relationship' existed among the BoE and the banks, and that all necessary information was made available to it.[1617]

The Great Depression did not have any significant impact upon the financial sector; its impact was more evident in the real economy than banks. Another important parameter was that traditionally, British bankers enjoyed greater popularity than their US counterparts, fact that allowed a relatively stable regulatory framework without 'regulatory waves' that usually come after crises and bank failures.[1618] The situation changed dramatically during the 1960s, especially in the US, when post war developments, with disintermediation being one of them, started changing the classic banking landscape.[1619] Disintermediation occurred both at the asset and liability side of a bank's balance sheet, in a period when upward growing oil prices forced central banks to raise interest rates. This global trend also entered the UK banking market with significant growth in banking outside the sectors controlled by the BoE.[1620] Moreover, the growth of Euromarkets[1621] provided the necessary liquidity and wholesale market funds to fuel the growth of a new, domestic banking market, mostly unregulated, lying outside the BoE traditional sphere of influence. The official reaction to this trend was further deregulation but, the always present bank failures, resulted in the creation of a statute-based system of financial regulation.[1622]

In the 1970s, the UK banking sector had two special characteristics. First, the increasing presence of foreign institutions and second, a constantly growing banking sector. The BoE responded to this situation by implementing a deregulatory policy that aimed at increasing competition, mostly through

---

1617 Ibid.

1618 Ibid.

1619 Banks in the US began to lose customers, which applied for commercial loans, to the commercial paper market, forcing banks to change their business models entering consumer and mortgage lending markets. These changes diminished the quality of banks' assets. See in H.M. Schooner and M. Taylor, 'Convergence and Competition: The Case of Bank Regulation in Britain and the United States' (1999) 20 *Michigan Journal of International Law*, p. 623.

1620 See in H.M. Schooner and M. Taylor, 'Convergence and Competition: The Case of Bank Regulation in Britain and the United States' (1999) 20 *Michigan Journal of International Law*, p. 623.

1621 In finance, the term 'Euromarkets' means the market for eurocurrencies: these are all currencies that are held as deposits by companies or individuals outside of their country of issue. The 'euro-' prefix in the term arose because originally such currencies were held in Europe, but that is no longer solely the case. A eurocurrency can now be held anywhere in the world that local banking regulations permit. The eurocurrency market is a major source of finance for international trade because of ease of convertibility and the absence of domestic restrictions on trading. Source: Investopedia.

1622 See in H.M. Schooner and M. Taylor, 'Convergence and Competition: The Case of Bank Regulation in Britain and the United States' (1999) 20 *Michigan Journal of International Law*, p. 624.

the 'Competition and Credit Control' (CCC) regime.[1623] The CCC regime was introduced in September 1971 and was implemented administratively, without the need for legislation, controlling credit supply through the manipulation of interest rates, as opposed to more quantitative techniques used in the past.[1624] Under the CCC regime, a wider range of banks were obliged to comply with the BoE's monetary and credit policy targets, especially by extending the reserve asset ratio to all 'statistical' banks.[1625] This extension was an attempt by the BoE to assert control over the new parts of banking sector, but it was too little and too late. The deregulation results and some governmental decisions over fiscal and monetary policies forced banks to increase sterling lending and when this inflationary bubble burst, secondary banks were left exposed to the real estate sector and forced BoE to engage in 'life-saving operations' by preparing a rescue package for these banks.

The 'Secondary Banking Crisis' of 1973-1974, put forward the creation of a statute-based regulation for the banking sector and some immediate changes applied to the BoE's supervision style. The first step was the creation of the new 'Banking and Money Markets Supervision Division' (BAMMS), to replace the Discount Office and its supervisory functions.[1626] BAMMS started placing more importance to the banks' capital ratios as opposed to the BoE's past practices that were targeted to the liquidity ratios.[1627] Moreover, extensive reporting requirements were imposed to the banks, with all British owned banks, foreign subsidiaries but not their UK branches, falling within the ambit of the requirement.[1628] Overall, the Secondary Banking Crisis highlighted four major deficiencies of the informal regulatory system. First, confusion existed regarding the status of banking recognitions; Second, several depository institutions were left unsupervised; Third, depositors were not protected from formal arrangements in case of failed banks; Fourth, it became clear that the BoE had failed to exercise its supervisory role, even where it had one.[1629] The clear bottom line of the Secondary Banking Crisis was the need for a robust regime of regulation, based on principles, despite the BoE's clear preference for maintaining the status quo.

1623 Ibid.

1624 Ibid.

1625 Under that requirement, all 'statistical' banks (i.e. the banks from which the BoE collected regular statistical reports containing balance sheet data and currency composition of their lending), were required to maintain interest free reserves within the BoE. This ratio was a specified ratio of their sterling denominated deposits.

1626 See in H.M. Schooner and M. Taylor, 'Convergence and Competition: The Case of Bank Regulation in Britain and the United States' (1999) 20 *Michigan Journal of International Law*, p. 626.

1627 Ibid.

1628 Ibid.

1629 Ibid., p. 629.

The UK's participation in the then European Economic Community (EEC) further pressed the system to adapt to the new legislative reality. The EECs' attempts to regulate banking and implement common standards obliged the UK to adapt its supervision and establish a formal system of licensing and regulation to its banking sector after almost 150 years.[1630] The reaction to this challenge was the enactment of the 1979 Banking Act,[1631] which created a new, two-tier system of banking supervision, separating between 'recognised banks' and 'licensed deposit takers' (LDTs), applying, under the influence of EEC law, minimum criteria to all banks. Another important aspect of the 1979 Banking Act was the creation of the 'Deposit Protection Scheme' (DPS) that was funded solely by bank contributions, through a dedicated levy, and included no access to public funds.[1632] Schooner and Taylor support that the separation between recognised banks and LDTs permitted the BoE to continue its informal style of regulation and supervision, mostly through the various regulatory requirements that were imposed to the two categories without making much sense, by continuing its 'flexible and case-by-case' approach that had always applied since the days of the Discount Office.[1633]

The Banking Act was once again amended in 1987, after major challenges to the BoE's traditional style of regulation demonstrated the limits of that system. The collapse of Johnson Matthey Bankers (JMB) in 1984, after losses that wiped out the entire bank's capital,[1634] exposed the BoE's inefficiencies regarding effective supervision and regulation. The implications from the demise of JMB were that the BoE did not manage to secure support from the big clearing banks, as it has done in the past, and that the JMB episode exposed

---

1630 Ibid., p. 630.

1631 Banking Act 1979, c 37 (UK).

1632 The initial protection was relatively small and up of only a 75% of a maximum £10,000 of an institution's sterling liability to an individual depositor. Obviously, the aim of the protection was to include only the small depositors and the 75% cap to introduce some sort of co-insurance. See in H.M. Schooner and M. Taylor, 'Convergence and Competition: The Case of Bank Regulation in Britain and the United States' (1999) 20 *Michigan Journal of International Law*, p. 630.

1633 See in H.M. Schooner and M. Taylor, 'Convergence and Competition: The Case of Bank Regulation in Britain and the United States' (1999) 20 *Michigan Journal of International Law*, p. 631.

1634 JMB was a subsidiary of Johnson Matthey gold refiners, one of the five London based gold dealing banks, recognized under the 1979 Act. The problems arose when JMB established a, rapidly growing, lending business onto its gold dealing activities. JMB's loan portfolio grew from £34 million to £450 million in just four years, with 1/3 of that expansion occurring during the last six months of that period. Moreover, the high concentration of the JMBs' exposures posed further risks that led the banks' accountants to recommend additional losses on 25 September 1984. Despite not being a significant bank, the BoE decided not to risk any instability in the gold market and bought JMB for £1 after its parent company Johnson Matthey injected £50 million of fresh capital.

BoE to an unprecedented level of public scrutiny, never seen before.[1635] The Leigh-Pemberton Committee (LPC), established with the aim to study the bank regulation system, made recommendations that were ultimately adopted through amendment to the Banking Act. LPC's most important recommendation was to abolish the two-tier system with a single system of 'authorised institutions' subject to certain statutory criteria, as defined in Schedule 3 of the Act. Among other things, the LPC Report proposed limits on large exposures, increased reporting requirements and finally, further requirements for the staffing of the BoE's Banking Supervision Division.[1636] The 1987 Banking Act, despite being unusually specific in its provisions, continued the practice of leaving the BoE with a substantial supervisory discretion to interpret and apply the rules. According to Schooner and Taylor, the extensive supervisory discretion enjoyed by the BoE not only precluded legal challenge to its rulemaking but also enabled her to maintain the flexible and institution specific approach to its supervisory duties in a way like that of the Japanese MoF.[1637]

The next bank failures that altered the regulatory and supervisory framework in the UK were the closure of the Bank of Credit and Commerce International (BCCI) on 5 July 1991, and the collapse of Barings Bank in 1995. The demise of BCCI hurt BoE's ability to maintain its reputation as a competent supervisor. An independent investigation and the subsequent 'Bingham Report' concluded that the BoE had the power to act effectively and revoke the institution's authorisation but demonstrated reluctance in using this power.[1638] The Bingham report did not suggest the adoption of new legislation but instead concluded that the BoE's overall style of supervision should remain the same. What needed to be improved was the level of cooperation between the BoE and the institutions that failed to be open and cooperative with their supervisors. What the Bingham Report added to the BoE was a 'Special Investigations Unit' in the Banking Supervision Division, staffed by fraud analysts and audit specialists.[1639]

[1635] See in H.M. Schooner and M. Taylor, 'Convergence and Competition: The Case of Bank Regulation in Britain and the United States' (1999) 20 *Michigan Journal of International Law*, p. 633.

[1636] The 1987 Act created the Board of Banking Supervision with the responsibility to oversee the BoE's execution of its supervisory duties and provide consultation, particularly in difficult cases. BoE could reject the Board's advice, but in that case had to inform the Chancellor of the Exchequer. In theory, the existence of the Supervisory Board was an added value to the supervision system but in practice proved to be dysfunctional since the Board had limited knowledge of the Supervisory Divisions' activities. See in H.M. Schooner and M. Taylor, 'Convergence and Competition: The Case of Bank Regulation in Britain and the United States' (1999) 20 *Michigan Journal of International Law*, p. 635.

[1637] See in H.M. Schooner and M. Taylor, 'Convergence and Competition: The Case of Bank Regulation in Britain and the United States' (1999) 20 *Michigan Journal of International Law*, p. 635.

[1638] Ibid., p. 637.

[1639] Ibid., p. 638.

While the collapse of the BCCI had a very limited impact on the UK's banking sector, this was not the case with the failure of Barings Bank, few years later. BCCI was perceived to be as a rogue institution, which helped to mitigate BoE's responsibilities, but Barings was a completely different story since the BoE was supervising Barings for more than a hundred years and this case was a clear red alarm signal that the system of supervision based on principles of trust, cooperation and candour was ineffective.[1640] BoE failed to supervise and question the large profits reported by the Barings' Singapore derivatives operations department[1641] and this was another luminous example of lack of inquisitiveness. Moreover, the BoE failed to timely identify serious management inadequacies that existed at all levels at Barings, that allowed the adoption and implication of internal processes not reflecting a bank's proper function. The final report on Barings failure was prepared by the BoE's Board of Banking Supervision and concluded that the BoE's approach towards more discretion and an institution-based supervision was of important premium 'on individual supervisors' ability to relate their judgements to the overall objectives of supervision'.[1642] Arthur Andersen, a consultancy company, also helped to prepare and implement a new style of supervision based on certain recommendations that favoured standardisation and more professionalism. Although the BoE accepted the recommendations and started adopting them, the newly elected Labor Government proposed a radical change in the supervision, through the establishment of an entirely new agency, the Financial Services Authority (FSA).

2.2. *The 'Big Bang' Financial (De)Regulatory Reforms*

The second most important event in the UK's history of financial (de) regulation was the radical capital markets reforms, introduced in the late 1980s, under the conservative Government of Margaret Thatcher. The reforms

---

1640 Ibid.

1641 Barings was brought down in 1995 by a massive trading loss caused by fraudulent trading. The bank permitted an internal situation where one of its employees, namely its head of derivatives trader in Singapore since 1992, Nick Leeson, assumed big bets on fraudulent trading. Leeson was supposed to be arbitraging, seeking to profit from differences in the prices of Nikkei 225 futures contracts listed on the Osaka Securities Exchange in Japan and on the Singapore International Monetary Exchange (SIMEX). However, Leeson, instead of buying on one market and immediately selling on another market for a small profit, using the strategy approved by his superiors bought on one market then held on to the contract, gambling on the future direction of the Japanese markets. When the Japanese market did not manage to recover from a series of losses, the bank was found severely exposed and assumed huge losses.

1642 See in H.M. Schooner and M. Taylor, 'Convergence and Competition: The Case of Bank Regulation in Britain and the United States' (1999) 20 *Michigan Journal of International Law*, p. 639.

were mostly aimed at increasing competition among the capital markets participants, since there were signals that London was lagging behind New York, in the competition for the best financial mega hub. Even though the reforms were not targeting solely the banks but rather the general function of capital markets, they had a profound impact on the banking sector since they increased the general level of competition between financial markets participants and propagated the growth of non-bank financial intermediation. Banks were forced to participate to follow their clients and offer them new services and new credit instruments that would better fit their needs. Mergers and acquisitions among the players helped banks to enter capital markets and create a new financial universe that characterises the UK financial sector still today. The phrase 'Big Bang' refers to a series of reforms that sought to eliminate perceived anticompetitive practices at the London Stock Exchange (LSE) and put London's financial markets on an equal competitive footing with its international rivals, particularly the US. From 1975 to 1985, the UK stock markets' turnover fell from almost 25% of the value of that of the US, to the remarkably low of 5%.[1643] Among other things, the reforms sought to remove price rigidities in the provision of securities transactions and dismantle barriers to entry onto the LSE. Two practices received particular attention: a) the fixed minimum commissions, and b) the so-called 'single capacity', which prevented both brokers from trading on their own account and market makers (jobbers) from acting for customers.

The abolition of minimum commissions changed the economics of brokerage and market-making, making joint-provision of these functions and foreign entry inevitable. Although the total number of institutions did not increase, there was a marked rise in the number of individual members of the Stock Exchange and there was also a wave of consolidation in the broking and market-making industry. On 27 October 1986, the Big Bang changes put London on tracks for a dramatic change, since brokers were able to compete on price rather than being abide by the fixed commissions.[1644] This small change in the regulatory framework had a profound impact on the market and far reaching effects, since it was the end of separation between brokers and jobbers, accompanied by a new trading platform and lifting of the rules that imposed the exclusion of foreign companies from the exchange.[1645] Despite the imminent success of the reforms, Schenk is of the view that the reforms

---

[1643] See in C. Schenk, 'Regulatory foundations of financialization: May Day, Big Bang and international banking, 1975–1990' (2020) 27(3) *Financial History Review*, p. 9. Since the 19th century, London has been the traditionally international equity market of the world, in terms of company listings. New York was mainly serving its large domestic market without enjoying the same reputation as London.

[1644] See in C. Schenk, 'Regulatory foundations of financialization: May Day, Big Bang and international banking, 1975–1990' (2020) 27(3) *Financial History Review*, p. 13.

[1645] Ibid.

were not as dramatic as many believed, an adaptation to longer-term forces than an immediate, shocking bang.[1646] With the abolition of fixed commissions, the separation between brokers and jobbers seemed at least not viable and a rush of mergers and acquisitions among the LSE members was perceived as a physical reaction of the markets, since there was a need of fresh capital and many non-members were preparing themselves for entering that market, after much anticipated lowering of entry requirements.[1647] Without doubt, the Big Bang reforms paved the way for conglomeration as it was one, among other reasons of course,[1648] for this trend. Conglomeration posed severe challenges for the supervisors since the institutions blurred the lines between the financial services and used the cross-border element to offer their services as much closer to their customers as they could. Supervisors, mostly used to operate on a local basis, found themselves in a highly competitive cross border environment, with mergers and acquisitions happening at a speed of light, forcing the adoption of the Basel Accords to mitigate the rising risks.[1649] Ultimately, the reforms helped the digitalisation of the trading IT systems by forcing banks to build their own dealing floors and requiring new premises for their expansion, reviving certain areas of London.[1650]

The big bang reforms undoubtedly had a positive impact but not the one many believe. The number of guilt market makers increased (from 3 to 27) and as a result the equity turnover increased sharply; average commissions fell for large trades (from £100,000 or more) while at the same time the price for small trades increased, leading to an indirect subsidisation of institutional investors from the individual ones; the number of individual shareholders increased but at the same time they possessed a declining proportion of the total shares; finally, the LSE membership increased resulting in a bigger market share but it was also subject to greater regulation through the 1986 Financial Services Act.[1651] We must see the Big Bang reforms must be seen as an example of self-regulation accompanied by tighten regulatory oversight and supervision and ultimately London did not close the gap with New York, despite an early

---

1646 Ibid., p. 14.

1647 Ibid., p. 18.

1648 Ibid., p. 19. In the 1980s, the trend towards further conglomeration was fortified by many other opportunities, such as the large corporate IPOs, privatizations wave that appeared across Europe, interest rate volatility and the surge in bond market. All these parameters forced financial intermediaries to combine their expertise to respond to an increased demand of investment banking services. Also, we must take into consideration the impact from the European Commission's White Paper on the completion of the internal market, which further signalled the down of new world and financial institutions had to be well positioned in advance.

1649 See in C. Schenk, 'Regulatory foundations of financialization: May Day, Big Bang and international banking, 1975–1990' (2020) 27(3) *Financial History Review*, p. 22.

1650 Ibid.

1651 Ibid., p. 23.

increase in turnover that could be sustained.[1652] The bottom line of Schenk's analysis is that London, despite the deregulatory effort, ended up with a stronger flavour of investment banking, since it was slowly turned into a market based financial system, where capital markets play a more important role than the more traditional bank lending function.[1653]

2.3. *The Creation of the UK Financial Services Authority (FSA)*

The creation of the Financial Services Authority (FSA), in 1998, was perhaps one of the most important events in the UK's financial history. Following the general trend at that time,[1654] the UK established a single financial regulator by merging into a new agency with all the previous regulators and supervisors of the financial industry. Although the debate around the benefits and drawbacks from adopting such a policy are well beyond the scope of the present book, for reasons of clarity and coherence we must briefly discuss this important policy decision. Furthermore, it reflected a general trend towards a more liberal financial services regime and a clear choice for lighter, but more effective regulation and supervision. It therefore had a profound effect on the way the financial and banking sectors in particular were regulated and supervised, since it contributed, to a certain extent, to the bank failures during the recent GFC.

On 1 May 1997, the Labor Party won the parliamentary elections for the first time since 1979. In the following days, the new Government moved fast to implement the new regime, opting for the single regulator model. On 6 May 1997, the then Chancellor of the Exchequer, Gordon Brown, announced that he was giving independence to the BoE regarding its monetary policy. A few days later, he announced that he was transferring the responsibility for banking regulation and supervision from the BoE to the 'Securities and Investment Board' (SIB)[1655] and further amendments to the regulatory framework introduced by

---

1652 Ibid.

1653 Ibid., p. 28.

1654 During that time, there was a global trend towards the unification of responsibility for the regulation and supervision of banking, capital markets and insurance sectors. Apart from the UK, many countries had adopted unified regulatory and supervisory agencies, with notable examples Japan, South Korea, and the Scandinavian countries the led the trend back in the late '80s and early '90s (Norway adopted the single regulator regime in 1986, Denmark in 1988 and Sweden in 1991). At the same time, at the EU level, the trend towards further integration was also evident and further propelled by the adoption of the Single European Act, in 1988. See in E. Ferran, 'Examining the United Kingdom's Experience in Adopting the Single Financial Regulator Model' (2003) 28 *Brooklyn Journal of International Law*, p. 257.

1655 The Securities and Investment Board (SIB) was a private company limited by guarantee and financed by a levy on the market participants. It set the overall regulatory framework but did not act itself as a direct regulator of most investment firms. See in E. Ferran, 'Examining the United Kingdom's Experience in Adopting the Single Financial Regulator Model' (2003) 28 *Brooklyn Journal of International Law*, p. 266.

the Financial Services Act of 1986.[1656] According to the Chancellor's official statement, the reform was necessary for three main reasons:[1657]

(1) The existing system was failing to deliver the standards of investor protection and supervision that the industry and the public had the right to expect,
(2) The two-tier system, created under the 1986 legislation was inefficient, confusing, and lacked accountability and a clear allocation of responsibilities, and
(3) There was a need for a regulatory structure that would better reflect the blurred nature of financial markets that offered products and services combining banking, insurance, and capital markets

For the new policy to run, the first step was the renaming of the SIB into 'Financial Services Authority' (FSA), on 28 October 1997. After that date, most of the existing regulatory agencies were absorbed by the FSA structure on an 'informal and ad hoc basis'.[1658] The new agency, FSA, had become the de facto single regulator of the financial system, becoming fully operational on 1 December 2001, after the relevant legislation, the 'Financial Services and Markets Act 2000' (FSMA) received its Royal Assent in June 2000. Until the end of that transitional period, FSA's powers were derived from the previous regime and old legislation. Banking regulation was a notable exception because the 1998 'Bank of England Act' officially transferred supervisory responsibility from the BoE to the FSA, without any significant changes to the framework. However, the FSMA contained only the general framework of the new regime, leaving the various details to be determined by the secondary legislation (Treasury and FSA's rules).[1659] FSA had its policy delineated by its four statutory objectives:[1660]

(1) Market confidence,
(2) Public awareness,
(3) Consumer protection, and
(4) Reduction of financial crime

1656 See in E. Ferran, 'Examining the United Kingdom's Experience in Adopting the Single Financial Regulator Model' (2003) 28 *Brooklyn Journal of International Law*, p. 270.

1657 Ibid., p. 271. See also in J. Silvia, 'Efficiency and Effectiveness in Securities Regulation: Comparative Analysis of the United States' Competitive Regulatory Structure and the United Kingdom's Single Regulator Model' (2008) 6 *DePaul Business & Commercial Law Journal*, p. 253.

1658 See in E. Ferran, 'Examining the United Kingdom's Experience in Adopting the Single Financial Regulator Model', (2003) 28 *Brooklyn Journal of International Law*, p. 273.

1659 Ibid., p. 275.

1660 See in J. Silvia, 'Efficiency and Effectiveness in Securities Regulation: Comparative Analysis of the United States' Competitive Regulatory Structure and the United Kingdom's Single Regulator Model' (2008) 6 *DePaul Business & Commercial Law Journal*, p. 254.

The above objectives inserted a hands-off approach, where the FSA operated under the belief that the firms who were committed to certain outcome-based principles were better positioned to decide by themselves how they were going to achieve these objectives.[1661]

The FSA was an 'integrated regulator' meaning that it regulated all financial institutions carrying on a wide range of investment businesses, including banking, dealing and managing financial instruments, and giving financial advice. It regulated both the manner in which they conduct their business and the robustness of their financial soundness. No person could engage in investment business without prior authorisation from the FSA, unless it was already authorised by another Member State in the European Economic Area (EEA), which it could benefit from the passporting provisions in the EU legislation.[1662] The FSA introduced a new style of regulation, primarily occupied by securing the ability of London to maintain its position as a financial mega hub, therefore supervision and regulation were oriented towards competition among the market participants so that the state could have a fruitful and well-functioning financial market. From the very beginning high-risk tolerance was unavoidable since greater risks are associated with greater returns, and the FSA was ready to assess only the risks that mattered most, implementing and accepting a 'non-zero failure regime'.[1663] The FSA was regulating through principles, with enforcement actions being the last resort, sacrificing certainty from legal rules for the sake of better competition and innovation. Unfortunately, the FSA did not manage to succeed in its role. Due to perceived regulatory failure of the banks during the global financial crisis of 2007–2009, the UK government decided to restructure financial regulation and supervision and decided to abolish the FSA. On 19 December 2012, the Financial Services Act 2012 received Royal Assent, abolishing the FSA with effect from 1 April 2013.[1664] Its responsibilities were split between two new agencies: the Financial Conduct Authority (FCA) and the Prudential Regulation Authority (PRA) within the BoE.

1661 Ibid.

1662 See in J. Black, 'Managing the Financial Crisis – the Constitutional Dimension, *LSE Working Papers*, 12/2010, London School of Economics, Law Department, December 2010, p. 6.

1663 See in J. Silvia, 'Efficiency and Effectiveness in Securities Regulation: Comparative Analysis of the United States' Competitive Regulatory Structure and the United Kingdom's Single Regulator Model' (2008) 6 *DePaul Business & Commercial Law Journal*, p. 254.

1664 Financial Services Act 2012, c 21 (UK).

3 THE 2007–2009 GLOBAL FINANCIAL CRISIS

Between September 2007 and February 2010, the UK Government had to adopt a series of extraordinary measures to face the imminent turmoil from the recent GFC. Within these months the UK Government:[1665]

- Nationalised in whole or in part, four banks,
- Arranged for the asset transfer of two building societies and two subsidiaries of Icelandic banks,
- Injected £37 billion into RBS and Lloyds Group through recapitalisations and in November 2009, further injected £39 billion in shares, mostly in RBS,
- Extended over £280 million in liquidity support,
- Created £200 billion of new money through 'quantitative easing' policy to support banks through UK gilts purchase,
- Agreed to guarantee up to £250 billion of banks' wholesale borrowing and to underwrite £281 billion of RBS's assets,
- Provided approximately £40 billion of loans and other types of funding to Bradford & Bingley and the Financial Services Compensation Scheme.

The UK Government was not alone in this public spending madness. Governments in the US and in the EU had similar tasks to contain the financial meltdown.[1666]

3.1. Bank Failures in the UK

3.1.1 The Case of Northern Rock

Northern Rock (NR) was a British bank based on the city of Newcastle upon Tyne, in the northeast UK. Originally established back in 1850s as a mutually owned building society, it demutualised and became the Northern Rock bank in 1997, when it floated in the stock exchange.[1667] In the period between 1997

[1665] See in J. Black, 'Managing the Financial Crisis – the Constitutional Dimension, *LSE Working Papers*, 12/2010, London School of Economics, Law Department, December 2010, p. 2.

[1666] According to Black, '[g]overnments in the US, the UK, and the rest of the EU were forced to inject US$ 4.89 trillion directly into banks and other financial institutions, equivalent to 6 percent GDP in each country / region and to issue guarantees on bank borrowing and bank assets which, if called upon, would equate to US$14 trillion gross: the equivalent of 50 percent of the GDP in each country/region'.

[1667] Northern Rock Building Society was formed in 1965 by the merger of two North East of England building societies: the *Northern Counties Permanent Building Society*, established in 1850, and the *Rock Building Society*, established in 1865. During the following 30 years, Northern Rock expanded through the acquisition of 53 smaller building societies and most notably the *North of England Building Society* in 1994. See in J. Black, 'Managing the Financial Crisis – the Constitutional Dimension, *LSE Working Papers*, 12/2010, London School of Economics, Law Department, December 2010, p. 2.

and 2007, NR grew at a very expansionary rate, almost 23% annually, and became the 5th largest mortgage bank by June 2007. This expansion was the result of an aggressive business strategy, particularly in the area of mortgage credit.[1668] According to the NR's business model, mortgages were offered at 'ultra-competitive rates' while also combining mortgage and personal lending up to the 125% of the total collateral value.[1669] As a result, traditional deposit funding was unable to catch up with such balance sheet growth and the cheap funding through wholesale markets used to close the funding gap and fund the bank's growth. NR issued and sold notes that gave their holder the right to the cash flows of the bank's loan portfolio while, at the same time, new loans were packaged and sold as asset backed securities (ABS).[1670]

NR exploited the loopholes in the regulatory framework, mostly regarding capital requirements, which started to degrade substantially, as early as of 1995. In 2005, the subordinated debt issued back in 2001 was recorded as equity, substantially dropping the level of leverage. Therefore, even though the official leverage ratio did not increase, 'narrowly defined leverage' skyrocketed to a factor beyond 90.[1671] On 13 September 2007, NR announced that needed assistance from the BoE. In the hearing of the bailout people started queuing in front of the NR's branches withdrawing their deposits, while the BoE announced emergency liquidity assistance to the bank. At first sight, it looked like a traditional bank run, where angry depositors were demanding their money, but reality was somehow different. The NR's collapse was the result of institutional investors' denial to rollover bank's short-term debts (credit lines) which became critical several weeks before 14 September 2007.[1672]

According to the Liikanen Report, the actual bank run took place in the wholesale market and not in the retail market, since the bank's funding model was based on short-term funding from wholesale markets, continuously rolled over when they became mature.[1673] In the case of NR, the key issue was the lack of trust among the banks participating in the interbank market, one of the most liquid markets that became completely illiquid, and the run of depositors occurred after the actual NR crisis events.[1674] The price of NR shares dropped from £12.50 in January 2007 to a low of £1 by year-end, leading to

1668 According to the Liikanen Report, the residential mortgage lending portfolio accounting for 90% of the outstanding loan portfolio and owning a market share of 40% of total UK gross mortgage lending in June 2007.

1669 See in High-Level Expert Group (HLEG), *Reforming the structure of the EU banking sector*, Brussels, 2 October 2012, p. 59.

1670 Ibid.

1671 Ibid.

1672 Ibid.

1673 Ibid.

1674 The retail deposits, despite the run on the bank by their owners, proved to be the most stable source of funding for Northern Rock throughout the entire liquidity crisis.

its nationalisation on 17 February 2008. The failure of NR therefore was not a default by its borrowers nor a run by its depositors but a run by its creditors.[1675] The Liikanen Report highlighted several key lessons that could be learned by the NR case:

(i) Banks balance sheets should be assessed as a whole and not merely by looking at individual parts which might be judged as prudent and at the same time the entire financial system should also be examined as a whole and not simply looking at its specific parts,[1676]

(ii) Modern banking crises may not be well explained and understood by using textbook retail deposit bank runs due to coordination failures as their main explanation,[1677]

(iii) Modern banking should be viewed together with capital markets and macro (economic) events that can have implications for banks,[1678]

(iv) NR was a bank that failed after a period of extremely rapid growth of activities, excessive reliance on short term funding sources and high leverage, three characteristics that are problematic according to the relevant literature.[1679]

3.1.2 The Case of the Royal Bank of Scotland

After the NR collapse, the turmoil spread across the UK and the next victim was the Royal Bank of Scotland (RBS). In October 2008, RBS in effect failed and was partially nationalised by the UK Government, since it was running with public support, both for liquidity and solvency assistance. Since 7 October 2008, RBS relied on the emergency liquidity assistance provided by the BoE to fund its business and since 13 October 2008, the UK Government announced that it would provide up to £20 billion of fresh equity to recapitalise the bank and restore its capital to the minimum levels.[1680] This amount was further increased to £25.5 billion thereby imposing a heavy burden to the taxpayers.[1681] The bank's capital position was far weaker than its published regulatory capital and its ability to absorb losses. This problem reflected the problematic regulatory definition of capital and a business model to operate with much less

[1675] See in High-Level Expert Group (HLEG), *Reforming the structure of the EU banking sector*, Brussels, 2 October 2012, p. 59.

[1676] Ibid.

[1677] Ibid.

[1678] Ibid.

[1679] Ibid., p. 60.

[1680] See in Financial Services Authority, *The failure of the Royal Bank of Scotland*, Financial Services Authority Board Report, December 2011, p. 40. The capital increase comprising a £15bn rights issue and a £5bn issue of preference shares but only 0.24% of the rights issue was subscribed by private investors. The rest entailed an injection of public funds.

[1681] See in High-Level Expert Group (HLEG), *Reforming the structure of the EU banking sector*, Brussels, 2 October 2012, p. 61.

capital than its peers did.[1682] Any measures adopted by the relevant authorities proved to be both ineffective and delayed.[1683] The FSA prepared a special report investigating the reasons for the RBS's collapse and according to that report, RBS's demise could be attributed to six main reasons:[1684]

(i) significant weaknesses in RBS's capital position during the Review Period, because of management decisions and permitted by an inadequate regulatory capital framework,
(ii) over-reliance on risky short-term wholesale funding,
(iii) concerns and uncertainties about RBS's underlying asset quality, which in turn was subject to little fundamental analysis by the FSA,
(iv) substantial losses occurred in credit trading activities, which eroded market confidence in the bank. Both RBS's strategy and the FSA's supervisory approach underestimated how bad losses associated with structured credit might be,
(v) the ABN AMRO acquisition, on which RBS proceeded without appropriate heed to the risks involved and with inadequate due diligence, and
(vi) an overall systemic crisis in which the banks in worse relative positions were extremely vulnerable to failure. RBS was one of these banks.

The FSA report further acknowledges that 'although poor capital and liquidity regulation made it more likely that there would be a systemic crisis and thus set the context for the failure, and while a flawed supervisory approach provided insufficient challenge, ultimate responsibility for poor decisions must lie with the firm. The multiple poor decisions that RBS made suggest, moreover, that there are likely to have been underlying deficiencies in RBS management, governance and culture which made it prone to make poor decisions'.[1685] Therefore, these underlying deficiencies in the RBS's management system could be viewed as a seventh reason of failure. The Liikanen Report is of the view that the immediate driver of RBS failure was not the inadequate capital but the unwillingness of wholesale market participants, driven by potential insolvency concerns, to refund the short-term debt that RBS had issued, and, but to a lesser extent, the retail depositors that were drawing their money. This liquidity run forced RBS to demand the ELA from the BoE, to cover the short-term funding gap, which was one of the biggest among its peers.[1686]

1682 According to the Liikanen Report, by the end of 2007, RBS had a CET1 ratio of just 2%. This amount was inadequate to absorb the global financial turmoil that erupted in 2008 autumn.

1683 According to the Liikanen Report, the FSA pushed RBS to raise capital from the markets in April 2008 but the amount of £12 billion that was issued back then turned out to be inefficient for the upcoming storm.

1684 See in Financial Services Authority, *The failure of the Royal Bank of Scotland*, Financial Services Authority Board Report, December 2011, p. 22.

1685 Ibid.

1686 See in High-Level Expert Group (HLEG), *Reforming the structure of the EU banking sector*, Brussels, 2 October 2012, p. 62.

RBS pursued a rapid expansion of its balance sheet together with its leverage, and its investment banking unit was the most rapidly expanding among the banks' units. At the same time, RBS also expanded fast its loan portfolio and this expansion led to heavy losses, particularly in the commercial lending division.[1687] Moreover, RBS had accumulated significant exposures containing credit risk in its trading portfolio, following its business decision to expand rapidly in the structured finance business, and the notorious acquisition of ABN AMRO bank further exposed RBS into this business exactly when it started to become less attractive for the rest participants.[1688] The ABN AMRO acquisition per se, was a major problem for RBS, which was the leader of the buying consortium. The acquisition was financed primarily with short-term debt instead of equity and eroded the bank's capital adequacy, increasing RBS's reliance on short-term debt market (overnight and unsecured funding) exponentially. Furthermore, ABN AMRO had a large portfolio of structured financial products, which suffered huge losses, all of which was assumed by the RBS, exposing her to further losses since the due diligence had proven extremely inadequate for such a large acquisition, both in scope and in depth.[1689] Therefore the overall bid was inappropriate and overvalued the target company's true value further exposing RBS's flawed management structure.

All the reports that analysed RBS's failure pointed out that it was a lethal combination of systemic failures and internal management processes that allowed the bank to exploit the various loopholes in the regulatory framework and act under bad supervision. In addition, the failure of the internal management system played an important role since it did not prevent the firm from engaging in risky activities and assuming risks without proper understanding of their destructive power. The overall function of the internal management system and the firm's corporate governance failed to prevent these actions and risky business models since it seemed not to be anyone capable of making sound business decisions.[1690]

3.1.3 The Case of HBOS and Lloyds TSB

The Halifax Bank of Scotland (HBOS) was created in 2001 resulting from the merger between Halifax plc and the Bank of Scotland, aiming at the creation of a 'fifth force' behind the established 'Big Four' in the UK's banking sector,

---

1687 Ibid. According to the Liikanen Report, during 2007-2010 period, losses from commercial lending reached a total of £32 billion when at the same time losses from the credit trading activities topped at £17.7 billion.

1688 See in High-Level Expert Group (HLEG), *Reforming the structure of the EU banking sector*, Brussels, 2 October 2012, p. 62.

1689 Ibid.

1690 Ibid.

as it would create a company of comparable size and stature.[1691] After the merger between Bank of Scotland and Halifax, HBOS became the UK's largest mortgage lender with around 20% market share, a strong presence in the insurance and investment business market, but it had minimal presence in wholesale treasury markets and international operations.[1692] HBOS adopted an aggressive post-merger strategy based on rapid growth and was a continuation of the two, pre-merger, entities' ambitions. By 2006, HBOS' profit had grown to almost £6 billion and reached a return on equity of 21%, with growth in international markets continuing and even accelerating in 2007. The bank was very active in some of the riskiest areas of the banking business: large real estate deals, lending to leverage buyouts, and speculative mortgage lending. In the real estate sector was particularly active since this sector was perceived as its natural centre of expertise and competence.[1693] At the same time, HBOS was also active in the US mortgage-backed securities market with an increasing investment in assets. In March 2008, HBOS shares fell 17% amid rumours that it had asked the BoE for emergency funding[1694] and on 17 September 2008, just after the demise of Lehman Brothers, its share price suffered again wild fluctuations, between 88p and 220p per share, despite FSA's assurances as to its liquidity and exposure to the wider credit crunch.

Following the liquidity crisis, the UK Government took a 43.4% stake in Lloyds TSB.[1695] On 8 October 2008, the UK government announced that it was making available new capital to UK banks, to assist them survive the global turmoil. On 13 October 2008, it indicated that it was making capital investments in RBS, and upon successful merger, HBOS, and Lloyds TSB, totalling £37 billion. In 2008, Lloyds TSB made a profit of £845 million, while in the same period HBOS recorded a loss of £7.4 billion. The total assets of Lloyds TSB and of HBOS at the end of 2008 amounted to £436 billion and to £690 billion respectively. Amid the turmoil and to prevent another bank failure, in September 2008, the UK government orchestrated a merger between HBOS and Lloyds TSB to prevent HBOS from failing and to create the biggest retail banking provider in the UK. The deal was made under pressure from the government, and the resulting entity became Lloyds Banking Group

---

1691 Halifax had been demutualized and floated four years prior to the 2001 merger. Although officially HBOS was not an acronym of any specific words, it is widely presumed to stand for 'Halifax Bank of Scotland'.

1692 See in A. Docherty and F. Viort, *Better Banking, Understanding and Addressing the Failures in Risk Management, Governance and Regulation*, Wiley Finance Series, Chicester, Wiley, 2014, p. 184.

1693 Ibid., p. 185.

1694 Source: The Guardian, available at: https://www.theguardian.com/business/2008/mar/20/creditcrunch.hbosbusiness.

1695 The European Commission ruled that LBG must sell a portion of its business by November 2013, as it categorised the stake purchase as state aid.

(LBG) in January 2009. Lloyds TSB announced the acquisition of HBOS on 18 September 2008. On 19 November 2008 (Lloyds TSB) and on 12 December 2008 (HBOS) the banks' shareholders approved the transaction, which formally took place in January 2009. On 19 January 2009, LBG received a £17 billion State recapitalisation split into £4 billion of preference shares and £13 billion of ordinary shares. After the finalisation of the deal, LBG has adopted additional measures since the acquisition of HBOS to reduce the risk of the business, with:

- the replacement of the senior management responsible for the collapse of HBOS: No ex-HBOS executives were accepted on the new LBG Board,
- extension of Lloyds TSB's prudent risk management philosophy, governance, and infrastructure across LBG,
- LBG's risk assets have passed an external review by PwC and
- Significant impairments have already been provisioned

For several years after the completion of the merger deal, the authorities were still grappling with the firm's losses and the findings of Parliamentary subcommittee's review was that the firm had adopted a 'flawed strategy, inappropriate culture and inadequate controls'.[1696]

3.1.4 The Case of UK's 'Icelandic banks'

Icelandic banks had built a strong presence in the UK. Their presence was focused on the retail market with significant deposit funded business mostly because of their higher interest rates.[1697] In the UK, back at that time, two Icelandic banks were operating: a) Kaupthing Singer & Friedlander, a UK-based banking subsidiary of Kaupthing Bank and b) Heritable, a UK subsidiary of Landsbanki Islands hf., a public limited bank company incorporated under the law of Iceland. Landsbanki operated also an internet-based deposit acceptance scheme under the brand name 'Icesave'. On 7–8 October 2008, the FSA founded the two Icelandic subsidiaries that no longer met the conditions for authorisation and were transferred to ING Direct, a wholly owned subsidiary of ING Group. The remainder of the two businesses were put into administration. Finally, the BoE agreed to provide a loan to the Financial Services Compensation Scheme, to compensate deposit holders in both the Icelandic subsidiaries and to Icesave. One of the most important parameters of the Icelandic banks issue, was that UK local authorities had over £900 million deposited in the failed Icelandic banks, of which £24.6 million belonged to fire and police authorities.[1698]

1696 See in A. Docherty and F. Viort, *Better Banking, Understanding and Addressing the Failures in Risk Management, Governance and Regulation*, Wiley Finance Series, Chichester, Wiley, 2014, p. 188.

1697 See in J. Black, 'Managing the Financial Crisis – the Constitutional Dimension, *LSE Working Papers*, 12/2010, London School of Economics, Law Department, December 2010, p. 35.

1698 Ibid., p. 9.

The UK Government decided to freeze the assets of Landsbanki in the UK, on 8 October 2008,[1699] following the freezing of its assets under the Icelandic government, since Landsbanki was placed into receivership in Iceland. The UK government based its decision on the provisions of the Anti-Terrorism Crime and Security Act of 2001, because the Treasury believed that 'actions to the detriment of the UK's economy had been or was likely to be taken by certain persons who are the government or resident of a country of territory outside the UK'.[1700] The decision for the freezing of the UK funds of Landsbanki was deemed necessary because 'the emergency legislation passed in Iceland on 7 October 2008 meant that UK creditors' rights could be prejudiced compared with other creditors. The Icelandic government had been unable to clarify the position of UK creditors in the administration process of Landsbanki and there was therefore a threat to UK economic interests. Landsbanki, through its UK branch and the Icesave deposit line has built up a substantial level of UK retail and wholesale depositors. The Icelandic action was likely to have a particularly significant unsettling effect on consumer confidence at a time of unprecedented disturbance of the financial sector.'[1701] On 9 October 2008, the HM Treasury issued a general license under the Landsbanki Freezing Order 2008 exempting certain activities from the prohibitions in Article 4 of the Order to avoid any detriment to third parties. The general license specified that a) payments must not be made to the Bank other than to the London Branch and b) that the London Branch is not to transfer funds to other parts of the Bank or to entities which form part of the same group of companies as the Bank. The blame game that followed the asset freeze between the governments of Iceland, UK and the Netherlands led to a referendum in Iceland, held on 6 March 2010 that ultimately rejected the proposed terms of the deal that was reached earlier between the countries. UK claimed €3.9 billion in compensation plus an interest of 5%.[1702] The events around the Icelandic banks issue demonstrated the problems of cooperation across regulators and supervisors in a fully interconnected financial system. The home-host supervisory approach had failed, and major losses occurred among the depositors who were not adequately protected by their respective jurisdictions.

1699 As required by the enabling Act, the Order was approved by both Houses of Parliament on 28 October 2008, which was 20 days after the Order had come into force.

1700 See in J. Black, 'Managing the Financial Crisis – the Constitutional Dimension, *LSE Working Papers*, 12/2010, London School of Economics, Law Department, December 2010, p. 36.

1701 Statutory Instrument 2008/2668: voluntary memorandum from HM Treasury, Landsbanki Freezing Order 2008 (S.I. 2008/2668), available at: https://publications.parliament.uk/pa/jt200708/jtselect/jtstatin/182/18210.htm.

1702 Although this might seem a relatively small number, back then was equivalent to almost 50 percent of Iceland's GDP.

4 THE POST CRISIS REFORMS IN THE UK FINANCIAL SECTOR

'Why did no one see this coming?', asked Queen Elisabeth on a visit to the prestigious London School of Economics, in November 2008, amid the crisis environment and the global turmoil produced by the failure of Lehman Brothers. The question, although rhetorical in meaning, needed a clear answer because it expressed the feeling of many people across UK. The Government decided to provide a clear response and took certain measures, the most important of which was the proposal to narrow the banking services and impose structural regulations, like the GSA in the US.

4.1. The Independent Commission on Banking (ICB)

UK's government established, in June 2010, the 'Independent Commission on Banking' (ICB), a government inquiry, with the task to consider structural and related non-structural reforms to the UK's banking sector to promote financial stability and competition. The ICB was comprised of five commissioners. The chairman was Sir John Vickers, and the other four commissioners were Clare Spottiswood, Bill Winters, Martin Taylor, and Martin Wolf. The commissioners were supported by a Secretariat of fourteen officials seconded by HM Treasury, the Department for Business, Innovation and Skills, the FSA, the BoE, and the Office of Fair Trading. The secretariat was headed by Sam Woods, and it delivered its final report and recommendations on 12 September 2011.

The most important aspect of the ICB's proposals is the ring-fencing of the retail deposit-taking services obligation but it's not the only proposal. These also included additional loss absorbency requirements for the banking sector generally, and discrete measures intended to improve competition in the retail banking market. The ICB's recommendations aim to:[1703]

(1) Reduce the probability and impact of systemic financial crises in the future,
(2) Maintain the efficient flow of credit to the real economy and the ability of households and businesses to manage their risks and financial needs over time, and
(3) Preserve the functioning of the payments system and guarantee capital certainty and liquidity for small savers including small and medium sized enterprises (SMEs).

[1703] See in Independent Commission on Banking (ICB), *Final Report – Recommendations*, September 2011, p. 20.

According to the final report, the above aims could be achieved by applying certain principles, within the context of a broader regulatory reform agenda applied both at a domestic and international level, by:[1704]

(1) curbing the incentives for excessive risk taking by neutralising subsidies and the unpriced risk of triggering financial crises, and by enabling the market to function more effectively,
(2) reducing the costs of systemic financial crises through increased resilience of institutions and the financial system as a whole, and through improved resolvability of institutions,
(3) promoting effective competition in the provision of banking services in the UK,
(4) having regard to any impact on GDP through the cycle, any fiscal implications, and the competitiveness of the UK financial and professional services sectors and the wider UK economy, and
(5) having regard to the possible impact of recommendations on non-bank parts of the financial system, and to the effects of wider regulatory reforms in the financial sector.

The ICB held numerous meetings and consultations, especially with all the relevant stakeholders. It produced an intermediate report for further consultation and prepared its final report, that contains the ring-fencing proposal. Although ring-fencing is not the only proposal of the final report, it is by far the most important since it created enormous implications for the banking sector. Therefore, the present book will delve into the ring-fencing measures and will only briefly present the rest of the proposals when will deem to be necessary.

4.1.1 The 'Retail Ring-Fencing' Proposal

The third chapter of the ICB's final report is dedicated to the ring-fencing recommendation. According to the ICB's wording: 'The purpose of the retail ring-fence is to isolate those banking activities where continuous provision of service is vital to the economy and to a bank's customers in order to ensure, first, that this provision is not threatened as a result of activities which are incidental to it and, second, that such provision can be maintained in the event of the bank's failure without government solvency support. A retail ring-fence should be designed to achieve the following objectives at the lowest possible cost to the economy:

- make it easier to sort out both ring-fenced banks and non-ring-fenced banks which get into trouble, without the provision of taxpayer-funded solvency support,

[1704] Ibid.

- insulate vital banking services on which households and SMEs depend from problems elsewhere in the financial system, and
- curtail government guarantees, reducing the risk to the public finances and making it less likely that banks will run excessive risks in the first place.'[1705]

This solution comes with the benefits of ultimately creating banks of simpler structure that could be easier to manage, monitor and regulate. Furthermore, the macro-prudential regulation would apply more 'precisely targeted' to the ring-fenced banks than to the existing structures.[1706] When designing the ring-fencing regime, the ICB specifically found that two key areas need to be considered:

(a) the 'location' of the fence, and
(b) the 'height' of the fence.[1707]

The location answers the question of which activities must or could take place within ring-fenced banks and which must or could take place within wholesale/investment banks or other financial institutions.[1708] The height of the fence answers the question which will be the degree of separation between ring-fenced banks and wholesale/investment banks within the same corporate group.[1709]

4.1.1.1 *The 'Location' of the Fence*

The ICB adopted the below three principles to specify the exact location of the fence:

(i) the services which should only take place within the ring-fenced entity, the so called 'mandated services',
(ii) the services which should not take place within the ring-fenced entity, the so called 'prohibited services', and lastly
(iii) the activities that are ancillary to the provision of the non-prohibited services, the so called 'ancillary activities'.

4.1.1.1.1 *The Principle of Mandated Services*

The ICB studied and considered the services that are of particular importance for the economy because a temporary suspension of these services, for resolution purposes, would create a serious disruption to the efficient performance of the broader economy and of the financial system as a whole. According to the ICB report, this occurs when the interruption of the service would come at a high economic cost and the affected customers do not have an alternative option

1705 Ibid., p. 35.
1706 Ibid.
1707 Ibid., p. 36.
1708 Ibid.
1709 Ibid.

available from another service provider. With these characteristics attached to the service, the governments feel obliged to step in and ensure that the service will continue to be provided even if the provider eventually fails. The ICB identified that in the banking sector, the customers that will suffer the most from the interruption of such a service, are those that are depended on such service to fulfil their day-to-day needs for money and concluded that the key services are deposits and overdraft facilities.[1710] The ICB further identified that the customers who largely do not have an alternative service provider and cannot reasonably be expected to plan for a service interruption event are individuals and the SMEs. The first principle, therefore, is the mandated services and according to the wording of the ICB final report:

> 'Only ring-fenced banks should be granted permission by the UK regulator to provide mandated services. Mandated services should be those banking services where: a) even a temporary interruption to the provision of service resulting from the failure of a bank has significant economic costs; and b) customers are not well equipped to plan for such an interruption. Mandated services currently comprise the taking of deposits from, and the provision of overdrafts to, individuals and small and medium-sized organisations.'[1711]

The first principle also described the scope of the ring-fencing regime. The ICB's report proposed that the requirement to comply with the ring-fencing regime should apply to anyone who wished to carry on a banking business, as a distinct legal entity, under the required permission from the UK regulator.[1712] The scope of the proposal would therefore include a) any standalone UK bank, b) any UK bank that was a subsidiary of a wider banking group having its headquarters in the UK and c) any UK bank that is a subsidiary of a wider banking group with its headquarters overseas.[1713] Moreover, the mandated services could also be provided in the UK from a foreign bank's branch.[1714] Finally, no other organisation could be allowed to provide mandated services in the UK and the foreign subsidiaries of UK headquartered banking groups would be exempted from the ring-fencing requirements, unless they were subsidiaries of a ring-fenced bank.[1715]

1710 Ibid., p. 37.

1711 Ibid., p. 38.

1712 Ibid., p. 39.

1713 Ibid.

1714 According to the ICB's report, any significant bank, based outside the European Economic Area (EEA), wishing to carry out mandated services in the UK, would be generally required to establish a UK subsidiary. See in Independent Commission on Banking (ICB), *Final Report – Recommendations*, September 2011, p. 39.

1715 Ibid.

Furthermore, the ICB examined the possibility of applying a de minimis rule, for banks having a balance sheet below certain threshold and took the view that such a rule was not based on a persuasive reasoning and therefore circumventing the ring-fencing rules was ultimately rejected,[1716] because:

- small and complex banks could still create major resolution challenges and impediments,
- exemption could create consumer confusion regarding the applicable regime to each bank,
- the risk of contagion from financial markets to the retail banking business would remain if a de minimis rule was in place for a large number of smaller banks that would operate below that level, and
- any such exemption below a certain size would disincentivise the universal banks to grow above de minimis level, distorting competition among the banks.

Finally, the ICB considered the idea of restricting mandated services by accepting only insured deposits, thereby leaving the option for both SMEs and individuals, to place their uninsured deposits outside the ring-fenced banks. This option would allow for an important proportion of services, where continuity was a necessity, to migrate outside the ring-fenced perimeter and therefore was also rejected.[1717]

4.1.1.1.2 *The Principle of Prohibited Services*

Having defined the mandated services and their perimeter, the ICB posed the question of which services should not be offered by a ring-fenced entity. Answering this question involved striking a balance between the costs associated with losing synergies and the benefits of improving financial stability through the separation regime.[1718] The debate was focused around three major questions:

(a) Should credit provision to individuals and SMEs be prohibited?
(b) Should wholesale and investment banking activities be prohibited?
(c) Should the provision of any commercial banking services to large companies and other organisations be permitted in ring-fenced banks? If so, which ones?

The first question, regarding credit provision to individuals and SMEs, actually brought up the idea of 'narrow banking' and of 'limited purpose banking'.[1719] Regarding narrow banking the ICB acknowledged the high economic costs associated with it and that the credit supply could not be stable

---

1716 Ibid.
1717 Ibid.
1718 Ibid., p. 41.
1719 Ibid., p. 44.

during times of distress. Simultaneously, limited purpose banking was equally rejected on the ground that some risk was tolerable to the bank intermediation role while at the same time relevant authorities were able to secure the credit supply without taxpayers' money.[1720] The narrow banking ideas added to the debate two important parameters that were considered by the ICB:

- Services that were not perceived as integral to the direct intermediation of funds or the provision of payments services should not be provided by the ring-fenced entities, because they would introduce unnecessary risk and complexity in the resolution procedure, thus increasing the bailout possibility,[1721] and
- In order to minimise the costs of the structural reform, it was important not to unnecessary restrict, without any available flexibility, both sides of a bank's balance sheet so to avoid the creation of inefficient mismatch of assets and liabilities.[1722]

Regarding the second question, the ICB took a different view, highlighting the differences between the US Volcker Rule and the ring-fencing regime proposed hereby. The main point was that the scope of ring-fencing measures would not be effectively supported by Volcker Rule-style prohibitions, because:[1723]

(i) Many other wholesale/investment banking activities make it harder for the competent authority to maintain the continuous provision of service without the need for taxpayer money,
(ii) In order to reduce the high degree of interconnection between the ring-fenced bank and the financial system the complete separation of trading activities was inevitable, since these activities, according to the ICB, were giving rise to market and counterparty credit risks,
(iii) The successful existence of banks that effectively conduct their intermediation role in the real economy, without at the same time participating in investment banking/wholesale banking operations, supports the argument that ring-fenced banks are viable, and
(iv) The crucial activities of monitoring, management and supervision of ring-fenced banks would be enhanced and guaranteed by removing from their business lines investment banking/wholesale banking operations.

Finally, regarding the third question, the ICB considered the need to provide services to large companies, a topic of great importance since the deposits from these entities are always a great source of liquidity and can also offer a higher degree of loss absorbing capacity. Moreover, the credit provision to these entities is accompanied by risks that the ring-fencing regime tries to

1720 Ibid., p. 45.
1721 Ibid.
1722 Ibid.
1723 Ibid.

mitigate and protect the banks from. Therefore, some restrictions were deemed necessary. The second principle is thus the prohibited services and according to the wording of the ICB's Report:

> 'Prohibited services. Ring-fenced banks should be prohibited from providing certain services. Prohibited services should be those banking services which meet any of the following criteria:
>
> a) make it significantly harder and/or more costly to resolve the ring-fenced bank;
>
> b) directly increase the exposure of the ring-fenced bank to global financial markets;
>
> c) involve the ring-fenced bank taking risk and are not integral to the provision of payments services to customers, or the direct intermediation of funds between savers and borrowers within the non-financial sector; or
>
> d) in any other way threaten the objectives of the ring-fence.
>
> As a result, prohibited services should include (though need not be limited to):
>
> a) any service which is not provided to customers within the EEA;
>
> b) any service which results in an exposure to a non-ring-fenced bank or a non-bank financial organisation, except those associated with the provision of payments services where the regulator has deemed this appropriate;
>
> c) any service which would result in a trading book asset;
>
> d) any service which would result in a requirement to hold regulatory capital against market risk;
>
> e) the purchase or origination of derivatives or other contracts which would result in a requirement to hold regulatory capital against counterparty credit risk; and
>
> f) services relating to secondary markets activity including the purchase of loans or securities.'[1724]

That principle would mean that the majority of retail and commercial activities of UK banks could be placed inside the ring-fenced entity, while the investment/wholesale banking activities would be excluded. Moreover, the above principle would be used as a compass by the competent authorities to define whether an activity should be placed inside or outside the ring-fenced entity. The ICB provides the authority with important room for manoeuvre since it requires to implement the second principle with the aim to protect the objectives of the ring-fencing and not with strict application of definitions in mind.[1725]

1724 Ibid., p. 51.
1725 Ibid., p. 53.

4.1.1.1.3 *The Principle of Ancillary Services*

The ICB then acknowledged that there are several activities which ring-fenced banks would need to do to deliver effectively those services that they would be permitted to provide. In particular, they would have to be able to manage their balance sheet against the variety of risks that arise during their business (risk management), manage their liquidity and raise funding. In banks, these needs are typically achieved through the 'treasury function'. Therefore, the third principle of ring-fencing would be the provision of ancillary services and according to the ICB report's wording:

> 'Ancillary activities. The only activities which a ring-fenced bank should be permitted to engage in are: the provision of services which are not prohibited; and those ancillary activities necessary for the efficient provision of such services. Ancillary activities should be permitted only to the extent they are required for this provision, and not as standalone lines of business.
>
> Ancillary activities would include, for example, employing staff and owning or procuring the necessary operational infrastructure. In particular, a ring-fenced bank should be permitted to conduct financial activities beyond the provision of non-prohibited services to the extent that these are strictly required for the purposes of its treasury function – i.e. for risk management, liquidity management, or in order to raise funding for the provision of non-prohibited services. In conducting ancillary activities, a ring-fenced bank may transact with and become exposed to non-ring-fenced banks and non-bank financial organisations.
>
> Backstop limits should be placed on the proportion of a ring-fenced bank's funding which is permitted to be wholesale funding and on its total exposures, secured and unsecured, to non-ring-fenced banks and other non-bank financial companies.'[1726]

What must be highlighted about these types of services is that the ancillary services, as defined above, shall only be allowed to complement the mandated services and not to be performed as standalone business from the ring-fenced banks.[1727]

4.1.1.2 *The 'Height' of the Fence*

The above-referred principles had to do with the location of the ring-fencing regime and which activities shall be included within or excluded from the ring-fenced bank. The second most important parameter of the ring-fencing solution is the height of the fence. The height of the ring-fence concerns the extent to which ring-fenced banks could be linked to other kinds of entities within any wider corporate group to which they belong, therefore their intragroup

[1726] Ibid., p. 62.
[1727] Ibid.

relations. Again, the Commission defined three important questions on this topic:

(a) Should a ring-fenced bank be allowed to be in the same corporate group as other companies, including those conducting prohibited activities, at all?
(b) If so, what legal and operational links should be permitted between a ring-fenced bank and its wider corporate group? and
(c) What economic links should be permitted between a ring-fenced bank and its wider corporate group?

Trying to answer the above questions, the ICB examined in depth the benefits that would arise from a complete separation regime that would also prohibit common ownership among the entities of a banking group. Therefore, the ring-fencing model seemed to be better positioned to fit within the EU legal framework, which according to the ICB's report would be difficult to accept restrictions on corporate control (banking groups' control). The ICB took the view that the ring-fenced entities shall be separate and standalone legal entities, in the sense that since it would be difficult to constantly monitor the various economic and operational links that are developed during normal operations. The regulators would face important impediments when they would try to impose constraints on the banking entities, because of exactly these various links.[1728] As a result, the ICB proposed the fourth ring-fencing principle, the legal and operational links and how these links could be structured within the banking groups. Therefore, according to ICB's report wording:

> 'Legal and operational links. Where a ring-fenced bank is part of a wider corporate group, the authorities should have confidence that they can isolate it from the rest of the group in a matter of days and continue the provision of its services without providing solvency support. As a result:
>
> a) ring-fenced banks should be separate legal entities – i.e. any UK regulated legal entity which offers mandated services should only also provide services which are not prohibited and conduct ancillary activities;
>
> b) any financial organisation owned or partly owned by a ring-fenced bank should conduct only activities permitted within a ring-fenced bank. This organisation's balance sheet should contain only assets and liabilities arising from these services and activities;
>
> c) the wider corporate group should be required to put in place arrangements to ensure that the ring-fenced bank has continuous access to all of the operations, staff, data and services required to continue its activities, irrespective of the financial health of the rest of the group; and

1728 Ibid., p. 66.

d) the ring-fenced bank should either be a direct member of all the payments systems that it uses or should use another ring-fenced bank as an agent.'[1729]

The above point (c) introduced the operational separability requirement to which the ring-fenced entity shall be complied. According to the ICB's report, a variety of models would apply to that requirement:

- All the relevant infrastructure could be supplied independently of the ring-fenced bank, either from a third party, or from the rest of the group, with appropriate service level agreements in place. These modalities would allow the ring-fenced entity to continue its operations even in the event of failure of other parts (entities) of the group.[1730]
- Another model would require the placement of the critical infrastructure needed for the ring-fenced bank to continue its operations to be put in a separate subsidiary, thereby insulating the operational capabilities of the group from any possible adverse event (failure) of any part of the group.[1731]
- Another model would require the ring-fenced bank to directly own the entire operational infrastructure leading to a complete ex ante operational separability. The main drawback of this approach would be the high costs associated with the maintenance and operation of duplicated systems and data warehouses, for the bank and the group.[1732]

Finally, the ICB concluded that the principle did not place additional restrictions on the sharing of information, expertise, and knowledge within the banking group. Particularly, information about individual customers would be shared so the ring-fenced bank could offer competitive products and exploit the synergies that arise. The 'one-stop shop' solution would be still available for the customers that require services from both the ring-fenced entity and the rest of the group, giving the option to sell products as an agent for the other group entities. The ICB took the view that similar arrangements, such as insurance products, were at place already so the experience existed and accepted.[1733] In reality, the ring-fenced entities belong to banking groups that are comprised of various entities across the globe, and as a result, their economic links are a crucial parameter of the project's success. Therefore, to be successful the structural reform, the economic links among the group members must be strictly controlled and regulated so that they will not jeopardise the stability of the ring-fenced entity. Considering these arguments, the ICB took the view that these intragroup links (economic relationships) must be regulated as the

1729 Ibid., p. 67.
1730 Ibid.
1731 Ibid.
1732 Ibid.
1733 Ibid., p. 68.

general third-party relationships.[1734] This approach was perceived as striking a balance and being a 'clear benchmark' to compare, contrast and judge the prices charged to the third parties for similar services. The ICB further understood that even though intragroup relationships give rise to risks that can be transmitted in the ring-fenced entity, a small level of risk was nonetheless tolerable and necessary to allow the bank to operate efficiently and exploit the synergies, while avoiding the migration of certain activities to less regulated sectors.[1735]

Ultimately, the fifth and final ring-fence principle had to do with the intragroup economic links and their limitation for the sake of the ring-fenced bank's stability. According to the report's wording:

> 'Economic links. Where a ring-fenced bank is part of a wider corporate group, its relationships with entities in that group should be conducted on a third-party basis and it should not be dependent for its solvency or liquidity on the continued financial health of the rest of the corporate group. This should be ensured through both regulation and sufficiently independent governance. Thus, where a ring-fenced bank is part of a wider corporate group:
>
> a) its relationships with any entities within the same group which are not ring-fenced banks should be treated for regulatory purposes no more favourably than third party relationships;
>
> b) all transactions (including secured lending and asset sales) with other parts of the group should be conducted on a commercial and arm's length basis in line with sound and appropriate risk management practices;
>
> c) where third party arm's length relationships are not ensured through the application of existing regulation, additional rules should be considered;
>
> d) assets should only be sold to and from the ring-fenced bank and other entities within the group at market value. The ring-fenced bank should not acquire any assets from other entities within the group unless such assets could have resulted from the provision of non-prohibited services;
>
> e) the ring-fenced bank should meet regulatory requirements, including those for capital, large exposures, liquidity and funding, on a solo basis;
>
> f) dividend payments and other capital transfers should only be made after the board of the ring-fenced bank is satisfied that the ring-fenced bank has sufficient financial resources to do so. In addition, any such payments which would cause the ring-fenced bank to breach any kind of capital requirement, including requirements to hold buffers above minimum requirements, should not be permitted without explicit regulatory approval;
>
> g) the board of the ring-fenced bank should be independent. The precise degree of independence appropriate would depend on the proportion of the banking group's assets outside the ring-fenced bank. Except in cases where the vast majority of the

[1734] Ibid., p. 70.

[1735] Ibid., p. 71.

group's assets were within the ring-fenced bank, the majority of directors should be independent non-executives of whom:
i. one is the Chair; and
ii. no more than one sits on the board of the parent or another part of the group;
h) a ring-fenced bank should make, on a solo basis, all disclosures which are required by the regulator of the wider corporate group and/or its other relevant substantial subsidiaries, and those which would be required if the ring-fenced bank were independently listed on the London Stock Exchange; and
i) the boards of the ring-fenced bank and of its parent company should have a duty to maintain the integrity of the ring-fence, and to ensure the ring-fence principles are followed at all times.'

The ICB's final report explicitly disconnected the ring-fencing principles from the ownership structure of the ring-fenced banks. Therefore, ring-fenced banks could be part of a broader banking group, usually under the 'holding company structure' or, alternatively, a ring-fenced bank could have a parent company, known as 'operating company'.[1736] Under the first option, the (banking) group is headed by a holding company which does not itself performs any business but simply owns other businesses, within the same group or not and usually coordinates their strategies. Under the second option, the ring-fenced bank could be directly owned by another bank or financial company, also including those who provide prohibited services, under the sole requirement that the ring-fencing principles would be followed.[1737] Ultimately, the ring-fenced bank could not be the parent company or have any equity interests (holdings) in any other entity, except for other ring-fenced banks.[1738]

For effective application of the arm's length requirement, this regulation shall apply to any transaction between the ring-fenced bank and the rest entities of the group, as they would apply to third parties. New regulations might be necessary to cover every possible aspect of the ring-fenced bank's operations, but they should include at least the following cases:

- exposures from the ring-fenced bank to the rest of the group, and vice versa, should be subject to the same large exposure limits as third parties, and no waivers should be granted. [...]
- additional limits should be placed around the level of total secured exposures between the ring-fenced bank and the rest of the group and the quality of collateral securing these exposures. [...] Without further restriction, this could lead to large intra-group exposures undermining the objectives of a ring-fence. Secured exposures (gross of the value of the collateral) between the ring-fenced bank and the rest of the group should be no more than twice

[1736] Ibid., p. 72.
[1737] Ibid.
[1738] Ibid.

the level of third-party unsecured limits and should include only assets of the highest quality

- the ring-fenced bank should not provide any form of unlimited guarantee, indemnity or similar commitment to the rest of the corporate group. Limited guarantees, and any other joint liabilities, should be captured within the third-party exposure limits
- limits should be placed on the total intraday exposures permitted between ring-fenced banks and the rest of the corporate group
- the ring-fenced bank should not be party to agreements which contain cross default clauses, or similar arrangements which are triggered by the default of entities in the rest of the corporate group unless it can satisfy the regulator that such clauses do not undermine the objectives of the ring-fence
- the ring-fenced bank should not receive a disproportionate amount of wholesale funding from the rest of the group
- asset sales or swaps between the ring-fenced bank and the rest of the group should be on a commercial and arm's length basis[1739]
- ring-fenced banks should be required to disclose all intra-group transactions and exposures on a regular basis and to demonstrate that these are taking place on a commercial and arm's length basis.

The report paid also particular attention regarding assets being sold to or from a ring-fenced bank to the rest of a corporate group. It concluded that these asset sales must also performed on a third-party basis – i.e. at market values – to avoid them being used as a mechanism for transferring subsidies from one entity to another through either inflated purchase prices or discounted sale prices. The ultimate scope of this practice is that asset sales must not result in the ring-fenced bank acquiring assets which it would not otherwise be permitted to acquire and/or hold. Moreover, the various business arrangements between ring-fenced banks and the rest of the group entities should also be on third party terms. For example, the ring-fenced bank should not provide any services to the rest of the group at unreasonably discounted rates and should not be required to give any preference to an entity within the group when purchasing risk-management products.[1740]

1739 The ICB's final report provided further explanation for the effective application of this specific requirement, where 'Commerciality' should be judged according to whether the terms are similar to comparable transactions with counterparties not in the same corporate group, and 'Arm's length' means that transactions should be valued as if they had been carried out between unrelated parties, each acting in his own best interest. See in Independent Commission on Banking (ICB), *Final Report – Recommendations*, September 2011, p. 73.

1740 See in Independent Commission on Banking (ICB), *Final Report – Recommendations*, September 2011, p. 74.

4.1.1.3 *Management Modalities*

The ICB's report links the project of ring-fenced banks with quality management. It is of utmost importance the banks to be governed by management boards that promote the efficient and effective management of ring-fenced entities. Otherwise, it would be very difficult for the regulators to face a management culture that opposes the general aim of ring-fencing. Therefore, alongside financial regulation and structural reforms, the governance of ring-fenced banks must apply, reflect, and encourage appropriate relationships with the rest of the group.[1741] Ring-fenced banks are expected to have a board composition that will ensure that all the above-mentioned ring-fencing principles will be implemented and ensured. The majority of directors shall be independent, non-executives, with minimal cross-over between these directors and the group's board members. Since the appropriate degree of independence depends on the proportion of banking group's assets held outside the ring-fenced banks, a necessary degree of flexibility shall be given to these groups where the ring-fenced banks comprise a (very) large part of the overall group. It is left for the directors and board members of both the group and the ring-fenced entity to comply with the spirit and the letter of the law.[1742]

The ICB's report contains further information regarding the payment of dividends from the ring-fenced bank; in normal times this can be anticipated, while in times of stress dividends shall not be paid if the payment could jeopardise the stability of the bank or the group. The viability of the ring-fenced bank must be assessed and prior approval from the competent authority must be obtained also considering any potential breach of capital and liquidity requirements.[1743] Moreover, the report contains proposals that would ensure market discipline since the 'workings of the ring-fencing should be clear and visible to market participants'.[1744]

4.1.2 ICB's Other Proposals

The ICB was given the mandate to consider whether the UK banking system needed structural and non-structural reforms, aiming at promoting financial stability and competition. Therefore, apart from the proposed reforms relevant to the structural reforms it also contains proposals in connection with further loss absorbency capacity and enhanced competition. Even though the rest of the ICB report's proposals are outside the scope of the present book, we are of the opinion that for reasons of coherence a very brief mention should be made on this point. Regarding the need for higher loss absorbency capacity

---

[1741] Ibid.

[1742] Ibid., p. 75.

[1743] Ibid.

[1744] Ibid.

by the banks, the ICB proposed the following measures in the fields of equity, leverage ratio, bail-in, depositor preference, primary loss absorbing capacity and resolution buffer:

Equity[1745]	• Ring-fenced banks with a ratio of risk-weighted assets (RWAs) to UK GDP of 3% or more should be required to have an equity-to-RWAs ratio of at least 10%. • Ring-fenced banks with a ratio of RWAs to UK GDP between 1% and 3% should be required to have a minimum equity-to-RWAs ratio set by a sliding scale from 7% to 10%.
Leverage ratio[1746]	• All UK-headquartered banks and all ring-fenced banks should maintain a Tier1 leverage ratio of at least 3%. • All ring-fenced banks with a RWAs-to-UK GDP ratio of 1% or more should have their minimum leverage ratio increased on a sliding scale (to a maximum of 4.06% at a RWAs-to-UK GDP ratio of 3%).
Bail-in[1747]	• The resolution authorities should have a primary bail-in power allowing them to impose losses on long-term unsecured debt (bail-in bonds) in resolution before imposing losses on other non-capital, non-subordinated liabilities. • The resolution authorities should have a secondary bail-in power to enable them to impose losses on all other unsecured liabilities in resolution, if necessary.
Depositor preference[1748]	• In insolvency (and in resolution), all insured depositors should rank ahead of other creditors to the extent that those creditors are either unsecured or only secured with a floating charge.
Primary loss-absorbing capacity[1749]	• UK-headquartered global systemically important banks (G-SIBs) with a 2.5% G-SIB surcharge, and ring-fenced banks with a ratio of RWAs to UK GDP of 3% or more, should be required to have capital and bail-in bonds (together, primary loss absorbing capacity) equal to at least 17% of RWAs. • UK G-SIBs with a G-SIB surcharge below 2.5%, and ring-fenced banks with a ratio of RWAs to UK GDP in between 1% and 3%, should be required to have primary loss-absorbing capacity set by a sliding scale from 10.5% to 17% of RWAs.
Resolution buffer[1750]	• The supervisor of any (i) G-SIB headquartered in the UK or (ii) a ring-fenced bank with a ratio of RWAs to UK GDP of 1% or more, should be able to require the bank to have additional primary loss-absorbing capacity of up to 3% of RWAs if, among other things, the supervisor has concerns about its ability to be resolved at minimum risk to the public purse. • The supervisor should determine how much additional primary loss-absorbing capacity (if any) is required, what form it should take, and which entities in a group the requirement should apply to, and whether on a (sub-) consolidated or solo basis.

1745 Ibid., p. 237.
1746 Ibid., p. 238.
1747 Ibid.
1748 Ibid.
1749 Ibid.
1750 Ibid.

Finally, several proposals were included in the report regarding market structure aspects, barriers to entry that may hamper the ability of new players to enter the business of banking in the UK, the switching of accounts for individuals and small businesses, as well as enhanced transparency requirements.[1751]

4.1.3 Assessment of the ICB's Report Proposals

The ICB's report tried to balance two almost controversial and non-compatible objectives. On the one hand, it tried to preserve the competitiveness of a well-established financial system that suffered a lot during the last financial crisis. On the other hand, it tried to secure that this system will be able, apart from being competitive, to perform crucial functions even in times of severe stress and when a credit crunch might appear again. The most difficult part of that delicate balance exercise is the complexity of the banking groups that are used to operate under the universal banking model, combining retail and investment/wholesale banking under a single entity.

The ring-fencing proposals, as defined in the final report, would stop this practice by separating the most important functions of a bank and protect them from the rest, more risky activities of the group. The new legal entities would have significantly constrained activities to be able to manage, monitor and supervise. This insulation from the rest of the financial system will protect them from shock transmission and from risks that are inherent in the modern financial system. Unless there is damage to the ring-fencing objectives, the structural reforms do not aim in reducing flexibility or impose a certain operating structure for the banks. On the contrary, banks will be able to operate according to their business models to the extent that they remain in compliance with the ring-fencing requirements. This view is fortified by the following elements:

- some services will be provided either from ring-fenced banks or from elsewhere. Non-banks would continue to be important providers of credit for all kinds of customers and corporate banking could be conducted either inside or outside the ring-fenced banks.[1752]
- Ring-fenced banks could be still parts of a wider corporate group, an alternative with lower costs compared to a full separation model, retaining the benefits that arise from the diversification of earning and financing.[1753]

As the report suggested, all the above structural measures must be complemented with further measures to address systematically the risks that arise in the economy, and particularly the risks from a potential failure of a large bank.

1751 Ibid., p. 239.
1752 Ibid., p. 77.
1753 Ibid.

4.2. The Legislation on Retail Ring-Fencing Introduced by the UK Government

The UK Government supported the findings of the ICB's final report and decided to enact the necessary legislation to implement the reports' proposals. Banking reform was the second key pillar of the UK Government's program for reform of the financial sector to address the weaknesses exposed by the financial crisis of 2007-09. The first pillar of this program, reforming the financial services regulation, has been legislated in the Financial Services Act that received Royal Assent in December 2012.[1754] The second pillar include the reform of the structure of the UK banking system, through the 'Financial Services (Banking Reform) Bill', which was introduced to UK's Parliament on 4 February 2013. Therefore, in 2013 the bill was adopted as an Act amending the 'Financial Services and Markets Act 2000' (FSMA). The 'Financial Services (Banking Reform) Act 2013'[1755] (Banking Reform Act) amended the FSMA, by introducing Sections 142A to 142ZI, to implement the ICB's proposals. The notion of ring-fencing was introduced to the UK regulatory landscape because of the above-mentioned amendment. The amendments further conferred power to the Treasury, the Financial Conduct Authority (FCA) and the Prudential Regulation Authority (PRA) to produce delegated acts that would clarify the basic legislation, the Banking Reform Act, thereby helping the industry to adapt to the various changes.

With this legislation, the largest UK banks were required by law to separate core retail banking services from their investment and international banking activities by 1 January 2019. Under the regime, banks are required to have separate legal entities to carry out different types of activities. To implement and effectively comply with ring-fencing requirements, banks needed to significantly restructure their activities during 2017 and 2018, with implications for their customers, counterparties, and suppliers. The implementation process of ring-fencing requirements has been closely managed by the banks and monitored by the PRA and the FCA respectively. The aim of the legislation is to ring-fence these core services on which customers rely from risks associated with other banking services.[1756] As of February 2025, a total of seven banking groups are subject to the ring-fencing regime: Barclays, HSBC, Lloyds Banking Group, NatWest Group, Santander UK, TSB Bank and Virgin Money.[1757]

[1754] Financial Services Act 2012, c. 21 (UK).

[1755] Financial Services (Banking Reform) Act 2013, c. 33 (UK).

[1756] See in K. Britton, L. Dawkes, S. Debbage and T. Idris, 'Ring-fencing: what is it and how will it affect banks and their customers?', *Bank of England Quarterly Bulletin*, Q4 2016, London, p. 164.

[1757] At the time when the £25 billion deposit threshold was decided, back in 2012-2013, TSB Bank and Virgin Money did not exist in their current form. After the February 2025 reforms, both TSB Bank and Virgin Money do not fall under the ring-fencing regime. For more

Figure 2.2: Total assets of UK banks at end-2020 (£bn)

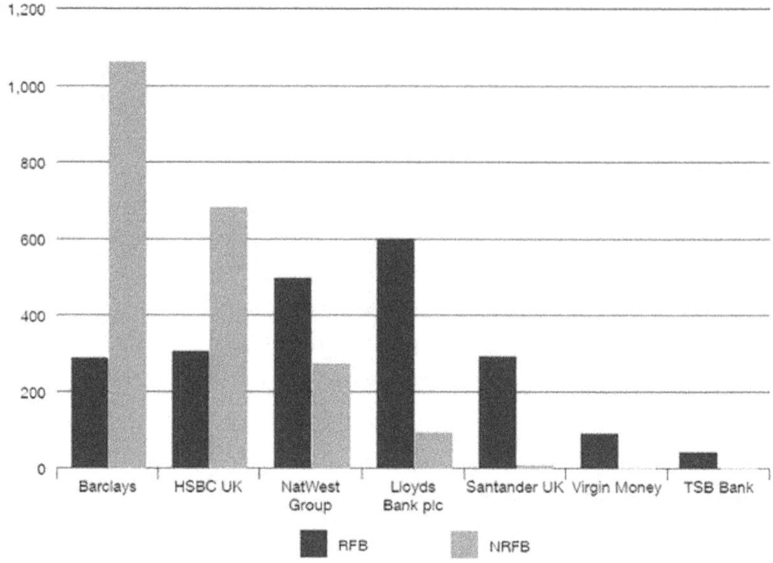

Source: *Ring-Fencing and Proprietary Trading Review* – RFPT, Independent Review, Final Report, March 2022, p. 27

The above diagram depicts how the UK banks have adapted their business models to the ring-fencing requirements. Barclays decided to create a small 'Ring-Fenced Body' (RFB) and a larger 'Non Ring-Fenced Body' (NRFB) to accommodate its international and investment banking activities; HSBC took a similar approach and created a large NRFB for its international investment banking activities while NatWest created a relatively large RFB as its focus in the UK is largely retail and commercial banking; Lloyds Banking Group similarly created a large RFB to accommodate its retail-focused strategy in the UK and Santander UK moved most of its corporate and investment banking activities to a UK branch of its parent company Banco Santander, placing its retail activities in its RFB. Finally, both TSB and Virgin Money, almost solely retail-focused banks, undertake only a minimal number of activities that are required to be provided in separate NRFBs. They placed almost all their activities in their RFBs. The basic legal documents that apply and explain the ring-fencing regime are:

(i) The FSMA 2000, as amended by the Banking Reform Act 2013 introducing the ring-fencing regime,

details see in Bank of England – PRA, 'Prudential Regulation Authority, Annual Report, 1 March 2024–28 February 2025, June 2025.

(ii) The statutory instruments issued by the HM Treasury in 2014 aiming at further explaining the regime's application:
   (a) 2014 No. 1960, The Financial Services and Markets Act 2000 (Ring-fenced Bodies and Core Activities) Order 2014, hereinafter referred to as the 'Ring-fenced Bodies and Core Activities Order 2014', and
   (b) 2014 No. 2080, The Financial Services and Markets Act 2000 (Excluded Activities and Prohibitions) Order 2014, hereinafter referred to as the 'Excluded Activities and Prohibitions Order 2014'
(iii) The 'Finalized Guidance on the FCA's approach to the implementation of ring-fencing and ring-fencing transfer schemes', issued by the Financial Conduct Authority on March 2016,
(iv) 'The implementation of ring-fencing: the PRA's approach to ring-fencing transfer schemes', issued by the Bank of England (Prudential Regulation Authority) in March 2016,
(v) 'The implementation of ring-fencing: prudential requirements, intragroup arrangements and use of financial market infrastructures', Policy Statement PS20/16, issued by the Bank of England (Prudential Regulation Authority) in July 2016, and
(vi) 'Ensuring operational continuity in resolution', issued by the Bank of England (Prudential Regulation Authority), Policy Statement PS21/16, in July 2016

Since the UK's regime is the strictest structural reform model, applying ring-fencing in a clearly articulated way, we will use the above-mentioned legal texts as the necessary compass to understand and discover this important regime. From now on any reference to the FSMA 2000 will be understood as a reference to the amended act by the Banking Reform Act 2013, unless explicitly stated otherwise.

4.2.1 The Location of the Fence

The UK retail ring-fencing legislation, as came into effect in April 2018, applies to banks with average total core deposits above £25 billion for a three-year period. Core deposits are those from individuals and small to medium businesses. The ring-fencing regime will not apply to 1) banks below the £25 billion limit, 2) to building societies, 3) foreign banks and 4) independent private banks.[1758] The Banking Reform Act 2013, build the ring-fence around the activities that cannot be even temporary interrupted without severe or systemic implications for the UK's financial system. The entity that will be ring-fenced is the 'ring-fenced body' (RFB)[1759] and these activities are the so

[1758] See in Section 142A(2) of the FSMA 2000.
[1759] See in Section 142A(1) of the FSMA 2000.

called 'core activities'. These are the mandated services that an RFB must provide and include only the acceptance of deposits from individuals and SMEs, whether carried in the UK or elsewhere. These core activities must be provided solely by the RFB and the RFB must provide only these core activities. Therefore, according to Section 142B (2) of the FSMA 2000: 'The regulated activity of accepting deposits (whether carried on in the United Kingdom or elsewhere) is a core activity unless it is carried on in circumstances specified by the Treasury by order.'

Furthermore, the Treasury has the ability to include in the ambit of the regulated activities other activities besides only deposit accepting, opening the door to an expansion of the regulated core activities.[1760] The provisions of Section 142C of FSMA 2000 provides that the notion of deposit acceptance services includes the following core services:

(a) facilities for the accepting of deposits or other payments into an account which is provided in the course of carrying on the core activity of accepting deposits;[1761]
(b) facilities for withdrawing money or making payments from such an account;[1762]
(c) overdraft facilities in connection with such an account.[1763]

The FSMA 2000 excludes certain activities from the RFB. These activities are designated as 'excluded activities' and according to the provisions of the FSMA: 'The regulated activity of dealing in investments as principal (whether carried on in the United Kingdom or elsewhere) is an excluded activity unless it is carried on in circumstances specified by the Treasury by order.'[1764]

The exemption of 'dealing in investments as a principal', inside or outside the UK, will affect the business area of both wholesale and investment banking activities[1765] while at the same time, the Treasury has the capacity to further exclude, via secondary legislation, other activities as well.[1766] With the 'Excluded Activities and Prohibitions Order 2014', the Treasury decided to expand the excluded activities by adding the activity of 'commodities trading': 'Dealing in commodities is an excluded activity, except where it is carried on in accordance with this article, or any of Articles 6, 8, 9, 10, 11 and 12.'[1767] Based on the that wording we understand that the exclusion is accompanied by an exception that ultimately allows the RFB to be involved in commodities trading but

---

1760 See in Section 142B(5) of the FSMA 2000.
1761 See in Section 142C(2)(a) of the FSMA 2000.
1762 See in Section 142C(2)(b) of the FSMA 2000.
1763 See in Section 142C(2)(c) of the FSMA 2000.
1764 See in Section 142D(2) of the FSMA 2000.
1765 See in K. Alexander, *Principles of Banking Regulation*, Cambridge, Cambridge University Press, 2019, p. 217.
1766 See in Section 142D(4) of the FSMA 2000.
1767 See in Article 5(1) of the Excluded Activities and Prohibitions Order 2014.

for specific purposes, '[...] where the commodities in question are required for its own use or consumption or for use or consumption by a subsidiary undertaking of the ring-fenced body'.[1768] The order further specifies the two cases where trading in commodities is not an excluded activity:[1769]

(a) 'to take a security interest over those commodities or to realise a security interest held over those commodities (including by selling the commodities), or',
(b) 'to enter into a title transfer collateral arrangement in relation to commodities, or acquire and hold equivalent commodities in accordance with the arrangement or enforce that arrangement (including by selling the commodities which are subject to that arrangement)'.

Furthermore, the Treasury's order introduces general exceptions that allow RFB to deal in excluded activities, under certain circumstances, and for specific reasons. According to the Order: 'A ring-fenced body does not carry on an excluded activity by entering into a transaction with another person (including a structured finance vehicle) if the sole or main purpose for which the ring-fenced body entered into the transaction, either by itself or in combination with other transactions, is that of limiting the extent to which [...] will be adversely affected by any of the factors specified in paragraph (2)'.[1770]

The factors specified in paragraph 2 are the following:[1771]

(a) changes in interest rates, exchange rates or commodity prices,
(b) changes in any index of retail prices or of residential or commercial property prices,
(c) changes in any index of the price of shares,
(d) default risk,
(e) liquidity risk

Therefore, the RFB can effectively engage in commodities trading with the aim of effectively managing its risks associated with its business and not for pure profit (proprietary trading). Another excluded activity is the 'securitisation and covered bonds', but the Treasury's Order further specifies that:

(a) 'A ring-fenced body does not carry on an excluded activity by selling investments to or buying investments from a sponsored structured finance vehicle of the ring-fenced body, or from a conduit vehicle of the ring-fenced body.'[1772]

[1768] See in Article 5(2) of the Excluded Activities and Prohibitions Order 2014.
[1769] See in Article 5(3) of the Excluded Activities and Prohibitions Order 2014.
[1770] See in Article 6(1) of the Excluded Activities and Prohibitions Order 2014.
[1771] See in Article 6(2) of the Excluded Activities and Prohibitions Order 2014.
[1772] See in Article 7(1) of the Excluded Activities and Prohibitions Order 2014.

(b) 'A ring-fenced body does not carry on an excluded activity by acquiring any instrument creating or acknowledging indebtedness issued by one or more of its sponsored structured finance vehicles.'[1773]

The Order provides for an exception to the excluded activities of dealing in investments as principal and commodities trading where the ring-fenced body is entering into a transaction with a central bank or a wholly owned subsidiary of a central bank.[1774] Further exceptions to the excluded activity of dealing in investments as a principal and commodities trading are applied, with respect to derivatives transactions, and Articles 9 to 12 set out the conditions that must be satisfied by a RFB, which wishes to deal in derivative instruments with its account holders. When the RFB complies with the relevant conditions it can sell currency and interest swaps, forward contracts (including futures) relating to currency, commodities or other property to its account holders,[1775] can sell certain options to its account holders, including interest rate caps and floors, and interest rate swaptions.[1776] Finally, Article 12 of the Treasury's Order sets out the conditions that must be satisfied by derivative transactions between a RFB and its account holders. Therefore, after the finalisation of structural reforms to the banks we have the following figure:

Ring-Fenced Body (RFB)	**Non-Ring-Fenced Body (NRFB)**
✓ Acceptance of individual (retail) and Small and Medium Size (SMEs) businesses deposits	✓ Trading and selling securities, commodities, and derivatives ✓ Having exposures to financial institutions other than building societies and other RFBs ✓ Having operations outside the EEA ✓ Underwriting securities ✓ Buying securitisations of other financial institutions

4.2.2 The Height of the Fence

The Banking Reform Act 2013 when amended the FSMA 2000, required the regulators to make rules that would ensure that the RFB would be able to act and operate independently from the rest of the group. This 'independence' shall be constructed in such a way that will allow the RFB to interact with the rest of the group on a 'third party basis' without compromising the ring-fencing

1773 See in Article 7(2) of the Excluded Activities and Prohibitions Order 2014.
1774 See in Article 8 of the Excluded Activities and Prohibitions Order 2014.
1775 See in Article 10 of the Excluded Activities and Prohibitions Order 2014.
1776 See in Article 11 of the Excluded Activities and Prohibitions Order 2014.

objectives while maintaining legal, operational, and economic independence.[1777] The ring-fencing purposes, as defined in Section 142H(4) are the following:

(a) 'ensuring as far as reasonably practicable that the carrying on of core activities by a ring-fenced body is not adversely affected by the acts or omissions of other members of its group'[1778],
(b) 'ensuring as far as reasonably practicable that in carrying on its business a ring-fenced body –
    (i) is able to take decisions independently of other members of its group, and
    (ii) does not depend on resources which are provided by a member of its group and which would cease to be available to the ring-fenced body in the event of the insolvency of the other member;'[1779],
(c) 'ensuring as far as reasonably practicable that the ring-fenced body would be able to continue to carry on core activities in the event of the insolvency of one or more other members of its group'[1780]

The above requirements will be analytically presented under three broader categories, aiming at a better understanding of the framework.

4.2.2.1 *Legal and Operational Links*

The banking groups that contain at least one RFB must comply with specific requirements regarding the legal and operational links between the RFB and the rest of the group entities. These requirements aim at securing the objectives of the ring-fencing regime.[1781] The PRA has set out its requirements regarding the legal structure of the banking groups that contain one or more RFB, particularly in relation to ownership structure and holdings of capital instruments within the group. The PRA's basic objective is to ensure the core services continuity by an RFB, in case of adverse events and on this ground[1782] has the right to impose requirements on such RFB or to give further directions to a qualifying parent undertaking respectively.[1783] Therefore, the PRA has formulated its expectations regarding the types of group entities in which an RFB may own or hold capital instruments according to:

[1777] See in K. Alexander, *Principles of Banking Regulation*, Cambridge, Cambridge University Press, 2019, p. 220.
[1778] Section 142H(4)(a).
[1779] Section 142H(4)(b).
[1780] Section 142H(4)(c).
[1781] See in Prudential Regulation Authority (PRA), 'Ring-Fenced Bodies (RFBs)', *Supervisory Statement*, SS8/16, Bank of England, December 2017, p. 5.
[1782] The PRA has this power under sections 55 and 192C of the FSMA 2000.
[1783] See in Prudential Regulation Authority (PRA), 'Ring-Fenced Bodies (RFBs)', *Supervisory Statement*, SS8/16, Bank of England, December 2017, p. 7.

- Holdings in excluded activity entities in the group
  'The PRA expects an RFB not to have ownership rights[1784] or hold capital instruments[1785] in an entity in its group that undertakes activities that, if it were an RFB, would contravene a prohibition or be excluded from activities under the Act. […] An RFB should also not hold capital instruments in a subsidiary of an excluded activity entity in its group.'[1786] The PRA will adopt this approach in a manner it considers to be proportionate to achieve the outcomes set out by the group ring-fencing purposes described by the FSMA 2000. In doing so, the PRA will assess, on a case-by-case analysis, the risks that such ownership stakes might pose to the resilience and resolvability of the RFB and to the general safety and soundness objective in relation to ring-fencing regime.[1787] The above-mentioned requirements are expected by the PRA to be met, where an RFB sub-group is formed, by all ring-fenced affiliates.[1788]
- Holdings in group entities that are not excluded activity entities
  'In principle, the PRA does not necessarily object to an RFB or its ring-fenced affiliates owning entities that are not excluded activity entities or holding the capital instruments of such entities.'[1789] Once again though the PRA will examine, on a case by case analysis, the risks that these holdings might pose for the RFB, aiming at securing its resilience and resolvability, the PRA's general safety and soundness objective in relation to ring-fencing and the ultimately the group ring-fencing purposes.[1790] Another important parameter of the RFB legal links with other group entities has to do with the expectations from the group entities that may own an RFB or hold capital instruments from the RFB. The PRA has articulated its expectations and 'Within a UK group […] the PRA does not expect an excluded activity entity, or a subsidiary of an excluded activity entity, to have ownership rights or hold capital instruments in an RFB or its ring-fenced affiliates.'[1791] This policy option, after taking into account the various exceptions and exemptions that may apply is consistent with the general ring-fencing purposes, as outlined in the FSMA 2000:
- the RFB's ability to take independent decisions,
- insulating the RFB from the acts or omissions of its group,

---

1784 Ibid. In this context, 'ownership rights' include voting rights and other rights to participate in the capital or profits of the relevant entity.

1785 Ibid. In this context 'capital instruments' are those instruments designed to provide loss absorbency to the issuer (i.e. those which qualify for recognition under the minimum requirement for own funds and eligible liabilities (MREL)).

1786 Ibid.

1787 Ibid.

1788 Ibid.

1789 Ibid., p. 8.

1790 Ibid.

1791 Ibid.

- limiting the reliance of the RFB on resources provided by other members of its group,
- reducing the complications of successfully resolving an RFB or its group

Proportionality will be again considered by the PRA when assessing the above parameters and a case-by-case analysis will support the final decision, balancing also the objectives of the ring-fencing regime. The PRA expects that the owner of an RFB may:[1792]

(i) maintain or establish a non-European Economic Area (EEA) branch,
(ii) have an ownership interest or hold capital instruments in a non-EEA undertaking,
(iii) have an ownership interest or hold capital instruments in an excluded activity entity,
(iv) have an ownership interest or hold capital instruments in an entity where the holding does not qualify as a participating interest.

Moreover, when assessing whether an entity, which is not an excluded activity entity, should be restricted from owning an RFB (or its ring-fenced affiliates) within the UK group, the PRA will consider, the resilience and resolvability of the RFB and the risks posed to the continuity of provision of core activities, by including in the assessment the extent to which:[1793]

(i) the RFB is able to take decisions independently of group entities where required by the Act,
(ii) the RFB is not reliant on resources in group entities which may cease to be available in the event of insolvency of that group entity, and
(iii) the RFB is sufficiently insulated from risks in the rest of the group, to ensure it is not adversely affected by the acts or omissions of the other group entities.

The RFB must be operational independent from the rest group entities. This independence is defined based on the following principles:[1794]

(i) Independent capitalisation and funding for any operational subsidiary,
(ii) Effective service level agreement between the group entities,
(iii) Provision of services by operational subsidiaries at an arm's length basis, and
(iv) The operational assets used for critical economic functions must be owned by the operational entity providing these services.

From the previously mentioned PRA's expectations we understand that FSMA 2000 has granted PRA a very broad mandate regarding the objectives of the ring-fencing with respect to the group structure and the legal links among the entities. PRA has a broad authority to assess each time whether an RFB

1792 Ibid.

1793 Ibid.

1794 See in K. Alexander, *Principles of Banking Regulation*, Cambridge, Cambridge University Press, 2019, p. 220.

or the rest of the group entities are allowed to perform specific action. On its analysis, the PRA should consider not only the specific issue but also the broader implications that this may have for the general ring-fencing objectives and the stability of the group. This allows for an *ad hoc* decision based on pragmatic and 'real time' evidence but obviously lacks the legal certainty that a rules-based approach would have.

4.2.2.2 *Economic Links*

The economic links between the RFB and the rest of the group entities shall be done under the 'third party principle' and a general 'third party rule' will apply. This general rule requires an RFB to apply the same standards when manages its exposures to, and arrangements with, group entities that are not members of the RFB sub-group as it would to third parties.[1795] The general third party rule is the embodiment of a key principle that should underpin an RFB's approach towards all transactions, arrangements and exposures with its wider group: 'that an RFB and its ring-fenced affiliates interact with the rest of the group as they would with a third party.'[1796] According to the PRA's updated supervisory statement, the ring-fencing rules do not necessarily prohibit the intragroup transactions 'on the sole basis that an RFB or its ring-fenced affiliates do not have identical transactions with a third party'.[1797] Furthermore, the PRA clarified that it does not require from the RFB or its ring-fenced affiliates to 'apply precisely the same policies and procedures to transactions with group entities that are not members of the RFB sub-group as they do to third party transactions'.[1798] It rather expects that the RFB and its ring-fenced affiliates will 'apply the same robust standards of assessment, risk management and oversight of intragroup transactions with group entities that are not members of the RFB sub-group as they would to third parties'.[1799]

The general third part rule sets out requirements how the intragroup counterparties are treated by the RFB or its ring-fenced affiliates, in relation to risk management, risk appetite and oversight. Under the arm's length rule, pricing, terms, and documentation of individual transactions are covered, with a special focus on the appropriate pricing, transparency and transactions' substitutability.[1800] The PRA provides further information regarding the intragroup transactions and other exposures that the RFB might engage in.[1801]

1795 See in Prudential Regulation Authority (PRA), 'Ring-Fenced Bodies (RFBs)', *Supervisory Statement*, SS8/16, Bank of England, December 2017, p. 24.
1796 Ibid.
1797 Ibid.
1798 Ibid.
1799 Ibid.
1800 Ibid.
1801 Ibid., p. 15.

In relation to secured intragroup exposures, the PRA clarified how the RFB should manage the collateral received from other group entities in accordance with the EU regulatory framework. Regarding the netting arrangements among the group members, PRA clarified that requires a RFB and its ring-fenced affiliates not to enter into netting arrangements that permit a counterparty to offset liabilities to the RFB or its ring-fenced affiliates against claims that the counterparty has on other group members outside the RFB sub-group in the event of default of one of the parties.[1802]

4.2.2.3 *The 'Arm's Length' Rule*

According to the PRA Rulebook, the RFBs must establish both an 'arm's length'[1803] policy and procedures. An RFB's arm's length policy must at least:[1804]

(i) establish robust means for identification, timely recording and monitoring of all transactions entered into with other group members which are not ring-fenced affiliates,
(ii) specify how the terms of a transaction will be determined, including pricing and settlement,
(iii) specify appropriate governance arrangements for amendments to the policy and procedures,
(iv) specify processes for approval and reporting of exceptions to the policy and procedures, and
(v) include procedures for dispute resolution between the ring-fenced body and members of its group which are not ring-fenced affiliates with which it transacts.

An RFB's arm's length procedures must include at least the following elements:[1805]

(1) approval of the arm's length policy by its governing body;
(2) review by the governing body of the arm's length policy at least annually considering the report of the internal audit function under (5) and the reports under (3);

1802 Ibid.

1803 The expression 'at arm's length' is commonly used to refer to transactions in which two or more unrelated and unaffiliated parties agree to do business, acting independently and in their self-interest. In transactions 'at arm's length', the parties involved should have equal bargaining power and symmetric information, leading the parties to agree upon fair market terms. In contrast, a transaction not conducted 'at arm's length' may happen between parties that may have a personal or close relationship. Usually, these transactions are concluded between family members, personal friends, or the parent company and its subsidiaries. [...] The 'arm's length' principle seeks to guarantee fair market conditions and that taxes are correctly allocated in those transactions in which potential conflicts of interest may arise. Source: Cornell Law School, Legal Information Institute, available at: https://www.law.cornell.edu/wex/arm%27s_length.

1804 PRA Rulebook 12.3.

1805 PRA Rulebook 12.4.

(3) the provision of internal reports to its governing body on the operation of the arm's length policy including the extent to which the ring-fenced body's transactions comply with its arm's length policy;
(4) assessment of the following matters by its internal audit function at least annually in relation to an appropriate subset of transactions:
 (a) the extent to which the arm's length policy complies with the requirements of this Chapter;
 (b) the effectiveness of the arm's length policy; and
 (c) the effectiveness of the procedures established in compliance with this Chapter.
(5) provision of a report from the internal audit function to the governing body at least annually on its assessment of the matters in 12.4(1)(d).

The above-mentioned requirements regarding the arm's length transactions apply in two different types of an RFB's transactions:

- Transactions with group entities that are not members of the RFB sub-group

According to the PRA's supervisory statement, '[t]he PRA does not object to an RFB or its ring-fenced affiliates putting in place framework agreements to aggregate transactions of a common type when meeting requirements under Ring-fenced Bodies 12 of the PRA Rulebook, provided that transactions are grouped in a meaningful way'.[1806] Where the PRA has concerns that the level of aggregation of transactions could be in any way inappropriate, it will consider taking appropriate action to address the risks associated with these transactions. When the RFB will decide to group together these transactions under framework agreements, this should be done in a way that: a) allows it to meet requirements under PRA rules, b) facilitates restructuring activity in recovery or resolution, and c) allows the RFB and its ring-fenced affiliates to disaggregate balances to individual transactions and individual entities if required.[1807]

- Intragroup transactions between an RFB and its ring-fenced affiliates

According to the PRA's supervisory statement, '[...] the PRA Rulebook does not require an RFB to transact with its ring-fenced affiliates only on arm's length terms'.[1808] From this wording we understand that the RFBs will be able to transact also on a non-arm's length terms, but the PRA expects from the RFBs to comply with their obligations under the ring-fencing regime, in

---

1806 See in Prudential Regulation Authority (PRA), 'Ring-Fenced Bodies (RFBs)', *Supervisory Statement*, SS8/16, Bank of England, December 2017, p. 27.
1807 Ibid.
1808 Ibid.

general. The PRA's Rulebook has many other provisions with requirements for the RFBs transactions with other ring-fenced affiliates:[1809]

- Fundamental Rules Part 2.1-2.8,
- Risk Control Part 2.1,
- Ring-fenced Bodies Part 3.1-3.3,
- Compliance Part 2.2 and Internal Audit Part 3.1,
- General Organizational Requirements Part 4.2,
- ICAA rules Part 2.1 and ILAA rules Part 2.1, and
- for RFB transactions with ring-fenced affiliates involving critical services, an RFB must comply with the requirements in Operational Continuity Parts 3.1 and 3.3.

Considering the above requirements, the PRA expects from an RFB that will maintain appropriate oversight of intragroup transactions with its ring-fenced affiliates and that will be able to identify and manage the risks to the RFB stemming from intragroup transactions with its ring-fenced affiliates. The statement further clarifies that where the PRA has concerns that an RFB is not appropriately managing its transactions with its ring-fenced affiliates, the PRA will consider the option of taking appropriate action to address the associated risks.[1810]

4.2.2.4 *Governance and Disclosure Requirements*

The RFB must be underpinned by strong governance that will defend the ring-fencing regime and its objectives.[1811] Strong governance must be reflected on the one hand by the RFB's board of directors' composition and on the other hand by a requirement for the board members to act in the interests of the RFB, as opposed to the group in general. According to the provisions of Section 142H(5)(d) of the FSMA 2000, the ring-fencing rules must include 'provision requiring a ring-fenced body to ensure that its board of directors (or if there is no such board, the equivalent management body) includes to a specified extent—(i) members who are treated by the rules as being independent of other members of the ring-fenced body's group, (ii) members who are treated by the rules as being independent of the ring-fenced body itself, and (iii) non-executive members;'. Therefore, the law has tried to impose the board composition requirements to secure that the ring-fencing objectives

1809 Ibid.
1810 Ibid.
1811 See in K. Alexander, *Principles of Banking Regulation*, Cambridge, Cambridge University Press, 2019, p. 221.

shall be met at any cost. Moreover, the PRA Rulebook has introduced further requirements regarding the RFB's board composition:

(i) An RFB must ensure that at least half of the members for the time being of its governing body are independent non-executive directors.[1812]

(ii) An RFB must ensure that the Chair of the Governing Body function is an independent non-executive director and does not chair the governing body of any other member of the ring-fenced body's group, other than a ring-fenced affiliate.[1813]

(iii) An RFB must ensure that no more than one-third of the members of its governing body are employees or directors of any other member of the ring-fenced body's group, other than of a ring-fenced affiliate.[1814]

(iv) An RFB must ensure that it publicly advertises every vacancy for an independent non-executive director to bring the existence of the vacancy to the notice of those members of the public who might reasonably be expected to seek nomination.[1815]

(v) An RFB must ensure that none of its senior management who is a member of its governing body is an executive member of the governing body of any other member of the ring-fenced body's group, other than a member that is a body corporate falling within section 192JA(2) of FSMA or a ring-fenced affiliate.[1816]

The above requirements ensure that legislation in place will permit the board members from the rest of the group to influence a more group-wide business strategy since any different approach would be able to veto any decision that would undermine the RFB's stability and prospects.[1817]

Regarding disclosure, the legislation requires 'the disclosure to the appropriate regulator of information relating to transactions between a ring-fenced body and other members of its group'.[1818] Together with the ICB's suggestion that the ring-fenced entity (RFB) must be able to publicly demonstrate that is independent from the rest group, in order to strengthen the reputation of the bank,[1819] disclosure requirements are very important tool for the regulator and the supervisory authority.

1812 PRA Rulebook 4.1.

1813 Ibid., 4.3.

1814 Ibid., 4.4.

1815 Ibid., 4.5.

1816 Ibid., 4.7.

1817 See in K. Alexander, *Principles of Banking Regulation*, Cambridge, Cambridge University Press, 2019, p. 221.

1818 Section 142H(5)(c) of the FSMA 2000.

1819 See in Independent Commission on Banking (ICB), *Final Report – Recommendations*, September 2011, p. 72.

4.2.2.5 *Capital Requirements, De Minimis Rule and Other Exemptions*

The initial proposal as articulated in the ICB's final report was to not accept any de minimis rule to the ring-fencing regime. The ICB took the view that even small and less complex banks a) perform the same vital services that need to be ring-fenced, and b) could still pose significant resolution challenges to the authorities.[1820] The associated risk of contagion was another important parameter that the ICB took into account, since small and less complex banks can still participate in the interbank market and consumers could be confused by an exemption to the uniform application of the ring-fencing regime. It was clear that from the ring-fencing, only the foreign subsidiaries of UK headquartered banking groups would be exempted, unless they were subsidiaries of a ring-fenced bank.[1821] The main fear was that many smaller banks operating under a certain de minimis level could still be a risk for the financial stability and at the same time create a distortive competition 'as universal banks might have a disincentive to grow beyond that level'.[1822] The ICB was not persuaded of the need for 'any de minimis exemption from the ring-fence principles'.[1823]

To the contrary, the Government did not agree with the Vickers Report proposal and decided to introduce a de minimis exemption, by applying ring-fencing only to banks with more than £25 billion of core retail deposits. The Government argued that applying ring-fencing to smaller banks may result in disproportionate costs and hinder competition. Therefore, ring-fencing does not include a) a building society, as defined in the Building Societies Act 1986[1824] or b) a UK institution of a class exempted by order made by the Treasury.[1825] The de minimis rule adopted by the Parliament, exempts from the ring-fencing requirements the banks that have less than £25 billion of core retail deposits and also the UK branches of foreign (non-EEA) institutions, unless they surpass the de minimis limit, where ring-fencing will apply.[1826] The UK's Government legislation applies higher capital requirements in the form of the systemic risk buffer to RFBs, as well as to the large building societies. This recognises that these institutions are systemically important to the domestic financial system and must comply with higher capital requirements exactly for their importance. In particular, the 'Other Systemically Important Institutions' (O-SII) buffer that applies additional capital requirements to banks with total

---

[1820] Ibid., p. 39.
[1821] Ibid.
[1822] Ibid.
[1823] Ibid.
[1824] See in Section 142A(2)(a) of the FSMA 2000.
[1825] See in Section 142A(2)(b) of the FSMA 2000.
[1826] See in K. Alexander, *Principles of Banking Regulation*, Cambridge, Cambridge University Press, 2019, p. 216.

assets above £175 billion is set with reference to banks in the ring-fencing regime and to some building societies.[1827]

4.2.3 Evaluation of the UK's Ring-Fencing Regime

The UK's ring-fencing regime has been into force since 1 January 2019. During previous years, the banks that were to comply with the new regulations prepared their structures and transferred their operations into the RFBs, while maintaining the non-core activities in the NRFBs. The ring-fencing regime is the only entity-based approach that has imposed such strict requirements on the banks and its impact must be analysed and understood. Up to date and to the best of the author's knowledge the most important publications that study the impact of the reforms in the post ring-fence environment are, from an economic perspective, that of Chavaz and Elliott (2020) and from an institutional perspective, as requested by the UK Parliament, the Independent Review of ring-fencing and proprietary trading (RFPT) in 2022. Combining these two publications, we will be able to analyse the effects of the structural reforms in the UK and better understand their impact.

4.2.3.1 *Economic Evaluation*

Chavaz and Elliott performed an analysis of the ring-fencing regime in the UK and its economic impact on banks. They documented implications for credit and liquidity supply, competition level among banks and risk taking via a funding structure channel, that of using deposits to fund universal banking operations, exactly what ring-fencing tries to avoid. They uncover a new mechanism under which structural separation affects credit supply, competition and risk taking, which was previously undocumented. The mechanism uncovered by Chavaz and Elliott is the 'deposit funding channel' which allows universal banks to use retail deposit to fund their presence in the capital markets (investment banking operations).[1828] The authors support the view that to the extent that retail deposits benefit from a safety or liquidity premium[1829] it acts as a constraint since it can change the relative funding costs of different activities and as a result affect the universal banks' incentives to engage in them.[1830] As a result, universal banks reduce their engagement in activities where their funding costs

[1827] See in *Ring-Fencing and Proprietary Trading Review* (RFPT), Independent Review, Final Report, March 2022, p. 103.

[1828] See in M. Chavaz and D. Elliott, 'Separating retail and investment banking: evidence from the UK', *Staff Working Paper* No. 892, Bank of England, November 2020, p. 2.

[1829] Safety premium is the explicit deposit guarantee, and the liquidity premium is the households' preference for liquidity, where they can easily access their deposits.

[1830] See in M. Chavaz and D. Elliott, 'Separating retail and investment banking: evidence from the UK', *Staff Working Paper* No. 892, Bank of England, November 2020, p. 2.

are relatively higher, because of the ring-fencing regime, and at the same time increase their presence in the retail credit markets. According to the authors, this alteration has knock on effects on the competition since the smaller banks now have to face tougher competition in their traditional everyday business.[1831] The results from the authors are consistent with industry comments that argue that ring-fencing has caused large banks to reduce syndicated lending and increase mortgage lending. Moreover, the authors observe that there exists a broader rebalancing of the universal banks' business model towards retail assets, to comply with the legislative requirements.[1832] This adjustment may have two potential side effects: a) an increased market concentration and b) that increased lending by the ring-fenced banks will diminish the smaller banks' market shares and their profit margins.[1833]

The Chavaz and Elliott paper's contribution is that the authors manage to enrich existing literature by observing the following:[1834]

(i) Ring-fencing creates an additional mechanism which can reduce corporate credit supply through banks' inability to use retail deposits to fund their capital markets activities,
(ii) Ring-fencing increases competition pressures in the capital markets since access to retail deposit funding is a competitive advantage,
(iii) Although the ring-fencing measures are believed to reduce moral hazard and risk taking, evidence by the two authors suggests that preventing the use of retail deposits to support the capital markets operations pushes banks towards retail markets and might further increase risk taking from smaller non-ring-fenced banks, thereby increasing systemic risk instead of decreasing it.

Theory holds that based on the ring-fencing legislation we observe a higher funding cost for the NRFB assets and a lower funding cost for the RFB assets, attributed to the deposit funding premium mentioned above and to the fact that absent ring-fencing the funding costs would be spread across the banks' assets.[1835] The results reported by the authors demonstrate that there is robust evidence for ring-fenced banks that they originate 'relatively larger mortgage volumes' gaining more market share.[1836] At the same time, we observe that universal banks adjust to the ring-fencing regime and the subsequent loss of deposit funding by 'reducing the supply of syndicated loans'.[1837] Apart from the business model, ring-fencing had an effect also on competition, since by calculating

---

1831 Ibid.
1832 Ibid., p. 6.
1833 Ibid.
1834 Ibid., p. 8.
1835 Ibid., p. 12.
1836 Ibid., p. 24.
1837 Ibid., p. 26.

the Herfindahl-Hirschman Index (HHI)[1838] for market concentration, based on market share increase, they observe that markets which are more exposed to ring-fenced banks have experienced a larger increase in concentration.[1839] This implies that smaller banks will respond to the competitive pressures by rebalancing towards riskier mortgages, thereby increasing the overall risk taking appetite because the pressure from the ring-fenced banks will reduce the value of the smaller banks incentivise the risk taking approach.[1840]

4.2.3.2 *Institutional Evaluation*

An institutional analysis of the ring-fencing regime's impact to the UK's banking sector was released in March 2022. The independent 'Ring-Fencing and Proprietary Trading (RFPT) Review' was set up by HM Treasury to examine how the ring-fencing regime operates for banks and, how banks undertake proprietary trading activities.[1841] HM Treasury appointed Keith Skeoch as Panel's Chairman, Betsy Nelson, John Flint, Linda Yueh, Patrick Honohan and Preben Prebensen to the independent review panel (the Panel). The RFPT Panel made a thorough analysis of the applicable ring-fencing regime, together with the banks' proprietary trading activities since they affirmed that these two are intrinsically coupled together.

4.2.3.2.1 *Ring-Fencing Regime*

The Panel decided to assess the impact of ring-fencing regime based on a) financial stability, b) competition and competitiveness, and c) operational challenges of the regime. With respect to financial stability the Panel took the view that the implementation of the overall reform package has made the (retail) banking sector safer than before the GFC. Ring-fencing has contributed to this safety through the creation of distinct retail deposit taking entities (RFBs) that are easier to manage, supervise and resolve. The RFBs are well capitalised, liquid and the regime is complemented by other reform measures that

---

1838 The Herfindahl-Hirschman Index (HHI) is a measure of market concentration, commonly used in economics to assess the level of competition in an industry or market. It helps determine how much market power is held by a few firms, which can indicate the likelihood of monopolistic or oligopolistic behaviour. The HHI is calculated by squaring the market share of each firm in the market and then summing the results. The interpretation of HHI is as follows:
i. HHI between 0 and 1,500: A market with low concentration and typically considered competitive.
ii. HHI between 1,500 and 2,500: A moderately concentrated market.
iii. HHI above 2,500: A market with high concentration, possibly dominated by a few firms (indicative of an oligopoly or monopoly).

1839 See in M. Chavaz and D. Elliott, 'Separating retail and investment banking: evidence from the UK', *Staff Working Paper* No. 892, Bank of England, November 2020, p. 31.

1840 Ibid., p. 34.

1841 See in *Ring-Fencing and Proprietary Trading Review* (RFPT), Independent Review, Final Report, March 2022, p. 20.

increase their overall safety.[1842] The Panel believes that it is difficult to directly quantify the contribution of the ring-fencing regime to the resilience of retail banking relative to other reforms that have been adopted and implemented in the sector. However, the Panel took the view that at a minimum, the ICB's recommendations paved the way for the widespread regulatory change since the GFC[1843] and discovered some occasions that the regime is not that successful and concluded that certain limitations persist. Most importantly:[1844]

(i) the ring-fencing regime has not increased the resilience of less complex banks within the regime,
(ii) the benefits of resilience, better supervision and protection are only attributed to the RFBs and not to the NRFBs or the wider group, and
(iii) based on certain evidence, the reduction in the implicit government guarantee and the progress in addressing too-big-to-fail is not attributable to ring-fencing regime

Another aspect of ring-fencing contribution to financial stability was the definition of 'critical functions'. The Panel found that critical functions, as defined by the PRA, also include investment banking, corporate banking and lending between financial institutions as well as other activities. Since the ring-fencing regime aims to insulate the RFBs from risks associated with some of these activities, they are prohibited from being offered by an RFB. This has resulted in being carried out in NRFBs, making NRFBs more essential than originally the ICB envisaged in its final report.[1845] The following table will provide us with an overview of the critical functions and the entity that offers them:

Critical functions provided by RFBs	**Critical functions provided by NRFBs**
• Retail & SME current accounts • Retail & SME savings accounts • Retail mortgages • Retail secured lending • Retail credit cards • Payments, settlement, & cash services • Corporate deposits & lending	• Corporate deposits & lending • Trade finance • Infrastructure lending • Credit card merchant services • Derivatives • Trading portfolios • Securities financing & lending • Payment services • Settlement services • Custody services

Source: *Ring-Fencing and Proprietary Trading Review* – RFPT, Independent Review, Final Report, March 2022, p. 39

[1842] Ibid., p. 35. Another important measure is the additional buffer to withstand losses (known as the '*Other Systemically Important Institutions*', O-SII buffer), which only applies to RFBs and building societies above a certain size.

[1843] See in *Ring-Fencing and Proprietary Trading Review* (RFPT), Independent Review, Final Report, March 2022, p. 35.

[1844] Ibid., p. 37.

[1845] Ibid., p. 38.

The Panel concluded that in case of an NRFB's failure, insolvency would not be a credible option since that entity provides critical functions to the public. Using the Panel's own words: 'If relying on the ring-fencing regime alone, the government would be faced with the unenviable choice of either providing taxpayer support or risking severe consequences for the wider financial system and economy. In that respect, the ring-fencing regime alone would not make it easier to manage a failing bank in an orderly manner without the need for taxpayer funds.'[1846] Therefore, the adoption of a credible resolution regime that will complement the undoubted success of the ring-fencing regime will further tap the loopholes that exist in a system with inherent crises. Since the ring-fencing explicitly gives priority to the RFB's resilience over NRFB's it creates an inconsistency between the two entities. This inconsistency is evident when both entities are considered to offer critical services to the public but only one is prioritised to survive. With critical functions provided both inside and outside the ring-fenced entities, resolution regime is extremely important since it seems that ring-fencing is not enough by itself to act as comprehensive and effective backstop mechanism.[1847]

The Panel believes that currently, the UK's financial system is not close to a failure but at the same time, it is acknowledged that UK does not operate 'a zero-failure regime' and therefore risks to public money remain, even theoretically, and must be properly addressed.[1848] Currently in the UK exist two different regulatory regimes, ring-fencing, and resolution, that have similar aims, namely ending too big to fail but are not aligned among them and most importantly have different priorities in case of bank failure. This inconsistency, according to the Panel's view, will add further complexity to the regulatory regime and will need to reorientate both regimes' priorities as the financial landscape evolves. Ring-fencing was an earlier attempt to address too big to fail issue based on a narrow banking approach. On the contrary, the resolution scheme has another, broader view, aiming at securing that every bank, irrespective of what business model has adopted, is able to be wound down without public spending.

With respect to competition and competitiveness issues, the Panel found that the RFBs have a liquidity surplus, attributed also to the special situations that the current COVID-19 pandemic has created.[1849] At the same time, findings suggest that banks outside the ring-fenced perimeter also have an

---

1846 Ibid., p. 39.

1847 Ibid., p. 41.

1848 Ibid., p. 10.

1849 Ibid., p. 11. According to the Panel's wording: 'Since the start of the Covid-19 pandemic, liquidity has increased substantially for banks globally, including RFBs in the UK whose retail deposits grew by £186 billion in the year to December 2020. Excess liquidity above internal liquidity targets held by the five largest RFBs was £120 billion as of September 2021, triple the pre-Covid-19 levels of £40 billion.'

excess liquidity that could be translated as a general characteristic and not a ring-fence specificity. Ring-fencing has also implications for the retail banking market competition. Large UK banks have a clear advantage over smaller banks already before the regime's application and according to the Panel's findings, it does not appear to have increase the RFBs market share across retail markets.[1850] This conclusion is in striking contrast with what Chavaz and Elliott have found on their economic analysis, presented above, but a possible explanation on that difference is beyond the scope of the present book. The same finding is also evidenced for the retail mortgage market, since the data demonstrate that RFBs have increased their mortgage value but have decreased their residential mortgages in terms of absolute numbers.[1851] Finally, it is generally assumed that NRFBs will need to have access only to wholesale funding, which is more costly than deposit funding, thereby raising their funding costs. The Panel believes that the current macroeconomic environment has a positive impact so far minimising the impacts for NRFBs. While is clear that ring-fencing will have an adverse effect in the future growth and competitiveness for NRFBs, up to date there is 'limited evidence' that this has occurred today.[1852] Finally, regarding the operational challenges of the ring-fencing regime, the Panel had to discover how many layers of regulatory legislation apply to this strict regime. For banks to comply with the regime's requirements they must navigate through a complex and strict framework with limited space for adjustments. The day-to-day implementation of ring-fencing has proven to be a very painful task since operational challenges are limitless.

Due to the strict requirements the UK Parliament had from the beginning, the fear that banks would try to undermine the regime's objectives by circumventing the restrictions. To address these concerns, the legislation had the option for the 'electrification of the fence' in cases where banks undermining the ring-fencing objectives. Electrification had the direct impact of fully separating the two entities (RFB and NRFB) of a bank, with each one of them becoming separately owned banks.[1853] The extreme policy option of electrification, that the supervisor has the power to use when deems appropriate, demonstrates the level of distrust among the political system and the banking sector and furthermore, how much afraid was the Parliament when adopting the ring-fencing measure, since it would like to have available more options to be used in extremis. The Panel reviewed the banks' practices and found no evidence that banks are trying to undermine the objectives of the ring-fencing

1850 See in *Ring-Fencing and Proprietary Trading Review* (RFPT), Independent Review, Final Report, March 2022, p. 11.

1851 Ibid., p. 12.

1852 Ibid.

1853 Ibid., p. 71.

regime.[1854] The PRA, according to the Panel, found that RFBs have complied with the regime's requirements except for a limited number of minor breaches, that banks managed to resolve them immediately or implemented remediation plans.[1855]

The constraints that are imposed on the RFBs are according to the Panel responsible for undesirable cliff edge effects. Since RFBs are prohibited from carrying out certain activities, as we seen earlier on, this means that they do not have the ability to offer certain financial products to their customers. In case they will offer an excluded or prohibited activity, regardless of its scale or volume, they are in breach of their regulatory obligations and since the restrictions are absolute, there is no way that a discretion on behalf of the authorities will be exercised.[1856] The cliff edge effects that banks faced are related to the disproportionate compliance costs that RFBs are facing in order to monitor and report every breach of the ring fencing requirements. The breaches, irrespective of their size, duration, and impact, must reported to the authorities as soon as possible, and the Panel concluded that 'These types of immaterial breaches do not promote the objectives of, nor adherence to, the ring-fencing regime […]'.[1857] This burdensome situation had led many banks to decide not to provide certain banking services and/or products to customers, even when they are not explicitly forbidden to do so, in order to avoid regulatory compliance costs and rigidity. The Panel concluded that it is a 'lose-lose situation' for both parties.[1858] 'Overall, the regime lacks proportionality, allowances, or a degree of flexibility for the authorities in their approach to enforcement. This has led to undesirable outcomes for customers.'[1859] The efficient and effective operation of the ring-fence regime requires compliance with the various regime's restrictions regarding available services. The excluded services, as we saw earlier, include dealing in investments as a principal and commodities trading. The restriction imposed on these two activities means

1854 Ibid., p. 72.

1855 Ibid., p. 72. For example, breaches in 2020 were reported as 'mostly of low materiality, and none were classed as severe'.

1856 See in *Ring-Fencing and Proprietary Trading Review* (RFPT), Independent Review, Final Report, March 2022, p. 72.

1857 Ibid.

1858 Ibid., p. 73. In this situation, the bank jeopardizes her relationship with the customer, since refuses to offer services not because she does not have the ability or the willingness to do so, but simply because the regulatory framework either does not allow it or is extremely burdensome. Especially, when servicing a corporate customer that requires the mixing of mandated and prohibited activities, the RFB is faced with additional complexity. At the same time, the customer must keep contact with both entities (RFB and NRFB) since its financing needs require cooperation among them. The Panel founds that this additional complexity and cost would incentivise customers to transact with banks lying outside of the ring-fencing regime, where the full range of services could be provided in one entity.

1859 See in *Ring-Fencing and Proprietary Trading Review* (RFPT), Independent Review, Final Report, March 2022, p. 73.

that RFBs cannot provide an important range of financial products and services to their customers. Although in most cases this does not cause any material problem, however, there is a group of business customers that would benefit from a wider range of product offerings from the RFB, especially if they are not sufficiently large enough and/or profitable enough to be banked by an NRFB. This situation results in inconvenience and undesirable outcomes both for banks and their customers, and in some cases these restrictions do not even improve financial stability.[1860]

Finally, the geographical restrictions which are imposed on the RFBs create further complexity since the logic behind the adoption of this measure has diminished over time. The rule is that RFBs are not allowed to open a branch or a subsidiary outside the UK or European Economic Area (EEA). The key concern behind this idea was the potential barriers to resolution that could be created from the branches and subsidiaries of the UK banks.[1861] Luckily, according to the Panel's report, the UK Government is in favour of a future amendment that could ease this restriction, provided though that cross-border resolution agreements with the relevant non-EEA countries will be signed. The Panel believes that retaining this provision is 'anachronistic' since it is not clear that banking business in EEA jurisdictions is necessarily safer than non-EEA jurisdictions.[1862] Furthermore, the Panel supports that while the legislation does not explicitly prohibit an RFB from providing services to customers that are based outside the UK/EEA (as long as the customers are serviced from the UK/EEA), it is clearly impractical, since it limits RFBs' ability to service their (UK) customers outside the EEA and further hampers the facilitation of international trade.[1863] When a bank notifies the PRA for a future expansion through branch or subsidiary in a third country, the PRA can under its current powers seek the bank's assessment of the risks and impact on resources and have a clear view over the proposed expansion. Overall, the Panel concluded emphatically that 'the PRA has developed sufficient oversight and supervisory tools to manage risks arising from an RFB opening a branch or subsidiary in a third country'.[1864]

4.2.3.2.2 *Proprietary Trading*

The Panel decided to study the impact on proprietary trading because, as referred earlier, it is perceived to be a very important parameter of the logic behind the ring-fencing regime. 'Classic' proprietary trading is where a firm

---

1860 Ibid., p. 75.
1861 Ibid., p. 78.
1862 Ibid.
1863 Ibid.
1864 Ibid., p. 79.

uses its own money to trade in financial instruments to make profit through speculation on the future prices.[1865] Since proprietary trading can expose banks to major losses, it has been seen by various commentators as one of the GFC causes and therefore was often referred as 'casino banking'.[1866] The Panel found that the FSBRA 2013, defined proprietary trading broadly, covering a wider range of activities than classic proprietary trading, to include market making, hedging activities and trading on behalf of customers.[1867]

In the current framework, as presented above, only RFBs are excluded from engaging in proprietary trading and NRFBs within the ring-fencing framework as well as other banks outside ring-fencing are free to engage in such activities.[1868] Further Panel findings confirm that UK operating banks do not engage in classic proprietary trading activities to any significant extent.[1869] Moreover, the Panel took the view that despite the risks arising from hedging and managing liquidity that require large trading positions, there certain benefits that can't be ignored.[1870] Apart from assessing banks' risk and liquidity management trading positions as prudent and beneficial, the Panel also concluded that PRA's supervisory method for mitigating proprietary trading risks is 'appropriate and comprehensive' and is based in three key principles: a) is judgement based, b) forward looking and c) focused on key risks.[1871]

The Panel discovered that classic proprietary trading is no longer performed by the UK banking sector and this has been attributed to increased capital requirements and liquidity, lower risk appetite from banks, the Senior Managers & Certification Regime (SM&CR) adopted by the FCA,[1872] and similar restrictions on other jurisdictions, most notably in the US.[1873] The risks remain though because non-banks that are engaged in proprietary trading have indirect links and exposures with UK banks and can transmit risk and

1865 Ibid., p. 85.

1866 Ibid.

1867 Ibid.

1868 Ibid., p. 86.

1869 Ibid., p. 87.

1870 Ibid.

1871 Ibid., p. 89.

1872 The 'Senior Managers and Certification Regime' (SM&CR) replaced the previously existed 'Approved Persons Regime' and changed how people working in financial services are regulated. SM&CR aims to reduce harm to consumers and strengthen market integrity by making individuals more accountable for their conduct and competence. The new regime is a catalyst for change – an opportunity to establish healthy cultures and effective governance in firms by encouraging greater individual accountability and setting a new standard of personal conduct. As part of this, the SM&CR aims to a) encourage a culture of staff at all levels taking personal responsibility for their actions, and b) make sure firms and staff clearly understand and can demonstrate where responsibility lies. For more information see in: https://www.fca.org.uk/firms/senior-managers-certification-regime.

1873 See in Ring-Fencing and Proprietary Trading Review (RFPT), Independent Review, Final Report, March 2022, p. 94.

turmoil. Hedge funds and principal trading firms undertake these activities, limiting banks to just 10% of total market share. Therefore, further monitoring is required in order to keep an eye on the proprietary trading activities and their associated risks.

4.2.3.2.3 *Panel's Final Recommendations*

The Panel concluded its analysis by making certain recommendations that aim at improving overall the ring-fencing regime. These recommendations are classified in two broad categories, as: a) ring-fencing recommendations and b) proprietary trading recommendations. Regarding the ring-fencing regime, the recommendations focus on the immediate issues faced by customers, banks, and regulators, as well as other possible options to address the ring-fencing regime's primary purpose of tackling too-big-to-fail, and consequently its alignment with the newly adopted resolution regime. Regarding proprietary trading, the recommendations reiterate the need to continue effectively monitoring related risks in banks, as well as the potential risks that may arise from activities undertaken in the non-bank sector.[1874] Overall, the Panel's recommendations are designed to achieve the following aims:[1875]

- Improve the outcomes for customers,
- Maintain financial stability benefits and minimise risks to public funds and
- Reduce the rigidity and unintended consequences of the ring-fencing regime.

Perhaps the Panel's most important recommendations are related to the scope of the ring-fencing regime. These recommendations stem from the Panel's analysis and conclusions that the financial stability related benefits of the ring-fencing regime are relevant and worthy only under the following conditions:[1876]

(a) When the ring-fencing regime is applied to large, complex banks,
(b) When banking services that are critical to the UK economy are undertaken by NRFBs, and
(c) that the resolution regime is now overtaking the ring-fencing regime in tackling too-big-to-fail.

While the Panel proposed maintaining the current level of £25 billion core deposits for entering the regime,[1877] deemed as proportional and in line with the general purposes of the ring-fencing, at the same time proposed to introduce another de minimis rule, regarding the excluded activities. Banks with deposits above the £25 billion level that do not undertake excluded activities above a certain (de minimis) level should be exempted from the ring-fencing

[1874] Ibid., p. 15.
[1875] Ibid., p. 98.
[1876] Ibid.
[1877] Ibid., p. 99.

requirement.[1878] According to the Panel's perception, the application of the ring-fencing regime to banks that do not undertake excluded activities does not produce financial stability benefits and therefore it would be more beneficial to introduce a certain level, just above zero, in order to avoid any cliff edge effects for banks that have already adapt to the regime.[1879] The banks with a total value of these excluded activities, which would be eligible for the de minimis test, below the de minimis level would be exempt from the ring-fencing requirement. To the contrary, '[a] bank with more than £25 billion deposits that moves above this de minimis level would then be subject to the requirements of the ring-fencing regime. To avoid cliff edges, the Panel suggests to only require the banks to place the excluded activities above the de minimis level into a separate legal entity – the NRFB'.[1880] Since banks within the regime's scope have already established their RFB and NRFB entities, with this proposal will be allowed to enter the excluded activities area and undertake some of them within the ring-fence, but only up to a certain de minimis limit. The activities whose value exceeds this de minimis limit would be placed in the NRFB entity, as discussed earlier. Therefore, a bank with more than £25 billion in core deposits would need to constantly keep the value of the excluded activities below the de minimis level or else it would be subject to the ring-fencing regime requirement. This is also important as it aims to ensure that banks remaining outside the ring-fencing regime would not have an unfair competitive advantage over the RFBs operating within the ring-fencing regime.[1881]

Ultimately, the Panel suggests that for banks, above the £25 billion deposit threshold, to be able to use this exemption and exit the ring-fencing regime, they should have to monitor and report all their excluded activities to demonstrate that these remain below the de minimis level. These additional monitoring and reporting requirements would require detailed oversight and monitoring of the risks while outside of the ring-fencing regime, mitigating any bank incentives to expand this kind of activity beyond what is deemed necessary. Obviously banks not using this exemption, such as those who far exceed the de minimis level or those who find themselves below the £25 billion deposit threshold, would not need to monitor and report these excluded activities.[1882] If RFBs choose to undertake certain excluded activities below the introduced de minimis level, they would need to monitor and report all the excluded activities within the RFB. This additional monitoring and reporting requirement would be prudent to mitigate the associated risks.[1883] The Panel's report concludes on this matter

1878 Ibid.
1879 Ibid.
1880 Ibid., p. 100.
1881 Ibid., p. 101.
1882 Ibid.
1883 Ibid.

by acknowledging that according to the Panel's assessment '[...] providing an exemption for banking groups with minimal levels of excluded activities would not undermine the resilience of the banks and would not increase financial stability risks [...]'[1884] because: a) banks' excluded activities would need to stay below the de minimis level and b) the PRA, FCA, and BoE have sufficient powers to exercise over UK subsidiaries of non-UK banking groups.[1885]

There are several potential benefits that could be realised from the package of recommendations' implementation. At the heart of the recommendations is the attempt to provide more flexibility to the authorities and banks, simultaneously, so that they can better adapt to customer needs while using a forward-looking, judgment-based approach, considering the associated risks as they evolve in a constantly changing financial sector and global economy. More importantly though, the package of recommendations lays the ground for future policy options to address the ring-fencing regime's primary purpose of tackling too-big-to-fail, and consequently its much-needed alignment with the resolution regime.[1886] In summary, the Panel's recommendations are stipulated in the table as follows:[1887]

Category	Recommendations
Ring-Fencing regime	(i) Change the scope of the ring-fencing regime to focus on large, complex banks: a. Banks with deposits below £25 billion should continue to be exempt from the ring-fencing regime, b. Banks with deposits above £25 billion that do not undertake excluded activities above a certain level should be exempt from the ring-fencing regime, c. Only excluded activities above that level should be required to be placed in an NRFB (ii) Align the ring-fencing regime with the resolution regime: a. HM Treasury should review the practicalities of how to align the ring-fencing and resolution regimes, with a view to introducing a new power for the authorities to remove banks from the ring-fencing regime that are judged to be resolvable. (iii) Adjust the restrictions on servicing relevant financial institutions (RFIs) a. An exemption should be introduced to allow RFBs to provide banking services to smaller RFIs, b. The definition of RFIs should be moved from legislation to the PRA Rulebook, and c. A grace period should be introduced for NRFBs to move customers that are no longer classified as an RFI to an RFB.

1884 Ibid., p. 102.
1885 Ibid.
1886 Ibid., p. 109.
1887 Ibid., p. 16.

	(iv) Improve the operation of the ring-fencing regime through technical amendments: a. Transitional periods for complying with ring-fencing rules should be introduced for mergers and acquisitions of banks, b. NRFBs should be enabled to service central banks outside of the UK, c. The status of trustees and insolvency practitioners should be clarified, and d. The notice of declaration onboarding requirements for NRFB customers should be removed. (v) Remove the blanket geographical restrictions from legislation that prevent RFBs from establishing operations or servicing customers outside of the EEA (vi) Review the excluded activities under the ring-fencing regime (vii) The BoE should ensure that sufficient plans are in place as part of its contingency planning to provide liquidity to NRFBs in a stress scenario
Proprietary trading	(i) Monitor risks from proprietary trading activities undertaken by banks in the UK (ii) Monitor and mitigate potential risks emanating from proprietary trading activities undertaken in the non-bank sector

Source: *Ring-Fencing and Proprietary Trading Review* – RFPT, Independent Review, Final Report, March 2022, p. 97

In case the above-mentioned amendments apply to the ring-fencing regime in the UK, the new landscape of available services to both RFBs and NRFBs would be as follows:

Only RFBs	Only NRFBs	Both RFBs/NRFBs
✓ Retail and small business deposit-taking	✓ Dealing in investments as principal ✓ Commodities trading ✓ Having exposure to financial institutions larger than SMEs	✓ Deposit taking for large corporates, building societies, and other RFBs ✓ Having exposure to building societies and other RFBs ✓ Lending to individuals and corporates ✓ Holding own securitisations ✓ Trade finance ✓ Payment services ✓ Hedging liquidity, interest rates, currency, commodity, and credit risks for itself ✓ Selling very simple derivatives to corporates, building societies, and other RFBs ✓ Exposure to financial institutions classed as SMEs ✓ Excluded activities below a *de minimis* level ✓ Operations outside of the EEA

Source: *Ring-Fencing and Proprietary Trading Review* – RFPT, Independent Review, Final Report, March 2022, p. 110

4.3. *Other Reforms*

The major regulatory change in the UK occurred in 2013, when the FSA was divided into the Prudential Regulation Authority (PRA), within the BoE and the Financial Conduct Authority (FCA). Currently, the PRA is responsible for the prudential regulation and supervision of around 1,500 deposit taking institutions (including banks, building societies and credit unions), insurance companies and designated investment firms. The FCA is the prudential supervisor for another 49,000 firms and is the conduct regulator for nearly 60,000 financial firms, including the firms prudentially supervised by the PRA ('dual-regulated firms').[1888] PRA's mandate is threefold: a) to promote the safety and soundness of the firms it regulates, b) to contribute to securing an appropriate degree of protection for insurance policyholders, and c) to facilitate effective competition between firms. The table below is extremely helpful at illustrating the current regulatory framework:

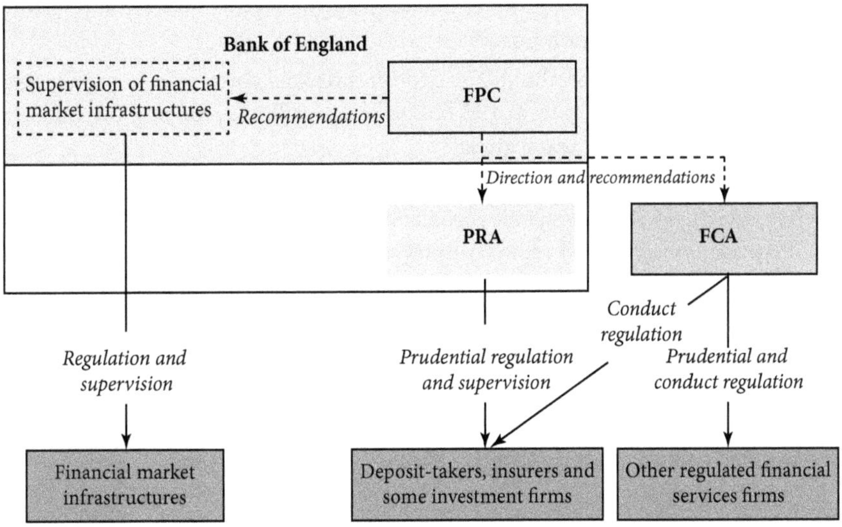

Source: Financial Stability Board (FSB), Peer Review of the United Kingdom, Review Report, 10 September 2013

1888 See in Financial Stability Board (FSB), *Peer Review of the United Kingdom, Review Report*, 14 April 2021, p. 7.

5 RECENT REFORMS OF THE RING-FENCING REGIME IN THE UK

5.1. *The Edinburgh Reforms (2022)*

The 'Edinburgh Reforms' are a comprehensive package of over 30 regulatory and tax reforms announced by the UK government on 9 December 2022, aimed at making the UK the world's most innovative and competitive financial center.[1889] The reforms focused on boosting investment and growth by updating financial services regulation to promote technological innovation, sustainable finance (ESG criteria), and to support the UK's global competitiveness. As part of the broader Edinburgh Reforms, the UK government confirmed that it will implement several of the RFPT's Final Report recommendations, aiming to modernise and streamline the ring-fencing framework:[1890]

- Exempt Retail-Focused Banks: Banking groups without significant investment banking operations would be removed from the regime entirely supporting smaller and challenger banks.[1891]
- Raise Applicability Threshold: The deposit threshold above which ring-fencing applies would increase from £25 billion to £35 billion, reducing the number of banks captured by the regime.[1892]
- Update 'Relevant Financial Institution' Definition: The definition would be updated to free up access for certain small businesses—like high street financial advisers—and reduce disproportionate compliance burdens.[1893]
- Relax Geographic Restrictions: The existing blanket ban that prevents RFBs from operating or servicing clients outside the EEA would be removed, aiming at promoting international competitiveness.[1894]
- Review Permitted/Restricted Activities: The list of activities of which RFBs are barred from conducting will be reviewed, with the potential to allow for more flexibility, such as hedging, project finance instruments, or selective equity stakes.[1895]
- Align with the Resolution Regime: A call for evidence was scheduled for Q1 2023 to explore aligning ring-fencing with the resolution framework,

---

1889 For more information on the Edinburgh Reforms, see the respective announcement from the HM Treasury: 'Edinburgh Reforms hail next chapter for UK Financial Services', December 2022, available at: https://www.gov.uk/government/news/edinburgh-reforms-hail-next-chapter-for-uk-financial-services.

1890 See in HM Treasury, 'Government response to the independent review on ring-fencing and proprietary trading', Policy Paper, December 2022.

1891 See in DLA Piper, 'The Edinburgh Reforms – Your guide to the proposals', December 2022.

1892 Ibid.

1893 Ibid.

1894 Ibid.

1895 Ibid.

including giving authorities the power to remove banks from ring-fencing if they are judged to be resolvable, drawing on the evolving resolution tools designed to manage bank failure safely.[1896]

These changes reflect a strategic shift toward a more flexible, growth-oriented ring-fencing regime. The goal is to reduce regulatory burden where risks are lower (e.g., in purely retail-focused banks), to enhance global competitiveness, and to synchronize ring-fencing with a more mature resolution framework.

5.2. The Leeds Reforms (2025)

The Leeds Reforms are a UK government initiative, announced in July 2025, to boost the financial services sector by streamlining regulations, attracting investment, and encouraging financial innovation.[1897] Key measures include allowing banks to alert customers about specific investment opportunities from April 2026, expanding Long Term Asset Funds, creating a new international investment support service, simplifying rules for raising capital, and streamlining the Senior Managers and Certification Regime. The goals of the reforms are:

- Boost Investment: Attract more capital into UK markets and drive finance into public markets.
- Encourage Innovation: Foster innovation within the financial sector and develop new products and services.
- Streamline Regulation: Simplify the financial regulatory framework by reducing red tape and complexity.
- Promote Competitiveness: Enhance the UK's position as a leading global financial center.
- Improve Consumer Access: Provide more access to financial advice and encourage public engagement with investment products.

With respect to our topic, the Leeds Reforms aim at freeing more capital for investments and this touches upon the ring-fencing regime, currently in place. 'The ring-fencing regime – which separates banks' retail and investment banking activities – will be reformed. The Economic Secretary will lead a review looking at how changes can strike the right balance between growth and stability, including protecting consumer deposits. This comes alongside a major review by the Financial Policy Committee of bank capital requirements. The review will inform work by the Government and Bank of England to ensure UK banks can compete internationally and provide vital investment

[1896] Ibid.

[1897] For more information on the Leeds Reforms see the respective announcement from the HM Treasury: 'Leeds Reforms to rewire financial system, boost investment and create skilled jobs across UK', July 2025, available at: https://www.gov.uk/government/news/leeds-reforms-to-rewire-financial-system-boost-investment-and-create-skilled-jobs-across-uk.

in the economy whilst maintaining the international regulatory standards which are crucial to securing financial stability.'[1898] The review of the ring-fencing regime is to be conducted by HM Treasury in collaboration with the BoE and aims to report by early 2026. The goal of the reforms is not to abolish the ring-fencing regime, but to undertake 'meaningful reform' that balances growth and competitiveness with the need to protect financial stability and depositors. Key areas under consideration include:[1899]

- Allowing RFBs to expand offerings, particularly enhancing their ability to serve UK businesses by offering a broader range of products and services.
- Addressing operational inefficiencies within the ring-fencing structure across banking groups.
- Allowing shared resources/services across the ring-fence, to improve operational flexibility and make the regime less burdensome.

Some changes though have already been implemented to the ring-fencing regime prior to the Leeds Reform announcement, based on the above-mentioned Edinburgh Reforms:

- The core deposit threshold for ring-fencing increased from £25 billion to £35 billion of 'core deposits',[1900]
- Introduction of a secondary exemption threshold (*de minimis*): banks with smaller trading businesses (trading assets < 10% of Tier 1 capital) can now be exempt even if they exceed the core deposit threshold,[1901]
- Removal of geographic limitations: RFBs may now establish operations outside the UK or EEA,[1902]
- Introduction of M&A transitional relief: four-year period before newly acquired banks fall under the ring-fencing rules,[1903]
- Expanded permitted activities for RFBs, which can now:[1904]
  - Have exposures up to £100,000 to a single relevant financial institution (RFI),
  - Invest in UK SMEs through funds or minority stakes, and
  - Engage in expanded trade finance, FX products, hedging longevity/mortality risks, and other core activities.

1898 Ibid.
1899 Ibid.
1900 See in Bank of England – PRA, *Prudential Regulation Authority, Annual Report, 1 March 2024 to 28 February 2025*, Bank of England, June 2025, p. 62.
1901 Ibid.
1902 Ibid.
1903 Ibid.
1904 See in LINKLATERS, *The UK ring-fencing regime: in the spotlight once again*, May 2025, p. 2.

6 CONCLUDING REMARKS

In comparison with other jurisdictions, the UK is an outlier when it comes to the implementation of structural separation. Most countries did not implement any form of structural separation for their banks, and the handful of countries did take a different, cautious and less rigid approach than the UK. Where other countries have implemented restrictions on what activities a bank can and cannot engage in, such as proprietary trading, the deposit-taking entities are still able to engage in a much wider scope of activities than RFBs in the UK.[1905] The RFPT's Panel report made some remarkable comments related to the ring-fencing regime. As presented above, the report illustrates the major difficulties that such a rigid regime brings to the everyday business of banking in the UK. Indeed, the banking business in the UK has become safer and much more liquid, but since the report concluded that the UK does not operate a 'zero failure banking system'[1906] the taxpayers' money is in danger and must be always bear in mind that in the future, public funds will be needed in extreme cases of system wide crises.[1907] Financial innovation, especially with the support of technology and Fintech solutions, is always one-step in front and the regulators/supervisors are lagging when it comes to implement new policies to old problems. Customers will always try to find what suits best their needs and the non-bank sector will always be willing to assume greater risks for greater returns, escaping the heavy regulatory burden of the ring-fencing. This was clearly acknowledged by the RFPT Panel's report and the UK Government reacted accordingly, by amending, albeit to a lesser extent, the ring-fencing regime. What remains to be seen is when and how the UK Government will further proceed with most recent proposals in order to restore the financial system's competitiveness. The industry wants an easing of the post-crisis restrictions that keep retail and investment banking operations apart and the pressure on the legislators will be of high power.

1905 See in *Ring-Fencing and Proprietary Trading Review* (RFPT), Independent Review, Final Report, March 2022, p. 29.

1906 Ibid., p. 112.

1907 Ibid., p. 45.

CHAPTER 5
EUROPEAN UNION: FROM UNIVERSAL BANKING TO... UNIVERSAL (?) BANKING

The European Union (EU) and Europe in general,[1908] have traditionally been bank dominated economies. The traditional model has been that of big universal banks that act as 'financial supermarkets' and, in some countries such as Germany, they actively participate in the corporate management through appointment of board members and shareholding. The close connection between corporations and banks gave Europe distinct characteristics regarding its banking sector and any type of structural reforms or similar measures were never a desirable solution to the sector's problems and to bank failures that happened from time to time. Only after the recent GFC, and the measures adopted in the US and in the UK, Europe started unwillingly to discuss a possible solution to its 'too big to fail' banks. Despite the efforts of the European Commission (the Commission) to organise and implement a proper solution to the structural reforms issue and discussions, up to date European banks remain almost entirely anchored around the universal banking model, offering the full spectrum of services that are available to them.[1909] Structural reforms at the EU level are very limited and only at national level there are some legislations that impose certain, light requirements to the banks, mostly in relation to their proprietary trading activities.

1908 Since the UK has been already discussed and analysed it is not included in our analysis at this Chapter. Although some numbers could include data and references to the UK, generally we do not consider the UK to be part of Europe for the purpose of the present book.

1909 See Annex I of Directive 2013/36/EU of the European Parliament and of the Council of 26 June 2013 on access to the activity of credit institutions and the prudential supervision of credit institutions, amending Directive 2002/87/EC and repealing Directives 2006/48/EC and 2006/49/EC, as it has been amended and currently into force.

1 A CURRENT OVERVIEW OF THE EU'S FINANCIAL SECTOR

The EU's financial sector could be characterised by two words: resilience and variety. Resilience, because despite the several socks that has navigated through remains robust and with a credible institutional framework that has been put in place after the recent GFC. The second word is variety, as in the EU we can see the dominance of bank versus market funding but adjusted to the particular aspects of each country. Based on the latest available data from the European Central Bank (ECB), the euro area financial sector has shrunk in absolute nominal terms since 2022 and despite a rise in nominal GDP, the total financial assets of the euro area financial sector have declined across sectors.[1910] Simultaneously, the composition of the euro area financial sector has remained broadly unchanged, with the share of banking sector assets in total financial system assets being stabilised at around one-third. Meanwhile, we observe a continuous growth of the share of non-bank financial intermediary (NBFI) assets from 2012 to nowadays.[1911] However, worsening asset quality, higher funding costs and limited consolidation of the banking sector creates headwinds for the future.[1912] Very helpful are also the available data from the European Banking Federation (EBF) Facts & Figures, based on their most recent publication, as of 2022. According to the EBF data, since 2009, Europe observed a downward trend in the number of credit institutions, with the number falling to 5,263 credit institutions in 2021.[1913] The amount of total assets is in an upward trend reaching €40.8 trillion in 2022 while total assets held by operating banks in the EFTA countries and the UK in 2021 was €4.5 trillion and €10.7 trillion respectively, totalling an amount equal to almost €60 trillion.[1914] The amount of deposit liabilities in the EU rose €25 trillion and the deposits from households (including non-profit institutions serving households), non-financial corporations (NFCs) and financial corporations which rose to €9.6 trillion, €3.8 trillion and €2.08 trillion respectively.[1915] The absence of a pan-European capital market that could offer an alternative source of funding to the bulk of enterprises (SMEs) in the EU forces banks to play an important intermediation role in Europe.

[1910] See in European Central Bank, *Financial Integration and Structure in the Euro Area*, ECB Committee of Financial Integration, June 2024, p. 25.

[1911] Ibid.

[1912] Ibid.

[1913] See in European Banking Federation (EBF), *Banking in Europe: EBF Facts & Figures 2022*, Brussels 2022, p. 4.

[1914] Ibid., p. 16.

[1915] Ibid., p. 12.

2 A HISTORICAL EVOLUTION OF THE BANKING BUSINESS IN EUROPE

Europe can be considered as the founding place of modern banking. The history of European banking is a fascinating evolution shaped by the rise of capitalism, the growth of empires and colonies, and the development of financial institutions blended with wars and crises. European banks were formed ab initio as universal banks, since they were accepting deposits from the public and were participating in the underwriting of government bonds, providing finance to the states. To facilitate our study, and given the many years of fascinating history, we will shorten our timeline and split the time before and after the important moment of the creation of the EU, also known as Economic Community, until the signing of the Lisbon Treaty in 2009. The initiative of the European integration project marks the beginning of a new era in the European banking sector because it was called upon to play an important role towards further integration among the various Member States.

2.1. The Era Before European Integration

From Italy, back in the 14th century where the first merchant banks started trading in commodities, also on their own account, until nowadays, European banks have been transformed into financial supermarkets financing the continent's growth.[1916] One of the first major European banks was the Medici Bank, established in Florence, Italy, in the late 14th century (1397). It played a pivotal role in European banking and the rise of Italian city-states. The Medici family also helped develop the practice of double-entry bookkeeping, a crucial innovation for modern banking. In cities like Venice and Genoa, Italian merchants and financiers developed sophisticated banking techniques, including the use of bills of exchange, which allowed for credit across borders. These cities became financial hubs in medieval Europe. Somehow northern, in Amsterdam, the Dutch Republic, a leading economic power of the time, created in 1609 the Bank of Amsterdam. This bank was one of the first institutions to offer the modern concept of a central bank with the ability to hold reserves and settle payments for international transactions. The Dutch were also influential in creating the modern concept of joint-stock banks, which allowed multiple investors to pool capital for large-scale ventures and investments. French banking in the 17th century also saw the rise of private institutions that lent to the monarchy. As we entered the period of industrial revolution, European

1916 See in K. Alexander, *Principles of Banking Regulation*, Cambridge, Cambridge University Press, 2019 and in C. Fohlin, 'A Brief History of Investment Banking from Medieval Times to the Present', in Y. Cassis, C.R. Schenk and S.R. Grossman (eds.), *The Oxford Handbook of Banking and Financial History*, Oxford, Oxford University Press, 2016.

banks also entered corporate financing business, mostly because in northern Europe, big corporations starved of capital to invest in the new technologies that were available for their expansion and increase of production. Alongside their traditional financing activities universal banks participated in the governance of non-financial corporations mostly through appointments of representatives in the boards of directors and ownership of equity stakes.[1917] This practice can be attributed to the fact that many universal banks participated in these entities by design or simply because they left with a big equity stake unsold after they had initially underwritten it. Moreover, European universal banks were also offering safekeeping services to their customers, related to their shares, so through their client relationships they were even exercising their clients' rights derived from the shares they were safekeeping for them.[1918] Banks in Belgium, Netherlands, Austria, Switzerland, France, and Germany provided their clients simultaneously with capital markets services and with loans thereby creating financial supermarkets to cover all their needs and as the industrialisation was moving forward, European universal banks were also increasing in size, following their clients' needs.

The need for central banks to manage national currencies, stabilise economies, and oversee financial markets became increasingly important and the development of large-scale international banking networks during the 19th century fostered economic integration across Europe. By the late 19th and early 20th centuries, European banking had become more complex and intertwined with the global economy. Leading European banks like Rothschilds, Barings, and Credit Lyonnais played key roles in financing European imperial projects, as well as the global spread of industrialisation. As the financial systems grew, many countries began to introduce regulations to control banking practices and reduce the risk of financial panics. With Europe entering World War I, the banking systems in many countries faced immense challenges, since governments borrowed heavily to finance the war, leading to an expansion of national government debts.

By the outbreak of World War I, Europe's banking systems had grown more interconnected and sophisticated, but the war would mark the beginning of a new era in financial history, with lasting impacts on global banking practices and institutions. This period marked a shift from relatively stable banking systems to wartime financial turmoil and in some cases, banks were nationalised or brought under more direct government control to facilitate war financing. The war led to inflation, the suspension of gold convertibility, and large deficits for many countries. After the end of World War I, European

---

1917 See in C. Fohlin, 'A Brief History of Investment Banking from Medieval Times to the Present', in Y. Cassis, C.R. Schenk and S.R. Grossman (eds.), *The Oxford Handbook of Banking and Financial History*, Oxford, Oxford University Press, 2016.

1918 Ibid.

economies were in dire strait since the war had devastated national economies, led to massive debts, and caused widespread inflation. The banking systems faced challenges such as currency devaluation and political instability, which shaped the financial landscape. Until World War II, this was the broad picture of the European banking sector. During the interwar years, some stability returned, but the economic recovery was uneven across Europe with some European countries nationalised key industries and financial institutions to stabilise their economies. The end of World War II left European economies in ruins, and the need for reconstruction was immediate. Banking systems in many countries were destroyed or heavily damaged, and the global financial system required a complete overhaul.

2.2. *From the European Integration to the recent Global Financial Crisis*

Thus, the period from the end of World War II to the establishment of the EU was marked by significant challenges and transformations in European banking and finance. Following the devastations of the war and economic upheaval, Europe gradually built a framework for economic cooperation that would culminate in the European Integration project, which aimed to foster peace, stability, and prosperity on the continent and the creation of the EU is a major milestone for the European banking system and its further integration. After the catastrophic Second World War, European states decided to converge with their economies and create an economic union that would progressively secure prosperity and peace in the continent. From the conceptual Economic Community to the current EU, the aim of this collective effort is to create 'an ever-closer union' among the Member States. Due to their importance, financial services are at the epicentre of this project and form one of the most critical parts of the single market. The freedom of capital movement and the freedom of (financial) services. At the EU level, liberalisation of capital movements across the EU Member States was closely linked with the fundamental freedom to provide (financial) services, since the very first steps of the EU. These efforts were concentrated in the completion of the internal market, as expressed in the famous Commission's 1985 White Paper.[1919] The creation of a unified banking market, necessary for the creation of the internal market, was based on the principle of mutual recognition was a prerequisite for a single banking license regime.[1920] The EU worked intensively towards the

1919 European Commission, *Completing the Internal Market,* White Paper from the Commission to the European Council (Milan, 28–29 June 1985), COM (85) 310 final, Brussels, 14 June 1985. See also in G. Zavos, 'Banking Integration in the European Community' (1989) 9 *Northwestern Journal of International Law & Business*, p. 572.

1920 See in G. Zavos, 'Banking Integration in the European Community' (1989) 9 *Northwestern Journal of International Law & Business*, p. 573.

direction of closer integration in the financial services sector based on three, crucial and equally important principles:[1921]

(i) The harmonisation of the essential aspects of banking integration,
(ii) The principle of mutual recognition of financial standards, and
(iii) The home country control principle.

The harmonisation of the essential aspects had been the long-term view of the Commission since the very first years. The main integration tools were the mutual recognition of supervisory standards and the harmonisation of the relevant banking legislation, mostly through directives. Together with the 'home country control' principle, the integration process accelerated since the EU was able to accept financial services easier and more effectively. The home country control principle has the meaning that all the activities of banks and other financial institutions carried out through branches or on a cross border provision of services on the EU's entire territory, in principle, will be supervised by the competent authorities of the Member States where the institution has its headquarters.[1922] All these tools were adopted in the Directive 89/646/EEC, better known as the 'Second Banking Directive' (2nd Banking Directive).[1923] What was truly revolutionary about that Directive was its Annex, containing a list of (financial) services that banks were allowed to offer based on their banking license, through the 'passporting' system.[1924] In order for the banks to benefit from the mutual recognition they had to comply with two, cumulative, requirements: a) they had to be authorised and supervised by the competent authorities of their home Member States, and b) they had to undertake activities that were included in the list attached to the Annex.[1925] The services included in the Annex were actually a 'product regulation', since they would contribute to the widespread of universal banking model. For reasons of coherence, the list was as follows:

(1) Acceptance of deposits and other repayable funds from the public.
(2) Lending.
(3) Financial Leasing.
(4) Money transmission services.
(5) Issuing and administering means of payment (e.g. credit cards, travellers' cheques, and bankers' drafts).
(6) Guarantees and commitments.

1921 Ibid.

1922 Ibid., p. 574.

1923 Second Council Directive 89/646/EEC of 15 December 1989 on the coordination of laws, regulations and administrative provisions relating to the taking up and pursuit of the business of credit institutions and amending Directive 77/780/EEC, [1989] *OJ* L 386/1.

1924 See in G. Zavos, 'Banking Integration in the European Community' (1989) 9 *Northwestern Journal of International Law & Business*, p. 574.

1925 Ibid., p. 575.

(7) Trading for own account or for account of customers in:
  (a) money market instruments (cheques, bills, CDs, etc.);
  (b) foreign exchange;
  (c) financial futures and options;
  (d) exchange and interest rate instruments;
  (e) transferable securities.
(8) Participation in share issues and the provision of services related to such issues.
(9) Advice to undertakings on capital structure, industrial strategy and related questions and advice and services relating to mergers and the purchase of undertakings.
(10) Money broking.
(11) Portfolio management and advice.
(12) Safekeeping and administration of securities.
(13) Credit reference services.
(14) Safe custody services, including inter alia:
  - consumer credit,
  - mortgage credit,
  - factoring, with or without recourse,
  - financing of commercial transactions (including forfeiting).

From the above annexed list is clear that a bank that wants to offer services in the EU territory practically has access to the full spectrum of available services. Universal banking was officially promoted by EU legislation, and a bank could offer services that were not allowed for the banks based on the host country. In a fictitious example, a Spanish bank could offer banking services to the Austrian market. Profiting from the above list, if the Spanish bank was allowed by the Spanish authorities to offer the full list of services in Spain, was able to do the same in Austria, even if the Austrian banks were not allowed by their respective authorities to offer certain services, let's say portfolio management and advice services. The annexed list contained not only the traditional banking activities, but also all forms of transactions in the securities field and this was mostly because of the blurring of demarcation between the traditional commercial banking and investment banking and that the market forces were shaping the banking sector, creating a new regulatory environment.[1926] With the second banking directive, the EU Member States were obliged to allow any credit institution established in another Member State to provide the full spectrum of the listed activities, as enumerated above, in a unified matter across the EU territory.

[1926] Ibid.

2.3. *The Post Crises Landscape: Tectonic Changes*

The result of the EU crises on banking and financial regulation was a 'cosmogony'.[1927] Just as the ancient Greek historian Hesiod[1928] who, thousands of years ago described the birth of the ancient world and the emergence of gods, 'cosmogony' accurately depicts the evolution of the EU regulatory framework after the recent GFC and the subsequent Eurozone crisis. The relevant legislation and the supporting academic literature are extremely vast, and the present book will refer only to what is deemed necessary for the coherent analysis of our subject. Therefore, in case a reader would like to have a deeper understanding of the legislative changes and of the relevant bibliography, especially for the EU, shall make use of other, more specialised academic work.

The most important change happened at the European financial regulatory architecture, that was radically changed and adapted to the lessons learned from the double crisis.[1929] The new architecture was based on the proposals of the so-called 'De Larosière Report'. The report, prepared by a high-level group at the request of the Commission, chaired by Jacques de Larosière, proposed the creation of a new financial architecture for the supervision in the EU. The new structure resulted in the creation of a new body, the European Systemic Risk Board (ESRB),[1930] tasked with the macroprudential oversight of the financial markets in the EU, and the creation of the European System of Financial Supervision (ESFS). The last one is not a body per se, but rather a coordinating structure for the three major micro-prudential, financial regulatory agencies of the EU, namely the European Banking Authority

---

1927 'Cosmogony', in astronomy science, studies the evolutionary behaviour of the universe and the origin of its characteristic features. See in Britannica: https://www.britannica.com/science/cosmogony.

1928 Hesiod (flourished c. 700 BC) was one of the earliest Greek poets, often called the 'father of Greek didactic poetry'. Two of his complete epics have survived, the 'Theogony', relating the myths of the gods, and the 'Works and Days', describing peasant life. See in Britannica: https://www.britannica.com/biography/Hesiod.

1929 See in E. Ludwig, *Lessons Learned from the 2008 Financial Crisis*, The William Taylor Memorial Lecture, The Group of Thirty, Washington D.C., where the basic lessons of the financial crisis are described. Moreover, in another important paper, Guillermo de la Dehesa described the inefficiencies that led to the global financial crisis.
See also in G. de la Dehesa, 'Twelve Market and Government Failures Leading to the 2008–2009 Financial Crisis', *Occasional Paper* No. 80, Group of Thirty, Washington.

1930 Regulation (EU) No 1092/2010 of the European Parliament and of the Council of 24 November 2010 on European Union macro-prudential oversight of the financial system and establishing a European Systemic Risk Board, [2010] *OJ* L 331/1.

(EBA),[1931] the European Securities and Markets Authority (ESMA),[1932] and the European Insurance and Occupational Pensions Authority (EIOPA),[1933] evolution of the previous committees; CEBS,[1934] CESR[1935] and CEIOPS.[1936] The three agencies, EBA, ESMA, and EIOPA have binding powers regarding the micro-prudential supervisory principles and practices,[1937] and currently ESMA is the supervisory authority for the credit rating agencies.[1938]

3 THE TWIN CRISES OF THE EUROPEAN UNION AND THEIR IMPACT

The EU suffered extensively from the GFC of 2007–2009. The initial banking crisis was quickly transformed into a sovereign debt crisis that hit harshly mostly the Mediterranean countries with unstable fiscal policies and banking

---

1931 Regulation (EU) No 1093/2010 of the European Parliament and of the Council of 24 November 2010 establishing a European Supervisory Authority (European Banking Authority), amending Decision No 716/2009/EC and repealing Commission Decision 2009/78/EC, [2010] OJ L 331/12.

1932 Regulation (EU) No 1095/2010 of the European Parliament and of the Council of 24 November 2010 establishing a European Supervisory Authority (European Securities and Markets Authority), amending Decision No 716/2009/EC and repealing Commission Decision 2009/77/EC, [2010] *OJ* L 331/84.

1933 Regulation (EU) No 1094/2010 of the European Parliament and of the Council of 24 November 2010 establishing a European Supervisory Authority (European Insurance and Occupational Pensions Authority), amending Decision No 716/2009/EC and repealing Commission Decision 2009/79/EC, [2010] *OJ* L 331/48.

1934 The *Committee of European Banking Supervisors* (CEBS) was an independent body in charge of advising and coordinating on banking regulation and supervision in the European Union (EU). Established by the European Commission in 2004, it was composed of senior representatives of bank supervisory authorities and central banks of the European Union. See in: https://www.eba.europa.eu/cebs-archive.

1935 The *Committee of European Securities Regulators* (CESR) was an independent body established by the European Commission to advise member state authorities' competent authorities on the technical details of securities legislation. See in: https://www.lexisnexis.co.uk/legal/glossary/committee-of-european-securities-regulators-cesr.

1936 The *Committee of European Insurance and Occupational Pensions Supervisors* (CEIOPS) was established on 5 November 2003 by the European Commission to advice in the fields of insurance, reinsurance and occupational pensions. See in: https://www.europeansources.info/record/committee-of-european-insurance-and-occupational-pensions-supervisors-ceiops/.

1937 See in J. Mitchell, P. Van Roy and C. Vespro, 'Ten Years After the Financial Crisis: Regulatory Reforms and The Belgian Banking Sector', *Reflets et perspectives de la vie économique*, 2017/1, Tome LVI, De Boeck Supérieur, p. 17.

1938 The three agencies, since they are not official bodies of the EU, written in the Treaty of the European Union (TEU), are binding by the effects of the Meroni Doctrine, and therefore have a very well-defined perimeter of action. For a deeper analysis on this special issue regarding the Meroni Doctrine and its application on the financial supervision in the EU, see in F. Annunziata, 'The Remains of the Day: EU Financial Agencies, Soft Law and the Relics of Meroni', Working Paper no. 106, *EBI Working Paper Series*, 2021, European Banking Institute.

sector exposed to the debt of its country. Moreover, it demonstrated in an emphatic way how unprepared the EU was for such a scenario and requested bold steps for the next day, steps that few years ago were unimaginable not to say even emphatically rejected. The impact of the recent GFC in the EU was twofold. On the one hand, many European banks collapsed, and others had to be saved by their respective governments. At the same time, these bailouts skyrocketed the public debt of these states into non-viable levels fuelling the next crisis, the Eurozone debt crisis. This double hit, on the banking sector per se and on the public finances paved the way for colossal changes in the banking regulation and supervision, and in the structure of the EU, with such radical changes that few years before could only be perceived as bad jokes.

Already struggling from the global financial turmoil that had washed up on its shores from the 2007–2009 collapse of the US subprime mortgage market, a new home-grown crisis erupted in Europe in 2010. Markets began to mistrust several countries, even members of the Eurozone, requiring ever-higher interest rates when they borrowed on the market, as a risk premium. They judged them as being increasingly risky: their governments had let their public deficits balloon, lost competitiveness, or allowed lax oversight of their national banking systems. Eventually, the unthinkable started to happen in 2010. Countries began to lose market access, finding themselves unable to refinance their government expenditure at acceptable borrowing costs. Greece was first country to ask for such help. The country received loans (Greek Loan Facility) from the other euro area countries on a bilateral basis. This situation demonstrated the faulty design of the Eurozone and the direct need to complement it with a stable mechanism that could protect the countries from predatory lending from global markets.

3.1. Bank Failures in the EU

During the period of 'Great Moderation' many European banks had heavily invested in the toxic US subprime loans and other complex financial products. With the burst of the housing bubble, they were left exposed, incurred losses and forced their respective governments to intervene and bail them out. Many prominent European banks failed during that period and because of the so-called bank sovereign nexus' the state of public finances in many Member States worsened, creating a feedback loop that was not able to break. Governments adopted nationalisation measures, arranged mergers among banks and sometimes even forced wind downs, together with public support schemes (state aids) channelled billions of euros to the European banking sector not to collapse. This constant supply of funds to the banking sector was under the review of the European Commission, since it violated the state aid rules as stipulated in the Treaty of the Functioning of the EU (TFEU). Legal interpretation and manoeuvring space were necessary for these extraordinary measures to be found compatible with the single market.[1939] Since the cases of the individual banks that failed during the turbulent years of the financial crisis are numerous and an exhaustive presentation is not feasible, we will present certain cases that have particular importance for the evolution of the crisis or were hit by the last waves of the financial crisis when it was transformed into the Eurozone debt crisis. We will present and discuss several cases of failed banks, and cases that had to do with Member States' entire banking systems, such as the Irish banks, the Greek and the Cypriot ones, which are used as indicative examples of bank failures during crisis times and are intended to populate our sample of cases, in order to have a more robust final result.

3.1.1 The Case of Irish Banks

Prior to the GFC, the Irish banking system had been in constant expansion. In a retrospective approach, from 2000 to 2007, the aggregate loan balances of Ireland's covered banks[1940] more than tripled, from €120 billion to €400 billion equalising a growth rate of almost 19% annually.[1941] As the Irish loan growth exceeded the economic growth and the available deposit funding, Irish banks funded this expansion through cheap borrowing from the wholesale markets taking into advantage the lower ECB interest rates and the ample market liquidity, mostly from foreign lenders.[1942] Ireland, according to economists, also suffered from a bubble in the housing market and therefore loans to construction, real estate and mortgages were funded by the Irish banks. These loans were collateralised by the underlying real estates and led to a notable risk concentration despite their initially increasing tendency that gave banks an extra security margin in their lending practice.[1943] Amid this crisis shaped environment, the Irish banking system was the first that collapsed in the EU. When the situation became critical, the (central) Bank of Ireland (BoI), the Department of Finance and the country's financial regulator started discussions about how the situation could be altered and preserve financial stability.

[1939] For a deeper analysis and understanding of the major issues at stake regarding the state aid measures and the competition rules applied at the EU level during the financial crisis of 2007–2009, see indicatively in L. Wagner, 'Aides d'État: l'art de la souplesse en temps de crise', *Cahiers de droit européen* (CDE), Vol. 47, n° 1, 2011, pp. 231–276 and in M. Reynolds, S. Macrory and M. Chowdhury, 'EU Competition Policy in the Financial Crisis: Extraordinary Measures' (2019) 33(6) *Fordham International Law Review*, Article 3, pp. 1670–1737.

[1940] As 'covered' banks were understood the six major Irish banks, and the smaller *Postbank*, that were covered by the governmental guarantee in September 2008. The banks covered were *Allied Irish Bank, Bank of Ireland, Anglo Irish Bank, Irish Life & Permanent, Irish Nationwide Building Society* and the *EBS* (Educational Building Society).

[1941] See in A.G. Zeissler, D. Ikeda and A. Metrick, 'Ireland and Iceland in Crisis D: Similarities and Differences' (2019) 1(3) *Journal of Financial Crises*, p. 47.

[1942] Ibid.

[1943] Ibid. New home prices in Ireland almost tripled between 1995 and 2007.

Since the collapse of Northern Rock, back in 2007, contingency planning and extraordinary measures were on the table and these discussions continued through the entire year.[1944] The belief among the Irish officials and executives was that the problem of Irish banks was one of liquidity rather than solvency and that a no-fail policy was mandated for the Irish banking sector.[1945] In late September 2008, within a single weekend various banks across Europe and the US were either nationalised or sold in deals arranged by governments and central banks. On Monday, 29 September 2008, Anglo Irish Bank (AIB), which was perceived as the weakest bank of all, saw its stock price to tumble, forcing BoI and Allied Irish Banks to request a meeting with the Prime Minister and the Minister of Finance to share their worries about potential future failure of AIB. Any possible bank failure would evaporate the rest of the banks' funding with adverse effects for them. This perspective forced the Irish government to introduce a blanket guarantee for almost all liabilities of the covered banks, including deposits (even those not eligible for guarantee), senior unsecured debt and subordinated debt with maturity date, excluding only undated (perpetual) subordinated debt.[1946] The estimated total amount of guarantees was up to €375 billion, more than double of the Irish GDP and none of the Irish banks were immediately nationalised as this happened, fully or partially, in 2009 and 2010.[1947] The following table provides a detailed analysis of the covered liabilities:

Type of liability	Amount in Euro (€)	Percentage of the package
Customer Deposits	€173.2 billion	47%
Senior Unsecured Debt	€124.2 billion	33%
Interbank Deposits	€49.1 billion	13%
Assets Covered Securities	€15.8 billion	4%
Dated Subordinated Debt	€12.2 billion	3%
Financial Instruments	€0.7 billion	0%

Source: A.G. Zeissler, D. Ikeda and A. Metrick, 'Ireland and Iceland in Crisis D: Similarities and Differences' (2019) 1(3) *Journal of Financial Crises*), p. 50

The decision of the Irish government to guarantee to such an extent all the liabilities, even though actually this guarantee was never activated, without immediate bank nationalisations was not very prudent. The constant

1944 Ibid., p. 49.
1945 Ibid.
1946 Ibid.
1947 Ibid., p. 50.

decrease in banks' asset values forced the government to assume control over banks and gave the wrong message to the markets: lack of credibility from the government's side.[1948] The Irish government required assistance from the EU and the IMF in November 2010, in exchange for strict restructuring and adaptation programs. The total amount of the financial assistance was €85 billion (€45 billion from the EU, €22.5 from the IMF and €17.5 billion from the Ireland's own pension reserve fund.[1949] Ireland has been characterised as the first country from the EU to face a crisis that evolved in the Eurozone sovereign debt crisis mostly because of the government's decision to issue that blanker guarantee of all banking sector's liabilities.

Ireland proceeded with a fast pace to restructure its failed banking system. The restructuring covered capital, liquidity, and asset quality, and was achieved through various steps that overlapped over time, in a painful process that involved bank rescuing, and banking sector's stabilisation and reorganisation.[1950] Two banks, AIB and INBS, were singled out for wind-down and several deleveraging plans were used to progressively reduce reliance on wholesale market funding. Moreover, a designated asset management company, the National Asset Management Agency (NAMA), was set up with the aim to remove certain commercial property and land loans from banks' balance sheets.[1951] The end of this process, found the Irish banking system emerged from the transformation and restructuring as smaller and more domestically and more retail-focused.[1952] Apart from restructuring the banking system, the Irish government adopted also a new financial supervisory policy. The Central Bank Reform Act of July 2010 established the BoI as a single fully integrated structure, with the purposes to 'enhance the system of regulatory control and to confer additional powers on the central bank, the governor and the Head of Financial Regulation to prevent potential serious damage to the financial system in the state, support the stability of that system and to protect users of financial services'.[1953] In addition to the above measure, banking regulation

1948 Ibid., p. 51.
1949 Ibid., p. 52.
1950 See in P. Baudino, D. Murphy and J.P. Svoronos, 'The banking crisis in Ireland', *FSI Crisis Management Series*, No. 2, Financial Stability Institute, Bank of International Settlements, Basel, 2020, p. 14.
1951 Ibid., p. 23. Created by legislation, NAMA, was established in November 2009 and its primary objective was to protect or even enhance the value of property development loans and maximize the state's return. What NAMA did, essentially was to replace the participating banks in their rights by controlling the relationship with the borrower and all associated decision-making and receipt of income from these loans. Moreover, since it was an agency partly owned by the state, NAMA also had been assigned with a secondary objective, that of making a positive contribution to society through the provision of social housing and by developing properties for investment.
1952 Ibid., p. 15, with a thorough analysis of the steps of the restructuring process.
1953 Ibid., p. 33.

has been overhauled through the introduction of the European legislation transposing the Basel III framework and by effective enforcement, forward-looking and risk-based supervision, which were introduced as part of the reforms adopted back in 2010.[1954]

3.1.2 The Case of Cypriot Banks

This case study is of particular importance and academic interest since it was the first time that resolution tools applied to certain banks, a year before the Banking Resolution and Recovery Directive (BRRD)[1955] was adopted by the EU. The Cypriot financial crisis was the product of multiple events that included the exposure of the Cypriot banks to the Greek sovereign bond crisis, exposure to overleveraged domestic property companies, the downgrading of the Cypriot government's bond to junk status by the credit rating agencies leading to an inability to fund the public expenditures from the international markets, as well as the overall reluctance of the Cypriot governments to restructure the financial sector.[1956] The events culminated in March 2013, where a seismic restructuring of the Cypriot banking system took place, reshaping permanently the financial landscape of the small Mediterranean island and breaking few taboos along the way.

Cyprus, prior to 2013, had accumulate macroeconomic imbalances through decreased tax revenues and increased social spending that increased the public deficit between 2009–2012. Banks took advantage from the entry in the Eurozone and the low interest rates, gathered deposits and increased their financing towards real estate development and private credit.[1957] Moreover, the banking sector suffered from inadequate risk management and corporate governance structures and had increased bank-sovereign nexus with both Greece and Cyprus. Based on the above macroeconomic situation it was evident that the time was running out for Cyprus. The situation worsened by a summer 2011 accident in a military camp, where an explosion in confiscated stored ammunition destroyed entirely the neighbouring and biggest power

---

1954 Ibid.

1955 Directive 2014/59/EU of the European Parliament and of the Council of 15 May 2014 establishing a framework for the recovery and resolution of credit institutions and investment firms and amending Council Directive 82/891/EEC, and Directives 2001/24/EC, 2002/47/EC, 2004/25/EC, 2005/56/EC, 2007/36/EC, 2011/35/EU, 2012/30/EU and 2013/36/EU, and Regulations (EU) No 1093/2010 and (EU) No 648/2012, of the European Parliament and of the Council, [2014] *OJ* L 173/190.

1956 See in N. Kleftouri, *Deposit Protection and Bank Resolution*, Oxford, Oxford University Press, 2015, p. 106.

1957 See in A. Michaelides, 'Cyprus; Bank of Cyprus (BOC) and Laiki: Resolution via Public Support and Bail-In, Including of Uninsured Depositors (2013)', in *Bank Resolution and Bail-In in the EU: Selected Case Studies Pre and Post BRRD*, Financial Sector Advisory Center, World Bank Group, 2016, p. 19.

plant of the island, leading to 13 deaths, major power cuts, and the resignation of Ministers of Economics and Foreign Affairs. Cyprus was in the spotlight and credit ratings altered reflecting downward future GDP and unsound public finances. In June 2012 Laiki Bank (also known as Cyprus Popular Bank – CPB) requested a bailout that absorb an amount equivalent to almost 10% of the Cypriot GDP.[1958] Since the Cypriot government bonds had rose above 7% access to international capital was almost prohibited and the government had to request help from the EU. Despite the urgent timing, the Cypriot government did not rush to negotiate a deal with the Troika and attempted for the next 18(!) months to manage the crisis internally.[1959] During this period, deposit outflows levelled up to an amount between €10-17 billion, mostly from the Cypriot banks' branches in Greece, until the final agreement in March 2013. The deposit outflow during a recession period can turn a solvent bank into insolvency.

In June 2012, the Central Bank of Cyprus (CBC) hired PIMCO to perform a stress test to Cypriot banks to determine the actual level of their capital needs. This procedure was not concluded until February 2013.[1960] PIMCO examined the banks' portfolios and estimated the capital needs to be at €5.8 billion. The main component of capital needs had to do with the 2012 Greek sovereign debt restructuring which resulted in severe losses for the two major banks, Bank of Cyprus (BoC) and Laiki Bank, because their portfolios were comprised from large holdings of Greek bonds.[1961] The concentration risk should had ring the alarm in the risk departments but the poor governance framework was not in position to change the bank's business decisions. The CBC continued to provide Emergency Liquidity Assistance (ELA) to Laiki Bank for the period until March 2013, based on the ECB's special permission. ELA was allowed to reach 60% of the GDP even though the ECB had opined that a resolution would have been a sounder solution for Laiki Bank, instead of the June 2012 bail out.[1962] Both the ECB and CBC justified their decision based on the assumption that Laiki Bank was 'dynamically solvent' under the condition that a reform program would be achieved after the negotiations.[1963]

[1958] Laiki Bank was one of the two largest banks in Cyprus and was nationalised in June 2012 to meet the requirements of the European Banking Authority. The cost of the bank's recapitalization has reached a total of €1.8 billion. As a result, the state obtained 84% of Laiki Bank's shares. Source: Eurofound, https://www.eurofound.europa.eu/observatories/emcc/erm/factsheets/laiki-bank.

[1959] See in A. Michaelides, 'Cyprus; Bank of Cyprus (BOC) and Laiki: Resolution via Public Support and Bail-In, Including of Uninsured Depositors (2013)', in *Bank Resolution and Bail-In in the EU: Selected Case Studies Pre and Post BRRD*, Financial Sector Advisory Center, World Bank Group, 2016, p. 19.

[1960] Ibid.

[1961] Ibid., p. 20.

[1962] Ibid.

[1963] Ibid.

On 16 March 2013, the Eurogroup agreed to a deal with the Cypriot government which included a horizontal, across all banks, tax of 6.75% for insured deposits up to €100.000 and a larger tax of 9.9% for uninsured deposits, higher than €100,000.[1964] This tax was actually a haircut, but since it was applied in a taxational form, prior Parliamentary approval was required. The Cypriot Parliament rejected the proposal for the horizontal tax on 19 March 2013, hoping for getting a better deal because the taboo of taxing insured deposits was unprecedented and worldwide criticism was provoked.[1965] The responsibility for such a decision and the associated political costs were enormous and no one had the willingness to vote in favour of such an experiment. This 'experimental therapy' of a classic disease shut down the Cypriot banking system for almost two weeks, from 18 to 28 March 2013, banning at the same time internet transactions to avoid any further capital flying. On 21 March 2013, the ECB announced its decision to maintain its current level of ELA for both Laiki and BoC, until 25 March 2013. 'Thereafter, Emergency Liquidity Assistance (ELA) could only be considered if an EU/IMF programme is in place that would ensure the solvency of the concerned banks' according to the official press release.[1966] The next day, the Parliament urgently approved a new legal act, that enabled the CBC to resolve insolvent institutions with a sound legal basis, and a new bailout plan was announced on 25 March 2013 that would not require parliament's approval.

According to the updated plan, Laiki Bank was resolved immediately with full contribution from its shareholders, bondholders, and uninsured depositors and further split into two parts, adopting a 'good/bad bank' approach. Certain assets, the 'good bank' (the Cypriot part), were transferred and merged into the BoC, including the insured deposits under €100,000 together with €9 billion of ELA.[1967] The 'bad bank' part (the legacy entity), holds all the overseas operations as well as all uninsured deposits above €100,000, old shares and bonds. The uninsured depositors were subject to a bail-in and became the new shareholders of the legacy entity. All the overseas operations, of the now defunct Laiki Bank, were also held by the legacy entity, until they were sold by the Special Administrator.[1968] The IMF performed a debt sustainability analysis

---

1964 Ibid.

1965 Ibid.

1966 See in European Central Bank (ECB), 'Governing Council decision on Emergency Liquidity Assistance requested by the Central Bank of Cyprus', 21 March 2013, Press Release, available at: https://www.ecb.europa.eu/press/pr/date/2013/html/pr130321.en.html.

1967 See in A. Michaelides, 'Cyprus; Bank of Cyprus (BOC) and Laiki: Resolution via Public Support and Bail-In, Including of Uninsured Depositors (2013)', in *Bank Resolution and Bail-In in the EU: Selected Case Studies Pre and Post BRRD*, Financial Sector Advisory Center, World Bank Group, 2016, p. 20.

1968 See in N. Kleftouri, *Deposit Protection and Bank Resolution*, Oxford, Oxford University Press, 2015, p. 114.

concluding that with a debt to GDP ratio at 90% the maximum amount that was available for its participation in Cyprus's program was no more than €10 billion.[1969] Therefore, the tax on deposits was supposed to provide for the rest amount, in a 'burden sharing' approach. The last piece of the Cypriot puzzle was the imposition of capital controls out of fears for flying capital from the bailed in BoC, and since the ELA from the ECB had reached sky levels and its extension was more of a dream, this measure was a necessity. Later that year, the CBC decided the final haircut level on BoC, and after a further independent review and evaluation, it was set at 47.5%. The resolution process was over but high levels of Non-Performing Loans and public frustration for the way resolution was implemented undermined the whole process.[1970]

To sum up the Cypriot case, the most important lessons that we can highlight are twofold. First, the Greek Private Sector Involvement (PSI) program wiped out from the two major Cypriot banks an amount almost equivalent to 25% of the Cyprus's GDP, creating literally a black hole in banks' capital base. Since there was no recourse to an external aid, as was the case for Greek banks, the effects were devastating. Second, the effects from delaying the deal conclusion for several months can be equally devastating from the financial stability's perspective. The Cypriot government procrastinated the deal with Troika, mostly for political reasons, in order to manage the crisis and avoid the high political costs associated with the previous Greek experience. Moreover, the Cypriot case is equally important for the bail in process as a resolution tool, were timely decision and implementation are of utmost importance and sound cooperation among all the participating actors is a prerequisite for its success.[1971]

3.1.3 The Case of Greek Banks

The Greek banks survived the global financial crisis almost untouched from the turmoil. Having stayed out from exotic financial products and from US subprime products only suffered from minor liquidity constraints due to the

1969 See in A. Michaelides, 'Cyprus; Bank of Cyprus (BOC) and Laiki: Resolution via Public Support and Bail-In, Including of Uninsured Depositors (2013)', in *Bank Resolution and Bail-In in the EU: Selected Case Studies Pre and Post BRRD*, Financial Sector Advisory Center, World Bank Group, 2016, p. 20.

1970 Ibid. The unexpected bail in of the Cypriot banks undermined the banking sector's credibility and depleted public trust. Among the public, there was a widespread belief that since they lost their deposits in an immoral and unfair process, their loans should also have to be bailed out by the government. Furthermore, many sound companies with their working capital deposited in the banks were bailed in, further undermining the recovery process, while at the same time pension funds and certain public sector entities were excluded from the bail in.

1971 See in N. Kleftouri, *Deposit Protection and Bank Resolution*, Oxford, Oxford University Press, 2015, p. 115.

frozen international interbank market, mostly after the Lehman Brothers collapse. Through the years the made one but serious mistake: they bought Greek government bonds, supporting the credit expansion and public spending, but since the international regulatory framework allowed government bonds a favourable capital treatment, this decision was also sound from a business perspective. Therefore, the bank sovereign nexus proved again a lethal combination for the Greek banking system and its effects were in newspapers' front paper for many years. Finally, before continuing our analysis, we must clarify that the Greece's financial assistance programs are well beyond the scope of the present book and we will only refer to them as a prerequisite to better understand the effects to the banking sector, therefore our analysis will be solely limited to the Greek banking sector, and the actions undertaken by the officials to restore it after the sovereign debt crisis and the subsequent PSI.

By late 2009, global markets were looking at Greece's poor economic performance, high public deficits, and distorted macroeconomic indicators. The Greek government, moving fast at securing financial stability, increased the level of deposit guarantee from €20,000 to €100,000 to avoid capital outflows and deposit withdrawals. The overall macroeconomic perspectives drove upwards the Greek government bonds' yields and after constant credit rating downgrades Greece was excluded from access to international markets.[1972] These developments inevitably drove the downgrading of Greek banks' credit ratings and since their access to wholesale market was already impaired by the global financial crisis, they started to feel the pressure on their balance sheets. Deposit withdrawals exacerbated the pressures and must be pointed out the Greek banks, in between 2010–2015 lost almost 45% of their deposit base.[1973] Constant supply of liquidity, through the ELA, came from the banks' access to the Eurosystem while at the same time the Greek government extended multiple times the guarantee program introduced in 2008. In April 2010, the Greek government requested financial assistance from the EU members and the IMF and in May 2010, the deal agreed through an adjustment program based on a Memorandum of Understanding (MoU). From 2010 to 2015, a total of three adjustment programs were agreed between Greece, the IMF, and the EU Member States, which included a total of €75 billion for the Greek banking sector.[1974] In late 2014, political uncertainty led to a radical left government which failed to find a compromise and the first half of 2015 was dramatically

---

[1972] See in M. Mavridou, A. Theodossiou, and T. Gklezakou, 'Greece; Several Greek Banks and Foreign Branches: Resolution via Public Recapitalization and Bail-In and State Aid Issues (2009–2015); Part 1: The Greek Experience of Restructuring and Recapitalization of Problem Banks', in *Bank Resolution and Bail-In in the EU: Selected Case Studies Pre and Post BRRD*, Financial Sector Advisory Center, World Bank Group, 2016, p. 30.

[1973] Ibid.

[1974] Ibid.

anxious for the Greek banks. The result of that delay was the imposition of capital controls and a banking holiday since the radical left government opted for a referendum, in historical moments of modern Greek state's history.

In between, the PSI as implemented by the Greek government, restructured the Greek public debt but at the same time wiped out the Greek banks' capital, since Greek banks were holding large amounts of government bonds. The PSI program affected almost €200 billion of Greek debt and resulted in almost €38 billion loss for Greek banks. The general macroeconomic conditions were not favourable for Greek banks amid high unemployment, increased taxation, and reduced wages. A sharp increase in non-performing loans rose the NPL ratio from 5% at the end of 2008 to 33% at the end of 2015, while the NPE ratio stood at 44% at the end of 2015.[1975] The following table is illustrative, regarding the evolution of Greek macroeconomic parameters:

Time period	GDP in € billion	GDP%	Unemployment	Housing prices
2008–2015	-66	-26.2%	7,8% → 24.9%	-39.9%

Source: M. Mavridou, A. Theodossiou, and T. Gklezakou, 'Greece; Several Greek Banks and Foreign Branches: Resolution via Public Recapitalization and Bail-In and State Aid Issues (2009–2015); Part 1: The Greek Experience of Restructuring and Recapitalization of Problem Banks', in *Bank Resolution and Bail-In in the EU: Selected Case Studies Pre and Post BRRD*, Financial Sector Advisory Center, World Bank Group, 2016, p. 31

The Greek banking sector was suffering and needed fresh capital to conclude its restructuring. Bank of Greece (BoG), the Greek central bank, performed in 2012 a strategic viability assessment to assess which banks were viable, meaning able to repay the funds they had received as assistance, and which not.[1976] The non-viable banks would be resolved, while the viable ones would be eligible for state assistance if they were unable to raise capital through private means. The banks deemed as 'non-viable' would avoid resolution under the condition of raising private capital. This examination was based on qualitative and quantitative criteria and had a certain timeframe, within which the banks were supposed to be able to repay the state funds.[1977] Overall, Greek banks underwent in total six stress tests to be able to access funds from the adjustment programs. These stress tests took under scrutiny the PSI effects and projections of future losses (expected losses) from banks' loan portfolios. Another set of actions undertook by Greek banks were the so-called 'Liability Management

[1975] Ibid., p. 31.
[1976] Ibid.
[1977] Ibid.

Exercises' (LMEs)[1978] and share capital increases to restore capital based on supervisor's directives and expectations.[1979] Under the LMEs, Greek banks exchanged previously issued Additional Tier 1 and Tier 2 instruments with Common Equity Tier 1 instruments. Until the end of 2015, Greek systemically important banks had raised €2.7 billion of capital through LMEs by offering a voluntary bond swap to their respective bondholders.[1980] Apart from private capital, state aid capital was provided through the participation of the Hellenic Financial Stability Fund (HFSF), which was established in 2010 under the first assistance program. The total amount of support provided by the HFSF reached €33 billion by the end of 2015[1981] and additional €5 billion was disbursed by the Greek government in the form of preference shares according to Law 3723/2008. Overall, the total amount disbursed to the banking sector topped at €63 billion and banks had to agree massive restructuring plans with the Commission with sale of foreign operations, layoffs, and consolidation of business lines.[1982]

The sector's consolidation was envisaged by the assistance programs and was particularly massive. Between 2010 and 2013, three subsidiaries of foreign banks were acquired by local banks and eight branches of foreign banks suspended their operations in Greece. Another major event was the purchase of the Greek branches of the three major Cypriot banks (Laiki Bank, BoC, and Elliniki Bank), from the Greek systemic bank, Piraeus Bank. This was an attempt to limit the contagion from the Cypriot banking crisis in the spring of 2013.[1983] At the same time, the BoG, acting as national resolution authority for

---

1978 A '*Liability Management Exercise*' (LME) is an action of balance sheet management. It can be an attractive tool for issuers, in our case banks, to either more efficiently use their cash resources or counteract stresses caused by such macroeconomic and industry conditions that make it difficult to access the debt capital markets. An issuer (bank) may consider performing an LME when: 1) the issuer is in trouble, 2) the issuer has spare liquidity, 3) the issuer wants to take advantage of better market conditions, 4) the issuer wants to alter unfavourable/restrictive terms, 5) for corporate restructuring reasons and 6) for adaptation in regulatory changes. Source: Norton Rose Fulbright, available at: https://www.nortonrosefulbright.com/en/knowledge/publications/94c08e07/ten-things-an-issuer-should-consider-when-conducting-a-liability-management-exercise-with-respect-to-its-bonds.

1979 See in M. Mavridou, A. Theodossiou, and T. Gklezakou, 'Greece; Several Greek Banks and Foreign Branches: Resolution via Public Recapitalization and Bail-In and State Aid Issues (2009–2015); Part 1: The Greek Experience of Restructuring and Recapitalization of Problem Banks', in *Bank Resolution and Bail-In in the EU: Selected Case Studies Pre and Post BRRD*, Financial Sector Advisory Center, World Bank Group, 2016, p. 31.

1980 The period from 2010 to 2015, the participation of private sector in the three share capital increases performed by Greek banks amounted to €25 billion. See in M. Mavridou, A. Theodossiou, and T. Gklezakou, 'Greece; Several Greek Banks and Foreign Branches: Resolution via Public Recapitalization and Bail-In and State Aid Issues (2009–2015); Part 1: The Greek Experience of Restructuring and Recapitalization of Problem Banks', in *Bank Resolution and Bail-In in the EU: Selected Case Studies Pre and Post BRRD*, Financial Sector Advisory Center, World Bank Group, 2016, p. 31.

1981 Ibid., p. 32.

1982 Ibid.

1983 Ibid.

Greece, order the resolution of 14 credit institutions (banks and cooperative banks), 13 of them before the enactment of BRRD and the last one after the enactment of the BRRD into Greek law. By the end of 2015, two resolution tools were used: a) the bridge bank and b) the sale of assets. Bridge banks were used twice, and the rest 12 cases were based on the sale of assets.[1984] The following table stipulates the resolution process for the 14 credit institutions:

Bank	Date of resolution	Resolution tool	Acquirer	Total resolution cost (in € million)
Proton Bank	9/10/2011	Bridge Bank	-	1,112
T-Bank	7/12/2011	Sale of Business	Hellenic Post Bank	677
Cooperative Lesvou - Limnou	23/03/2012	Sale of Business	National Bank of Greece	56
Achaiki Cooperative	23/03/2012	Sale of Business	National Bank of Greece	209
Cooperative of Lamia	23/03/2012	Sale of Business	National Bank of Greece	55
Agricultural Bank of Greece (ATE - Bank)	27/03/2012	Sale of Business	Piraeus Bank	7,471
Hellenic Post Bank	18/01/2013	Bridge Bank	Eurobank	3,733
First Business Bank	10/5/2013	Sale of Business	National Bank of Greece	457
Probank	26/07/2013	Sale of Business	National Bank of Greece	563
Cooperative of Western Macedonia	8/12/2013	Sale of Business	Alpha Bank	95
Cooperative of Evia	8/12/2013	Sale of Business	Alpha Bank	105
Cooperative of Dodecanese	8/12/2013	Sale of Business	Alpha Bank	259
Panellinia Bank	17/04/2015	Sale of Business	Piraeus Bank	297
Cooperative of Peloponnese	18/12/2015	Sale of Business	National Bank of Greece	93

Source: O. Andruszkiewicz,, J. Mathis, C. Wilkinson, M. Vassiliadis, K. Peppas and G. Gatopoulos, 'Study on the Financial Sector in Greece during the Economic Adjustment Programmes: 2010–2018', European Commission Final Report, June 2020, p. 67

[1984] Ibid.

Before each of the above-mentioned resolutions, the BoG, acting under its capacity as the national resolution authority, determined the perimeter of the assets and liabilities of the bank under resolution that would be transferred to the bridge bank or to the acquirer.[1985] When the 'Sale of Business' tool was about to be used, an informal and confidential bidding process was conducted. In the case of commercial banks, the aim was to define the perimeter of the transferred assets and liabilities based on a case-by-case analysis, focusing mostly on the assets that were deemed to be 'healthy and viable'.[1986] In contrast, cooperative banks had only their deposits transferred due to the general low quality loan portfolios they had and the limited interest from bidders in acquiring their assets.[1987] In all the 14 resolution cases, shareholders were entirely written off and in the case of cooperative banks, the shareholders were mostly retail investors suffering losses. In two cases, holders of subordinated debt were also wiped out during the resolution process.[1988]

As a conclusion to the Greek case, we must focus on the fact that the resolution process that applied to 14 banks had solely the aim to protect the uncovered depositors. The process's main objective was the protection of financial stability through cautious application of resolution tools that have a minimum impact on potential bank runs and deposit outflows.

3.1.4 The Case of Spanish Banks

The Spanish economy was suffering from a devastating real estate bubble. Because of the recent GFC and the Eurozone crisis, real estate prices have fallen sharply, and non-performing loans rose significantly. Spanish financial institutions were especially vulnerable due to dependence on wholesale funding, bad lending practices, a weak national regulatory framework, and poor choices by the government and of the Bank of Spain (BoS). The asset deterioration had a profound impact on those banks that were domestically oriented and grew significantly during the pre-crisis years based on expanding their domestic lending portfolios. Among the credit institutions that took advantage of the credit growth were the so-called cajas (saving & loans banks).[1989]

1985 Ibid.

1986 Ibid.

1987 Ibid.

1988 Ibid., p. 33.

1989 Despite the fact the throughout the Spanish economic history many crises hit the country, with the most severe being the 1866 and the 1977 banking crises where almost half of the existing institutions were dissolved and merged with other banks in both cases, the history of cajas shows no record of any serious crisis event after the establishment of the first institution back in 1835. See also in P. Martín-Aceña, 'The savings banks crisis in Spain: When and How?', in *The Aftermaths of Crises Savings and Savings Banks: Elements of Stability in Times of Crises?*, Perspectives, 66, WSBI (World Savings and Retail Banking Institute) – ESBG (European Savings and Retail Banking Group), December 2013, p. 86.

Cajas were institutions founded based on a particular structure: their capital accrued from retained earnings and governance was assumed by a mixture of depositors, employees, and local politicians.[1990] Non-retained, generated profits were distributed to local and socially oriented purposes but their business model was mostly driven by local political concerns and not always based on sound business decisions and practices.[1991] Originally small in size and with domestically focused activities, cajas were allowed to expand nationally and franchise nationwide only after the 1997 Royal Decree. Another important parameter that fuelled their growth was the easier access to the international capital flows and to financial products (such as covered bonds, securitisations, etc.) that were necessary to fund their activities.[1992] Cajas adopted an aggressive strategy model that helped them continuously gain market share from the large, listed banks, mainly focused on the real estate sector. With the unfolding of the crisis, cajas had to cope with three challenges: a) the deterioration of their loan portfolio as both activity and prices in the real estate sector began to deteriorate, b) a structural problem based on their institutional structure that did not allow them to increase their capital, together with general concerns regarding their governance structure, and c) their weak financial structure based almost solely on the wholesale funding markets, at a time when these markets started to shrink significantly.[1993] The process of restructuring the Spanish banking sector aimed at: a) achieving an institutional transformation which required the transfer of all assets and liabilities into new incorporated entities having the legal form of a bank b) restructuring and downsizing of activities so as to eliminate the excessive capacity in the banking sector and c) recognising asset deterioration in portfolios and simultaneous capital increases in selected institutions to enhance their solvency.[1994]

The difficulties began in 2009 when the BoS rescued the first cajas, Caja de Castilla – La Mancha. The Savings Banks Deposit Guarantee Fund (FGDCA in the Spanish language) intervened and acquired almost €600 million of distressed (non-performing) assets. Later the sale of the caja required another €2,5 billion in additional aid and this was the moment when financial

1990 See in High-Level Expert Group (HLEG), *Reforming the structure of the EU banking sector*, Brussels, 2 October 2012, p. 65.

1991 Ibid., p. 66.

1992 Ibid.

1993 Ibid., p. 66.

1994 Ibid. As of September 2012, only 13 banking groups remained active. Back in 2010 there were 45 non-listed cajas that shared approximately 45% of the Spanish financial system. Since the process of consolidation begun 43 of those cajas took part in the sector's consolidation. As of September 2012, the average size of these institutions has increased from €29 billion in December 2009 to €102 billion by June 2012, because of the sector's consolidation.

authorities discovered that the problem might be worse and systemic.[1995] According to various studies performed back then, major cajas, such as the giants Bancaja, Catalunya, Caja del Mediterraneo and Caixa Galicia required recapitalisation. In 2010 there were four merging operations and three outright purchases of smaller institutions by larger and financially sound entities.[1996] The BoS intervened again in May 2010 to rescue another caja institution, Cajasur, and at the same time the European authorities performed a series of stress tests to examine the Spanish banking system's strength. The stress tests revealed that five big cajas were in a fragile position with very low capital ratios and in dire need of capitalisation. 2011 was also a horrible year and FROB[1997] had to engage in four bail outs drying out immense quantities of public funds. The general mistrust for the Spanish economy had as a result the closing of the international markets for Spanish banks further aggravating their situation. Next year, 2012 was even more complicated with a constant pressure towards Spanish banks that lead to another stress test, this time for the entire financial sector.[1998]

The Spanish government realised the pressures and decided to ask for external assistance from its European partners. On 25 June 2012, the Spanish government submitted a formal request for financial assistance and on 20 July 2012, a MoU was signed between the EFSF and the government of Spain according to which the latter was to receive €100 billion in financial aid to capitalise institutions that needed core resources. Furthermore, it was also agreed to establish a special asset management company with public and private capital, that would assume foreclosed real estate assets from the financial entities subject to the recapitalisation and restructuring process.[1999] This 'bad bank', under the name SAREB, was tasked with the mandate to clean banks' balance sheets and recover as much as possible from the distressed assets. The financial aid came from three sources: a) the FGD (Deposit Guarantee Fund of Credit Institutions), b) the FROB and c) the ESM, successor of the EFSF.[2000]

1995 See in P. Martín-Aceña, 'The savings banks crisis in Spain: When and How?', in *The Aftermaths of Crises Savings and Savings Banks: Elements of Stability in Times of Crises?*, Perspectives, 66, WSBI (World Savings and Retail Banking Institute) – ESBG (European Savings and Retail Banking Group), December 2013, p. 92.

1996 Ibid.

1997 FROB stands for '*Fondo para la Reestructuración Ordenada Bancaria*' (Fund for the Orderly Restructuring of the Banking Sector) created in July 2009.

1998 See in P. Martín-Aceña, 'The savings banks crisis in Spain: When and How?', in *The Aftermaths of Crises Savings and Savings Banks: Elements of Stability in Times of Crises?*, Perspectives, 66, WSBI (World Savings and Retail Banking Institute) – ESBG (European Savings and Retail Banking Group), December 2013, p. 93.

1999 Ibid.

2000 Ibid. At the end of 2012, the Spanish financial system received a total of €61.2 billion of which 63,5% came from the ESM contribution. From a technical standpoint, Spain had initially signed a deal with the EFSF because, at the time, the ESM was not expected to begin operations in October. The ESM took over the Spanish program in November 2012,

Spain, exited the financial assistance program of the ESM on 31 December 2013.[2001]

3.1.5 The Case of Dexia Bank

By 2009, Dexia was one of the 20 largest banks in Europe with more than €500 billion in assets. The Dexia Group was formatted back in 1996, when '*Crédit Communal de Belgique*' (CCB), a Belgian institution founded in 1860 to provide financing to local administrations, merged with '*Crédit Local de France*' (CLF), a French institution established in 1987 to also service local governments.[2002] Following the 1996 merger, Dexia Group 'became one of the first pan European financial institutions'.[2003] The rapid expansion of Dexia came through both organic expansion and acquisitions and in 2000, Dexia acquired 'Financial Security Assurance' (FSA), a US company that provided credit enhancement for municipal bond issuers and insurance.[2004] At the same time, also expanded its services (retail market, asset management and insurance services) in Belgium, France and Germany, leading to a dual listing in both Paris and Belgium stock exchanges.[2005] Dexia operated two business lines, a universal banking line and a public/project finance line. The first was centred in Europe and Turkey offering retail, asset management, investor, and capital markets services to more than 55 million customers as well as institutions of all sizes. The second business line operated in more than 30 countries and accounted for almost half of its profits, offering a wide range of innovative products and services to build infrastructures (basic lending, bonds, highly structured products, credit enhancement, insurance and credit and asset

just before Spain negotiated its first instalment. That made Spain the first client of the permanent firewall. The role of the IMF had to be limited, as it has not the capacity to provide any loans to specific sectors, such as banking. Instead, the IMF took part in an advisory capacity, without offering Spain any money.

2001 According to the ESM website, Spain was the first, and so far, the only, euro area Member State to request a rescue program tailored only for the financial sector. One of the euro area's largest economies, it didn't require a full macroeconomic adjustment program because of reforms implemented earlier and because it was still able to borrow on capital markets.

2002 Both CCB and CLF, before their merger had expanded their services and geographic presence well beyond their initial markets. CCB had begun to also accept retail deposits from individuals back in 1947 and by 1990 had entered the Luxembourgish market. CLF had expanded its business internationally, both to several EU countries and to the US market. Also in 1991, it underwent an IPO on the Paris Stock Exchange.

2003 See in R.Z. Wiggins, N. Tente and A. Metrick, 'European Banking Union D: Cross-Border Resolution-Dexia Group' 2019) 1(3) *Journal of Financial Crises*, p. 174.

2004 Through this acquisition, Dexia became the world's leader in offering financial services for the public sector. See in R.Z. Wiggins, N. Tente and A. Metrick, 'European Banking Union D: Cross-Border Resolution-Dexia Group' (2019) 1(3) *Journal of Financial Crises*, p. 174.

2005 Ibid.

management).[2006] In 2005–2006 Dexia adopted a new business plan and a new management structure aiming to better integrate its operations and support a further growth strategy. The new 10-year strategic plan had a two-pillar strategy, based on developing both its universal banking operations and its traditional operation through geographic expansion. Overall, the bank would aim to take advantage of the new common currency in the European Union and exploit the synergies among its operations.[2007]

The problems started from its US subsidiary due to the breaking of the housing market bubble and the subsequent subprime market crisis. Dexia had exposure to the US housing market mainly through its subsidiary, FSA. This monoline insurer operated two business lines: a) a financial guarantee business line offering credit enhancement and insurance services related to residential mortgage-backed securities and b) a financial products business which offered guaranteed investment contracts to municipal issuers.[2008] FSA, like many of its peers, borrowed short term to finance its long term lending and when the interbank market collapsed driving the overnight credit market completely frozen, faced severe difficulties to roll over its debt. Even though FSA was not engaged in the more exotic collateralised debt obligations and managed to retain its triple-A rating from Moody's the general market turmoil obliged Dexia to provide on 23 June 2008, a $5 billion standby line of credit to FSA, in an attempt to quell the negative rumours regarding its liquidity.[2009] FSA continued struggling and Dexia decided to sold the company to Assured Guarantee Ltd.[2010] In 2008 Dexia recorded total losses amounted to €3.3 billion with the total loss from the FSA resulting in €1.66 billion and the rest arising from impairments and value deterioration from certain counterparties in its investment portfolio.[2011] Dexia was also exposed to Hypo Real Estate AG, a German bank and particularly its Dublin based subsidiary, 'Deutsche Pfandbriefbank' (commonly known as 'Depfa')[2012] since it had extended a

2006 Ibid., p. 175.

2007 Ibid.

2008 Ibid., p. 176.

2009 Ibid., p. 177.

2010 The deal of selling FSA, announced on 14 November 2008, was facilitated by $16.9 billion in support from the French and Belgian governments respectively, which assumed responsibility for FSA's risks and liabilities. Since this transaction constituted a state aid scheme, the European Commission had to give its prior approval.

2011 See in R.Z. Wiggins, N. Tente and A. Metrick, 'European Banking Union D: Cross-Border Resolution-Dexia Group' (2019) 1(3) *Journal of Financial Crises*, p. 177. Of the total amount of loses, €810 million came from adjustments to its investment's portfolios, including exposures of €473 million to Lehman Brothers, €174 million to the Icelandic Banks and of €57 million to Washington Mutual.

2012 Depfa was a competitor to Dexia in the public finance arena and had sold CDOs and German bonds backed by loans and securities issued by municipalities. When these bonds were downgraded, Depfa experienced difficulties in raising funds to buy them back as was required to do so. This liquidity problem of Depfa became a great concern of Hypo,

multimillion euro loan. On 30 September 2008, Dexia failed to raise the cash needed to operate and sought government assistance. On 9 October 2008, the governments of France, Luxembourg and Belgium provided €6.4 billion on capital injection and a guarantee of Dexia's liabilities and bonds, up to €150 billion, forcing both its CEO and Chairman of the Board to resign. Dexia was also eligible for assistance, up to an amount of almost $60 billion, under the Fed, since it had a New York bank subsidiary.[2013] Since the above governmental intervention, under the EU law was state aid, the Commission approved the rescue plan under the following conditions:[2014]

- Dexia would reorient its operations and would focus on its core banking activities and its traditional markets (Belgium, France, and Luxembourg),
- Dexia would reduce its public sector lending activity outside these markets and its bond portfolio, ring fencing it in a specific division within the bank, in line with a predefined write down plan,
- Dexia would reduce its market activities and cease proprietary trading, and finally
- Dexia would make a significant contribution to the restructuring costs by suspending, for a two-year period, dividend payments on cash equities and interest payments on instruments constituting own funds.

Dexia's bad luck continued by entering the next storm, that of the Eurozone debt crisis, just when the restructuring plan seemed to have worked. A bank run on deposits was averted and the refocus on its core business reduced its balance sheet allowing the bank to announce the exit from the liquidity framework provided by the three governments four months earlier. Moreover, the bank managed to raise €35.5 billion in medium- and long-term debt and passed the EU stress tests 'with flying colours'.[2015] Since Dexia was engaged in public finance activities, it is well understood that it was exposed to the sovereign debt of the Eurozone countries, especially to Greece, Spain, Portugal, and Italy.[2016] In the summer of 2011, Dexia started losing access to funding and on 4 October 2011, reported the biggest loss in its history, amounting to €4 billion, largely due to writing down the Greek debt. Once again, Dexia asked for help from the French, Belgian and Luxembourgish governments, further

---

the parent bank that had similar difficulties from her real estate operations. This domino situation forced the German government to support Hypo with a consortium of other banks and provide a €50 billion bailout fearing that a general instability was ante portas.

[2013] See in R.Z. Wiggins, N. Tente and A. Metrick, 'European Banking Union D: Cross-Border Resolution-Dexia Group' (2019) 1(3) *Journal of Financial Crises*, p. 178.

[2014] Ibid., p. 179.

[2015] Ibid., p. 182.

[2016] Ibid. Wiggins, Tente and Metrick claim that based on the EU stress test documentation, Dexia had an exposure to Greece's sovereign debt amounting to almost €8.5 billion (direct and through credit risk exposure) and an additional amount of up to €20 billion to the debt of Spain, Italy, Portugal, and other EU countries.

shanking its shares by 22%. Customers withdrew around €300 million from the bank and the share's price closed just above €1.[2017] On 5 October, trading in Dexia's shares halted at the request of its Belgian regulator and a resolution was applied as follows:[2018]

- The Belgian governments would purchase Dexia Bank Belgium, a retail bank for €4 billion,
- A Qatari investment group would purchase its Luxembourg based private banking unit and
- The rest of the group would be wounded down.

The majority of Dexia's trouble assets, apart from any assets and operations that could possibly be sold, would be isolated on a bad bank entity, supported by €90 billion 10-year governments guarantees, split among the three countries.[2019] The in-depth investigation from the Commission granted permanent approval on 21 December 2012, after a temporary approval granted in October 2011. Dexia continued to post enormous losses from its assets and particularly from its Greek debt exposures. On the aftermath of this resolution process, Dexia Group remained a state-owned entity from both the Belgian and French governments. The retail bank, purchased by the Belgian state continued its operation under a new brand name, Belfius Bank, and is subject to prudential supervision by the newly created Single Supervisory Mechanism, with former Dexia being the only bank under resolution that came under the direct supervision of the SSM.[2020]

3.1.6 The Case of Fortis Bank

The case of Fortis, Belgium's largest bank, can be seen as the archetype of failed resolution attempt during the global turmoil and before the creation of the resolution mechanism in the banking union. The EU Member States failed in establishing a common resolution approach and instead pursued different and even contradictory approaches that ultimately gave wrong meaning to the markets.

The Fortis Group was created in 1990 when AMEV merged with VSB Group and later that same year joined with AG Group. AMEV was a large Dutch insurance company, VSB was a Dutch banking group and AG Group was also a Belgian insurance company. After the mergers, the new company operated in both Belgium and the Netherlands through a complex structure

---

2017 Ibid.

2018 Ibid., p. 184.

2019 The government guarantees were assigned to Belgium (€54.45 billion or 60.5%), France (€32.85 billion or 36.5%) and Luxembourg (€2.7 billion or 3%).

2020 See in R.Z. Wiggins, N. Tente and A. Metrick, 'European Banking Union D: Cross-Border Resolution-Dexia Group' (2019) 1(3) *Journal of Financial Crises*, p. 185.

of holding company with various subsidiaries.[2021] In the coming years, Fortis grew organically through a series of aggressive acquisitions and was seen as an EU single market realisation. In 1998, the two parent companies adopted identical structures in an attempt to streamline internal processes and operations. Several initiatives followed until the adoption of single Board of Directors in 2000, the single Fortis share in December 2001 and the 2004 amendment of the two parent companies' Articles of Association to create a more internationally oriented Board of Directors.[2022] By 2006, Fortis operated as a unified multinational business but the two parent companies, Fortis SA/NV (Belgium) and Fortis N.V. (the Netherlands) retained their independent status. Each parent company was registered in its home country publishing their financial statements under the legal and regulatory requirements of their home countries. The group published a consolidated financial statement, as required by the Belgian legislation and a joint report of both parent companies.[2023] Fortis's base and strongest markets were the Benelux countries but by 2007 Fortis had operations in more than 50 countries, operating two business lines: a) banking and b) insurance. Banking operations included retail banking services (deposit, credit, investment financial services to individuals and small businesses), merchant and private banking services to a wide variety of clients (large international companies, medium sized enterprises, public sector entities and high net worth individuals). Insurance operations offered a variety of products (life, healthcare, and disability insurance products) as well as mortgage and savings instruments, through an expanded network of channels.[2024] Fortis's complex structure was not only a problem for the internal coordination of its operations but also for the efficient regulation and supervision of the group. Regulatory supervision was applied at both consolidated level and at the individual operating company level. Since the banking operations, headquartered in Brussels, were the largest part of the group, the Belgian authority, Belgian Banking, Finance, and Insurance Commission (BBFIC) was the consolidating and coordinating supervisor for EU purposes and its subsidiaries had to comply with the regulations in the countries they operated.[2025] Fortis was of systemic importance in the Benelux countries, not only because of its large market shares but also because of

[2021] See in R.Z. Wiggins, N. Tente and A. Metrick, 'European Banking Union C: Cross-Border Resolution-Fortis Group' (2019) 1(3) *Journal of Financial Crises*, p. 152.

[2022] Ibid. In particular, the single Fortis share was a new financial instrument that was combining the shares of the two parent companies. This 'Twin Share Principle' allowed investors to participate in both companies, Belgian and Dutch, and therefore be able to choose a wholly Belgian or a wholly Dutch sourced dividend.

[2023] Ibid.

[2024] Ibid.

[2025] Ibid., p. 154.

its function as a clearing member at several major domestic and foreign exchanges.[2026]

The turning point in Fortis's history was the ABN AMRO acquisition in October 2007. At that time, ABN AMRO was the second largest Dutch bank and Fortis, together with the Royal Bank of Scotland (RBS) and the Spanish bank Banco Santander, formed a consortium to make a hostile takeover bid.[2027] The total amount of €71 billion that the consortium paid for the acquisition was considered by many analysts as too high, and Fortis contributed with €24 billion. This participation was financed by a wide variety of instruments: issuance of new shares, convertible bonds, hybrid instruments, divestment, and capital relief transactions. Moreover, Fortis arranged a borrowing facility of €10 billion as bridge financing.[2028] Fortis took over the Dutch banking operations of ABN AMRO, its private banking and asset management functions and the commercial loan and mortgage loan divisions, resulting in a strengthen market share.[2029] These increased market shares forced the Dutch authorities to have a closer look on the terms of the deal since both Fortis and ABN AMRO were of systemic importance for the Netherlands. The Dutch central bank found potential problems at both institutions could create system wide problems by at the end found no legal basis for halting the conclusion of the deal and instead of objecting the deal imposed several conditions on the consortium. On the contrary, the Commission, when assessing the deal, concluded that the acquisition by Fortis presented competitive issues centred around the concentration on commercial banking and requested Fortis to divest certain of its commercial banking units before proceeding with the deal. This resulted in a €300 million loss for Fortis.[2030]

Apart from competition issues, a difficult integration process accompanied the deal and soon after the deal, Fortis started to struggle integrating the new components into its operating module. The integration process delayed for several reasons: a) Fortis had acquired a great amount of intangible assets that could not put on its balance sheet and would have to write them

---

2026 Ibid.

2027 Ibid. At the same time, Barclays also made a bid to acquire ABN AMRO, and its offer was preferred by the ABN AMRO's board mainly due to the Barclays's intent to maintain most of the bank intact. At that time, ABN AMRO was the 15th largest bank in the world with operations in 63 countries employing more than 100.000 employees. When the exclusive period that Barclays had available expired without success, the consortium made a higher bid but with the proposal of breaking the bank. A hedge fund, which was a major shareholder in the ABN AMRO, favoured the consortium's proposal, thereby securing a favourable vote in the assembly.

2028 See in R.Z. Wiggins, N. Tente and A. Metrick, 'European Banking Union C: Cross-Border Resolution-Fortis Group' (2019) 1(3) *Journal of Financial Crises*, p. 155.

2029 Ibid.

2030 Ibid., p. 156.

off,[2031]and b) if fully integrated, ABN AMRO would lower significantly the capital requirements and Fortis would be in danger of breaching the minimum capital requirements.[2032] Moreover, the €300 million loss from the selling of its commercial banking assets had to be recognised adding further pressure on its balance sheet. At the same time, the US subprime crisis started to appear on Fortis's balance sheet with losses on its subprime mortgages' portfolio.[2033] Fortis's situation became worse by June 2008 where the bank announced that it had to fortify its capital base, due to the impact from the financial crisis, by raising additional €8.3 billion and paying its dividend in stock rather than cash, in a move that was to save €1.5 billion. Since the dividend was one of the main selling points of the new shares, it provoked an uproar among its shareholders, further dropping its share price to €10 on 26 June 2008.[2034] Fortis finally managed to issue 150 million shares to large investors at a €10 price per share, placing them with Libyan and Chinese investors, offering them a 25% discount and preventing Belgian shareholders from participating. During this stressful situation, Fortis's CEO resigned, and customers continued to withdraw their funds leading the bank to a worsening liquidity crisis that by September 2008 was already at the brink of collapse. The defaults of Lehman Brothers and Northern Rock spread the turmoil in the markets and made investors highly suspicious regarding who the next victim would be.

It became clear that Fortis required resolution and coordination needed among the major government-stakeholders: Belgium, Luxembourg and Netherlands. According to the first resolution plan, the governments decided to inject €11.2 billion into the bank each one buying the parts operating in the respective country.[2035] The first allocation of Fortis's funds upset the Dutch government that believed that Belgians had a better deal and were acquiring the best parts of the group. Therefore, few hours after the initial deal pursued a different strategy by nationalising Fortis's Dutch assets in an attempt to reassure Dutch depositors safeguarding at the same time the country's financial market.[2036] After the Dutch actions, Belgium and Luxembourg regrouped

2031 Ibid., p. 157.
2032 Ibid.
2033 Ibid.
2034 Ibid. On 26 June, the credit rating agency Standard & Poor's changed Fortis rating into 'negative implications' and after further review, on 17 July, lowered again Fortis's ratings on its core operating groups and subsidiaries.
2035 Ibid., p. 158. Belgium would pay €4.7 billion to acquire 49% of the Belgian holding company including the Belgian bank and insurance businesses, the Netherlands would pay €4 billion to acquire 49% of the Dutch banking subsidiary and finally Luxembourg would contribute with €2.5 billion to acquire 49% of its banking subsidiary in Luxembourg.
2036 Ibid., p. 159.

together and on 5 October 2008, announced a revamped rescue plan through 'additional measures':

- An additional capital injection amounted of €4.7 billion leading the Belgian government to acquire almost 100% of the share capital,
- The Belgian government agreed to transfer 75% of its interest in the Fortis Belgian Bank and 67% of the Luxembourgish bank to the French bank BNP Paribas for €8.25 billion in stock (later renegotiated to €11 billion),
- The Luxembourgish government would acquire a 1,1% share in BNP Paribas, and
- BNP Paribas would purchase the Belgian insurance activities of the Fortis group,
- Because of the BNP Paribas's denial to acquire Fortis's toxic assets, a portfolio with them would be transferred to a special purpose vehicle that would be financed and owned by the Belgian government (24%), BNP Paribas (10%) and Fortis Group (66%).

The Fortis Group would continue to own Fortis Insurance International and the above-mentioned 66% of the structured products vehicle, benefiting at the same time from the sale of Fortis Insurance Netherlands and Fortis Insurance Belgium.[2037] The state aid scheme, reviewed under the Commission, was approved under the light of saving the banks and safeguarding financial stability since there existed a threat to the financial markets. Finally, on 12 March 2009, the Fortis shareholders' general assembly approved the deal, after changes applied because of judicial review from Brussels Courts.[2038] Key deal changes included:[2039]

- Increased price from BNP Paribas to €11.2 billion,
- Belgium retained a 25% blocking vote in Fortis Belgium,
- Instead of acquiring all of Belgium insurance services, Belgium acquired only 25%,
- The costs of the structured products SPV, now valued at €11.8 billion, were allocated as follows:
    - 11.76% share by BNP Paribas,
    - 43.53% share by the Belgian Government,
    - 44.71% share by Fortis Group

Fortis continues to operate under the BNP Paribas group still to date. Its trouble resolution has been analySed by the Basel Committee on Banking Supervision (BCBS), sitting the various shortcomings that prevented the sound resolution of the group on a cross-border dimension. Together with Dexia, there were the two seminal cases of bank resolution in the EU that

2037 Ibid.
2038 Ibid., p. 160.
2039 Ibid.

demonstrated the need to apply common rules and procedures, paving the way for the creation of the banking union.

3.1.7 The Case of the German Landesbank

The Landesbank have been traditionally the third pillar of the German banking system, which comprised of private banks, savings banks, and cooperative banks.[2040] The private sector is dominated by the so-called 'Big Four' banks (Deutsche Bank, Commerzbank, UniCredit and Postbank). The savings bank sector comprised of locally oriented savings banks, the so-called Sparkassen, nine regionally oriented 'Landesbanken' (LBs) and some specialised institutions. The cooperative banking sector has a structure similar to the savings banks sector.[2041] Especially the LBs, originally had two main purposes: a) acting as bankers to the regional state and b) representing central institutions for the savings banks in their regional states, acting as clearing houses, holding their excess liquidity reserves, providing marketing services and access to capital markets and moreover, they developed a wide range of commercial and investment banking activities, by offering to clients of savings banks related services with access to foreign markets and credit on larger scale.[2042] Through their size and international activities, the LBs, largely complement the activities offered by the Sparkassen, providing to mid and large capitalisation corporations necessary services. Due to their role, the LBs were extremely important for regional growth and economic development and were seen by the local governments as the necessary vehicles to implement their economic policies. There existed a long-established tradition of Länder governments' interference in LBs lending decisions and overall public sector ownership far exceeded that in comparable economies.[2043] Therefore, in such complex structure, the savings banks are the owner of the LBs and a major investor in their debt. Due to the gradual transformation of the German financial system, the LBs role as central institutions for the savings banks had decreased over time and they expanded in similar ways as the private banks.[2044] What is interesting about the LBs is the fact that they have a complex ownership structure. LBs are mostly owned by their regional Sparkassen associations and

2040 See in D. Detzer, 'Financial Systems in Financial Crisis: An analysis of banking systems in the EU' (2014) 49(2) *Intereconomics*, p. 57.

2041 Ibid., p. 58.

2042 See in High-Level Expert Group (HLEG), 'Liikanen Report', 'Reforming the structure of the EU banking sector', Brussels, 2 October 2012, p. 64.

2043 See in I. Hardie and D. Howarth, 'Die Krise but not La Crise? The financial crisis and the transformation of German and French banking systems', *Journal of Common Market Studies*, November 2009, 47:5, p. 1019.

2044 See in High-Level Expert Group (HLEG), 'Liikanen Report', 'Reforming the structure of the EU banking sector', Brussels, 2 October 2012, p. 64.

the local State (Land). In some cases, they are cross-owned by other LBs, the national Sparkassen association and by some private equity.[2045] Due to their public ownership, LBs and savings banks enjoyed a guarantee in the event of default by the local public founding entity (known as 'Gewährträgerhaftung'), as well as a maintenance guarantee whereby the owner ensures that the bank can meet its financial obligations at all times (known as 'Anstaltslast').[2046] This guarantee was not of much importance for the savings banks, since they funded themselves with stable deposits, but was of extreme importance for the LBs since they relied extensively on the wholesale market to refinance their debt. These guarantees forced the Lands to intervene during the financial crisis and bail out the LBs and their creditors.

German banks were heavily exposed to the US real estate bubble and the subprime crisis through their asset holdings. This exposure led to a general write-off between 2007 and August 2009 up to €102 billion.[2047] By the end of 2008, three LBs (Sachsen LB, Bayern LB, and West LB) were already in need of recapitalisation. Since LBs were characterised by low profitability, attributed mostly to low revenue generation and high operational costs, their expansive growth came from the accumulation of funding reserves before the loss of their state guarantees in July 2005. According to the Liikanen report, the amount of that funding was based on very optimistic projections regarding the future customer business and also a result of loose governance control that often ignored the rapid exposure to foreign asset classes.[2048] With all these accumulated funds, the LBs helped finance the asset bubbles in other countries by lending to other banks and buying foreign securities including those generated from complex structured transactions. Several LBs were hit hard from the global financial turmoil. Favoured by these state guarantee schemes, expanded rapidly into the international and investment banking sector exposing themselves to risks that proven to be disastrous. The massive bail outs triggered investigations by the Commission to verify that state aid rules were not breached and demanded restructuring of the recipient banks. LBs adapted their business models to a more regionally oriented activity as originally defined by the various state laws.

2045 Ibid.

2046 Ibid.

2047 See in D. Detzer, 'Financial Systems in Financial Crisis: An analysis of banking systems in the EU' (2014) 49(2) *Intereconomics*, Vol. 49, Issue 2, 2014, p. 61.

2048 See in High-Level Expert Group (HLEG), 'Liikanen Report', 'Reforming the structure of the EU banking sector', Brussels, 2 October 2012, p. 65.

3.1.8 The Case of Icelandic Banks

The 2007-2009 GFC hit particularly hard Iceland, since all three of the country's major banks failed, following: i) difficulties in refinancing their short-term debt, and ii) a run deposits in Netherlands and the UK.[2049] The Icelandic banking system was dominated by three banks: Glitnir,[2050] Kaupthing,[2051] and Landsbanki,[2052] combined owned more than 90% of the banking system's total assets. Asset growth in Iceland exceeded economic growth and banks were funding themselves mostly through the wholesale markets. Most of these funds were short-term loans from other financial institutions based on the US, the UK, and the EU. Moreover, these loans were denominated on each country's national currency (pound, dollar, and euro) and were accompanied

---

2049 See in N. Kleftouri, *Deposit Protection and Bank Resolution*, Oxford, Oxford University Press, 2015, p. 106.

2050 Glitnir was an international Icelandic bank formed in 1990 through the state-directed merger of three private banks—Alþýðubanki (Union Bank), Verzlunarbanki (Bank of Commerce), and Iðnaðarbanki (Industrial Bank)—and the failing public Útvegsbanki (Fisheries Bank) to create Íslandsbanki. Íslandsbanki was the only major privately held commercial bank in Iceland and was publicly listed on the Iceland Stock Exchange in 1993. In 2000, it merged with FBA Icelandic Investment Bank. Operating as a financial group, Glitnir offered universal banking services and specialized in three global sectors: seafood/food, sustainable energy, and offshore supply vessels. It had branches in London and Copenhagen, with representative offices in Halifax, Canada, and Shanghai, China. Glitnir also owned a bank in Luxembourg and financial companies in Norway, treating Iceland and Norway as its home markets. Its services included retail, corporate, and investment banking, stock trading, and capital management.

2051 Established in 1982 as a small agency for financial advisory and securities brokerage, Kaupthing became a major player in the changes in the Icelandic financial market, continually setting trends and being one of the five founding partners of the Icelandic Stock Exchange. In the mid-1990s, Kaupthing widened its focus to include opportunities abroad, and became the first Icelandic financial institution to operate outside Iceland. Kaupthing was listed on the Icelandic Stock Exchange in October 2000, at which point the original owners of the bank, the savings banks in Iceland, reduced their holdings, and individuals and institutional investors replaced them as shareholders. Few years later, in 2002, Kaupthing Bank shares were listed on the Stockholm Stock Exchange. Prior to its collapse, Kaupthing Bank operated in thirteen countries, including all the Nordic countries, the Netherlands, Belgium, Luxembourg, Switzerland, the UK, and the US. It was the seventh largest bank in the Nordic countries in terms of market capitalization.

2052 Landsbanki, once one of Iceland's largest banks, had assets of ISK 3,058 billion and a market capitalization of ISK 383 billion by December 2007. Founded in 1885, it played a key role in Iceland's economic growth. From 1927 to 1961, it served as Iceland's central bank, primarily issuing currency until replaced by the Central Bank of Iceland. The bank was state-owned until privatization between 1998 and 2003. Landsbanki was Iceland's leading provider of financial services for individuals, companies, and institutions, boasting the country's largest branch network with 40 locations. By 2006, it financed nearly 40% of corporate loans in Iceland and was the principal bank for about 60% of companies listed on the OMX Iceland Stock Exchange. It was also the top provider of mergers and acquisitions, derivatives, equity, and fixed income services. Starting in 2000, Landsbanki expanded internationally through acquisitions and organic growth. This global expansion included the creation of its Icesave subsidiary in 2006, which later played a critical role in the bank's collapse.

by the respective foreign exchange risk.[2053] In February 2006, the Iceland's overall economic outlook was downgraded by the credit rating agencies and Icelandic banks had to replace their source of funding, since many investors denied rolling over the loans extended to the Icelandic banks, by rapidly and aggressively gathering retail deposits from across Europe.[2054] Iceland was experiencing a stock market boom and its banks were providing loans that were collateralised by stock belonging to companies listed on the Icelandic stock exchange. This proved to be a bad business model since in July 2008 Icelandic stock prices have lost almost half their value within a year, setting in motion a downward spiral (lower stock prices, lower collateral values, lower loan values, etc.).[2055]

When the interbank market frozen up due to the Lehman effect, Icelandic banks faced a liquidity concern since their short term borrowed debt had to be rolled over and withdrawn without any prior notice. The 'Icelandic D-Day' was Monday, 29 September 2008. On that day, the Icelandic government announced that it would contribute €600 million to Glitnir in exchange for the bank's 75% capital. This move aimed at securing Glitnir's payment of large debts due on 15 October 2008 ($750 million) since the bank was not in the position to fulfil its contractual obligations.[2056] However, the proposed nationalisation of Glitnir never went through, as it was placed in receivership by the FME before the initial plan of the Icelandic government to purchase the 75% stake had been approved by the banks' shareholders. Rather than restoring confidence in the market this planed action made investors suspicious about the financial health of the other two major banks, Landsbanki and Kaupthing, and accelerated outflows were the result of that turmoil.[2057] The UK financial regulator and the ECB demanded additional funds and margin respectively from Landsbanki to continue its operations forcing the bank to demand foreign currency by the Central Bank of Iceland. This request was rejected because the central bank had already loaned to Kaupthing its remaining foreign currency reserves to tap its liquidity bleeding. On Monday, 6 October, the Icelandic parliament passed the 125/2008 Emergency Act, which gave the country's Financial Supervisory Authority the necessary power to take over the operations of a failing bank. Iceland was preparing herself for a hard landing.[2058] After the UK authorities closed down Landsbanki's UK deposit taking branch on the evening of 6 October 2008, the Icelandic financial supervisory authority took over control

---

2053 See in A.G. Zeissler, D. Ikeda and A. Metrick, 'Ireland and Iceland in Crisis D: Similarities and Differences' (2019) 1(3) *Journal of Financial Crises*, p. 47.

2054 Ibid

2055 Ibid., p. 49.

2056 Ibid., p. 50.

2057 Ibid.

2058 Ibid.

in Landsbanki on 7 October 2008, based on the newly enacted Emergency Act. Glitnir surrender control on the same day, 7 October and Kaupthing on 9 October. The three Icelandic banks that previously controlled up to 90% of all banking assets in Iceland became state owned within a single week in a loud collapse.[2059] Particularly the events around the Landsbanki's asset freezing in the UK exposed the Icelandic banking system and demonstrated to the rest of the world that the situation was much more crucial than originally perceived.

What must be credited to the Icelandic authorities though is the effective way in which they acted to preserve financial stability and continuation of critical banking services. Iceland took over its major banks timely and guaranteed only part of its banks' liabilities (domestic deposits) requiring from private creditors to participate in the losses.[2060] Moreover, the small island had not the ability and the resources to stand behind its banking system, which had grown more than twice of the country's GDP, therefore a loss distribution among the creditors and frustrated investors was inevitable but it also did not prove to be extremely burdensome for the public finances. In this end the currency sovereignty of Iceland was at the same time a curse and a blessing: in the beginning hastened the problems because creditors and investors demanded repayment in dollars but at the end the option for devaluation against other currencies helped the country to secure cheaper exports for its products, therefore recovering easier that other countries members of the Eurozone (Ireland).[2061]

3.2. *The European Banking Union: 'Breaking the Vicious Circle'*

Within this environment and amid bailouts and a sovereign debt crisis, the EU decided to move forward with the creation of a 'European Banking Union' since it was '... imperative to break the vicious circle between banks and sovereigns'.[2062] The basic idea behind the banking union was that if the banking sector was cut from the sovereign stability would be again prevailed and banks would not need constant state interventions that increased public debt. The Commission was tasked with the assignment of presenting a time binding road map on how a banking union would be feasible within the EU framework. On 12 September 2012, the Commission presented its road map.[2063] According to

2059 Ibid.

2060 Ibid., p. 51.

2061 Ibid.

2062 See in European Council, *EURO AREA SUMMIT STATEMENT*, 29 June 2012, p. 1, available at: https://www.consilium.europa.eu/uedocs/cms_data/docs/pressdata/en/ec/131359.pdf.

2063 See in European Commission, Communication from the Commission to the European Parliament and the Council, A Roadmap towards a Banking Union, COM (2012) 510 final, Brussels, 12.9.2012.

Prof. Gortsos '... the establishment of the EBU should lead to the creation of a 'Europeanised bank safety net' consisting of three pillars:

- a 'Single Supervisory Mechanism' (the 'SSM') exclusively for the banking sector (i.e. not for the other two sectors of the financial system, insurance and securities) and mainly for credit institutions legally incorporated in euro area Member States, with regard to their micro-prudential supervision (the 'first pillar'),
- a 'Single Resolution Mechanism' (the 'SRM') for unviable credit institutions (also mainly incorporated in euro area Member States) and a Single Resolution Fund (the 'SRF') to cover any resulting funding gaps, provided that a decision is made on the resolution of such credit institutions (the 'second pillar'), and
- a single deposit guarantee scheme, which coupled with the 'Single Resolution Board' (the 'SRB', a part of the SRM) could form a 'European Deposit Insurance and Resolution Authority' ('EDIRA') (the 'third pillar').'[2064]

This construction has been further fortified with a 'Single Rulebook' and a 'Single Handbook'. The single rulebook contains the substantive rules on all the previous aspects and is an integral part of the single market for financial services and is developed either by the EU institutions (legislative acts falling under the ambit of Article 289 TFEU) or by the EU institutions with the direct involvement and contribution of the European Banking Authority (EBA), the so called delegated and implementing acts (legislative acts falling under the ambit of Articles 290-291 TFEU).[2065] The single handbook contains the common supervisory practices that are adopted and applied by the relevant bodies of the banking union and are published under legal bases that are contained in the founding regulations of each body.[2066]

On 13 November 2013, the 'Single Supervisory Mechanism' (SSM) went into effect,[2067] providing for a system of supervision of the largest and systemically important banks (credit institutions in the EU law) in the EU Member States that have adopted the euro as their single currency.[2068] As of 4 November 2014, the ECB has ultimate authority over all banks subject to the SSM's supervision. The SSM is responsible for the supervision of credit institutions only, and that means that are excluded from its perimeter insurance and reinsurance firms,

---

2064 See in C.V. Gortsos, 'A brief overview of the European Banking Union', *L'Europe en formation*, 2017/2, n°383-384, Summer - Autumn 2017, p. 62.

2065 Ibid., p. 63.

2066 See in R.Z. Wiggins, M. Wedow and A. Metrick, 'European Banking Union A: The Single Supervisory Mechanism' (2019) 3(1) *Journal of Financial Crises*, p. 117.

2067 See in C.V. Gortsos, 'A brief overview of the European Banking Union', *L'Europe en formation*, 2017/2, n° 383-384, Summer - Autumn 2017, p. 64. The legal basis of the SSM is Council Regulation (EU) No 1024/2013 of 15 October 2013 '*conferring specific tasks on the European Central Bank concerning policies relating to the (micro-) prudential supervision of credit institutions*' (the 'SSMR'), which became operative on 4 November 2014.

2068 See in R. Wiggins, M. Wedow and A. Metrick, 'European Banking Union A: The Single Supervisory Mechanism' (2019) 1(3) *Journal of Financial Crises*, p. 114.

hedge funds, investment firms and central counterparties (CCPs).[2069] Under the SSM's ambit fall all the banks that are operating in the EU, but at this point a very important distinction must be made: a) the ones deemed as 'significant institutions' are directly supervised by the SSM, whereas b) the rest institutions that are deemed to be 'less significant' will continue to be supervised by their National Supervisory Authorities (NSAs) under the ECB's oversight.[2070]

The banking union's second pillar is the 'Single Resolution Mechanism' (SRM)[2071] which is based on a 'Single Resolution Fund' (SRF)[2072] feed by annual levies imposed on banks. Since the latter is based on an Intergovernmental Agreement, it is an instrument of public international law and, as such, all the rights and obligations laid down therein are subject to the principle of reciprocity.[2073] It applies to the Contracting Parties whose institutions are subject to the SSM and the SRM also from 1 January 2016. Under the SRF Agreement, the Contracting Parties are committed to transfer the contributions raised annually at national level to the SRF in accordance with the BRRD and the SRMR.[2074] The SRF is planned to reach a target level of at least 1% of the amount of 'covered deposits' of all credit institutions authorised in all participating Member States (which is about €55 billion). In principle, it is being financed by the participating institutions' ex-ante contributions, while the EU budget or the national budgets may not be held liable for any expenses or losses incurred by the SRF.[2075]

The missing third and last pillar of the banking union is, unfortunately, still under construction. The prospect of establishing a pan-European deposit guarantee scheme, as the third main component of the EBU, has only been discussed in terms of principles and high-level politics. The prospective of

2069 Ibid., p. 117.

2070 Ibid. For a deeper analysis of the distinction between the significant and the less significant institutions, see also in C.V. Gortsos, *The Single Supervisory Mechanism (SSM)*, Nomiki Vivliothiki, Athens, 2015, p. 113 onwards.

2071 See in C.V. Gortsos, 'A brief overview of the European Banking Union', *L' Europe en formation*, 2017/2, n° 383-384, Summer - Autumn 2017, p. 66. The SRM was established by Regulation (EU) No 806/2014 of the European Parliament and of the Council of 15 July 2014 '*establishing uniform rules and a uniform procedure for the resolution of credit institutions and certain investment firms in the framework of a Single Resolution Mechanism and a Single Resolution Fund [...]*' (the 'SRMR'), which became applicable from 1 January 2016.

2072 See in C.V. Gortsos, 'A brief overview of the European Banking Union', *L'Europe en formation*, 2017/2, n° 383-384, Summer - Autumn 2017, p. 67. The SRF was established by Articles 67-69 of the SRMR and is also based on the Intergovernmental Agreement (No. 8457/14) by twenty-six EU Member States 'on the transfer and mutualization of contributions to the Single Resolution Fund' (the 'SRF Agreement'). Available at: https://data.consilium.europa.eu/doc/document/ST%208457%202014%20INIT/EN/pdf.

2073 The principle of reciprocity is the equivalent performance of those rights and obligations by all contracting Parties.

2074 See in C.V. Gortsos, 'A brief overview of the European Banking Union', *L'Europe en formation*, 2017/2, n° 383-384, Summer - Autumn 2017, p. 67.

2075 Ibid., p. 68.

creating a 'European Deposit Insurance Scheme' (EDIS) was laid down in the famous 'Five Presidents Report' of 22 June 2015.[2076] Based on this report, the European Commission tabled a proposal for a regulation of the European Parliament and of the Council 'amending Regulation EU No 806/2014 in order to establish a European Deposit Insurance Scheme'.[2077] According to the proposal, the EDIS should be introduced gradually, in a three-phase approach:[2078]

- Phase 1 – re-insurance: During the first three-year phase (2017-2019), the 're-insurance approach' should apply, whereby a national DGS will have access to EDIS funds under two conditions: a) only when all its own resources are exhausted and b) if it fully complies with the DGS Directive[2079]
- Phase 2 – co-insurance: As of 2020, the EDIS would become a progressively mutualised system ('co-insurance') but still would be subject to appropriate limits and safeguards against potential abuses.
- Phase 3 – full insurance: The EDIS should fully insure national DGSs as of 2024, the same year when the SRF and the requirements of the DGS Directive will be fully phased in.

Unfortunately, due to the extremely debatable issue of deposit guarantees the legislative process is far from being finalised and the so-called third pillar of the banking union will remain under construction for the foreseeable future.

4 RIDING THE WAVE OF STRUCTURAL REFORMS: THE EU WAY

In light of the earlier mentioned bank failures at European and EU level, demanding extensive public spending for the banks' bail-out, leading therefore to the vicious circle between banks and sovereign states, Commissioner Michel Barnier,[2080] established a High-Level Expert Group (HLEG) on bank structural

---

2076 See in European Commission, *The Five President's Report: Completing Europe's Economic and Monetary Union*, Report, 22 June 2015, available at: https://ec.europa.eu/info/sites/default/files/5-presidents-report_en.pdf.

2077 See in European Commission, Proposal for a REGULATION OF THE EUROPEAN PARLIAMENT AND OF THE COUNCIL amending Regulation (EU) 806/2014 in order to establish a European Deposit Insurance Scheme, COM (2015) 586 final, Strasbourg, 24 November 2015.

2078 See in C.V. Gortsos, 'A brief overview of the European Banking Union', *L'Europe en formation*, 2017/2, nº 383-384, Summer - Autumn 2017, p. 71.

2079 Directive 2014/49/EU of the European Parliament and of the Council of 16 April 2014 on deposit guarantee schemes, [2014] *OJ* L 173/149.

2080 Michel Barnier (born in 1951) is a French politician that served as European Commissioner for Internal Market and Services, in the Juncker Commission from 2009 to 2014. During his tenure, Barnier handled many important issues, such as the reform of the financial sector (40 pieces of legislation between 2010 and 2014), the banking union (starting with the Single Supervisory Mechanism) and the digital single market.

reforms in February 2012. President of the HLEG was appointed Mr. Erkki Liikanen, back then Governor of the (Central) Bank of Finland. HLEG's task has been to assess whether additional reforms, specially targeted at the individual banks' structure, would create safer banking and financial system by further reducing the probability and impact of failure and better protecting vulnerable retail clients.[2081] The HLEG's mandate was therefore very similar to that of the ICB in the UK, a few years earlier. Moreover, the HLEG acknowledged that major structural related reforms, based on related initiatives, have been adopted or are in the process of being adopted by many other countries. The HLEG, to draft its final report, organised a series of hearings with various stakeholders, including policy makers, investors, academics, consumers and providers of financial services.

4.1. The 'Liikanen Report'

The HLEG released its final report in October 2012 and contained five measures that 'augment and complement the set of regulatory reforms already enacted by the EU, the Basel Committee and national governments'.[2082] In a nutshell these measures are stipulated in the Final Report as follows:

(i) Mandatory separation of proprietary trading activities and other significant trading activities,[2083]
(ii) Additional separation of activities conditional on the recovery and resolution plan,[2084]
(iii) Possible amendments to the use of bail-in instruments as a resolution tool,[2085]
(iv) A review of capital requirements on trading assets and real estate related loans,[2086]
(v) Strengthening the governance and control of banks.[2087]

Of the above proposed measures, the most important is the first measure that calls for a mandatory separation of proprietary and other trading activities. Therefore, our analysis will focus on this measure.

The HLEG's proposal is that 'proprietary trading and all assets or derivative positions incurred in the process of market-making, other than the activities exempted below, must be assigned to a separate legal entity, which can be an investment firm or a bank [...] within the banking group. Any loans,

2081 See in High-Level Expert Group (HLEG), *Reforming the structure of the EU banking sector*, Brussels, 2 October 2012, p. i.
2082 Ibid., p. iii.
2083 Ibid., p. v.
2084 Ibid., p. vii.
2085 Ibid., p. viii.
2086 Ibid.
2087 Ibid., p. x.

loan commitments or unsecured credit exposures to hedge funds (including prime brokerage for hedge funds), SIVs and other such entities of comparable nature, as well as private equity investments, should also be assigned to the trading entity. The requirements apply on the consolidated level and the level of subsidiaries'.[2088] The separation would be mandatory only if the activities to be separated amount to a significant share of the bank's business, or if the volume of these type of activities will be perceived as significant from a financial stability perspective.[2089] Therefore, it was suggested that the decision requiring the mandatory separation of certain activities should proceed in a two-stage approach:

(a) In the first stage, if a bank had assets that were held for trading and available for sale exceeding either 1) a relative threshold of 15-25% of the bank's total assets or 2) an absolute threshold of €100 billion, the bank would automatically proceed to the second stage.[2090]
(b) In the second stage, the relevant supervisors would determine the need for separation of activities based on the share of assets to which the separation requirement would apply.[2091] It left for the European Commission to calibrate that level appropriately, aiming at ensuring that the mandatory separation requirement will apply to all banks for which the activities to be separated are significant, compared to their balance sheet.

The result of the above-mentioned process would be the transfer of all the activity concerned to the legally separated trading entity, once the bank exceeds the predefined final threshold. The HLEG proposes an appropriate transition period to phase in the structural reforms and a proportional approach for the smaller and less complex banks that would even be fully excluded from the structural reforms.[2092] The HLEG suggests that only the previously mentioned banking activities would be required to be transferred to the trading entity, while all the rest banking activities would remain under the roof of deposit funded entity (the deposit bank). Obviously, if any firm specific recovery and resolution plans require other measures, new requirements will apply, and exempted banking activities will be reviewed under the new approach.[2093] These permitted activities include, but need not be limited to, lending to large as well as small and medium-sized companies, trade finance and consumer lending, mortgage and interbank lending, participation in loan syndications and plain vanilla securitisation for funding purposes, private wealth management and

2088 Ibid., p. 101.
2089 Ibid.
2090 Ibid.
2091 Ibid.
2092 Ibid.
2093 Ibid.

asset management services and, exposures to regulated money market (UCITS) funds.[2094] According to the final report, also the use of derivatives for own asset and liability management purposes, as well as sales and purchases of assets to manage the assets in the liquidity portfolio, would also be permitted for deposit banks. Finally, only the deposit bank would be allowed to supply retail payment services.[2095]

Moreover, the HLEG clarified that the provision of hedging services to non-banking clients (for example using forex and interest rate options and swaps) which fall within narrow position risk limits in relation to own funds, would be defined in regulation, and securities underwriting and related activities do not have to be separated. These activities could thus be carried out by the deposit bank.[2096] The HLEG acknowledged the inherent risks that are associated with these activities and suggests that the supervisory authorities shall remain alerted for the risks that would be arisen from such activities.[2097] The trading entity would be allowed to engage in all other banking activities, apart from the ones mandated specifically to the deposit bank and cannot fund itself with insured deposits and will not be allowed to supply retail payment services. The legally separate deposit bank and trading entity can operate within a bank holding company structure, but the deposit bank must be 'sufficiently insulated' from the risks assumed by the trading entity.[2098] In order to ensure the resilience of the two types of entities, both the deposit bank and the trading entity would each individually be subject to all the (prudential) regulatory requirements, such as those imposed by the CRR/CRD provisions, and consolidated supervision, which pertain to EU financial institutions.[2099] Based on the HLEG's opinion, the specific objectives of structural separation are to:[2100]

- limit a banking group's both incentives and ability to take excessive risks with insured deposits,
- prevent the coverage of losses incurred in the trading entity by the funds of the deposit bank, and hence limit the taxpayers' and deposit insurance system's liability,
- avoid the excessive allocation of lending from the deposit bank to other financial activities, thereby to the detriment of the non-financial sectors of the economy,

---

2094 Ibid.
2095 Ibid.
2096 Ibid.
2097 Ibid.
2098 Ibid., p. 102.
2099 Ibid.
2100 Ibid.

- reduce the interconnectedness between both banks and the shadow banking system, which has been a source of contagion in a system-wide banking crisis and
- level the playing field in investment banking activities between banking groups and stand-alone investment banks, as it would improve the risk-sensitivity of the funding cost of trading operations by limiting the market expectations of public protection of such activities.

Apart from pursuing the obvious target of safeguarding financial stability, the separation also aims at maintaining the banks' ability to provide a wide range of financial services to their customers and to their tailored needs. Therefore, the separation is allowed within the banking group so that the same entity can be used to cover customer needs and maintain customers' benefits from the existence of various business lines.[2101] This is an indirect acceptance of the theory in favour of the existence of scope and scale synergies from the combination of business lines under the same roof, retaining the benefits of universal banking model. Finally, the HLEG proposes that any transfer of funds and/or risks between the trading entity and the deposit bank within the same group, shall be done at market terms and restricted under the normal rules that apply to large exposures on interbank exposures.[2102] Furthermore, any transfer of risks and/or funds from the deposit bank to the trading entity, directly or indirectly would not be allowed, to the extent that such a transaction would endanger the deposit bank's capital adequacy, together with the additional capital buffers that may apply on top of the minimum capital requirements.[2103] Dividend payment restrictions will apply at both entities in case they do not fulfil their capital adequacy requirements, both minimum and additional buffers.

Another possibility for separation is supported by the HLEG through the recovery and resolution mechanism, proposed back then by the European Commission. During the assessment of the resolution and recovery capacity, the competent authority will have the possibility to assess whether the credit institution will be able to comply with the recovery and resolution requirements. To that end, the competent authority may require a greater scope of separation compared to the mandatory one, as described above.[2104] The HLEG supports the view that the effectiveness and credibility of the recovery and resolution mechanism is linked with the ability of the competent authority to require broader reforms in each case believes this would be necessary. Therefore, based on this view, the recovery and resolution plan shall be deemed adequate and credible only when the competent authority approves it, and the bank must be

---

2101 Ibid.
2102 Ibid.
2103 Ibid.
2104 Ibid., p. 103.

prepared to adopt broader structural reforms than originally scheduled. The ability of banks to draw, adopt and implement realistic and effective recovery and resolution plans is of utmost importance for the financial stability of the system and the HLEG views them as a necessary tool that supports the proposed structural reforms. On the other hand, though it must be pointed out that this necessity for credible recovery and resolution planning means that the structural reforms are not per se panacea and cannot be viewed as a standalone tool. Therefore, it seems that, by definition, the HLEG report understands the reduced importance of this measure and tries to couple it with a more credible resolution and recovery tool.

4.2. *The Proposed Structural Reforms' Regulation*

On 29 January 2014, the European Commission, after considering the HLEG's final report proposals, tabled its proposal for a regulation introducing structural reforms to the banking sector.[2105] Although this legislative proposal was not successful and was later withdrawn, it is very important to be properly understood not only because it was EU's response to the 'breaking the banks' saga, but also because it was the first and to the best of our knowledge last attempt, at the EU level, to regulate the structure of the banking sector. The aim of the legislative proposal (hereinafter the proposed regulation or the draft regulation) was to 'prevent [...] systemic risk, financial stress or failure of large, complex and interconnected entities in the financial system, in particular credit institutions, and at meeting the following objectives:

(a) to reduce excessive risk taking within the credit institution;
(b) to remove material conflicts of interest between the different parts of the credit institution;
(c) to avoid misallocation of resources and to encourage lending to the real economy;
(d) to contribute to undistorted conditions of competition for all credit institutions within the internal market;
(e) to reduce interconnectedness within the financial sector leading to systemic risk;
(f) to facilitate efficient management, monitoring and supervision of the credit institution;
(g) to facilitate the orderly resolution and recovery of the group.'[2106]

[2105] See in European Commission, Proposal for a Regulation Of The European Parliament And Of The Council on structural measures improving the resilience of EU credit institutions, COM (2014) 43 final, Brussels, 29 January 2014.

[2106] Ibid., Article 1 of the proposed regulation.

The proposed regulation, based on the proposals of the Liikanen Report and influenced also by the structural reforms enacted in the US (the Volcker Rule), the UK and in other countries in the EU, contained rules for a twofold proposal regarding the: a) prohibition of proprietary trading and b) the separation requirement for certain trading activities.[2107] The proposed perimeter of regulation's scope was defined both positively and negatively. Based on the positive definition of the proposal's scope, we found the following financial entities:

(a) 'any credit institution or an EU parent, including all branches and subsidiaries irrespective of where they are located, when it is identified as a global systemically important institution (G-SIIs) in application of Article 131 of Directive 2013/36/EU',[2108] and
(b) 'any of the following entities that for a period of three consecutive years has total assets amounting at least to EUR 30 billion and has trading activities amounting at least to EUR 70 billion or 10 percent of its total assets:
    (i) any credit institution established in the Union which is neither a parent undertaking nor a subsidiary, including all its branches irrespective of where they are located;
    (ii) an EU parent, including all branches and subsidiaries irrespective of where they are located, where one[2109]of the group entities is a credit institution established in the Union;
    (iii) EU branches of credit institutions established in third countries.'.

The negative scope of the proposed regulation was defined based on which entities were not falling under the ambit of the proposed regulation. Therefore, the proposed regulation would not be applied to:

- 'EU branches of credit institutions established in third countries if they are subject to a legal framework deemed equivalent in accordance with Article 27(1);'[2110]
- 'subsidiaries of EU parents established in third countries if they are subject to a legal framework deemed equivalent in accordance with Article 27(1);'[2111] and
- 'entities referred to in points (2) to (23) of Article 2(5) of Directive 2013/36/EU.'[2112]

[2107] Ibid., Article 2 of the proposed regulation.
[2108] Ibid., Article 3, para. 1(a) of the proposed regulation.
[2109] Ibid., para. 1(b) of the proposed regulation.
[2110] Ibid., Article 4, para. 1(a) of the proposed regulation.
[2111] Ibid., para. 1(b) of the proposed regulation.
[2112] Ibid., para. 1(c) of the proposed regulation.

The proposed ban would apply to EU banks, EU parent banks, their branches and subsidiaries, as well as to the EU branches of non-EU banks, provided that the above referred thresholds and requirements were applicable.[2113] An interesting exemption was available for a competent authority when it could exempt from the requirements of Chapter III subsidiaries of EU parents established in third countries where there are no rules deemed equivalent to Articles 10 to 16 and 20, if that competent authority is satisfied that:

- 'there is a resolution strategy agreed upon between the group level resolution authority in the Union and the third country host authority;'[2114] and
- 'the resolution strategy for the subsidiary of an EU parent established in a third country has no adverse effect on the financial stability of the Member State(s) where the EU parent and other group entities are established.'[2115]

Another important aspect of the proposed regulation was the definition of proprietary trading as 'using own capital or borrowed money to take positions in any type of transaction to purchase, sell or otherwise acquire or dispose of any financial instrument or commodities for the sole purpose of making a profit for own account, and without any connection to actual or anticipated client activity or for the purpose of hedging the entity's risk as result of actual or anticipated client activity, through the use of desks, units, divisions or individual traders specifically dedicated to such position taking and profit making, including through dedicated web-based proprietary trading platforms'.[2116] The proposed regulation, introduced therefore a more narrow ban on proprietary trading, at least compared with the similar ban in the US, and on specific investment banking transactions that do not qualify, per se, as proprietary trading. From the wording of proprietary trading's definition, however, were excluded the activities of securities underwriting, market making, and transactions destined to hedge risks resulting from client's activity.[2117] Moreover, the Commission's proposed regulation introduced a prohibition on certain trading activities for the entities referred to in Article 3 (entities falling under the ambit of the regulation). Specifically, these entities were not allowed to:

- 'engage in proprietary trading'[2118] and

2113 See in K. Alexander, *Principles of Banking Regulation*, Cambridge, Cambridge University Press, 2019, p. 224.

2114 See in European Commission, Proposal for a Regulation Of The European Parliament And Of The Council on structural measures improving the resilience of EU credit institutions, COM (2014) 43 final, Brussels, 29 January 2014, Article 4, para. 2(a) of the proposed regulation.

2115 Ibid., para. 2(b) of the proposed regulation.

2116 Article 5, point (4) of the proposed regulation.

2117 See in K. Alexander, *Principles of Banking Regulation*, Cambridge, Cambridge University Press, 2019, p. 223.

2118 See in European Commission, Proposal for a Regulation Of The European Parliament And Of The Council on structural measures improving the resilience of EU credit institutions, COM (2014) 43 final, Brussels, 29 January 2014, Article 6, para. 1(a) of the proposed regulation.

- 'with their own capital or borrowed money and for the sole purpose of making a profit for own account'[2119]:
  - 'acquire or retain units or shares of AIFs as defined by Article 4(1)(a) of Directive 2011/61/EU',[2120]
  - 'invest in derivatives, certificates, indices or any other financial instrument the performance of which is linked to shares or units of AIFs,'[2121] and
  - 'hold any units or shares in an entity that engages in proprietary trading or acquires units or shares in AIFs'[2122].

Exemptions from the general prohibition on certain trading activities were foreseen on:

- 'financial instruments issued by Member States central governments or by entities listed in point (2) of Article 117 and in Article 118 of Regulation (EU) No 575/2013',[2123]
- 'a situation where an entity referred to in Article 3 meets all of the following conditions'[2124]:
  - 'it uses its own capital as part of its cash management processes'[2125],
  - 'it exclusively holds, purchases, sells, or otherwise acquires or disposes of cash or cash equivalent assets. Cash equivalent assets must be highly liquid investments held in the base currency of the own capital, be readily convertible to a known amount of cash, be subject to an insignificant risk of a change in value, have maturity which does not exceed 397 days and provide a return no greater than the rate of return of a three-month high quality government bond'[2126]
- ' [...] to closed-ended and unleveraged AIFs as defined in Directive 2011/61/EU where those AIFs are established in the Union or, if they are not established in the Union, they are marketed in the Union according to Articles 35 or 40 of Directive 2011/61/EU, to qualifying venture capital funds as defined in Article 3(b) of Regulation (EU) No 345/2013, to qualifying social entrepreneurship funds as defined in Article 3(b) of Regulation (EU) No 346/2013, and to AIFs authorised as ELTIFs [...]'.[2127]

Overall, the prohibited activities were a) the proprietary trading in financial instruments and commodities, b) investments and participations in hedge funds and c) investments and participations in entities that undertake the previous

2119 Ibid., para. 1(b) of the proposed regulation.
2120 Ibid., para. 1(b)(i) of the proposed regulation.
2121 Ibid., para. 1(b)(ii) of the proposed regulation.
2122 Ibid., para. 1(b)(iii) of the proposed regulation.
2123 Ibid., para. 2(a) of the proposed regulation.
2124 Ibid., para. 2(b) of the proposed regulation.
2125 Ibid., para. 2(b)(i) of the proposed regulation.
2126 Ibid., para. 2(b)(ii) of the proposed regulation.
2127 Ibid., para. 3 of the proposed regulation.

activities. The exemptions to the prohibitions set above are on transactions: a) on money market instruments with cash management purposes, b) on trading in EU Member States' government bonds (this exemption could also be extended to other governments' bonds through the necessary delegated acts) and c) to unleveraged and close ended funds, including inter alia private equity, venture capital and social entrepreneurship funds.

The next important aspect of the Commission's legislative proposal was the requirement for separation. The Commission took the view that since banks are about to continue engaging in other trading and investment banking activities (including market making, lending to venture capital and private equity funds, investment and sponsorship of risky securitisation, sales and trading of derivatives etc.), they will be allowed to do so subject to the discretion of the competent authority who will be obliged to review the trading activities and will have the power as well as an obligation under certain circumstances, to separate a subset of activities (such as market making, risky securitisation, complex derivatives, etc.) if certain metrics are exceeded.[2128] Once again the perimeter of the separation requirement is defined negatively, by what activities shall not be included in the trading activities. Therefore, the trading activities shall include activities other than the following:[2129]

(i) Accepting deposits that are eligible under the Deposit Guarantee Scheme,
(ii) lending activities including, consumer credit, credit agreements relating to immovable property, factoring with or without recourse, financing of commercial transactions (including forfeiting),
(iii) financial leasing,
(iv) payment services,
(v) issuing and administering other means of payment such as travellers' cheques and bankers' drafts insofar as such activity is not covered by the previously mentioned payment services,
(vi) money brokering, safekeeping, and administration of securities,
(vii) credit reference services,
(viii) safe custody services, and
(ix) issuing electronic money

From the above requirements, trading in sovereign bonds is excluded ([…] buying or selling of financial instruments issued by Member States' central governments […])[2130] and also the European Commission was empowered to further exclude or include any financial instruments from the separation

2128 See in European Commission, Proposal for a Regulation Of The European Parliament And Of The Council on structural measures improving the resilience of EU credit institutions, COM (2014) 43 final, Brussels, 29 January 2014, p. 8.

2129 Ibid., Article 8, para. 1(a)–(i) of the proposed regulation.

2130 Ibid., para. 2 of the proposed regulation.

requirements.[2131] Competent authority's duty to review the trading activities was articulated in Article 9 of the proposed regulation and includes at least the following activities: '[...] market making, investments in and acting as a sponsor for securitisation, and trading in derivatives [...]'.[2132] The entities that must be reviewed by the competent authority are the following:

- 'a core credit institution established in the Union, which is neither a parent undertaking nor a subsidiary, including all its branches irrespective of where they are located',[2133]
- 'an EU parent, including all branches and subsidiaries irrespective of where they are located, where one of the group entities is a core credit institution established in the Union',[2134]
- 'EU branches of credit institutions established in third countries'.[2135]

When assessing the trading activities, the competent authority shall be based on the following metrics:[2136]

(a) 'the relative size of trading assets, as measured by trading assets divided by total assets',
(b) 'the leverage of trading assets as measured by trading assets divided by core Tier 1 capital',
(c) 'the relative importance of counterparty credit risk, as measured by the fair value of derivatives divided by total trading assets',
(d) 'the relative complexity of trading derivatives, as measured by level 2 and 3 trading derivatives assets divided by trading derivatives and by trading assets',
(e) 'the relative profitability of trading income, as measured by trading income divided by total net income',
(f) 'the relative importance of market risk, as measured by computing the difference between trading assets and liabilities in absolute value and dividing it by the simple average between trading assets and trading liabilities',
(g) 'the interconnectedness, as measured by the methodology referred to in Article 131(18) of Directive 2013/36/EU', and
(h) 'Credit and liquidity risk arising from commitments and guarantees provided by the core credit institution'.

The above-mentioned metrics would have been elaborated by the EBA based on delegated acts (regulatory technical standards – RTS and implementing technical standards – ITS), specifying how these metrics shall be measured

2131 Ibid., para. 3 of the proposed regulation.
2132 Ibid., Article 9, para. 1 of the proposed regulation.
2133 Ibid., para. 1(a) of the proposed regulation.
2134 Ibid., para. 1(b) of the proposed regulation.
2135 Ibid., para. 1(c) of the proposed regulation.
2136 Ibid., para. 2(a)–(h) of the proposed regulation.

and where appropriate specifying how these metrics would be produced based on already existed supervisory data.[2137] From the above analysis is clear that the 'deposit taking entities' within banking groups can only engage in these activities as long as the competent authority does not decide that they need to be performed within a distinct 'trading entity'.[2138]

The Commission's proposal results in a structure where a 'core credit (bank) institution'[2139] shall undertake the activities which a 'trading entity' is not allowed to perform. At the same time, the trading entity will be assigned with these activities that are prohibited for a core bank entity. Moreover, the competent authority, based on the provisions of Article 10, has been granted the power to require the separation of certain trading activities when 'the limits and conditions linked to the metrics referred to in points (a) to (h) of Article 9(2) [...] are met [...] and it therefore deems that there is a threat to the financial stability of the core credit institution or to the Union financial system as a whole, taking into account the objectives referred to in Article 1 [...]'.[2140] This decision is based on a dynamic process since the competent authority is obliged to constantly monitor the specific metrics that demonstrate the need to require the separation of the certain trading activities. If the bank succeeds in demonstrating, to the satisfaction of the competent authority, that these activities do not endanger the European Union's financial stability, the competent authority may decide not to require the separation.[2141] Finally, the proposed regulation was giving the competent authority the power to require the separation of a particular trading activity if it considered that the activity in question threatened the financial stability of the bank or of the European Union as a whole.[2142] Even after the separation, the deposit bank would have been able to prudently manage its own risks. To achieve that requirement, the proposed regulation allowed 'to carry out trading activities to the extent that the purpose is limited to only prudently managing its capital, liquidity and funding'.[2143] To this end only certain financial products would have been available for that purpose: interest rate derivatives, foreign exchange derivatives and credit derivatives eligible for central counterparty clearing. Furthermore, the 'core credit institution shall demonstrate to the competent supervisor that the hedging activity is designed to reduce, and demonstrably

2137 Ibid., para. 4 of the proposed regulation.
2138 Ibid., p. 10.
2139 As defined in Article 5, point 16 of the proposed regulation.
2140 See in European Commission, Proposal for a Regulation Of The European Parliament And Of The Council on structural measures improving the resilience of EU credit institutions, COM (2014) 43 final, Brussels, 29 January 2014, Article 10, para. 1 of the proposed regulation.
2141 Ibid., para. 3 of the proposed regulation.
2142 Ibid., para. 2 of the proposed regulation.
2143 Ibid., Article 11, para. 1 of the proposed regulation.

reduces or significantly mitigates, specific, identifiable risks of individual or aggregated positions of the core credit institution'.[2144] It seems therefore that with the proposed regulation, the European Commission tried to control, to a great extent, the available hedging options for the deposit taking entities in order to avoid a blurring of the lines between hedging activities and trading in derivatives for own account. Liquidity management by the credit institution might be perceived as market making or proprietary trading because inevitably the actions by the credit institution will lead to the building of certain speculative positions, therefore this should be associated with certain safeguards provided above.[2145] At the same time the credit institution shall be able to offer risk management services to its clients. It is desirable that the core credit institution is still able to sell certain risk management products (derivatives) to non-financial, non-banking clients to cover their business needs. However, by selling these derivatives to clients exposes the bank to more risks, which in turn may notably hinder its ability to apply credible resolution plan, making its resolution more complex and therefore it will be subject to different degrees of safeguards and controls.[2146] To avoid such situations, the proposed regulation took the view that 'interest rate, foreign exchange, credit, emission allowance and commodity derivatives eligible for central counterparty clearing can be sold by the core credit institution to its non-financial clients, insurance undertakings and institutions for occupational retirement provision, but only to hedge interest rate, foreign exchange and credit risk, commodity risk and emission allowance risk and subject to caps on the resulting position risk'.[2147] The proposed regulation specifies in Article 12 the conditions under which such a sell would be available:

- 'the sole purpose of the sale is to hedge interest rate risk, foreign exchange risk, credit risk, commodity risk or emissions allowance risk'[2148] and
- 'The core credit institution's own funds requirements for position risk arising from the derivatives and emission allowances does not exceed a proportion of its total risk capital requirement to be specified in a Commission delegated act [...]'[2149]

It is important to clarify at this point that in case the requirement in point (b) above is not fulfilled, 'the derivatives and emission allowances may neither be sold by the core credit institution nor be recorded on its balance sheet'.[2150]

2144 Ibid.
2145 Ibid., p. 9.
2146 Ibid.
2147 Ibid., p. 10.
2148 Ibid., Article 12, para. 1(a) of the proposed regulation.
2149 Ibid., para. 1(b) of the proposed regulation.
2150 Ibid., para. 1 of the proposed regulation.

When the competent authorities demand the separation of certain trading activities from a core credit institution, based on the decision described above, and the trading activities remain within the same banking group, then these trading activities '[...] may be carried out only by a group entity that is legally, economically and operationally separate ("trading entity") from the core credit institution'.[2151] These requirements remind us the similar requirement imposed by the ring fencing regulation in the UK, but here applies to the trading entity and not to the core credit institution. The aim if this measure is to control and certify, anytime, that the separation is effective and mitigates all the risks associated with the trading entity. Article 13 articulated the necessary requirements both for the parent company and trading entity to comply with in order to secure the effectiveness of the separation. More in detail, the EU parent company shall ensure that:

- 'a group containing core credit institutions and trading entities shall be structured so that on a sub-consolidated basis two distinct sub-groups are created, only one of which contains core credit institutions',[2152] and
- 'To the extent necessary [...] the core credit institution can carry on its activities in the event of the insolvency of the trading entity'.[2153]

  At the same time also,
- 'The core credit institution shall not hold capital instruments or voting rights in a trading entity',[2154]
- 'The core credit institution and the trading entity shall issue their own debt on an individual or sub-consolidated basis provided that this is not inconsistent with the resolution plan agreed by the relevant resolution authorities in accordance with the BRRD',[2155]
- 'All contracts and other transactions entered into between the core credit institution and the trading entity shall be as favourable to the core credit institution as are comparable contracts and transactions with or involving entities not belonging to the same sub-group',[2156]
- 'A majority of the members of the management body of the core credit institution and of the trading entity respectively shall consist of persons who are not members of the management body of the other entity. No member of the management body of either entity shall perform an executive function in both entities with the exception for the risk management officer of the parent undertaking',[2157]

2151 Ibid., Article 13, para. 1 of the proposed regulation.
2152 Ibid., para. 3 of the proposed regulation.
2153 Ibid., para. 4 of the proposed regulation.
2154 Ibid., para. 5 of the proposed regulation.
2155 Ibid., para. 6 of the proposed regulation.
2156 Ibid., para. 7 of the proposed regulation.
2157 Ibid., para. 8 of the proposed regulation.

- "The management body of the core credit institution, of the trading entity and of their parents shall have a duty to uphold the objectives of the separation',[2158]
- '[...] the name or the designation of the trading entity and of the core credit institution shall be such that the public can easily identify which entity is a trading entity and which entity is a core credit institution',[2159]
- The structurally separated entities shall comply with the necessary requirements, as stipulated in the Regulation (EU) 275/2013 and the Directive 2013/36/EU, both at consolidated and at sub consolidated level[2160]

When the competent authority, by applying the procedure described in Article 10 para. 3 for the separation of certain trading activities, the core credit institution or its EU parent company must submit to the competent Authority a separation plan within a 6-month period from the date of the decision for the separation.[2161] The separation plan must contain at least the following:

(a) 'specification of assets and activities that will be separated from the core credit institution',[2162]

(b) 'details on how the rules referred to in Article 13 are applied',[2163] and

(c) 'a timeline for the separation'[2164]

The competent authority would have had the power to demand further adaptations to the separation plan within 6 months from the date of their submission or to finally approve the proposed separation plan.[2165] Article 18 further describes the process when adaptations to the separation plan are demanded or when the institution fails to submit a separation plan as demanded by the competent authority.[2166] Finally, the institution and its management body must prove that they have applied the separation plan and that the institution is fully complied with competent authority's requirements.[2167] Article 20 of the proposed regulation sets the clear framework for the activities that are restricted for the trading entity. Specifically, the trading entity shall not: a) accept deposits that are eligible under the Deposit Guarantee Scheme, and b) provide payment services, as defined in the then Payment Services Directive (PSD), unless 'the said payment services are ancillary and strictly necessary for the exchange of collateral relating to trading activities'.[2168] Apart from the above measures, the regulation established also limits to the large exposures,

---

2158 Ibid., para. 9 of the proposed regulation.
2159 Ibid., para. 10 of the proposed regulation.
2160 Ibid., paras. 11–13 of the proposed regulation.
2161 Ibid., Article 18, para. 1 of the proposed regulation.
2162 Ibid., para. 2(a) of the proposed regulation.
2163 Ibid., para. 2(b) of the proposed regulation.
2164 Ibid., para. 2(c) of the proposed regulation.
2165 Ibid., para. 3 of the proposed regulation.
2166 Ibid., paras. 4–7 of the proposed regulation.
2167 Ibid., paras. 8–9 of the proposed regulation.
2168 Ibid., Article 20, point (b) of the proposed regulation.

both on intra group and on extra group exposures. Regarding intra-group exposures, the limit was set on 25% of own eligible capital and for extra-group exposures the limit was set: a) to 200% for the whole financial sector, and b) to 25% for any individual financial entity.

Maybe the most important parameter of the proposed regulation was the option to grant derogations from the requirements provided in Chapter III of the proposed regulation. This derogation shall be granted when the institutions are subject to legislation that is deemed to be equivalent to the EU's framework. The European Commission shall grant the said derogation after the Member State submits such an application, under the prerequisite that the legislation of the Member State has been adopted before 29 January 2014.[2169] The application for the derogation must be submitted by a Member State but the decision for the derogation is granted on the name of the institution concerned.[2170] In order to grant the derogation, the European Commission shall examine whether the national legislation is equivalent to the EU's and, if fulfil the following criteria:

(a) 'it aims at preventing financial stress or failure and systemic risk referred to in Article 1',[2171]
(b) 'it prevents credit institutions taking eligible deposits from individuals and SMEs from engaging in the regulated activity of dealing in investments as principal and holding trading assets',[2172]
(c) 'if the credit institution taking eligible deposits from individuals and SMEs belongs to a group, it ensures that the credit institution is legally separated from group entities that engage in the regulated activity of dealing in investments as a principal or hold trading assets, and the national legislation specifies the following:
    (i) the credit institution taking eligible deposits from individuals and SMEs is able to make decisions independently of other group entities,
    (ii) the credit institution taking eligible deposits from individuals and SMEs has a management body that is independent of other group entities and independent of the credit institution itself,
    (iii) the credit institution taking eligible deposits from individuals and SMEs is subject to capital and liquidity requirements in its own right

2169 See also in K. Alexander, *Principles of Banking Regulation*, Cambridge, Cambridge University Press, 2019, p. 227. This date was proposed on the draft regulation to include the legislations enacted by France, Belgium, Germany, and the UK, so they could claim for the equivalence regime.

2170 See in European Commission, Proposal for a Regulation Of The European Parliament And Of The Council on structural measures improving the resilience of EU credit institutions, COM (2014) 43 final, Brussels, 29 January 2014, Article 21, para. 1 of the proposed regulation.

2171 Ibid., para. 1(a) of the proposed regulation.

2172 Ibid., para. 1(b) of the proposed regulation.

(iv) the credit institution taking eligible deposits from individuals and SMEs may not enter into contracts or transactions with other group entities other than on terms similar to those referred to in Article 13(7).'[2173]

The procedure for the granting of derogation is specified in para. 2 of Article 21 of the proposed regulation and the European Commission had the power to ask for further information in order to assess whether the granting of the derogation will be in the Union's interests.

Summing up the draft proposal, we can observe that the Commission went beyond the Liikanen Report's proposals. According to Prof. Alexander, the draft regulation 'linked separation requirements not to proprietary trading [...] but to trading activities in general'[2174] and by defining in a negative way the trading activities kept an extremely large pool of potentially 'dangerous' services out of a credit institution's operating ability. Since proprietary trading was subject to an outright ban, the negative definition of trading activity would potentially allow the competent authority to include any activity that according to her is dangerous for financial stability, thus expanding the perimeter of the activities that require a separation from the core credit institution. Should the metrics, based on which the supervisor will evaluate and examine the necessity for separation, remain below the predefined thresholds, the separation is not obligatory and remains under the authority's discretion. Once the separation will be triggered, the trading activities under question shall only be carried out by a specially designated entity, the trading entity, which is legally, economically, and operationally separated from the core credit bank (deposit taking institution).[2175] This could result in an institution that since it would accept deposits, it would only had the possibility to engage in trading activities for the sole purpose of managing its capital, liquidity and funding, and continue to sell derivative instruments only under certain conditions.[2176] The draft proposal, as it was tabled by the Commission, was not calling for a breakup of the big European universal banking groups. They could have continued to serve their clients with a broad set of services and products and at the same time would have a more simplified and resolvable structure, supposed to limit the too big to fail effects.[2177]

2173 Ibid., para. 1(c) of the proposed regulation.

2174 See in K. Alexander, *Principles of Banking Regulation*, Cambridge, Cambridge University Press, 2019, p. 227.

2175 Ibid.

2176 Ibid.

2177 Ibid.

4.3. *The Outcome: 'Universal Banking is Dead! Long Live Universal Banking?'*

We mentioned earlier that Europe is dominated by large universal banks and is predominantly a bank based financial system. The universality of banking services has been well embedded for many centuries and introducing structural reforms to the banking sector would be an extremely demanding and difficult to implement task. The banking sector used all its influence and political pressure to alleviate the burden of such regulatory reforms either by adopting lighter versions of the original plans or by suffocating from the very beginning such initiatives. Since the adoption of the Volcker Rule in the US and the Vickers Report in the UK, everyone thought that Europe's time had come after the Liikanen's final report.

The Commission's draft regulation was perceived by many as the last nail in universal banking's coffin. Instead of adopting a blanket structure through a regulation, at the EU level, European universal banks opted for targeted amendments at national, Member State level, through local laws that were ultimately seriously watered down, at least compared to the EU draft proposal. To many commentators' surprises, Europe, and particularly the EU, remains a strong proponent of universal banking system, either on its purest form (one roof - many services) or through a light version of holding company's structure. Therefore, any reports over the future 'death' of universal banking in Europe proved to be like the famous premature reports of Marc Twain's death: 'greatly exaggerated'.[2178]

4.3.1 The Failure of the Proposed Regulation

From the very beginning, the Commissions' draft regulation was an ambitious project that had serious deficiencies to come over. The most important and at the same time controversial issue was that of the derogation regime. France, Germany, and Italy were opposed to the proposal from the beginning, in support of the universal banking regime, and the UK was highly concerned both about the Volcker rule style prohibition on proprietary trading and for the process to obtain the derogation regime from the Commission.[2179] The derogation, as

[2178] Mark Twain, famously joked about the rumours of his own death. In 1897, a newspaper mistakenly reported that he had died, prompting Twain to quip, 'The report of my death was an exaggeration.' Ironically, when he actually passed away on 21 April 1910, it was shortly after the appearance of Halley's Comet, which he had been born under in 1835. Twain once predicted he would 'go out with it', and indeed, he died the day after the comet's closest approach to Earth — a poetic and fitting end for the legendary humourist.

[2179] See in A. Carr, 'Bank structural reform: too big to fail, too big to save and too complex to manage, supervise and resolve?', in M. Haentjens and B. Wessels (eds.), *Research Handbook on Crisis Management in the Banking Sector*, Cheltenham, Edward Elgar Publishing, 2015, p. 16.

provided by the draft regulation, allows for a credit institution that is subject to a national legislation deemed as equivalent to the EU legislation, not to be subject to the draft regulation. Exemption shall be granted by the Commission, upon previous application by the Member State concerned. For the national legislation to be deemed as equivalent to the EU, it must have the same effect with the EU legislation.[2180] In essence the national legislation must ensure that the deposit taking entity:

- Has the capacity to take decisions independently from the rest of the group entities,[2181]
- Has a management body which is independent from the rest of the group entities and from the deposit taking entity,[2182]
- It is subject to capital and liquidity requirements that are sufficient for her own right,[2183] and
- Enters into contracts with the trading entity at arm's length (third party basis).[2184]

The above requirements shall form the basis for the Commission's assessment of whether derogation will be granted to the credit institution that is subject to an equivalent regime. Based on the draft proposal, only the UK, France and Germany would have been granted such a derogation, and not Belgium which had adopted its own legislation later than the initial date contained in the draft legislation.[2185] These requirements were criticised by the Council's Legal Service (CLS) through a valid legal argumentation. In particular, the derogation regime seemed to be in controversy with the EU law since a regulation, which is of direct application in all Member States, is of general application and binding in its entirety should not contain any derogations, exemptions, waivers, or options.[2186] Moreover, the CLES's argument is even more strengthen if we examine it under the light of the legal basis of the draft regulation. Article 114 of the Treaty of the Functioning of the EU (TFEU) provides for the European Parliament and for the Council to '[...] adopt the measures for the approximation of the provisions laid down

---

2180 Ibid., p. 7.

2181 See in European Commission, Proposal for a Regulation of the European Parliament and of the Council on structural measures improving the resilience of EU credit institutions, COM (2014) 43 final, Brussels, 29 January 2014, Article 21, para. 1(c), point (i) of the proposed regulation.

2182 Ibid., point (ii) of the proposed regulation.

2183 Ibid., point (iii) of the proposed regulation.

2184 Ibid., point (iv) of the proposed regulation.

2185 See in A. Carr, 'Bank structural reform: too big to fail, too big to save and too complex to manage, supervise and resolve?', in M. Haentjens and B. Wessels (eds.), *Research Handbook on Crisis Management in the Banking Sector*, Cheltenham, Edward Elgar Publishing, 2015, p. 7. Belgium adopted its legislation for the structural reforms on 25 April 2014 and thus was not able to benefit from a derogation.

2186 Ibid.

by law, regulation or administrative action in Member States which have as their object the establishment and functioning of the internal market'.[2187] Since these measures have as their objective the establishment and functioning of the internal market, it is possible to have certain derogations or options but only under the condition that the EU legislation contains specific criteria for its application.[2188] Certain elements of the draft regulation were incompatible with the Article 114 TFEU requirements. Specifically, the fact that the derogation would apply only to certain Member States, the cut-off date of 29 January 2014, and the proposal that the Commission would decide on the derogation's permissibility were highly problematic if the same legal basis would have been retained.[2189] If the Commission would like to keep the derogation option available, then a more suitable legal tool could have been preferred, such as a directive, which is binding only as to the result which is to be reached.[2190] According to Carr, the directive would be a more suitable legal instrument since it could satisfy the directly competing demands of France and Germany on the one side and of the UK on the other. Back then, the UK's ring-fencing regime was already well advanced, and the UK government wouldn't be in favour of an EU attempt that would require to 'dismantle its carefully designed regime'.[2191] Furthermore, the EU draft regulation was seen as a threat to the universal banking model by the French and German banks and their respective governments, a position also expressed by the significantly less ambitious and onerous structural reforms legislations that were adopted by the two countries and we will examine shortly after.

According to Massoc, as soon the acute phase of the financial crisis was controlled, European governments soon began to revive the idea of promoting their global 'too-big-to-fail' universal banks. They perceived the growth of these banks as a fundamental element of their economy's global competitiveness and sought to implement legislation that would not hinder and even allow

2187 See in Article 114, para. 1 of the Treaty of the Functioning of the European Union (TFEU).

2188 See in A. Carr, 'Bank structural reform: too big to fail, too big to save and too complex to manage, supervise and resolve?', in M. Haentjens and B. Wessels (eds.), *Research Handbook on Crisis Management in the Banking Sector*, Cheltenham, Edward Elgar Publishing, 2015, p. 7.

2189 Ibid.

2190 For an excellent analysis and deeper understanding of the various EU legal instruments and the differences between them see indicatively in P. Craig and G. de Búrca, *EU law: Text, cases, and materials*, 6th ed., Oxford, Oxford University Press, 2015, p. 105 onwards, and in J.P. Jacqué, *Droit Institutionnel de l'Union Européenne*, Paris, Dalloz, 2018, p. 601 onwards.

2191 See in A. Carr, 'Bank structural reform: too big to fail, too big to save and too complex to manage, supervise and resolve?', in M. Haentjens and B. Wessels (eds.), *Research Handbook on Crisis Management in the Banking Sector*, Cheltenham, Edward Elgar Publishing, 2015, p. 7.

these banks to expand.[2192] Furthermore, the banking union managed to cope with the big universal banks and now even supports the plans to promote competitiveness through the expansion of the big European banking groups.[2193] The creation of national financial champions was a political choice for France and Germany and the structural reforms agenda didn't find solid support among national parliaments.[2194]

4.3.2 Structural Reforms at the Member State Level

Shortly after the Liikanen final report, France, Germany, and Belgium, adopted legislations that introduced structural reforms to their respective banking systems. All the three legislations were less harsh and onerous compared to UK's ring-fencing legislation and to the Commission's draft regulation, simply because their (hidden) aim was also to prevent the universal banking model without compromising much of its efficiency and operating know how. Thus, before the Commission would table its own proposal, the three countries moved fast and adopted relevant legislation.

4.3.2.1 *France*

The French reforms[2195] followed the EU draft regulation spirit and subjects credit institutions and financial holding companies to a subsidiarisation requirement, under the condition that their trading activity exceeds certain limits.[2196] The legislative bill was formally presented in December 2012 and was enacted in July 2013, requiring the transfer of specific trading activities to separate trading entities within the same group by 1 July 2015.[2197] The French legislation defines proprietary trading in such a way as to explicitly exclude,

---

2192 See in E. Massoc, 'Banks, power, and political institutions: the divergent priorities of European states towards "too-big-to-fail" banks: The cases of competition in retail banking and the banking structural reform' (2020) 22(1) *Business and Politics*, p. 155.

2193 Ibid., p. 156.

2194 Massoc, in her article, makes an excellent analysis on how banks' power shapes the agenda and state priorities regarding bank structural reforms legislation, by presenting the French banking-political nexus among the top executives of both public and private sector and how the political power and influence of local German coalitions shaped, silently, the structural reforms agenda to be as much fruitless as possible, after having secure their own benefits.

2195 Loi n° 2013-672 du 26 juillet 2013 de séparation et de régulation des activités bancaires, available at: https://www.legifrance.gouv.fr/download/pdf?id=5DybqNo80gkatRTyFJP7R01tUE4pff_NWtPY0T-2KIM=.

2196 See in K. Alexander, *Principles of Banking Regulation*, Cambridge, Cambridge University Press, 2019, p. 225; in J-H. Binder, 'Ring-Fencing: An Integrated Approach with Many Unknowns' (2015) 16 *European Business Organization Law Review*, p. 112; and in E. Fernandez-Bollo, 'Structural Reform and Supervision of The Banking Sector in France' (2013) 2013(1) *OECD Journal: Financial Market Trends*.

2197 See in J-H. Binder, 'Ring-Fencing: An Integrated Approach with Many Unknowns' (2015) 16 *European Business Organization Law Review*, p. 112.

among others, a) the provision of investment services to clients, b) hedging and c) market making activities.[2198] For these activities, no subsidiarisation is required. By the moment the subsidiarisation will be realised, the trading entity is prohibited from accepting deposits.[2199] Within the ambit of the French legislation fall all credit institutions, financial companies, and mixed financial holding companies but only if the certain thresholds will be exceeded.[2200] According to the French legislation, the separated trading entity:[2201]

- Must be subject to specific licensing from the French regulator,
- Must be distinguished from the rest banking group,
- Must not be consolidated with its banking group, from a prudential perspective and
- It is not allowed to carry out high frequency trading or enter into OTC derivatives transactions on agricultural commodities.

4.3.2.2 *Germany*

The German reforms legislation was introduced as government bill in February 2012 and enacted in August 2013.[2202] It applies to credit institutions, as defined in the Regulation (EU) 575/2013. These credit institutions may carry out certain treading activities only through a legally, economically, and operationally separated 'financial trading institution' (*finanzhandelsinstitut*). According to the German law, the subsidiarisation applies when a) certain thresholds are reached or b) the competent authority deems the trading activities to be risky and pose a threat to the credit institution's solvency.[2203] Prima facie, the German legislation seems to have a broad scope since it captures deposit taking/credit institutions and all the entities within a group that contains a deposit taking institution.[2204] Under the new framework, credit

2198 Article 2, para. 1(a)–(f) of the French LOI no. 2013-672.

2199 See in K. Alexander, *Principles of Banking Regulation*, Cambridge, Cambridge University Press, 2019, p. 225.

2200 See in A. Carr, 'Bank structural reform: too big to fail, too big to save and too complex to manage, supervise and resolve?', in M. Haentjens and B. Wessels (eds.), *Research Handbook on Crisis Management in the Banking Sector*, Cheltenham, Edward Elgar Publishing, 2015, p. 11.

2201 Ibid., p. 15.

2202 The German Banking Act (Kreditwesengesetz – KWG), sections 3 and 25f, as they have been amended by the '*Gesetz zur Abschirmung von Risiken und zur Planung der Sanierung und Abwicklung von Kreditinstituten und Finanzgruppen*', of 7 August 2013, Bundesgesetzblatt, Part I, p. 3090.

2203 See in K. Alexander, *Principles of Banking Regulation*, Cambridge, Cambridge University Press, 2019, p. 225.

2204 See in A. Carr, 'Bank structural reform: too big to fail, too big to save and too complex to manage, supervise and resolve?', in M. Haentjens and B. Wessels (eds.), *Research Handbook on Crisis Management in the Banking Sector*, Cheltenham, Edward Elgar Publishing, 2015, p. 11.

institutions operating above specific quantitative thresholds are prohibited from engaging in proprietary trading and funding through equity positions or through loans or guarantees, hedge funds and other alternative investment funds.[2205] Certain exemptions apply with respect to inter alia transactions that qualify as market making or as hedging transactions and for the firms that found themselves below the thresholds, the supervisory authority retains the power to impose similar restrictions if deemed necessary.[2206]

What is interesting in the German legislation is that the two previously mentioned requirements lead to two distinct options. In the case of reaching the predefined threshold of €100 billion in trading activities or the entity group's balance sheet totalled for the last three business years at least €90 billion and trading activities accounted for no less than 20% of such total,[2207] the subsidiarisation requirement applies to transactions for the institution's own account and can be only carried out in a trading subsidiary entity and the market making activity with transactions aimed at hedging client activity are excluded from the requirement.[2208] In case that the subsidiarisation is required by the competent authority, this applies not only to transactions for own account but also to 'any financial transaction deemed to entail comparable risks'.[2209]

4.3.2.3 *Belgium*

Belgium adopted relevant legislation in 2014[2210] that imposed restrictions on the activities of banking groups and credit institutions. Following the publication of the Volcker Rule and Vickers Report, the Belgian government requested that the National Bank of Belgium (NBB) explore and analyse the desirability and feasibility of introducing similar structural reforms in Belgium.[2211] In response to Belgian government's request, the NBB published an interim report in

---

2205 See in J-H. Binder, 'Ring-Fencing: An Integrated Approach with Many Unknowns' (2015) 16 *European Business Organization Law Review*, p. 113.

2206 Ibid.

2207 See in A. Carr, 'Bank structural reform: too big to fail, too big to save and too complex to manage, supervise and resolve?', in M. Haentjens and B. Wessels (eds.), *Research Handbook on Crisis Management in the Banking Sector*, Cheltenham, Edward Elgar Publishing, 2015, p. 11.

2208 See in K. Alexander, *Principles of Banking Regulation*, Cambridge, Cambridge University Press, 2019, p. 225.

2209 Ibid.

2210 'Act of 25 April 2014 on the legal status and supervision of credit institutions', *Belgisch Staatsblad*, 07 May 2014, Ed. 2, p. 36794.

2211 See in J. Mitchell, 'Structural Banking Reforms', *Financial Stability Review*, National Bank of Belgium (NBB), 2014, p. 100 and in J-H. Binder, 'Ring-Fencing: An Integrated Approach with Many Unknowns' (2015) 16 *European Business Organization Law Review*, p. 112.

June 2012, and its final report appeared in July 2013.[2212] The Belgian Banking Act introduces a prohibition in principle of proprietary trading activities, as of 1 January 2015.[2213] However, the prohibition is not a blanket one and some proprietary trading activities are excluded from the ambit of the Article 119 of the said law.[2214] Permitted proprietary trading activities (including market-making, hedging, treasury management, and long-term investments) are capped, and these types of activities must comply with strict requirements on reporting, internal governance, and risk-management. The prohibited activities for credit institutions and their subsidiaries will have to be transferred to a legally separate entity outside the consolidated credit institution.[2215]

2212 For a detailed analysis of the proposed measures see in National Bank of Belgium (NBB), *Structural banking reforms in Belgium: final report*, July 2013.

2213 Article 119 of the Belgian Banking Law: 'Art. 119. À partir du 1er janvier 2015, il est interdit à tout établissement de crédit d'exercer des activités de négociation pour compte propre, que ce soit directement ou par l'intermédiaire de filiales belges ou étrangères.'

2214 Article 121 of the Belgian Banking Law: 'Art. 121. § 1er. Sous réserve de l'article 123, l'interdiction prévue à l'article 119 ne s'applique pas aux opérations sur instruments financiers qui font partie des activités suivantes, pour autant que ces opérations répondent aux conditions prévues au paragraphe 2:
1° la fourniture aux clients de services d'investissement et services auxiliaires, tels que définis à l'article 46, 1°, 1., 2. et 4. à 8., et 2°, de la loi du 6 avril 1995, visant à répondre aux besoins de financement, de couverture ou d'investissement des clients;
2° les activités de tenue de marché consistant en la présence régulière et continue, sur un marché réglementé ou dans un système multilatéral de négociation dont il est membre, d'un intervenant qui offre des prix d'achat et de vente fermes pour des instruments financiers, assortis d'un engagement de sa part de se porter contrepartie à ces prix sur des quantités minimales, aux fins d'apporter de la liquidité au marché concerné, pour autant que cet intervenant soit certifié en tant que teneur de marché par l'entreprise de marché ou l'entreprise d'investissement qui exploite le marché ou le système multilatéral de négociation en question;
3° les activités de couverture des risques propres de l'établissement de crédit ou de ses filiales, en ce compris les risques liés aux activités visées aux 1°, 2°, 4° et 5°;
4° la gestion saine et prudente des liquidités de l'établissement de crédit et de ses filiales;
5° l'achat et la vente d'instruments financiers acquis dans l'intention de les conserver durablement.
§ 2. Pour être exemptées de l'interdiction prévue à l'article 119, les opérations sur instruments financiers visées au paragraphe 1er doivent répondre aux conditions suivantes:
1° elles doivent s'effectuer à l'intérieur des limites de risque et dans le respect des mesures d'encadrement fixées en application de l'article 122;
2° s'agissant des opérations effectuées dans le cadre des activités visées au paragraphe 1er, 1° à 3°, l'établissement de crédit doit démontrer qu'elles sont nécessaires pour qu'il puisse remplir son rôle d'intermédiaire auprès de ses clients;
3° s'agissant des opérations effectuées dans le cadre des activités visées au paragraphe 1er, 4° et 5°, l'établissement de crédit doit démontrer qu'elles sont nécessaires en vue d'une gestion saine et prudente des liquidités ou investissements en question.'

2215 See in J-H. Binder, 'Ring-Fencing: An Integrated Approach with Many Unknowns' (2015) 16 *European Business Organization Law Review*, p. 112.

5 STRUCTURAL REFORMS IN THE EU BANKING SECTOR: A MISSED OPPORTUNITY?

The Belgian, French, and German financial reform proposals share several important characteristics, largely inspired by the Liikanen Report. A central feature is the segregation of certain high-risk trading activities, aligning with broader European efforts to regulate such practices, while still aiming to preserve the universal banking model widely supported in Continental Europe. This reflects a clear political preference for maintaining the integrated structure of universal banks rather than moving toward narrow banking as the sirens of separation advocate.[2216]

A second shared feature is how these national-level proposals define and regulate proprietary trading and market-making. While all three frameworks acknowledge the importance of allowing credit institutions to engage in market-making, they frame it as a potential subcategory of proprietary trading; This allows regulators to intervene and restrict market-making if it becomes overly significant within a bank's trading portfolio. Compared to the more rigid European Commission proposal, the Belgian, French, and German approaches are more flexible and allow for gradual regulatory adjustment based on data collected during implementation.[2217]

Thirdly, although these reforms were introduced in conjunction with early efforts to implement resolution planning requirements (ahead of the EU's BRRD), they fall short in effectively linking the goals of reducing trading risks and improving banks' resolvability. In France and Germany, resolution planning is treated as a separate issue, with little integration between risk containment and group structure simplification. While Belgium's central bank did consider both aspects together in its preparatory study, even the resulting legislation failed to fully integrate them.[2218] Lastly, a significant limitation of all three national initiatives is the lack of solid empirical evidence to support their policy choices. Apart from the Belgian central bank's study, which provided a more granular analysis of bank balance sheets, most proposals are based on limited data. Though some impact studies estimate implementation and operational costs, they often focus narrowly –such as the cost of setting up separate trading entities – potentially underestimating the broader implications for financial institutions' structures and strategies.[2219]

From the preceding analysis one question inevitably arises: Was the structural reform movement a missed opportunity for the European Union? Again, the famous British sitcom, Yes Minister, provides us with an appropriate

2216 Ibid., p. 113.
2217 Ibid.
2218 Ibid., p. 114.
2219 Ibid.

answer; The proverbial answer given to Minister Jim Hacker by his Permanent Secretary, Sir Humphrey Appleby, each time the minister was asking a difficult question: 'Well, yes and no Minister'. Yes, because it was a chance to create a more stable and easier to resolve banking structure, at least for the G-SIBs, that operate in Europe and no, because the adoption of the BRRD, few months later, gave the EU a very powerful weapon, that can deliver a stable, robust, and credible framework for the orderly resolution of banks. Moreover, the derogation issue was a very difficult political compromise that would have been unacceptable for the rest of the EU Member States to accept it. On the other hand, it would have been extremely difficult for the UK to accept such legislation since it had already started to apply the transfer schemes for its ring-fencing legislation.[2220] To the present author's view, the structural reforms agenda in the EU was just an idea to calm the angry taxpayers from the recent bank bailouts and its implementation was a red line for the traditional universal banking system in the EU. Despite the examples of France, Germany and Belgium, Europe remains up to date a solid castle of universal banking and even these efforts are not as extreme as those adopted in the UK and the US in the aftermath of the global financial crisis. On the other hand, the EU remains with the BRRD legislation to control the resolution process of the big universal banks and finally with the SSM, that is expected to deliver a new approach to the banking supervision.

[2220] See in A. Carr, 'Bank structural reform: too big to fail, too big to save and too complex to manage, supervise and resolve?', in M. Haentjens and B. Wessels (eds.), *Research Handbook on Crisis Management in the Banking Sector*, Cheltenham, Edward Elgar Publishing, 2015, p. 16.

PART III.

Analysis of the Interplay between the Structural Reforms and the Findings from the Case Study Jurisdictions

CHAPTER 1
STRUCTURAL REFORMS REGULATION AND FINANCIAL STABILITY: INTERACTIONS AND IMPLICATIONS

1 INTRODUCTION

Broadly speaking, the rationale behind the initiatives to introduce structural reforms in the banking sector has been based on four major building blocks:

(a) The first block has to do with tackling the so called 'Too-Big-to-Fail' (TBTF) phenomenon by aiming to, first, limit the size of big universal banks, and second, by reducing their interconnectedness;[2221]

(b) The second block has to do with eliminating the transmission of risks between the 'traditional banks' (those engaged in deposit taking and other traditional commercial banking activities) and the more volatile investment banking activities, with the last being exposed to speculative capital market operations, with the aim of protecting depositors from losses arising from the investment banking activities;[2222]

(c) The third block has to do with removing the funding subsidies that investment banks enjoy by having access to the deposits, usually protected by deposit insurance schemes, to fund their speculative operations in the capital markets, by curbing the size of such speculative activities;[2223] and

(d) The final block has to do with enabling appropriate resolution tools that will ensure the orderly wound down of smaller and less diversified banks;[2224]

Moral outrage also played an important role in the battle for the introduction of structural reforms.[2225] This moral outrage originated structural

---

[2221] See in R. Cranston, E. Avgouleas, K. van Zwieten, C. Hare and T. van Sante, *Principles of Banking Law*, Oxford, Oxford University Press, 2017, p. 71.

[2222] Ibid.

[2223] Ibid.

[2224] Ibid.

[2225] Ibid.

reform initiatives were based on two facts: a) a minority of big, internationally active and multifunctional banks, had accumulated tremendous losses due to their 'careless engagement with speculative markets, especially purchases of structured credit products that later turned loss-making'[2226] and b) the discovery of 'widespread abuse of public trust by big banks in a series of morally repulsive incidents which were economically detrimental, per se, only occasionally'.[2227] These events ranged from product miss-selling accusations,[2228] alleged money laundering assistance,[2229] competition infringements (Euribor and LIBOR manipulations,[2230] foreign exchange trading markets distortions) as well as other poorly designed investment decisions that had an impact on market's integrity (JPMC's 'London Whale' incident).[2231]

In response to these problems, the structural reforms initiative tried to introduce a separation between, on the one hand these banking activities that were perceived as risky (investment banking and capital markets activities) and those that were perceived as safe (deposit taking, retail lending and payments).[2232] Such reforms either took the form of functional separation (separation across different types of business activities) or geographical separation, requiring the subsidiarisation of significant domestic operations of foreign banks. Functional separation has been the preferred way forward for advanced economies, with reforms been implemented either through outright ban of certain operations either through 'ring-fencing' requirements for activities that have a special interest.[2233]

2226 Ibid., p. 72.

2227 Ibid.

2228 For example, Wells Fargo, one of the biggest US banks, was involved in certain cases were miss-selling practices were publicly revealed (charging higher costs to African American and Hispanic borrowers, overdraft fees anti-consumer practices, cross-selling scandal that allowed its employees to create fake accounts, and various other consumer-based discriminations).

2229 See indicatively, 'Credit Suisse bank found guilty over money-laundering charges', *BBC*, 27 June 2022, available at: https://www.bbc.com/news/business-61957774.

2230 See in European Commission, 'AMENDED - Antitrust: Commission fines banks €1.49 billion for participating in cartels in the interest rate derivatives industry', Press Release, Brussels, 4 December 2013, available at: https://ec.europa.eu/commission/presscorner/detail/en/IP_13_1208.

2231 See indicatively, 'The London Whale', Bloomberg, 26 February 2016, available at: https://www.bloomberg.com/opinion/quicktake/the-london-whale.

2232 See in R. Cranston, E. Avgouleas, K. van Zwieten, C. Hare and T. van Sante, *Principles of Banking Law*,Oxford, Oxford University Press, 2017, p. 72.

2233 Ibid.

2 ENDING THE 'TOO-BIG-TO-FAIL' (TBTF) PROBLEM?

The basic rationale for adopting structural reforms, nowadays, is to end the TBTF problem. A simple question arises naturally: What exactly is the meaning of the TBTF problem? While it is obvious that all banks benefit from a safe and sound financial system, banks differ in their systemic importance. The events from the recent GFC remind us that during the financial meltdown, governments siphoned enormous amounts of money to stabilise the trembling system and mitigate the negative spillover consequences for the real economy. According to the FSB 'implicit subsidies turned into explicit subsidies' with such subsidies affecting the funding costs of banks, thereby distorting competitiveness, and altering their incentives to take on risks.[2234] According to Prof. Omarova, the TBTF problem is by no means a new phenomenon, since it arose from the crisis that involved the Continental Illinois National Bank and Trust Company, back in 1984. The TBTF phrase though is even older since it first appeared to the governmental rescue of the Lockheed Corporation.[2235]

Financial institutions may become so large, complex, and interconnected that their potential distress would cause significant harm to the financial system and the economy. More importantly a disorderly insolvency of such a financial institution it is believed that it will lead to great value destruction because of fire sale liquidation of assets and the loss of franchise value.[2236] Moreover, protracted and costly litigation will arise, and possible contagion and side effects will force other market participants to take defensive measures in order to deal with such an unexpected situation. At this crucial point governments will need to intervene with bailouts that usually take the form of capital injections into the distressed banks, usually in exchange for an equity stake or an explicit guarantee of some or all its liabilities.[2237] According the FSB, the knowledge that a bank may be bailed out 'represents an implicit government subsidy, which had implications for the behaviour of banks and markets'[2238] and this may incentivise investors to fund the global systemically important banks (G-SIBs) at significantly lower rates compared to other non G-SIBs. As a result of such implicit subsidies, banks and their shareholders may take risks that are beyond the limits of the institution knowing that in case everything goes wrong the state will 'do the laundry'. Such moral hazard may create distortions in the market since bank managers and shareholders

---

[2234] See in Financial Stability Board (FSB), *Peer Review of the United Kingdom, Review Report*, 14 April 2021, p. 11.

[2235] See in S.T. Omarova, 'The "Too Big to Fail" Problem' (2019) 103 *Minnesota Law Review*, p. 2495.

[2236] See in Financial Stability Board (FSB), *Peer Review of the United Kingdom, Review Report*, 14 April 2021, p. 11.

[2237] Ibid.

[2238] Ibid.

will take decisions that might seem to be rational from a business point of view, but which have negative consequences from a social point of view.[2239] Therefore, in absence of credible resolution regimes, public authorities are not able to credibly commit to allowing systemically important banks to fail, giving thereby to such banks a funding cost advantage and market discipline may fail to exercise effective risk limitation, leading to further market and competition distortions.

The TBTF reforms aim at reducing both the probability and costs of financial crises, generating large social benefits, such as improved resource allocation, higher productivity growth, more resilient financial system and ultimately less risk to the taxpayers.[2240] According to the FSB's report, the objectives of the TBTF reforms are a) to shield taxpayers from losses by increasing loss-absorbing capacity, b) to mitigate risk taking incentives and c) to facilitate orderly resolution of those institutions.[2241] For the reforms to be effective, the FSB is of the view that:

- 'Governments must have the powers, the information, and the incentives to move from bailout to bail-in. Banks must have financial resources and legal and operational structures that facilitate the effective use of resolution tools by the resolution authorities.'[2242]
- 'The behaviour of banks must be affected by the prospect of resolution rather than bailout, together with capital surcharges and enhanced supervision.'[2243]
- 'Market participants must have sufficient information to price these changes and to exert market discipline.'[2244]
- 'These mechanisms must be sufficiently strong to affect aggregate outcomes, for example by reducing risk in the financial system.'[2245]

The post crisis TBTF reforms are mostly driven by the FSB, which was called upon to deliver a solid and credible framework to deal with the issue. The FSB's policy framework comprises:

(a) standards for higher loss absorbency capacity through capital surcharges and the tool of Total Loss Absorbency Capacity (TLAC),[2246]
(b) recommendations for enhanced supervision and heightened supervisory expectations and,[2247]

2239 Ibid.
2240 Ibid., p. 13.
2241 Ibid.
2242 Ibid.
2243 Ibid.
2244 Ibid.
2245 Ibid.
2246 Ibid., p. 15.
2247 Ibid.

(c) policies to put in place effective resolution regimes and resolution planning coupled with assessment and improvement of firms' structures and operations.[2248]

The FSB required that systemically important banks, in a global context, should have higher loss absorbency capacity than the minimum Basel III levels. The rationale behind this requirement is that such banks must be able to absorb crises without restricting the provision of financial services, including credit supply and market functioning. The FSB, with the active support of the Basel Committee on Banking Supervision (BCBS), produced a methodology in 2011 for assessing the systemic importance of banks.[2249] The FSB uses this methodology to identify the systemically important banks (SIBs) and to separate them in two categories: a) the Global Systemically Important Banks (G-SIBs), and b) the Domestic Systemically Important Banks (D-SIBs). In this category, banks are not significant from a global perspective but are still important from a domestic one since their distress or failure could have a significant impact on their domestic financial system and economy. Such effects could also be felt on a cross-border basis even if the banks are not systemically important from a global perspective.[2250] D-SIBs are identified by their national authorities who are better placed to evaluate the impact of a potential distress or failure on the local financial system and economy, compared to international bodies (BCBS, FSB, etc.). Higher loss absorbency requirements are another tool to make SIBs more robust to shocks. The aim is to allow such banks to absorb losses both on a going concern and in a resolution phase. In 2011, the BCBS published the relevant methodology for the calculation of capital surcharges to G-SIBs, a buffer that must be met with Common Equity Tier – 1 (CET-1), the highest quality of capital.[2251] On the contrary, the BCBS framework regarding D-SIBs, includes only principles on how to calculate the relevant buffer but does not propose any specific percentage. Finally, in December 2017, the BCBS issued the finalised package of Basel III reforms, which among other things, introduced a leverage ratio buffer requirement for the G-SIBs, equivalent to 50% of the risk weighted capital buffer, which will come into effect in 2023.[2252]

Another element of the post crisis TBTF reforms was the decision to enhance the intensity and effectiveness of the supervision of Systemically Important Financial Institutions (SIFIs). The aim behind this decision is that with more intense supervision, moral hazard shall be reduced by the time supervisors will

---

2248 Ibid.

2249 The BCBS's assessment methodology was based on five aspects of a bank's systemic impact: a) size, b) interconnectedness, c) lack of substitutes, d) international activity, and e) complexity.

2250 See in Financial Stability Board (FSB), *Peer Review of the United Kingdom, Review Report*, 14 April 2021, p. 16.

2251 Ibid., p. 17.

2252 Ibid.

intervene to influence the behaviour of managers. The BCBS delivered in 2012 the 'Basel Core principles for Effective Banking Supervision',[2253] incorporating also some recommendations based on a consultation between the IMF and the FSB, back in 2010.[2254] The last major building block in the TBTF reforms was the introduction of robust resolution mechanisms that should reduce the probability of bank failure by mitigating again the moral hazard issue. Such measures allow authorities to resolve financial institutions in an orderly manner, thus avoiding cliff edge effects such as those that appeared after the Lehman Brothers failure. Simultaneously, taxpayers will not face such heavy burdens while they will continue to have access to vital financial activities and credit supply.[2255] In 2011, the FSB issued the 'Key Attributes of Effective Resolution Regimes for Financial Institutions' (the Key Attributes) that was updated in 2014, and sets out 'the responsibilities, instruments and powers that resolution authorities should have at their disposal for firms that could have a systemic impact of they fail'.[2256] Apart from that, the key attributes set also the standards for recovery and resolution planning as well as on resolvability assessments, with further guidance being issued by the FSB on the matters. The Key Attributes provide that resolution should be initiated when a firm is no longer viable or likely to be no longer viable (failing or likely to fail) and has no reasonable prospect of becoming so, with the resolution aiming at ensuring that the firm will timely and early enter into resolution before the entire capital will be wiped out and before the firm will become balance sheet insolvent.[2257] The Key Attributes require clear standards or suitable indicators of non-viability to help guide the decisions on whether firms meet the conditions for entry into resolution and that the national competent authorities tasked with the implementation of the resolution process have a range of powers that is necessary to resolve the firm that has entered into the resolution process aiming at achieving international financial stability, protection of depositors, and minimisation of the overall resolution costs.[2258]

The question arises naturally: how did banks adapt to the post crisis TBTF reforms? According to the FSB, '[...] analysis suggests that the profitability of SIBs, and in particular of G-SIBs, has fallen relative to that of other banks,

---

2253 The BCBS Core Principles (BCPs) are the de facto minimum standards for sound prudential regulation and supervision of banks and banking systems, and compliance with them is assessed by the IMF and the World Bank within the context of the 'Financial Sector Assessment Program' (FSAP). The BCPs were complemented in 2013 by the 'Principles for Effective Risk Data Aggregation and Risk Reporting' and in 2014 by the 'Principles for Supervisory Colleges'.

2254 See in Financial Stability Board (FSB), *Peer Review of the United Kingdom, Review Report*, 14 April 2021, p. 17.

2255 Ibid., p. 18.

2256 Ibid.

2257 Ibid.

2258 Ibid.

reflecting higher capital, lower implicit funding subsidies, and lower risk'.[2259] Moreover, '[o]rganizational complexity, measured by number of subsidiaries, was high before the crisis and has remained so. However, the number of subsidiaries is only one factor that may influence organizational complexity. Other important dimensions could not be analyzed, owing to the lack of data'.[2260] The FSB's report shows that the overall TBTF post crisis reforms, under conservative assumptions, have produced positive net benefits.[2261] According to the Report's wording: 'Observed changes suggest increases in resilience, no material increases in the costs of funding, and more market discipline. Potentially negative side effects, such as a fall in aggregate lending or greater unintended fragmentation of financial markets, have not been observed. Where SIBs have reduced their activities, other suppliers of financial services have stepped in. Systemically important banks have lost domestic market share and market concentration has fallen. A reallocation of business away from SIBs to other firms is an expected outcome of TBTF reforms. On average, SIBs have lost domestic market share, but these trends differ across countries and regions.'[2262]

What is clear from the above analysis is that in principle, the TBTF reforms, at least those evaluated by the FSB's reports, demonstrate a certain de-risking and deleveraging process within the financial system, on behalf of banks. What though remains unclear is to what extent the structural reforms a) can be evaluated for contributing to that trend, and b) if they were indeed necessary. Prima facie, it seems that the FSB does not include the structural reforms within the final report, and the present author is of the view that this is mostly attributed to the intrinsic difficulty of measuring the impact of the structural measures adopted globally and have an impact on the G-SIBs and D-SIBs. According to the FSB, all the rest TBTF reforms have a countable and measurable impact on the social level, but this does not seem to be the case with the structural reforms. The ring-fencing, the Volcker Rule, and all the rest similar measures do contribute to the system's general stability, do decrease the social costs but it seems that we cannot quantify by how much. Therefore, we are unable to have a clear view to what extent these reforms are actually beneficial or simply create more burden than what they try to resolve. Despite the necessity of the rest of the TBTF reforms, the structural reforms seem to be an extra complication for both banks and competent authorities. The present book author's view is that the resolution regimes are the most important

2259 Ibid., p. 54.
2260 Ibid.
2261 Ibid., p. 75.
2262 Ibid.

tool and must be complemented with structural reforms only under certain circumstances that will be based on clear assumptions for their necessity.[2263]

Contrary to the FSB's report, Prof. Omarova, deconstructs the TBTF problem on its two basic ingredients/factors: a) the 'F factor' for the failure of the banks and b) the 'B factor' for the size of the banks that are perceived to be TBTF.[2264] The F factor stands for the failure of a particular financial institution and denotes bailouts or various forms of government rescue of financial firms that are on the brink of insolvency[2265] while the B factor denotes an ambiguity since it is unclear whether it means 'big' or 'bigness'.[2266] The F factor solutions to the TBTF problem include those policies and regulatory measures that target explicitly the firm failure aspect of the TBTF problem and all currently adopted measures seek to either a) minimise the broader fallout from any individual firm's failure, and b) to minimise individual financial firms' chances of failing.[2267] This is to be achieved through special tools:

(i) capital and liquidity regulation and stress tests, and
(ii) resolution planning and designation of competent authorities for the implementation of the resolution.

The B factor solutions to the TBTF problem include those policies and regulations that explicitly deal with and address the 'bigness' aspect of the TBTF problem, and only a small number of post crisis regulatory reforms belong to them.[2268] Also these reforms are considered 'highly controversial and difficult to implement',[2269] a view that we fully endorsed in this book. The B factor solutions are generally divided into two broad categories:

(a) regulatory measures that directly target the financial firms' balance sheet size,[2270] and
(b) structural reforms that restrain the growth and reduce the systemic significance of TBTF firms, by subjecting them to various activity-based limitations[2271]

In the first category, the size limitations, we found regulatory measures that impose direct limits on a firm's size and such measures are the most obvious but also the least common type of measures of a B factor solution. Size limits are a traditional antitrust tool and as a practical matter they usually apply only to the context of regulatory approval of mergers, in our case between

2263 More analysis of the issue will be provided in the specific subsection of the present chapter.
2264 See in S.T. Omarova, 'The "Too Big to Fail" Problem' (2019) 103 *Minnesota Law Review*, p. 2499.
2265 Ibid.
2266 Ibid., p. 2502.
2267 Ibid., p. 2505.
2268 Ibid., p. 2510.
2269 Ibid.
2270 Ibid.
2271 Ibid.

banks and other financial firms.[2272] Within this framework, Section 622 of Dodd-Frank Act prohibits mergers and acquisitions if they would result in a firm with total liabilities that exceed 10% of the total liabilities of all financial firms,[2273] however, it must be pointed out that these concentration limits do not preclude the organic growth of the firm.

Prof. Omarova discussed a second potential source of size limits that exist in the US regulatory framework. Section 121 of the Dodd-Frank Act grants the Fed the authority to require from any BHC with at least $250 billion in assets to terminate any activities and to sell any assets, if such a BHC poses 'a grave threat' to the US financial stability.[2274] However, the exercise of this authority is subject to strict procedural requirements and is reserved for cases in extremis, with the Fed not being able to order the divestment of a firm's assets simply because of its 'bigness'.[2275] The available mitigatory actions of the Section 121 include the following list of measures:

- 'Limit the ability of the company to merge with, acquire, consolidate with, or otherwise become affiliated with another company,[2276]
- 'Restrict the ability of the company to offer a financial product or products',[2277]
- 'Require the company to terminate one or more activities',[2278]
- 'Impose conditions on the manner in which the company conducts 1 or more activities',[2279] and finally
- 'If the Board of Governors determines that the actions described in paragraphs (1) through (4) are inadequate to mitigate a threat to the financial stability of the United States in its recommendation, require the company to sell or otherwise transfer assets or off-balance-sheet items to unaffiliated entities.'[2280]

The second category is the activity-based limitations, also known as 'structural reforms'. The term 'structural reforms' is a broad one, including measures that aim to limit the universe of legally permissible activities and investments of certain financial firms', banks in our case, further limiting it on the, publicly insured, deposit taking institutions.[2281] At the same time,

2272 Ibid.
2273 12 U.S.C. § 1852(b).
2274 12 U.S.C. § 5331(a).
2275 See in S.T. Omarova, 'The "Too Big to Fail" Problem' (2019) 103 *Minnesota Law Review*, p. 2511.
2276 12 U.S.C. § 5331(a)(1).
2277 12 U.S.C. § 5331(a)(2).
2278 12 U.S.C. § 5331(a)(3).
2279 12 U.S.C. § 5331(a)(4).
2280 12 U.S.C. § 5331(a)(5).
2281 See in S.T. Omarova, 'The "Too Big to Fail" Problem' (2019) 103 *Minnesota Law Review*, p. 2511. The same view is also supported by Guynn and Kenadjian (R.D. Guynn and P.S. Kenadjian, 'Structural Solutions: Blinded by Volcker, Vickers, Liikanen, Glass Steagall and Narrow Banking', in A. Dombret and P.S. Kenadjian (eds.), *Too Big to Fail III:*

structural reforms are also, as mentioned earlier, a tool of macro-prudential regulation and also the most 'politically salient and controversial' reforms.[2282] While the F factor solutions generally aim at shaping financial firms' economic incentives to better align them with the general public interest and public interest perceptions, the B factor solutions operate differently, by 'redrawing directly the key legal and economic boundaries within financial markets' and their bluntness and high impact character of this regulatory type of intervention in the financial system renders structural reforms 'inherently more salient and politically controversial' compared to the F factor solutions.[2283]

3 NON-BANK FINANCIAL INTERMEDIATION AND STRUCTURAL REFORMS

'Risks arising from the shift of credit intermediation to non-bank financial intermediaries should continue to be closely monitored. As non-bank financial institutions have picked up market share, some risks have moved outside the banking system. This shift may enhance the stability of the financial system, not only because it may lead to a diversification of funding sources. However, it could also be a source of financial instability.'[2284] The wording from the FSB's report is clear and it must be seriously considered before structural reforms are adopted as 'eye candy' measures. The danger is real and exists. The report simply confirms what experts have already warned about: structural reforms may create incentives for the migration of certain financial services to non-bank and less regulated entities.[2285] This trend is captured by the popular term 'shadow banking' that describes a diverse ecosystem of entities that offer banking services without being authorised as banks, financial activities

Structural Reform Proposals - Should We Break Up the Banks?, Volume 16, Institute for Law and Finance Series, Berlin, De Gruyter, 2015,) who describe structural reforms as 'illusory' and 'complementary to other more targeted reforms' and by D.J. Elliott, 'Ten Arguments Against Breaking Up the Big Banks', in A. Dombret and P.S. Kenadjian (eds.), *Too Big to Fail III: Structural Reforms Proposals, Should We Break Up the Banks?*, Volume 16, Institute for Law and Finance Series, Berlin, De Gruyter, 2015, who believes that arguments against structural reforms are more compelling to him and need for more analysis than already exists.

2282 See in S.T. Omarova, 'The "Too Big to Fail" Problem' (2019) 103 *Minnesota Law Review*, p. 2511.

2283 Ibid., p. 2515.

2284 See in Financial Stability Board (FSB), *Peer Review of the United Kingdom, Review Report*, 14 April 2021, p. 76.

2285 See in R.D. Guynn and P.S. Kenadjian, 'Structural Solutions: Blinded by Volcker, Vickers, Liikanen, Glass Steagall and Narrow Banking', in A. Dombret and P.S. Kenadjian (eds.), *Too Big to Fail III: Structural Reform Proposals - Should We Break Up the Banks?*, Volume 16, Institute for Law and Finance, Berlin, De Gruyter, 2015, p. 140.

and infrastructures.[2286] This non-bank financial intermediation (NBFI) ecosystem, comprising investment funds, insurance companies, pension funds and other financial intermediaries with different business models, balance sheets specificities and governance structures, is subject to distinct regulatory frameworks within and across jurisdictions. These NBFIs play an increasingly important role in financing the real economy, in managing the savings of households and corporates and in offering credible alternatives to consumers of financial and financial related activities.[2287] They are a valuable alternative to bank financing and help to support real economic activity, taking also advantage of the explosive growth of Fintech environment. This type of non-bank financing may become a source of systemic risk if it involves maturity/liquidity transformation or leads to the build-up of leverage and the diversity and growing involvement of NBFIs in credit provision has led to even more interconnections, including on a cross-border basis; this simply means that stress in certain parts of the financial system can be transmitted more widely to other healthy parts and to the broader economy.[2288]

The traditional legal approach is that if it provides a banking service, then it is a bank. Non-bank entities that offer banking services pose a risk to the financial system in exactly the same way as traditional banks do: a) funding and liquidity risk, if the NBFI will suffer a loss of confidence and experiences a period of customers' withdrawals (bank run), b) solvency risk, if it has a leveraged balance sheet and its asset exposures will decrease in value, and c) contagion risk, if it is interconnected with other NBFI entities, with the regulated financial system and has similar exposures with other shadow bank entities.[2289] There is no diminution of such risks simply by sifting activity onto new entities that have different name but operate in the same way and under the same, or even similar, business model targeting the same clients as traditional banks do. Since NBFI entities tend to be less regulated compared to traditional banks, regulatory arbitrage will certainly be a driving force behind the demand for services from NBFI entities; the increasing regulatory requirements imposed on traditional banks will inevitably force certain activities outside the safe perimeter of traditional, regulated, banks. If NBFI is driven solely by regulatory arbitrage purposes, then financial stability of the

---

2286 Although the term 'shadow banking' is commonly known as the term covering all the non-bank financial related entities, the FSB has changed its definition and now the correct term is 'Non-Bank Financial Institutions'.

2287 See in Financial Stability Board (FSB), *Peer Review of the United Kingdom, Review Report*, 14 April 2021, p. 76.

2288 Ibid.

2289 See in A. Docherty and F. Viort, *Better Banking, Understanding and Addressing the Failures in Risk Management, Governance and Regulation*, Wiley Finance Series, Chichester, Wiley, 2014, p. 245 and in K. Alexander, *Principles of Banking Regulation*, Cambridge, Cambridge University Press, 2019, p. 301.

NBFI sector will not represent a public good, as is the case with traditional banking stability.[2290] On the contrary, when NBFI is not driven solely by purposes of regulatory arbitrage it can constitute a public good since it helps to achieve efficiencies by offering services with significant economic value outside the traditional banking system.[2291] NBFI is merely the development of new, specialised business models that are more efficient or effective than the classic banking models. However, in several cases, NBFI entities exploit the opportunity for regulatory arbitrage provided by the absence of or from inefficient regulation or from the existence of an alternative regulatory regime (e.g. insurance).[2292]

The recent GFC showed us that many of the entities in need of a bail out were part of what was then considered as the shadow banking sector (currently NBFI); Bear Stearns, Lehman Brothers, AIG, the two GSEs, commercial paper conduits and the MMMFs to name but a few. Also, regulated commercial banks that failed were heavily exposed through loans to the NBFI sector, both for financing and from investments in the form of CDOs.[2293] Many of their problems resulted from their inability to fully understand, assess and manage the interconnections or the risks of those interconnections to the NBFI entities. Moreover, the regulatory approaches varied significantly between the EU and the US. Certain authors argue that the conversation for the imposition of structural reforms in the banking sector 'detracts valuable attention and resources from dealing with the very real issues arising from the shift of maturity transformation from the official banking sector to the shadow banking sector that has taken place and will continue to take place despite and in part because of the so-called structural solutions'.[2294] We fully endorse the above view. As the NBFI entities are expected to increase their market share, so will the danger of contagion in the event one of them fails, thus increasing the chances of a publicly funded bail out, unless of course those entities are also subject to a resolution system like the one that applies to the official banking groups. Although in theory NBFI does not require public funding for bail out and NBFI entities shall bear their own costs, the possibility of a public money-based bail out comes from the fact that since those entities will offer similar to banking services, the potential systemic risk and the interconnections between the regulated banking sector increases substantially in our view that possibility.

2290 See in K. Alexander, *Principles of Banking Regulation*, Cambridge, Cambridge University Press, 2019, p. 301.

2291 Ibid., p. 302.

2292 See in A. Docherty and F. Viort, *Better Banking, Understanding and Addressing the Failures in Risk Management, Governance and Regulation*, Wiley Finance Series, Chichester, Wiley, 2014, p. 245.

2293 See in Financial Stability Board (FSB), *Peer Review of the United Kingdom, Review Report*, 14 April 2021, p. 141.

2294 Ibid., p. 142.

We firmly believe therefore that the final result will only be the migration of some prohibited activities from the official banking sector to the NBFI system forcing the first to engage in riskier and riskier activities to remain competitive. Obviously, as NBFI entities can only grow bigger and account for a larger percentage of the financial system, the possibility for a bail out in a stressful event can only grow.[2295]

At the same time, it would also be highly problematic to try to prohibit NBFI entities from offering banking like services and competing with the traditional banks. Authors Guynn and Kenadjian support that history is littered with attempts by governments to grant monopoly powers over the money creation process to certain institutions or groups of institutions that were specially licensed for that. The well-known attempt by the US government to grant a monopoly over the creation of paper money only to the newly established national banking system in 1864 and drive the state-chartered banks out of existence was *ab initio* ill fated.[2296] The state-chartered banks responded by offering to their customers checking accounts instead of bank notes. The checking accounts proved to be as efficient as bank notes, and in some cases more efficient than them when considered as a means of storing and exchanging value – money. This story teaches us that just like state banks found their way to survive amid an existential crisis, nowadays the NBFI entities will always explore new ways to offer banking like services and products without being obliged to adapt to such onerous regulations as traditional banks do.[2297] Innovation finds a fertile ground in the financial services sector; we saw earlier in our analysis how technological advances in the means of communication and financial products' engineering paved the way for further (de)regulation in the US financial sector with the creation of new services and products.

During the recent GFC, traditional banks were not at the epicentre of the turmoil. On the contrary, NBFIs, including investment banks, GSEs and insurance companies were at the heart of the turmoil. The interbank linkages spread the risks across the world and the financial products infected other parts of the financial system. Structural reforms do not tackle the ill connection between the 'official' banking sector and the NBFI entities. On the contrary they reinforce this connection by simply offering more freedoms to the NBFIs to enter new markets where traditional banks had been well established. As a result, NBFI will compete with traditional banking intermediation in market segments that have no previous experience, thereby giving rise to concerns about possible adverse effects, and will assume risks that are not familiar with how they work or how they will be effectively managed. Concurrently,

2295 Ibid., p. 143.
2296 Ibid.
2297 Ibid., p. 144.

traditional banks will lose access to certain business markets, and they will have to replenish the lost income, usually by increasing their presence in other market segments and/or by increasing their assumed risks. The solution is to regulate creatively the NBFI sector with the aim to maximise its benefits while at the same time minimising its risks.[2298] When NBFI will be subject to regulation, tailor made to its particular nature, the banking activities that will migrate will not pose a threat to the financial system and it can continue to provide the benefits it has been associated with. Therefore, the optimal solution is not to allow such activities to migrate into uncharted and unregulated areas of the financial system but to regulate NBFI in such a manner that it could be both a safe and alternative option for funding.

4 BANKING RESOLUTION REGIMES AND STRUCTURAL REFORMS: AN INCONVENIENT MARRIAGE?

A critical component of the post crisis TBTF reforms was the introduction and implementation of a globally accepted resolution framework for financial institutions and particularly banks. The interaction between the structural reforms and the resolution framework is of utmost importance since one of the most important reasons behind the adoption of structural reforms is the enhanced resolvability of the systemically important financial institutions (SIFIs). Structural reforms and resolution reforms must work in tandem to provide for a smooth and operable resolution of SIFIs without requiring taxpayers' money.

But how exactly do the resolution regimes interact with the bank group structures? The question is of extreme importance because it has side effects on the way the resolution regimes are used to resolve troubled institutions and ultimately safeguard financial stability. So, in order to think about the impact that structural regulations have on the resolution regimes, we must first understand how the resolution regimes are conducted in practice. The resolution of financial groups can be conducted in one of two ways: a) the 'Single Point of Entry' (SPoE), and b) the 'Multiple Point of Entry' (MPoE).[2299] Based on the FSB's definitions the SPoE involves the application of resolution powers at the top parent or holding company level by a single resolution authority. Most probably this authority oversees the global consolidated supervision

[2298] See in K. Alexander, *Principles of Banking Regulation*, Cambridge, Cambridge University Press, 2019, p. 306.

[2299] See in S. Gleeson, 'Structural Separation and Bank Resolution', in A. Dombret and P.S. Kenadjian (eds.), *Too Big to Fail III: Structural Reform Proposals - Should We Break Up the Banks?*, Volume 16, Institute for Law and Finance Series, Berlin, De Gruyter, 2015, p. 156.

of a financial group and the SPoE strategy operates through the absorption of losses incurred within the group by the top parent or holding company through the write down and/or the mandatory conversion of unsecured debt issued by that top level company in equity (the tool of bail in). Provided that enough loss absorbency capacity is available at the top parent or holding company, operating subsidiaries are expected to continue on a going concern basis without entering into resolution.[2300] The MPoE involves the application of resolution powers by two or more resolution authorities to different parts of the group and is likely to result in the breaking up of the group in two or more separate parts. The group might be split across national or regional basis, along business lines, or a combination of each, with the resolution powers being applied to the separate parts need not be the same and could include various resolution options (bail in, bridge entity, transfer of business or wind down).[2301]

There is no binary choice between the two approaches and in practice, a combination might be necessary to accommodate the structure of a firm and the local regimes in the key jurisdictions where it operates with the choice of the strategy needs to take account of the existing structure and business model of the individual firm and the firm's particular characteristics.[2302] Gleeson makes an important point by reminding that SPoE and MPoE are 'names of resolution approaches, not types of corporate structure' and as a result, some banks are structured in a way that facilitates the implementation of an SPoE resolution approach while others are structured in a way that facilitates the MPoE model of resolution.[2303] However there can be no guarantee that an SPoE oriented bank will be resolved by the home supervisor of the holding company and simultaneously the same applies for an MPoE oriented bank, that will be resolved by the closure of a ring-fenced entity, because in practice the resolution authority will decide its approach based on the specific circumstances of the crisis concerned.[2304] An SPoE resolution strategy may represent the most effective option in case the debt issued at the top of the group is sufficient to absorb the group's losses and ensure the viability of the operating subsidiaries and it may be more suitable option to a firm that operates in a highly integrated manner (centralised liquidity management,

---

2300 See in Financial Stability Board (FSB), *Recovery and Resolution Planning for Systemically Important Financial Institutions: Guidance on Developing Effective Resolution Strategies*, 16 July 2013, p. 13.

2301 Ibid.

2302 Ibid.

2303 See in S. Gleeson, 'Structural Separation and Bank Resolution', in A. Dombret and P.S. Kenadjian (eds.), *Too Big to Fail III: Structural Reform Proposals - Should We Break Up the Banks?*, Volume 16, Institute for Law and Finance Series, Berlin, De Gruyter, 2015, p. 157.

2304 Ibid.

trading, hedging and risk management).[2305] On the other side of the fence, an MPoE strategy may be suitable for firms that operate based on a decentralised structure and enjoy greater financial, legal and operational separation along national or regional lines, with various sub-groups of relatively independent, capitalised and separately funded subsidiaries, particularly if different parts of the group can continue on a standalone basis. What is clear though is that in some cases, a group may need to be restructured to make itself amenable to an SPoE or MPoE resolution strategy.[2306]

The SPoE approach will involve the recapitalisation of a bank group at the holding company level through either writing down debt issued directly by the holding company or by writing down debt elsewhere in the group and forwarding upstream the proceeds based on the belief that the group usually is worth more than the sum of its parts and by dealing with resolution at the group level minimum value destruction can be achieved.[2307] By contrast, an MPoE approach is based on the idea that a troubled member of the group will be hived off and allowed to fail while the rest of the group will continue to operate. MPoE is underpinned by a group structure that minimises interdependence across the group members aiming at ensuring that one part of the group is not able to drag down the rest of the group.[2308] In the SPoE proceedings the aim and object of the process is to avoid any formal process being commenced in relation to any of the other operating entities of the holding company. What Gleeson therefore supports is that it is completely indifferent to the supervising resolution authority, how the bank has structured its business and what business is undertaken by each entity or how these entities are divided in terms of their business model and roles. 'If the purpose of the exercise is not to touch the legal entities, the distribution of business between those entities cannot, by definition, be relevant to the conduct of the resolution' he concludes.[2309] What becomes clear from the above analysis and Gleeson's statement is that in order to support that functional separation within a banking group facilitates and improves resolvability we need to make a necessary assumption by accepting that the banking group concerned will be resolved using an MPoE approach rather than an SPoE. Therefore, since the vast majority of GSIBs have adopted resolution plans based on an SPoE

2305 See in Financial Stability Board (FSB), *Recovery and Resolution Planning for Systemically Important Financial Institutions: Guidance on Developing Effective Resolution Strategies*, 16 July 2013, p. 13.

2306 Ibid.

2307 See in S. Gleeson, 'Structural Separation and Bank Resolution', in A. Dombret and P.S. Kenadjian (eds.), *Too Big to Fail III: Structural Reform Proposals - Should We Break Up the Banks?*, Volume 16, Institute for Law and Finance Series, Berlin, De Gruyter, 2015, p. 157.

2308 Ibid.

2309 Ibid., p. 158.

approach, this alone suggests that separating entities and/or activities does not guarantee that will be an optimal policy option to enhance resolvability and ultimately guarantee financial stability, at least based on an SPoE approach.[2310]

The same issue is more complex when viewed from the side of an MPoE approach. Complexity arises from the fact that an MPoE friendly structure does not mean that every single entity within the group will be resolved separately since MPoE friendly banking groups usually operate under clusters of legal entities rather than completely separate standalone entities.[2311] As a result, when we speak about an MPoE approach most probably we will end up meaning multiple SPoE approaches that in many cases might also be dozens. Usually, banks that have adopted MPoE resolution approaches were those that had a significant amount of their activities established in emerging markets with their operations be conducted through separately established and capitalised subsidiaries, mostly for two reasons.[2312] The first reason is that national governments require domestic operations to be conducted through a locally established subsidiary because this option gives the government more control over domestic banking activities and provides also for a mechanism to control effectively any national currency outflows. The second reason is that local activities are very exposed to a credit crunch of the government in the country concerned and a local activity can fail either by a local bank failure or by other means. In such a case it is useful for the banking group to be able to ring-fence the local creditors of the failed bank subsidiary instead of allowing the banking group to become a de facto guarantor of sovereign credit.[2313] To the above, classic, factors, we must add a more recent one that also exercises influence on the MPoE approach. The collapse of trust and confidence between the home and the host resolution authorities and to a certain extent between the governments of the home and host authorities, which resulted from the recent GFC. Such lack of confidence inevitably leads to ring-fencing efforts, usually by requiring banks to operate through separately capitalised subsidiaries and not through branches, since for the national resolution authorities this structure ensures that the bank will be able to be resolved locally without external cooperation and dependency. More importantly though, 'ensures that any national taxpayer funding which is provided is clearly applied to the payment of the local creditors and is not sent abroad for the potential benefit of foreigners'.[2314]

With such pressure on the universal banking model, as illustrated by the earlier mentioned SPoE approach, a bank with an MPoE structure will be divided

2310 Ibid.
2311 Ibid.
2312 Ibid., p. 159.
2313 Ibid.
2314 Ibid.

across national lines and the question that arises is to what extent a functional separation will assist its resolvability. Within this context, national regulators and supervisors will pay great attention to the interconnections between the various group entities, and especially for the subsidiary in their territory, with the aim to ensure that national individual subsidiaries of the wider banking group will be able to continue unaffected their operations if problems arise elsewhere in the group.[2315] The same approach is endorsed by the FSB, in its guidance on MPoE strategies, by saying that: 'Material subsidiaries or regional blocs should have in place funding arrangements that make it possible for them to be separated and continue operating should other parts of the group enter resolution. Intra-group financial interdependencies (for example, guarantees and contingent claims) and other exposures between group entities that would hamper a clean separation or risk the spread of contagion through the group should be limited. For example, exposures between group entities may need to be reduced and any intra-group funding should be provided at "arm's length" and subject to appropriate large exposures limits.'[2316] Therefore, the issue is how the structural reforms within an MPoE structured bank will interact with a predominantly national subsidiary structure as is currently the case. Volcker Rule style separation is group wide straight forward solution which effectively applies at the group wide level, subject to exemptions for the overseas operations of the BHC, while Vickers style structural reforms aim at protecting depositors in one country and therefore are seen as a more nationalistic approach with the UK being the only, up to date, country with such a view. Ultimately, Liikanen style separation aims at separating an activity that is perceived to be risky from an activity that is perceived to be less risky, and as a result, they also operate at a group wide level. Their effect would be that the group, which is already horizontally separated across national subsidiaries, will be also required to be vertically separated, since these subsidiaries will be now required to be split between a market and a non-market business department.[2317]

Gleeson supports the above view by also saying that a structural separation regime can be seen as assisting a resolution regime only when the resolution will be executed on a SPoE basis.[2318] He further supports that banking groups which are to be resolved on a MPoE basis, the typical approach is based on

---

[2315] Ibid., p. 161.

[2316] See in Financial Stability Board – FSB (2013a), 'Recovery and Resolution Planning for Systemically Important Financial Institutions: Guidance on Developing Effective Resolution Strategies', 16 July 2013, available at: https://www.fsb.org/wp-content/uploads/r_130716b.pdf, p. 18.

[2317] See in S. Gleeson, 'Structural Separation and Bank Resolution', in A. Dombret and P.S. Kenadjian (eds.), *Too Big to Fail III: Structural Reform Proposals - Should We Break Up the Banks?*, Volume 16, Institute for Law and Finance Series, Berlin, De Gruyter, 2015, p. 161.

[2318] Ibid., p. 162.

separation by jurisdiction and not by banking functions.[2319] This overlaying functional separation will be added on top of country by country separation requirements may well have adverse effects, since it will force existing MPoE groups away from their current models, in a development that will interfere with the clean brake concepts that are the essence of the MPoE resolution. Since the application of the MPoE will be harder, Gleeson concludes that 'we have been unable to identify a resolution strategy that which would benefit from structural separation within the group to be resolved'.[2320] The final result of the above structural measures will be that many national market businesses will be unable to survive as standalone units on grounds of their size and the groups' challenge will be to decide either to close down entirely their business or to aggregate their national activities into a larger multinational markets with sufficient scale business that will allow operating profits and the contested economies of scale.[2321]

Despite all the above, obstacles to resolvability remain and evidence from the FSB's report demonstrates that systemically important banks have more financial resources to absorb losses in resolution, have improved their resolvability, have improved technical and operational capabilities to execute resolution, 'but more needs to be done'.[2322] The structural reforms complement the resolution regimes and may, under certain circumstances, facilitate the resolution of a systemically important financial institution but in no way can replace a resolution regime. The optimal solution would be to create a modus operandi in which structural reforms, when adopted, will credibly reinforce the resolution regime by allowing even the biggest and most complex financial institutions to become resolvable within a time framework and a process that will not jeopardise the entire system's stability.

4.1. Interaction with the EU BRRD Legislation

The EU's Bank Recovery and Resolution Directive (BRRD),[2323] effective from 1 January 2016, provides a legally binding, transnational, bank resolution regime by requiring the resolution authorities of the EU Member States to have

2319 Ibid.
2320 Ibid.
2321 Ibid., p. 161.
2322 See in Financial Stability Board (FSB), *Peer Review of the United Kingdom, Review Report*, 14 April 2021, p. 33.
2323 Directive 2014/59/EU of the European Parliament and of the Council of 15 May 2014 establishing a framework for the recovery and resolution of credit institutions and investment firms and amending Council Directive 82/891/EEC, and Directives 2001/24/EC, 2002/47/EC, 2004/25/EC, 2005/56/EC, 2007/36/EC, 2011/35/EU, 2012/30/EU and 2013/36/EU, and Regulations (EU) No 1093/2010 and (EU) No 648/2012, of the European Parliament and of the Council, [2014] *OJ* L 173/190.

four resolution tools available for use by the national competent authorities. These tools are:[2324]

(a) the sale of business tool,
(b) the bridge institution tool,
(c) the asset separation tool, and
(d) the bail-in tool,

The national resolution authorities enjoy discretion over whether or not to use the available resolution tools, or in what combination they will use them, including the use of the bail-in tool to impose losses on bank liabilities when an institution is deemed to be 'failing or likely to fail'.[2325] The design of the BRRD bail-in tool requires from covered institutions to issue special loss absorbent capital, the so-called Minimum Required Eligible Liabilities (MREL). The bail-in tool must be seen as a response to one of the main causes of the 2007–2009 global financial crisis, that banks and other financial institutions had not engaged in adequate resolution planning and as a result when the market frozen in 2007 and in 2008, the public authorities were left with only the traditional insolvency proceedings to allocate losses to an institution's creditors when it was experiencing financial difficulties.[2326] The BRRD requires a list of factors to be fulfilled before the resolution authorities can make use of the resolution tools available. Based on these factors, the resolution authority must determine that the bank is:

(i) considered failing or likely to fail,[2327]
(ii) there is no other alternative solution from the private sector that could effectively provide a similar solution,[2328] and
(iii) There is public interest in the bank's resolution.[2329]

Moreover, the BRRD refers to the general principles of law that apply to resolutions so that Member States must ensure that any resolution action or measure which imposes losses to creditors and shareholders is subject to the general constraints of the BRRD legal framework and the EU law in general, including the EU Treaties.[2330]

The important question that arises is whether the EU resolution regime under the BRRD makes the structural reforms necessary. Both the UK Banking Act of 2013 and the withdrawn European Commission's proposal emphasised

---

2324 Ibid., Art. 37, para. 3.

2325 See in K. Alexander, *Principles of Banking Regulation*, Cambridge, Cambridge University Press, 2019, p. 193.

2326 Ibid.

2327 Directive 2014/59/EU of the European Parliament and of the Council of 15 May 2014 establishing a framework for the recovery and resolution of credit institutions and investment firms [...], [2014] *OJ* L 173/ 190, Art. 32, para. 3(a).

2328 Ibid., Art. 32, para. 3(b).

2329 Ibid., Art. 32, para. 3(c).

2330 Ibid., Art. 34.

that ring-fencing was an important tool that will enhance the resolvability of the large complex banking organisations. Ring-fencing is perceived to be beneficial for two reasons: a) it may make post bail in restructuring easier to execute because the financial group will be more transparent, since the ring-fencing regime will allow the bail in to apply firstly on the investment banking liabilities before touching the retail banking liabilities,[2331] and b) may provide for a fall back option for the resolution authority where losses are greater than the gone concern loss absorbing capacity of the holding company.[2332] The post bail-in restructuring may be facilitated by the ring-fencing regime by providing 'separability between the core business lines and functions' that are performed by the ring-fenced body (RFB) compared to those performed by the non-ring-fenced body (NRFB).[2333] The separability's effectiveness will depend on ring-fencing delivering some or all of the following requirements:

- The RFB and the NRFB should not depend on each other operationally,[2334]
- They do not book risk onto each other's balance sheets,[2335]
- They each have distinct franchise values and maintain distinct client relationships,[2336]
- They each have standalone access to the necessary financial markets infrastructures (including their access to payment and settlement systems),[2337] and
- They each have separate human resources and governance arrangements[2338]

However, the above considerations are not unique to banks subject to ring-fencing requirements since there are ways to deliver the above requirements without imposing ring-fencing regimes. Moreover, the post bail-in restructuring process may require splitting business lines and functions between the RFB and the NRFB and ring-fencing might not be the best available solution.[2339]

The second reason why the ring-fencing solution might be beneficial for the resolution authorities is that it provides fall-back options in cases where losses are greater than the gone concern loss absorbency capacity of the banking group's holding company.[2340] In case where the losses are greater than the

2331 See in K. Alexander, *Principles of Banking Regulation*, Cambridge, Cambridge University Press, 2019, p. 231.
2332 Ibid.
2333 Ibid.
2334 Ibid.
2335 Ibid.
2336 Ibid.
2337 Ibid.
2338 Ibid.
2339 Ibid.
2340 Ibid.

holding company's GLAC, but are confined to either the RFB or the NRFB, the ring-fencing solutions might be beneficial for two reasons:

(i) by insulating or, in certain circumstances, transferring to a bridge bank or a private sector purchaser (PSP), the healthy (non-loss generating) part of the group,[2341] and

(ii) in respect of bailing in operating liabilities of the loss-generating part of the group, whether the RFB or the NRFB, it should be relatively less disruptive to bail-in operating liabilities of either the RFB or the NRFB than to bail in those operating liabilities had both the RFB and NRFB functions been conducted out of a single legal entity.[2342]

However, both options are likely to be highly disruptive and lead to a disorderly resolution outcome. Moreover, ring-fencing is highly unlikely to deliver a stand-alone viability of either the RFB or NRFB entities, particularly in the case where the other part of the group is failing, although meeting, the above listed, separability conditions should help to mitigate such risk. In the case where losses are spread more evenly across both the RFB and NRFB entities, ring-fencing measures may not deliver much in the way of fallback resolution options and their positive effects may simply reduce the likelihood that both the RFB and NRFB are simultaneously loss making.[2343] The view from the other side of the fence is that the SPoE resolution approach can achieve the key outcomes that ring-fencing was initially designed to achieve. Notably, SPoE ensures continuity of the core retail functions, along with all other critical functions in a banking group without considering whether they are located within the RFB, NRFB or other parts of the group. Therefore, 'by reducing the TBTF subsidy for a bank as a whole, it achieves the same outcome as trying to reduce, through ring-fencing measures, the TBTF subsidy derived from the integration of the wholesale and investment banking businesses with the retail banking business',[2344] where the retail business is also deemed as a TBTF business. Furthermore, it is highly doubtful whether these outcomes could be achieved by ring-fencing measures alone, without being complemented by a credible group-wide resolution strategy. Nevertheless, ring-fencing measures may also have certain side benefits for resolution. The transfer of debt from the bank subsidiary to the top-level holding company that may become cheaper if the bank subsidiary is separated into ring-fenced and non-ring-fenced entities is an illustrative example. Such separation may also simplify any collateral arrangements, therefore making liquidity provision to the ring-fenced bank

---

2341 See in K. Alexander, 'Regulating the Structure of the EU Banking Sector' (2015) 16 *European Business Organization Law Review*, p. 248.

2342 Ibid., p. 249.

2343 Ibid.

2344 Ibid.

more manageable and stable in case the rest of the group or other group entities are in resolution proceedings.

A particular aspect of the EU Member States structural reforms, related to the resolution, is that the efficacy of structural reforms can be questioned if the sole purpose of the reforms is to facilitate the resolution of the banking group. This stems from the fact that the BRRD provides broad powers for the resolution authorities to require banks or banking groups to change their organisational structure if the competent authority determines ex ante that the bank or the banking group's structure is a substantial impediment to the resolution of the bank or the banking group as a whole.[2345] Article 17 para. 5 of the BRRD, provides that the resolution authority is empowered to conduct a resolvability assessment in order to identify if and to what extent there are any substantial impediments to the implementation of a feasible and credible resolution plan on behalf of the bank or the banking group. In case the relevant authority determines that there are substantial impediments to the resolution plan of the firm and its resolvability is under question it may order the firm to remove such impediments, including changing its organisational structure or business activities. According to Prof. Alexander, this could involve changes to the legal, operational, and financial structure of the institution or the group itself and to their business activities.[2346] The resolution authority has the power to adopt the following, non-exhaustive, available measures:

(i) 'Require the entity to revise any intragroup financing agreements or review the absence thereof, or draw up service agreements, whether intra-group or with third parties, to cover the provision of critical functions',[2347]
(ii) 'Require the entity to limit its maximum individual and aggregate exposures',[2348]
(iii) 'Impose specific or regular additional information requirements relevant for resolution purposes',[2349]
(iv) 'Require the entity to divest specific assets',[2350]
(v) 'Require the entity to limit or cease specific existing or proposed activities',[2351]

2345 Directive 2014/59/EU of the European Parliament and of the Council of 15 May 2014 establishing a framework for the recovery and resolution of credit institutions and investment firms [...], [2014] *OJ* L 173/190, Art. 17, para. 5.

2346 See in K. Alexander, *Principles of Banking Regulation*, Cambridge, Cambridge University Press, 2019, p. 233.

2347 Directive 2014/59/EU of the European Parliament and of the Council of 15 May 2014 establishing a framework for the recovery and resolution of credit institutions and investment firms [...], [2014] *OJ* L 173/190, Art. 17, para. 5(a).

2348 Ibid., para. 5(b).

2349 Ibid., para. 5(c).

2350 Ibid., para. 5(d).

2351 Ibid., para. 5(e).

(vi) 'Restrict or prevent the development of new or existing business lines or sale of new or existing products',[2352]

(vii) 'Require changes to legal or operational structures of the entity or any group entity, either directly or indirectly under its control, so as to reduce complexity in order to ensure that critical functions may be legally and operationally separated from other functions through the application of the resolution tools',[2353]

(viii) 'Require an entity or a parent undertaking to set up a parent financial holding company in a Member State or a Union parent financial holding company,[2354]

(ix) 'require an institution or an entity referred to in point (b), (c) or (d) of Article 1(1) of this Directive to submit a plan to restore compliance with the requirements of Articles 45e or 45f of this Directive, expressed as a percentage of the total risk exposure amount calculated in accordance with Article 92(3) of Regulation (EU) No 575/2013 and, where applicable, with the combined buffer requirement and with the requirements referred to in Article 45e or 45f of this Directive, expressed as a percentage of the total exposure measure referred to in Articles 429 and 429a of Regulation (EU) No 575/2013',[2355]

(x) 'Require an institution or entity referred to in point (b), (c) or (d) of Article 1(1) to issue eligible liabilities to meet the requirements of Article 45e or Article 45f',[2356]

(xi) 'require an institution or entity referred to in point (b), (c) or (d) of Article 1(1), to take other steps to meet the minimum requirement for own funds and eligible liabilities under Article 45e or Article 45f, including in particular to attempt to renegotiate any eligible liability, additional Tier 1 instrument or Tier 2 instrument it has issued, with a view to ensuring that any decision of the resolution authority to write down or convert that liability or instrument would be effected under the law of the jurisdiction governing that liability or instrument',[2357]

(xii) 'for the purpose of ensuring ongoing compliance with Article 45e or Article 45f, require an institution or entity referred to in point (b), (c) or (d) of Article 1(1), to change the maturity profile of: (i) own funds instruments, after having obtained the agreement of the competent

2352 Ibid., para. 5(f).
2353 Ibid., para. 5(g).
2354 Ibid., para. 5(h).
2355 Ibid., para. 5(ha).
2356 Ibid., para. 5(i).
2357 Ibid., para. 5(j).

authority, and (ii) eligible liabilities referred to in Article 45b and in point (a) of Article 45f(2)',[2358] and

(xiii) 'where an entity is the subsidiary of a mixed-activity holding company, requiring that the mixed-activity holding company set up a separate financial holding company to control the entity, if necessary in order to facilitate the resolution of the entity and to avoid the application of the resolution tools and the exercise of the powers referred to in Title IV having an adverse effect on the non-financial part of the group'.[2359]

Similarly, the Single Resolution Mechanism Regulation (SRMR)[2360] for the Member States that participate in the EU Banking Union, requires from the Single Resolution Board (SRB) to draw up resolution plans, in consultation with the national competent authorities and the national resolution authorities, including the group resolution authority. SRMR's Article 10 para. 11 is equivalent to Article 17 para. 5 of the BRRD to the extent that the SRB, when drafting and assessing the resolution plans submitted by the banks and the banking groups has the power and shall use that power to identify any potential, material impediments to resolvability, proposes relevant measures to the resolution authorities to address such impediments, after taking into account the EU legal principles of necessity and proportionality.[2361] The SRB has the power to require the relevant national resolution authority to adopt specific measures to order the institution to remove the identified impediments if the institution subject to resolution powers can be potentially entitled to draw on funds from the Single Resolution Fund (SRF).[2362] The national resolution authorities are allowed to take any of the following measures:

(a) 'to require the entity to revise any intragroup financing agreements or review the absence thereof, or draw up service agreements (whether intra-group or with third parties) to cover the provision of critical functions',[2363]

2358 Ibid., para. 5(ja).

2359 Ibid., para. 5(k).

2360 Regulation (EU) No 806/2014 of the European Parliament and of the Council of 15 July 2014 establishing uniform rules and a uniform procedure for the resolution of credit institutions and certain investment firms in the framework of a Single Resolution Mechanism and a Single Resolution Fund and amending Regulation (EU) No 1093/2010, [2014] *OJ* L 225/1.

2361 See in K. Alexander, *Principles of Banking Regulation*, Cambridge, Cambridge University Press, 2019, p. 234.
See also the wording of SRMR, Article 10, para. 10: 'The Board shall also take into account the need to avoid any impact on the institution or the group concerned which would go beyond what is necessary to remove the impediment to resolvability or would be disproportionate.'

2362 Ibid.

2363 Regulation (EU) No 806/2014 of the European Parliament and of the Council of 15 July 2014 establishing uniform rules and a uniform procedure for the resolution of credit institutions and certain investment firms in the framework of a Single Resolution Mechanism and a Single Resolution Fund and amending Regulation (EU) No 1093/2010, [2014] *OJ* L 225/1, Art. 10, para. 11(a).

(b) 'to require the entity to limit its maximum individual and aggregate exposures',[2364]
(c) 'to impose specific or regular additional information requirements relevant for resolution purposes',[2365]
(d) 'to require the entity to divest specific assets',[2366]
(e) 'to require the entity to limit or cease specific existing or proposed activities',[2367]
(f) 'to restrict or prevent the development of new or existing business lines or sale of new or existing products',[2368]
(g) 'to require changes to legal or operational structures of the entity or any group entity, either directly or indirectly under their control, so as to reduce complexity in order to ensure that critical functions may be legally and operationally separated from other functions through the application of the resolution tools',[2369]
(h) 'to require an entity to set up a parent financial holding company in a Member State or a Union parent financial holding company,[2370]
(i) 'to require an entity to issue eligible liabilities to meet the requirements of Articles 12f and 12g',[2371]
(j) 'to require an entity to take other steps to meet the requirements referred to in Articles 12f and 12g, including in particular to attempt to renegotiate any eligible liability, Additional Tier 1 instrument or Tier 2 instrument it has issued, with a view to ensuring that any decision of the Board to write down or convert that liability or instrument would be effected under the law of the jurisdiction governing that liability or instrument',[2372]
(k) 'to require an entity to submit a plan to restore compliance with the requirements of Articles 12f and 12g of this Regulation, expressed as a percentage of the total risk exposure amount calculated in accordance with Article 92(3) of Regulation (EU) No 575/2013 and, where applicable, with the combined buffer requirement and with the requirements of Article 12f or 12g of this Regulation expressed as a percentage of the total exposure measure referred to in Articles 429 and 429a of Regulation (EU) No 575/2013',[2373]

2364 Ibid., para. 11(b).
2365 Ibid., para. 11(c).
2366 Ibid., para. 11(d).
2367 Ibid., para. 11(e).
2368 Ibid., para. 11(f).
2369 Ibid., para. 11(g).
2370 Ibid., para. 11(h).
2371 Ibid., para. 11(i).
2372 Ibid., para. 11(j).
2373 Ibid., para. 11(k).

(l) 'for the purpose of ensuring ongoing compliance with Article 12f or 12g, to require an entity to change the maturity profile of: (i) own funds instruments, after having obtained the agreement of the competent authorities, including the ECB, and (ii) eligible liabilities referred to in Article 12c and point (a) of Article 12g(2)'.[2374]

Based on the abovementioned provisions of the BRRD and SRMR, we understand that the *raison d'être* of the Commission's structural regulation proposal was highly doubtful. If the primary purpose of the draft Regulation was to facilitate bank recovery and resolution by proposing or permitting a particular set of pre-bail-in organisational structures for banking groups, then the utility of this proposal was substantially undermined by the broad powers granted to Member State resolution authorities to require banking groups to reorganise themselves or to change their institutional structures in any way that the resolution authority believes is necessary to promote a more effective resolution of the banking group during times of distress.[2375] This results in a potentially direct conflict between the legal requirements of a Member State's ring-fence law and the power of the Member State's resolution authority to impose on a bank or on a banking group reorganisation requirements to ensure its resolvability under the resolution framework. In other words, a banking group, fully compliant with its jurisdiction's requirements for structural regulation, can be ordered by its resolution authority—at any time prior to a resolution or restructuring event—to change its organisational structure to enhance its resolvability. This created significant legal uncertainty for the banking group and limited the effectiveness of the Member State's structural regulation law, since the regulated entity must comply with two requirements, stemming from different legal bases, and be contradictory among them. These substantial powers for resolution authorities certainly raise questions about the need for any EU legislation permitting or disallowing certain pre-bail-in organisational structures for banks and banking groups and were probably among the most important reasons why the European Commission had to withdraw its proposal back in 2018.[2376]

2374 Ibid., para. 11(l).

2375 See in K. Alexander, 'Regulating the Structure of the EU Banking Sector' (2015) 16 *European Business Organization Law Review*, p. 252, and in K. Alexander, *Principles of Banking Regulation*, Cambridge, Cambridge University Press, 2019, p. 234.

2376 See in K. Alexander, *Principles of Banking Regulation*, Cambridge, Cambridge University Press, 2019, p. 234.

4.2. Interaction with the International Resolution Regimes

Apart from the EU resolution regime, structural reforms must cooperate and work in tandem with other resolution regimes adopted across the world. Given the high level of interconnection among the internationally active financial institutions and the fact that their operations are spread across the world, the reality is that those institutions face severe compliance costs with various resolution regimes that in some cases are also contradicting between them. The importance of effective resolution regimes is also endorsed from important academic cycles vis a vis the traditional bankruptcy schemes; such traditional schemes are insufficient to protect financial stability for at least two reasons: a) bankruptcy laws are inherently micro-prudential in nature since they focus on protecting individual firms, not the smooth functioning of entire systems (financial system)[2377] and b) the result from the Lehman Brothers bankruptcy demonstrated the limited ability of national bankruptcy laws to reorganise the capital structure of a large and complex financial firm.[2378] From the countries we used as case studies in our analysis, within this subpart we will only examine the US and the UK, since their structural reforms are the most important, both from a theoretical and practical standpoint. To the contrary, this does not diminish the importance of the Canadian and the Japanese resolution frameworks, but their coexistence with the structural reforms' regulation seems not to pose important issues, at least to the same extent as the US and UK regimes do.

The US bank resolution regime underwent significant changes with the Dodd-Frank Act, with the purpose to ensure the financial stability of the US and to put a permanent end to the practices by the governments and the central banks to bail out financial firms that were about to fail.[2379] Section II of the Dodd-Frank Act established the Orderly Liquidation Authority (OLA) which is operated and administered by the FDIC. OLA's purpose is to maintain financial stability threatened from institutions that pose a significant risk to it and minimise the moral hazard caused by the bail outs that are funded from the taxpayers' funds by requiring the orderly liquidation of a failing bank[2380] in a matter that a) 'creditors and shareholders will bear the losses of the financial company,[2381] b) 'management responsible for the condition of the financial company will not be retained',[2382] and c) 'the Corporation and other appropriate

2377 See in S.L. Schwarcz, 'Beyond Bankruptcy: Resolution as a Macroprudential Regulatory Tool' (2018) 94 *Notre Dame Law Review*, p. 717.

2378 Ibid.

2379 See in K. Alexander, *Principles of Banking Regulation*, Cambridge, Cambridge University Press, 2019, p. 186.

2380 12 U.S.C. § 5384(a).

2381 Ibid., § 5384(a)(1).

2382 Ibid., § 5384(a)(2).

agencies will take all steps necessary and appropriate to assure that all parties, including management, directors, and third parties, having responsibility for the condition of the financial company bear losses consistent with their responsibility, including actions for damages, restitution, and recoupment of compensation and other gains not compatible with such responsibility'.[2383] The FDIC may serve as the receivership for large, interconnected financial institutions that are categorised as systemically important and within the regulatory perimeter we find bank holding companies, non-bank financial companies that are deemed to be SIFIs, subsidiaries of bank holding companies and non-bank SIFIs, and broker dealer firms that are registered under the SEC provisions and are also members of the Securities Investor Protection Corporation (SIPC).[2384] The OLA relies heavily on the idea that the FDIC should enjoy an almost complete discretion in making high stakes decisions about whether banks should enter receivership (resolution) and what type of resolution this should be. The judicial review in OLA is existent but is also minimal and thus the OLA has not been tested before the US Courts.[2385]

Even though the OLA far from clearly articulates what will happen in practice, the FDIC's SPoE strategy is designed to fill this gap. To implement effectively its SPoE strategy, the FDIC shall be appointed as a receivership only of the top-tier US holding companies and subsidiaries would remain open to continue their operations. The FDIC will organise a bridge financial company to which it will transfer assets from the receivership estate, primarily the covered entities investments and loans to subsidiaries.[2386] With the receivership will remain losses, which would be apportioned according to the statutory priority among the former equity holders and unsecured creditors, together with their equity, both subordinated and unsecured. Through a security for claims exchange the claims of creditors in the receivership would be satisfied by issuance of securities representing debt and equity of the new holding company or holding companies.[2387] In such a manner, debt in the failed company would be converted into equity that would serve to secure that the new operations are well capitalised so that the newly formed bridge financial company will continue to operate and provide the holding company with services of the covered financial company. The subsidiaries would remain open and operating,

2383 Ibid., § 5384(a)(3).

2384 See in R.S. Carnell, J.R. Macey, G.P. Miller, and P. Conti-Brown, *The Law of Financial Institutions*, 7th ed., Aspen Casebook Series, New York, Wolters Kluwer, 2021, p. 392.

2385 Ibid., p. 393. The only case before the US Courts to test the judicial limits of the OLA was the 2015, *State National Bank of Big Spring v. Lew*, 795 F.3d 48 (DC Cir. 2015), and is not an important banking case since it didn't announce a major new principle in the federal banking law, but it still is the only case that in relation to the OLA.

2386 See in R.S. Carnell, J.R. Macey, G.P. Miller, and P. Conti-Brown, *The Law of Financial Institutions*, 7th ed., Aspen Casebook Series, New York, Wolters Kluwer, 2021, p. 396.

2387 Ibid.

allowing them to continue the supply of critical operations to the financial system and avoiding the disruption that would otherwise accompany their closing, minimising the potential spillover effects and the risks to the financial system.[2388] The benefit of this process is that since the subsidiaries would continue to operate as going concerns, and any financial obligations would have been transferred to the bridge financial company, counterparties to most of the financial firms' derivatives contracts would have no legal right to request the termination of their contracts, preventing in this way the fire sale of assets and the disorderly termination of these contracts.[2389]

Once again, the question that arises is identical with the one in relation to the EU resolution regime. Since we have a credible resolution regime with clear procedures and mandates why we need to adopt, extra burdensome regulations that separate certain activities, completely ban others, and require compliance with complex regimes? Since the target of the SPoE strategy and the OLA is to secure financial stability through an orderly resolution mechanism, adopting structural reforms seems to go beyond what it is necessary. Moreover, the Dodd-Frank Act requires BHCs to submit to their supervisors 'living wills' (aka resolution plans) which contain detailed information about their plan to avoid financial calamity and how they will deal with such calamity should it appears.[2390] Should the supervisors assess that these living wills are not well articulated and pose significant threats to the US financial stability they have the power to require amending actions that will ensure the acceptance of such plans from them. The same logic behind our analysis regarding the EU resolution applies also to the US. Structural reforms may help an already established and credible resolution scheme to work better and more effectively but cannot replace it or be the first violin in the financial stability orchestra. Structural reforms, especially in the US, were a long-term reality that was surpassed by the evolving nature of financial markets and their needs.

In the UK, back in 2009, the Parliament received the Royal Assent for the Banking Act of 2009 that granted the Treasury and the BoE sweeping powers to restructure failing banks and to transfer their shares to the UK government own bridge bank or to a private purchaser. The Financial Services Act of 2012 amended the 2009 Banking Act to expand the use of resolution powers to systemically important investment banks.[2391] The Banking Act Special Resolution Regime applies to UK incorporated banks and investment banks that have permission from the UK regulator to accept deposits and to banking group holding companies incorporated in the UK which own bank

---

2388 Ibid.

2389 Ibid.

2390 Ibid., p. 405.

2391 See in K. Alexander, *Principles of Banking Regulation*, Cambridge, Cambridge University Press, 2019, p. 184.

subsidiaries operating in other jurisdictions. The regime does not apply to foreign owned branches of banks incorporated in other European Economic Area countries.[2392] The BoE, as the UK resolution authority, is tasked with managing bank failure in pursuit of its statutory resolution objectives. These objectives include protecting and enhancing the stability of the UK financial system, ensuring the continuity of banking services and critical functions, and also protecting public funds from being used for bail outs.[2393] Similar to the EU resolution regime, the BoE may only place a firm into resolution when a number of statutory conditions are met: a) the bank must be 'failing or likely to fail', b) it is not reasonably likely that action can or will be taken to change this, and c) bank resolution is also only used if it is in the public interest. It must be noted that if the public interest test is not met, banks may be placed instead into the relevant statutory insolvency regime.[2394] Overall, the resolution decision is followed by 3 stage phase: a) stabilisation phase, b) restructuring phase, and c) exit from the resolution regime.

The resolution regime has evolved significantly, especially since the introduction of the BRRD back in 2015. Around the same time, the Banking Act was amended once again, this time to introduce a new objective for the BoE to ensure the continuity of all critical functions regardless of whether they sit in the RFB or NRFB. This amendment in the Banking Act reflects the importance of the NRFB and the services it provides to the economy.[2395] The panel that reviewed the ring-fencing regime highlighted the fact that while the ring-fencing regime remains silent on the critical functions provided by NRFBs, the resolution regime acknowledges the importance of NRFBs and of their services and aims to manage the failure of an NRFB alongside the RFB. As a result, the resolution regime provides 'a more comprehensive solution to tackling the failure of a large UK banking group that contains both an RFB and an NRFB'.[2396] This view is supported by the evidence regarding the impact of the resolution regime in reducing the implicit government guarantees (TBTF) outlined earlier in commission's final review. The review panel concluded that without the existence of a robust resolution regime, and with critical (banking) functions on both sides of the ring-fence, 'taxpayers would remain financially exposed if forced to rely on the ring-fencing regime alone to manage the failure of a bank. In other words, the ring-fencing regime does not act as a comprehensive backstop if the resolution regime is unable to manage a bank

2392 Ibid.

2393 See in *Ring-Fencing and Proprietary Trading Review* (RFPT), Independent Review, Final Report, March 2022, p. 130.

2394 Ibid.

2395 Ibid., p. 40.

2396 Ibid.

failure'.[2397] Finally, the review panel tried to avoid a blame game towards the initial approach of the Vickers Report and adopted a softer language by stating that '[w]hilst it could not have been foreseen by the ICB in the aftermath of the GFC, the evolving regulatory landscape throughout the past decade has resulted in two regimes that are not aligned in the way they aim to address too-big-to-fail, adding complexity to regulation in the UK. In essence, the ring-fencing regime was an earlier attempt at addressing too-big-to-fail with a focus on a narrow set of critical functions. But it is the resolution regime that is now better placed to provide a comprehensive solution for tackling this issue.'[2398]

The UK's ring-fencing regime explicitly prioritises the resilience of the RFBs over NRFBs. In contrast, the resolution regime also recognises the importance of NRFBs and aims to manage the failure of both entities. This stance creates a clear inconsistency between the two regimes, where the resilience of an RFB is prioritised over an NRFB, but in a failure situation, the critical functions of both are recognised as being important.[2399] Based on a thorough examination of the relevant data and the submitted resolution plans from the UK banks, the Panel concluded that ring-fencing does not play an important role in improving the resolvability of banks, because:

- the resolution regime is mostly 'structure-agnostic'. The only 'structural' requirement seems to be that banks who are required to hold the MREL levels above minimum capital requirements need to structurally subordinate MREL by setting up a clean holding company.[2400]
- The ring-fencing regime is not a pre-requisite for achieving resolvability. For a bank to be considered resolvable, it must meet three resolvability outcomes: a) financial resilience; b) continuity and restructuring; and c) coordination and communication. To achieve these outcomes, the bank must meet expectations set out in eight underlying BoE's statements of policy[2401] and the only area where the Panel found ring-fencing as relevant is 'Restructuring Planning'.[2402]
- in a resolution situation, it is even possible that provisions of the ring-fencing regime may have to be disapplied from the competent authorities,[2403] so that they do not become an impediment to an orderly resolution. The orderly

---

[2397] Ibid.

[2398] Ibid.

[2399] Ibid.

[2400] Ibid., p. 41.

[2401] These eight Policy Statements are dealing with: 1) MREL; 2) Valuations; 3) Funding in resolution; 4) Continuity of financial contracts in resolution; 5) Operational continuity in resolution; 6) Continuity of access to Financial Market Infrastructure; 7) Restructuring planning; and 8) Management, governance, and communications.

[2402] See in *Ring-Fencing and Proprietary Trading Review* (RFPT), Independent Review, Final Report, March 2022, p. 41.

[2403] The BoE intends to carry out the bail-in resolution strategy at the financial holding company level, not the individual RFB/NRFB entity level. Therefore, it might be necessary to disapply key ring-fencing provisions to facilitate an orderly resolution of the bank.

resolution of a large banking group might need the deployment of capital, liquidity, and resources in a way different and incompatible with how the ring-fencing regime would operate in normal circumstances.[2404]

Overall, the review Panel recognised that the ring-fencing regime:

- has the potential to facilitate resolvability in so far as it could reduce the time and cost of the post-resolution restructuring process,[2405] and
- the benefit of structural separation under the ring-fencing regime is time limited.[2406]

Regarding the facilitation of resolvability, during the restructuring phase of resolution, ring-fencing can, at least theoretically, provide the optionality to handle different parts of a bank separately, and adopt different strategies for each one of them. If an issue arises in one part of a banking group, for example in the NRFB entity, the ring-fencing regime may reduce the reputational damage for the other, healthy parts of the group.[2407] Taking into account the existing separation of management and business lines, ring fencing could also increase the value for potential buyers interested in purchasing RFB assets and liabilities, since buyers may be less likely to take retail assets and deposits that are in the same legal entity as the 'bad assets' that caused the failure. Ring-fencing could prevent this 'tainting' of the RFB entity, by making the resolution process more orderly. Equally, the rigidity of the ring-fencing regime may mean the assets are mainly attractive to another RFB entity rather than any buyer outside the regime, so attractiveness may be limited.[2408] The panel review, further found that in any case, this potential benefit is limited only to a narrow set of scenarios, as it would only be realised where the failure of a bank was caused by activities which were taking place in an NRFB entity only. Given the realities of modern banking and the exposures of banks subject to ring-fencing, it is not certain that a failure would be attributed solely to NRFB activities. Obviously, 'there are more scenarios where banks could fail across multiple business lines and across the ring-fence, and this would result in requiring restructuring involving both the RFB and NRFB entities. In such scenarios, the structural benefits of ring-fencing separation are not relevant'.[2409] Regarding the time limitation of the ring-fencing regime and in order to meet the objective of continuity and restructuring requirements under the Resolvability Assessment Framework (RAF), banks must maintain robust restructuring planning capabilities rather than a form of ex-ante separation.

2404 See in *Ring-Fencing and Proprietary Trading Review* (RFPT), Independent Review, Final Report, March 2022, p. 41.

2405 Ibid.

2406 Ibid.

2407 Ibid.

2408 Ibid.

2409 Ibid.

In simpler words, the resolution regime does not require banks to undertake any restructuring or structural separation measures as long as they are able to plan and execute restructuring effectively and in a timely way in the event of a resolution and the Panel's view is that after the point at which the restructuring capabilities of banks are assessed as robust, by the competent authorities 'the theoretical benefit of ex-ante separation under the ring-fencing regime falls away'.[2410]

5 PRUDENTIAL SUPERVISION

Structural reforms must also complement the applicable general prudential supervision requirements. Broadly speaking, prudential supervision requirements include the capital requirements, calibrated by the BCBS and adopted by the member jurisdictions, and processes that the BCBS has defined as also applicable; the SREP processes. In a nutshell, the prudential supervision framework is defined by the three pillars structure, articulated by the BCBS. The first pillar covers the minimum capital requirements for the banks based on their risk weighted assets (Pillar 1 requirements), the second pillar includes the SREP process and any capital add-ons to cover risks not directly addressed by the first pillar (Pillar 2 requirements) and the third pillar is the market discipline through extensive disclosure requirements (Pillar 3 requirements). Structural reforms are a particular type of financial regulation and their interaction with the framework of prudential supervision has not been in depth studied and understood. The question that primarily arises is whether structural reforms are necessary if we have in place a robust framework of prudential requirements that cover correctly the risks associated with financial intermediation. In the following pages we will try to discover and briefly explain the interaction between prudential requirements and structural reforms and possibly evaluate the need for their adoption with reference to the BCBS's three pillar structure.

5.1. Capital Requirements and Structural Reforms

Bank capital serves four main purposes: 1) to absorb losses arising from declines in asset value, 2) to provide start-up funding for a bank's early operations, 3) to reduce losses to deposit insurance schemes by providing a means to repay the claims of depositors and creditors of a failed bank, and 4) to create incentives for shareholders, directors, and managers of the bank

[2410] Ibid.

to exercise more prudence when overseeing banks' operations.[2411] Another type of regulatory capital is the so-called 'bail-inable debt', which is often used in bank resolution situations and converts to capital if bank capital falls below some contractually or regulatory determined trigger point.[2412] The bail-inable debt is also known as 'Total Loss Absorbency Capacity' (TLAC) and the FSB expected countries to hold a minimum amount of TLAC of 18% by 2022.[2413]

Higher capital requirements than the minimum internationally accepted, usually through the adoption of country specific buffers and other capital add-ons, can be a viable alternative solution to the rigid structural reforms and separation doctrines. Canada is a brilliant example of such approach and the fact that the Canadian banking system does not suffer from banking crises is a widely accepted persuasive explanation for the effectiveness of that solution. If we believe that through capital requirements, of any level, we can effectively address the associated risks with financial intermediation then why we should impose rigid and strict structural requirements that might prove to be impediments to the efficient use of capital even in times of stress. Such extreme solutions should be well calibrated and should keep a balance between safety and soundness and the financial system's ability to effectively perform its tasks. Equally important is the need to implement a coherent system of prudential regulation through capital requirements in the sense that even the medium sized banks of a country should be bound by these capital requirements in order to eliminate the risks from spreading a turmoil that will start from smaller banks while at the same time the bigger and most important banks will be healthy. The 2023 banking turmoil in the US is an illustrative example of how medium sized banks that are not deemed of systemic importance can fail and create turmoil in the market.[2414] The failure of SVB during the March 2023 turmoil, offers a number of lessons that arose mostly from the failure (or the policy choice) not to extend the Dodd-Frank architecture to those banks that were seen as less significant/systemic; SVB, as a smaller, but still very large bank, was not subject to capital regulation applicable to the large banks, was not required to engage in stress testing and resolution planning and the bankruptcy of its holding company was anything but orderly.[2415]

2411 See in K. Alexander, *Principles of Banking Regulation*, Cambridge, Cambridge University Press, 2019, p. 87.

2412 Ibid., p. 89.

2413 In addition to Tier 1 and Tier 2 capital requirements, the TLAC standard requires banks to hold at a minimum additional loss absorbent capital consisting of subordinated bonds and convertible capital instruments (CoCos).

2414 See in E.J. Janger, 'Equity for Intermediaries: The Resolution of Financial Firms in Bankruptcy and Bank Resolution' (2024) 41 *Yale Journal on Regulation*, p. 995.

2415 Ibid.

5.2. SREP Processes and Structural Reforms

The active engagement on behalf of supervisors to the banking operations is another important parameter for ensuring financial stability. Bank supervisors should be active, evaluate and assess both bank risk management practices and banking operations in a way that ensures that banks do not take excessive risks and at the same time, they have capital of good quality to ensure their viability and resolvability, if needed. The current international framework of prudential supervision is mostly based on the framework agreed under the auspices of the BCBS and its three pillars structure. Since Pillar 1 represents the minimum capital requirements, presented in the previous section, Pillar 2 contains the supervisory review process. The Pillar 2 supervisory review process ensures that banks have adequate capital and liquidity to support all the risks in their business, especially with respect to risks not fully captured by the Pillar 1 process and encourages good risk management. Under Pillar 2, states enjoy a level of discretion in imposing a further range of measures on individual institutions or groups of institutions to address corporate governance weaknesses and risk management practices which are deemed to be unsound.[2416] Under Pillar 2, bank supervisors can adjust capital to be additive to the minimum capital requirements calculated under Pillar 1. Therefore, supervisors enjoy the discretion to increase total capital requirements by imposing higher capital requirements through the Pillar 2 discretion if they believe that the bank or the banking group has in place inadequate risk management processes and governance structures. This extra amount of capital must reflect the quality of the bank's governance deficiency and shall be assessed through the Supervisory Review Enhancement Process (SREP), a crucial component of Basel's Pillar 2 requirements.[2417] The BCBS has identified four key principles of supervisory review under Pillar 2:

(a) Principle 1: Banks should have a process for assessing their overall capital adequacy in relation to their risk profile and a strategy for maintaining their capital levels.
(b) Principle 2: Supervisors should review and evaluate banks' internal capital adequacy assessments and strategies, as well as their ability to monitor and ensure their compliance with regulatory capital ratios. Supervisors should take appropriate supervisory action if they are not satisfied with the result of this process.
(c) Principle 3: Supervisors should expect banks to operate above the minimum regulatory capital ratios and should have the ability to require banks to hold capital in excess of the minimum requirements.

2416 See in K. Alexander, *Principles of Banking Regulation*, Cambridge, Cambridge University Press, 2019, p. 108.

2417 Ibid.

(d) Principle 4: Supervisors should seek to intervene at an early stage to prevent capital from falling below the minimum levels required to support the risk characteristics of a particular bank and should require rapid remedial action if capital is not maintained or restored.

Therefore, it is understood that supervisors have a great chance to review the risks assumed by banks, assess their potential impact, and determine ab initio the optimum level of capital by recalculating the risks that are assessed through the SREP tool. Should they discover that a bank has assumed more risk than what they perceive as acceptable, they can impose higher capital requirements that will reflect the new risk level. Moreover, they can ask the bank to explain in depth the incentives and the business motives behind total risk appetite, reassess the bank's capital planning and impose governance reforms that will ensure a better understanding of the bank's own risks. Pillar 2 capital requirements and the SREP process can offer an alternative solution to the structural reforms' rigidity, since they will allow the bank to engage in all types of banking activities but at the cost of higher capital requirements that will reflect the risks assumed. Moreover, the SREP process will help supervisors to better understand the associated risks and calibrate the capital requirements as well as the way they supervise in order to offer flexibility but mostly an appropriate environment to the banks and other financial institutions in order to support economic growth. Therefore, we do not see again how the rigidity of structural reforms would add more certainty to the regulators and supervisors with respect to their duties and how we would have a safer financial system without hindering the ability of banks to fruitfully engage in the entire spectrum of financial activities.

6 CROSS BORDER/INTERNATIONAL COOPERATION AND STRUCTURAL REFORMS

Banks operate across various jurisdictions with various business models. Implemented simultaneously, these national proposals represent a combination of materially different rules and requirements applying to institutions that are active in all their markets. Differences among the various structural regulation regimes might provide scope for cross border regulatory arbitrage by large, internationally active and systemically important banking groups, further exacerbating the burden on consolidated supervision and jeopardising the efficiency of cross border resolution.[2418] Moreover, the combined impact of different national rules may force global banking groups to move their business

[2418] See in J. Vinals, C. Pazarbasioglu, J. Surti, A. Narain, M. Erbenova and J. Chow, 'Creating a Safer Financial System: Will the Volcker, Vickers, and Liikanen Structural Measures Help?', *IMF Staff Discussion Note*, SDN/13/4, May 2013, International Monetary Fund, Washington D.C., p. 21.

to the 'highest common denominator' leading to even higher costs that would have incurred through compliance with any of such measures, should be taken in isolation.[2419] Side effects in competitiveness from structural reforms, and particular from ring fencing regimes, may have cumulative adverse effects for real economies and financial sectors in countries where such measures will be adopted. In a fictitious case, the same bank may operate as a universal bank in Europe, as RFB in the UK and be subject to the Volcker Rule in the US, at the same time. The holding company structure allows for various entities to be set up and subsidiarisation is necessary to effectively control a truly complex structure. It is obvious that cross border cooperation between the home and the host country, the various authorities and relevant bodies is an important step towards ensuring financial stability.

Given the potentially significant costs, which can permeate the global economy, there is a clear need for evaluation of structural reforms' implications for other jurisdictions. By developing certain principles for the evaluation of implications, policymakers would thus be able to facilitate cooperation, perform necessary adjustments, and ultimately mitigate any adverse effects.[2420] Thus, a pragmatic and global approach is necessary to avoid such unintended implications. Certain researchers, tried to define the basic elements that such principles should incorporate:

(a) 'A clear articulation of the objectives of structural measures',[2421] so that authorities should find a way to close any gaps between the different sets of measures, to the extent that the objectives are similar across countries.
(b) 'An analysis of their implications for internationally agreed reform of prudential regulation, supervision, and resolution',[2422] so that we can have a clear view of how the implications will interact with the Basel framework, the resolution mechanisms, and the shadow-banking sector.
(c) 'An assessment of the implication of these measures on risk-based supervision',[2423] so that we can measure both the risks that will be reduced after the introduction of structural reforms and the risks that will be born from the increased costs of compliance with these new regimes.
(d) 'The assignment of the monitoring of extra-territorial implications of national structural measures to an international body such as the FSB', so that we can estimate the real impact on other jurisdictions, avoid any negative spillover effects, and offer a forum of interaction among the regulators, with periodical evaluations.[2424]

2419 Ibid.
2420 Ibid., p. 24.
2421 Ibid.
2422 Ibid.
2423 Ibid.
2424 Ibid., p. 25.

We will therefore examine how cross-border cooperation in resolution and supervision will assist the implementation of structural reforms, since as we have already explained they must be combined in order to produce the optimal result.

6.1. In Resolution

Building on the analysis of the two resolution approaches, presented earlier, the Single Point of Entry (SPoE) and the Multiple Point of Entry (MPoE), it is equally important to secure a proper level of coordination and cooperation between the relevant resolution authorities so that resolution process will be executed effectively and under a common understanding, without nationalistic approaches impeding the process. Significant moves have been made towards the coordination of the resolution authorities regarding both the ex-ante design of the resolution plans and the ex-post processes that execute the resolution.[2425] The FSB encourages countries to enter into cooperation agreements which tailor made for the SIFIs with multinational operations, specifying how in the event of crisis resolution powers will be allocated and exercised among the national resolution authorities.[2426] For these two models, coordination between the national resolution authorities is equally important. The SPoE would greatly reduce the complexity of banking groups by allowing one resolution authority to exercise its powers at the highest company level, increasing the chances of a successful resolution because companies operating in diverse jurisdictions would not need to be restructured. The MPoE implies distinct resolution processes that must be well coordinated, since the most obvious result would be the breaking up of the group into constituent parts. This approach is more suitable for entities for which the internal recapitalisation under the SPoE would not work or for which breakup of the group is deemed more appropriate.[2427]

Such a coordination example is provided by the EU's resolution framework as established by the BRRD that requires the Member States to establish group

2425 See in J. Armour, 'Making Bank Resolution Credible', in N. Moloney, E. Ferran, and J. Payne (eds.), *The Oxford Handbook of Financial Regulation*, Oxford, Oxford University Press, 2015, p. 469.

2426 Obviously, the appropriate delineation of such agreements and their content depends on the interaction between the national authorities and the nature and content of the living wills prepared by the institutions themselves. Each institution will prepare the living wills based on its business model and the specificities that apply. At the same time, the home national resolution authority has a deep knowledge on the living wills of the institutions under its authority and can share its experience with the host national authority for better coordination.

2427 See in J. Armour, 'Making Bank Resolution Credible', in N. Moloney, E. Ferran, and J. Payne (eds.), *The Oxford Handbook of Financial Regulation*, Oxford, Oxford University Press, 2015, p. 470.

level resolution colleges responsible for information gathering, assessing the resolution plans, and execute any resolution when deemed necessary.[2428] The banking group resolution plans are drawn up and implemented on the basis of consensus between the national resolution authority, responsible for each of the subsidiaries, and the group level resolution authority.[2429] In the absence of consensus between the home and the host resolution authorities, national resolution authorities responsible for the subsidiaries remain free to pursue their own plans. The EBA is assigned with the task to participate and assist the coordination of these resolution colleges, acting as a conciliator if consensus cannot be achieved.[2430] Multinational coordination in Europe can be seen as two concentric circles, with their ambit being defined by the BRRD and the Single Resolution Mechanism for those Member States that belong in the banking union, respectively. The outer circle, which comprises all EU Member States, falls within the ambit of the BRRD and requires each country to transpose to its national legislation common rules regarding the powers available to national authorities for bank resolution.[2431] The inner circle, which falls under the ambit of the banking union's Single Resolution Mechanism and is comprised of all the Eurozone Member States and any non-Eurozone Member States which will decide to opt in.

From the preceding analysis it becomes clear that for structural reforms to be efficient solution, coordination in terms of resolution regimes is more than necessary, since the two regulatory measures must work in tandem in order to safeguard financial stability. The challenge of implementing cross-border banking resolution has been historically associated with coordination failures, which ultimately resulted in disorderly resolutions with devastating consequences and dangerous systemic effects.[2432] These are exactly the rationales for enhanced cross-border cooperation since the global banking reality is cross-border by its nature and can lead to regulatory arbitrage between the regimes.

2428 Directive 2014/59/EU of the European Parliament and of the Council of 15 May 2014 establishing a framework for the recovery and resolution of credit institutions and investment firms […], [2014] *OJ* L 173/190, Art. 88.

2429 Ibid., Arts. 13 and 92.

2430 See in J. Armour, 'Making Bank Resolution Credible', in N. Moloney, E. Ferran, and J. Payne (eds.), *The Oxford Handbook of Financial Regulation*, Oxford, Oxford University Press, 2015, p. 469.

2431 Ibid., p. 470.

2432 For an excellent analysis on the matter of international coordination in cross border resolution proceedings see in F. Lupo-Pasini and R.P. Buckley, 'International Coordination in Cross-Border Bank Bail-ins: Problems and Prospects' (2015) 16 *European Business Organization Law Review*, pp. 203–226.

6.2. In Supervision

Cooperation in cross border supervision of banking groups is more than necessity. After the global financial crisis, the regulatory focus shifted towards the largest, more complex financial institutions bringing them into the spotlight. These institutions were supposed to be the most sophisticated, at least in terms of risk management, but at the end of the day, regulators viewed them as those that pose the biggest risks to financial stability, domestically, regionally, and internationally.[2433] Now, international coordination is more enhanced and supported by various international fora that promote cooperation, dialogue, and common practices. Despite all these, structural reforms do not reach consensus among international regulators and different approaches, as have been presented earlier in the present book, create impediments both to regulators and banks. Regulators cannot agree on a common approach regarding structural reforms since these are based on historical, cultural, and business-related reasons that may justify or not their adoption. Simultaneously, banks, because of the same reasons, do not follow common business models and may engage, or not, in the full spectrum of financial activities or simply in part of them. Therefore, supervisors must follow the banking models and adapt their supervision to them. Coordination and cross border cooperation among the supervisors is therefore a critical part for ensuring financial stability, since sometimes supervisors must examine different banking models in the same country, or similar banking models in different countries that have fundamentally different economic characteristics.[2434]

From the regulatory and supervisory standpoint, internationally active financial institutions face now a completely different regulatory environment than prior to the crisis. They are obliged to restructure their business models, activities, operations, and presence to respond to the intentional implementation of policies that aim to treat the underlying causes of the international financial crisis. However, at the same time, conflicts have emerged between major regulators that implement common approaches in 'differing and often conflicting matters'.[2435] This raises concerns for financial institutions that must comply with competing and differentiated regimes, often aim to different targets, ultimately creating new risks that negatively impact financial stability, albeit hypothetically. Structural reforms in the banking sector ultimately seem to be a national campaign and do not have global support, not even at the highest level (G-7). In the UK, the Panel that undertook to review the ring-fencing

2433 See in D.W. Arner, 'Cross-Border Supervision of Financial Institutions', in N. Moloney, E. Ferran, and J. Payne (eds.), *The Oxford Handbook of Financial Regulation*, Oxford, Oxford University Press, 2015, p. 500.

2434 Ibid., p. 501.

2435 Ibid., p. 502.

regime concluded that: 'In comparison with other jurisdictions, the UK is an outlier when it comes to the implementation of structural separation. Most countries did not implement any form of structural separation for their banks, and the handful of countries that did took a different, less rigid approach than the UK.'[2436] The failure of the European Commission's legislative proposal for a structural reforms' regulation demonstrated also that universal banking model is well embedded in the European continent and the domestic attempts to tame the megabanks became a legislative reality only in a handful of countries. Even in Switzerland, which is not examined in light of the present book case studies, Swiss national laws do not impose explicit structural separation requirements, ban proprietary trading, specify the exclusion of certain services, or place any other restrictions on deposit takers regarding the type of customers that they can bank. In that sense, there is no ring-fencing regime in Switzerland.[2437] At the same time, Canada continues to support an almost universal banking model coupled with enhanced supervisory requirements that seems to perform more than well. Ultimately, Japan still has a separation regime, but it is far milder than the US and UK respectively. Recent voices of tearing down the firewalls will probably find their way through the Japanese Diet.

This short review of the separation regimes simply reminds us that international coordination is extremely important for the efficient adoption of structural reforms. Structural reforms are just any other financial regulatory reforms; they will perform well only when they are globally accepted as an optimal solution and will be globally applied. Instead of adopting rigid solutions that harm financial innovation and do not deal effectively with the TBTF problem, international cooperation has more to offer. Regulators and supervisors from across the globe have the chance to meet, exchange ideas and practices, reflect on optimal solutions and engage in fruitful dialogues that will inevitably promote financial stability, since obviously this is what everybody truly wants: a financial system, globally connected that will perform its tasks, efficiently and safely, without putting in danger the taxpayers' money. There is a continuous need for enhancement of the international regulatory standards and the development of new tools and mechanisms to address any conflicting situations as they emerge from the implementation of the various reforms. This will enable banks, and financial institutions in general, to manage their compliance with credible regulatory regimes that seek to promote financial stability and economic growth, while at the same time they will fulfil their central functions within a healthy financial system: to provide credit for an

2436 See in *Ring-Fencing and Proprietary Trading Review* (RFPT), Independent Review, Final Report, March 2022, p. 29.

2437 Ibid., p. 31.

ever-growing global economy.[2438] The challenges to efficient and effective cooperation are not minimal. We could broadly delineate them in the following categories:

(a) concerns about sovereignty: Some countries tend to resist outside influence on their financial systems.
(b) concerns about uneven implementation: Not all countries follow international standards equally and this might lead to either 'gold plating' or 'cherry picking' practices.
(c) rising geopolitical tensions: Rivalries among countries, and particularly of the most powerful and financially important ones (e.g. US–China), can undermine trust among them and further impede coordination at international level.
(d) Regulatory divergence: National priorities among the countries can conflict (e.g. growth vs. stability) and further create frictions.

While international cooperation is widely acknowledged as essential for ensuring global financial stability, it faces several structural and political challenges that constrain its efficacy. Chief among these is the enduring tension between national sovereignty and supranational regulatory coordination, as states are often reticent to align fully with international standards when doing so may limit their discretion over domestic financial policy, particularly under conditions of economic and/or political stress. Furthermore, heterogeneity in economic development, institutional capacity, tradition and cultural parameters and regulatory priorities between advanced and emerging economies create asymmetries that complicate consensus-building and uniform implementation of proposed or even agreed reforms. Emerging economies, in particular, may perceive global regulatory frameworks as reflecting the interests and institutional biases of developed countries, thereby undermining legitimacy and buy-in. In addition, geopolitical competition, especially among major economic powers, often impedes collaboration, fostering strategic mistrust and fragmented responses to systemic risks such as cyber threats, climate finance, or digital asset regulation. Finally, regulatory divergence – driven by differences in legal traditions, financial architectures, and domestic mandates – further hampers the harmonisation of rules, potentially leading to arbitrage and regulatory blind spots. These challenges underscore the complex interplay between global interdependence and national autonomy in the governance of financial stability.

[2438] See in D.W. Arner, 'Cross-Border Supervision of Financial Institutions', in N. Moloney, E. Ferran, and J. Payne (eds.), *The Oxford Handbook of Financial Regulation*, Oxford, Oxford University Press, 2015, p. 504.

CHAPTER 2
CONCLUDING REMARKS
Answering the Important Question: Is Regulation through Structural Reforms An Effective Way to Prevent the Financial System from Instability Events and Turmoil?

1 INTRODUCTION

In this final part of the book, we will try to provide a clear answer on the research question: is regulation through structural reforms an effective way to prevent the financial system from instability events and turmoil? Are these measures an optimal solution to safeguard financial stability? In order to give an answer as clear and coherent as possible, it is important to proceed with the findings of our research in a two-step analysis, as follows: as a first step we will evaluate the findings from the countries we used as case studies by making a comparison between them and their specifications so that we can have the full picture of the various specificities, and the second and final step will be to compare the findings from the special parameters examined in part D of the present book. The case studies will allow us to understand how the structural reforms are combined across countries, and the comparison of the special parameters will allow us to understand the interplay between these parameters, which are common to the case study countries, and the structural reforms per se.

2 COMPARISON AND ANALYSIS OF THE FINDINGS FROM PART II (JURISDICTIONS' SPECIFICATIONS)

We will start our comparative analysis of the findings from the jurisdictions' specifications we examined earlier on, in Part C of the present book. We will start from the lighter regime towards the stricter one so by escalating the level of separation we will try to understand the level of complexity and assess the current situation and to what extent financial stability is safeguarded by such framework.

2.1. Canada

The Canadian framework, in our view the lighter and more flexible one, allows for the six largest banks to account for approximately 90% of total assets among Canada's federally regulated deposit taking institutions. Their diversified business lines extend beyond traditional deposit-taking and lending activities into trading, investment banking, wealth management and insurance. The remaining 10% of Canadian banking assets are held by smaller institutions with niche focus and business strategies, such as mortgage lending, commercial real estate, or credit cards. The Canadian quasi universal banking style has been praised as the best model since no major banking crises have been recorded in Canada for more than a century. The secret of such success is simple: Canada has an integrated system of financial supervision anchored around the Office of the Superintended of Financial Institutions (OSFI) which has a broad view of the entire financial system. Moreover, the Basel framework is always timely adopted and adapted to the Canadian market specificities, usually with higher capital requirements and other country specific add-ons, but most importantly is combined with a robust and active supervision from the Canadian authorities. On 31 January 2022, the OSFI adopted the Basel III framework for the Canadian banks and according to the press release 'OSFI's implementation of these rules reflects three key principles: introducing rules that are fit for Canada, setting the right incentives, and tailoring capital and liquidity requirements to better reflect the unique nature of small and medium-sized banks'.[2439] The spirit of the OSFI's policy is that the Canadian requirements are tailored to the banks' needs within the Basel framework and will protect banks from any adverse events. Higher capital requirements for Canadian banks, compared to the minimum levels agreed at the BCBS, are an important tool for financial stability since banks have a greater loss absorbing capacity. At the same time, the concentrated banking market provides a controlled level playing field, largely protected from outsiders that want to enter the Canadian market. It is a clear 'quid pro quo' situation that seems to work perfectly for the Canadian society, since the crises are almost unknown.

Another important parameter which must be considered when assessing the Canadian 'miracle of financial stability' is that the system of financial supervision is producing greater benefits at a lower cost, when compared to their US counterparties. In the US the fragmented system of financial supervision and regulation has left the worst from both worlds: costing a lot

[2439] See in Office of the Superintendent of Financial Institutions (OSFI), O*SFI completes Basel III reforms, releases final capital and liquidity rules to protect Canadians*', Press Release, 31 January 2022.

and offering very little.[2440] Clear allocation of tasks and clear structures within the Canadian system facilitates the accountability for failure, overcoming the similar collective action problems that are endemic to its south neighbour, and allow regulators to take potentially unpopular and difficult decisions, thereby opposing lobbyists and policy makers that seek different policy options.[2441] Finally, Canada has a different culture compared to the US, but this cannot be an attribute of its own, since when Canadian banks operate in the US have run into the same regulatory and compliance issues as their American counterparts.[2442] From the above it is well demonstrated that regulatory structure and supervisory attitude rather than simple cultural differences have altered the behaviour in Canadian banking industry.

2.2. European Union

Our next case study is the EU and most importantly the European Commission's failed proposal for a regulation introducing structural reforms, based on the proposal of the 2012 Liikanen Report. Europe has been a universal banking proponent and the structural separation of certain activities that were perceived to be riskier than others was impossible to reconcile with the strong tradition. Moreover, the introduction of the resolution regime through the BRRD and the creation of the banking union were seen as far more effective ways to safeguard financial stability. The EU's paradox though is that despite the withdrawal of the Commission's legislative proposal, a few Member States, namely France, Germany, and Belgium, adopted national laws which enacted structural separation between the commercial and investment banking activities. This policy option can only be understood if we examine the bank failures that occurred in these countries, with Belgium and Germany being hard hit by the global financial crisis and their banking systems facing serious problems. France didn't face direct problems with its banks but the involvement of the French government in the bail out of the French parts of neighbouring banks (Dexia and Fortis) surely influenced to a certain extent the enactment of the national legislation.

2440 See in L.E. Breydo, 'Structural Foundations of Financial Stability: What Canada Can Teach America About Building a Better Regulatory System' (2015) 17 *University of Pennsylvania Journal of Business Law*, p. 1025.

2441 Ibid., p. 1030.

2442 In 2011, the Royal Bank of Canada (RBC) paid to the SEC a $30.4 million settlement because its securities division sold complex securities products to unsuitable clients without properly informing them for the associated risks. Subsequently, in March 2014, RBC's investment banking unit was found guilty of aiding and abetting fiduciary duties violations with a hospital buyout transaction back in 2011 (*In re Rural/Metro Corp. S'holders Litig.*, 88 A.3d 54 (Del. Ch. 2014)).

Despite the failed proposal from the European Commission and the Member State level national legislation that imposes some level of structural reforms, the EU remains faithful to the universal banking model, and this can be certainly attributed to the advantages attached to the single market, where the passporting provisions of the Treaties allow banks to offer the full spectrum of services through branching, and to the strong bank-based funding tradition. Moreover, the German model of universal banking is strongly embedded in the financial sector and Europe has neither much power nor willingness to abandon it.

2.3. *Japan*

The findings from Japan are extremely interesting. The severe banking crisis that occurred on the aftermath of the liberalisation efforts as well as the particular structure of its banking (and financial) system make Japan a textbook example of how irrelevant the separation requirement can become, when discussed as a standalone obsession. Japan had to adapt its banking system on the aftermath of its banking crisis in the mid-1990s where many bank failures and mounting non-performing loans forced the economy to contract and economists to describe that period as 'the lost decade'. The strict compartmentalisation and segmentation, imposed for many years in the financial sector, impeded Japanese banks from evolving and provide tailor made solutions to their clients. The gradual loss of this competitive advantage led to an outdated business model which under certain macroeconomic conditions proved to be lethal for the economy. The Japanese authorities, out of fear for the protection of their sacred competition rules, finally allowed banks to merge and expand their activities but kept certain separation lines that still today prevent the full blend of banking and capital markets activities, the so called 'firewall regulations'. After Japanese banks were allowed to enter the securities business through the use of holding company structure and subsidiaries in 1993, these firewall regulations prohibiting the transfer of customer information between banks and their securities affiliates have remained in place. The firewall regulations separating securities, banking and insurance businesses are aimed at preventing harmful events caused by conflicts of interest and curbing any potential abuse of the dominant position of Japanese banks. Banks are subject to these regulations that prohibit banks and securities firms from sharing their non-public customer information (limited to certain material information) with their affiliates without a customer's prior approval. However, it must be noted that the sharing of non-public customer information for internal management purposes is permitted, and the sharing of non-public corporate customer information is permitted if the relevant bank provides a corporate customer with an opt-out opportunity in advance. After recent amendments in the relevant legislation, the sharing of foreign corporate customer information is now permitted, albeit certain exemptions apply.

The rationale behind such separation is that banks can't be left to grow beyond certain limits so that can be a healthy competition regime in place, in contrast to the US regime that the separation doctrine is based on the premise that banks cannot jeopardise the deposit insurance scheme. Protection of competition is a legitimate policy objective which can justify certain interventions in the structure of the firms that harm the consumer welfare but its application on the Japanese case study was not completely successful. The financial sector was left in a situation where banks were relatively small compared to their international counterparts and the expansion possibilities almost non-existent. Moreover, the services they offered couldn't match efficiently the needs of the economy and when the asset bubble hit the consequences were devastating. The Japanese authorities completely failed to supervise the activities of the banks despite the very strict segmentation of services and in theory simple business models. Overall, the fact that banks were not allowed to offer capital market-related services, at least to the full extent possible, was not sufficient to avoid an almost ten-year banking crisis.

2.4. United States

The US is the holy grail of the structural reforms' regulation movement. The historical evolution, the importance and severity of separation, but most importantly the fierce academic debates on the need for those measures on the aftermath of every crisis highlight its importance for our analysis. With a long history in separating banking business from capital markets related services, the US adopted the Volcker Rule on the aftermath of the recent GFC, as a solution to the TBTF problem. The GFC demonstrated that the New Deal era-based system of financial regulation was insufficient to protect a financial system that included large financial conglomerates that might nest a bank, an investment bank and an insurance company within the same group.[2443]

Technically known as Section 619 of the Dodd-Frank Act, Volcker Rule focuses on prohibiting deposit taking institutions and their separately incorporated non deposit taking affiliates from engaging in proprietary trading in certain financial instruments and from acquiring or retaining ownership interests in, sponsoring, or entering into certain lending and other covered transactions with hedge funds, private equity funds and many other vehicles, including securitisation funds, which are defined as 'covered funds'.[2444]

2443 See in E.J. Janger, 'Equity for Intermediaries: The Resolution of Financial Firms in Bankruptcy and Bank Resolution' (2024) 41 *Yale Journal on Regulation*, p. 968.

2444 See in R.D. Guynn and P.S. Kenadjian, 'Structural Solutions: Blinded by Volcker, Vickers, Liikanen, Glass Steagall and Narrow Banking', in A. Dombret and P.S. Kenadjian (eds.), *Too Big to Fail III: Structural Reform Proposals - Should We Break Up the Banks?*, Volume 16, Institute for Law and Finance Series, Berlin, De Gruyter, 2015, p. 126.

In connection with understanding the Volcker Rule, two things are important to know. First, the Volcker Rule is by large a prohibition on activities and does not require any reforms to the structure of the banking institution in a way similar to that of the UK (ring-fencing structure) and second, is important to understand that the prohibitions on activities contained in the rule apply not only to the deposit taking institutions but also to their affiliates, parents and subsidiaries of such institutions.[2445] The broader picture therefore is that the Volcker Rule prohibitions apply not only to banking institutions covered by it but also to their parents and affiliates on a worldwide basis. This intended(?) extraterritorial effect of the Volcker Rule provides for an additional layer of complexity in the banks that operate on a transnational business model and have significant trading activity with or in the US.

The final rule, released on 10 December 2013, with an originally effective date of 1 April 2014, was 71 pages length but the preamble which provides supplementary information explaining the rule runs close to 900 pages. Complexity therefore is inherent in the Volcker Rule and when a bank needs to read so many pages to understand the rationale behind a rule it is obvious that the rule is ill based and compliance will be a very challenging process.[2446] The Volcker Rule requires such transactions to be entirely out of the banking groups, forcing thereby a total separation of such activities from the rest, in contrast to the Liikanen proposal, which opted for a separate entity within the same group, and the Vickers Report's ring fencing which required certain activities to be ring fenced within the same banking group.[2447] Guynn and Kenadjian support the view that the Volcker Rule and the total separation regime that it introduced was not based on empirical evidence that either proprietary trading transaction or investing in, sponsoring, or entering into covered transactions with hedge funds or private equity funds had any significant impact on the financial firms' failures during the global financial crisis.[2448] Rather it was based on a theoretical, cultural, and ideological perception that certain activities are

---

2445 See in D. Stone, 'The Volcker Rule', in A. Dombret and P.S. Kenadjian (eds.), *Too Big to Fail III: Structural Reform Proposals - Should We Break Up the Banks?*, Volume 16, Institute for Law and Finance Series, Berlin, De Gruyter, 2015, p. 96.

2446 According to a Los Angeles Times 2019 article, the Volcker Rule '...had forced banks to include all trades that they intended to be short-term to be covered under the rule and required an explanation for each one. JPMorgan Chase & Co. Chief Executive Jamie Dimon famously quipped that each trader would need a psychologist and a lawyer by his side to comply'.
Available at: https://www.latimes.com/business/story/2019-08-20/volcker-rule-revisions-land-on-a-changed-wall-street.

2447 See in R.D. Guynn and P.S. Kenadjian, 'Structural Solutions: Blinded by Volcker, Vickers, Liikanen, Glass Steagall and Narrow Banking', in A. Dombret and P.S. Kenadjian (eds.), *Too Big to Fail III: Structural Reform Proposals - Should We Break Up the Banks?*, Volume 16, Institute for Law and Finance Series, Berlin, De Gruyter, 2015, p. 128.

2448 Ibid.

not appropriate for 'officially licensed deposit taking institutions and their separately capitalised non deposit taking affiliates'.[2449] We tend to agree with this position given that the most important aspect of the global financial crisis was the misprice of the risks associated with certain structured products and not the trading activities per se of the institutions that failed.

Volcker Rule is also perceived to be in striking contrast with the rest of the Dodd – Frank Act, since it violates a core principle of the act which is also a key lesson of the recent GFC. The lesson is that 'activities should be regulated according to their nature and not according to the type of charter or license that the institution has in which they are conducted. If fund sponsoring and proprietary trading are dangerous, why are they dangerous only for commercial banks and their affiliates?'[2450] Proponents of structural reforms usually reply to this allegation but saying that credit supply to SMEs and consumers is a socially beneficial activity whereas proprietary trading and hedge funds and private equity funds activities are not. Moreover, commercial banks and their affiliates benefit from the public safety net that provides commercial banks with deposit insurance and central banking lender of last resort. Thereby, banks use this advantage to benefit from lower funding costs and finance their riskier activities with funds that are benefited from that public subsidy, jeopardising at the end of the day financial stability and public money.[2451] Given that the US's financial regulation system suffers from chronicle 'regulatory overlap' - the joint use of multiple legal rules to address a common market failure - it is rather doubtful how structural regulation will help to prevent a financial crisis, since on top of an already complex system of financial regulation the Congress imposed another burdensome legislation that requires a general ban on certain activities, only when are performed for own account.[2452] The 2023 event of bank collapses in the US and the need for intervention from the Federal Reserve demonstrated that crises are always present and can arise from aspects that are not related to the structural reforms discussions. More importantly, the 2023 banking turmoil demonstrated that the decision from the Trump administration to lower the regulatory standards by accepting the lobbying efforts from certain banks to be outside the Dodd-Frank bank safety net perimeter was not the wisest one. Some commentators argue that banks can become systemically important, and therefore too-big-to-fail, before the regulators notice but more importantly 'a campfire can start a forest fire' in

---

2449 Ibid.

2450 Ibid.

2451 Ibid., p. 132.

2452 For a broader discussion on the matter, see indicatively in M.C. Turk, 'Overlapping Legal Rules in Financial Regulation and the Administrative State' (2020) 54 *Georgia Law Review*, pp. 791–868.

the sense that leaving medium sized banks outside the Dodd-Frank perimeter had unfortunate consequences.[2453]

2.5. United Kingdom

Finally, in our view, the most severe regime has been adopted in the UK. The 'ring-fencing' legislation was the result of the Vickers Report, back in 2011 which proposed the separation of trading activities and underwriting from commercial banking and lending to SMEs but allowed them to coexist within the same banking group as long as they are in separately capitalised entities which can transact with each other under 'arm's length' basis. Vickers Report introduced a regime similar to the US's when the GLBA was in place but nevertheless before the Volcker Rule. Furthermore, it added a requirement for the commercial banking entity to apply higher capital and lower leverage requirements than those applicable under the Basel Agreements.[2454] The UK authorities took the view that ring-fencing allows differential capital and loss absorbency requirements to be imposed on different parts of banking groups, tailor made to their systemic importance and other considerations, while seeking to minimise the impact on cross-border wholesale banking activities.[2455] The most important aspect of the proposal and later of the law, is that it significantly narrowed the range of banking activities which are compatible with the ring fenced entity. The bank's focus is to be on consumer, real estate, and SMEs lending and while it can lend to larger corporate clients and deal in certain derivatives products, the RFB cannot offer any more sophisticated products to its customers. At the same time the NRFB is not allowed to accept deposits from individuals or from SMEs from within the EEA or to operate any payment systems.[2456] As a result of this approach, the RFB will face higher costs because of the capital and leverage requirements, will be focused on traditionally risky banking businesses (consumer, real estate

---

[2453] See in E.J. Janger, 'Equity for Intermediaries: The Resolution of Financial Firms in Bankruptcy and Bank Resolution' (2024) 41 *Yale Journal on Regulation*, p. 996.

[2454] See in R.D. Guynn and P.S. Kenadjian, 'Structural Solutions: Blinded by Volcker, Vickers, Liikanen, Glass Steagall and Narrow Banking', in A. Dombret and P.S. Kenadjian (eds.), *Too Big to Fail III: Structural Reform Proposals - Should We Break Up the Banks?*, Volume 16, Institute for Law and Finance Series, Berlin, De Gruyter, 2015, p. 128.

[2455] See in Financial Stability Board (FSB), *Structural Banking Reforms, Cross-border consistencies and global financial stability implications*, Report to G20 Leaders for the November 2014 Summit, 27 October 2014, p. 7.

[2456] See in R.D. Guynn and P.S. Kenadjian, 'Structural Solutions: Blinded by Volcker, Vickers, Liikanen, Glass Steagall and Narrow Banking', in A. Dombret and P.S. Kenadjian (eds.), *Too Big to Fail III: Structural Reform Proposals - Should We Break Up the Banks?*, Volume 16, Institute for Law and Finance Series, Berlin, De Gruyter, 2015, p. 129.

and SMEs lending) and will be completely cut off from other lucrative, and sometimes less risky, fee based activities.[2457]

A striking feature of the UK's structural reforms is that the apparently safer ring-fenced entity will be required to focus solely on lending areas which are traditionally seemed risky, and the BCBS therefore has assigned higher risk weightings for the calculation of capital requirements under the Basel Agreements.[2458] Guynn and Kenadjian further support that the demises of WaMu and Wachovia in the US and of Northern Rock in the UK are highly attributed to real estate lending practices, while that of Lehman Brothers and Bear Stearns were attributed to the lack of a stable deposit funding base that forced them to rely extensively on the repo market for funding.[2459] Finally, according to their view, the UK's ring-fencing regime recreates the conditions which applied in the US, in 2007–2009 period, under the provisions of Sections 16 and 21 of the GSA that survived the repeal from the GLBA and required the separation of deposit taking institutions and investment banks under the common roof of a BHC. These entities were also required to transact at arm's length but even that regime did not prevent the failures across both sides of the separation line.[2460] Moreover, the Panel set up to review the ring-fencing regime and the proprietary trading ban considered the impacts of the ring-fencing regime on financial stability relative to the original aims of the ICB and HM Treasury and found that while some of these have been achieved as previously outlined, further analysis has identified a number of areas where the regime has been less successful, including a) 'ring-fencing has not increased the resilience of less complex banks within the regime',[2461] b) 'the benefits of increased resilience, better supervision, and better protection are relevant only for RFBs, not NRFBs and the wider group'[2462] and c) 'evidence suggests that the reduction in the implicit government guarantee and the progress in addressing too-big-to-fail is not attributable to ring-fencing'.[2463] As a result, the ring-fencing regime is currently under criticism in the UK, since it seems unable to fulfil, at least clearly, the basic aims of its conception.

The draconian regime has serious flaws in its post implementation phase and on top of that, it seems at odds with the resolution regime, as has been previously analysed. The fact that the UK recently amended the ring-fencing regime, following the suggestions of the Panel Report, denotes the uncertainty of the regime with respect to securing also the competitiveness of the banking

[2457] Ibid.
[2458] Ibid.
[2459] Ibid.
[2460] Ibid.
[2461] See in *Ring-Fencing and Proprietary Trading Review* (RFPT), Independent Review, Final Report, March 2022, p. 37.
[2462] Ibid.
[2463] Ibid.

sector. Furthermore, the previously mentioned 'Leeds Reforms' aim at further enhancing the UK financial system's competitiveness and target new reforms of the regime, especially with respect to the resolution approach and its interaction with the regime.

The theoretical background of these three proposals, is the older idea of 'narrow banking', as it was presented to President Roosevelt by a distinguished group of economists, from Chicago University. The so-called 'Chicago Plan'[2464] required the splitting of banks' two main functions, accepting deposits and providing loans, and banks would have had to keep 100% of their deposits readily available. Lending would have been funded by equity or by bank liabilities, other than insured deposits, or from private investors.[2465] The Chicago Plan ultimately succumbed to alternative, less stringent, measures that were embodied in the Banking Act of 1935, but its principles (e.g. restricting bank assets, and limiting taxpayers' liability from the Federal deposit insurance) have reemerged in the contemporary debate over banking reform in the US: after all, there has been a rejuvenation of the 100% reserve plan via 'narrow banking' or 'core banking' proposals. Though the early New Deal legislation must be considered as an overall success, since it remained relatively unchanged for almost fifty years, a formidable challenge is posed in devising a financial system that will last well into the 21st century. The recent incarnation of such ideas has been mostly associated with the academic work of John Kay in the UK[2466] and Laurence Kotlikoff in the US[2467] albeit they are not the only ones who advocate similar approaches.[2468] Kotlikoff's proposal for narrow banking, known as 'Limited Purpose Banking' (LPB), aims to eliminate financial crises by fundamentally restructuring the banking system. Under this model, banks would no longer lend or take on risk but would instead function like mutual funds, holding only safe, liquid assets such as government securities. All financial intermediation – such as lending – would occur through fully-backed mutual funds, where investors, not depositors or taxpayers, bear the

---

2464 During the 1930s, there were numerous proposals put forth to modify the financial system. The 1933 proposal was put forward in a series of memoranda by economists at the University of Chicago to abolish the fractional reserve system and impose 100% reserves on demand deposits. The proposal was known to the Roosevelt administration prior to the passage of the Banking Act of 1933 and later led directly to legislation introduced by Senator Bronson Cutting of New Mexico, and other Progressives, as part of the debate over the Banking Act of 1935.

2465 See in R.D. Guynn and P.S. Kenadjian, 'Structural Solutions: Blinded by Volcker, Vickers, Liikanen, Glass Steagall and Narrow Banking', in A. Dombret and P.S. Kenadjian (eds.), *Too Big to Fail III: Structural Reform Proposals - Should We Break Up the Banks?*, Volume 16, Institute for Law and Finance Series, Berlin, De Gruyter, 2015, p. 130.

2466 See in J. Kay, *Narrow Banking: The Reform of Banking Regulation*, Report, September 2009.

2467 See in L.J. Kotlikoff, *Jimmy Stewart is dead: Ending the world's ongoing financial plague with limited purpose banking*, Hoboken, Wiley, 2010.

2468 See in A. Levitin, 'Safe Banking: Finance and Democracy' (2016) 83 *The University of Chicago Law Review*, pp. 357-455.

risk. The system would be overseen by a single regulatory authority ensuring transparency and full disclosure. By separating deposits from risky lending, Kotlikoff's model seeks to eliminate the possibility of bank runs, remove the need for deposit insurance or bailouts, and create a stable, transparent financial system.[2469] Common criticisms against this proposal are the transition issues towards the new system, that this system might restrict credit to small businesses or individuals, since mutual funds may not lend as freely as banks and that Traditional banking is arguably more efficient at maturity transformation (turning short-term deposits into long-term loans). Kay is another strong proponent of narrow banking, but his approach is less radical than Kotlikoff's. His main argument is that we should separate the 'utility function' of banking from the 'casino function', meaning, separate safe deposit-taking and payments from risky financial speculation. Under his model, utility banks would hold deposits fully backed by safe, liquid assets, with no involvement in lending or investment, ensuring depositors' funds are always secure and eliminating the need for deposit insurance or bailouts. Riskier financial activities would be conducted by separate institutions that cannot access depositors' money and would be allowed to fail without threatening the financial system. Kay's approach aims to reduce systemic risk and increase financial stability through structural reform, not complex regulation, by quarantining financial risk away from the core functions people rely on daily.[2470]

While their proposals differ in certain aspects, the main idea is the same: to create institutions which separate the utility functions of running payments systems and taking deposits from individuals and SMEs, from the rest, casino functions, which include everything else banks do, including anything in relation to the investment banking services.[2471] Banks would be also required to hold 100% of their deposits, primarily if not entirely, in cash and government bonds. The differences between these proposals are targeted at exactly what else banks can do, with Kotlikoff seeing them as providing mutual fund-style investments for their customers, and the extent to which the activities that are pushed out from within the bank must be regulated. However, both variations have the same scope: to gradually push out of the banks the activities that are seen as risky, radically narrowing the scope of banks in the most 'utility activities'.[2472]

2469 See in L.J. Kotlikoff, *Jimmy Stewart is dead: Ending the world's ongoing financial plague with limited purpose banking*, Hoboken, Wiley, 2010.

2470 See in J. Kay, *Narrow Banking: The Reform of Banking Regulation*, Report, September 2009.

2471 See in R.D. Guynn and P.S. Kenadjian, 'Structural Solutions: Blinded by Volcker, Vickers, Liikanen, Glass Steagall and Narrow Banking', in A. Dombret and P.S. Kenadjian (eds.), *Too Big to Fail III: Structural Reform Proposals - Should We Break Up the Banks?*, Volume 16, Institute for Law and Finance Series, Berlin, De Gruyter, 2015, p. 130.

2472 Ibid.

Neither Kay's proposal nor Kotlikoff's were adopted as legislation or regulation, therefore any further analysis of the two radical proposals is beyond the scope of the present book. Guynn and Kenadjian offer three, very short, remarks about these proposals that we believe they must be cited here. The first remark is that tying the banks' credit to their sovereigns' credit was turn out to be a very dangerous policy option, as demonstrated by the Eurozone crisis.[2473] The second remark is that these proposals present many 'definitional problems' since they do not explain, for example, why lending to SME's, a traditional risky business, is seen as an activity that belongs to utility banking functions and therefore is perceived to be less risky than underwriting highly rated corporate bonds.[2474] Finally, the third remark is a citation from Charles Goodhart's observation on the matter, which is indeed remarkably to the point: 'A problem with proposals of this kind is that they run counter to the revealed preferences of savers for financial products that are both liquid and safe, and of borrowers for loans that do not have to be repaid until some future date. It is one of the main functions of financial institutions to intermediate between the desires of savers and borrowers, i.e. to create financial mismatch. To make such a function illegal seems draconian.'[2475]

All the three structural reform proposals target certain activities (proprietary trading, hedge funds and private equity funds) without providing credible explanation on how these activities contributed to the recent GFC and the bail outs of financial institutions that were not commercial banks. Vickers and Liikanen would recreate in Europe and the UK, the situation which existed in the US under the Sections 16 and 21 of the GSA, as amended by the GLBA, on the eve of the GFC. According to Guynn and Kenadjian, when WaMu and Wachovia failed and Citigroup and BofA had to be bailed out, it does not appear to be a good policy option to be adopted by the EU. If this policy did not work in the US, how exactly was supposed to work in Europe, with a very different model of banking operations?[2476] Moreover, none of these structural reform proposals do anything to prevent the massive migration of trading and hedge funds related activities to the shadow banking system and for the shadow banking system to compete for the same retail funds, that might otherwise be stored in deposit accounts and used for payments through the official banking system, to be used through other channels and systems that offer money like

---

[2473] Ibid., p. 131.

[2474] Ibid.

[2475] See in C.A.E. Goodhart, 'The Optimal Financial Structure', *LSE Financial Markets Group Paper Series*, Special Paper 222, London School of Economics, March 2013, p. 5.

[2476] See in R.D. Guynn and P.S. Kenadjian, 'Structural Solutions: Blinded by Volcker, Vickers, Liikanen, Glass Steagall and Narrow Banking', in A. Dombret and P.S. Kenadjian (eds.), *Too Big to Fail III: Structural Reform Proposals - Should We Break Up the Banks?*, Volume 16, Institute for Law and Finance Series, Berlin, De Gruyter, 2015, p. 132.

substitutes (digital currencies, apple pay, google pay, etc.).[2477] The Volcker Rule has already led to significant relocation of proprietary trading and hedge funds and private equity related activities to the shadow banking industry, and the Rule per se has nothing to say about how such relocation of services would have solved the problems of the last crisis.

3 COMPARISON AND ANALYSIS OF THE FINDINGS FROM THE INTERACTION OF STRUCTURAL REFORMS AND FINANCIAL STABILITY

The TBTF issue was revived during and after the recent GFC, mostly to describe the need to bail out a large non-bank financial institution, Bear Stearns, in March 2008, and a few months later the failure of Lehman Brothers, another non-bank financial institution. From the Bear Stearns case onwards, it was created a perception that financial institutions above a certain size, regardless of their nature (banks or non-banks), would not be allowed to fail at any cost. After the demise of Lehman Brothers, the US government saved an insurance conglomerate, AIG, and the entire MMMF industry, accompanied by a generous bail out of the US car industry, expanding thereby the public safety net to non-financial firms. None of these entities had insured deposits nor had access to the Fed's lender of last resort system, the so-called 'discount window'. Furthermore, none of them run a payments system or provide substantial amounts of credit to consumers or to SMEs, outside the debt capital markets. With this historical background in mind, it is difficult to explain why the TBTF issue has been associated that much with the systemically important banking groups. Moreover, it is even harder to understand why the preferred way to solve the TBTF issue is through the adoption of (structural) separation measures between the various financial activities.

The problems associated with the failure of a financial institution can be solved in two ways: a) ex ante, by reducing the likelihood of a failure per se and b) ex post, by reducing the loss given failure.[2478] On the ex-ante side, the prudential supervision requirements suffice to prevent crises and ultimately guarantee financial stability. The Basel III framework, as finalised in December 2017,[2479] seeks to address shortcomings of the pre-crisis regulatory framework and provides a regulatory foundation for a resilient banking system that supports the real economy. It provides a tighter framework of minimum capital and liquidity requirements, on which participating states can build up

2477 Ibid.

2478 Ibid., p. 135.

2479 See in Basel Committee on Banking Supervision (BCBS), '*Basel III: Finalising post-crisis reforms*', Press Release, 7 December 2017, available at: https://www.bis.org/press/p171207.htm.

and impose their own, higher requirements, with Canada being one example. A key objective of the revisions incorporated into the Basel framework is to reduce the excessive variability of risk-weighted assets (RWA), because at the peak of the global financial crisis, a wide range of stakeholders lost faith in banks' reported risk-weighted capital ratios. The Committee's own empirical analyses highlighted a worrying degree of variability in banks' calculation of RWAs and the agreed revisions to the regulatory framework will help restore credibility in the calculation of RWAs by:

- 'Enhancing the robustness and risk sensitivity of the standardised approaches for credit risk and operational risk, which will facilitate the comparability of banks' capital ratios',[2480]
- 'Constraining the use of internally modelled approaches',[2481] and
- 'Complementing the risk-weighted capital ratio with a finalised leverage ratio and a revised and robust capital floor'[2482].

Yet the interaction between the Basel based prudential regulation and the national based structural regulation measures is unclear since the two approaches differ in scope and approach. The Basel framework takes banks' business models as given and imposes capital and liquidity requirements based on the riskiness of the banking groups' activities, while structural regulation imposes (hard) constraints on the activities that a bank may engage, therefore shapes its business model.[2483] Viewed from this angle, the two approaches may be perceived as complementary, since certain aspects of structural regulation may reinforce the Basel framework and ensure that it will act more effectively when needed.

On the ex-post side, the attempt to reduce the losses of a given failure relies heavily on the existence, use, and expansion of credible resolution regimes, tailored to the needs and specificities of the financial and banking sector.[2484] The major problem that public authorities had to face during the recent GFC was the absence of appropriate tools to handle the failures in an orderly manner, forcing them to choose between a disorderly sale of the entities through the liquidation of assets, in fire sale prices amid a financial panic, and a prolonged and value destroying reorganisation process, where the institution involved loses most of its value by the time the reorganisation

---

2480 Ibid.

2481 Ibid.

2482 Ibid.

2483 See in L. Gambacorta and A. van Rixtel, 'Structural bank regulation initiatives: approaches and implications', *BIS Working Papers*, no. 412, April 2013, Basel, Bank of International Settlements, p. 5.

2484 See in R.D. Guynn and P.S. Kenadjian, 'Structural Solutions: Blinded by Volcker, Vickers, Liikanen, Glass Steagall and Narrow Banking', in A. Dombret and P.S. Kenadjian and (eds.), *Too Big to Fail III: Structural Reform Proposals - Should We Break Up the Banks?*, Volume 16, Institute for Law and Finance Series, Berlin, De Gruyter, 2015, p. 137.

was approved and completed.[2485] The similarities of the second option with the prolonged time that the Japanese government needed to solve the banking crisis are remarkable and the short period of time between the two experiences is a clear example of how history is often repeated with tragic consequences if the lessons are not actually learned. The interaction between resolution regimes and structural reforms is very important for financial stability. Experience from the Lehman Brothers' demise on both sides of the Atlantic crystallised that ordinary bankruptcy proceedings or traditional insolvency laws were highly inefficient tools to reduce the loss associated with the failure of a financial institution for several reasons. The first reason is that traditional bankruptcy laws and proceedings are very slow and cannot prevent the evaporation of a financial institution's value, unless there can be used quickly to separate the bad from the good assets.[2486] Second, traditional bankruptcy laws are based on a general 'stay of claims' against the bankrupt, which interferes with banking's essence, that is the ability to commit to pay and bankruptcy courts tend not to understand their role as including a broader mandate to safeguard financial stability and depositors' confidence.[2487] The initiation of ordinary bankruptcy proceedings against Lehman Brothers especially in the UK, resulted in a messy situation where repercussions spread across the Atlantic and multiple uncoordinated national bankruptcy and insolvency proceedings were seeking to liquidate assets for the benefit of local creditors and to the detriment of almost everyone else. The Courts' mandate was solely to impose a blanket-style protection on national creditors without considering general stability concerns.[2488] Structural reforms, at least as were in place in the US before the recent GFC, did little to prevent such situations, since they were not combined with appropriate resolution planning or anything similar to that.

Moreover, the evidence from the recent, March 2023 banking turmoil, indicates that the failed banks suffered from flaws that were well known to the competent authorities. This means that the authorities did little or nothing in some cases, to prevent the collapse of those banks. Again the business models were not necessarily flawed or risky; they were risky up to the point where the risk management systems the banks had in place were inadequate to handle them and to the point where the competent authorities failed to timely and properly understand and take adequate measures to tame them. The major difference between the disastrous recent GFC and the March 2023 turmoil was that the resolution regimes in place, no matter how efficient are, worked properly and to a certain extent without major issues. Undoubtedly, they must be further strengthened before a worst-case scenario might occur.

2485 Ibid., p. 138.
2486 Ibid.
2487 Ibid.
2488 Ibid., p. 139.

Ultimately, we must highlight the following concern: although the idea of breaking up the big banking groups has many advocates, few of them have actually come forward with concrete measures on how this should be implemented properly, without any detrimental effects for economic growth, innovation and access to state-of-the-art financial services. Theoretical approaches and policy option seem to collide with the hard reality of financial markets and their evolving nature. UK's ring-fencing regime is the only attempt, that has been already reviewed, and the results are not much encouraging to say at least. Lack of competitiveness and fears that big banks remain TBTF, despite the adopted solutions, are supporting a very different view. There are a lot of questions related to how the structural reforms will be implemented; these questions must be answered by any structural separation proposal:

- Who will determine when and how a bank will be broken up?
- On what grounds will the decision to break up a bank be based?
- What is the optimal size for a banking group? The answer changes if we are discussing about a universal bank?
- Are only domestic assets counted when assessing a breakup solution?
- Will banks be allowed to grow beyond a certain size and if yes will there be any further restrictions associated with their size?
- Will the thresholds be adapted over time to reflect any material changes in RWAs in risk management practices and financial engineering methods?
- Who will decide where different customers will end up after a bank break up?
- How will resolution processes operate in tandem with structural separation regimes?
- Over what time period will the breakup be implemented and in what context? Will it be in the context of a resolution process or will it be associated with the SREP process and early supervisory warnings about possible instability events?

None of the above-mentioned structural reforms proposals, apart from the UK's regime, which as stated earlier has many drawbacks in retrospect, provide credible answers to the questions above. Although there are some arguments in favour of breaking the banks, which deserve further discussion, the lack of credible answers from the proponents of narrow banking and the structural separation allows us to conclude that structural separation measures are difficult to implement, with serious drawbacks on the performance of both banks and financial markets, and therefore of the broader economy.[2489] Ring-fencing solutions of any kind have implications for both the banking group

[2489] See in D.J. Elliott, 'Ten Arguments Against Breaking Up the Big Banks', in A. Dombret and P.S. Kenadjian (eds.), *Too Big to Fail III: Structural Reforms Proposals, Should We Break Up the Banks?*, Volume 16, Institute for Law and Finance Series, Berlin, De Gruyter, 2015, p. 124.

and financial stability. The banking group, in general, will be worse off because of the ring-fencing measures since capital and liquidity trapped in individual subsidiaries will increase funding and liquidity costs. Accordingly, the banking group can exploit a few mitigating factors such as:[2490]

(i) less centralised business model where individual operations are more self-sufficient,
(ii) ring fencing decisions that are permanently adopted, or
(iii) banking groups with sound liquidity contingency planning.

A banking group with a relatively high percentage of domestic assets and profits generated in the home country will also be less vulnerable to similar ring-fencing measures. Global banking groups also face implications from ring fencing measures as they need to adapt their business models to operate efficiently across different borders/markets. These entities are global market players that benefit from assets and risk diversification as they are less exposed to a single domestic market or to regional markets.[2491] Moreover, they play a central role in the allocation of funds across jurisdictions and the existence of 'trapped pools of resources', containing liquidity and capital, in different jurisdictions makes the financial system as a whole less efficient, more fragmented and less resilient; simply reduces the ability of such banking groups to mobilise resources and respond quickly to problems in particular locations.[2492] There is a broad consensus that group wide mobility of resources, both capital and liquidity, can help to mitigate the effects of shocks in financial stability and act as a stabiliser mechanism, a shock absorbing buffer or as a source of systemic stability.[2493]

Ring-fencing measures also impact both home and host countries. In home countries, whose interests are more or less aligned with the banking group's interests, the ring-fencing regime would be a benefit for a home supervisor with limited fiscal resources if the troubled entity is not the parent bank. The decision for ring fencing would reduce the fiscal burden for the home country in case the bank's foreign operations become distressed, provided that they will be organised as a subsidiary entity.[2494] Another case where the home supervisor would happily accept, and even encourage, the decision for ring fencing by the host country's regulator would be when he (the home country supervisor) cast doubts over the adequacy of supervisory cooperation agreements, the stability of the regime or the economic condition of the host country.[2495] For the host

2490 See in K.D'Hulster and I. Otker-Robe, 'Ring-Fencing Cross-Border Banks: An Effective Supervisory Response?' (2018) 5(1) *Journal of Financial Perspectives*, p. 13.
2491 Ibid.
2492 Ibid.
2493 Ibid., p. 14.
2494 Ibid., p. 13.
2495 Ibid.

country, the benefits here are more straightforward. Its financial system will be less vulnerable to contagion from other countries and will be better protected should the parent company has any problems, at least in a short-term horizon. At the same time though, credit availability for large institutional clients will be diminished and the banking system will be less diversified. Especially in countries with underdeveloped economies, shallow capital markets and weak deposit base, self-sufficiency measure based on a ring fencing regime will result in increased cost of funding further translated in increased cost of lending; therefore consumers are automatically worse off with such a regime.[2496] In the long term, host countries are facing the risk that global banking groups faced with increased ring-fencing measures will need to adapt their business models to comply with the ring fencing requirements, adopting more inward looking approaches and ultimately leaving the host jurisdiction. Such decisions will ultimately put under heavy pressure the global banking operations and will accelerate deleveraging trends that emerged on the aftermath of the recent GFC.[2497]

4 FINAL ASSESSMENT AND CONCLUDING REMARKS

Perhaps the most challenging task of our research and analysis was to formulate the concluding remarks' part. The above analysis, far from being a complete one, tries to present the broad picture of the banking separation debate. Despite the present author's attempts to present the topic as complete and cohesive as possible, further analysis is required, particularly with respect to the relation between the structural reforms and the various resolution regimes, in order to have a better understanding of how the structural reforms can ultimately exist and work effectively in preserving financial stability, in tandem with an effective and credible resolution regime.[2498] Moreover, equally important is the relation between structural reforms and the economic implications that might deteriorate credit availability and increase the costs of other, market related banking operations, such as market making and proprietary trading, derivatives trading and hedging operations. The available evidence presented

---

[2496] Ibid.

[2497] Ibid.

[2498] See in M. de la Mano, 'Bank Structural Reform and Too-Big-to-Fail', in A. Dombret and P.S. Kenadjian (eds.), *Too Big to Fail III: Structural Reform Proposals - Should We Break Up the Banks?*, Volume 16, Institute for Law and Finance Series, Berlin, De Gruyter, 2015, p. 70.

so far is to the best of our knowledge of a mixed nature and does not favour either universal or separated/narrow banking initiatives.[2499]

The author of the present book shares the view that, unfortunately, it is far from clear whether the structural reforms' initiative is an effective measure to prevent the financial system from experiencing crises. Since (financial) crises are inherent in the financial systems, it seems to be inevitable that we will experience them even if we are going to adopt extremely 'narrow banking' approaches or semi-effective structural reforms. The very nature of banking business is about assuming and effectively managing risks (liquidity, credit, operational, cyber, etc.); therefore, in our view it seems extremely difficult to simply exonerate risk from the banking business, at least in the way supporters of separation regimes propose. While such approaches aim at creating a safe banking environment, nonetheless, tend to forget or at best not fully recognise that risk remains even on the simplest (safest) banking operations, such as providing fully secured mortgages and in the case study of Japan, fully secured mortgages only to the members of a bank (fishermen, lumberjacks, etc.) or of certain areas (regional banks, city banks, etc.) or special type of banks (long term credit banks, Jusen, etc.). By not allowing banks to enter certain business, of course under certain regulatory requirements, and combine services, innovation and credit supply, and further diversify their risks, inevitably we will end up with a banking system that will be rigid, restricted, unproductive and expensive but most importantly those activities that will be deemed as riskier will move to new service providers; outside the 'bank safety net' and the regulatory perimeter, without the experience of the banking industry, the pilling of traditional bank risks might end up creating similar crises, not to say even worse than the ones we try to avoid. Previously regulated but risky activities, now migrate to non-bank financial entities which lie outside the bank regulatory perimeter and offer services that were traditionally offered by banks, which at the same time are struggling to provide efficient financing to the economy.

To make things even worse, we are afraid that banks will gradually lose market share from even more traditional banking activities, such as lending, from other, less regulated players, that have different characteristics compared to classic banks. The current bank disintermediation trend we observe, is only one example of the situation that we are afraid of. The competition from the growing private equity solutions is an illustrative example of such a situation. The transfer of credit supply to structures like private equity and investment funds that constantly adapt to the market needs, exploiting the loopholes in

2499 See also in P. Staikouras, 'Universal Banks, Universal Crises? Disentangling Myths from Realities in Quest of a New Regulatory and Supervisory Landscape', *Journal of Corporate Law Studies*, Vol. 11, Part I, for a detailed presentation of the relevant economic analyses that support each of the debated sides.

the international regulatory regime is already present. Is it a threat for the traditional banks? Only time will show how this 'battle' will end up. For the moment, we observe the trend and the rapid change in technological advances, that dominates the discussion on financial and banking regulation.

We are of the opinion that the best solution is not to break up the 'megabanks' but instead to adopt credible resolution regimes, even for the biggest financial institutions, that will be capable of orderly liquidating or winding down any type of bank, irrespective of how complex, how important, how interconnected or how global it will be. The same is supported also by Prof. Schwarcz, who argues that traditional bankruptcy law, which focuses on protecting individual firms (micro-prudential regulation), is insufficient for safeguarding the broader financial system (macroprudential regulation).[2500] Prof. Schwarcz concludes that resolution-based regulation should aim not only to protect individual firms but also to safeguard the financial system as a whole, including markets and infrastructure, thereby serving as an additional macroprudential regulatory tool.

Resolution schemes will also put indirect pressure on shareholders to actively participate in the management and oversight of their invested capital, when the danger of whipping it out will be credible. The existence of credible resolution regimes is unfortunately only the one side of the coin. The other side also requires a supervision regime that will be both 'active' and 'proactive'. Active in a sense that will act accordingly when the crisis is acute and present, paving the way for solutions that have a positive impact on financial stability while minimising any losses to both shareholders and society (public funds). At the same time, supervision must also be proactive, in the sense that the competent authority must have in advance all the necessary tools, capacity, resources, powers and information, to evaluate the status quo timely and decide if there are any proactive measures to be taken that will prevent any crisis from happening. Securing active supervision that will complement effective resolution in a way that financial systems will be able to perform safely at an optimum level shall be the pinnacle of every financial regulatory system. However, we must not forget that financial regulation is a quasi-art. It is the art of taking the most benefits from a system while using the least cost regulatory intervention, aiming at ensuring the constant well-being of the system and of its users. It is a very difficult exercise for competent authorities that must constantly balance different policies with different outcomes. Financial stability policies, for good or for bad, go hand to hand with competition policy, innovation, efficient credit supply to fuel economic growth, monetary and exchange policies and other policies, that create a complex picture and pose a difficult exercise for

---

2500 For a more detailed analysis of his opinion see in S.L. Schwarcz, 'Beyond Bankruptcy: Resolution as a Macroprudential Regulatory Tool' (2018) 94 *Notre Dame Law Review*, pp. 709–749.

the national states. Failures might also be part of the optimum solution when they do not trigger turmoil pushing up to the limits of the system. Failures are part of the game and must be part of a healthy competition market. Financial stability is considered a public good and no one has anything contrary to say about that. Structural reforms are indeed a way to safeguard it but come at a high cost, both countable and uncountable. Countable because we can measure how much contraction we observe in the financial markets (liquidity, market making, proprietary trading, etc.) and uncountable because until today we do not know how the NBFIs have evolved and engulfed the activities that are banned for traditional banks.

The introduction of resolution reforms on the aftermath of the recent GFC, to complement the regulatory overhaul of financial system, poses existential questions to the structural reforms' supporters. Unfortunately, none of them has a very persuasive explanation why we must keep adopting structural reforms, with their pros and cons, when at the same time, we have adopted credible resolution regimes that can deal with bank failures and the *ultimum refugium* of preventing financial instability has certain limits that are better served by other initiatives. Structural reforms have also their limits. Maybe they are more suitable for less sophisticated financial systems with needs completely different from those of modern and more sophisticated financial systems that operate on a global and interconnected scale. The post war reconstruction needs of Japan is a perfect example of such a less sophisticated financial system, with special needs, that were better served by narrow banking entities, rigid structures, and strict compartmentalisation under a well-controlled competition policy. When such systems reach their predestined limits and if certain actions to modernise and adapt are not effectively adopted, then crisis is inevitable, and other tools must be used to clean the mess when the party is over. The same logic applied also to the US financial system under the strict separation regime of the Glass-Steagall reforms era. This model was a necessity when adopted but reached its limits when technological advances and market forces (of various forms) circumvented the walls erected and forced US banks to lose competitiveness. This rung the bell of further liberalisation of the US financial system, that was unfortunately combined with an unexpected lack of effective supervision, thus fuelling the crisis and demonstrated the structural problems that plague the US financial system from its conception. With our respective analysis earlier in this book, we demonstrated also that legal complexity in the US banking sector further impedes its efficiency. In Europe, though the story is somehow different since the structural reforms failed at the EU level but were adopted by a handful of countries at national level and frankly, we do not understand the rationale behind such a policy option. Lack of coordination among the Member States of the EU and the adoption of different measures tend to increase the regulatory costs and create an uneven playing field that in the long run will prove to be ineffective. On the other hand, the creation of the EU Banking Union and the resolution regime seems to have succeeded in securing stability, at least for the foreseen future. In Canada, the efficiency of the supervisory regime offsets any risks assumed by banks and there seems to be no need for further structural separation in the banking sector; a model that must undoubtedly be used as a compass to any further discussion in the subject, as we believe that the supervision performed by the Canadian authorities complements a banking system that is tightly regulated in terms of competition. Finally, the UK, adopted a strict ring-fencing model and the Panel review, that to the best of our knowledge is the first and only review of such reforms globally, concluded that even though banks seem to be safer the drawbacks are significantly higher than originally anticipated and further legislative actions must be taken to preserve financial stability and efficiency of financial markets.

Even though the sirens of banking separation, under any of its proposed forms, are not satisfied with the present level of structural separation and continue to advocate for further curtail of the universal banking model, the present book's author argues that it is far from being convinced that such reforms will help establish a safer banking and financial system. At the end of the day, the banking business is about managing effectively and efficiently the inherent risks of such business and even in the simplest banking operations risks are inherent and remain since we cannot eliminate them completely. While it is true that these risks might become simpler, be reduced in quantity or be better understood, still they will remain risks that have to be effectively managed. The experiences from banking crises around the world, such as the US savings and loan crisis in the 1980s, the Nordic banks' crisis in the early 1990s and the collapse of the UK banks during the recent GFC (Northern Rock, Bradford & Bingley, and Alliance and Leicester) and of the 2023 banking turmoil, suggest that banking crises can arise from traditional banking activities (poor underwriting and weak regulation in traditional bank lending) and not only from riskier securities' and derivatives' trading practices. It is an error to think that systemic risk lives on a single entity, even if this entity is a big universal bank. According to Janger, '[t]he hallmark of systemic risk is not the failure of one bank, but the ensuing contagion. A run on one institution may spread to other institutions, and then to the larger economy. As a result, there is no guaranty that the spark that starts the fire will be a TBTF institution'.[2501] Structural reforms and separation measures between the various banking activities have nothing to say about that; they do not offer us any added value regarding the simple and traditional banking business risks that created severe

[2501] See in E.J. Janger, 'Equity for Intermediaries: The Resolution of Financial Firms in Bankruptcy and Bank Resolution' (2024) 41 *Yale Journal on Regulation*, p. 996.

crises, credit crunches and ill-fated economic prospects; the cases of S&L bank failures and that of the Japanese banking crisis remain an illustrative example of how 'simple banks' can fail and destroy economic value.

Bank regulation cannot and should not seek to create a safe bubble, an environment where no bank failures take place, but rather an environment where any bank failure, either systemically important or not, big or medium sized bank, can be effectively and efficiently managed (resolved) in such a way that it will not endanger the stability of the entire financial system and create market dislocation or credit crunch in the real economy.[2502] At the end of the day, the solution to such a complex problem for sure will not be a radical one and as Prof. Staikouras suggested, right after the crisis: 'modesty should be the guiding principle as only some of them appear suitable to serve financial stability without stifling innovation and hampering growth.'[2503] In our view, there is no better way to summarise and conclude our analysis than Andreas Dombret's own words: 'To ensure financial stability, we have to apply a wide range of measures. We have to adjust capital requirements, we have to implement liquidity requirements, we have to make banks resolvable to name but a few. Breaking up the banks might shield commercial banking and thereby the real economy to a certain degree. But it cannot, on its own, ensure financial stability. And when it comes to cutting the guardian knot might mutate into a tedious exercise of splitting hairs.'[2504]

2502 See in R. Cranston, E. Avgouleas, K. van Zwieten, C. Hare and T. van Sante, *Principles of Banking Law*, Oxford, Oxford University Press, 2017, p. 28.

2503 See in P. Staikouras, 'Universal Banks, Universal Crises? Disentangling Myths from Realities in Quest of a New Regulatory and Supervisory Landscape' (2011) 11 *Journal of Corporate Law Studies*, Part I, p. 172.

2504 See in A. Dombret, 'Cutting the Guardian Knot or splitting hairs – The debate about breaking up the banks', in A. Dombret and P.S. Kenadjian (eds.), *Too Big to Fail III: Structural Reforms Proposals, Should We Break Up the Banks?*, Volume 16, Institute for Law and Finance Series, Berlin, De Gruyter, 2015, p. 10.

REFERENCES & BIBLIOGRAPHY

1. PRIMARY SOURCES

Treaties

1. Treaty on European Union (Consolidated version 2016), *Official Journal of the European Union*, C 202, Volume 59, 7 June 2016, p. 13
2. Treaty on the Functioning of the European Union (Consolidated version 2016), *Official Journal of the European Union*, C 202, Volume 59, 7 June 2016, p. 47

2. CASE LAW

2.1. Canada

1. Reference re Securities Act, 2011 SCC 66, [2011] 3 SCR 837 [Securities Reference]
2. Reference re Pan-Canadian Securities Regulation, 2018 SCC 48

2.2. United States

2.2.1. US Supreme Court

1. *McCulloch v. Maryland*, 17 U.S. (4 Wheat.) 316 (1819)
2. *Veazie Bank v. Fenno*, 75 U.S. (8 Wall.) 533 (1869)
3. *Munn v. Illinois*, 94 U.S. 113 (1876)
4. *Nebbia v. New York*, 291 U.S. 502 (1934)
5. *West Coast Hotel Co. v. Parrish*, 300 U.S. 379 (1937)
6. *Lochner v. New York*, 198 U.S. 45 (1905)
7. *Gade v. National Solid Wastes Management Association*, 505 US 88, 108 (1992)
8. *Florida Lime & Avocado Growers, Inc. v. Paul*, 373 U. S. 132, (1963)
9. *Hines v. Davidowitz*, 312 U. S. 52, 67 (1941)
10. *Barnett Bank of Marion Cty., N. A. v. Nelson*, 517 U.S. 25 (1996)
11. *Skidmore v. Swift & Co.*, 323 U.S. 134 (1944)
12. *Seila Law LLC v. Consumer Financial Protection Bureau*, 591 U.S. 197 (2020)
13. *Securities Industry Association v. Board of Governors of Federal Reserve System*, 839 F. 2d 47 (2nd Circuit), cert. denied, 486 U. S. 1059 (1988)
14. *Chevron U.S.A. Inc. v. Natural Resources Defense Council, Inc.*, 467 U. S. 837, 842 (1984)
15. Securities *Industry Assn. v. Board of Governors*, FRS, (Bankers Trust I) 468 U. S. 137 (1984)
16. *Investment Co. Inst. v. Camp*, (ICI v. Camp) 401 U.S. 617 (1971)
17. NationsBank *of North Carolina v. Variable Annuity Life Insurance Co. (VALIC)*, 513 U.S. 251 (1995)

2.2.2. US Federal & District Courts

1. *SEC v. Levine*, 689 F. Supp. 317 (S.D.N.Y. 1988)
2. *SEC v. Drexel Burnham Lambert Inc.*, 837 F. Supp. 587 (S.D.N.Y. 1993)
3. *Slade v. Shearson, Hammill Co., Inc.*, 517 F.2d 398 (2d Cir. 1974)
4. *Wells Fargo Bank of Texas NA v. James*, 321 F.3d 488 (5th Cir. 2003)
5. *Monroe Retail, Inc. v. RBS Citizens, N.A.*, 589 F.3d 274 (6th Cir. 2009)
6. *Rose v. Chase Bank* USA, N.A., 513 F.3d 1032, 1038 (9th Cir. 2008)
7. *Gutierrez v. Wells Fargo Bank, NA*, 704 F.3d 712 (9th Cir. 2012)
8. *Ind. Community Bankers v. Bd. of Governors*, 195 F.3d 28 (D.C. Cir. 1999)
9. *Securities Ind. Ass'n v. Board of Governors*, 900 F.2d 360 (D.C. Cir. 1990)
10. *Securities Industry Assn. v. Board of Governors, FRS*, (Bankers Trust II) 807 F.2d 1052 (D.C. Cir. 1986), cert. denied, 483 U.S. 1005 (1987)
11. *National Courier Association v. Board of Governors of Federal Reserve System*, 516 F. 2d 1229 (D.C. Circuit)

3. SECONDARY SOURCES

Laws, Regulations and Directives

3.1. United States

1. Emergency Economic Stabilization Act of 2008
2. National Currency Act of 1863
3. National Bank Act of 1864
4. Federal Reserve Act of 1913
5. McFadden Act of 1927
6. Banking Act of 1932
7. Federal Home Loan Bank Act of 1932
8. Banking Act of 1933 (Glass – Steagall Act)
9. Securities Act of 1933
10. Securities Exchange Act of 1934
11. Investment Company Act of 1940
12. Investment Advisers Act of 1940
13. Bank Holding Company Act of 1956
14. Bank Holding Company Act Amendments of 1970
15. Commodity Exchange Act of 1974
16. Riegle-Neal Interstate Banking and Branching Efficiency Act of 1994
17. Financial Institutions Reform, Recovery and Enforcement Act of 1989
18. Federal Deposit Insurance Corporation Improvement Act of 1991
19. Depository Institutions Deregulation and Monetary Control Act of 1980
20. Garn-St Germain Depository Institutions Act of 1982
21. National Securities Markets Improvement Act of 1996
22. Gramm Leach Bliley Act of 1999
23. Sarbanes-Oxley Act of 2002
24. Dodd-Frank Wall Street Reform and Consumer Protection Act of 2010
25. Economic Growth, Regulatory Relief, and Consumer Protection Act of 2017
26. Federal Reserve Board's Regulation Q
27. Federal Reserve Board's Regulation W

3.2. United Kingdom

1. 1826 Joint Stock Bank Act
2. 1844 Join Stock Bank Act
3. 1879 Companies Act
4. 1986 Financial Services Act
5. 1979 Banking Act
6. 1986 Financial Services Act
7. 1998 Bank of England Act
8. 2000 Financial Services and Markets Act
9. Anti-Terrorism Crime and Security Act of 2001
10. Financial Services Act 2012
11. Financial Services (Banking Reform) Act 2013

3.3. European Union

1. Second Council Directive 89/646/EEC of 15 December 1989 on the coordination of laws, regulations and administrative provisions relating to the taking up and pursuit of the business of credit institutions and amending Directive 77/780/EEC, [1989] *OJ* L 386/1
2. Directive 2013/36/EU of the European Parliament and of the Council of 26 June 2013 on access to the activity of credit institutions and the prudential supervision of credit institutions and investment firms, amending Directive 2002/87/EC and repealing Directives 2006/48/EC and 2006/49/EC, [2013] *OJ* L 176/338
3. Regulation (EU) No 1092/2010 of the European Parliament and of the Council of 24 November 2010 on European Union macro-prudential oversight of the financial system and establishing a European Systemic Risk Board, [2010] *OJ* L 331/1
4. Regulation (EU) No 1093/2010 of the European Parliament and of the Council of 24 November 2010 establishing a European Supervisory Authority (European Banking Authority), amending Decision No 716/2009/EC and repealing Commission Decision 2009/78/EC, [2010] *OJ* L 331/12
5. Regulation (EU) No 1095/2010 of the European Parliament and of the Council of 24 November 2010 establishing a European Supervisory Authority (European Securities and Markets Authority), amending Decision No 716/2009/EC and repealing Commission Decision 2009/77/EC, [2010] *OJ* L 331/84
6. Regulation (EU) No 1094/2010 of the European Parliament and of the Council of 24 November 2010 establishing a European Supervisory Authority (European Insurance and Occupational Pensions Authority), amending Decision No 716/2009/EC and repealing Commission Decision 2009/79/EC, [2010] OJ L 331/48
7. Council Regulation (EU) No 1024/2013 of 15 October 2013 conferring specific tasks on the European Central Bank concerning policies relating to the prudential supervision of credit institutions, [2013] OJ L 287/63
8. Regulation (EU) No 806/2014 of the European Parliament and of the Council of 15 July 2014 establishing uniform rules and a uniform procedure for the resolution of credit institutions and certain investment firms in the framework of a Single Resolution Mechanism and a Single Resolution Fund and amending Regulation (EU) No 1093/2010, [2014] *OJ* L 225/1
9. Directive 2014/49/EU of the European Parliament and of the Council of 16 April 2014 on deposit guarantee schemes, [2014] *OJ* L 173/149

10. Directive 2014/59/EU of the European Parliament and of the Council of 15 May 2014 establishing a framework for the recovery and resolution of credit institutions and investment firms and amending Council Directive 82/891/EEC, and Directives 2001/24/EC, 2002/47/EC, 2004/25/EC, 2005/56/EC, 2007/36/EC, 2011/35/EU, 2012/30/EU and 2013/36/EU, and Regulations (EU) No 1093/2010 and (EU) No 648/2012, of the European Parliament and of the Council, [2014] *OJ* L 173/190

3.4. Canada

1. Bank Act (S.C. 1991, c. 46)
2. Bank of Canada Act (R.S.C., 1985, c. B-2)
3. Canada Deposit Insurance Corporation Act (R.S.C., 1985, c. C-3)
4. Office of the Superintendent of Financial Institutions Act (R.S.C., 1985, c. 18 (3rd Supp.), Part I)

3.5. Japan

1. Act for Establishment of the Financial Services Agency (Act No. 57 of 2000, Japan)
2. Act on Emergency Measures for Early Strengthening of the Financial System (Act No. 132 of 1998, Japan)
3. Act on Prohibition of Private Monopolization and Maintenance of Fair Trade (Act No. 54 of 1947, Japan)
4. Act on Special Measures for Strengthening Financial Functions (Act No. 111 of 1998, Japan)
5. Act on Temporary Measures for Strengthening Financial Functions (Act No. 99 of 1998, Japan)
6. Bank of Japan Act (Law No. 89 of 1997, Japan)
7. Banking Act (Act No. 59 of 1981, Japan)
8. Companies Act (Act No. 86 of 2005, Japan)
9. Convertible Bank Note Act of 1884 or Convertible Bank-Note Ordinance (Ordinance No. 18 of May 6, 1884, Japan)
10. Corporate Reorganization Act (Act No. 154 of 2002, Japan)
11. Deposit Insurance Act (Act No. 59 of 1971, Japan)
12. Financial Instruments and Exchange Act (Act No. 25 of 1948, Japan)
13. Financial System Reform Act (Act No. 87 of 1993, Japan)
14. Financial System Reform Law (Law No. 87 of 1992, Japan)
15. Fisheries Cooperatives Law (Act No. 242 of 1948, Japan)
16. Law Concerning Emergency Measures for the Reconstruction of the Functions of the Financial System (Financial Reconstruction Law) (Law No. 132 of 1998, Japan)
17. Law on Preparation of Financial Acts Accompanying Cancellation of Prohibition of Holding Companies (Act No. 120 of 1997, Japan)
18. Long-Term Credit Bank Act (Act No. 61 of 1952, Japan)
19. Mutual Banking Law (Law No. 187 of 1952, Japan)
20. National Bank Act of 1872 (Japan)
21. Norinchukin Bank Law (Law No. 93 of 2001, Japan)
22. Secured Bond Trust Act (Act No. 52 of 1905, Japan)
23. Securities and Exchange Act (Act No. 25 of 1948, Japan)
24. Stock Transaction Ordinance of 1874 (Japan)
25. Supplementary Provisions to Bank of Japan Act (Act No. 121 of 1997, Japan)

4. BOOKS & BOOK CHAPTERS

1. ALEXANDER, K., *Principles of Banking Regulation*, Cambridge, Cambridge University Press, 2019
2. ANAND, A. and PEIHANI, M., 'Regulating Systemic Risk in Canada', in D. ARNER et al. (eds.), *Systemic Risk in the Financial Sector: Ten Years After the Great Crash*, Waterloo, Centre for International Governance Innovation, 2019
3. ARMOUR, J., 'Making Bank Resolution Credible', in N. MOLONEY, E. FERRAN, and J. PAYNE (eds.) *The Oxford Handbook of Financial Regulation*, Oxford, Oxford University Press, 2015
4. ARNER, D.W., 'Cross-Border Supervision of Financial Institutions', in N. MOLONEY, E. FERRAN and J. PAYNE (eds.), *The Oxford Handbook of Financial Regulation*, Oxford, Oxford University Press, 2015
5. BALL, L.M., *The Fed and Lehman Brothers: Setting the Record Straight on a Financial Disaster*, Studies in Macroeconomic History, Cambridge, Cambridge University Press, 2018
6. CARR, A., 'Bank structural reform: too big to fail, too big to save and too complex to manage, supervise and resolve?', in M. HAENTJENS and B. WESSELS (eds.), *Research Handbook on Crisis Management in the Banking Sector*, Cheltenham, Edward Elgar Publishing, 2015
7. CARNELL, R.S., MACEY, J.R., MILLER, G.P. and CONTI-BROWN, P., *The Law of Financial Institutions*, 7th ed., Aspen Casebook Series, New York, Wolters Kluwer, 2021
8. CRAIG, P. and DE BÚRCA, G., *EU law: Text, cases, and materials*, 6th ed., Oxford, Oxford University Press, 2015
9. CRANSTON, R., AVGOULEAS, E., VAN ZWIETEN, K., HARE, C. and VAN SANTE, T., *Principles of Banking Law*, Oxford, Oxford University Press, 2017
10. COPELOVITCH, M. and SINGER, D.A., *Banks on the Brink, Global Capital, Securities Markets, and the Political Roots of Financial Crises*, Cambridge, Cambridge University Press, 2020
11. DELLIS, G., *An Economic Analysis of Public Law, Demos and Agora*, Cheltenham, Edward Elgar Publishing, 2021
12. DOCHERTY, A. and VIORT, F., *Better Banking, Understanding and Addressing the Failures in Risk Management, Governance and Regulation*, Wiley Finance Series, Chichester, Wiley, 2014
13. DOMBRET, A., 'Cutting the Guardian Knot or splitting hairs – The debate about breaking up the banks', in A. DOMBRET and P.S. KENADJIAN (eds.), *Too Big to Fail III: Structural Reforms Proposals, Should We Break Up the Banks?*, Volume 16, Institute for Law and Finance Series, Berlin, De Gruyter, 2015
14. ELLIOTT, D.J., 'Ten Arguments Against Breaking Up the Big Banks', in A. DOMBRET and P.S. KENADJIAN (eds.), *Too Big to Fail III: Structural Reforms Proposals, Should We Break Up the Banks?*, Volume 16, Institute for Law and Finance Series, Berlin, De Gruyter, 2015
15. FOHLIN, C., 'A Brief History of Investment Banking from Medieval Times to the Present', in Y. CASSIS, C.R. SCHENK and S.R. GROSSMAN (eds.) *The Oxford Handbook of Banking and Financial History*, Oxford, Oxford University Press, 2016
16. GLEESON, S., 'Structural Separation and Bank Resolution', in A. DOMBRET and P.S. KENADJIAN (eds.), *Too Big to Fail III: Structural Reform Proposals - Should We Break Up the Banks?*, Volume 16, Institute for Law and Finance Series, Berlin, De Gruyter, 2015

17. Goodhart, C.A.E., *The Regulatory Response to the Financial Crisis*, Cheltenham, Edward Elgar Publishing, 2009
18. Gortsos, C.V., *Introduction to International Financial Law*, Athens, Nomiki Vivliothiki, 2011
19. Gortsos, C.V., *The Single Supervisory Mechanism (SSM)*, Athens, Nomiki Vivliothiki, 2015
20. Guynn, R.D. and Kenadjian, P.S., 'Structural Solutions: Blinded by Volcker, Vickers, Liikanen, Glass Steagall and Narrow Banking', in A. Dombret and P.S. Kenadjian (eds.) *Too Big to Fail III: Structural Reform Proposals - Should We Break Up the Banks?*, Volume 16, Institute for Law and Finance Series, Berlin, De Gruyter, 2015
21. Herring, R.J., 'Conflicts Between Home and Host Country Prudential Supervisors', in D. Evanoff, G. Kaufman and J. LaBrosse (eds.) *International Financial Instability, Global Banking and National Regulation*, Vol. 2, World Scientific Studies in International Economics, October 2007
22. Himino, R., *The Japanese Banking Crisis*, Singapore, Palgrave Macmillan, 2021
23. Iannotta, G., *Investment Banking, A Guide to Underwriting and Advisory Services*, Berlin, Springer, 2010
24. Jacqué, J.P., *Droit institutionnel de l'Union européenne*, Paris, Dalloz, 2018
25. Kay, J., 'Narrow Banking: The Reform of Banking Regulation', Report, September 2009, electronically available at: https://www.johnkay.com/wp-content/uploads/2009/12/JK-Narrow-Banking.pdf
26. Kleftouri, N., *Deposit Protection and Bank Resolution*, Oxford, Oxford University Press, 2015
27. Kobrak, C. and Martin, J., *From Wall Street to Bay Street, The Origins and Evolution of American and Canadian Finance*, Toronto, University of Toronto Press, 2018
28. Kotlikoff, L.J., *Jimmy Stewart is dead: Ending the world's ongoing financial plague with limited purpose banking*, Hoboken, Wiley, 2010
29. Lastra, R.M., 'Systemic Risk and Macro-prudential Supervision', in N. Moloney, E. Ferran and J. Payne, (eds.), *The Oxford Handbook of Financial Regulation*, Oxford, Oxford University Press, 2015
30. de la Mano, M., 'Bank Structural Reform and Too-Big-to-Fail', in A. Dombret and P.S. Kenadjian (eds.) *Too Big to Fail III: Structural Reform Proposals - Should We Break Up the Banks?*, Volume 16, Institute for Law and Finance Series, Berlin, De Gruyter, 2015
31. Meredith, P. and Darroch, J.L., *Stumbling Giants, Transforming Canada's Banks for the Information Age*, Toronto, University of Toronto Press, 2017
32. Mishkin, F.S., *The Economics of Money, Banking, and Financial Markets*, 7th ed., The Addison-Wesley Series in Economics, Boston, Pearson, 2004
33. Mishkin, F.S. and Eakins, S.G., *Financial Markets and Institutions*, 5th ed., The Addison-Wesley Series in Economics, Boston, Pearson, 2006
34. Norberg, J., *Financial Fiasco, How America's Infatuation with Homeownership and Easy Money Created the Economic Crisis*, Washington D.C., Cato Institute, 2009
35. Omarova, S.T., 'Central Banks, systemic risk and financial sector structural reform', in R.M. Lastra and P. Conti-Brown (eds.), *Research Handbook on Central Banking*, Cheltenham, Edward Elgar Publishing, 2018
36. Oppolzer, K., *Ring-Fencing in Europe, The EU's Bank Structural Reform and a Legal Comparative Look at National Legislation in Europe's Three Financial Capitals*, Baden-Baden, Nomos Verlagsgesellschaft mbH & Co. KG, 2019

37. POSNER, R., *The crisis of capitalist democracy*, Cambridge, Harvard University Press, 2010
38. POSNER, E.A., *Last Resort, The Financial Crisis and the Future of Bailouts*, Chicago, The University of Chicago Press, 2018
39. RAJAN, R.G., *Fault Lines: How Hidden Fractures Still Threaten the World Economy*, Princeton, Princeton University Press, August 2011
40. REINHART, C.M. and ROGOFF, K.S., *This Time Is Different, Eight Centuries of Financial Folly*, Princeton, Princeton University Press, 2009
41. SAUNDERS, A. and WALTER, I., *Universal Banking in The United States-What Could We Gain? What Could We Lose?*, New York, Oxford University Press, 1994
42. STONE, D., 'The Volcker Rule', in A. DOMBRET and P.S. KENADJIAN (eds.) *Too Big to Fail III: Structural Reform Proposals - Should We Break Up the Banks?*, Volume 16, Institute for Law and Finance Series, Berlin, De Gruyter, 2015
43. WILMARTH Jr., A.E., *Taming the Megabanks, Why We Need a New Glass-Steagall Act*, New York, Oxford University Press, 2020

5. JOURNAL ARTICLES & PAPERS

1. ALLEN, H.J., 'What is "Financial Stability"? The Need for Some Common Language in International Financial Regulation' (2014) 45 *Georgetown Journal of International Law*, pp. 929–952
2. ALLEN, W.A. and WOOD, G., 'Defining and Achieving Financial Stability', Special Paper No. 160, Special Paper Series, LSE Financial Markets Group, London School of Economics, April 2005
3. ALEXANDER, K., 'Regulating the Structure of the EU Banking Sector' (2015) 16 *European Business Organization Law Review*, pp. 227–253
4. ANNUNZIATA, F., 'The Remains of the Day: EU Financial Agencies, Soft Law and the Relics of Meroni', Working Paper no. 106, EBI Working Paper Series, 2021, European Banking Institute
5. BAILEY, D.K., 'A Defense of The Doctrine of Preemption: Revealing the Fallacy That Federal Preemption Contributed to The Financial Crisis' (2014) 16(4) *Journal of Constitutional Law*, pp. 1041–1108
6. BEBENROTH, R., DIETRICH, D. and VOLLMER, U., 'Bank Regulation and Supervision in bank-dominated financial systems: a comparison between Japan and Germany' (2009) 27(2) *European Journal of Law and Economics*, pp. 177-209, 2009
7. BENS, J. and KUMHOF, M. (2012), 'The Chicago Plan Revisited', WP/12/202, IMF Working Paper, International Monetary Fund, Washington D.C., 2012
8. BENJENK, R., 'Quixotic Regulation: Section 23A of the Federal Reserve Act and Containment of the Federal Safety Net Subsidy' (2012) 2 *Harvard Business Law Review*, pp. 461–485
9. BENSTON, G., 'Universal Banking' (1994) 8(3) *Journal of Economic Perspectives*, pp. 121–134
10. BINDER, J-H., 'Ring-Fencing: An Integrated Approach with Many Unknowns' (2015) 16 *European Business Organization Law Review*, pp. 97–119
11. BLACK, J., 'Managing the Financial Crisis – the Constitutional Dimension', LSE Working Papers, 12/2010, London School of Economics, Law Department
12. BODANSKY, D., 'What's in a Concept? Global Public Goods, International Law, and Legitimacy' (2012) 23(3) *The European Journal of International Law*

13. Bogert, E.A., 'Anti – Federalist Banking Policy Under Dodd-Frank: The Case for the Liberal Pre-Emption of State Banking Law' (2020) 6(2) *University of Pennsylvania Journal of Law & Public Affairs*, pp. 309–345
14. Bordo, M.D., 'An Historical Perspective on The Crisis Of 2007-2008', Working Paper 14569, NBER Working Paper Series, National Bureau of Economic Research (NBER), 2008, available at: http://www.nber.org/papers/w14569
15. Bordo, M.D., 'The Operation and Demise of the Bretton Woods System; 1958 to 1971', Economics Working Paper, Hoover Institution, February 2017, available at: https://www.hoover.org/sites/default/files/research/docs/16116-bordo.pdf
16. Bossone, B., 'Should Banks Be Narrowed?', IMF Working Paper, WP/01/159, International Monetary Fund, Washington D.C., 2001
17. Breydo, L.E., 'Structural Foundations of Financial Stability: What Canada Can Teach America About Building a Better Regulatory System' (2015) 17 *University of Pennsylvania Journal of Business Law*, pp. 973–1080
18. Brown, R.J. Jr., 'Japanese Banking Reform and the Occupation Legacy: Decompartmentalization, Deregulation, and Decentralization' (1993) 21(2) *Denver Journal of International Law & Policy*, pp. 361–399
19. Buckley, R.P., Avgouleas, E. and Arner, D.W., 'Three Decades of International Financial Crisis, What Have We Learned and What Still Needs to Be Done?', ADB Economics Working Paper Series, No. 615, Asian Development Bank, June 2020
20. Burcu Avci, S., Schipani, C.A., Nejat Seyhun, H., 'Eliminating Conflicts of Interests in Banks: The Significance of the Volcker Rule' (2018) 35 *Yale Journal on Regulation*, pp. 343–381
21. Calomiris, C.W., 'Universal Banking American Style' (1998) 154 *Journal of Institutional and Theoretical Economics (JITE)*, pp. 44–57
22. Calomiris, C.W. and Mason, J.R., 'Fundamentals, Panics, and Bank Distress During the Depression' (2003) 93(5) *American Economic Review* pp. 1615–1647
23. Chavaz, M. and Elliott, D., 'Separating retail and investment banking: evidence from the UK', Staff Working Paper No. 892, Bank of England, November 2020
24. Chen, D., 'Acute Symptoms of Chronic Problems: Japan's Procrastination in Solving Its Banking Crisis, the Current Situation and a Future Perspective' (2000) 9 *Minnesota Journal of Global Trade*, pp. 269–297
25. Chow, J.T.S. and Surti, J., 'Making Banks Safer: Can Volcker and Vickers Do It?', IMF Working Paper, WP/11/236, International Monetary Fund, Washington D.C., 2011
26. Coval, J.D., Jurek, J. and Stafford, E., 'The Economics of Structured Finance', Working Paper, 09–060, Harvard Business School, 2009
27. Crockett, A. (1997), 'Why is Financial Stability a Goal of Public Policy?', *Economic Review*, Fourth Quarter 1997, Kansas City Federal Reserve, 1997
28. D'Hulster, K. and Otker-Robe, I., 'Ring-Fencing Cross-Border Banks: An Effective Supervisory Response?' (2018) 5(1) *Journal of Financial Perspectives*
29. de la Dehesa, G., 'Twelve Market and Government Failures Leading to the 2008–2009 Financial Crisis', Occasional Paper No. 80, Group of Thirty, Washington D.C.
30. Detzer, D., 'Financial Systems in Financial Crisis: An analysis of banking systems in the EU', (2014) 49(2) *Intereconomics*, pp. 56–87
31. Eichengreen, B., 'The origins and nature of the Great Slump revisited' (1992) 45(2) *Economic History Review*, pp. 213–239
32. Felsenfeld, C., 'The Bank Holding Company Act: Has It Lived Its Life?' (1993) 38(1) *Villanova Law Review*, pp. 1–101

33. Fernandez-Bollo, E., 'Structural Reform and Supervision of The Banking Sector in France' (2013) 2013(1) *OECD Journal: Financial Market Trends*
34. Ferran, E., 'Examining the United Kingdom's Experience in Adopting the Single Financial Regulator Model' (2003) 28 *Brooklyn Journal of International Law*, pp. 257–307
35. Frankel, J., 'The Plaza Accord, 30 Years Later', Working Paper 21813, NBER Working Paper Series, National Bureau of Economic Research (NBER), December 2015, available at: https://www.nber.org/papers/w21813
36. Gambacorta, L. and van Rixtel, A., 'Structural bank regulation initiatives: approaches and implications', BIS Working Papers, no. 412, April 2013, Bank of International Settlements
37. Goodhart, C.A.E., 'The Optimal Financial Structure', LSE Financial Markets Group Paper Series, Special Paper 222, London School of Economics, March 2013
38. Gordon, J.N. and Gandia, C.M., 'Money Markets Funds Run Risk: Will Floating Net Asset Value Fix the Problem?' (2014) 2014(2) *Columbia Business Law Review*, pp. 313–370
39. Gorman, C.M., 'Are Chinese Walls the Best Solution to the Problems of Insider Trading and Conflicts of Interest in Broker-Dealers?' (2004) 9 *Fordham Journal of Corporate & Financial Law*, pp. 475–499
40. Gorton, G. and Metrick, A., 'Regulating the Shadow Banking System', Brookings Papers on Economic Activity, Fall 2010, pp. 261–312
41. Gorton, G. and Metrick, A., 'Securitized banking and the run on repo' (2012) 104(3) *Journal of Financial Economics*, pp. 425–451
42. Gortsos, C.V., 'The Basel Committee on Banking Supervision through the lens of its 2013 Charter', 2017, available at SSRN: https://ssrn.com/abstract=2900107
43. Gortsos, C.V., 'A brief overview of the European Banking Union', Centre international de formation européenne 'L'Europe en formation', 2017/2, n° 383-384, pp. 61–83, Summer - Autumn 2017
44. Gren, J., 'The Eurosystem and the Single Supervisory Mechanism: institutional continuity under constitutional constraints', Legal Working Paper Series, No. 17, European Central Bank – ECB, Frankfurt, July 2018
45. Gutwillig, J.H., 'Glass versus Steagall: The fight over federalism and American banking' (2014) 100 *Virginia Law Review*, Note, pp. 771–815
46. Hardie, I. and Howarth, D., 'Die Krise but not La Crise? The financial crisis and the transformation of German and French banking systems' (2009) 47(5) *Journal of Common Market Studies*, pp. 1015–1036
47. Hockett, R., 'The Macroprudential Turn: From Institutional "Safety and Soundness" to Systematic "Financial Stability" in Financial Supervision' (2015) 9(2) *Virginia Law and Business Review*, pp. 201–256
48. Hofmann, C., 'A Legal Analysis of the Eurozone Crisis' (2013) 18(3) *Fordham Journal of Corporate & Financial Law*, pp. 518–564
49. Janger, E.J., 'Equity for Intermediaries: The Resolution of Financial Firms in Bankruptcy and Bank Resolution' (2024) 41 *Yale Journal on Regulation*, pp. 965–1010
50. Jones, C.P.A, 'Japanese Banking Reform: A Legal Analysis of Recent Developments' (1993) 3(2) *Duke Journal of Comparative & International Law*, pp. 387–440
51. Kamikawa, R., 'The Interaction between Financial Regulation and Financial Crisis in Japan: Change in Financial Administration and Two Financial Crises from 1980 to 2010' (2012) 59 *Osaka University Law Review*, pp. 1–26
52. Kanda, H., 'Developments in Japanese Securities Regulation: An Overview' (1995) 29(3) *The International Lawyer*, pp. 599–614

53. Kawai, M. and Takagi, S., 'Why was Japan Hit So Hard by the Global Financial Crisis?', Working Paper No. 153, ADBI Working Paper Series, October 2009, Asian Development Bank Institute
54. Khair Alshaleel, M. and Hoekstra, J., 'A Decade after the Global Financial Crisis: New Regulatory Challenges to Financial Stability' (2021) 32(1) *European Business Law Review*, pp. 117–156
55. Kobayashi, K., 'Effects of Japanese Financial Regulations and Keiretsu Style Groups on Japanese Corporate Governance' (2020) 43(2) *Hastings International and Comparative Law Review*, Article 7, pp. 340–364
56. Kress, J.C., 'Solving Banking's "Too Big to Manage" Problem' (2019) 104 *Minnesota Law Review*, pp. 171–241
57. Kroszner, R.S. and Rajan, R.G., 'Is the Glass-Steagall Act Justified? A Study of the U.S. Experience with Universal Banking Before 1933' (1994) 84(4) *The American Economic Review*, pp. 810–832
58. Levitin, A., 'Safe Banking: Finance and Democracy' (2016) 83 *The University of Chicago Law Review*, pp. 357–455
59. Lupo-Pasini, F., 'Financial Stability in International Law' (2017) 18 *Melbourne Journal of International Law*, pp. 1–26
60. Lupo-Pasini, F. and Buckley, R.P., 'International Coordination in Cross-Border Bank Bail-ins: Problems and Prospects' (2015) 16 *European Business Organization Law Review*, pp. 203–226
61. Macey, J.R. and Miller, G.P., 'Corporate Governance and Commercial Banking: A Comparative Examination of Germany, Japan, and the United States' (1995) 48 *Stanford Law Review*, pp. 73–111
62. Massoc, E., 'Banks, power, and political institutions: the divergent priorities of European states towards "too-big-to-fail" banks: The cases of competition in retail banking and the banking structural reform' (2020) 22(1) *Business and Politics*, pp. 136–160
63. McNamara, C. and Metrick, A., 'Restructuring and Forgiveness in Financial Crises D: The Japanese Financial Crisis of the 1990s' (2020) 2(1) *The Journal of Financial Crises*, pp. 122–144
64. Menand, L. and Ricks, M., 'Federal Corporate Law and the Business of Banking' (2021) 88(6) *The University of Chicago Law Review*, pp. 1361–1418
65. Menand, L. and Ricks, M., 'Rebuilding Banking Law: Banks as Public Utilities' (2024) 41 *Yale Journal on Regulation*, pp. 591–651
66. Milhaupt, C.J., 'Japan's Experience with Deposit Insurance and Failing Banks: Implications for Financial Regulatory Design?' (1999) 77 *Washington University Law Quarterly*, pp. 399–431
67. Mishkin, F.S., 'Anatomy of a financial crisis', Working Paper No. 3934, NBER Working Paper Series, National Bureau of Economic Research (NBER), December 1991,
68. Mishkin, F.S. and White, E.N., 'Unprecedented Actions: The Federal Reserve's Response to the Global Financial Crisis in Historical Perspective', Working Paper 20737, NBER Working Paper Series, National Bureau of Economic Research (NBER), December 2014, available at: https://www.nber.org/papers/w20737
69. Mitchell, J., Van Roy, P. and Vespro, C., 'Ten Years After The Financial Crisis: Regulatory Reforms And The Belgian Banking Sector' *Reflets et perspectives de la vie économique*, 2017/1, Tome LVI, pp. 9–28, available at: https://www.cairn.info/revue-reflets-et-perspectives-de-la-vie-economique-2017-1-page-9.htm
70. McLaughlin, P.A., Sherouse, O., Febrizio, M. and Scott King, M., 'Is Dodd-Frank the Biggest Law Ever?' (2021) 7 *Journal of Financial Regulation*, pp. 149–174

71. Nakaso, H., 'The financial crisis in Japan during the 1990s: how the Bank of Japan responded and the lessons learnt', BIS Papers, No. 6, Bank of International Settlements, October 2001

72. Napolitano, G., 'Il nuovo Stato salvatore: strumenti di intervento e assetti istituzionali', *Giornale di diritto amministrativo*, N. 11, pp. 1083–1094, 2008

73. Omarova, S.T., 'The Quiet Metamorphosis: How Derivatives Changed the "Business of Banking"' (2009) 63(4) *University of Miami Law Review*, pp. 1041–1109

74. Omarova, S.T., 'From Gramm-Leach-Bliley to Dodd-Frank: The Unfulfilled Promise of Section 23A of the Federal Reserve Act' (2011) 89 *North Carolina Law Review*, pp. 1683–1776

75. Omarova, S.T. and Tahyar, M.E., 'That Which We Call a Bank: Revisiting the History of Bank Holding Company Regulations in the United States' (2012) 31 *Review of Banking and Financial Law*, pp. 113–198

76. Omarova, S.T., 'The Merchants of Wall Street: Banking, Commerce, and Commodities' (2013) 98 *Minnesota Law Review*, pp. 265–355

77. Omarova, S.T., 'The "Too Big to Fail" Problem' (2019) 103 *Minnesota Law Review*, pp. 2495–2541

78. Omarova, S.T., 'Public Banking as an Institutional Design Project' (2024) 41 *Yale Journal on Regulation*, pp. 1128–1184

79. Palhau Mora, P., 'The "Too Big to Fail" Subsidy in Canada: Some Estimates', Staff Working Paper, Bank of Canada, 2018

80. Patrikis, E., 'Japan's Big Bang Financial Reforms', Essay, Brooklyn Journal of International Law, 1998, Vol. XXIV, No. 2, pp. 577–592

81. Philips, R.J., 'The Regulation and Supervision of Bank Holding Companies: A Historical Perspective', Working Paper No. 116, Jerome Levy Economics Institute of Bard College and Colorado State University, May 1994

82. Pomper, B.A., 'The Japanese Financial Reform of 1993: Will Reform Spark Innovation?' (1995) 28 *Cornell International Law Journal*, pp. 525–567

83. Puri, P. and Nichol, A., 'Developments in Financial Services Regulation: A Canadian Perspective' (2014) 55(2) *Canadian Business Law Journal*, pp. 455–488

84. Ratnovski, L. and Huang, R., 'Why Are Canadian Banks More Resilient?', IMF Working Paper, WP/09/152, International Monetary Fund, Washington D.C., 2009

85. Rhee, J. and Metrick, A., 'Guarantees and Capital Infusions in Response to Financial Crises A: Haircuts and Resolutions' (2020) 2(1) *Yale Journal of Financial Crises*, pp. 33–50

86. Rhee, J. and Metrick, A., 'Guarantees and Capital Infusions in Response to Financial Crises B: U.S. Guarantees During the Global Financial Crisis' (2020) 2(1) *Yale Journal of Financial Crises*, pp. 51–68

87. Reynolds, M., Macrory, S. and Chowdhury, M., 'EU Competition Policy in the Financial Crisis: Extraordinary Measures' (2011) 33(6) *Fordham International Law Review*, Article 3, pp. 1670–1737

88. Sibbitt, E.C., 'A Brave New World for M&A of Financial Institutions in Japan: Big Bang Financial Deregulation and the New Environment for Corporate Combinations of Financial Institutions' (1998) 19(4) *University of Pennsylvania Journal of International Economic Law*, pp. 965–1027

89. Silvia, J., 'Efficiency and Effectiveness in Securities Regulation: Comparative Analysis of the United States' Competitive Regulatory Structure and the United Kingdom's Single Regulator Model' (2008) 6 *DePaul Business & Commercial Law Journal*, pp. 247–263

90. Schenk, C., 'Regulatory foundations of financialization: May Day, Big Bang and international banking, 1975–1990' (2020) 27(3) *Financial History Review*, pp. 397–417
91. Schinasi, G.J., 'Defining Financial Stability', IMF Working Paper, WP/04/187, International Monetary Fund, 2004, Washington D.C.
92. Schooner, H.M. and Taylor, M., 'Convergence and Competition: The Case of Bank Regulation in Britain and the United States' (1999) 20 *Michigan Journal of International Law*, pp. 595–655
93. Schwarcz, S.L., 'Systemic Risk' (2008) 97 *Georgetown Law Journal*, pp. 193–249
94. Schwarcz, S.L., 'Regulating Shadow Banking' (2012) 31 *Review of Banking and Financial Law*, pp. 619–642
95. Schwarcz, S.L., 'What Is Securitization? And For What Purpose?' (2012) 85 *Southern California Law Review*, pp. 1283–1299
96. Schwarcz, S.L., 'Ring-Fencing' (2013) 87 *Southern California Law Review*, pp. 69–110
97. Schwarcz, S.L., 'Beyond Bankruptcy: Resolution as a Macroprudential Regulatory Tool' (2018) 94 *Notre Dame Law Review*, pp. 709–749
98. Staikouras, P., 'Universal Banks, Universal Crises? Disentangling Myths from Realities in Quest of a New Regulatory and Supervisory Landscape' (2011) 11 *Journal of Corporate Law Studies*, Part I, pp. 139–175
99. Tarullo, D.K., 'Bank Supervision and Administrative Law' (2022) 1 *Columbia Business Law Review*, pp. 279–401
100. Thorson, A.H. and Siegfanz, F., 'The 1997 Deregulation of Japan's Holding Companies' (1999) 8(2) *Pacific Rim Law & Policy Journal*, pp. 261–349
101. Tirado, I., 'Banking Crises and the Japanese Legal Framework', Discussion Paper No. 2017-E-2, Institute for Monetary and Economic Studies, Bank of Japan, Tokyo, 2017
102. Turk, M.C., 'Overlapping Legal Rules in Financial Regulation and the Administrative State' (2020) 54 *Georgia Law Review*, pp. 791–868
103. Vickers, J., 'Some Economics of Banking Reform', Discussion Paper Series, No. 632/2012, Department of Economics, University of Oxford
104. Vollmer, U. and Bebenroth, R., 'The Financial Crisis in Japan: Causes and Policy Reactions by the Bank of Japan' (2012) 9(1) *The European Journal of Comparative Economics*, pp. 51–77
105. Walter, I., 'Universal Banking: A Shareholder Value Perspective', New York University Working Paper No. FIN-96-040, 1996
106. Walter, I., 'Universal Banking and Financial Architecture' (2012) 52 *The Quarterly Review of Economics and Finance*, pp. 114–122
107. Wagner, L., 'Aides d'État: l'art de la souplesse en temps de crise', *Cahiers de droit européen (CDE)*, 2011, vol. 47, n° 1, pp. 231–276
108. White, A. (2016), 'Banks as Utilities' (2016) 90 *Tulane Law Review*, pp. 1241–1283
109. Wiggins, R.Z., Piontek, T. and Metrick, A., 'The Lehman Brothers Bankruptcy A: Overview' (2019) 1(1) *Journal of Financial Crises*, pp. 39–62
110. Wiggins, R.Z., Tente, N. and Metrick, A., 'European Banking Union C: Cross-Border Resolution–Fortis Group' (2019) 1(3) *Journal of Financial Crises*, pp. 150–171
111. Wiggins, R.Z., Tente, N. and Metrick, A., 'European Banking Union D: Cross-Border Resolution—Dexia Group' (2019) 1(3) *Journal of Financial Crises*, pp. 172–188
112. Wiggins, R.Z., Wedow, M. and Metrick, A., 'European Banking Union A: The Single Supervisory Mechanism' (2019) 1(3) *Journal of Financial Crises*, pp. 113–129

113. Wilmarth Jr., A.E., 'The Dark Side of Universal Banking: Financial Conglomerates and the Origins of the Subprime Financial Crisis' (2009) 41(4) *Connecticut Law Review*, pp. 963–1050
114. Wilmarth Jr., A.E., 'The Dodd-Frank Act's Expansion of State Authority to Protect Consumers of Financial Services' (2011) 36(4) *The Journal of Corporation Law*, pp. 895–954
115. Wilmarth Jr., A.E., 'Prelude to Glass-Steagall: Abusive Securities Practices by National City Bank and Chase National Bank During the "Roaring Twenties"' (2016) 90(5) *Tulane Law Review*, pp. 1285–1329
116. Wilmarth Jr., A.E., 'The Road to Repeal of the Glass-Steagall Act' (2017) 17(4) *Wake Forest Journal of Business and Intellectual Property Law*, pp. 441–548
117. Zavos, G., 'Banking Integration in the European Community' (1989) 9 *Northwestern Journal of International Law & Business*, pp. 572–587
118. Zeissler, A.G., Ikeda, D. and Metrick, A., 'Ireland and Iceland in Crisis D: Similarities and Differences' (2019) 1(3) *Journal of Financial Crises*

6. INSTITUTIONAL PUBLICATIONS & REPORTS / FINAL REPORTS

1. Adrian, T. and Shin, H.S., 'The Shadow Banking System: Implications for Financial Regulation', Staff Report no. 382, Federal Reserve Bank of New York Staff Reports, July 2009
2. Andruszkiewicz, O., Mathis, J., Wilkinson, C., Vassiliadis, M., Peppas, K., and Gatopoulos, G. 'Study on the Financial Sector in Greece during the Economic Adjustment Programmes: 2010–2018', European Commission Final Report, June 2020
3. Bank of England – PRA, 'Prudential Regulation Authority, Annual Report, 1 March 2024–28 February 2025, June 2025, available at: https://www.bankofengland.co.uk/-/media/boe/files/annual-report/2025/pra-2024-25.pdf
2. Basel Committee on Banking Supervision - BCBS, 'Report on the 2023 banking turmoil', October 2023, available at: https://www.bis.org/bcbs/publ/d555.pdf
3. Baudino, P., Murphy, D. and Svoronos, J.P., 'The banking crisis in Ireland', FSI Crisis Management Series, No. 2, Financial Stability Institute, Bank of International Settlements
4. Britton, K., Dawkes, L., Debagge, S. and Idris, T., 'Ring-fencing: what is it and how will it affect banks and their customers?', Bank of England Quarterly Bulletin 2016 Q4, 2016, available at SSRN: https://ssrn.com/abstract=2898735
5. Brown, E., 'Consolidated Financial Regulation: Six National Case Studies and the Experience of the European Union', Background Paper no. 2, The Volcker Alliance, 2015, available at: https://www.volckeralliance.org/sites/default/files/attachments/Background%20Paper%202_Consolidated%20Financial%20Regulation%20-%20Six%20National%20Case%20Studies%20and%20the%20Experience%20of%20the%20European%20Union.pdf
6. Carpenter, D.H., Murphy, E.V., Murphy, M.M., 'The Glass-Steagall Act: A Legal and Policy Analysis', Congressional Research Service, Report, R44349, 16 January 2016, available at: https://sgp.fas.org/crs/misc/R44349.pdf
7. Committee on Banking and Currency (CBC) – the 'Pecora Committee', 'Stock Exchange Practices', Final Report, No. 1455, Senate – US Congress, 16 June 1934, available at: https://www.senate.gov/about/resources/pdf/pecora-final-report.pdf
8. Daniel, F., 'Recent Changes to Canada's Financial Sector Legislation', Bank of Canada Review, Winter 2002-2003, Bank of Canada

9. European Banking Federation – EBF, 'Possible reform of the structure of the EU Banking sector', EBF Liikanen Task Force Report, June 2012, Brussels, available at: https://www.france-post-marche.fr/wp-content/uploads/2021/04/FBE-Study-on-on-the-issue-of-possible-reforms-to-the-structure-of-the-EU-Banking-Sector-EBF-Liikanen-Task-Force-Report.pdf
10. European Banking Federation – EBF: 'Banking in Europe: EBF Facts & Figures 2022', Brussels, 2022, available at: https://www.ebf.eu/wp-content/uploads/2022/12/Banking-in-Europe-EBF-Facts-and-Figures-2022.-FINAL.pdf
11. European Central Bank – ECB, 'Financial Integration and Structure in the Euro Area', ECB Committee of Financial Integration, June 2024, available at: https://www.ecb.europa.eu/pub/pdf/fie/ecb.fie202406~c4ca413e65.en.pdf
12. Financial Crisis Inquiry Commission – FCIC, 'THE FINANCIAL CRISIS INQUIRY REPORT', Final Report of the National Commission on the Causes of the Financial and Economic Crisis in the United States, January 2011, available at: https://www.govinfo.gov/content/pkg/GPO-FCIC/pdf/GPO-FCIC.pdf
13. Financial Services Authority – FSA, 'The failure of the Royal Bank of Scotland', Financial Services Authority Board Report, December 2011, available at: https://www.fca.org.uk/publication/corporate/fsa-rbs.pdf
14. Financial Stability Board – FSB, 'Peer Review of Canada, Review Report', 30 January 2012, available at: https://www.fsb.org/wp-content/uploads/r_120130.pdf
15. Financial Stability Board – FSB, 'Recovery and Resolution Planning for Systemically Important Financial Institutions: Guidance on Developing Effective Resolution Strategies', 16 July 2013, available at: https://www.fsb.org/wp-content/uploads/r_130716b.pdf
16. Financial Stability Board – FSB, 'Peer Review of the United States, Review Report', 27 August 2013, available at: https://www.fsb.org/wp-content/uploads/r_130827.pdf
17. Financial Stability Board – FSB, 'Peer Review of the United Kingdom, Review Report', 10 September 2013, available at: https://www.fsb.org/uploads/r_130910.pdf
18. Financial Stability Board – FSB, 'Structural Banking Reforms, Cross-border consistencies and global financial stability implications', Report to G20 Leaders for the November 2014 Summit, 27 October 2014, available at: https://www.fsb.org/wp-content/uploads/r_141027.pdf
19. Financial Stability Board – FSB, 'Peer Review of Japan, Review Report', 21 December 2016, available at: https://www.fsb.org/wp-content/uploads/Japan-peer-review-report.pdf
20. Financial Stability Board – FSB, 'Evaluation of the Effects of Too-Big-To-Fail Reforms', Final Report, 1 April 2021, available at: https://www.fsb.org/wp-content/uploads/P010421-1.pdf
21. Financial Stability Board – FSB, 'Peer Review of the United Kingdom, Review Report', 14 April 2021, available at: https://www.fsb.org/wp-content/uploads/P140421.pdf
22. Freedman, C., 'The Canadian Banking System', Technical Report No. 81, Staff Research, Bank of Canada, 1998, available at: https://www.bankofcanada.ca/wp-content/uploads/2010/01/tr81.pdf
23. High-Level Expert Group (HLEG), 'Liikanen Report', 'Reforming the structure of the EU banking sector', Brussels, 2 October 2012
24 HM Treasury, 'Government response to the independent review on ring-fencing and proprietary trading', Policy Paper, December 2022, available at: https://www.gov.uk/government/publications/ring-fencing-reforms/government-response-to-the-independent-review-on-ring-fencing-and-proprietary-trading

24. Independent Commission on Banking (ICB), 'Vickers Report', 'Final Report – Recommendations', September 2011, available at: https://webarchive.nationalarchives.gov.uk/ukgwa/20131003105424/https:/hmt-sanctions.s3.amazonaws.com/ICB%20final%20report/ICB%2520Final%2520Report%5B1%5D.pdf
25. Institute of International Finance (IIF), 'Making Resolution Robust – Completing the Legal and Institutional Frameworks for Effective Cross-Border Resolution of Financial Institutions', June 2012, Washington D.C., available at: https://www.iif.com/portals/0/files/private/Making_Resolution_Robust_20120607.pdf
26. International Monetary Fund (IMF), 'United Kingdom, Financial Sector Assessment Program, Financial System Stability Assessment', IMF Country Report No. 16/167, June 2016, Washington D.C., available at: https://www.imf.org/en/Publications/CR/Issues/2016/12/31/United-Kingdom-Financial-Sector-Assessment-Program-Financial-System-Stability-Assessment-43978
27. Ludwig, E., 'Lessons Learned from the 2008 Financial Crisis', The William Taylor Memorial Lecture, The Group of Thirty, Washington D.C., available at: https://group30.org/images/uploads/publications/G30_LessonsLearned2008FinancialCrisis.pdf
28. McDonald, O., 'The Repeal of the Glass-Steagall Act, Myth and Reality', Policy Analysis, No. 804, November 2016, Cato Institute, Washington D.C.
29. Mitchell, J., 'Structural Banking Reforms', Financial Stability Review, p. 99–111, National Bank of Belgium, 2014
30. National Bank of Belgium – NBB, 'Structural banking reforms in Belgium: final report', July 2013, available at: https://www.nbb.be/doc/ts/publications/nbbreport/2013/structuralbankingreformsen.pdf
31. Office of the Comptroller of the Currency – OCC, 'Activities Permissible for National Banks and Federal Savings Associations, Cumulative', October 2017, available at: https://www.occ.gov/publications-and-resources/publications/banker-education/files/pub-activities-permissible-for-nat-banks-fed-saving.pdf
32. Prudential Regulation Authority – PRA, 'The implementation of ring-fencing: the PRA's approach to ring-fencing transfer schemes', Statement of Policy, March 2016, available at: https://www.bankofengland.co.uk/-/media/boe/files/prudential-regulation/statement-of-policy/2016/the-implementation-of-ring-fencing-the-pras-approach-to-ring-fencing-transfer-schemes-sop.pdf
33. Prudential Regulation Authority – PRA, 'The Implementation of ring-fencing: prudential requirements, intragroup arrangements and use of financial markets infrastructures', Policy Statement, PS20/16, Bank of England, July 2016, available at: https://www.bankofengland.co.uk/-/media/boe/files/prudential-regulation/policy-statement/2016/ps2016
34. Prudential Regulation Authority – PRA, 'Ring-Fenced Bodies (RFBs)', Supervisory Statement, SS8/16, Bank of England, December 2017, available at: https://www.bankofengland.co.uk/-/media/boe/files/prudential-regulation/supervisory-statement/2017/ss816update2.pdf
35. Prudential Regulation Authority – PRA, 'Proprietary Trading Review', Bank of England, September 2020, available at: https://www.bankofengland.co.uk/-/media/boe/files/prudential-regulation/report/proprietary-trading-review-2020.pdf?la=en&hash=5CE09780161C55C63253ABB18FA659021287E522
36. Ring-Fencing and Proprietary Trading Review – RFPT, Independent Review, Final Report, March 2022, available at: https://rfpt.independent-review.uk/uploads/CCS0821108226-006_RFPT_Web%20Accessible.pdf
37. Sykes, J.B., 'Banking Law: An Overview of Federal Preemption in the Dual Banking System', Congressional Research Service, Report, R45081, 23 January 2018, available at: https://sgp.fas.org/crs/misc/R45081.pdf

38. Sykes, J.B., 'Federal Preemption in the Dual Banking System: An Overview and Issues for the 116th Congress', Congressional Research Service, Report, R45726, 17 May 2019, available at: https://sgp.fas.org/crs/misc/R45726.pdf
39. Vinals, J., Pazarbasioglu, C., Surti, J., Narain, A., Erbenova, M. and Chow, J., 'Creating a Safer Financial System: Will the Volcker, Vickers, and Liikanen Structural Measures Help?', IMF Staff Discussion Note, SDN/13/4, May 2013, International Monetary Fund, Washington D.C.

7. SPEECHES

1. Lane, T., 'Financial Stability in One Country?', Remarks by Tim Lane, Deputy Governor of the Bank of Canada, Weatherhead Center for International Affairs, Harvard University, 11 February 2013, Cambridge, Massachusetts, available at: https://www.bankofcanada.ca/wp-content/uploads/2013/02/remarks-110213.pdf
2. Mishkin, F., 'How Should We Respond to Asset Price Bubbles?', Speech, at the Wharton Financial Institutions Center and Oliver Wyman Institute's Annual Financial Risk Roundtable, Philadelphia, Pennsylvania, 15 May 2008, available at: https://www.federalreserve.gov/newsevents/speech/mishkin20080515a.htm

8. MISCELLANEOUS

1. Akagami, H. and Watanabe, Y., 'The Banking Regulation Review: Japan', *The Law Reviews*, 4 May 2021, available at: https://thelawreviews.co.uk/title/the-banking-regulation-review/japan
2. Anderson Mori & Tomotsune, 'Easing of Firewall Regulations under the Financial Instruments and Exchange Act of Japan', September 2014, (AMT) available at: https://www.amt-law.com/asset/pdf/bulletins2_pdf/140930.pdf
3. DLA Piper, 'The Edinburgh Reforms – Your guide to the proposals', December 2022, available at: https://www.dlapiper.com/en/insights/publications/2022/12/the-edinburgh-reforms-your-guide-to-the-proposals
4. LINKLATERS, 'The UK ring-fencing regime: in the spotlight once again', May 2025, available at: https://www.linklaters.com/knowledge/publications/alerts-newsletters-and-guides/2025/may/27/the-uk-ring-fencing-regime-in-the-spotlight-again
5. Martin, J., 'The Toronto-Dominion Bank and Canada's "Little Bang" of 1987', Case Study, Rotman School of Management, University of Toronto, 2012
6. Martín-Aceña, P., 'The savings banks crisis in Spain: When and How?', in 'The Aftermaths of Crises Savings and Savings Banks: Elements of Stability in Times of Crises?', Perspectives, 66, WSBI (World Savings and Retail Banking Institute) – ESBG (European Savings and Retail Banking Group), December 2013
7. Mavridou, M., Theodossiou, A. and Gklezakou, T., 'Greece; Several Greek Banks and Foreign Branches: Resolution via Public Recapitalization and Bail-In and State Aid Issues (2009–2015); Part 1: The Greek Experience of Restructuring and Recapitalization of Problem Banks', in 'Bank Resolution and Bail-In in the EU: Selected Case Studies Pre and Post BRRD', Financial Sector Advisory Center, World Bank Group, 2016
8. McDaniel, L., 'Reference re Securities Act (2011): Does Parliament Have the Power to Establish a Canada-wide Securities Regulator?', Article, Centre for Constitutional Studies, University of Alberta, 2012, available at: https://www.constitutionalstudies.ca/2012/07/reference-re-securities-act-2011-does-parliament-have-the-power-to-establish-a-canada-wide-securities-regulator/
9. Michaelides, A., "Cyprus; Bank of Cyprus (BOC) and Laiki: Resolution via Public Support and Bail-In, Including of Uninsured Depositors (2013)", in "Bank Resolution

and Bail-In in the EU: Selected Case Studies Pre and Post BRRD", Financial Sector Advisory Center, World Bank Group, 2016

10. Ono, S., 'Japan's firewall regulation – a crackdown on undisclosed information transfer', IFLR, 1 February 2023, available at: https://www.iflr.com/article/2b847pmp7anohuvj206ps/local-insights/japans-firewall-regulation-a-crackdown-on-undisclosed-information-transfer
11. Reinhardt, C., 'Why Canada hates the Volcker Rule, the landmark U.S. financial reform imposes high costs north of the border, say Canadians. Americans don't think so.', article in MACLEANS' Business column, February 2013, available at: https://www.macleans.ca/economy/business/why-canada-hates-the-volcker-rule/
12. Sotelino, F. and Gonzalez, R., 'Universal Banking Post Crisis: Past and Future of International Corporate and Personal Banking', 2012, available at SSRN: https://papers.ssrn.com/sol3/papers.cfm?abstract_id=2102863

www.ingramcontent.com/pod-product-compliance
Ingram Content Group UK Ltd.
Pitfield, Milton Keynes, MK11 3LW, UK
UKHW051906290926
8980IPUK00018B/1799

9 781839 70577